P9-DFF-040

THE REPUBLIC OF REASON

THE REPUBLIC OF REASON

The Personal Philosophies of the Founding Fathers

Selected, Edited, and with Commentary
by
NORMAN COUSINS

PERENNIAL LIBRARY

HARPER & ROW, PUBLISHERS, SAN FRANCISCO
Cambridge, Hagerstown, New York, Philadelphia, Washington
London, Mexico City, São Paulo, Singapore, Sydney

134155

A hardcover edition of this work was published by Harper & Row in 1958, under the title 'In God We Trust.'

THE REPUBLIC OF REASON: *The Personal Philosophies of the Founding Fathers.* Copyright © 1958, 1988 by Norman Cousins. Foreword copyright © 1988 by Richard B. Morris. All rights reserved. Printed in the United States of America. No part of this book may be used or reproduced in any manner whatsoever without written permission except in the case of brief quotations embodied in critical articles and reviews. For information address Harper & Row, Publishers, Inc., 10 East 53rd Street, New York, NY 10022. Published simultaneously in Canada by Fitzhenry & Whiteside, Limited, Toronto.

FIRST PAPERBACK EDITION

Library of Congress Cataloging-in-Publication Data

[In God we Trust]
  The Republic of reason.

  Bibliography: p.
  Includes index.
  1. Church and state—United States—Early works to 1800. 2. Christianity—Early works to 1800. 3. Religion—Early works to 1800. 4. Free throught—Early works to 1800. 5. United States—Religion—To 1800—Early works to 1800. I. Cousins, Norman.
  BR516.15 1988   277.3'07'0922   87-45695
  ISBN 0-06-250161-5

---

88 89 90 91 92 MPC 10 9 8 7 6 5 4 3 2 1

For AMY LOVEMAN
and those who loved her

ACKNOWLEDGMENTS

The editor wishes to express his deep sense of appreciation to Professors Allan Nevins and Merrill Jensen, who have helped him to avoid important errors in the opening chapter; to Professor Richard B. Morris, for his detailed criticisms and suggestions on the entire manuscript; to his assistant, Miss Sallie Lou Parker, whose inexhaustible energy in helping to bring the research materials together figured so largely in the making of this book; and to Mrs. Anne Slavitt and Alfred Williams, for their assistance. He also wishes to thank Georgia Haugh and the staff of the William L. Clements Library at the University of Michigan, Joseph C. Mask of the New York Public Library, and the staff of the Library of Congress. It goes without saying that the editor is solely responsible for any errors or shortcomings in the book.

Contents

FOREWORD BY RICHARD B. MORRIS ix

INTRODUCTION 1

1. BENJAMIN FRANKLIN 16
   "I Never Was Without Some Religious Principles"

2. GEORGE WASHINGTON 44
   ". . . The Path of True Piety Is so Plain as to Require But Little Political Direction"

3. JOHN ADAMS 74
   "I Have Been a Church-Going Animal for Seventy-Six Years . . . And This Has Been Alleged as One Proof of My Hypocrisy"

4. THOMAS JEFFERSON 114
   "I Never Told My Own Religion, nor Scrutinized That of Another"

5. THE JEFFERSON-ADAMS LETTERS 217
   "Sentiments of Respect and Affectionate Attachment"

6. JAMES MADISON 295
   "What Is Here a Right Towards Men Is a Duty Towards the Creator"

7. ALEXANDER HAMILTON 326
   "Fly to the Bosom of Your God, and Be Comforted"

8. SAMUEL ADAMS 344
"Revelation Assures Us That Righteousness Exalteth a Nation"

9. JOHN JAY 358
"We Differ in Opinion; and, I Am Persuaded, with Equal Sincerity"

10. THOMAS PAINE 389
"I Consider Myself in the Hands of My Creator"

EDITOR'S NOTES 444

GUIDE TO FURTHER READING AND RESEARCH 445

INDEX 451

Foreword

"THERE is no country in the world where the Christian religion retains a greater influence over the souls of men than America." So Tocqueville observed, while conceding elsewhere that in his stay in America he had met "nobody, lay or cleric," who did not agree about the complete separation of church and state. The astute French observer had put his finger on an American paradox, for, despite the general obeisance to religious values by the American people, divided as they were by numerous sects, there was no country where one could find a greater degree of religious toleration or where government exercised less authority over religious life.

The comprehension of this American paradox is the central theme of Norman Cousins's *The Republic of Reason*, wherein explanations are sought by probing the religious views of the Founding Fathers. What gives special pertinence to Norman Cousins's illuminating documentary is the fact that this attitude held by Americans toward the relation of their government to religion was not confined to the age of the Founding Fathers but still remains both paradoxical and complex.

Debates are being currently waged in courts and legislatures, on the federal level and in state and town governments, in pulpits and the media over the degree to which the First Amendment forbids government aid to religion. Advocates of some form of prayer in the schools (even "a moment of silence") and a variety of devices to fund parochial and private education have argued that "the wall of separation" between church and state that Jefferson described was a "metaphor" that few of the Founding Fathers shared with him. Similarly the "creationists," who demand equal space or time in textbooks and classroom teaching with the advocates of evolution, pose a test to the government's neutrality in the conflict between science and revealed religion.

In his examination of the religious ideas of the Founding Fathers, Norman Cousins discovers areas of diversity and those of common accord.

Although governed by Enlightenment thinking, the Founding Fathers, unlike their European counterparts, the *philosophes*, failed to manifest overt hostility to traditional Christianity (with Thomas Paine the special exception). Deists like Franklin and Jefferson had no difficulty in reconciling their private skepticism with public orthodoxy. Jefferson declared that "religion belonged solely to man and God" and defined the nonestablishment clause of the First Amendment as erecting a wall of separation between state and church. Yet he devoted considerable time in later life to writing a book on the teachings of Jesus, whose moral ideas he endorsed while questioning his divine nature. At the other end of the religious spectrum one finds Samuel Adams, John Jay, and Benjamin Rush, all devout observers, unquestioning in their acceptance of revealed religion.

Varied though the Founding Fathers may have been in the degree to which they paid obeisance to rational currents and in their display of outward piety, they were nonetheless in general accord in their support of religious toleration. Where we do find subtle differences, as Norman Cousins has demonstrated, is in their attitude toward the separation of church and state.

In a postrevolutionary era marked by the disestablishment of the Church of England and the upthrust of religious pluralism, the issue was no longer whether government, state or federal, should support one preferred church. Rather, did people see the issue as between strict neutrality on the part of government (a neutrality that would take the form of providing support for all Christian denominations) or complete abstention from support for religion?

That issue was central to church-state debates in Virginia beginning with the outbreak of the American Revolution and continuing down through the following decade. Since these debates provide essential background to the First Amendment, they justify special examination. The controversy may be said to have begun when George Mason, the chief architect of Virginia's Bill of Rights as well as the state's Constitution of 1776, had drafted a section providing "that all men should enjoy the fullest toleration in the exercise of religion according to the dictates of conscience, unpunished, and unrestrained by the magistrate, unless, under colour of religion, any man disturb the peace, the happiness, or safety of society, or of individuals."

That did not go far enough for James Madison, who persuaded the Virginia Convention to replace Mason's words "fullest toleration in the exercise of religion" with "free exercise of religion," a more sweeping phrase, implying an inherent personal right rather than a limit upon state action, and without any exceptions. The movement for religious freedom coincided with an initiative by Thomas Jefferson to disestablish the Church of England. In the postwar period, when Jefferson was at his diplomatic post in Paris, James Madison espoused his sponsor's cause. In the Virginia legislature he managed to block the effort of the Protestant Episcopal Church, the successor in the States to the Church of England, to have a general assessment levied for the support of religion and to incorporate the clergy of their denomination.

Recognizing that in its proposed form the assessment bill would have little chance of passing, Patrick Henry and other proponents of church support broadened the scope of the bill to require people to pay a tax "for the support of the Christian religion or of some Church, denomination or communion of Christians or of some form of Christian worship." The bill precipitated a great debate between Henry and Madison. The former argued that the decline of religion went hand in hand with the decline of the state. Madison denied that religion was necessary to the state and questioned whether religious establishments were necessary even for religion itself. If one wishes to improve morals, Madison insisted, then improve the administration of justice, set a personal example by moral behavior and by suitable provisions for the education of young people.

What is especially noteworthy is that the debate could hardly be considered to be challenging the values of religion but as centering on the issue of what kind of Christian society the state needed or should support. Madison, while pointing out the inherent dangers of leaving it to the courts to decide what Christianity really was, what parts of the Scripture were canonical or apocryphal, and whether one should obtain salvation alone or in conjunction with good works, avoided a frontal attack on Christianity.

Now the pro-assessment delegates countered with a proposal to include all religions in the assessment plan and also to permit the incorporation of all Christian societies desiring it. In fact, however, when the bill was finally presented to the legislature it confined incorporation to the Episcopal Church. Hoping to stem a rising tide of opposition to the bill, its proponents camouflaged it by including a clause providing that money not allocated for any particular sect of taxpayers should be disposed of "for the encouragement of seminaries of learning within the counties whence such sums shall arise." Since most education was in the hands of parish schools, the proposition was in diametrical opposition to Jefferson's free public school system proposed back in 1779. The incorporation bill, as it went through various revisions, was finally defeated in large measure due to the opposition of the Episcopal laity who found it seriously defective from the point of view of their control.

With church incorporation dead, Madison was now free to rally opinion against the assessment measure in the Piedmont and the dissenting interior counties. Back in June of 1785, he had scored a great propaganda coup by drafting a "Memorial and Remonstrance against Religious Assessments." The "Memorial" elicited so extraordinary a popular response that the assessment bill never even came up for a vote. The results must have pleased George Washington, who deplored the political divisions that the bill might raise and had expressed the hope that it "would die an easy death."

It would be fair to say that few state papers framed in the revolutionary era had so momentous an impact on American constitutional law as did Madison's "Memorial and Remonstrance." It was the principal authority for the scholarly dissenting opinion of Justice Rutledge in a 1947 decision of the Supreme Court in which a five-to-four majority upheld reimbursing parents with public funds for costs of transportation to parochial schools. Madison's "Memorial" is the great omnipresence overhanging every court confronted with the variety of subterfuges that are being continually proposed to provide tax support for church or private schools.

In his "Memorial and Remonstrance," Madison declared that the right of every man to exercise religion according to his own conviction and conscience is a right guaranteed by the Virginia Declaration of Rights and deemed inalienable. Arguing that religion was wholly exempt from the authority of society at large and *a fortiori* from a legislative body, he denounced as "tyrants" those rulers who would encroach on the right of the people and denigrated as "slaves" the people who would submit to such encroachments.

This was strong language indeed, but Madison regarded the move toward establishment and assessments as constituting the first serious challenge to America's liberties. Citing the American Revolution as an example, he declared, "The freemen of America did not wait till usurped power had strengthened itself by exercise, and entangled the question in precedents." Who does not see, he asked, that "the same authority which can force a citizen to contribute three pence only of his property for the support of any one establishment, may force him to conform to any other establishment in all cases whatsoever?" As in the case of the popular resistance to the tea tax, Madison, a true revolutionary, looked beyond the trivial levy that was contemplated to aid religious teachers and saw as its logical consequence the imposition of church control upon the state. To Madison the issue posed by assessment constituted a test of the fundamental rights guaranteed by Virginia's Declaration of Rights. If the legislature could demolish this right, then they could control the freedom of the press, abolish trial by jury, and, indeed, deprive the people of the suffrage and even establish "an independent and hereditary assembly." Such authority Madison denied to his state's legislative body.

Madison may have been puzzled by the inconsistency of the Confederation Congress on this issue when legislating for the territories. Just a few months before he drew up his "Memorial and Remonstrance," Congress, in voting a plan for the government of the western territories, retained a clause setting aside one section in each township for the support of public schools while striking out the provision reserving a section for the support of religion. Madison's comment: "How a regulation so unjust in itself, so foreign to the authority of Congress, and so hurtful to the sale of public land and smelling strongly of an antiquated bigotry, could have received the countenance of a committee is truly a matter of astonishment."

What must he have thought when he learned that Congress, sitting in New York during July of 1787, while Madison was attending the Constitutional Convention in Philadelphia, sought in its justly celebrated Northwest Ordinance to provide in Article I for liberty of conscience while asserting at the same time that "religion, morality, and knowledge being necessary for good government and the happiness of mankind," schools and the means of education shall forever be encouraged. Following its passage, Congress then authorized the sale by the Board of Treasury of large tracts of land to the Ohio Company with the provision that lot number 29 of each township be given for the support of religion. Significantly, Congress in 1789, while reenacting the Northwest Ordinance, omitted the arrangement for setting aside a lot in each township for the support of religion.

Among some states, however, political discrimination against non-Christians continued to prevail. Not knowing what was transpiring at the secret Constitutional Convention in Philadelphia, the Jews of that city memorialized the Convention to avoid including in the federal Constitution the objectionable test oath in the existing Pennsylvania Constitution that required members of the assembly of that state to subscribe to a declaration acknowledging both the Old and the New Testament "to be given by divine inspiration." Some weeks earlier, however, Charles Cotesworth Pinckney had submitted to the Convention, for reference to the Committee of Detail, a number of propositions, among them: "No religious test or qualification shall ever be annexed to any oath or office under authority of the United States." This proposition was referred to the Committee of Detail without debate or further consideration. When the committee reported back, Pinckney then moved to amend the article with the addition of these words: "but no religious test shall ever be required as a qualification to any office of public trust under the authority of the United States." Roger Sherman thought the clause unnecessary, "the prevailing liberality being a sufficient security against such tests." But Gouverneur Morris and General Pinckney backed the motion, which was agreed to unanimously.

The entire article was adopted, with only North Carolina voting "no" and Maryland divided.

Although the Constitution was signed with this enlightened provision and although that document enumerates no power to the federal government to establish religion or interfere with its free exercise, its silence on those latter subjects, among other criticisms of the document at the various state ratifying conventions, prompted the first Congress under Madison's prodding to propose twelve amendments, the ten finally ratified being known as the Bill of Rights. It was Madison's version of the first guaranty of the First Amendment—the nonestablishment clause—that survived in its final form, along with a provision forbidding Congress from making any law "prohibiting the free exercise thereof." Madison would have prohibited the states as well as Congress from infringing on freedom of conscience, speech, press, and trial by jury in criminal cases, but Congress overruled him, and it was not until the Fourteenth Amendment that the Constitution would impose significant limits upon state powers to infringe individual liberties.

On its face the record suggests complete abstention of the federal government from religion, but the politicians were too knowledgeable of the depth of public religiosity to cut the state off from all connection with religion and morality. The years in which the Constitution was created and put into early operation were a time of deep faith. Many citizens embraced a civil religion based on morality and public virtue, while in these very same years church membership burgeoned and Protestant sects multiplied. Indeed, a religious revival had preceded the American Revolution, and a second one, even more sweeping in character, would grip the nation after the founding of the federal government. The appearance of the latter coincided with deistic and rational currents and advances in science. While in America toleration in religion was the rule, not the exception, the public expected the federal government or its officials to avow some regard for religion. The Constitution merely requires the president at his inauguration to take an oath or affirm faithfully to execute his office and to the best of his ability "preserve, protect, and defend the Constitution of the United States." But beginning with George Washington that oath has been customarily taken on the Bible (which the first President kissed), although two presidents have exercised their privilege of so affirming. Congress chooses and pays chaplains. Chaplains are provided for the armed services and federal prisons. Congress, under its taxing power, has made exceptions for churches and clergy members. Under its power to raise armies, Congress has exempted conscientious objectors and clergy members. Beginning with the first president (Thomas Jefferson excepted),

Thanksgiving Day proclamations have been customarily issued. The dollar bill avows "In God We Trust," and the pledge of allegiance, since President Eisenhower, contains the phrase "under God." Indeed, while repeatedly affirming our conviction of the need for a strict separation of state and church, we have constantly associated our various governments with religious and moral values and, as a nation, invoked divine help in times of crisis.

These compromises would hardly come as a shock to the principled Founding Fathers, whose religious views Norman Cousins illuminates. They were rationalists and products of the Enlightenment, but they were also successful politicians who were not prepared to affront public opinion. Hence, in recognizing the paradoxes and complexities that characterized American society in their day, they left us with deeply abiding problems still unresolved.

Richard B. Morris
Columbia University

Introduction

ALMOST every schoolchild can recite the basic facts about Columbus's discovery of America. Very few of them, however, know that Spain received title to the New World as a result of a decision in 1494 by Pope Alexander VI. Portugal had laid claim to the lands discovered by Columbus, but the pope ruled that Spain should be given possession of everything west of the Azores and Cape Verde islands, which is to say, North America. Everything east of the line would go to Portugal. In 1495, seeking to mollify Portugal, the pope moved the dividing line further west. Thus it was that Brazil became a Portuguese possession.

The fact that religious authority dictated not just affairs within nations but among them may come as a surprise to modern generations of Americans, whose view of history is shaped largely by their own "past"—a past symbolized by independence from outside authority. For most of the earth's inhabitants, however, religion has been a predominant political force throughout history. The influence of Confucianism in China; of Hinduism in the Indian subcontinent; of Moslem belief in the Near East, Southeast Asia, and Africa; of Buddhism and Shintoism in the Far East; and of Christianity throughout the world—all these basic religious ingredients have been at the center of political history for hundreds of years. More than four hundred years after the Magna Carta, King Charles I contended that the High Court of Justice had no authority to try him on charges of having violated the basic freedoms of English citizens. His defense was that his authority came not from Parliament but from God. This argument was not without historical substance or precedent; the divine right of kings was a standard feature of monarchy in England and elsewhere.

The abuses that proceeded out of the fixed idea that political rulers were God's agents on earth were a prime reason for the migration of English citizens to the New World. In seeking escape from religious tyranny, however, the new settlers did not leave behind all religious control of political activities.

The Founding Fathers could ponder the paradox that many thousands of settlers had come to this country to escape from the oppressive religious

1

atmosphere of England and other nations in Europe and had promptly established similar repressions in their new surroundings. It is one of the ironies of human history that what was to be a religious haven in the New World turned into an arena of fierce religious competition and discrimination. Puritans, whose beliefs were similar in many ways to those of the Quakers, found nothing in their creed to keep them from legislating against members of the Society of Friends. Indeed, Puritan Massachusetts in colonial America banished Quakers from their state on pain of death. And when Quakers persisted in returning in defiance of law and in practicing their religious faith, the Puritans made good the threat. Quaker women were burned at the stake. The anti-Quaker law adopted by the Pilgrims of Plymouth Colony in 1658 declared that "No Quaker Rantor or any other such corrupt person shall be a freeman of this Corporation." No doubt the Puritans felt they had every right to maintain their own religious community, but, as Jefferson and Madison pointed out later, religious monopoly and religious oppression are not far apart.

In Virginia, where the Church of England was accepted as the prevailing religion of the people, restrictions against dissenters were hardly less severe than in England itself. Baptists, Quakers, and Catholics were specific targets. Any Quaker who was discovered inside the state was jailed without bail. The laws prohibited the publication or distribution of any book of pamphlets containing articles of Quaker faith.

In Virginia, too, all sorts of penalties or restrictions were imposed on the unorthodox. At the beginning of the eighteenth century, a law was passed that virtually defined the nature of belief for Christians. Denial of the authority of the Old and New Testaments was illegal. Offenders who were judged guilty could be barred from public office. Repeated offenders risked jail. Little wonder that Virginians such as Washington, Jefferson, and Madison believed the situation to be intolerable.

Even in Quaker Pennsylvania during the colonial period, all citizens were subjected to religious restrictions. An act passed in 1700, for example, required all citizens to attend church on Sunday or prove they had been at home reading the Scriptures. Failure to do so was subject to fines.

Prejudice against Catholics in most of the states was especially severe. It was not unusual for the Catholic church to be attacked from the Puritan pulpit in New England. Anti-Catholicism flared up time and again in pamphlets and in political activity. In the early colonial period, Catholics flocked to Maryland, which had been assured freedom of religious worship by its founder, Lord Baltimore. Catholics wrote the early laws of Baltimore and administered a state that for a time had one of the finest records for religious freedom among the colonies. But when the Protestants came into authority, especially after 1689, Catholics felt the weight of repressive legislation.

In Massachusetts and Connecticut—and, in fact, in varying degrees throughout the colonies—there was mounting resentment because of the favored position given members of the clergy. These privileges led to specific abuses. It was not only the substantial wealth and property holdings of some clergymen that gave rise to public concern but the extent to which ecclesiastical authority spilled over into the political. Such abuses were believed by many to constitute more of a threat to religion than any of the activities of the dissenters. It was pointed out that many of the reforms preached by Jesus were again in urgent demand.

It was against this background that the Founding Fathers were determined that a person's religious beliefs were his private concern and an inviolate right. The Constitution-makers were students of history; they were also students of human behavior. Nothing to them was more certain than that the same conditions and circumstances that produced tyranny or persecution in one place would, if repeated, produce them in another place. It was not that the Founding Fathers were cynical. They believed in the natural goodness of human beings and in the capacity of the human being to build tall edifices of nobility and decency. But they also knew that this natural goodness had to be protected if it was to be developed. They knew, too, that a poorly constructed society—that is, a society in which laws can be altered or improvised by those on or close to the seat of power—is a society that scorns natural rights and tends to have contempt for the individual human being.

What especially troubled the Founding Fathers were the religious requirements for public office in many of the states. New Hampshire, New Jersey, North Carolina, South Carolina, and Georgia required members of their state legislatures to be Protestants. Pennsylvania required a belief in God and in the inspiration of the Scriptures. Unitarians, Jews, and Catholics did not qualify for public office in most of the states.

Charles Pinckney of South Carolina proposed at the Constitutional Convention that such restrictions be prohibited. Pinckney's text stated: "No religious test or qualification shall ever be annexed to any oath of office under the authority of the United States." Later, Pinckney sharpened the proposal in these words: "No religious test shall ever be required as a qualification to any office or public trust under the authority of the United States." The Constitutional Convention adopted the motion unanimously.

One of the common misconceptions of the American past is that the colonies, having won their revolution against Great Britain, proceeded immediately to consolidate that victory by organizing themselves into the

United States of America as we know it today. But as numerous histories make clear, victory in the War for Independence led to a period of confusion and disintegration in the relationships of the former colonies. Conflicting territorial claims, interstate trade rivalries, and different currencies, to say nothing of complications arising out of different customs, languages, and religions, threatened to dissolve the gains of independence.

After the treaty with Great Britain in 1783 formalizing the end of the war, the absence of workable authority on the collective level disfigured the relationships among the states. The debates of the Philadelphia Constitutional Convention, therefore, focused on much more than the need to institutionalize the separation from Great Britain. Those debates were directed to the need to make independence work. Of equal importance were basic philosophical and historical issues. What, essentially, constituted a nation? If the biblical injunction—render unto God that which is God's and unto Caesar that which is Caesar's—was to serve as a governing principle, how were God and Caesar to be defined? How was authority to be divided between the central government and the government of the states? A collective entity was necessary if the former colonies were to function without conflict or disintegration; but how to create such an entity? How to create a working balance between the authority of the states and the authority of the national government? And, of equal importance, what about the relationship of the individual citizen to the state and to the collective unit of the states?

What about human rights? The men who met at Philadelphia in 1787 believed that human beings possessed natural rights just in the act of being born. There was no clear line of agreement at Philadelphia, however, as to how natural rights were to be manifested or upheld. Finally, what was to be learned from human experience?

One of the primary gifts of the Founding Fathers to the American people was to endow their nation with historical memory. James Madison's records of the constitutional debates and the *Federalist Papers* reflect the respect of the American Founding Fathers for historical experience. The rise and fall of nations served as their classroom. The questions that had to be resolved touched off fascinating discussions. There was hardly a subject that did not evoke some reference to an historical event or historical principle.

In a literal sense, the Founding Fathers would include everyone who had a vital part in establishing the American colonies and in molding American freedoms and independence. Every signer of the Declaration of Independence and the Constitution of the United States—indeed every governor and every member of every ratifying state legislature—could with varying degrees of justification be represented.

Over the years, however, there has been a logical tendency to use the term more selectively. Out of the many hundreds of names a few are now generally regarded as the principal founders. These are the key figures in setting America free and in building a new nation. This book uses the term "Founding Fathers" in that sense. It deals with the personal philosophies of George Washington, Benjamin Franklin, Thomas Jefferson, John Adams, Samuel Adams, James Madison, Alexander Hamilton, Thomas Paine, and John Jay. There are others—John Dickinson, Patrick Henry, Benjamin Rush, James Otis, Philip Freneau, Charles Pinckney, James Wilson, Roger Sherman, and Gouverneur Morris among them—who have legitimate claims to inclusion, but the group discussed in this book is supremely representative of the composite leadership of the period.

It has often been asked how, within a short span of time on the east coast of the North American continent, there should have sprung up such a rare array of genius—men who seemed in command of historical experience and who combined moral imagination with a flair for leadership. Part of the answer is that these men invested their combined strength in a great idea. James Madison, for example, had urgent thoughts about what people had to do to become free and remain free; but he did not feel he had relieved himself of his obligation to serve those ideas when he set them down in the public prints. It was also necessary for him to join his concerns to those of other men who were in a position to exert leadership. Madison wanted to prove his ideas in direct contact with minds he respected.

The young men who designed the government of the United States— many of them were in their thirties—were a talented and influential group of joiners. They were joiners not in the sense that they belonged to any band or group that came forward. They were the kind of working joiners who, like the philosopher-statesmen of early Greece, sought perfection through an integrated wholeness. The young American giants knew how to put men and ideas together. They connected their spiritual beliefs to political action. They saw no walls separating science, philosophy, religion, and art.

The term "whole man" has become somewhat frayed in our time through endless argument over its essential meaning: exactly what is a "whole man"? To the extent that example has the power to settle an argument, it may be rewarding to scrutinize the human display case of the revolutionary period of our history. The youthful Founding Fathers were, many of them, dramatic examples of whole men. What was most remarkable about this was that they themselves saw nothing remarkable about it. They believed it entirely natural that a human being should seek and achieve the broadest possible personal development. Indeed it was unnatural for a person to be shut off from anything inside him capable of growth. For natural rights were not limited to the political. Natural rights had something to do with the place of the individual in the world and the stretching power of individual spirit and talent. The end of government, therefore, was to translate freedom into creative growth. The whole men it helped to produce understood the difficult business of operating a complex society.

I must not make it seem that we are dealing here with men who were so preoccupied with grand designs and abstractions that they knew little about the enjoyment of living. Far from it. They had a zest for life. It grew out of a conviction that life must be lived at its fullest, whether for the individual or the society itself. An exciting life was more than high adventure or fancy diversions. It depended not at all on the standardized situations that were supposed to stimulate or satisfy. A truly exciting life was connected to high sensitivity. For awareness came with the gifts of life. In order to mean anything, awareness had to be sharpened and put to work.

The letters the Founding Fathers wrote to each other reflected a rounded view of life and a sensitivity to the needs and potentialities of human beings. There was respect for the growing universe of knowledge and the possibilities of progress. But these letters also tell us a great deal about the kind of men who wrote them. They make it clear that they helped to educate one another. They shared in an adventure of mutual growth, pooling their observations about life, their insights into behavior, and their convictions about government.

Most of the Founding Fathers carried on a vast correspondence—much of it with one another—long after the Revolution was won and the United States of America had become an established government. They considered letter writing an essential part of the intellectual diet of a rounded person. The exchange between Thomas Jefferson and John Adams, for example, has few equals for depth, range of subject matter, literary style, and general intellectual achievement in recorded correspondence. Philosophy, religion, science, literature, economics, history, anthropology, music, politics—nothing in human experience or attainment was alien to them. And all the strands of their multiple interests were woven together into a single smooth texture. Adams and Jefferson were dealing with the nature of human life and its basic needs. Any great area of human achievement was therefore a logical and important part of their total concern.

George Washington and Benjamin Franklin registered their main impact on their contemporaries through the force of their personalities rather than through any detailed exposition of their political ideas and philosophy. They had declared their allegiance to certain fundamental principles. Others might analyze and refine those principles and project them against the historical background or become their inspired advocates before the public. Washington and Franklin were concerned with the larger design and the need to keep it intact. Washington's sense of timing was excellent. He permitted just enough play of debate to bring out the full color of an issue; but he generally stepped in when the momentum of argument threatened a costly showdown. Franklin, too, was the architect of consent, more interested in helping to create an atmosphere in which meaningful agreement was possible than in advancing fixed ideas of his own. All these men were part of the total process of mutual education that figured so largely in the intellectual achievements of the group as a whole.

Washington's role as a personal court of appeals was not an easy one, especially as it concerned the exchanges between Jefferson and Hamilton in the early years of the republic. Each found it necessary to come to him with long detailed arguments against the position of the other. But it was the mark of Washington's genius that for a considerable time he was able to retain both men in the service of the nation. This was a prodigious asset for a young nation that needed the spirit of freedom that Jefferson helped to give it and the constitutional framework that Hamilton helped to build.

Students of American history have tended over the years to divide themselves into opposing camps on the Jefferson-Hamilton issue. Yet it is possible to define a third position—one that regards both men as a unit and champions their joint contribution. For the emphasis of Hamilton on the form of free government was joined to the emphasis of Jefferson on the substance of free government.

The American Constitution is not a compromise between the ideas of the Jeffersonians and Hamiltonians. It is actually a working combination of these ideas. And it may help us to blunt the cutting edge of the competition between the two if we remind ourselves that Jefferson gave the place of honor inside his home at Monticello, just inside the front door, to the bust of Hamilton.

Thomas Paine's relation to the other Founding Fathers was perhaps not as intimate or as sustained as the relations of the other men to one another. He helped to create a climate of necessity for the kind of leadership that Washington and Jefferson had to offer. But he tended, often at moments of triumph, to draw off by himself or to become involved elsewhere. Even so, he cannot be considered apart from the joint enterprise that characterized this period of American history.

No man of the time felt more deeply about the issue of national and personal freedom than did Paine. No one worked harder than Paine to ignite the minds of the people on the issues of the Revolution. He believed

that the struggle against England was actually a summing up of the great
test facing the people of the Western world. He saw this struggle as a
laboratory that might prove to people everywhere that freedom could be
the portion of all. The universalism of his concerns accounted for his
remarkable power outside America. But inside America he tended to operate on his own.

Any attempt to view the Founding Fathers against the religious background of their times must begin with the fact that the background was
highly varied. The religions of the colonies, like the peoples themselves,
had neither a common origin nor a dominant evolving character. The
main differences in religion were regional, but even within the regions
themselves there were interesting mixtures.

In New England, for example, the religious situation changed during
different periods of its development. The seventeenth and eighteenth centuries produced changes both in the nature and direction of religious
organizations. While New England went by the general description of
Puritan, that term is much too broad to define the religious or social
complexion of the region. Ralph Barton Perry, in his *Puritanism and
Democracy*, describes Puritanism as a "theocratic, Congregational, Presbyterian, Calvinistic, Protestant, medieval Christianity. . . . Each of these
five factors comprises a set of ideas, and they compose an orderly succession in which each in turn qualifies its predecessor. Thus Protestantism,
Presbyterianism and Congregationalism are forms of Calvinism, and Puritan theocracy a form of Presbyterianism and Congregationalism."

Calvinism was more than a series of fixed points on a theological
compass; it was a way of life that embraced and affected politics, economics, social outlook, and, to be sure, individual behavior. It insisted on
vigorous denial of worldly pleasures and natural weakness. It quoted scriptural
authority to ban a wide variety of human activities, including theatergoing
and dancing. But agencies can take just so much joy out of life before they
create powerful counterforces. And, as usually happens in reform movements, the reaction was directed not against the institution or the name
but against its unwanted manifestations. Just as Christianity split itself into
countless contrasting and often conflicting movements, each of them retaining the name of Christ, so in a more limited way Calvinism in New
England had its divergent groups, each professing Calvinism and seeking
to keep it pure.

New England was a reflection of the crosscurrents that gave motion and
unpredictability to all sections of America. New York and Pennsylvania
were both the main melting pots and the main population distribution
centers. The favorite regions for the non-English-speaking peoples after

New York and Pennsylvania seemed to be the Carolinas, Virginia, and Maryland. French Huguenots who fled persecution came to Massachusetts, Virginia, New York, and South Carolina. There was a major German migration to Pennsylvania, already the home of Quakers and the related German sects. There were also Mennonites and some Anabaptists and Waldenses. The Dunkers, a German Baptist group, arrived almost in their total membership in Pennsylvania. Other Germans settled in New York and the Carolinas.

Jewish settlers came from Spain by way of Holland and found a haven in New York and Rhode Island. Perhaps the largest exodus of all at the time was represented by the migration of Presbyterian settlers from Ulster, Ireland, most of whom came to Pennsylvania in the mountain country west of the Susquehanna River. The large numbers of Dutch people who created a New Amsterdam added to the color, the wealth, and the variety of the human mixture that was the new America.

All these groups had their own religious experiences and outlooks, divisions and subdivisions, branches and subbranches. Far from representing any weakness of the whole, they provided strength. As Jefferson and various others have pointed out, what was true of America politically was true in the reverse spiritually. In politics it was thus: United we stand, divided we fall. In religion: Divided we stand, united we fall.

Considering the fact of this mixture, one might wonder how it would be possible for any great ideas to take hold and what the magic was that enabled a varied society to be affected by a new set of values or directions. The answer is to be found in the history of ideas. An idea does not have to find its mark in the minds of large numbers of people in order to create an incentive for change. Ideas have a life of their own. They can be nourished and brought to active growth by a small number of sensitive, vital minds that somehow respond to the needs of a total organism, however diffused the parts of that organism may be. These minds sense both the need for change and the truth of ideas that define the nature of change. When the ideas are articulated and advocated, the popular response is not merely the product of logic reaping its gains but of a dormant awareness coming to life. In a large sense this is what happened in the period of the Great Awakening in New England. Edwin Scott Gaustad has shown how from 1740 to 1742, widespread change and upheaval took place. Religion was made less forbidding, less complicated and detached, more responsive to human temper and weakness.

Similarly, the general impact of the Enlightenment on a varied America did not take the form of a unified mass movement that swept aside all contrary institutions. What happened was a new infusion of intellectual energy, a rising sense of conviction that there were wrongs that had to be set right, that sacrifice was essential, and that the moment was now. People did not have to pursue the words that would give meaning to the big ideas; the words were there all the time, waiting to be discovered and used. Thus, the precise phrases of the Declaration of Independence occurred to many people almost at the same time, all of them experiencing the shock of recognition when they discovered they were not alone. Jefferson threw the grand loop; he brought the words, the need, and the moment together.

To say that the Founding Fathers were the product of the Age of Enlightenment does not mean that they had a uniform view of religion or philosophy or anything else. All the Enlightenment did—and this was enough—was to give people greater confidence than before in the reach of human intelligence. It provided new vitality and scope for the free will in the shaping of society. People could still be different in their approach to life, government, or religion. But at least they had a new sense of the possibilities of effective action based on thought and a respect for each other's rights in the adventure of change.

What was most significant about the Enlightenment was that its impact was felt throughout a large part of the Western world. For many generations, inspiring things had been said about natural rights or the natural reaches of human intelligence. Men like Francis Bacon, Newton, Galileo, Copernicus, Comenius, Sir John Harrington, Leibnitz, Locke, Hobbes, Montesquieu, and Quesnay provided the theory. The Jesuits who returned from their mission in China made an historic contribution to the philosophy of freedom when they brought back with them new insights into natural law and the inalienable rights of human beings. These insights influenced the thinking of the Physiocrats in France, who in turn influenced people in the new world and eventually would hold it together.

The soil of an Age of Enlightenment had been carefully prepared. Then, in the latter half of the eighteenth century and early nineteenth century, all the seeds of the free mind seemed to sprout at the same time. Jefferson and Madison and Adams did not exist in splendid geographical isolation. England vibrated with the new spirit of intellectual emancipation. Throughout almost all Europe, in fact, the air was alive with ideas. Joseph Priestly (so admired by Franklin and Jefferson), Richard Price, Arthur Young, Jeremy Bentham, and William Godwin in Great Britain; Lessing and Goethe in Germany; Voltaire, Diderot, Turgot, and Condorcet in France; Henry Grattan and John Philpot Curran in Ireland; David Hume in Scotland—all these and many more were taking part in the same intellectual adventure. The same things were being said throughout the Western world about human rights and the human potential. Some years later, Daniel Webster summed it up:

The whole world is becoming a common field for intellect to act in. Energy of mind, genius, power, wheresoever it exists, may speak out in any tongue, and the world will hear it. A great chord of sentiment and feeling runs through two continents, and vibrates over both. Every breeze wafts intelligence from country to country; every wave tolls it; all give it forth and all in turn receive it. There is a vast commerce of ideas; there are marts and exchanges for intellectual discoveries, and a wonderful fellowship of those individual intelligences which make up the mind and opinion of the age.

Mind is the great lever of all things; human thought is the process by which human ends are ultimately answered; and the diffusion of knowledge, so astonishing in the last half-century, has rendered innumerable minds, variously gifted by nature, competent to be competitors or fellow-workers on the theater of intellectual cooperation.

All in all, it was an exciting time to be alive. Human suffering and submission to tyranny—whatever the source—were no longer to be accepted supinely as the natural form of political existence. The divine right of kings was to be reexamined and resisted. The aim was to develop habits of critical thinking that would give arbitrary government a hard time. Human beings questioned their religions as they did everything else. Not that there was an inevitable and stern conflict between reason and faith. As Carl Becker points out in *The Heavenly City of the Eighteenth Century Philosopher*, it was unfortunate that the term "rationalist" took on the connotation of an unbeliever in contrast to the term "man of faith." Such misuse, he said, "obscures the fact that reason may be used to support faith as well as to destroy it."

The American Founding Fathers—to the extent that they can be regarded as a group—believed deeply in the ability of human beings to take part in self-government; in the capacity of people to make sense of their lives if given reasonable conditions within society itself; in the responsive power of people when exposed to great ideas; in the ability of people to stand upright spiritually without ornate or complicated props; in due process of law; in the right of human beings to make basic decisions concerning their religions or anything else—again given the proper conditions.

It was inevitable, perhaps, that the intellectual momentum generated in so many places over so many years would carry society far beyond what had been considered possible limits only a short time earlier. Theology became an especially inviting arena for lay inquiry and exploration. For the more people probed the universe and the more they became acquainted with the wonder of life itself, the more interested they became in a first cause. They wanted an unobstructed outlet for their contemplations or their speculations. When they questioned denominational religion, it was not because they questioned the spiritual urge in human beings but because they felt that the evolution of religion should keep pace with the expanding horizons of human intellect and progress. Most of all, they respected the right of people to attach spiritual significance to the great questions and great mysteries. They were opposed to legislation that sought literal acceptance of biblical interpretation of the universe and humanity's place in it. Similarly, they were opposed to laws—which actually existed in several of the American states—making church attendance compulsory. Man's approach to God, they believed, was as personal as his own soul. And they objected, too, to the kind of privileges that enabled some members of the clergy to enjoy the perquisites and authority of royalty.

Jefferson in particular sought to rescue religious belief from the kind of state sponsorship or entanglement that often led to injustice and discrimination. His argument was not against faith but against monopoly and political power under religious auspices. Indeed, he believed that faith could best survive when relieved of the burden of governing through enforced belief. He was convinced that the more people knew about science, the greater would be their respect for the Deity. To him, the universe was far more mysterious and grandiose than the fundamentalist view claimed.

It is significant that most of the Founding Fathers grew up in a strong religious atmosphere; some had Calvinist family backgrounds. In reacting against it, they did not react against basic religious ideas or what they considered to be the spiritual nature of humanity. Most certainly they did not turn against God or lose their respect for religious belief. Indeed, it was their very concern for the conditions under which free religious belief was possible that caused them to invest so much of their thought and energy into the cause of human rights.

As a group, they reflected a fair degree of diversity in their individual creeds. Certainly, Samuel Adams's Puritanism was in stark contrast with Thomas Paine's Deism. Where we find a large measure of unity is in the position or attitudes of the Founding Fathers toward religion in general. It is therefore necessary to make a distinction between their personal articles of faith and their historical role with reference to the development of religion in America.

The pages that follow have much to say on both scores. It is important to emphasize here, however, that one of the causes that brought the founders together was the relationship of government to religion and the place of the individual with reference to both. For the founders believed that religious experience was intensely personal; they were mindful of the ease with which religions tended to be arrayed against each other, often at the expense of religion itself. Therefore, if the natural right to religious beliefs was to be upheld, the individual had to be protected against both the authoritarian anti-religious state and religious monopoly.

For confirmation, the founders had only to consult history. Many denominations, in a clear position of authority, were unable to resist the temptation of monopoly. Hence the need to guarantee the religious freedom of all as the best way of serving the spiritual needs of the individual. Rights were "God-given"; man was "endowed by his Creator"; there were "natural laws" and "natural rights"; freedom was related to the "sacredness" of humanity. The development of a free man was not divorced from the idea of moral man, any more than religious man could be separated from moral man. There was also strong spiritual content in the confidence of the American founders in the capacity of man to govern his own affairs, to hold the ultimate power in the operation of his society, and to be able to decide correctly when given access to vital information.

Hence the emphasis of the founders on the need to keep the power centers of government under careful scrutiny and control. No man—no matter how high his position in government—could exempt himself from laws that applied to all. This made more than one principal branch of government necessary, preventing those who enacted the laws from enforcing them and those who enforced them from interpreting them. It also made for a certain cumbersomeness in the operation of government, but even this was not without its advantages, especially when it tended to protect the people from the kinds of short cuts that stressed greater efficiency as the justification for greater power. Much later, when America was confronted by grave economic problems and by massive external threats, it was to become necessary to increase the federal authority substantially beyond that envisioned in 1787–89, but the system of checks and balances survived the transition and indeed became strengthened.

In any event, the men who brought this nation into being were determined to design a structure in which, so far as was possible, human error in the operation of government would occur in the open and its effects carefully contained. They were utterly disdainful of the best-man theory of government; i.e., get the right people into positions of authority and the government will take care of itself. History was littered with the wreckage of governments headed by good people gone wrong.

Similarly, as it concerned the Constitution of a free people, the Founding Fathers were concerned with the built-in protections and conditions that made such institutions possible. Constitutional provisions might not provide absolute guarantees, but they at least defined the standard and fixed the responsibility of the state. In the relationship of government to religion, for example, there was a solid ring of conviction that tied the Founding Fathers to each other. The government was not to take upon itself the responsibility to determine the religion of its people.

The fact that there was to be no state church did not mean that the Founding Fathers did not respect the right to spiritual belief. They were aware of the persecution and discrimination that had existed in the colonies whenever the state sponsored its own church and arrogated to itself the right to legislate against dissenters. As a practical matter, it therefore became necessary to underwrite religious freedom for all. How, otherwise, to avoid an almost inevitable contest for power among the various denominations? The right of an individual to worship in his or her own way or not to worship at all was part of the protection to be afforded in a free society. If worship became compulsory, it would be only a matter of time before the state could decide what the form and place of worship were to be.

In addition to the erroneous notion that our religious freedoms are the sole reaction to the tyrannies of the Old World, there is yet another fallacy concerning the establishment of religious freedom in America. This is the fallacy that holds that most of the Founding Fathers were essentially agnostics or atheists. George Washington has been criticized over the years for his lack of formal belief. Thomas Jefferson has been described on occasion as a foe of organized religion. And familiar to all is the remark attributed to Theodore Roosevelt that Thomas Paine was a "filthy little atheist." But as the pages in this book seek to make clear, each of these men had highly developed personal beliefs. There was nothing unsubstantial or uninspired about their personal articles of faith. Such criticisms as they may have had of religious institutions were based less on theological than political grounds. It was only when a church, demanding freedom for itself, sought to deny it to others that they expressed opposition to religious organization. And even in the case of Thomas Paine, as may be observed in this volume, his main energies in the religious area were devoted to proving the existence of God and a universal design.

Recurrently, the question of religion in public life has been a major American political issue. Most frequently, the question has centered on the place of religion in public schools. As might be expected, this question has manifested itself in a wide variety of ways—all the way from the controversy over the teaching of evolution, going back to the twenties, to the debate over prayer in the classroom, up through the eighties. The arguments roll on endlessly—and the Constitution is generally invoked by opposite sides as justification for their positions. Is the U.S. Constitution so ambiguous on religion as to permit conflicting interpretations? The language of the Constitution is clear enough—at least on two points. No one who aspires to public office should be required to hold any particular religious affiliation or conform to any particular religious views. Also, no official seal of approval is to be placed on any religion. These two principles are clear enough. The difficulty arises over particular situations that are not expressly covered by the phrasing of constitutional provisions. For example, does classroom prayer run counter to the constitutional clause barring an "establishment of religion"? Similarly, if the theory of evolution is taught in biology classes, are the schools obligated (or permitted) to teach the biblical theory of creation?

If the arguments cannot be definitively resolved by reference to documents, then the obvious recourse must be to the intentions of those who inspired the documents. What were the religious views of the American Founding Fathers? How much is known about their personal beliefs that would throw light on the specific religious issues being debated today?

The materials for answering these questions are not meager or elusive. Thousands of letters, papers, memoirs, and documents exist on the philosophical and religious beliefs of the Founding Fathers. It is not necessary to interpret the thrust or significance of these materials; they provide an explicit and comprehensive account of ideas and attitudes bearing on religion in general and the role in particular of government in the religious life of the American people. Obviously, these materials are not uniform. But they do provide a clear view of the kind of thinking that resulted in such documents as the U.S. Constitution and the statutes of the individual states prior to federal union.

The purpose of this volume is to bring together in one place a representative account of the personal philosophies of the Founding Fathers. Thousands of letters, papers, memoirs, and documents have been examined. The attempt has been not to interpret but to record in their own words such materials as have a bearing on articles of personal faith or explorations into that vital and meaningful area where philosophy and religion meet.

The assembled materials would have made possible separate books rather than chapters on each of the individuals, certainly in the cases of Benjamin Franklin, Thomas Jefferson, and John Adams. It was essential, therefore, to use excerpts from letters, papers, and documents rather than the complete text in each case. In doing so, the editor has attempted to avoid any deletions that would change the context. In any event, students and researchers are asked to take note of the fact that most of the material is in the form of excerpts that are not to be mistaken for or used as complete statements. The editor also calls attention to the fact that punctuation and spelling have been adapted to the contemporary form in some of the selections for maximum reading facility.

1. BENJAMIN FRANKLIN

"I Never Was Without Some Religious Principles"

BENJAMIN FRANKLIN was a human prism who showed glittering lights no matter from what side he was viewed. Whether as philosopher, statesman, printer, scientist, mathematician, inventor, medical investigator, navigator, or agriculturist, he had something important to add to the store of the world's knowledge; and he did it with zest, charm, and a gift for the clear view. In an age known for its varied talents, he was easily America's most composite man. As such he won the respect and affection of Europe for himself and, to an almost equal extent, for his country. He was rounded in interests without being polished; aristocratic in intellect without being undemocratic in thought; daring in ideas without being impractical in their execution; perennially youthful in outlook but consistently mature in approach.

Of religion, he asked only that he be allowed to pay his respect to all— his way of saying that he did not want any denomination to be awarded authority over all others. "I have ever let others enjoy their religious sentiments," he wrote in his eighty-fourth year, "without reflecting on them for those who appeared to me unsupportable and even absurd."

His early religious education was as a Presbyterian, but it carried strong dissenter influences. The earlier family background had been Calvinist. He started to think for himself almost as soon as he learned to write, a habit which became increasingly pronounced as he got older and which gave him as much delight as it imposed demands. He fell in love with the printed word, both in terms of the artistry of a well-designed page and the possibilities for using it to stretch the human mind.

At the age of twenty-two he wrote his *Articles of Belief and Acts of Religion*. He expressed his belief in the existence of a Supreme Being and listed what he considered the spiritual virtues, among them his hope that he would "refrain from censure, calumny, and detraction; that I may avoid and abhor deceit and envy, fraud, flattery, and hatred, malice, lying, and ingratitude." Also, "That I may possess integrity and eveness of mind, resolution in difficulties, and fortitude under affliction. . . . That I may have tenderness for the weak and reverent respect for the ancient; that I may be kind to my neighbors, good-natured to my companions, and hospitable to strangers. . . ."

It did not take him long to chart an open course in life. By the time he was twenty-six he was expressing views in the seasoned, witty, knotty-pine style that was to win him such a wide following in later years. But *Poor Richard's Almanac* was deceptively simple and homespun. It had a genuine philosophical core that belonged to the family of ideas in which Emerson, William James, and Oliver Wendell Holmes were later to be at home.

His education was in the nature of a chain reaction of discovery. After only a few years of formal elementary schooling, he began his explorations in thought and knowledge. One book pointed the way to sundry others; each subject had its own continuing mysteries and its challenges.

The advantage of self-education in Franklin's case was clear. There were no boundary lines or terminal rituals, as in formal schooling, to mislead a person into thinking that he had completed his education. It never occurred to him that there was any point at which he could say that his learning was adequate for his life's work or for life itself. He could no more conceive of cutting his mind off from its natural food, knowledge, than he could expect to function physically in a starved condition. There was nothing phenomenal to him in the ability to think creatively and competently in so many fields; this was how the human mind was supposed to work.

Knowledge by itself, of course, could be meaningless unless it was tied to a proper attitude toward people and life in general and to a sense of responsibility. Franklin enlisted himself, therefore, in service to the cause of man. With it went a profound belief in the capacity of an individual to become effective. "I have always thought that one man of tolerable abilities may work great changes and accomplish great affairs among mankind, if he first forms a good plan and . . . makes the execution of that same plan his sole study and business."

Franklin's own plan is revealed in his contribution to the art of government and the art of living. During the Philadelphia Constitutional Convention, his knowledge of the chemistry of human emotions and his rustic charm prevented numberless explosions. Thirty years earlier he had advocated federation. And now, at Philadelphia, he moved mightily but quietly to see that a group of men who had it in their power to create the necessary federation would not turn away from their historic work. Once, when breakdown in the constitutional debates seemed imminent, he cooled the passions and restored the perspective of the delegates:

"Our different sentiments on almost every question," he said, ". . . is methinks a melancholy proof of the imperfection of human understanding.

We indeed seem to feel our own want of political wisdom, since we have been running about in search of it. . . . I have lived, Sir, a long time, and the longer I live, the more convincing proofs I see of this truth—that God governs in the affairs of men. And if a sparrow cannot fall to the ground without his notice, is it probable that an empire can rise without his aid? We have been assured, Sir, in the sacred writings, that 'except the Lord building the House they labour in vain that build it.' I firmly believe this; and I also believe that without his concurring aid we shall succeed in this political building no better than the Builders of Babel: We shall be divided by our little partial local interests; our projects will be confounded, and we ourselves shall become a reproach and bye word down to future ages. And what is worse, mankind may hereafter from this unfortunate instance, despair of establishing governments by human wisdom and leave it to chance, war, and conquest.

"I therefore beg leave to move—that henceforth prayers imploring the assistance of Heaven, and its blessings on our deliberations be held in this Assembly every morning before we proceed to business. . . ."

Some of the delegates thought it strange that this proposal should have come from a man not infrequently criticized as a free-thinker or atheist and infidel who had expressed his doubts about Christian doctrines of revelation. But Franklin was absolutely sincere; he regarded prayer not as a convenient special-delivery system by which to receive favors from the Deity but as an essential way of knitting oneself together and achieving a sympathetic resonance with a more majestic force than man could control or comprehend.

Once he wrote to his sister: "There are some things in your New England doctrine and worship which I do not agree with; but I do not therefore condemn them, or desire to shake your belief or practice of them." His respect for the religions of others was in itself an article of his faith.

Vernon Parrington quotes Sainte-Beuve about Franklin—with and without blemishes: "There is a flower of religion, a flower of honor, a flower of chivalry, that you must not require of Franklin." Then Parrington adds: "In his modesty, his willingness to compromise, his open-mindedness, his clear and luminous understanding, his charity—above all, in his desire to subdue the ugly facts of society to some more rational scheme of things—he proved himself a great and useful man, one of the great and most useful whom America has produced."

A few weeks before he died, Franklin wrote to Ezra Stiles, president of Yale University: "Here is my creed. I believe in one God, Creator of the Universe. That He governs it by His providence. That He ought to be worshipped. That the most acceptable service we render Him is doing good to His other children. That the soul of man is immortal, and will be treated with justice in another life respecting its conduct in this. These I take to be the principal principles of sound religion, and I regard them as you do in whatever sect I meet with them. As to Jesus of Nazareth, my opinion of whom you particularly desire, I think the system of morals and his religion, as he left them to us, the best the world ever saw or is likely to see; but I apprehend it has received various corrupt changes, and I have, with most of the present dissenters in England, some doubts as to his divinity; though it is a question I do not dogmatize upon, having never studied it, and think it needless to busy myself with it now, when I expect soon an opportunity of knowing the truth with less trouble. I see no harm, however, in its being believed, if that belief has the good consequence, as probably it has, of making his doctrines more respected and better observed; especially as I do not perceive that the Supreme [Being] takes it amiss, by distinguishing the unbelievers in His government of the world with any peculiar marks of His displeasure. . . .

"All sects here, and we have a great variety, have experienced my good will in assisting them with subscriptions for building their new places of worship; and, as I have never opposed their doctrines, I hope to go out of the world in peace with them all. . . ."

Franklin died on April 17, 1790, at the age of eighty-four in the city of Philadelphia to which he had given so much of himself and which, since then, has given to much of itself to him.

Benjamin Franklin was fifty-eight when he wrote this letter to his daughter. He had not yet attained the widespread recognition that gave him so much influence in his later years. Indeed, his letter reflects acute concern about his unhappy position.

LETTER TO HIS DAUGHTER, NOVEMBER, 1764

My dear child, the natural prudence and goodness of heart God has blessed you with, make it less necessary for me to be particular in giving you advice. I shall therefore only say, that the more attentively dutiful and tender you are towards your good mamma, the more you will recommend yourself to me. But why should I mention *me*, when you have so much higher a promise in the commandments, that such conduct will recommend you to the favor of God. You know I have many enemies, all indeed on the public account, (for I cannot recollect, that I have in a private capacity given just cause of offense to any one whatever,) yet they are enemies, and very bitter ones; and you must expect their enmity will extend in some degree to you, so that your slightest indiscretions will be magnified into crimes, in order the more sensibly to wound and afflict me. It is, therefore, the more necessary for you to be extremely circumspect in all your behaviour, that no advantage may be given to their malevolence.

Go constantly to church, whoever preaches. The act of devotion in the Common Prayer Book is your principal business there, and, if properly attended to, will do more towards amending the heart than sermons generally can do. For they were composed by men of much greater piety and wisdom, than our common composers of sermons can pretend to be; and therefore I wish you would never miss the prayer days; yet I do not mean you should despise sermons, even of the preachers you dislike; for the discourse is often much better than the man, as sweet and clear waters come through very dirty earth. I am the more particular on this head, as you seemed to express, a little before I came away, some inclination to leave our church, which I would not have you do.

Like Thomas Jefferson, Benjamin Franklin was attracted to the idea of making the Scripture more accessible. In a letter to Benjamin Vaughan, he explains the background for his own version of the Lord's Prayer.

LETTER TO BENJAMIN VAUGHAN, NOVEMBER 9, 1779

It was addressed to Mr. J. R., that is, James Ralph, then a youth of about my age, and my intimate friend; afterwards a political writer and historian. The purport of it was to prove the doctrine of fate, from the supposed attributes of God; in some manner as this. That in erecting and governing the world, as he was infinitely wise, he knew what would be best; infinitely good, he must be disposed, and infinitely powerful, he must be able, to execute it. Consequently *all is right.*

There were only a hundred copies printed, of which I gave a few to friends; and afterwards disliking the piece, as conceiving it might have an ill tendency, I burnt the rest, except one copy, the margin of which was filled with manuscript notes by Lyons, author of the *Infallibility of Human Judgment,* who was at that time another of my acquaintances in London. I was not nineteen years of age when it was written. In 1730, I wrote a piece on the other side of the question, which began with laying for its foundation this fact; *"That almost all men in all ages and countries have at times made use of* Prayer." Thence I reasoned, that, if all things are ordained, prayer must among the rest be ordained. But, as prayer can procure no change in things that are ordained, praying must then be useless, and an absurdity. God would therefore not ordain praying if every thing else was ordained. But praying exists, therefore all other things are not ordained, &c. This pamphlet was never printed, and the manuscript has been long lost. The great uncertainty I found in metaphysical reasonings disgusted me, and I quitted that kind of reading and study for others more satisfactory.

Like Thomas Jefferson, who was captivated with the idea of preparing his own version of the New Testament, Benjamin Franklin conceived the idea of a more supple rendition of the Lord's Prayer.

THE LORD'S PRAYER REVISED (UNDATED)

Old Version	New Version, by B. Franklin
1. Our Father which art in heaven,	1. Heavenly Father,
2. Hallowed be thy name.	2. May all revere thee,
3. Thy kingdom come,	3. And become thy dutiful children and faithful subjects.
4. Thy will be done on earth, as it is in heaven.	4. May thy laws be obeyed on earth, as perfectly as they are in heaven.
5. Give us this day our daily bread.	5. Provide for us this day, as thou hast hitherto daily done.
6. Forgive us our debts, as we forgive our debtors.	6. Forgive us our trespasses, and enable us to forgive those who offend us.
7. And lead us not into temptation, but deliver us from evil.	7. Keep us out of temptation, and deliver us from evil.

Reasons for the Change of Expression.

Old Version.—*Our Father which art in Heaven.*

New Version.—*Heavenly Father* is more concise, equally expressive, and better modern English.

Old Version.—*Hallowed be thy name.* This seems to relate to an observance among the Jews not to pronounce the proper or peculiar name of God, they deeming it a profanation so to do. We have in our language no *proper name* for God; the word *God* being a common, or general name, expressing all chief objects of worship, true or false. The word *hallowed* is almost obsolete. People now have but an imperfect conception of the meaning of the petition. It is therefore proposed to change the expression into

New Version.—*May all revere thee.*

Old Version.—*Thy kingdom come.* This petition seems suited to the then condition of the Jewish nation. Originally their state was a theocracy; God was their king. Dissatisfied with that kind of government, they desired a visible, earthly king, in the manner of the nations around them. They had such kings accordingly; but their happiness was not increased by the change, and they had reason to wish and pray for a return of the theocracy, or government of God. Christians in these times have other ideas, when they speak of the kingdom of God, such as are perhaps more adequately expressed by the

New Version.—*Become thy dutiful children and faithful subjects.*

Old Version.—*Thy will be done on earth, as it is in heaven;* more explicitly.

New Version.—*May thy laws be obeyed on earth, as perfectly as they are in heaven.*

Old Version.—*Give us this day our daily bread.*—Give us what is *ours* seems to put in a claim of right, and to contain too little of the grateful acknowledgment and sense of dependence that become creatures, who live on the daily bounty of their Creator. Therefore it is changed to

New Version.—*Provide for us this day, as thou hast hitherto daily done.*

Old Version.—*Forgive us our debts, as we forgive our debtors.* (Matthew). *Forgive us our sins, for we also forgive every one that is indebted to us.* (Luke). Offerings were *due* to God on many occasions by the Jewish law, which, when people could not pay, or had forgotten, as debtors are apt to do, it was proper to pray that those debts might be forgiven. Our Liturgy uses neither the *debtors* of Matthew, nor the *indebted* of Luke, but instead of them speaks of *those that trespass against us.* Perhaps the considering it as a Christian duty to forgive debtors was by the compilers thought an inconvenient idea in a trading nation. There seems, however, something presumptuous in this mode of expression, which has the air of proposing ourselves as an example of goodness fit for God to imitate. *We hope you will at least be as good as we are;* you see we forgive one another, and therefore we pray that you would forgive us. Some have considered it in another sense. *Forgive us as we forgive others.* That is, if we do not forgive others, we pray that thou wouldst not forgive us. But this, being a kind of conditional *imprecation* against ourselves, seems improper in such a prayer; and therefore it may be better to say humbly and modestly

New Version.—*Forgive us our trespasses, and enable us likewise to forgive those who offend us.* This, instead of assuming that we have already in and of ourselves the grace of forgiveness, acknowledges our dependence on God, the Fountain of Mercy, for any share we may have of it, praying that he would communicate it to us.

Old Version.—*And lead us not into temptation.* The Jews had a notion, that God sometimes tempted, or directed, or permitted, the tempting of people. Thus it was said, he tempted Pharaoh, directed Satan to tempt Job, and a false prophet to tempt Ahab. Under this persuasion, it was natural for them to pray, that he would not put them to such severe trials. We now suppose that temptation, so far as it is supernatural, comes from the Devil only; and this petition continued conveys a suspicion, which, in our present conceptions, seems unworthy of God; therefore it might be altered to

New Version.—*Keep us out of temptation.*

It is doubtful whether any of the Founding Fathers left behind as full an account of his early religious development and ideas as did Benjamin Franklin. The following material is drawn directly from his Autobiography, *much of it written in 1781 when Franklin was seventy-five.*

AUTOBIOGRAPHY

This obscure family of ours was early in the Reformation, and continued Protestants through the reign of Queen Mary, when they were sometimes in danger of trouble on account of their zeal against popery. They had got an English Bible, and to conceal and secure it, it was fastened open with tapes under and within the cover of a joint-stool. When my great-great grandfather read it to his family, he turned up the joint-stool upon his knees, turning over the leaves then under the tapes. One of the children stood at the door to give notice if he saw the apparitor coming, who was an officer of the spiritual court. In that case the stool was turned down again upon its feet, when the Bible remained concealed under it as before. This anecdote I had from my uncle Benjamin. The family continued all of the Church of England till about the end of Charles the Second's reign, when some of the ministers that had been ousted for non-conformity holding conventicles in Northamptonshire, Benjamin and Josiah adhered to them, and so continued all their lives: the rest of the family remained with the Episcopal Church.

Josiah, my father, married young, and carried his wife with three children into New England, about 1682. The conventicles having been forbidden by law, and frequently disturbed, induced some considerable men of his acquaintance to remove to that country, and he was prevailed with to accompany them thither, where they expected to enjoy their mode of religion with freedom. By the same wife he had four children more born there, and by a second wife ten more, in all seventeen; of which I remember thirteen sitting at one time at his table, who all grew up to be men and women, and married; I was the youngest son, and youngest child but two, and was born in Boston, New England. My mother, the second wife, was Abiah Folger, daughter of Peter Folger, one of the first settlers of New England, of whom honorable mention is made by Cotton Mather, in his church history of that country, entitled Magnalia Christi Americana, as *"a godly, learned Englishman,"* if I remember the words rightly. I have heard that he wrote sundry small occasional pieces, but only one of them was printed, which I saw now many years since. It was written in 1675, in the home-spun verse of that time and people, and addressed to those then concerned in the government there. It was in favor of liberty of conscience, and in behalf of the Baptists, Quakers, and other sectaries that had been under persecution, ascribing the Indian wars, and other distresses that had befallen the country, to that persecution, as so many judgments of God to punish so heinous an offense, and exhorting a repeal of those uncharitable laws. The whole appeared to me as written with a good deal of decent plainness and manly freedom. The six concluding lines I remember, though I have forgotten the two first of the stanza; but the purport of them was, that his censures proceeded from good-will, and, therefore, he would be known to be the author.

> Because to be a libeller (says he)
>   I hate it with my heart;
> From Sherburne town, where now I dwell
>   My name I do put here;
> Without offense your real friend,
>   It is Peter Folger.

My elder brothers were all put apprentices to different trades. I was put to the grammar-school at eight years of age, my father intending to devote me, as the tithe of his sons, to the service of the Church. My early readiness in learning to read (which must have been very early, as I do not remember when I could not read), and the opinion of all his friends, that I should certainly make a good scholar, encouraged him in this purpose of his. My uncle Benjamin, too, approved of it, and proposed to give me all his short-hand volumes of sermons, I suppose as a stock to set up with, if I would learn his character.

*   *   *

My parents had early given me religious impressions, and brought me through my childhood piously in the Dissenting way. But I was scarce fifteen, when, after doubting by turns of several points, as I found them disputed in the different books I read, I began to doubt of Revelation itself. Some books against Deism fell into my hands; they were said to be the substance of sermons preached at Boyle's Lectures. It happened that they wrought an effect on me quite contrary to what was intended by them; for the arguments of the Deists, which were quoted to be refuted, appeared to me much stronger than the refutations; in short, I soon became a thorough Deist. My arguments perverted some others, particularly Collins and Ralph; but, each of them having afterwards wronged me greatly without the least compunction, and recollecting Keith's conduct towards me (who was another freethinker), and my own towards Vernon and Miss Read, which at times gave me great

trouble, I began to suspect that this doctrine, though it n
not very useful. My London pamphlet, which had for its
of Dryden:

> Whatever is is right. Though purblind
> Sees but a part o' the chain, the nearest
> His eyes not carrying to the equal beam,
> That poises all above;

and from the attributes of God, his infinite wisdom, goodness and power,
concluded that nothing could possibly be wrong in the world, and that vice
and virtue were empty distinctions, no such things existing, appeared now
not so clever a performance as I once thought it; and I doubted whether
some error had not insinuated itself unperceived into my argument, so as to
infect all that followed, as is common in metaphysical reasonings.

I grew convinced that *truth*, *sincerity* and *integrity* in dealings between
man and man were of the utmost importance to the felicity of life; and I
formed written resolutions, which still remain in my journal book, to practice
them ever while I lived. Revelation had indeed no weight with me, as such;
but I entertained an opinion that, though certain actions might not be bad
because they were forbidden by it, or good *because* it commanded them, yet
probably these actions might be forbidden *because* they were bad for us, or
commanded *because* they were beneficial to us, in their own natures, all the
circumstances of things considered. And this persuasion, with the kind hand
of Providence, or some guardian angel, or accidental favorable circumstances
and situations, or all together, preserved me, through this dangerous time of
youth, and the hazardous situations I was sometimes in among strangers,
remote from the eye and advice of my father, without any willful gross
immorality or injustice, that might have been expected from my want of
religion. I say willful, because the instances I have mentioned had something
of *necessity* in them, from my youth, inexperience, and the knavery of others.
I had therefore a tolerable character to begin the world with; I valued it
properly, and determined to preserve it.

* * *

I had been religiously educated as a Presbyterian; and though some of the
dogmas of that persuasion, such as *the eternal decrees of God, election, rep-
robation, etc.*, appeared to me unintelligible, others doubtful, and I early
absented myself from the public assemblies of the sect, Sunday being my
studying day, I never was without some religious principles. I never doubted,
for instance, the existence of the Deity; that he made the world, and governed
it by his Providence; that the most acceptable service of God was the doing
good to man; that our souls are immortal; and that all crime will be pun-

and virtue rewarded, either here or hereafter. These I esteemed the essentials of every religion; and, being found in all the religions we had in our country, I respected them all, though with different degrees of respect, as I found them more or less mixed with other articles, which, without any tendency to inspire, promote, or confirm morality, served principally to divide us, and make us unfriendly to one another. This respect to all, with an opinion that the worst had some good effects, induced me to avoid all discourse that might tend to lessen the good opinion another might have of his own religion; and as our province increased in people, and new places of worship were continually wanted, and generally erected by voluntary contribution, my mite for such purpose, whatever might be the sect, was never refused.

Though I seldom attended any public worship, I had still an opinion of its propriety, and of its utility when rightly conducted, and I regularly paid my annual subscription for the support of the only Presbyterian minister or meeting we had in Philadelphia. He used to visit me sometimes as a friend, and admonish me to attend his administrations, and I was now and then prevailed on to do so, once for five Sundays successively. Had he been in my opinion a good preacher, perhaps I might have continued, notwithstanding the occasion I had for the Sunday's leisure in my course of study; but his discourses were chiefly either polemic arguments, or explications of the peculiar doctrines of our sect, and were all to me very dry, uninteresting, and unedifying, since not a single moral principle was inculcated or enforced, their aim seeming to be rather to make us Presbyterians than good citizens.

At length he took for his text that verse of the fourth chapter of Philippians, *"Finally, brethren, whatsoever things are true, honest, just, pure, lovely, or of good report, if there be any virtue, or any praise, think on these things."* And I imagined, in a sermon on such a text, we could not miss of having some morality. But he confined himself to five points only, as meant by the apostle, viz.: 1. Keeping holy the Sabbath day. 2. Being diligent in reading the holy Scriptures. 3. Attending duly the public worship. 4. Partaking of the Sacrament. 5. Paying a due respect to God's ministers. These might be all good things; but, as they were not the kind of good things that I expected from that text, I despaired of ever meeting with them from any other, was disgusted, and attended his preaching no more. I had some years before composed a little Liturgy, or form of prayer, for my own private use (viz., in 1728), entitled, *Articles of Belief and Acts of Religion*. I returned to the use of this, and went no more to the public assemblies. My conduct might be blameable, but I leave it, without attempting further to excuse it; my present purpose being to relate facts, and not to make apologies for them.

It was about this time I conceived the bold and arduous project of arriving at moral perfection. I wished to live without committing any fault at any time; I would conquer all that either natural inclination, custom, or company might lead me into. As I knew, or thought I knew, what was right and wrong, I did not see why I might not always do the one and avoid the other. But I soon found I had undertaken a task of more difficulty than I had imagined. While my care was employed in guarding against one fault, I was often surprised by another; habit took the advantage of inattention; inclination was sometimes too strong for reason. I concluded, at length, that the mere speculative conviction that it was our interest to be completely virtuous, was not sufficient to prevent our slipping; and that the contrary habits must be broken, and good ones acquired and established, before we can have any dependence on a steady, uniform rectitude of conduct. For this purpose I therefore contrived the following method.

In the various enumerations of the moral virtues I had met with in my reading, I found the catalogue more or less numerous, as different writers included more or fewer ideas under the same name. Temperance, for example, was by some confined to eating and drinking, while by others it was extended to mean the moderating every other pleasure, appetite, inclination, or passion, bodily or mental, even to our avarice and ambition. I proposed to myself, for the sake of clearness, to use rather more names, with fewer ideas annexed to each, than a few names with more ideas; and I included under thirteen names of virtues all that at that time occurred to me as necessary or desirable, and annexed to each a short precept, which fully expressed the extent I gave to its meaning.

These names of virtues, with their precepts, were:

1. TEMPERANCE.

Eat not to dullness; drink not to elevation.

2. SILENCE.

Speak not but what may benefit others or yourself; avoid trifling conversation.

3. ORDER.

Let all your things have their places; let each part of your business have its time.

4. RESOLUTION.

Resolve to perform what you ought; perform without fail what you resolve.

5. FRUGALITY.

Make no expense but to do good to others or yourself; i.e., waste nothing.

6. INDUSTRY.

Lose no time; be always employed in something useful; cut off all unnecessary actions.

7. SINCERITY.

Use no hurtful deceit; think innocently and justly, and, if you speak, speak accordingly.

8. JUSTICE.

Wrong none by doing injuries, or omitting the benefits that are your duty.

9. MODERATION.

Avoid extremes; forbear resenting injuries so much as you think they deserve.

10. CLEANLINESS.

Tolerate no uncleanliness in body, clothes, or habitation.

11. TRANQUILLITY.

Be not disturbed at trifles, or at accidents common or unavoidable.

12. CHASTITY.

Rarely use venery but for health or offspring, never to dullness, weakness, or the injury of your own or another's peace or reputation.

13. HUMILITY.

Imitate Jesus and Socrates.

My intention being to acquire the *habitude* of all these virtues, I judged it would be well not to distract my attention by attempting the whole at once, but to fix it on one of them at a time; and, when I should be master of that, then to proceed to another, and so on, till I should have gone through the thirteen; and, as the previous acquisition of some might facilitate the acquisition of certain others, I arranged them with that view, as they stand above. Temperance first, as it tends to procure that coolness and clearness of head, which is so necessary where constant vigilance was to be kept up, and guard maintained against the unremitting attraction of ancient habits, and the force of perpetual temptations. This being acquired and established, Silence would be more easy; and my desire being to gain knowledge at the same time that I improved in virtue, and considering that in conservation it was obtained rather by the use of the ears than of the tongue, and therefore wishing to break a habit I was getting into of prattling, punning, and joking, which only made me acceptable to trifling company, I gave *Silence* the second place. This and the next, *Order*, I expected would allow me more time for attending to my project and my studies. *Resolution*, once become habitual, would keep me firm in my endeavors to obtain all the subsequent virtues; *Frugality* and Industry freeing me from my remaining debt, and producing affluence and independence, would make more easy the practice of Sincerity and Justice, etc., etc. Conceiving then that, agreeably to the advice of

Pythagoras in his Golden Verses, daily examination would be necessary, I contrived the following method for conducting that examination.

TEMPERANCE.

EAT NOT TO DULNESS;
DRINK NOT TO ELEVATION.

	S.	M.	T.	W.	T.	F.	S.
T.							
S.	*	*		*		*	
O.	**	*	*		*	*	*
R.			*			*	
F.		*			*		
I.			*				
5.							
J.							
M.							
C.							
T.							
C.							
H.							

I made a little book, in which I allotted a page for each of the virtues. I ruled each page with red ink, so as to have seven columns, one for each day of the week, marking each column with a letter for the day. I crossed these columns with thirteen red lines, marking the beginning of each line with the first letter of one of the virtues, on which line and in its proper column, I might mark, by a little black spot, every fault I found upon examination to have been committed respecting that virtue upon that day.

I determined to give a week's strict attention to each of the virtues successively. Thus, in the first week, my great guard was to avoid even the least offence against *Temperance*, leaving the other virtues to their ordinary chance, only marking every evening the faults of the day. Thus, if in the first week I could keep my first line, marked T, clear of spots, I supposed the habit of that virtue so much strengthened, and its opposite weakened, that I might venture extending my attention to include the next, and for the following week keep both lines clear of spots. Proceeding thus to the last, I could go through a course compleat in thirteen weeks, and four courses in a year. And like him who, having a garden to weed, does not attempt to eradicate all the bad herbs at once, which would exceed his reach and his strength, but works on one of the beds at a time, and, having accomplished the first, proceeds to a second so I should have, I hoped, the encouraging pleasure of seeing on my pages the progress I made in virtue, by clearing successively my lines of their spots, till in the end, by a number of courses, I should be happy in viewing a clean book, after a thirteen weeks' daily examination.

This my little book had for its motto these lines from Addison's *Cato:*

> Here will I hold. If there's a power above us
> (And that there is, all nature cries aloud
> Through all her works), He must delight in virtue;
> And that which he delights in must be happy.

Another from Cicero,

> O vitae Philosophia dux! O virtutum indagatrix expultrixque vitiorum! Unus dies, bene et ex praeceptis tuis actus, peccanti immortalitati est anteponendus.[1]

Another from the Proverbs of Solomon, speaking of wisdom or virtue:

> "Length of days is in her right hand, and in her left hand riches and honour. Her ways are ways of pleasantness, and all her paths are peace." iii. 16, 17.

And conceiving God to be the fountain of wisdom, I thought it right and necessary to solicit his assistance for obtaining it; to this end I formed the following little prayer, which was prefixed to my tables of examination, for daily use.

> "*O powerful Goodness! bountiful Father! merciful Guide! Increase in me that wisdom which discovers my truest interest. Strengthen my resolutions to perform what that wisdom dictates. Accept my kind offices to thy other children as the only return in my power for thy continual favours to me.*"

I used also sometimes a little prayer which I took from Thomson's Poems, viz.:

> Father of light and life, thou Good Supreme!
> O Teach me what is good; teach me Thyself!

---

[1] [O philosophy the leader of life! O she who explores virtue and casts out faults! One day, living well and according to your own precepts, is to be preferred to an immortality of sinning.—ED.]

LIBRARY
BRYAN COLLEGE
DAYTON, TENN. 37321

Save me from folly, vanity, and vice,
From every low pursuit; and fill my soul
With knowledge, conscious peace, and virtue pure;
Sacred, substantial, never-fading bliss!

The precept of *Order* requiring that *every part of my business should have its allotted time,* one page in my little book contained the following scheme of employment for the twenty-four hours of a natural day.

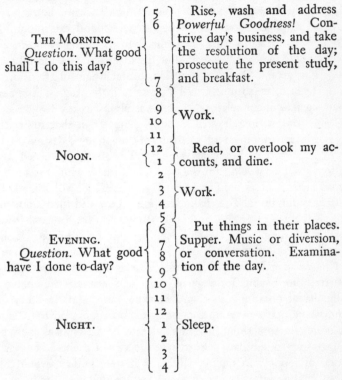

THE MORNING. *Question.* What good shall I do this day?	5 6 7	Rise, wash and address *Powerful Goodness!* Contrive day's business, and take the resolution of the day; prosecute the present study, and breakfast.
	8 9 10 11	Work.
NOON.	12 1	Read, or overlook my accounts, and dine.
	2 3 4	Work.
EVENING. *Question.* What good have I done to-day?	5 6 7 8 9	Put things in their places. Supper. Music or diversion, or conversation. Examination of the day.
NIGHT.	10 11 12 1 2 3 4	Sleep.

I entered upon the execution of this plan for self-examination, and continued it with occasional intermissions for some time. I was surprised to find myself so much fuller of faults than I had imagined; but I had the satisfaction of seeing them diminish. To avoid the trouble of renewing now and then my little book, which, by scraping out the marks on the paper of old faults to make room for new ones in a new course, became full of holes, I transferred my tables and precepts to the ivory leaves of a memorandum book, on which the lines were drawn with red ink, that made a durable stain, and on those lines I marked my faults with a black-lead pencil, which marks I could easily wipe out with a wet sponge. After a while I went through one course only in a year, and afterward only one in several years, till at length I omitted them entirely, being employed in voyages and business abroad, with a multiplicity of affairs that interfered; but I always carried my little book with me.

My scheme of ORDER gave me the most trouble; and I found that, though it might be practicable where a man's business was such as to leave him the disposition of his time, that of a journeyman printer, for instance, it was not possible to be exactly observed by a master, who must mix with the world, and often receive people of business at their own hours. *Order*, too, with regard to places for things, papers, etc., I found extremely difficult to acquire. I had not been early accustomed to it, and, having an exceeding good memory, I was not so sensible of the inconvenience attending want of method. This article, therefore, cost me so much painful attention, and my faults in it vexed me so much, and I made so little progress in amendment, and had such frequent relapses, that I was almost ready to give up the attempt, and content myself with a faulty character in that respect, like the man who, in buying an ax of a smith, my neighbour, desired to have the whole of its surface as bright as the edge. The smith consented to grind it bright for him if he would turn the wheel; he turned, while the smith pressed the broad face of the ax hard and heavily on the stone, which made the turning of it very fatiguing. The man came every now and then from the wheel to see how the work went on, and at length would take his ax as it was, without farther grinding. "No," said the smith, "turn on, turn on; we shall have it bright by-and-by; as yet, it is only speckled." "Yes," says the man, *"but I think I like a speckled ax best."* And I believe this may have been the case with many, who, having, for want of some such means as I employed, found the difficulty of obtaining good and breaking bad habits in other points of vice and virtue, have given up the struggle, and concluded that *"a speckled ax was best"*; for something that pretended to be reason, was every now and then suggesting to me that such extreme nicety as I exacted of myself might be a kind of foppery in morals, which, if it were known, would make me ridiculous; that a perfect character might be attended with the inconvenience of being envied and hated; and that a benevolent man should allow a few faults in himself, to keep his friends in countenance.

In truth, I found myself incorrigible with respect to Order; and now I am grown old, and my memory bad, I feel very sensibly the want of it. But, on the whole, though I never arrived at the perfection I had been so ambitious of obtaining, but fell far short of it, yet I was, by the endeavour, a better and a happier man than I otherwise should have been if I had not attempted it; as those who aim at perfect writing by imitating the engraved copies, though they never reach the wished-for excellence of those copies, their hand is mended by the endeavour, and is tolerable while it continues fair and legible.

It may be well my posterity should be informed that to this little artifice, with the blessing of God, their ancestor owed the constant felicity of his life, down to his 79th year, in which this is written. What reverses may attend the remainder is in the hand of Providence; but, if they arrive, the reflection on past happiness enjoyed ought to help his bearing them with more resignation. To Temperance he ascribes his long-continued health, and what is still left to him of a good constitution; to Industry and Frugality, the early easiness of his circumstances and acquisition of his fortune, with all that knowledge that enabled him to be a useful citizen, and obtained for him some degree of reputation among the learned; to Sincerity and Justice, the confidence of his country, and the honorable employs it conferred upon him; and to the joint influence of the whole mass of the virtues, even in the imperfect state he was able to acquire them, all that evenness of temper, and that cheerfulness in conversation, which makes his company still sought for, and agreeable even to his younger acquaintance. I hope, therefore, that some of my descendants may follow the example and reap the benefit.

It will be remarked that, though my scheme was not wholly without religion, there was in it no mark of any of the distinguishing tenets of any particular sect. I had purposely avoided them; for, being fully persuaded of the utility and excellency of my method, and that it might be serviceable to people in all religions, and intending some time or other to publish it, I would not have any thing in it that should prejudice any one, of any sect, against it. I purposed writing a little comment on each virtue, in which I would have shown the advantages of possessing it, and the mischiefs attending its opposite vice; and I should have called my book THE ART OF VIRTUE,[2] because it would have shown the means and manner of obtaining virtue, which would have distinguished it from the mere exhortation to be good, that does not instruct and indicate the means, but is like the apostle's man of verbal charity, who only without showing to the naked and hungry how or where they might get clothes or victuals, exhorted them to be fed and clothed.—James ii. 15, 16.

But it so happened that my intention of writing and publishing this comment was never fulfilled. I did, indeed, from time to time, put down short hints of the sentiments, reasonings, etc., to be made use of in it, some of which I have still by me; but the necessary close attention to private business in the earlier part of my life, and public business since, have occasioned my postponing it; for, it being connected in my mind with *a great*

---

[2] Nothing so likely to make a man's fortune as virtue [*Marginal note*].

and extensive project, that required the whole man to execute, and which an unforeseen succession of employs prevented my attending to, it has hitherto remained unfinished.

In this piece it was my design to explain and enforce this doctrine, that vicious actions are not hurtful because they are forbidden, but forbidden because they are hurtful, the nature of man alone considered; that it was, therefore, every one's interest to be virtuous who wished to be happy even in this world; and I should, from this circumstance (there being always in the world a number of rich merchants, nobility, states, and princes, who have need of honest instruments for the management of their affairs, and such being so rare), have endeavored to convince young persons that no qualities were so likely to make a poor man's fortune as those of probity and integrity.

My list of virtues contained at first but twelve; but a Quaker friend having kindly informed me that I was generally thought proud; that my pride showed itself frequently in conversation; that I was not content with being in the right when discussing any point, but was overbearing, and rather insolent, of which he convinced me by mentioning several instances; I determined endeavouring to cure myself, if I could, of this vice or folly among the rest, and I added *Humility* to my list, giving an extensive meaning to the word.

I cannot boast of much success in acquiring the *reality* of this virtue, but I had a good deal with regard to the *appearance* of it. I made it a rule to forbear all direct contradiction to the sentiments of others, and all positive assertion of my own. I even forbid myself, agreeably to the old laws of our Junto, the use of every word or expression in the language that imported a fixed opinion, such as *certainly, undoubtedly*, etc., and I adopted, instead of them, *I conceive, I apprehend*, or *I imagine* a thing to be so or so; or *it so appears to me at present*. When another asserted something that I thought an error, I denied myself the pleasure of contradicting him abruptly, and of showing immediately some absurdity in his proposition; and in answering I began by observing that in certain cases or circumstances his opinion would be right, but in the present case there *appeared* or *seemed* to me some difference, etc. I soon found the advantage of this change in my manner; the conversations I engaged in went on more pleasantly. The modest way in which I proposed my opinions procured them a readier reception and less contradiction; I had less mortification when I was found to be in the wrong, and I more easily prevailed with others to give up their mistakes and join with me when I happened to be in the right.

And this mode, which I at first put on with some violence to natural inclination, became at length so easy, and so habitual to me, that perhaps for these fifty years past no one has ever heard a dogmatical expression escape me. And to this habit (after my character of integrity) I think it principally owing that I had early so much weight with my fellow-citizens when I proposed new institutions, or alterations in the old, and so much influence in public councils when I became a member; for I was but a bad speaker, never eloquent, subject to much hesitation in my choice of words, hardly correct in language, and yet I generally carried my points.

In reality, there is, perhaps, no one of our national passions so hard to subdue as *pride*. Disguise it, struggle with it, beat it down, stifle it, mortify it as much as one pleases, it is still alive, and will every now and then peep out and show itself; you will see it, perhaps, often in this history; for, even if I could conceive that I had compleatly overcome it, I should probably be proud of my humility.

*   *   *

I put down, from time to time, on pieces of paper, such thoughts as occurred to me respecting it [lessons learned from the reading of history—ED.]. Most of these are lost; but I find one purporting to be the substance of an intended creed, containing, as I thought, the essentials of every known religion, and being free of every thing that might shock the professors of any religion. It is expressed in these words, viz.:

"That there is one God, who made all things.

"That he governs the world by his providence.

"That he ought to be worshiped by adoration, prayer, and thanksgiving.

"But that the most acceptable service of God is doing good to man.

"That the soul is immortal.

"And that God will certainly reward virtue and punish vice, either here or hereafter."

My ideas at that time were, that the sect should be begun and spread at first among young and single men only; that each person to be initiated should not only declare his assent to such creed, but should have exercised himself with the thirteen weeks' examination and practice of the virtues, as in the before-mentioned model; that the existence of such a society should be kept a secret, till it was become considerable, to prevent solicitations for the admission of improper persons, but that the members should each of them search among his acquaintance for ingenuous, well-disposed youths, to whom, with prudent caution, the scheme should be gradually communicated; that the members should engage to afford their advice, assistance, and support to each other in promoting one another's interests, business, and advancement in life; that, for distinction, we should be called *The Society of the Free and Easy*: free, as being, by the general practice and habit of the virtues, free from the dominion of vice; and particularly by the practice of industry and frugality, free from debt, which exposes a man to confinement, and a species of slavery to his creditors.

This is as much as I can now recollect of the project, except that I communicated it in part to two young men, who adopted it with some enthusiasm; but my then narrow circumstances, and the necessity I was under of sticking close to my business, occasioned my postponing the further prosecution of it at that time; and my multifarious occupations, public and private, induced me to continue postponing, so that it has been omitted till I have no longer strength or activity left sufficient for such an enterprise; though I am still of opinion that it was a practicable scheme, and might have been very useful, by forming a great number of good citizens; and I was not discouraged by the seeming magnitude of the undertaking, as I have always thought that one man of tolerable abilities may work great changes, and accomplish great affairs among mankind, if he first forms a good plan, and, cutting off all amusements or other employments that would divert his attention, makes the execution of that same plan his sole study and business.

* * *

About the year 1734 there arrived among us from Ireland a young Presbyterian preacher, named Hemphill, who delivered with a good voice, and apparently extempore, most excellent discourses, which drew together considerable numbers of different persuasions, who joined in admiring them. Among the rest, I became one of his constant hearers, his sermons pleasing me, as they had little of the dogmatical kind, but inculcated strongly the practice of virtue, or what in the religious stile are called good works. Those, however, of our congregation, who considered themselves as orthodox Presbyterians, disapproved his doctrine, and were joined by most of the old clergy, who arraigned him of heterodoxy before the synod, in order to have him silenced. I became his zealous partisan, and contributed all I could to raise a party in his favour, and we combated for him a while with some hopes of success. There was much scribbling pro and con upon the occasion; and finding that, tho' an elegant preacher, he was but a poor writer, I lent him my pen and wrote for him two or three pamphlets, and one piece in the Gazette of April, 1735. These pamphlets, as is generally the case with controversial writings, though eagerly read at the time, were soon out of vogue, and I question whether a single copy of them now exists.

During the contest an unlucky occurrence hurt his cause exceedingly. One of our adversaries having heard him preach a sermon that was much admired, thought he had somewhere read the sermon before, or at least a part of it. On search, he found that part quoted at length, in one of the British Reviews, from a discourse of Dr. Foster's. This detection gave many of our party disgust, who accordingly abandoned his cause, and occasioned our more speedy discomfiture in the synod. I stuck by him, however, as I rather approved his giving us good sermons composed by others, than bad ones of his own manufacture, though the latter was the practice of our common teachers. He afterward acknowledged to me that none of those he preached were his own; adding, that his memory was such as enabled him to retain and repeat any sermon after one reading only. On our defeat, he left us in search elsewhere of better fortune, and I quitted the congregation, never joining it after, though I continued many years my subscription for the support of its ministers.

* * *

In 1739 arrived among us from Ireland the Reverend Mr. Whitefield, who had made himself remarkable there as an itinerant preacher. He was at first permitted to preach in some of our churches; but the clergy, taking a dislike to him, soon refused him their pulpits, and he was obliged to preach in the fields. The multitudes of all sects and denominations that attended his sermons were enormous, and it was matter of speculation to me, who was one of the number, to observe the extraordinary influence of his oratory on his hearers, and how much they admired and respected him, notwithstanding his common abuse of them, by assuring them they were naturally *half beasts and half devils*. It was wonderful to see the change soon made in the manners of our inhabitants. From being thoughtless or indifferent about religion, it seemed as if all the world were growing religious, so that one could not walk through the town in an evening without hearing psalms sung in different families of every street.

And it being found inconvenient to assemble in the open air, subject to its inclemencies, the building of a house to meet in was no sooner proposed, and persons appointed to receive contributions, but sufficient sums were soon received to procure the ground and erect the building, which was one hundred feet long and seventy broad, about the size of Westminster Hall; and the work was carried on with such spirit as to be finished in a much shorter time than could have been expected. Both house and ground were vested in trustees, expressly for the use of any preacher of any religious persuasion who might desire to say something to the people at Philadelphia; the design in building not being to accommodate any particular sect, but the inhabitants in general; so that even if the Mufti of Constantinople were to send a missionary to preach Mohammedanism to us, he would find a pulpit at his service.

Mr. Whitefield, in leaving us, went preaching all the way through the colonies to Georgia. The settlement of that province had lately been begun, but, instead of being made with hardy, industrious husbandmen, accustomed to labor, the only people fit for such an enterprise, it was with families of broken shop-keepers and other insolvent debtors, many of indolent and idle habits, taken out of the jails, who, being set down in the woods, unqualified for clearing land, and unable to endure the hardships of a new settlement, perished in numbers, leaving many helpless children unprovided for. The sight of their miserable situation inspired the benevolent heart of Mr. White-field with the idea of building an Orphan House there, in which they might be supported and educated. Returning northward, he preached up this charity, and made large collections, for his eloquence had a wonderful power over the hearts and purses of his hearers, of which I myself was an instance.

I did not disapprove of the design, but, as Georgia was then destitute of materials and workmen, and it was proposed to send them from Philadelphia at a great expense, I thought it would have been better to have built the house there, and brought the children to it. This I advised; but he was resolute in his first project, rejected my counsel, and I therefore refused to contribute. I happened soon after to attend one of his sermons, in the course of which I perceived he intended to finish with a collection, and I silently resolved he should get nothing from me. I had in my pocket a handful of copper money, three or four silver dollars, and five pistoles in gold. As he proceeded I began to soften, and concluded to give the coppers. Another stroke of his oratory made me ashamed of that, and determined me to give the silver; and he finished so admirably, that I emptied my pocket wholly into the collector's dish, gold and all. At this sermon there was also one of our club, who being of my sentiments respecting the building in Georgia, and suspecting a collection might be intended, had, by precaution, emptied his pockets before he came from home. Towards the conclusion of the discourse, however, he felt a strong desire to give, and applied to a neighbor, who stood near him, to borrow some money for the purpose. The application was unfortunately [made] to perhaps the only man in the company who had the firmness not to be affected by the preacher. His answer was, "*At any other time, Friend Hopkinson, I would lend to thee freely; but not now, for thee seems to be out of thy right senses.*"

Some of Mr. Whitefield's enemies affected to suppose that he would apply these collections to his own private emolument; but I, who was intimately acquainted with him (being employed in printing his Sermons and Journals, etc.), never had the least suspicion of his integrity, but am to this day decidedly of opinion that he was in all his conduct a perfectly *honest man*; and methinks my testimony in his favour ought to have the more weight, as we had no religious connection. He used, indeed, sometimes to pray for my conversion, but never had the satisfaction of believing that his prayers were heard. Ours was a mere civil friendship, sincere on both sides, and lasted to his death.

The following instance will show something of the terms on which we stood. Upon one of his arrivals from England at Boston, he wrote to me that he should come soon to Philadelphia, but knew not where he could lodge when there, as he understood his old friend, and host, Mr. Benezet, was removed to Germantown. My answer was, "You know my house; if you can make shift with its scanty accommodations, you will be most heartily welcome." He replied, that if I made that kind offer for Christ's sake, I should not miss of a reward. And I returned, *"Don't let me be mistaken; it was not for Christ's sake, but for your sake."* One of our common acquaintance jocosely remarked, that, knowing it to be the custom of the saints, when they received any favour, to shift the burden of the obligation from off their own shoulders, and place it in heaven, I had contrived to fix it on earth.

The last time I saw Mr. Whitefield was in London, when he consulted me about his Orphan House concern, and his purpose of appropriating it to the establishment of a college.

He had a loud and clear voice, and articulated his words and sentences so perfectly, that he might be heard and understood at a great distance, especially as his auditors, however numerous, observed the most exact silence. He preached one evening from the top of the Court-house steps, which are in the middle of Market-street, and on the west side of Second-street, which crosses it at right angles. Both streets were filled with his hearers to a considerable distance. Being among the hindmost in Market-street, I had the curiosity to learn how far he could be heard, by retiring backwards down the street towards the river; and I found his voice distinct till I came near Front-street, when some noise in that street obscured it. Imagining then a semicircle, of which my distance should be the radius, and that it were filled with auditors, to each of whom I allowed two square feet, I computed that he might well be heard by more than thirty thousand. This reconciled me to the newspaper accounts of his having preached to twenty-five thousand people in the fields, and to the ancient histories of generals haranguing whole armies, of which I had sometimes doubted.

By hearing him often, I came to distinguish easily between sermons newly composed, and those which he had often preached in the course of his travels. His delivery of the latter was so improved by frequent repetitions that every accent, every emphasis, every modulation of voice, was so perfectly well turned and well placed, that, without being interested in the subject, one could not help being pleased with the discourse; a pleasure of much the same kind with that received from an excellent piece of music. This is an advantage itinerant preachers have over those who are stationary, as the latter cannot well improve their delivery of a sermon by so many rehearsals.

Benjamin Franklin was welcome wherever he went on the Continent. He had an audience with Pope Pius VI in 1784, one eventual result of which was that John Carroll became the first Roman Catholic bishop in the United States. In 1776, Father Carroll had joined Franklin on a special mission to Canada. During the mission, Franklin became ill; Father Carroll helped to care for him. The immediate background of this letter was that Franklin had heard reports that French circles were intriguing to have the Catholic Church in America placed under a French vicar-apostolic responsible to the papal nuncio in Paris. Benjamin Franklin paid a call on the Pope. Father Carroll was named prefect-apostolic in 1784. He became bishop on November 14, 1789.

FRANKLIN DIARY, JULY 1, 1784

The Pope's Nuncio called, and acquainted me that the Pope had, on my recommendation, appointed Mr. John Carroll, superior of the Catholic clergy in America, with many of the powers of a bishop; and that probably he would be made a bishop *in partibus* before the end of the year. He asked me which would be most convenient for him, to come to France, or go to St. Domingo, for ordination by another bishop, which was necessary. I mentioned Quebec as more convenient than either. He asked whether, as that was an English province, our government might not take offence at his going thither? I thought not, unless the ordination by that bishop should give him some authority over our bishop. He said, not in the least; that when our bishop was once ordained, he would be independent of the others, and even of the Pope; which I did not clearly understand. He said the Congregation *de Propagandâ Fide* had agreed to receive, and maintain and instruct, two young Americans in the languages and sciences at Rome; (he had formerly told me that more would be educated *gratis* in France). He added, they had written from America that there are twenty priests, but that they are not sufficient; as the new settlements near the Mississippi have need of some.

The Nuncio said we should find, that the Catholics were not so intolerant as they had been represented; that the Inquisition in Rome had not now so much power as that in Spain; and that in Spain it was used chiefly as a prison of state. That the Congregation would have undertaken the education of more American youths, and may hereafter, but that at present they are overburdened, having some from all parts of the world. He spoke lightly of their New Bostonian convert Thayer's conversion; that he had advised him not to go to America, but settle in France. That he wanted to go to convert his countrymen; but he knew nothing yet of his new religion himself, &c.

Received a letter from Mr. Bridgen of London, dated the 22nd past, acquainting me, that the Council of the Royal Society had voted me a gold medal, on account of my letter in favor of Captain Cook. Lord Howe had sent me his Journal, 3 vols. 4to, with a large volume of engravings, on the same account, and, as he writes, "*with the King's approbation.*"

BENJAMIN FRANKLIN

Two weeks after his audience with Pope Pius VI on the matter of Jᶜ Carroll, Franklin has another matter for disposition by the Vatican.

FRANKLIN DIARY, JULY 16, 1784

Received a letter from two young gentlemen in London, who are come from America for ecclesiastical orders, and complain that they have been delayed there a year, and that the Archbishop will not permit them to be ordained unless they will take the oath of allegiance; and desiring to know if they may be ordained here. Inquired, and learned that, if ordained here, they must vow obedience to the Archbishop of Paris. Directed my grandson to ask the Nuncio, if their bishop in America might not be instructed to do it literally?

FRANKLIN DIARY, JULY 18, 1784

A good abbé brings me a large manuscript containing a scheme of reformation of all churches and states, religion, commerce, laws, &c., which he has planned in his closet, without much knowledge of the world. I have promised to look it over, and he is to call next Thursday. It is amazing the number of legislators that kindly bring me new plans for governing the United States.

Ezra Stiles, Congregational minister, president of Yale College, and fighter for the abolition of slavery, maintained a correspondence with many of the most important men in the Revolutionary period of American history. Some of the questions he put in his letters were concerned with the religious beliefs of the recipients.

LETTER TO EZRA STILES, MARCH 9, 1790

I received your kind letter of January 28, and am glad you have at length received the portrait of Governor Yale from his family, and deposited it in the College Library. He was a great and good man, and had the merit of doing infinite service to your country by his munificence to that institution. The honor you propose doing me by placing mine in the same room with his, is much too great for my deserts; but you always had a partiality for me, and to that it must be ascribed. I am however too much obliged to Yale College, the first learned Society that took notice of me and adorned me with its honors, to refuse a request that comes from it through so esteemed a friend. But I do not think any one of the portraits you mention, as in my possession, worthy of the place and company you propose to place it in. You have an excellent artist lately arrived. If he will undertake to make one for you, I shall cheerfully pay the expense; but he must not delay setting about it, or I may slip through his fingers, for I am now in my 85th year, and very infirm.

1 this a very learned work, as it seems to me, on the ancient
ns, lately printed in Spain, and at least curious for the beauty
ion. Please accept it for your College Library. I have subscribed
opedia now printing here, with the intention of presenting it
. I shall probably depart before the work is finished, but shall
leave directions for its continuance to the end. With this you will receive
some of the first numbers.

You desire to know something of my religion. It is the first time I have
been questioned upon it. But I cannot take your curiosity amiss, and shall
endeavor in a few words to gratify it. Here is my creed. I believe in one God,
Creator of the Universe. That he governs it by his Providence. That he ought
to be worshipped. That the most acceptable service we render to him is doing
good to his other children. That the soul of man is immortal, and will be
treated with justice in another life respecting its conduct in this. These I take
to be the fundamental principles of all sound religion, and I regard them
as you do in whatever sect I meet with them.

As to Jesus of Nazareth, my opinion of whom you particularly desire, I
think the system of morals and his religion, as he left them to us, the best
the world ever saw or is likely to see; but I apprehend it has received various
corrupting changes, and I have, with most of the present dissenters in England, some doubts as to his divinity; though it is a question I do not dogmatize
upon, having never studied it, and think it needless to busy myself with it
now, when I expect soon an opportunity of knowing the truth with less
trouble. I see no harm, however, in its being believed, if that belief has the
good consequence, as probably it has, of making his doctrines more respected
and better observed; especially as I do not perceive, that the Supreme takes
it amiss, by distinguishing the unbelievers in his government of the world
with any peculiar marks of his displeasure.

I shall only add, respecting myself, that having experienced the goodness
of that Being in conducting me prosperously through a long life, I have no
doubt of its continuance in the next, though without the smallest conceit of
meriting such goodness. My sentiments on this head you will see in the
copy of an old letter enclosed,[3] which I wrote in answer to one from a zealous
religionist, whom I had relieved in a paralytic case by electricity, and who,
being afraid I should grow proud upon it, sent me his serious though rather
impertinent caution. I send you also the copy of another letter,[4] which will
show something of my disposition relating to religion. With great and sincere

---

[3] [Probably a letter written to Joseph Huey.—ED.]
[4] [This is possibly a reference to a letter to Thomas Paine.—ED.]

esteem and affection, I am, your obliged old friend and most obedient humble servant

B. FRANKLIN

P.S. Had not your College some present of books from the King of France? Please to let me know, if you had an expectation given you of more, and the nature of that expectation? I have a reason for the enquiry.

I confide, that you will not expose me to criticism and censure by publishing any part of this communication to you. I have ever let others enjoy their religious sentiments, without reflecting on them for those that appeared to me unsupportable and even absurd. All sects, here, and we have a great variety, have experienced my good will in assisting them with subscriptions for building their new places of worship; and, as I have never opposed any of their doctrines, I hope to go out of the world in peace with them all.[5]

FRANKLIN'S HOPE FOR MANKIND

God grant that not only the Love of Liberty but a thorough knowledge of the rights of man may pervade all the nations of the earth, so that a philosopher may set his feet anywhere on its surface and say, "This is my country."

---

[5] [This letter was written in reply to the following query in a letter from Ezra Stiles (January 28, 1790):

"You know, sir, that I am a Christian, and would to Heaven all others were such as I am, except my imperfections and deficiencies of moral character. As much as I know of Dr. Franklin, I have not an idea of his religious sentiments. I wish to know the opinion of my venerable friend concerning Jesus of Nazareth. He will not impute this to *impertinence* or improper curiosity, in one, who for so many years has continued to love, estimate, and reverence his abilities and literary character, with an ardor and affection bordering on adoration. If I have said too much, let the request be blotted out, and be no more; and yet I shall never cease to wish you that happy Immortality, which I believe Jesus alone has purchased for the virtuous and truly good of every religious denomination in Christendom, and for those of every Age, Nation, and Mythology, who reverence the Deity, and are filled with integrity, righteousness and benevolence. Wishing you every blessing, I am, dear Sir, your most obedient servant,

EZRA STILES."—ED.]

2. GEORGE WASHINGTON

"... The Path of True Piety Is So Plain as to Require But Little Political Direction"

THE end of the American War for Independence brought freedom from outside rule, but it also brought uncertainty and upheaval. The states became insecure in their relationships with each other. There were those in Connecticut who feared the expansionist aims of Massachusetts, and vice versa. New York and New Jersey, with a common harbor, became involved in tariff wrangling. Currency was not uniform throughout the states. The states were strengthening their militia.

It was for the purpose of averting a total breakdown that a call was issued for a conference at Philadelphia that might explore ways of strengthening the Articles of Confederation, under which states were then organized. It was realized that the success of the conference or convention would depend in substantial part on the man who would serve as its head. There was only one man who had the unanimous support of the entire convention. It was the general who had held the American forces together during the victorious Revolution. George Washington had succeeded in turning back the British largely because he was able to keep the military coalition of the states from breaking off into fragments. Washington had the stature and the singleness of purpose that gave the states the confidence, the rallying power, and the tenacity needed for victory. He was a man of good will and absolute integrity, in whom all Americans could believe regardless of party.

It was this combination of abilities that saved the Federal Constitutional Convention. Washington did exactly what was expected of him. He stayed outside the range of frequently bitter debate, using his authority sparingly so that he could apply his full prestige before the people of all the states in the biggest job of all, which was to get the Constitution ratified. This ability to stand symbolically before the nation with arms fully outstretched in order to appeal to and embrace all groups and parties caused many people to regard him as a national father. And when it became necessary to elect the first

President under the United States Constitution, the choice of the electors was automatic.

George Washington carried with him into the Presidency the belief that he could be above the give-and-take of party strife and political debate. He appointed a Cabinet in which opposing political views would be both represented and balanced. He apparently felt that good will and the overview would enable him to reconcile any differences. For a time the symbol of Washington was strong enough to make the system work; but it was inevitable perhaps that the political rough-and-tumble would emerge sooner or later. In a republic one party has to take the responsibility for creating a program and doing everything in its power to develop the popular support to get it accepted. The luster of Washington's reputation could not indefinitely sustain a nonpolitical approach to hard political questions. The attacks on him grew increasingly bitter. Some in his own party felt that he had never really been one of them, and there were those in the opposition who could hardly wait for him to become a legitimate political target. The result was a period of brutal criticism the like of which the country has seldom seen since. Washington was even lampooned as the "Stepfather of his Country." He became progressively embittered; in 1793 he permitted himself to say before his Cabinet that he would rather be in his grave than in the present situation.

Whatever Washington's difficulties as President, the fact remains that he was superbly equipped for the job of leadership during the Revolution, at the Philadelphia Convention, and for the symbolic requirements of the first Presidency. In his retirement he regained the high standing he had once enjoyed; his detractors became silent.

Washington was born in Virginia in 1732. His parents were well placed socially. His religious education was Episcopalian. His formal schooling was limited to about five years. When he was eleven, his father died and his older half-brother Lawrence, a devout churchman, became his guardian. At fifteen George became a surveyor. This led to some interest in real estate. When he was seventeen, he invested his accumulated earnings—$500—in the purchase of large tracts. In this way he met people who lived close to the land; many of them were freemen and dissenters. They, in turn, came to respect the young man who was so restrained in manner, fair in his dealings, genuinely interested in their well-being. Repeatedly, they elected him as their representative. At the age of twenty-four, Washington was elected to the Virginia House of Burgesses. He served in the state militia. His military rise was rapid. At forty-four he became commander in chief of the Continental Army.

Not all the decisions Washington had to make as military leader were concerned with purely military affairs. As a number of the following items indicate, the attitudes and dispositions of his soldiers were of considerable importance. On several occasions he found it necessary to deal with religious prejudice. Anti-Catholicism during the Revolutionary period of American history was particularly rife. "No Popery" banners flew in various parts of New England. Tory Loyalists tried to frighten their fellow Americans into giving up the fight against England by holding up the threat of domination by the Catholic Church. "An absolute dominion over you will be set up by your late protectors," a Tory pamphlet declared. "An American Bastille will be erected; the Romish religion will be established; the maxims and proceedings . . . of the Romish inquisition will be your reward for your infinite ingratitude and folly in casting off the enlightened, humane, and equitable authority of your rightful sovereign."

The Army was not immune from such fears, some of which were related to what was happening in Canada. In June, 1774, Parliament passed the Quebec Act, a liberal piece of legislation, certainly so far as the French Canadians were concerned. The act was an effort to retain the loyalty of the Canadians. It restored many of the French laws which had previously been revoked and it granted full scope for religious belief and activity. Since most of the beneficiaries were Catholics, the Quebec Act was regarded most uneasily in the states. It was not difficult for agitators to whip up anti-Catholic frenzy by talking about the growing threat of Catholicism in the New World. In New York, a young radical named Alexander Hamilton wrote against the Quebec Act. In Boston, Samuel Adams was denouncing the act in terms that were on a par with the condemnation of Great Britain for closing the port of Boston and annulling self-government in Massachusetts. Hamilton and Adams, of course, were extremely sensitive on the religious issue in view of their abhorrence of what had happened in European history. But the specific things they said against the Quebec Act erased the important dividing line between legitimate concern over special privilege in religion and harmful appeals to religious prejudice.

Anxiety over Canada was intensified by another provision in the Quebec Act, under which territory north of the Ohio River was to be annexed to the Province of Quebec. In June, 1775, a Connecticut militia officer, Benedict Arnold, persuaded Congress to authorize a military expedition into Canada for the purpose of bringing it into the military union. By this time, however, anti-Catholic bigotry in the States had become an issue in Canada; the Catholic hierarchy in Canada was loyal to the Crown.

The attitude of the American expeditionary force in Canada toward Catholics and Catholicism was of profound concern to General Washington, as his order to Colonel Arnold makes clear. His instructions to guard against religious bigotry were explicit and effective. One of the measures he took to indicate his own position was to issue an Army order calling for the commemoration of St. Patrick's Day. Washington was well aware of religious abuses that caused people to react politically; but he was also aware of the dangers of fancied abuse and bigotry. In his command of the Army and in his Presidency of the United States, he was constantly vigilant in the cause of religious freedom. He was also careful to avoid any seeming partiality.

This may help to explain why Washington has been chosen as one of their own by various denominations—and, for that matter, why he has been claimed by nonbelievers. His broad, generous public positions were apparently interpreted differently by different groups. Some controversy arose as to whether he was even a Christian.

Washington's early biographers were convinced that he was a devout practitioner of orthodox Christianity. Jared Sparks quotes friends of Washington who accompanied him to church in various parts of the United States. Sparks also quotes a letter in which Washington said he was "sure there never was a people who had more reason to acknowledge a divine interposition in their affairs than those of the United States; and I should be pained to believe that they have forgotten that agency, which was so often manifested during our revolution, or that they failed to consider the omnipotence of that God, who is alone able to protect them." From another letter quoted by Sparks: "Ours is a kind of struggle designed by Providence, I dare say, to try the patience, fortitude, and virtue of men."

The frequent references to the Deity, as well as the character and actions of Washington, convinced Sparks that Washington was a believing and practicing Christian: "If a man who spoke, wrote, and acted as a Christian through a long life, who gave numerous proofs of his believing himself to be such, and who was never known to say, write, or do a thing contrary to his professions—if such a man is not to be ranked among the believers of Christianity, it would be impossible to establish the point by any train of reasoning."

There were many men of good will and good faith, however, who have used substantially the same evidence to support their belief that Washington, like Jefferson and Franklin, was nondenominational in his spiritual views. They point out, as Thomas Cumming Hall has done in *The Religious Background of American Culture*, that Washington attended church without formal affiliation. They are convinced that Washington was profoundly affected by the morals and teachings of Jesus and that he was certainly a Christian in this sense, augmenting his natural Deism.

Whatever the precise facts, it is most certainly untrue that Washington was an atheist, as was charged during his Presidency and at various times since. The fact that he took no communion once the American Revolution started may have greater political than religious significance; his earlier connection with the Church of England may have been a factor.

If there is ambiguity about his specific views, this is doubtless a reflection of the fact that he had a strong sense of privacy about certain things and permitted no intrusion. He was completely gracious when the question would come up, however, as may be apparent in the material that follows. And he went to considerable trouble to assure all denominations that he had nothing but the highest respect for their particular beliefs. His approbation, however, was nearly identical in all instances. It is also clear that, like most of the other political leaders of his time, he felt he could best serve religion by ensuring that no single denomination be given government authority over the others. He wrote to the Reformed German Congregation in New York that "the establishment of Civil and Religious Liberty was the Motive which induced me to the Field [the American Revolution]." And to the members of the New Church in Baltimore he wrote:

"We have abundant reason to rejoice that in this Land the light of truth and reason has triumphed over the power of bigotry and superstition, and that every person may here worship God according to the dictates of his own heart. In this enlightened Age and in this land of equal liberty it is our boast that a man's religious tenets will not forfeit the protection of the laws, nor deprive him of the right of attaining and holding the highest offices that are known in the United States."

Washington died at the age of sixty-seven. There is some question whether his death might not have been caused by poor medical treatment. He had a severe respiratory ailment and fever. Four times during the day blood was drawn from him, in accordance with contemporary medical practice. It is possible that he lost two quarts of blood in this manner. In addition, he was made to drink powerful potions that almost choked him; plasters of various sorts added not at all to his comfort. Toward the end he was aware that he was dying. He was completely calm about the fact and dictated various memoranda to make sure that all his affairs would be put in order. When a secretary at his bedside expressed the devout hope that he would recover, Washington smiled, saying that his death was near and that it was a "debt which we must all pay." A few minutes later, he summoned his secretary. "I am just going," he said. "Have me decently buried; and do not let my body be put into the vault in less than three days after I am dead. Do you understand me?" The secretary said he did, and Washington said, " 'Tis well." These were his last words.

The first two items that follow were addressed to Colonel Benedict Arnold, then in charge of the military expedition in Canada. There were reports of anti-Catholic sentiment in the Continental forces. Supposedly, a "Pope's Night" was to be staged in which the Pope would be burned in effigy. This was hardly the way to persuade the Catholic French Canadians to join the American Union. In any event, it was religious bigotry and General Washington acted to stop it. The first item is an excerpt from an explanatory letter to Colonel Arnold. The second consists of the pertinent section from the official order. It is made clear that rights of conscience in religious matters are to be protected.

LETTER TO BENEDICT ARNOLD, SEPTEMBER 14, 1775

You are intrusted with a command of the utmost consequence to the interest and liberties of America. Upon your conduct and courage and that of the officers and soldiers detached on this expedition, not only the success of the present enterprise, and your own honor, but the safety and welfare of the whole continent may depend. I charge you, therefore, and the officers and soldiers under your command, as you value your own safety and honor and the favor and esteem of your country, that you consider yourselves as marching, not through an enemy's country; but that of our friends and brethren, for such the inhabitants of Canada and the Indian Nations have proved themselves in this unhappy contest between Great Britain and America. That you check by every motive of duty and fear of punishment, every attempt to plunder or insult any of the inhabitants of Canada. Should any American soldier be so base and infamous as to injure any Canadian or Indian, in his person or property, I do most earnestly enjoin you to bring him to such severe and exemplary punishment as the enormity of the crime may require. Should it extend to Death itself it will not be disproportional to its guilt at such a time and in such a cause: But I hope and trust, that the brave men who have voluntarily engaged in this expedition, will be governed by far different views; that order, discipline, and regularity of behavior will be as conspicuous, as their courage and valour.

I also give it in charge to you to avoid all disrespect to or contempt of the religion of the country and its ceremonies. Prudence, policy, and a true Christian spirit, will lead us to look with compassion upon their errors without insulting them. While we are contending for our own liberty, we should be very cautious of violating the rights of conscience in others, ever considering that God alone is the judge of the hearts of men, and to him only in this case, they are answerable. Upon the whole, sir, I beg you to inculcate upon the officers and soldiers, the necessity of preserving the strictest order during their march through Canada; to represent to them the shame, disgrace and ruin to themselves and country if they should by their conduct turn the hearts of our brethren in Canada against us. And on the other hand, the honors and rewards which await them, if by their prudence and good behavior, they conciliate the affections of the Canadians and

Indians, to the great interests of America, and convert those favorable dispositions they have shown into a lasting union and affection. Thus wishing you and the officers and soldiers under your command all honor, safety, and success, I remain, sir, etc.

INSTRUCTIONS TO ARNOLD, SEPTEMBER 14, 1775

As the Contempt of the Religion of a Country by ridiculing any of its Ceremonies or affronting its Ministers or Votaries has ever been deeply resented, you are to be particularly careful to restrain every Officer and Soldier from such Imprudence and Folly and to punish every Instance of it. On the other Hand, as far as lays in your power, you are to protect and support the free Exercise of the Religion of the Country and the undisturbed Enjoyment of the rights of Conscience in religious matters, with your utmost Influence and Authority. Given under my Hand, at Head Quarters, Cambridge, this 14th Day of September one Thousand seven Hundred and seventy-five.

The next five items are drawn from Washington's General Orders, from 1775 to 1779. These orders stress the need for religious influence and outlook. They also take up the matter of cursing and drunkenness. Things were bad enough in the Continental Army—low pay, severe physical discomfort, inadequate equipment, poor food—without having to worry about disorderliness. Washington presided over the Army the way he presided over his own household, with fatherly firmness.

GENERAL ORDERS, 1775-79

HEADQUARTERS, CAMBRIDGE, JULY 4, 1775

The General most earnestly requires, and expects, a due observance of those articles of war, established for the government of the army which forbid profane cursing, swearing and drunkenness; and in like manner requires and expects, of all officers, and soldiers, not engaged on actual duty, a punctual attendance on divine service, to implore the blessings of heaven upon the means used for our safety and defence.

HEADQUARTERS, NEW YORK, JULY 9, 1776

The Hon. Continental Congress having been pleased to allow a Chaplain to each Regiment, with the pay of Thirty-three Dollars and one third per month—The Colonels or commanding officers of each regiment are directed to procure Chaplains accordingly; persons of good Characters and exemplary lives—To see that all inferior officers and soldiers pay them a suitable respect and attend carefully upon religious exercises. The blessing and protection of Heaven are at all times necessary but especially so in times of public distress and danger—the General hopes and trusts, that every officer and man will endeavor to so live, and act, as becomes a Christian Soldier defending the dearest Rights and Liberties of his country.

HEADQUARTERS, NEW YORK, AUGUST 3, 1776

Parole Uxbridge. Countersign Virginia.

That the Troops may have an opportunity of attending public worship, as well as take some rest after the great fatigue they have gone through; The General in future excuses them from fatigue duty on Sundays (except at the Ship Yards, or special occasions) until further orders. The General is sorry to be informed that the foolish, and wicked practice, of profane cursing and swearing (a Vice heretofore little known in an American Army) is growing into fashion; he hopes the officers will, by example, as well as influence, endeavour to check it, and that both they, and the men will reflect, that we can have little hopes of the blessing of Heaven on our Arms, if we insult it by our impiety, and folly; added to this, it is a vice so mean and low, without any temptation, that every man of sense, and character, detests and despises it.

HEADQUARTERS, VALLEY FORGE, MAY 2, 1778

While we are zealously performing the duties of good Citizens and Soldiers we certainly ought not to be inattentive to the higher duties of Religion. To the distinguished Character of Patriot, it should be our highest Glory to add the more distinguished Character of Christian. The signal Instances of providential Goodness which we have experienced and which have now almost crowned our labours with complete success, demand from us in a peculiar manner the warmest returns of Gratitude and Piety to the Supreme Author of all Good.

HEADQUARTERS, MOORES HOUSE, JULY 29, 1779

Many and pointed orders have been issued against that unmeaning and abominable custom of *Swearing*, notwithstanding which, with much regret the General observes that it prevails, *if possible*, more than ever; His feelings are continually wounded by the Oaths and Imprecations of the soldiers whenever he is in hearing of them.

The Name of That Being, from whose bountiful goodness we are permitted to exist and enjoy the comforts of life is incessantly imprecated and profaned in a manner as wanton as it is shocking. For the sake therefore of religion, decency and order the General hopes and trusts that officers of every rank will use their influence and authority to check a vice, which is as unprofitable as it is wicked and shameful.

If officers would make it an invariable rule to reprimand, and if that does not do punish soldiers for offences of this kind it could not fail of having the desired effect.

This letter to George Washington's stepson, John Parke Custis, was written on January 22, 1777. A few weeks earlier, General Washington had crossed the Delaware, unhinging the British position along the river. The British retreated to New Brunswick and Washington began the arduous job of rebuilding his forces.

LETTER TO JOHN PARKE CUSTIS, JANUARY 22, 1777

. . . In a word, I believe I may with truth add, that I do not think any officer since the creation ever had such a variety of difficulties and perplexities to encounter as I have. How we shall be able to rub along till the new army is raised, I know not. Providence has heretofore saved us in a remarkable manner, and on this we must principally rely.

The successful operation of a revolution was not the only thing General Washington had to worry about. When his brother Samuel died, the estate was in a terrible tangle; George had the job of straightening it out. Not long before Samuel died, his wife passed away. The following letter of condolence was written by George to his brother on August 10, 1777.

LETTER TO SAMUEL WASHINGTON, AUGUST 10, 1777

I most sincerely condole with you on your late loss; and doubt not your feeling it in the most sensible manner; nor do I expect that human Fortitude, and reason, can so far overcome natural affection, as to enable us to look with calmness upon losses which distress us although they are acts of Providence, and in themselves unavoidable, yet acquiescence to the divine will is not only a duty, but is to be aided by every manly exertion to forget the causes of such uneasiness.

One of George Washington's friends, distantly related by marriage, was Bryan Fairfax, of Virginia. Fairfax was a conservative and a loyalist. He felt certain in 1774 that he could persuade George Washington of the unreasonableness of the growing movement against Great Britain. In particular, he wanted Washington to send a conciliatory message to Parliament. Washington politely refused. The same year Washington presented county resolutions calling for rebellion and offered to raise a thousand men for this purpose, pay for them himself, and march them to Boston. Fairfax became increasingly unpopular in Virginia and found it expedient to leave. Later, he wrote Washington a letter saying how fairly he, Fairfax, had been treated by Washington. ". . . At a time your popularity was at the highest and mine at the lowest," Fairfax wrote, "and when it is so common for men's resentments to run high against those that differ from them in opinion . . . you [acted] with your wonted kindness towards me. [This] hath affected me more than any favour I have received; and could not be believed by some in New York, it being above the run of common minds." Washington wrote a characteristically gracious reply.

LETTER TO BRYAN FAIRFAX, MARCH 1, 1778

Your favor of the 8th of Decr. came safe to my hands after a considerable delay in its passage. The sentiments you have expressed of me in this Letter are highly flattering, meriting my warmest acknowledgments, as I have too good an Opinion of your sincerity and candour to believe that you are capable of unmeaning professions and speaking a language foreign from your Heart. The friendship I ever professed, and felt for you, met with no diminution from the difference in our political Sentiments. I know the rectitude of my own intentions, and believing in the sincerity of yours, lamented, though I did not condemn, your renunciation of the creed I had adopted. Nor do I think any person, or power, ought to do it, whilst your conduct is not opposed to the general Interest of the people and the measures they are pursuing; the latter, that is our actions, depending upon ourselves, may be controlled, while the powers of thinking originating in higher causes, cannot always be moulded to our wishes.

The determinations of Providence are all ways wise; often inscrutable, and though its decrees appear to bear hard upon us at times is nevertheless meant for gracious purposes; in this light I cannot help viewing your late disappointment; for if you had been permitted to have gone to England, unrestrained even by the rigid oaths which are administered on those occasions your feelings as a husband, Parent, and etc. must have been considerably wounded in the prospect of a long, perhaps lasting separation from your nearest relatives. What then must they have been if the obligation of an oath had left you without a Will? Your hope of being instrumental in restoring Peace would prove as unsubstantial as mist before the Noon days Sun and would as soon dispel: for believe me, Sir, great Britain understood herself perfectly well in this dispute but did not comprehend America. She meant as Lord Campden in his late speech in Parliament clearly, and explicitly declared, to drive America into rebellion that her own purposes might be more fully answered by it but take this along with it, that this Plan originating in a firm belief, founded on misinformation.

George Washington never failed to ascribe a result to the will of Providence, nor did he ever fail to work for a desired result to the point of exhaustion, if necessary—as the following excerpt from a letter may indicate. It was a classical instance of "Praise the Lord and pass the ammunition." The recipient of this letter, Brigadier General Thomas Nelson, had once commanded the Old Dominion militia in front of Yorktown, was a signer of the Declaration of Independence, and was a delegate at the Constitutional Convention. When General Nelson died, he left a widow and eleven children, and was £35,000 in debt. Hearing of this and knowing that General Nelson had given his entire fortune to the Revolutionary cause, Washington did everything he could to help, including the appointment of young Thomas Nelson to a place on his secretarial staff. This letter was written from Washington's field camp in White Plains.

LETTER TO THOMAS NELSON, AUGUST 20, 1778

It is not a little pleasing, nor less wonderful to contemplate, that after two years manoeuvring and undergoing the strangest vicissitudes that perhaps ever attended any one contest since the creation, both armies are brought back to the very point they set out from and, that that which was the offending party in the beginning is now reduced to the use of the spade and pick axe for defence. The hand of Providence has been so conspicuous in all this, that he must be worse than an infidel that lacks faith, and more than wicked, that has not gratitude enough to acknowledge his obligations but, it will be time enough for me to turn preacher when my present appointment ceases; and therefore I shall add no more on the Doctrine of Providence; but make a tender of my best respects to your good Lady; the Secretary and other friends, and assure you that with the most perfect regard I am &c.

The Indians of the Delaware tribe had gone out of their way to be amicable toward the colonists. Their natural bent was peaceful—so much so, in fact, that they had stayed as far away from the turmoil of revolution as they could, identifying themselves at the beginning of the war with the loyal colonists. But now, in 1779, the chiefs of the Delaware Indians decided to pay a call on Congress and stopped off at Washington's headquarters, where he addressed them after their custom. Many years earlier, the tribe had endorsed Christianity. In 1782, a Christian settlement of the Delaware Indians was set upon and its people massacred. The meaning of Christianity apparently had not been fully understood by all of its own advocates.

SPEECH TO DELAWARE CHIEFS, MAY 12, 1779

Brothers: I am glad you have brought three of the Children of your principal Chiefs to be educated with us. I am sure Congress will open the arms of love to them, and will look upon them as their own Children, and will have them educated accordingly. This is a great mark of your confidence and of your desire to preserve the friendship between the Two Nations to the end of time, and to become One people with your Brethren of the United States. My ears hear with pleasure the other matters you mention. Congress will be glad to hear them too. You do well to wish to learn our arts and way of life, and above all, the religion of Jesus Christ. These will make you a greater and happier people than you are. Congress will do every thing they can to assist you in this wise intention; and to tie the knot of friendship and union so fast, that nothing shall ever be able to loose it.

The demobilization of the Army after victory had its intense strains for Washington. What troubled him particularly was that the discharged soldiers were not being given their accumulated back pay. Congress agreed with Washington that at least three months' back pay should be provided— in theory. In practice, the question was academic; there was not enough money. Then an idea was developed under which the states would assume part of the obligation. Washington wanted to do everything possible to cement good relations with the states.

FROM A CIRCULAR LETTER TO THE GOVERNORS OF THE STATES ON DISBANDING THE ARMY, HEADQUARTERS, NEWBURGH, JUNE 8, 1783

The free cultivation of letters, the unbounded extension of commerce, the progressive refinement of manners, the growing liberality of sentiment, and, above all, the pure and benign light of Revelation, have had a meliorating influence on mankind, and increased the blessings of society. At this auspicious period the United States came into existence as a Nation, and if their citizens should not be completely free and happy, the fault will be entirely their own. . . .

I now make it my earnest prayer that God would have you and the State over which you preside, in his holy protection, that he would incline the hearts of the citizens to cultivate a spirit of subordination and obedience to government; to entertain a brotherly affection and love for one another, for their fellow citizens of the United States at large, and particularly for their brethren who have served in the field; and, finally, that he would be most graciously pleased to dispose us all to do justice, to love mercy, and to demean ourselves with that charity, humility, and pacific temper of mind, which were *the characteristics of the Divine Author* of our blessed religion, and without an humble imitation of whose example in these things we can never hope to be a happy nation.

The Reverend John Rodgers, a Presbyterian clergyman who had served in both New York and Connecticut, wrote a letter to George Washington on May 30, 1783, suggesting that Congress give a Bible to each soldier in the Continental Army. Washington's reply was written from his headquarters.

LETTER TO JOHN RODGERS, JUNE 11, 1783

Your proposition respecting Mr. Aikins Bibles would have been particularly noticed by me, had it been suggested in Season; but the late Resolution of Congress for discharging part of the Army, taking off near two thirds of our Numbers, it is now too late to make the Attempt. It would have pleased me, if Congress should have made such an important present, to the brave fellows, who have done so much for the Security of their Country's Rights and Establishment.

Now that the war was over—both on the battlefield and at the treaty tables —George Washington wrote a note that had been on his mind for some time.

ADDRESS TO CONGRESS, DECEMBER 23, 1783

I consider it an indispensable duty to close this last solemn act of my official life by commending the interests of our dearest country to the protection of Almighty God, and those who have the superintendence of them, to his holy keeping.

Having now finished the work assigned me, I retire from the great theatre of action; and bidding an affectionate farewell to this august body under whose orders I have so long acted, I here offer my commission, and take my leave of all the employments of public life.

President Washington's correspondence with religious bodies is impressively voluminous. It is also somewhat repetitious—inevitably so, since it was an article of faith with Washington to show equal solicitude and respect toward all faiths. Washington was equally determined to keep his own religion a private matter and avoided any indication of affiliation in his letters. However, the extreme cordiality of the letters, as mentioned earlier, led some groups to make the identification themselves. Now follows a representative selection of letters and messages, all excerpted, written during the period 1782–97.

LETTERS TO RELIGIOUS BODIES, 1782–97

TO THE MINISTER, ELDERS, AND DEACONS OF THE REFORMED PROTESTANT DUTCH CHURCH IN KINGSTON, NOVEMBER 16, 1782

I am happy in receiving this public mark of the esteem of the Minister, Elders and Deacons of the Reformed Protestant Dutch Church in Kingston.

Convinced that our Religious Liberties were as essential as our Civil my endeavors have never been wanting to encourage and promote the one, while I have been contending for the other; and I am highly flattered by finding that my efforts have met the approbation of so respectable a body.

In return for your kind concern for my temporal and eternal happiness, permit me to assure you that my wishes are reciprocal; and that you may be enabled to hand down your Religion pure and undefiled to a Posterity worthy of their Ancestors is the fervent prayer of Gentlemen.

TO THE MINISTER, ELDERS, AND DEACONS OF THE TWO UNITED DUTCH RE-FORMED CHURCHES OF HACKENSACK AND SCHALENBURGH AND THE INHAB-ITANTS OF HACKENSACK, NOVEMBER 10, 1783

Your affectionate congratulations on the happy conclusion of the War, and the glorious prospect now opening to this extensive Country, cannot but be extremely satisfactory to me.

Having shared in common, the hardships and dangers of the War with my virtuous fellow Citizens in the field, as well as with those who on the Lines have been immediately exposed to the Arts and Arms of the Enemy, I feel the most lively sentiments of gratitude to that divine Providence which has graciously interposed for the protection of our Civil and Religious Liberties.

In retiring from the field of Contest to the sweets of private life, I claim no merit, but if in that retirement my most earnest wishes and prayers can be of any avail, nothing will exceed the prosperity of our common Country, and the temporal and spiritual felicity of those who are represented in your Address.

TO THE MINISTER, ELDERS, DEACONS, AND MEMBERS OF THE REFORMED GER-MAN CONGREGATION OF NEW YORK, NOVEMBER 27, 1783

The illustrious and happy event, the end of the War, on which you are pleased to congratulate and welcome me to this City, demands all our gratitude; while the favorable sentiments you have thought proper to express of my conduct, entitles you to my warmest acknowledgments.

Disposed, at every suitable opportunity to acknowledge publicly our infinite obligations to the Supreme Ruler of the Universe for rescuing our Country from the brink of destruction; I cannot fail at this time to ascribe all the honor of our late successes to the same glorious Being. And if my humble exertions have been made in any degree subservient to the execution of the divine purposes, a contemplation of the benediction of Heaven on our righteous Cause, the approbation of my virtuous Countrymen, and the testimony of my own Conscience, will be a sufficient reward and augment my felicity beyond anything which the world can bestow.

The establishment of Civil and Religious Liberty was the Motive which induced me to the Field; the object is attained, and it now remains to be my earnest wish and prayer, that the Citizens of the United States would make a wise and virtuous use of the blessings, placed before them; and that the reformed German Congregation in New York; may not only be conspicuous for their religious character, but as examplary, in support of our inestimable acquisitions, as their reverend Minister has been in the attainment of them.

IN REPLY TO AN ADDRESS FROM THE CLERGY, GENTLEMEN OF THE LAW, AND PHYSICIANS OF PHILADELPHIA, DECEMBER 13, 1783

Conscious of no impropriety in wishing to merit the esteem of my fellow Citizens in general; I cannot hesitate to acknowledge that I feel a certain pleasing sensation in obtaining the good opinion of men eminent for their virtue, knowledge and humanity; but I am sensible at the same time, it becomes me to receive with humility the warm commendations you are pleased to bestow on my conduct: for I have been led to detest the folly and madness of unbounded ambition if I have been induced from other motives to draw my sword and regulate my behaviour, or if the management of the War has been conducted upon purer principles: let me not arrogate the merit to human imbecility, but rather ascribe whatever glory may result from our successful struggle to a higher and more efficient Cause. For the re-establishment of our once violated rights; for the confirmation of our Independence; for the protection of Virtue, Philosophy and Literature: for the present flourishing state of the Sciences, and for the enlarged prospect of human happiness, it is our common duty to pay the tribute of gratitude to the greatest and best of Beings.

REPLY TO AN ADDRESS SENT BY THE GENERAL COMMITTEE OF THE UNITED BAPTIST CHURCHES IN VIRGINIA, MAY, 1789.

If I could have entertained the slightest apprehension, that the constitution framed in the convention, where I had the honor to preside, might possibly endanger the religious rights of any ecclesiastical society, certainly I would never have placed my signature to it; and if I could now conceive that the general government might ever be so administered as to render the liberty of conscience insecure, I beg you will be persuaded, that no one would be more zealous than myself to establish effectual barriers against the horrors of spiritual tyranny, and every species of religious persecution. For you doubtless remember, that I have often expressed my sentiments that every man, conducting himself as a good citizen, and being accountable to God alone for his religious opinions, ought to be protected in worshipping the Deity according to the dictates of his own conscience.

REPLY TO AN ADDRESS SENT BY THE GENERAL ASSEMBLY OF PRESBYTERIAN CHURCHES IN THE UNITED STATES (ADDRESS DATED MAY 26, 1789; WASHINGTON'S REPLY UNDATED)

While I reiterate the professions of my dependence upon Heaven as the source of all public and private blessings; I will observe that the general prevalence of piety, philanthropy, honesty, industry and economy seems, in the ordinary course of human affairs, particularly necessary for advancing and confirming the happiness of our country. While all men within our territories are protected in worshipping the Deity according to the dictates of their consciences; it is rationally to be expected from them in return, that they will be emulous of evincing the sanctity of their professions by the innocence of their lives and the beneficence of their actions; for no man, who is profligate in his morals, or a bad member of the civil community, can possibly be a true Christian, or a credit to his own religious society.

I desire you to accept my acknowledgments for your laudable endeavors to render men sober, honest, and good Citizens, and the obedient subjects of a lawful government.

MESSAGE TO THE BISHOP OF THE METHODIST CHURCH OF NEW YORK, MAY 29, 1789

I trust the people of every denomination, who demean themselves as good citizens, will have occasion to be convinced that I shall always strive to prove a faithful and impartial patron of genuine, vital religion.

REPLY TO AN ADDRESS SENT BY THE GENERAL CONVENTION OF BISHOPS, CLERGY, AND LAITY OF THE PROTESTANT EPISCOPAL CHURCH IN NEW YORK, NEW JERSEY, PHILADELPHIA, DELAWARE, MARYLAND, VIRGINIA, AND NORTH CAROLINA, AUGUST 19, 1789

On this occasion it would ill become me to conceal the joy I have felt, in perceiving the fraternal affection, which appears to increase every day among the friends of *genuine religion*. It affords edifying prospects, indeed, to see Christians of different denominations dwell together in more charity, and conduct themselves in respect to each other with a more *Christian-like spirit* than ever they have done in any former age, or in any other nation.

REPLY TO AN ADDRESS SENT BY THE RELIGIOUS SOCIETY CALLED QUAKERS FROM THEIR YEARLY MEETING FOR PENNSYLVANIA, NEW JERSEY, DELAWARE, AND THE WESTERN PARTS OF MARYLAND AND VIRGINIA, SEPTEMBER 28, 1789 (REPLY UNDATED)

Government being, among other purposes, instituted to protect the persons and consciences of men from oppression, it certainly is the duty of rulers, not only to abstain from it themselves, but according to their stations, to prevent it in others.

The liberty enjoyed by the people of these States, of worshipping Almighty God agreeably to their consciences, is not only among the choicest of their *blessings*, but also of their *rights*. While men perform their social duties faithfully, they do all that society or the state can with propriety demand or expect; and remain responsible only to their Maker for the religion, or modes of faith, which they may prefer or profess.

Your principles and conduct are well known to me; and it is doing the people called Quakers no more than justice to say, that (except their declining to share with others the burthen of the common defense) there is no denomination among us, who are more exemplary and useful citizens.

I assure you very explicitly, that in my opinion the conscientious scruples of all men should be treated with great delicacy and tenderness; and it is my wish and desire, that the laws may always be as extensively accommodated to them, as a due regard to the protection and essential interests of the nation may justify and permit.

REPLY TO AN ADDRESS BY THE SYNOD OF THE DUTCH REFORMED CHURCH IN NORTH AMERICA ON OCTOBER 9, 1789 (REPLY UNDATED)

I readily join with you that "while just government protects all in their religious rights, true religion affords to government its surest support."

REPLY TO AN ADDRESS FROM MINISTERS AND ELDERS REPRESENTING THE MASSACHUSETTS AND NEW HAMPSHIRE CHURCHES BELONGING TO THE FIRST PRESBYTERY OF THE EASTWARD, NEWBURYPORT, OCTOBER 28, 1789

I am persuaded, you will permit me to observe, that the path of true piety is so plain as to require but little political direction. To this consideration we ought to ascribe the absence of any regulation, respecting religion, from the Magna-Carta of our country. To the guidance of the ministers of the gospel this important object is, perhaps, more properly committed. It will be your care to instruct the ignorant, and to reclaim the devious, and, in the progress of morality and science, to which our government will give every furtherance, we may confidently expect the advancement of true religion, and the completion of our happiness.

REPLY TO A CONGRATULATORY ADDRESS BY A COMMITTEE OF ROMAN CATHO-
LICS WAITING UPON THE PRESIDENT, MARCH 15, 1790, ACCORDING TO THE
MARYLAND JOURNAL AND BALTIMORE ADVERTISER

I feel that my conduct in War and in Peace has met with more general approbation than could reasonably have been expected; and I find myself disposed to consider that fortunate circumstance, in a great degree, resulting from the able support and extraordinary candor of my fellow-citizens of all denominations.

As mankind become more liberal, they will be more apt to allow, that all those who conduct themselves as worthy members of the community are equally entitled to the protection of civil government. I hope ever to see America among the foremost nations in examples of justice and liberality. And I presume, that your fellow-citizens will not forget the patriotic part which you took in the accomplishment of their revolution, and the establishment of their government; or the important assistance, which they received, from a Nation in which the Roman Catholic religion is professed . . . May the members of your Society in America, animated alone by the pure spirit of Christianity, and still conducting themselves as the faithful subjects of our free government, enjoy every temporal and spiritual felicity.

REPLY TO MOSES SEIXAS, SEXTON OF THE HEBREW CONGREGATION OF NEW-
PORT, WHO SENT WASHINGTON A LETTER OF WELCOME ON HIS VISIT TO THE
TOWN OF NEWPORT, AUGUST 17, 1790

The citizens of the United States of America have a right to applaud themselves for having given to Mankind examples of an enlarged and liberal policy, a policy worthy of imitation. All possess alike liberty of conscience and immunities of citizenship. It is now no more that toleration is spoken of, as if it was by the indulgence of one class of people that another enjoyed the exercise, of their inherent natural rights. For happily the Government of the United States, which gives bigotry no sanction, to persecution no assistance requires only that they who live under its protection should demean themselves as good citizens, in giving it on all occasions their effectual support.

It would be inconsistent with the frankness of my character not to avow that I am pleased with your favorable opinion of my administration, and fervent wishes for my felicity. May the Children of the Stock of Abraham, who dwell in this land, continue to merit and enjoy the good will of the other Inhabitants, while every one shall sit in safety under his own vine and fig-tree, and there shall be none to make him afraid. May the father of all mercies scatter light and not darkness in our paths, and make us all in our several vocations useful here, and in his own due time and way everlastingly happy.

MESSAGE TO THE HEBREW CONGREGATIONS OF PHILADELPHIA, NEW YORK, CHARLESTON, AND RICHMOND, DECEMBER, 1790

The liberal sentiment towards each other which marks every political and religious denomination of men in this country stands unrivalled in the history of nations. The affection of such people is a treasure beyond the reach of calculation; and the repeated proofs which my fellow citizens have given of their attachment to me, and approbation of my doings form the purest source of my temporal felicity. The affectionate expressions of your address again excite my gratitude, and receive my warmest acknowledgments.

The power and goodness of the Almighty were strongly manifested in the events of our late glorious revolution, and his kind interposition in our behalf has been no less visible in the establishment of our present equal government. In war he directed the sword and in peace he has ruled in our councils, my agency in both has been guided by the best intentions, and a sense of the duty which I owe my country: and as my exertions hitherto have been amply rewarded by the approbation of my fellow-citizens, I shall endeavor to deserve a continuance of it by my future conduct. . . .

LETTER TO THE MEMBERS OF THE NEW CHURCH IN BALTIMORE, JANUARY 27, 1793

We have abundant reason to rejoice that in this Land the light of truth and reason has triumphed over the power of bigotry and superstition, and that every person may here worship God according to the dictates of his own heart. In this enlightened Age and in this Land of equal liberty it is our boast, that a man's religious tenets will not forfeit the protection of the Laws, nor deprive him of the right of attaining and holding the highest Offices that are known in the United States.

Your prayers for my present and future felicity are received with gratitude; and I sincerely wish, Gentlemen, that you may in your social and individual capacities taste those blessings, which a gracious God bestows upon the Righteous.

LETTER TO THE RECTOR, CHURCH WARDENS, AND VESTRYMEN OF THE UNITED EPISCOPAL CHURCHES OF CHRIST CHURCH AND ST. PETER'S OF PHILADELPHIA, MARCH 2, 1797

To this public testimony of your approbation of my conduct and affection for my person I am not insensible, and your prayers for my present and future happiness merit my warmest acknowledgments. It is with peculiar satisfaction I can say that, prompted by a high sense of duty in my attendance on public worship, I have been gratified, during my residence among you, by the liberal and interesting discourses which have been delivered in your Churches.

Believing that that Government alone can be approved by Heaven, which promotes peace and secures protection to its Citizens in every thing that is dear and interesting to them, it has been the great object of my administration to insure those invaluable ends; and when, to a consciousness of the purity of intentions, is added the approbation of my fellow Citizens, I shall experience in my retirement that heartfelt satisfaction which can only be exceeded by the hope of future happiness.

LETTER TO THE CLERGY OF DIFFERENT DENOMINATIONS RESIDING IN AND NEAR THE CITY OF PHILADELPHIA, MARCH 3, 1797

Believing, as I do, that *Religion* and *Morality* are the essential pillars of Civil society, I view, with unspeakable pleasure, that harmony and brotherly love which characterizes the Clergy of different denominations, as well in this, as in other parts of the United States; exhibiting to the world a new and interesting spectacle, at once the pride of our Country and the surest basis of Universal Harmony.

That your labours for the good of Mankind may be crowned with success; that your temporal enjoyments may be commensurate with your merits; and that the future reward of good and faithful Servants may be yours, I shall not cease to supplicate the Divine Author of life and felicity.

Major General Henry Knox had the favor of Washington's admiration and friendship. He served under Washington in the Revolutionary War. In the first of the three letters that follow, Washington writes from Mt. Vernon and reflects some of his feelings about the war just ended. In the second letter he sends his condolences to General Knox, whom he had appointed to his Cabinet as Secretary of War. In the third, he expresses his confidence about the American future.

LETTERS TO HENRY KNOX

FEBRUARY 20, 1784

I feel now, however, as I conceive a wearied traveller must do, who, after treading many a painful step, with a heavy burden on his shoulders, is eased of the latter, having reached the goal to which all the former were directed; and from his house top is looking back, and tracing with a grateful eye the meanders by which he escaped the quicksands and mires which lay in his way; and into which none but the All-powerful guide, and great disposer of human events could have prevented his falling. . . .

MARCH 2, 1797

Amongst the last acts of my political life, and before I go hence into retirement, *profound*, will be the acknowledgment of your kind and affectionate letter from Boston, dated the 15th of January.

From the friendship I have always borne you, and from the interest I have ever taken in whatever related to your prosperity and happiness, I participated in the sorrows which I know you must have felt for your late and heavy losses.[1] But [it] is not for man to scan the wisdom of Providence. The best he can do is to submit to its decrees. Reason, Religion, and Philosophy, teaches us to do this, but 'tis time alone that can ameliorate the pangs of humanity and soften its woes.

MARCH 27, 1798

Cruel must these reports be, if unfounded; and if well founded, what punishment can be too great for the Actors in so diabolical a Drama? The period is big with events, but what will it produce is beyond the reach of human ken. On this, as upon all other occasions, I hope the best. It has always been my belief that Providence has not led us so far in the path of Independence of one Nation, to throw us into the Arms of another. And that the machinations of those, who are attempting it, will sooner or later recoil upon their own Heads. Heaven grant it may soon happen upon all those whose conduct deserve it.

A bill was introduced in the Virginia legislature under which citizens would be taxed to pay the salaries of teachers who taught the Christian religion. George Mason, a Jefferson liberal and one of the leaders in the campaign to add a Bill of Rights to the Constitution, was alarmed at the idea of assessing people for religious education and sought Washington's support. Washington's position was that any denomination had the right to provide for its own religious instruction, and that a public assessment would be "impolitic."

LETTER TO GEORGE MASON, OCTOBER 3, 1785

I have this moment received yours of yesterday's date, enclosing a memorial and remonstrance against the Assessment Bill. . . .

Although, no man's sentiments are more opposed to *any kind* of restraint upon religious principles than mine are; yet I must confess that I am not amongst the number of those who are so much alarmed at the thoughts of

---

[1] [The death of three children.—ED.]

making people pay towards the support of that which they profess, if of the denomination of Christians; or declare themselves Jews, Mahomitans or otherwise, and thereby obtain proper relief. As the matter now stands, I wish an assessment had never been agitated, and as it has gone so far, that the Bill could die an easy death; because I think it will be productive of more quiet to the State, than by enacting it into a Law; which, in my opinion, would be impolitic, admitting there is a decided majority for it, to the disquiet of a respectable minority. In the first case the matter will soon subside; in the latter, it will rankle and perhaps convulse, the State. The Dinner Bell rings, and I must conclude with an expression of my concern for your indisposition.

Benjamin Lincoln was a Revolutionary War general who was wounded in the Saratoga campaign. Lincoln was also a delegate at the Federal Constitutional Convention. Washington wrote this letter from Mt. Vernon.

LETTER TO BENJAMIN LINCOLN, FEBRUARY 11, 1788

As you must be convinced that whatever affects your happiness or welfare cannot be indifferent to me I need not tell you that I was most sensibly affected by your letter of the 20th of January. Yes, my dear sir, I sincerely condole with you the loss of a worthy, amiable and valuable son! Although I had not the happiness of a personal acquaintance with him, yet the character he sustained, and his near connexion with you are, to me, sufficient reasons to lament his death. It is unnecessary for me to offer any consolation on the present occasion; for to a mind like yours it can only be drawn from that source which never fails to give a bountiful supply to those who reflect justly. Time *alone* can blunt the keen edge of afflictions; Philosophy and our Religion holds out to us such hopes as will, upon proper reection, enable us to bear with fortitude the most calamitous incidents of life and these are all that can be expected from the feelings of humanity; is all which they will yield.

The morning of April 30, 1789, George Washington rose even earlier than usual. So did a number of other people in New York City. It was to be a busy day, starting with prayers in the churches, followed by a full-dress military parade through the heart of the city, an official reception by both houses of Congress assembled in New York, and a special ceremony on the steps of the Federal Hall in Wall Street. To attend this ceremony people had come from all the thirteen states. The event was the inauguration of the first President of the United States of America. George Washington, with characteristic thoroughness, had worked for many weeks on a statement he might read to the group. He had thought he would present his detailed ideas concerning much-needed legislation. But then he changed his mind and decided to deal primarily with the big and symbolic meaning of the event, and the major challenges before the new nation. He wanted to keep the talk within twenty minutes, and to read in unhurried fashion. It is not known definitely how much help Washington received in the preparation of the First Inaugural Address. Johnathan Trumbull (son of the governor of Connecticut) and David Humphries, two deeply religious men, assisted Washington with his various messages and papers at this time. It is also believed that James Madison did some helpful editorial work on the draft. Following the inauguration, the official group attending the inauguration left for a special service in St. Paul's Chapel.

FROM THE FIRST INAUGURAL ADDRESS, APRIL 30, 1789

It would be peculiarly improper to omit in this first official Act, my fervent supplications to that Almighty Being who rules over the Universe, who presides in the Councils of Nations, and whose providential aids can supply every human defect, that his benediction may consecrate to the liberties and happiness of the People of the United States, a Government instituted by themselves for these essential purposes: and may enable every instrument employed in its administration to execute with success, the functions allotted to his charge. In tendering this homage to the Great Author of every public and private good, I assure myself that it expresses your sentiments not less than my own; nor those of my fellow-citizens at large, less than either. No People can be bound to acknowledge and adore the invisible hand, which conducts the Affairs of men more than the People of the United States. Every step, by which they have advanced to the character of an independent nation, seems to have been distinguished by some token of providential agency. And in the important revolution just accomplished in the system of their United Government, the tranquil deliberations and voluntary consent of so many distinct communities, from which the event has resulted, cannot be compared with the means by which most Governments have been established, without some return of pious gratitude along with an humble anticipation of the future blessings which the past seem to presage. These reflections, arising out of the present crisis, have forced themselves too strongly on my mind to be suppressed. You will join me I trust in thinking that there are none under the influence of which, the proceedings of a new and free Government can more auspiciously commence.

Sir Edward Newenham was born in Cork County, Ireland, and represented Dublin County in Parliament from 1776 to 1797. He was voluble and prolific; he spoke and wrote with vast energy on abuses of government power, and he was the father of eighteen children. He corresponded with President Washington on the religious disputes inside Ireland.

LETTERS TO SIR EDWARD NEWENHAM, 1792

PHILADELPHIA, JUNE 22, 1792

I have now before me your letters of the 9 of January and 12 of February to which it will not be in my power to reply so fully as my inclination would lead me to do if I had no avocation but those of a personal nature.

I regret exceedingly that the disputes between the Protestants and Roman Catholics should be carried to the serious alarming height mentioned in your letters. Religious controversies are always productive of more acrimony and irreconcilable hatreds than those which spring from any other cause; and I was not without hopes that the enlightened and liberal policy of the present age would have put an effectual stop to contentions of this kind.

PHILADELPHIA, OCTOBER 20, 1792

Where your letter of the 21st of December last has been travelling since it left you, I cannot tell; but it did not get to my hands till within a few weeks past; when I likewise received yours of the 15th of July, introducing Mr. Anderson. I was sorry to see the gloomy picture which you drew of the affairs of your Country in your letter of December; but I hope events have not turned out so badly as you then apprehended. Of all the animosities which have existed among mankind, those which are caused by a difference of sentiments in religion appear to be the most inveterate and distressing, and ought most to be deprecated. I was in hopes, that the enlightened and liberal policy, which has marked the present age, would at least have reconciled *Christians* of every denomination so far, that we should never again see their religious disputes carried to such a pitch as to endanger the peace of Society.

The next three items are addressed to William Pearce, whom Washington had engaged as manager of his Mt. Vernon homestead in 1794. President Washington wrote these letters from Philadelphia and Germantown. Mr. Pearce was troubled by the elements at Mt. Vernon. Washington, as will be observed, was more than merely philosophical about such matters.

LETTERS TO WILLIAM PEARCE, 1794

PHILADELPHIA, MAY 25, 1794

I learnt with concern from your letter of the 18th instant, that your crops were still labouring under a drought, and most of them very much injured. At disappointments and losses which are the effects of Providential acts, I never repine; because I am sure the alwise disposer of events knows better than we do, what is best for us, or what we deserve. Two or three fine rains have fallen here in the course of the past week; some of which I hope (though I fear the showers were partial) may have extended to Mount Vernon.

SEPTEMBER 14, 1794

I am sorry to hear of the heavy rains you have had, on many accounts; but on none more than throwing you backward in the Mill swamps, and the hard and unfit condition it will put them grounds for the reception of the grass seeds even if it should not have gullied and washed the soil off in places. I know too, that besides stopping your ploughs on Acct. of the wetness of the land, that such rains are apt to gully the fields already sown with Wheat and to render those which have not received in the Seed in a much worse condition for this purpose; but as these are the effects of Providential dispensations resignation is our duty. I am persuaded you will render the disadvantage as light as possible, and that is all I can expect.

MARCH 27, 1796

I am sorry to find by it [his letter of the 20th] that your winter grain has changed its appearance for the worse; and that your fences have been so much deranged by the high wind you have had, in a greater degree I think than it was here, tho' it was very violent with us also. These being acts of Providence and not within our control, I never repine at them; but if the Roller will be of any use to the grain, I beg it may be applied. Let the damage which the Cupulo, and other things, have sustained from the wind be repaired as soon as possible.

President Washington had no desire to continue in office beyond his first term. Vast problems had to be faced almost daily, especially for a new government; but Washington had achieved his primary objective, which was to create faith in the federation and to establish a sound pulse beat for the government itself. He had the adulation of the American people; it was a good time to step down. But the pressure applied to him by his party was greater than he could withstand or resist. His victory was overwhelming, but the results of his second administration somewhat less so. He had been the grand architect of coalition in the attainment of a common cause. The cause having been achieved, however, there came a point where each of the elements he had brought together became less interested in co-operation than in its own postponed desires. All sorts of political ruptures occurred. Washington, the sainted figure during his first term, became a target for attack and abuse on a scale that was as disillusioning to him as it was educational. Toward the end of his first term, he had asked James Madison to suggest the draft of a Presidential message on his retirement. But now, four years later, Madison was no longer in the inner circle. But Alexander Hamilton was—Hamilton whose influence with and access to Washington had grown all this time. Hamilton worked from the original Madison draft and turned over his own draft to the President for his work on the final copy. The portion of the Farewell Address that follows has to do with the place of religion and ethics in a free republic.

FAREWELL ADDRESS, SEPTEMBER 19, 1796

Of all the dispositions and habits which lead to political prosperity, Religion and Morality are indispensable supports. In vain would that man claim the tribute of Patriotism, who should labour to subvert these great Pillars of human happiness, these firmest props of the duties of men and citizens. The mere politician, equally with the pious man ought to respect and to cherish them. A volume could not trace all their connections with private and public felicity. Let it simply be asked where is the security for property, for reputation, for life, if the sense of religious obligation *desert* the oaths, which are the instruments of investigation in Courts of Justice? And let us with caution indulge the supposition, that morality can be maintained without religion. Whatever may be conceded to the influence of refined education on minds of peculiar structure, reason and experience both forbid us to expect that National morality can prevail in exclusion of religious principle.

'Tis substantially true, that virtue or morality is a necessary spring of popular government. The rule indeed extends with more or less force to every species of free Government. Who that is a sincere friend to it, can look with indifference upon attempts to shake the foundation of the fabric. . . .

Observe good faith and justice towards all Nations. Cultivate peace and harmony with all. Religion and morality enjoin this conduct; and can it be that good policy does not equally enjoin it? It will be worthy of a free, enlightened, and at no distant period, a great Nation to give to mankind the magnanimous and too novel example of a People always guided by an exalted justice and benevolence. Who can doubt that in the course of time and things the fruit of such a plan would richly repay any temporary advantages which might be lost by a steady adherence to it? Can it be, that Providence has not connected the permanent felicity of a Nation with its virtue? The experiment, at least, is recommended by every sentiment which ennobles human Nature. Alas! is it rendered impossible by its vices?

Jonathan Trumbull was governor of Connecticut, one of the first states to ratify the new U.S. Constitution. In view of the bitter opposition to the new form of government, especially in Virginia, New York, Rhode Island, and North Carolina, it was a cause of rejoicing when a state decided to join the federation.

LETTER TO JONATHAN TRUMBULL, JULY 20, 1788

Your friend Colo. Humphreys informs me, from the wonderful revolution of sentiment in favor of federal measures, and the marvellous change for the better in the elections of your state, that he shall begin to suspect that miracles have not ceased; indeed, for myself, since so much liberality has been displayed in the construction and adoption of the proposed General Government, I am almost disposed to be of the same opinion. Or at least we may, with a kind of grateful and pious exultation, trace the finger of Providence through those dark and mysterious events, which first induced the states to appoint a general convention and then led them one after another (by such steps as were best calculated to effect the object) into an adoption of the system recommended by that general Convention; thereby, in all human probability, laying a lasting foundation for tranquility and happiness; when we had but too much reason to fear that confusion and misery were coming rapidly upon us. That the same good Providence may still continue to protect us and prevent us from dashing the cup of national felicity just as it has been lifted to our lips, is the earnest prayer of, my dear sir, your faithful friend, etc.

Washington maintained a correspondence with his friend the Marquis de Lafayette after the latter returned to France, then in the developing throes of its own struggle against monarchy. It was apparent to Washington that all mankind was tied together in a community of aspiration.

LETTERS TO THE MARQUIS DE LAFAYETTE

AUGUST 15, 1786

Although I pretend to no peculiar information respecting commercial affairs, nor any foresight into the scenes of futurity; yet as the member of an infant empire, as a philanthropist by character, and (if I may be allowed the expression) as a citizen of the great republic of humanity at large; I cannot help turning my attention sometimes to this subject. I would be understood to mean, I cannot avoid reflecting with pleasure on the probable influence that commerce may hereafter have on human manners and society in general. On these occasions I consider how fond, perhaps an enthusiastic idea, that as the world is evidently much less barbarous than it has been, its melioration must still be progressive; that nations are becoming more humanized in their policy, that the subjects of ambition and causes for hostility are daily diminishing, and, in fine, that the period is not very remote, when the benefits of a liberal and free commerce will, pretty generally, succeed to the devastations and horrors of war.

AUGUST 15, 1787

Newspaper accounts inform us that the Session of the Assembly of Notables is ended, and you have had the goodness (in your letter of the 5th of May) to communicate some of the proceedings to me, among which is that of the interesting motion made by yourself respecting the expenditure of public money by Monsieur de Callonne, and the consequence thereof.

The patriotism, by which this motion was dictated throws a lustre on the action, which cannot fail to dignify the Author, and I sincerely hope with you, that much good will result from the deliberations of so respectable a Council, I am not less ardent in my wish that you may succeed in your plan of toleration in religious matters. Being no bigot myself to any mode of worship, I am disposed to indulge the professors of Christianity in the church, that road to Heaven, which to them shall seem the most direct plainest easiest and least liable to exception.

Thanksgiving Day was first proclaimed by William Bradford, Governor of the Plymouth Colony, in 1621. The first time it was proclaimed for the United States under its new Constitution was for Thanksgiving, 1789. President Washington issued his Proclamation on October 3, 1789. He attended St. Paul's Chapel of Trinity Parish Episcopal on Thanksgiving Day. Bad weather kept many people at home.

THE FIRST THANKSGIVING DAY PROCLAMATION UNDER THE CONSTITUTION, NEW YORK CITY, OCTOBER 3, 1789

Whereas it is the duty of all Nations to acknowledge the providence of Almighty God, to obey his will, to be grateful for his benefits, and humbly to implore his protection and favor, and Whereas both Houses of Congress have by their joint Committee[2] requested me to "recommend to the People of the United States a day of public thanks-giving and prayer to be observed

---

[2] [The Senate concurred in the House resolve to this effect, September 26.—ED.]

by acknowledging with grateful hearts the many signal favors of Almighty God, especially by affording them an opportunity peaceably to establish a form of government for their safety and happiness."

Now therefore I do recommend and assign Thursday the 26th day of November next to be devoted by the People of these States to the Service of that great and glorious Being, who is the beneficent Author of all the good that was, that is, or that will be. That we may then all unite in rendering unto him our sincere and humble thanks, for his kind care and protection of the People of this country previous to their becoming a Nation, for the signal and manifold mercies, and the favorable interpositions of his providence, which we experienced in the course and conclusion of the late war, for the great degree of tranquility, union, and plenty, which we have since enjoyed, for the peaceable and rational manner in which we have been enabled to establish constitutions of government for our safety and happiness, and particularly the national One now lately instituted, for the civil and religious liberty with which we are blessed, and the means we have of acquiring and diffusing useful knowledge and in general for all the great and various favors which he hath been pleased to confer upon us.

And also that we may then unite in most humbly offering our prayers and supplications to the great Lord and Ruler of Nations and beseech him to pardon our national and other transgressions, to enable us all, whether in public or private stations, to perform our several and relative duties properly and punctually, to render our national government a blessing to all the people, by constantly being a government of wise, just and constitutional laws, discreetly and faithfully executed and obeyed, to protect and guide all Sovereigns and Nations (especially such as have shown kindness unto us) and to bless them with good government, peace and concord. To promote the knowledge and practice of true religion and virtue, and the increase of science among them and us, and generally to grant unto all Mankind such a degree of temporal prosperity as he alone knows to be best.

The following quotation attributed to Washington is from James K. Paulding's Life of Washington, *published in 1835. Paulding was a naval official and officer who wrote prolifically in a wide variety of fields.*

ATTRIBUTED QUOTATION (Undated)

The Existence of a Supreme Being

It is impossible to account for the creation of the universe, without the agency of a Supreme Being.

It is impossible to govern the universe without the aid of a Supreme

Being. It is impossible to reason without arriving at a Supreme Being. Religion is as necessary to reason, as reason is to religion. The one cannot exist without the other. A reasoning being would lose his reason, in attempting to account for the great phenomena of nature, had he not a Supreme Being to refer to; and well has it been said, that if there had been no God, mankind would have been obliged to imagine one.

3. JOHN ADAMS

"I Have Been a Church-Going Animal for Seventy-Six Years . . . And This Has Been Alleged as One Proof of My Hypocrisy"

"ASK me not, then, whether I am a Catholic or Protestant, Calvinist or Arminian. As far as they are Christians, I wish to be a fellow-disciple with them all."

The key to this statement is the opening clause of the second sentence: "As far as they are Christians . . ." For John Adams had some fairly well-defined ideas of what merited the term Christian. He could be as eloquent and rhapsodic about the principles of Christianity as he could be scathing about the abuses carried on in its name. As a definition of faith, Christianity to him was the "brightness of the glory and the express portrait of the character of the eternal, self-existent, independent, benevolent, all powerful and all merciful creator, preserver and father of the universe, the first good, first first, and first fair."

But on the administration of Christianity, he could swing just as strongly in the opposite direction: ". . . ever since the Reformation, when or where has existed a Protestant or dissenting sect who would tolerate A Free Inquiry? The blackest billingsgate, the most ungentlemanly insolence, the most yahooish brutality is patiently endured, countenanced, propagated, and applauded. But touch a solemn truth in collision with a dogma of sect, though capable of the clearest proof, and you will soon find you have disturbed a nest, and the hornets will swarm about your legs and hands and fly into your face and eyes."

Unlike George Washington, whose writings or statements having to do with religion caused various groups to claim him as their own, John Adams was fairly successful in convincing most religious bodies that he and they were on opposite sides. The Deists might go along with his criticism of church organization, but they would immediately be confronted with a caustic attack by Adams on Thomas Paine, one of the most prominent

74

Deists of the age. Or the orthodox would be attracted by his statement that he "had never known any better people than the Calvinists," among them his own ancestors. But then Adams would turn around and say that Calvinism was not to his own taste and ask how it "happened that millions of fables, tales, legends have been blended with both Jewish and Christian revelation that have made them the most bloody religion that ever existed?"

To be called a Puritan, Deist, Orthodox Christian, and Humanist in one lifetime was no small achievement, but Adams was easily equal to it and certainly untroubled by it. Whatever others might think, he was confident of his convictions. They were perfectly consistent as he saw them; all he had done was to separate the principles from the practices. Though he criticized ritual he insisted on the importance of going to church; he reconciled the two because he got out of church exactly what he felt it should give him, nothing more or less. And despite his frequent tartness, his settled view was that "all good men are Christians, and I believe . . . there are good men in all nations, sincere and conscientious." He identified himself with and became one of the leading Unitarians in America.

John Adams was an exponent of the natural inequality of man and a whole host of other ideas which astounded the liberal thinkers of his time. At all events, Adams was not a man to be taken for granted. He unblushingly claimed credit for Jefferson's political development: "I am bold to say I was his preceptor in politics and taught him everything that was good and solid in his whole political conduct." But there were long periods when he was Jefferson's bitterest opponent and critic. He was even more opposed to Alexander Hamilton. It is difficult to say whether Benjamin Franklin reflected the view of any considerable number of his contemporaries when he is supposed to have said: "John Adams is always honest, sometimes great, but often mad."

If it seems strange that such fierce independence, if that is the word for it, could have led to the Presidency, one possible answer may be found in the fact that while few liked him, almost all respected him. "He is vain, irritable, and a bad calculator of the force and probable effect of the motives which govern men," Thomas Jefferson wrote. "This is all the ill which can possibly be said of him. He is as disinterested as the being who made him; he is profound in his views and accurate in his judgment, except where knowledge of the world is necessary to form a judgment. He is so amiable, that I pronounce you will love him if ever you become acquainted with him. He would be, as he was, a great man in Congress."

John Adams was the second President of the United States but not the first Adams to achieve prominence in America. Four generations earlier his ancestor Henry Adams emigrated to America. And John Adams lived long enough to see his son, John Quincy, become President of the United States (1824) and receive the kind of support and public adulation that he himself had only rarely known.

John Adams was born in Braintree, Massachusetts, in 1735, of parents he described as pious and churchgoing in the main. He had a general education at Harvard College in preparation for what he had long felt was his natural calling, the ministry. Some disinclinations set in, however, and he veered into law. He had seen something of the life of a minister in the local parish, attended as it was with all sorts of theological and operational difficulties. "Very strong doubts arose in my mind, whether I was made for a pulpit in such times, and I began to think of other professions." Besides, "frigid John Calvin" inspired in him a lack of appropriate zeal.

Therefore the law. Also, the beginning of his public career. He had a series of minor public offices, all the while writing essays, articles, books. His blistering independence and integrity did not always win him party backing, but they did win him the kind of public support that gave him a forward thrust in politics. Of all the famed Massachusetts insurgents, Adams was probably the most industrious, learned, persistent, and effective. He served in the Massachusetts Assembly and Council, and in the Continental Congress, distinguishing himself in the committee charged with the preparation of a Declaration of Independence. Jefferson marveled at his ability as advocate of the Declaration "against the multifarious assaults it encountered."

During the Revolution, he held some dozens of posts, in all of which he was effective though not always popular. He represented the states at crucial negotiations abroad. And all the while he continued his writing. When the United States came into being, he was elected its first Vice-President. "My country has in its wisdom," he later wrote to his wife, "contrived for me the most insignificant office that ever the invention of man contrived or his imagination conceived."

The country also saw fit to raise him from that modest station, and he became Washington's successor as President. Some political observers at the time commented that this might have been more the result of bungling by Hamilton inside the Federalist party than of overwhelming sentiment for Mr. Adams. Be that as it may, a man fairly free of political obligations or ties moved into the White House. It was a stormy administration internally. Externally, it did its main job, which was to keep a young country on its course.

In retirement, John Adams mellowed somewhat. His old quarrels no longer seemed so important and his early friendship with Thomas Jefferson was revived. His correspondence shows that, although he may have softened in his manner in his declining years, his convictions lost none of their tang and he retained the air of a glorious curmudgeon.

This excerpt from John Adams' Autobiography covers some of the early religious influences. It also reveals a clarity of expression and simplicity of style that made him one of the most effective writers of his day.

ADAMS' AUTOBIOGRAPHY

Between the years 1751, when I entered, and 1754, when I left college, a controversy was carried on between Mr. Bryant, the minister of our parish, and some of his people, partly on account of his principles, which were called Arminian, and partly on account of his conduct, which was too gay and light, if not immoral. Ecclesiastical councils were called, and sat at my father's house. Parties and their acrimonies arose in the church and congregation, and controversies from the press between Mr. Bryant, Mr. Niles, Mr. Porter, Mr. Bass, concerning the five points.

I read all these pamphlets and many other writings on the same subjects, and found myself involved in difficulties beyond my powers of decision. At the same time, I saw such a spirit of dogmatism and bigotry in clergy and laity, that, if I should be a priest, I must take my side, and pronounce as positively as any of them, or never get a parish, or getting it must soon leave it. Very strong doubts arose in my mind, whether I was made for a pulpit in such times, and I began to think of other professions.

I perceived very clearly, as I thought, that the study of theology, and the pursuit of it as a profession, would involve me in endless altercations, and make my life miserable, without any prospect of doing any good to my fellow-men.

The last two years of my residence at college produced a club of students (I never knew the history of the first rise of it) who invited me to become one of them. Their plan was to spend their evenings together in reading any new publications, or any poetry or dramatic compositions that might fall in their way. I was as often requested to read as any other, especially tragedies, and it was whispered to me and circulated among others that I had some faculty for public speaking, and that I should make a better lawyer than divine.

This last idea was easily understood and embraced by me. My inclination was soon fixed upon the law. But my judgment was not so easily determined. There were many difficulties in the way. Although my father's general expectation was that I should be a divine, I knew him to be a man of so thoughtful and considerate turn of mind, to be possessed of so much candor and moderation, that it would not be difficult to remove any objections he might make to my pursuit of physic or law, or any other reasonable course.

My mother, although a pious woman, I knew had no partiality for the life of a clergyman. But I had uncles and other relations, full of the most illiberal prejudices against the law. I had, indeed, a proper affection and veneration for them but as I was under no obligation of gratitude to them, which could give them any color of authority to prescribe a course of life to me, I thought little of their opinions.

Other obstacles more serious than these presented themselves. A lawyer must have a fee for taking me into his office. I must be boarded and clothed for several years. I had no money; and my father, having three sons, had done as much for me, in the expenses of my education, as his estate and circumstances could justify, and as my reason or my honor would allow me to ask. I therefore gave out that I would take a school, and took my degree at college undetermined whether I should study divinity, law, or physic.

In the public exercises at commencement, I was somewhat remarked as a respondent, and Mr. Maccarty of Worcester, who was empowered by the selectmen of that town to procure them a Latin master for their grammar-school, engaged me to undertake it. About three weeks after commencement, in 1755, when I was not yet twenty years of age, a horse was sent me from Worcester, and a man to attend me. We made the journey, about sixty miles, in one day, and I entered on my office. For three months, I boarded with one Green, at the expense of the town, and by the arrangement of the selectmen. Here I found Morgan's "Moral Philosopher," which I was informed had circulated with some freedom in that town, and that the principles of deism had made a considerable progress among several persons in that and other towns in the county.

Three months after this, the selectmen procured lodgings for me at Dr. Nahum Willard's. This physician had a large practice, a good reputation for skill, and a pretty library. Here were Dr. Cheyne's works, Sydenham, and others, and Van Swieten's Commentaries on Boerhaave. I read a good deal in these books and entertained many thoughts of becoming a physician and a surgeon. But the law attracted my attention more and more; and, attending the courts of justice, where I heard Worthington, Hawley, Trowbridge, Putnam, and others, I felt myself irresistibly impelled to make some effort to accomplish my wishes.

I made a visit to Mr. Putnam, and offered myself to him. He received me with politeness, and even kindness, took a few days to consider of it, and then informed me that Mrs. Putnam had consented that I should board in his house, that I should pay no more than the town allowed for my lodgings, and that I should pay him a hundred dollars when I should find it convenient. I agreed to his proposals without hesitation, and immediately took possession of his office. His library, at that time, was not large; but he had all the most essential lawbooks.

Immediately after I entered with him, however, he sent to England for a handsome addition of law books, and for Lord Bacon's works. I carried with me to Worcester, Lord Bolingbroke's "Study and Use of History" and his "Patriot King." These I had lent him, and he was so well pleased with them that he added Bolingbroke's works to his list, which gave me an opportunity of reading the posthumous works of that writer, in five volumes.

Mr. Burke once asked, who ever read him through? I can answer that I read him through before the year 1758, and that I have read him through at least twice since that time. But I confess, without much good or harm. His ideas of the English constitution are correct, and his political writings are worth something; but, in a great part of them, there is more of faction than of truth. His religion is a pompous folly; and his abuse of the Christian religion is as superficial as it is impious. His style is original and inimitable; it resembles more the oratory of the ancients than any writings of speeches I ever read in English.

The next twelve items are all drawn from John Adams' diary for the year 1756. Some identifications: Major Gardiner was a personal friend. The Reverend Dr. Mayhew was a Harvard graduate who published a series of sermons in 1749 which analyzed Calvinistic doctrines and found them wanting. He declared that overscrupulous and zealous bigots were un-Christian. James Putnam, a Worcester, Massachusetts, lawyer, accompanied John Adams on long evening walks. In the late summer of 1756, Adams decided to study law under Putnam. It was a vital decision and a good one. All Adams' talents seemed to come into focus in his study of the law.

ADAMS' DIARY

FEBRUARY 13, 1756

Supped at Major Gardiner's, and engaged to keep school at Bristol, provided Worcester people at their ensuing March meeting should change this into a moving school,[1] not otherwise. Major Greene this evening fell into some conversation with me about the Divinity and satisfaction of Jesus Christ. All the argument he advanced was, "that a mere creature or finite

---

[1] [The instructor walked around the class, somewhat in the Greek peripatetic manner.—ED.]

being could not make satisfaction to infinite justice for any crimes," and that "these things are very mysterious." Thus mystery is made a convenient cover for absurdity.

FEBRUARY 16, 1756

The Church of Rome has made it an article of faith that no man can be saved out of their church, and all other religious sects approach to this dreadful opinion in proportion to their ignorance, and the influence of ignorant or wicked priests.

Oh! That I could wear out of my mind every mean and base affectation; conquer my natural pride and self-conceit; expect no more deference from my fellows than I deserve; acquire that meekness and humility which are the sure mark and characters of a great and generous soul; subdue every unworthy passion and treat all men as I wish to be treated by all. How happy should I then be in the favor and good will of all honest men and the sure prospect of a happy immortality!

FEBRUARY 18, 1756

Spent an hour in the beginning of the evening at Major Gardiner's where it was thought that the design of Christianity was not to make men good riddle-solvers, or good mystery-mongers, but good men, good magistrates, and good subjects, good husbands and good wives, good parents and good children, good masters and good servants. The following questions may be answered some time or other, namely—Where do we find a precept in the Gospel requiring Ecclesiastical Synods? Convocations? Councils? Decrees? Creeds? Confessions? Oaths? Subscriptions? and whole cartloads of other trumpery that we find religion encumbered with in these days?

FEBRUARY 21, 1756

Snow about ankle deep. I find, by repeated experiment and observation in my school, that human nature is more easily wrought upon and governed by promises, and encouragement, and praise, than by punishment, and threatening and blame. But we must be cautious and sparing of our praise, lest it become too familiar and cheap, and so, contemptible; corporal as well as disgraceful punishments depress the spirits, but commendation enlivens and stimulates them to a noble ardor and emulation.

FEBRUARY 22, 1756

Suppose a nation in some distant region should take the Bible for their only law-book, and every member should regulate his conduct by the precepts there exhibited! Every member would be obliged, in conscience, to temperance and frugality and industry; to justice and kindness and charity towards his fellow men; and to piety, love and reverence towards Almighty God. In this commonwealth, no man would impair his health by gluttony, drunkenness, or lust; no man would sacrifice his most precious time to cards or any other trifling and mean amusement; no man would steal, or lie, or in any way defraud his neighbor, but would live in peace and good will with all men; no man would blaspheme his Maker or profane his worship; but a rational and manly, a sincere and unaffected piety and devotion would reign in all hearts. What a Utopia; what a Paradise would this region be!

MARCH 2, 1756

Began this afternoon my third quarter. The great and Almighty author of nature, who at first established those rules which regulate the world, can as easily suspend those laws whenever his providence sees sufficient reason for such suspension. This can be no objection, then, to the miracles of Jesus Christ. Although some very thoughtful and contemplative men among the heathen attained a strong persuasion of the great principles of religion, yet the far greater number, having little time for speculation, gradually sunk into the grossest opinions and the grossest practices. These, therefore, could not be made to embrace the true religion till their attention was roused by some astonishing and miraculous appearances. The reasoning of philosophers, having nothing surprising in them, could not overcome the force of prejudice, custom, passion, and bigotry. But when wise and virtuous men commissioned from heaven, by miracles awakened men's attention to their reasonings, the force of truth made its way with ease to their minds.

MARCH 7, 1756

Heard Mr. Maccarty all day. Spent the evening and supped at Mr. Greene's with Thayer. Honesty, sincerity, and openness I esteem essential marks of a good mind. I am, therefore, of opinion that men ought (after they have examined with unbiased judgments every system of religion, and chosen one system, on their own authority, for themselves), to avow their opinions and defend them with boldness.

MARCH 17, 1756

A fine morning. Proceeded on my journey towards Braintree. Stopped to see Mr. Haven,[2] of Dedham, who told me, very civilly, he supposed I took

---

[2] The Reverend Jason Haven, then just ordained as pastor of the first parish in Dedham.

my faith on trust from Dr. Mayhew, and added, that he believed the doctrine
of the satisfaction of Jesus Christ to be essential to Christianity, and that he
would not believe this satisfaction unless he believed the Divinity of Christ.
Mr. Balch was there too, and observed, that he would not be a Christian
if he did not believe the mysteries of the gospel; that he could bear with
an Arminian, but when, with Dr. Mayhew, they denied the Divinity and
satisfaction of Jesus Christ, he had no more to do with them; that he knew
not what to make of Dr. Mayhew's two discourses upon the expected
dissolution of things. They gave him an idea of a cart whose wheels wanted
greasing; it rumbled on in a hoarse, rough manner; there was a good deal of
ingenious talk in them, but it was thrown together in a jumbled, confused
order. He believed the doctor wrote them in a great panic. He added further
that Arminians, however stiffly they maintain their opinions in health,
always, he takes notice, retract when they come to die, and choose to die
Calvinists. Set out for Braintree and arrived about sunset.

APRIL 15, 1756

Drank tea and spent the evening at Mr. Putnam's in conversation concerning Christianity. He is of opinion that the apostles were a company of
enthusiasts. He says that we have only their word to prove that they spoke
with different tongues, raised the dead, and healed the sick.[3]

APRIL 25, 1756

Astronomers tell us with good reason, that not only all the planets and
satellites in our solar system, but all the unnumbered worlds that revolve
around the fixed stars are inhabited, as well as this globe of earth. If this
is the case, all mankind are no more in comparison of the whole rational
creation of God, than a point to the orbit of Saturn. Perhaps all these
different ranks of rational beings have in a greater or less degree committed
moral wickedness. If so, I ask a Calvinist whether he will subscribe to this
alternative, "Either God Almighty must assume the respective shapes of all
these different species and suffer the penalties of their crimes in their stead,
or else all these beings must be consigned to everlasting perdition?"

---

[3] At breakfast, dinner and tea, Mr. Putnam was commonly disputing with me
upon some question of religion. He had been intimate with one Peasley Collins, the
son of a Quaker in Boston, who had been to Europe, and came back, a disbeliever
of every thing; fully satisfied that religion was a cheat, a cunning invention of priests
and politicians; that there would be no future state, any more than there is at present
any moral government. Putnam could not go these whole lengths with him. Although
he would argue to the extent of his learning and ingenuity to destroy or invalidate
the evidences of a future state, and the principles of natural and revealed religion,
yet I could plainly perceive that he could not convince himself that death was an
endless sleep.

APRIL 26, 1756

The reflection that I penned yesterday appears upon the revision to be weak enough. For first, we know not that the inhabitants of other globes have sinned. Nothing can be argued in this manner till it is proved at least probably that all these species of rational beings have revolted from their rightful Sovereign. When I examine the little prospect that lies before me, and find an infinite variety of bodies in one horizon of, perhaps, two miles diameter, how many millions of such prospects there are upon the surface of this earth, how many millions of globes there are within our view, each of which has as many of these prospects upon its own surface as our planet; great and marvellous are thy works!

MAY 1, 1756

If we consider a little of this our globe, we find an endless variety of substances mutually connected with and dependent on each other. In the wilderness we see an amazing profusion of vegetables, which afford sustenance and covering to the wild beasts. The cultivated plains and meadows produce grass for the cattle, and herbs for the service of man. The milk and the flesh of other animals afford a delicious provision for mankind.

A great part of the human species are obliged to provide food and nourishment for other helpless and improvident animals. Vegetables sustain some animals; these animals are devoured by others, and these others are continually cultivating and improving the vegetable species. Thus, nature upon our earth is in a continual rotation.

If we rise higher, we find the sun and moon, to a very great degree, influencing us. Tides are produced in the ocean; clouds in the atmosphere; all nature is made to flourish and look gay by these enlivening and invigorating luminaries. Yea, life and cheerfulness is diffused to all other planets, as well as ours, upon the sprightly sunbeams.

No doubt, there is as great a multitude and variety of bodies upon each planet, in proportion to its magnitude, as there is upon ours. These bodies are connected with, and influenced by each other. Thus, we see the amazing harmony of our solar system.

The minutest particle, in one of Saturn's satellites, may have some influence upon the most distant regions of the system. The stupendous plan of operation was projected by Him who rules the universe, and a part assigned to every particle of matter, to act in this great and complicated drama. The Creator looked into the remotest futurity, and saw his great designs accomplished by this inextricable, this mysterious complication of causes. But to rise still higher, this solar system is but one very small wheel in the great, the astonishing machine of the world. Those stars, that twinkle in the heavens, have each of them a choir of planets, comets, and satellites, dancing round them, playing mutually on each other, and all, together, playing on the other systems that lie around them.

Our system, considered as one body hanging on its center of gravity, may affect and be affected by all the other systems within the compass of creation. Thus it is highly probable every particle of matter influences and is influenced by every other particle in the whole collected universe.

At the age of thirty, John Adams was considered one of the most promising young lawyers in Boston. He was invited to join the prestige-carrying Sodalitas Club, the members of which met every Thursday evening to read papers dealing with specialized aspects of the law. In the early spring of 1865, John Adams presented a paper titled "Dissertation on the Canon and Feudal Law," a portion of which follows. This was Adams' first sustained literary effort, and it was well received. In the next few months Adams enlarged on the essay. It was printed in the Boston Gazette *in August, 1765; later in the year it was reprinted in* The London Chronicle *and there were confident predictions that young Adams would soon be at the top of his profession. Omitted for some reason from the published version in the* Gazette *was the following opening sentence: "I always consider the settlement of America with reverence and wonder, as the opening of a grand scene and design in Providence for the illumination of the ignorant and the emancipation of the slavish part of mankind all over the earth."*

A DISSERTATION ON THE CANON AND FEUDAL LAW, "BOSTON GAZETTE," AUGUST, 1765

It may be thought polite and fashionable by many modern fine gentlemen, perhaps, to deride the characters of these persons [Puritans] as enthusiastical, superstitious, and republican. But such ridicule is founded in nothing but foppery and affectation, and is grossly injurious and false. Religious to some degree of enthusiasm it may be admitted they were; but this can be no peculiar derogation from their character; because it was at that time almost the universal character not only of England, but of Christendom. Had this, however, been otherwise their enthusiasm, considering the principles on which it was founded and the ends to which it was directed, far from being a reproach to them, was greatly to their honor; for I believe it will be found universally true, that no greater enterprise for the honor or happiness of mankind was ever achieved without a large mixture of that noble infirmity.

Whatever imperfections may be justly ascribed to them, which, however, are as few as any mortals have discovered, their judgment in framing their policy was founded in wise, humane and benevolent principles. It was founded in revelation and in reason too. It was consistent with the principles of the best and greatest and wisest legislators of antiquity.

Tyranny in every form, and shape, and appearance was their disdain and abhorrence; no fear of punishment, nor even of death itself in exquisite tortures, had been sufficient to conquer that steady, manly, pertinacious spirit with which they had opposed the tyrants of those days in church and state.

They were very far from being enemies to monarchy; and they knew as well as any men, the just regard and honor that is due the character of a dispenser of the mysteries of the gospel of grace. But they saw clearly, that popular powers must be placed as a guard, a control, a balance, to the powers of the monarch and the priest, in every government, or else it would soon become the man of sin, the whore of Babylon, the mystery of iniquity, a great and detestable system of fraud, violence, and usurpation.

Their greatest concern seems to have been to establish a government of the church more consistent with the Scriptures, and a government of the state more agreeable to the dignity of human nature, than any they had seen in Europe, and to transmit such a government down to their posterity, with the means of securing and preserving it forever. To render the popular power in their new government as great and wise as their principles of theory, that is, as human nature and the Christian religion require it should be, they endeavored to remove from it as many of the feudal inequalities and dependencies as could be spared, consistently with the preservation of a mild limited monarchy. And in this they discovered the depth of their wisdom and the warmth of their friendship to human nature. But the first place is due to religion. They saw clearly, that of all the nonsense and delusion which had ever passed through the mind of man, none had ever been more extravagant than the notions of absolutions, indelible characters, uninterrupted successions, and the rest of those fantastical ideas, derived from the canon law, which had thrown such a glare of mystery, sanctity, reverence, and right reverend eminence and holiness, around the idea of a priest, as no mortal could deserve, and as always must, from the constitution of human nature, be dangerous in society.

For this reason, they demolished the whole system of diocesan episcopacy; and, deriding, as all reasonable and impartial men must do, the ridiculous fancies of sanctified effluvia from episcopal fingers, they established sacerdotal ordination on the foundation of the Bible and common sense. This conduct at once imposed an obligation on the whole body of the clergy to industry, virtue, piety, and learning, and rendered the whole body infinitely more independent on the civil powers, in all respects, than they could be where they were formed into a scale of subordination, from a pope down to priests and friars and confessors—necessarily and essentially a sordid, stupid, and wretched herd—or than they could be in any other country, where an archbishop held the place of a universal bishop, and the vicars and curates that of the ignorant, dependent, miserable rabble aforesaid,—and infinitely more sensible and learned than they could be in either.

This subject has been seen in the same light by many illustrious patriots, who have lived in America since the days of our forefathers, and who have adored their memory for the same reason. And methinks there has not appeared in New England a stronger veneration for their memory, a more penetrating insight into the grounds and principles and spirit of their policy, nor a more earnest desire of perpetuating the blessings of it to posterity, than that fine institution of the late Chief Justice Dudley, of a lecture against popery, and on the validity of presbyterian ordination. This was certainly intended by that wise and excellent man, as an eternal memento of the wisdom and goodness of the very principles that settled America. But I must again return to the feudal law.

John Adams arrived in the cosmopolitan city of Philadelphia on August 29, 1774, in order to attend the Continental Congress. The wide thoroughfares, impressive public buildings, large stores, and elegant houses were in strong contrast with the Boston he had just left. But he thought that morals and manners in Boston were better. He was also somewhat troubled by the speech of the Philadelphians, a difficulty that was no doubt mutual. In any event, Adams soon had other things to think about. Some religious questions came up in the Congress that engaged his attentions and also his emotions. Besides, 1774 was an eventful year in Philadelphia: all sorts of issues were being debated; great events were in the making.

ADAMS' DIARY, OCTOBER 14, 1774

Went in the morning to see Dr. Chovet and his skeletons and wax-works —most admirable, exquisite representations of the whole animal economy. Four complete skeletons; a leg with all the nerves, veins and arteries injected with wax; two complete bodies in wax, full grown; waxen representations of all the muscles, tendons, etc., of the head, brain, heart, lungs, liver, stomach, etc. This exhibition is much more exquisite than that of Dr. Shippen at the hospital. The Doctor reads lectures for two half joes [sic] a course, which takes up four months. These wax-works are all of the Doctor's own hands. Dined with Dr. Morgan, an ingenious physician and an honest patriot. He showed us some curious paintings upon silk which he brought from Italy, which are singular in this country and some bones of an animal of enormous size found upon the banks of the river Ohio. Mr. Middleton, the two

Rutledges, Mr. Mifflin, and Mr. William Barrell dined with us. Mrs. Morgan is a sprightly, pretty lady. In the evening were invited to an interview, at Carpenters' Hall, with the Quakers and Anabaptists. Mr. Backus is come here from Middleborough with a design to apply to the Congress for a redress of grievances of the anti-pedobaptists in our Province. The cases from Chelmsford, the case of Mr. White of Haverhill, the case of Ashfield and Warwick were mentioned by Mr. Backus. Old Israel Pemberton was quite rude, and his rudeness was resented; but the conference, which held till eleven o'clock, I hope will produce good.

There is an anecdote which ought not to be omitted, because it had consequences of some moment at the time, which have continued to operate for many years, and, indeed, are not yet worn out, though the cause is forgotten, or rather was never generally known. Governor Hopkins and Governor Ward, of Rhode Island, came to our lodgings and said to us, that President Manning, of Rhode Island College, and Mr. Backus, of Massachusetts, were in town, and had conversed with some gentlemen in Philadelphia who wished to communicate to us a little business, and wished that we would meet them at six in the evening at Carpenters' Hall. Whether they explained their affairs more particularly to any of my colleagues, I know not; but I had no idea of the design. We all went at the hour, and to my great surprise found the hall almost full of people, and a great number of Quakers seated at the long table with their broad-brimmed beavers on their heads. We were invited to seats among them, and informed that they had received complaints, from some Anabaptists and some Friends in Massachusetts, against certain laws of that Province, restrictive of the liberty of conscience, and some instances were mentioned in the General Court, and in the courts of justice, in which Friends and Baptists had been grievously oppressed. I know not how my colleagues felt, but I own I was greatly surprised and somewhat indignant, being, like my friend Chase, of a temper naturally quick and warm, at seeing our State and her delegates thus summoned before a self-created tribunal, which was neither legal nor constitutional.

Israel Pemberton, a Quaker of large property and more intrigue, began to speak, and said that Congress was here endeavoring to form a union of the Colonies; but there were difficulties in the way, and none of more importance than liberty of conscience. The laws of New England, and particularly of Massachusetts, were inconsistent with it, for they not only compelled men to pay to the building of churches and support of ministers, but to go to some known religious assembly on first days, etc.; and that he and his friends were desirous of engaging us to assure them that our State would repeal all those laws and place things as they were in Pennsylvania.

A suspicion instantly arose in my mind, which I have ever believed to have been well founded, that this artful Jesuit, for I had been before apprized of his character, was endeavoring to avail himself of this opportunity to break up the Congress, or at least to withdraw the Quakers and the governing part of Pennsylvania from us; for, at that time, by means of a most unequal representation, the Quakers had a majority in their House of Assembly, and, by consequence, the whole power of the State in their hands. I arose, and spoke in answer to him. The substance of what I said, was, that we had no authority to bind our constituents to any such proposals; that the laws of Massachusetts were the most mild and equitable establishment of religion that was known in the world, if indeed they could be called an establishment; that it would be in vain for us to enter into any conferences on such a subject, for we knew beforehand our constituents would disavow all we could do or say for the satisfaction of those who invited us to this meeting. That the people of Massachusetts were as religious and conscientious as the people of Pennsylvania; that their consciences dictated to them that it was their duty to support those laws, and therefore the very liberty of conscience, which Mr. Pemberton invoked, would demand indulgence for the tender consciences of the people of Massachusetts, and allow them to preserve their laws; that it might be depended on, this was a point that could not be carried; that I would not deceive them by insinuating the faintest hope, for I knew they might as well turn the heavenly bodies out of their annual and diurnal courses, as the people of Massachusetts at the present day from their meeting-house and Sunday laws. Pemberton made no reply but this: "Oh! sir, pray don't urge liberty of conscience in favor of such laws!" If I had known the particular complaints which were to be alleged, and if Pemberton had not broken irregularly into the midst of things, it might have been better, perhaps to have postponed this declaration. However, the gentlemen proceeded, and stated the particular cases of oppression, which were alleged, in our general and executive courts. It happened that Mr. Cushing and Mr. Samuel Adams had been present in the General Court when the petitions had been under deliberation, and they explained the whole so clearly that every reasonable man must have been satisfied. Mr. Paine and I had been concerned at the bar in every action in the executive courts which was complained of, and we explained them all to the entire satisfaction of the impartial men, and showed that there had been no oppression or injustice in any of them. The Quakers were not generally and heartily in our cause; they were jealous of independence; they were then suspicious, and soon afterwards became assured, that the Massachusetts delegates, and especially John Adams, were advocates for that obnoxious measure, and they conceived prejudices which were soon increased and artfully inflamed and are not yet worn out.

When John Adams returned in 1774 to Boston from Philadelphia with its quiet private homes and noisy public controversies, he had no time to settle back at his country place. Articles were appearing over the name "Massachusettensis" that were attracting wide attention. The articles argued the British position. It developed that they were written by Daniel Leonard, with whom Adams had been friendly. Leonard was a wealthy lawyer of strong loyalist convictions. Adams replied to these articles over the name "Novanglus" in the Boston Gazette. After the Declaration of Independence, Leonard was banished and spent the rest of his life in England, Canada, and the Bahamas. The following excerpt is from one of the "Novanglus" papers, subtitled: "A History of the Dispute with America, from its Origin, in 1754, to the Present Time."

"NOVANGLUS" PAPER, 1774

Massachusetts is then seized with a violent fit of anger at the clergy.[4] It is curious to observe the conduct of the tories towards this sacred body. If a clergyman, of whatever character, preaches against the principles of the revolution, and tells the people that, upon pain of damnation, they must submit to an established government, the tories cry him up as an excellent man and a wonderful preacher, invite him to their tables, procure him missions from the society and chaplainships to the navy, and flatter him with the hopes of lawn sleeves.

But if a clergyman preaches Christianity, and tells the magistrates that they were not distinguished from their brethren for their private emolument, but for the good of the people; that the people are bound in conscience to obey a good government, but are not bound to submit to one that aims at destroying all the ends of government,—oh sedition! treason!

The clergy in all ages and countries, and in this in particular, are disposed enough to be on the side of government as long as it is tolerable. If they have not been generally in the late administration on that side, it is a demonstration that the late administration has been universally odious.

---

[4] "All our dissenting ministers were not inactive on this occasion. When the clergy engage in a political warfare, religion becomes a most powerful engine, either to support or overthrow the state. What effect must it have had upon the audience, to hear the same sentiments and principles, which they had before read in a newspaper, delivered on Sundays from the sacred desk, with a religious awe, and the most solemn appeals to Heaven, from lips which they had been taught from their cradles to believe could utter nothing but eternal truths!"—*Massachusettensis*.

The clergy of this province are a virtuous, sensible, and learned set of men, and they do not take their sermons from newspapers, but the Bible; unless it be a few, who preach passive obedience. These are not generally curious enough to read Hobbes. It is the duty of the clergy to accommodate their discourses to the times, to preach against such sins as are most prevalent, and recommend such virtues as are most wanted. For example,—if exorbitant ambition and venality are predominant, ought they not to warn their hearers against those vices? If public spirit is much wanted, should they not inculcate this great virtue? If the rights and duties of Christian magistrates and subjects are disputed, should they not explain them, show their nature, ends, limitations, and restrictions, how much soever it may move the gall of Massachusettensis?

Almost twenty years before the Revolution, John Adams anticipated the shift in the center of national power from Great Britain to America. He also knew the thing the American people had most to fear. This excerpt is from a letter to Nathan Webb, a friend. It was written while Adams was teaching Latin in a grammar school in Worcester, Massachusetts.

LETTER TO NATHAN WEBB, OCTOBER 12, 1755

All that part of creation which lies within our observations, is liable to change. Even mighty states and kingdoms are not exempted.

If we look into history, we shall find some nations rising from contemptible beginnings, and spreading their influence till the whole globe is subjected to their sway. When they have reached the summit of grandeur, some minute and unsuspected cause commonly affects their ruin, and the empire of the world is transferred to some other place. Immortal Rome was at first but an insignificant village, inhabited only by a few abandoned ruffians; but by degrees it rose to a stupendous height, and excelled, in arts and arms, all the nations that preceded it. But the demolition of Carthage, (what one should think would have established it in supreme dominion) by removing all danger, suffered it to sink into a debauchery, and made it at length an easy prey to barbarians.

England, immediately upon this, began to increase (the particular and minute causes of which I am not historian enough to trace) in power and magnificence, and is now the greatest nation upon the globe. Soon after the Reformation, a few people came over into this new world for conscience sake. Perhaps this apparently trivial incident may transfer the great seat of empire into America. It looks likely to me: for if we can remove the turbulent Gallicks, our people, according to the exactest computations, will in another century become more numerous than England herself.

Should this be the case, since we have, I may say, all the naval stores of the nation in our hands, it will be easy to obtain the mastery of the seas; and then the united force of all Europe will not be able to subdue us. The only way to keep us from setting up for ourselves is to disunite us. *Divide et impera.* Keep us in distant colonies, and then, some great men in each colony desiring the monarchy of the whole, they will destroy each other's influence and keep the country *in equilibrio.*

Be not surprised that I am turned politician. This whole town is immersed in politics. The interests of nations, and all the *dira* of war, make the subject of every conversation. I sit and hear, and after having been led through a maze of sage observations, I sometimes retire, and by laying things together, form some reflections pleasing to myself. The produce of one of these reveries you have read above. Different employments and different objects may have drawn your thoughts other ways. I shall think myself happy, if in your turn you communicate your lucubrations to me.

It was not easy for John Adams to make up his mind to enter the law; not only his parents but his friends had views on the matter. One of his best friends, Richard Cranch, thought he should hold to his earlier intention to be a minister. They amicably debated the matter in a series of letters. Cranch later married Polly Smith. Adams married Polly's sister Abigail.

LETTER TO RICHARD CRANCH, OCTOBER 18, 1756

I am set down with a design of writing to you. But the narrow sphere I move in, and the lonely, unsociable life I lead, can furnish a letter with little more than complaints of my hard fortune. I am condemned to keep school two years longer. This I sometimes consider as a very grievous calamity, and almost sink under the weight of woe. But shall I dare to complain and to murmur against Providence for this little punishment, when my very existence, all the pleasure I enjoy now, and all the advantages I have of preparing for hereafter, are expressions of benevolence that I never did and never could deserve?

Shall I censure the conduct of that Being who has poured around me a great profusion of those good things that I really want, because He has kept from me other things that might be improper and fatal to me if I had them?

That Being has furnished my body with several senses, and the world around it with objects suitable to gratify them. He has made me an erect figure, and has placed in the most advantageous part of my body the sense of sight. And he has hung up in the heavens over my head, and spread out in the fields of nature around me, those glorious shows and appearances with which my eyes and my imagination are extremely delighted.

I am pleased with the beautiful appearance of the flower, and still more pleased with the prospect of forests and of meadows, of verdant fields and mountains covered with flocks; but I am thrown into a kind of transport when I behold the amazing concave of heaven, sprinkled and glittering with stars.

That Being has bestowed upon some of the vegetable species a fragrance that can almost as agreeably entertain our sense of smell. He has so wonderfuly constituted the air we live in, that, by giving it a particular kind of vibration, it produces in us as intense sensations of pleasure as the organs of our bodies can bear, in all the varieties of harmony and concord. But all the provision that He has made for the gratification of my senses, though very engaging instances of kindness, are much inferior to the provision for the gratification of my nobler powers of intelligence and reason. He has given me reason, to find out the truth and the real design of my existence here, and, has made all endeavors to promote that design agreeable to my mind and attended with a conscious pleasure and complacency. On the contrary, He has made a different course of life, a course of impiety and injustice, of malevolence and intemperance, appear shocking and deformed to my first reflection.

He has made my mind capable of receiving an infinite variety of ideas, from those numerous material objects with which we are environed; and of retaining, compounding, and arranging the vigorous impressions which we receive from these into all the varieties of picture and of figure.

By inquiring into the situation, produce, manufactures, &c., of our own, and by travelling into or reading about other countries, I can gain distinct ideas of almost every thing upon this earth at present; and by looking into history, I can settle in my mind a clear and a comprehensive view of the earth at its creation, of its various changes and revolutions, of its progressive improvement, sudden depopulation by a deluge, and its gradual re-peopling; of the growth of several kingdoms and empires, of their wealth and commerce, their wars and politics; of the characters of their principal leading men; of their grandeur and power; their virtues and vices; of their insensible decays at first, and of their swift destruction at last.

In fine, we can attend the earth from its nativity, through all the various turns of fortune; through all its successive changes; through all the events that happen on its surface, and all the successive generations of mankind, to the final conflagration, when the whole earth, with its appendages, shall be consumed by the furious element of fire. And after our minds are furnished with this ample store of ideas, far from feeling burdened or overloaded, our thoughts are more free and active and clear than before, and we are capable of spreading our acquaintance with things much further.

Far from being satiated with knowledge, our curiosity is only improved and increased; our thoughts rove beyond the visible diurnal sphere, range through the immeasurable regions of the universe, and lose themselves among a labyrinth of worlds. And not contented with knowing what is, they run forward into futurity, and search for new employment there. There they can never stop. The wide, the boundless prospect lies before them! Here alone they find objects adequate to their desires. Shall I now presume to complain of my hard fate, when such an ample provision has been made to gratify all my senses, and all the faculties of my soul? God forbid. I am happy, and I will remain so, while health is indulged to me, in spite of all the other adverse circumstances that fortune can place me in.

I expect to be joked upon, for writing in this serious manner, when it shall be known what a resolution I have lately taken. I have engaged with Mr. Putnam to study law with him two years, and to keep school at the same time. It will be hard work; but the more difficult and dangerous the enterprise, a brighter crown of laurel is bestowed on the conqueror. However, I am not without apprehensions concerning the success of this resolution, but I am under much fewer apprehensions than I was when I thought of preaching.

The frightful engines of ecclesiastical councils, of diabolical malice and Calvinistical good-nature never failed to terrify me exceedingly whenever I thought of preaching. But the point is now determined, and I shall have liberty to think for myself without molesting others or being molested myself. Write to me the first good opportunity, and tell me freely whether you approve my conduct.

John Adams was admitted to the bar in 1758. By 1761, when this letter was written, his community standing was of a high order. He had been chosen "surveyor of highways," ostensibly something of an honor, but in practice not too inspiring. His work did not interfere with his thinking and writing. In the following letter to a strong personal friend, Samuel Quincy, John Adams has some things to say about human genius and eternal life.

LETTER TO SAMUEL QUINCY, APRIL 22, 1761

The review of an old letter from you upon original composition and original genius has raised a war in my mind. "Scraps of verse, sayings of philosophers," the received opinion of the world, and my own reflections upon all, have thrown my imagination into a turmoil like the reign of a rumor in Milton, or the jarring elements in Ovid, where

> nulli sua forma manebat.
> Obstabatque aliis aliud,[5]

a picture of which I am determined to draw.

---

[5] [To no one did his own form remain. And each was getting in the other's way. —Ed.]

Most writers have represented genius as a rare phenomenon, a Phoenix. Bolingbroke says: "God mingles sometimes, among the societies of men, a few and but a few of those on whom he is graciously pleased to bestow a larger portion of the ethereal spirit than in the ordinary course of his providence he bestows on the sons of men." Mr. Pope will tell you that this *"vivida vis animi* [vigorous force of mind] is to be found in very few, and that the utmost stretch of study, learning, and industry can never attain to this." Dr. Cheyne shall distinguish between his quick-thinkers and slow-thinkers, and insinuate that the former are extremely scarce.

We have a becoming reverence for the authority of these writers, and of many others of the same opinion; but we may be allowed to fear that the vanity of the human heart had too great a share in determining these writers to that opinion. The same vanity which gave rise to that strange religious dogma, that God elected a precious few (of which few, however, every man who believed the doctrine is always one) to life eternal, without regard to any foreseen virtue, and reprobated all the rest, without regard to any foreseen vice. A doctrine which, with serious gravity, represents the world as under the government of humor and caprice, and which Hottentots and Mohawks would reject with horror.

If the orthodox doctrine of genius is not so detestable as that of unconditional election, it is not much less invidious nor much less hurtful. One represents eternal life as an unattainable thing without the special favor of the Father, and even with that, attainable by very few, one of a tribe, or two of a nation, and so tends to discourage the practice of virtue. The other represents the talents to excel as extremely scarce, indulged by nature to very few, and unattainable by all the rest, and therefore tends to discourage industry. You and I shall never be persuaded or frightened either by Popes or councils, poets or enthusiasts, to believe that the world of nature, learning and grace is governed by such arbitrary will or inflexible fatality. We have much higher notions of the efficacy of human endeavors in all cases.

John Adams wrote this letter from Holland, where he was obtaining recognition of the United States, to Robert R. Livingston, Secretary of Foreign Affairs under the Continental Congress.

LETTER TO ROBERT R. LIVINGSTON, OCTOBER 8, 1782

. . . I am an enemy to every appearance of restraint in a matter so delicate and sacred as the liberty of conscience; but the laws here do not permit Roman Catholics to have steeples to their churches, and these laws could not be altered. I shall be impatient to receive the ratification of Congress. . . .

John Adams was in Paris when he wrote this letter to Dr. Richard Price, author of the book Observations on the Importance of the American Revolution, *which had been given Adams by Benjamin Franklin. Mr. and Mrs. Adams were eager to get back to the United States; but the next month John Adams was informed that Congress had appointed him the first United States Minister to the Court of St. James.*

LETTER TO RICHARD PRICE, APRIL 7, 1785

I think it may be said in praise of the citizens of the United States, that they are sincere inquirers after truth in matters of government and commerce; at least that there are among them as many in proportion, of this liberal character, as any other country possesses. They cannot, therefore, but be obliged to you, and any other writers capable of throwing light upon these objects, who will take the pains to give them advice.

I am happy to find myself perfectly agreed with you, that we should begin by setting conscience free. When all men of all religions consistent with morals and property, shall enjoy equal liberty, property or rather security of property, and an equal chance for honors and power, and when government shall be considered as having in it nothing more mysterious or divine than other arts or sciences, we may expect that improvements will be made in the human character and the state of society. But what an immense distance is that period! Notwithstanding all that has been written from Sidney and Locke down to Dr. Price and the Abbé de Mably, all Europe still believes sovereignty to be a divine right, except a few men of letters. Even in Holland their sovereignty, which resides in more than four thousand persons, is all divine.

But I did not intend to enter into details. If you will permit, I should be glad to communicate with you concerning these things.

The "M. Genêt" to whom John Adams is writing here is the father of the famous Edmond Charles Édouard ("Citizen") Genêt who caused such commotion in the United States in his role as Minister from France. M. Genêt was secretary-interpreter at the Ministry of Foreign Affairs in France. His son Edmond succeeded him in that post at the age of eighteen. Adams came to Paris in 1780 with a wide variety of delicate missions to perform for the United States. He became involved in all sorts of diplomatic complications having to do with the American-French alliance. Adams defended the basic concept of the alliance against critics. This letter to his friend discusses the nature of amity or enmity among nations.

LETTER TO M. GENÊT, MAY 17, 1780

General Conway, in his speech in the house of Commons, on the 6th of May, affirms that the alliance between France and the United States is not natural. Whether it is or not is no doubt a great question. In order to determine whether it is or not, one should consider what is meant by a natural alliance; and I know of no better general rule than this,—when two nations have the same interests in general, they are natural allies; when they have opposite interests, they are natural enemies.[6] . . .

Religion is the fourth part of the barrier. But let it be considered, first, that there is not enough of religion of any kind among the great in England to make the Americans very fond of them. Secondly, that what religion there is in England, is as far from being the religion of America as that of France. The hierarchy of England is quite as disagreeable to America as that of any other country. Besides, the Americans know very well that the spirit of propagating any religion by conquest, and of making proselytes by force or by intrigue is fled from all other countries of the world in a great measure, and that there is more of this spirit remaining in England than anywhere else. And the Americans had, and have still, more reason to fear the introduction of a religion that is disagreeable to them, at least as far as bishops and hierarchy go, from a connection with England, than with any other nation of Europe. The alliance with France has no article respecting religion. France neither claims nor desires any authority or influence over America in this respect; whereas, England claimed and intended to exercise authority and force over the Americans; at least, so far as to introduce bishops; and the English Society for Propagating Religion in Foreign Parts, has, in fact, for a century sent large sums of money to America to support their religion there, which really operated as a bribe upon many minds, and was the principal source of toryism. So that upon the whole, the alliance with France is in fact more natural, as far as religion is concerned, than the former connection with Great Britain or any other connection that can be formed.

Any serious critic of the Revolution or the U.S. Government could expect to hear from John Adams. His voluminous Defence of the Constitutions of Government of the United States of America *consists of specific replies to specific observations. This excerpt from Volume III reflects John Adams' basic faith in education for freedom.*

---

[6] [General Conway contended there were various barriers.—ED.]

DEFENCE OF THE CONSTITUTIONS OF GOVERNMENT OF THE UNITED STATES
OF AMERICA, 1788

The world has been too long abused with notions, that climate and soil decide the characters and political institutions of nations. The laws of Solon and the despotism of Mahomet have, at different times, prevailed at Athens; consuls, emperors, and pontiffs have ruled at Rome. Can there be desired a stronger proof, that policy and education are able to triumph over every disadvantage of climate? Mankind have been still more injured by insinuations, that a certain celestial virtue, more than human, has been necessary to preserve liberty. Happiness, whether in despotism or democracy, whether in slavery or liberty, can never be found without virtue. The best republics will be virtuous, and have been so; but we may hazard a conjecture, that the virtues have been the effect of the well ordered constitution, rather than the cause. And, perhaps, it would be impossible, to prove that a republic cannot exist even among highwaymen, by setting one rogue to watch another; and the knaves themselves may in time be made honest men by the struggle.

John Adams became the first Vice-President of the United States of America in 1788. There seems to be some evidence that the office did not tax his full abilities. He was not a man to stay out of an important debate, but his job in the Senate limited him to the manipulation of the gavel and a chance to break tie votes. In any event, he had time during his first year in office to write a series of long philosophical essays called Discourses on Davila. *It is doubtful that there exists anywhere a finer exposition of his views on the problems of economic disparity as they affect the individual. This excerpt is drawn from one of the early essays.*

DISCOURSES ON DAVILA, 1790-91

In Machiavel's History of Florence, we read: "It is given from above, that in all republics there should be fatal families, who are born for the ruin of them; to the end that in human affairs nothing should be perpetual or quiet." (Lib. 3)

If, indeed, this were acknowledged to be the will of Heaven, as Machiavel seems to assert, why should we entertain resentments against such families? They are but instruments, and they cannot but answer their end. If they are commissioned from above to be destroying angels, why should we oppose or resist them? As to "the end," there are other causes enough, which will forever prevent perpetuity or tranquility, in any great degree, in human affairs. Animal life is a chemical process, and is carried on by unceasing motion. Our bodies and minds, like the heavens, the earth, and the sea, like all animal, vegetable, and mineral nature, like the elements of earth, air, fire, and water, are continually changing.

The mutability and mutations of matter, and much more of the intellectual and moral world, are the consequences of laws of nature, not less without our power than beyond our comprehension.

While we are thus assured that, in one sense, nothing in human affairs will be perpetual or at rest, we ought to remember, at the same time, that the duration of our lives, the security of our property, the existence of our conveniences, comforts, and pleasures, the repose of private life and the tranquility of society, are placed in very great degrees in human power.

Equal laws may be ordained and executed; great families, as well as little ones, may be restrained. And that policy is not less pernicious, than that philosophy is false, which represents such families as sent by Heaven to be judgments. It is not true in fact. On the contrary, they are sent to be blessings; and they are blessings, until, by our own obstinate ignorance and imprudence, in refusing to establish such institutions as will make them always blessings, we turn them into curses.

There are evils, it is true, which attend them as well as other human blessings, even government, liberty, virtue, and religion. It is the province of philosophy and policy to increase the good and lessen the evil that attends them as much as possible. But it is not surely the way, either to increase the good or lessen the evil which accompanies such families, to represent them to the people as machines, as rods, as scourges, as blind and mechanical instruments in the hands of divine vengeance, unmixed with benevolence. Nor has it any good tendency or effect, to endeavor to render them unpopular; to make them objects of hatred, malice, jealousy, envy, or revenge to the common people.

The way of wisdom to happiness is to make mankind more friendly to each other. The existence of such men or families is not their fault. They created not themselves. We, the plebeians, find them the workmanship of God and nature, like ourselves. The constitution of nature, and the course of providence, has produced them as well as us; and they and we must live together; it depends on ourselves, indeed, whether it shall be in peace, love, and friendship, in war or hatred. Nor are they reasonably the objects of censure or aversion, of resentment, envy, or hatred, for the gifts of fortune, any more than for those of nature.

Conspicuous birth is no more in a man's power to avoid than to obtain. Hereditary riches are no more a reproach than they are a merit. A paternal estate is neither a virtue nor a fault. He must, nevertheless, be a novice in this world, who does not know that these gifts of fortune are advantages in society and life, which confer influence, popularity, and power. The distinction that is made between the gifts of nature and those of fortune appears to be not well founded. It is fortune which confers beauty and strength, which are called qualities of nature, as much as birth and hereditary wealth, which are called accidents of fortune; and, on the other hand, it is nature which confers these favors as really as stature and agility.

Narrow and illiberal sentiments are not peculiar to the rich or the poor. If the vulgar have found a Machiavel to give countenance to their malignity, by his contracted and illiberal exclamations against illustrious families as the curse of Heaven, the rich and the noble have not infrequently produced sordid instances of individuals among themselves, who have adopted and propagated an opinion, that God hates the poor, and that poverty and misery on earth are inflicted by Providence in its wrath and displeasure.

This noble philosophy is surely as shallow and as execrable as the other plebeian philosophy of Machiavel; but it is countenanced by at least as many of the phenomena of the world. Let both be discarded, as the reproach of human understanding, and a disgrace to human nature. Let the rich and the poor unite in the bands of mutual affection, be mutually sensible of each other's ignorance, weakness, and error, and unite in concerting measures for their mutual defence against each other's vices and follies, by supporting an impartial mediator.

All through the early part of 1796, there was speculation about President Washington and a third term. The man who was going to be President stayed far outside the political tumult. He was attending to his reading—Tacitus and Homer—he had some friends to see, and he was keeping up with his diary, from which the following short notes are drawn. His feelings about Thomas Paine are explicit. Three months after he wrote the second of these notes he was elected President of the United States.

ADAMS' DIARY, JULY 26, 1796

Cloudy . . .
The Christian religion is, above all the religions that ever prevailed or existed in ancient or modern times, the religion of wisdom, virtue, equity, and humanity, let the blackguard Paine say what he will; it is resignation to God, it is goodness itself to man.

ADAMS' DIARY, AUGUST 14, 1796

One great advantage of the Christian religion is that it brings the great principle of the law of nature and nations—Love your neighbor as yourself, and do to others as you would that others should do to you,—to the knowledge, belief, and veneration of the whole people. Children, servants, women, and men, are all professors in the science of public and private morality. No other institution for education, no kind of political discipline, could diffuse this kind of necessary information, so universally among all ranks and descriptions of citizens. The duties and rights of the man and the citizen are thus taught from early infancy to every creature. The sanctions of a future life are thus added to the observance of civil and political, as well as domestic and private duties. Prudence, justice, temperance, and fortitude, are thus taught to be the means and conditions of future as well as present happiness.

Some of President Adams' sentiments about what was happening in France toward the end of the period of the Revolutionary War are apparent in this reply to an address from the Grand Jurors of the County of Hampshire, Massachusetts.

LETTER TO THE GRAND JURORS OF THE COUNTY OF HAMPSHIRE, MASSACHUSETTS, OCTOBER 3, 1798

I have received with much pleasure your address of the 28th of September from Northampton.

The manifestations of your respect, approbation, and confidence are very flattering to me, and your determination to support the Constitution and laws of your country is honorable to yourselves. If a new order of things has commenced, it behooves us to be cautious, that it may not be for the worse. If the abuse of Christianity can be annihilated or diminished, and a more equitable enjoyment of the right of conscience introduced, it will be well; but this will not be accomplished by the abolition of Christianity and the introduction of Grecian mythology, or the worship of modern heroes or heroines, by erecting statues of idolatry to reason or virtue, to beauty or to taste. It is a serious problem to resolve, whether all the abuses of Christianity even in the darkest ages, when the Pope deposed princes and laid nations under his interdict, were ever so bloody and cruel, ever bore down the independence of the human mind with such terror and intolerance, or taught doctrines which required such implicit credulity to believe, as the present reign of pretended philosophy in France.

The Presidency of John Adams brought him little personal glory and much anguish. He was a Federalist, but many in his own party did not look to him for leadership; they looked to Alexander Hamilton. The battles with Hamilton over foreign policy were especially bitter. It was during Adams' administration that Congress passed the Alien and Sedition Acts that disgraced the Federalist party. In 1800 Adams ran for a second term but was routed by Jefferson. Adams returned to Quincy, Massachusetts, in a mood of total defeat. He had built a tall ladder; every rung but the top one had supported his weight. Now, at the age of sixty-five, he had to pick himself off the ground and make the rest of his life come to something. His intellectual regeneration was steady. After a while, his reading and writing were giving him the pleasure they once did. He was seeing his old friends again. He had a quarter of a century to live. Dr. Benjamin Rush was a joy to hear from and write to. It was Rush who helped to repair the rift with Thomas Jefferson. In the following two letters to Dr. Rush, John Adams is back in full stride, turning the full play of his mind on such familiar subjects as Thomas Paine, religion, virtue, and John Adams.

LETTERS TO BENJAMIN RUSH, 1810-11

JANUARY 21, 1810

I have not seen, but am impatient to see, Mr. Cheetham's life of Mr. Paine. His political writings, I am singular enough to believe, have done more harm than his irreligious ones. He understood neither government nor religion. From a malignant heart he wrote virulent declamations, which the enthusiastic fury of the times intimidated all men, even Mr. Burke, from answering as he ought. His deism, as it appears to me, has promoted rather than retarded the cause of revolution in America, and indeed in Europe. His billingsgate, stolen from Blount's Oracles of Reason, from Bolingbroke, Voltaire, Bérenger, &c., will never discredit Christianity, which will hold its ground in some degree as long as human nature shall have any thing moral or intellectual left in it. The Christian religion, as I understand it, is the brightness of the glory and the express portrait of the character of the eternal, self-existent, independent, benevolent, all powerful and all merciful creator, preserver, and father of the universe, the first good, first perfect, and first fair. It will last as long as the world. Neither savage nor civilized man, without a revelation, could ever have discovered or invented it. Ask me not, then, whether I am a Catholic or Protestant, Calvinist or Arminian. As far as they are Christians, I wish to be a fellow-disciple with them all.

AUGUST 28, 1811

I agree with you in sentiment, that religion and virtue are the only foundations, not only of republicanism and of all free government, but of social felicity under all governments and in all the combinations of human society. But if I should inculcate this doctrine in my will, I should be charged with hypocrisy and a desire to conciliate the good will of the clergy towards my family, as I was charged by Dr. Priestley and his friend Cooper, and by Quakers, Baptists, and I know not how many other sects, for instituting a national fast, for even common civility to the clergy, and for being a church-going animal.

If I should inculcate those "national, social, domestic, and religious virtues" you recommend, I should be suspected and charged with an hypocritical, machiavelian, jesuitical, pharisaical attempt to promote a national establishment of Presbyterianism in America; whereas I would as soon establish the Episcopal Church, and almost as soon the Catholic Church.

If I should inculcate "fidelity to the marriage bed," it would be said that it proceeded from resentment to General Hamilton, and a malicious desire to hold up to posterity his libertinism. Others would say that it is only a vainglorious ostentation of my own continence. For among all the errors, follies, failings, vices, and crimes, which have been so plentifully imputed to me, I cannot recollect a single insinuation against me of any amorous intrigue, or irregular or immoral connection with woman, single or married, myself a bachelor or a married man.[7]

If I should recommend the sanctification of the sabbath, like a divine, or even only a regular attendance on public worship as a means of moral instruction and social improvement, like a philosopher or statesman, I should be charged with vain ostentation again, and a selfish desire to revive the remembrance of my own punctuality in this respect; for it is notorious enough that I have been a church-going animal for seventy-six years, from the cradle. And this has been alleged as one proof of my hypocrisy.

Even in retirement, Adams found it difficult to stay out of political and intellectual controversy. At the time he wrote this letter to Judge F. A. Van der Kemp, he had recently read Dieu et les Hommes, *some essays by Lord Bolingbroke;* Guenee's Letters, *defending the Bible and the Jews against Voltaire; and various writings by Voltaire dealing with his attacks on religion in general and Christianity in particular.*

LETTERS TO F. A. VAN DER KEMP, 1809-1816

FEBRUARY 16, 1809

. . . in spite of Bolingbroke and Voltaire, I will insist that the Hebrews have done more to civilize men than any other nation. If I were an atheist,

---

[7] August 31, 1811. I had forgot the story of the four English girls whom General Pinckney was employed to hire in England, two for me and two for himself. J. A.

and believed in blind eternal fate, I should still believe that fate had ordained the Jews to be the most essential instrument for civilizing the nations. If I were an atheist of the other sect, who believe or pretend to believe that all is ordered by chance, I should believe that chance had ordered the Jews to preserve and propagate to all mankind the doctrine of a supreme, intelligent, wise, almighty sovereign of the universe, which I believe to be the great essential principle of all morality, and consequently all civilization. I cannot say that I love the Jews very much neither, nor the French, nor the English, nor the Romans, nor the Greeks. We must love all nations as well as we can, but it is very hard to love most of them.

JULY 13, 1815

My friend, what opportunities have I had to do good things, and how few have I done! I am ashamed, I grieve, I am mortified and humiliated, at the recollection of what I have been and where I have been. Yet, I have done nothing to reproach myself with. I have done all in my power to do, and have been overwhelmed by a dispensation, uncontrollable by any talents or virtues I possessed.

My friend, again! the question before mankind is,—how shall I state it? It is, whether authority is from nature and reason, or from miraculous revelation; from the revelation from God, by the human understanding, or from the revelation to Moses and to Constantine, and the council of Nice. Whether it resides in men or in offices. Whether offices, spiritual and temporal, are instituted by men, or whether they are self-created and instituted themselves. Whether they were or were not brought down from Heaven in a phial of holy oil, sent by the Holy Ghost, by an angel incarnated in a dove, to anoint the head of Clovis, a more cruel tyrant than Frederic or Napoleon. Are the original principles of authority in human nature, or in stars, garters, crosses, golden fleeces, crowns, sceptres, and thrones? These profound and important questions have been agitated and discussed, before that vast democratical congregation, mankind, for more than five hundred years. How many crusades, how many Hussite wars, how many powder plots, St. Bartholomew's days, Irish massacres, Albigensian massacres, and battles of Marengo have intervened! *Sub judice lis est* [The dispute is still being judged]. Will Zingendorf, Swendenborg, Whitefield, or Wesley prevail? Or will St. Ignatius Loyola inquisitionize and jesuitize them all? Alas, poor human nature! Thou are responsible to thy Maker and to thyself for an impartial verdict and judgment.

"Monroe's treaty!" I care no more about it than about the mote that floats in the sunbeams before my eyes. The British minister acted the part of a *horse-jockey*. He annexed a *rider* that annihilated the whole treaty.

You are "a dissenter from me in politics and religion." So you say, I cannot say that I am a dissenter from you in either, because I know not your sentiments in either. Tell my plainly your opinions in both, and I will tell you, as plainly, mine. I hate polemical politics and polemical divinity as cordially as you do, yet my mind has been involved in them for sixty-five years at least. For this whole period I have searched after truth by every means and by every opportunity in my power, and with a sincerity and impartiality, for which I can appeal to God, my adored Maker. My religion is founded on the love of God and my neighbor; on the hope of pardon for my offences; upon contrition; upon the duty as well as the necessity of supporting with patience the inevitable evils of life; in the duty of doing no wrong, but all the good I can, to the creation, of which I am but an infinitesimal part. Are you a dissenter from this religion? I believe, too, in a future state of rewards and punishments, but not eternal.

DECEMBER 27, 1816

Jesus is benevolence personified, an example for all men. Dupuis has made no alteration in my opinions of the Christian religion, in its primitive purity and simplicity, which I have entertained for more than sixty years. It is the religion of reason, equity, and love; it is the religion of the head and of the heart. . . .

But to leave Dupuis to be answered or reviewed in Edinburgh or London, I must inquire into the attributes given by the ancient nations to their divinities; gods with stars and new moons in their foreheads or on their shoulders; gods with heads of dogs, horns of oxen, bulls, cows, calves, rams, sheep, or lambs; gods with the bodies of horses; gods with the tails of fishes; gods with the tails of dragons and serpents; gods with the feet of goats. The bull of Mithra; the dog of Anubis; the serpent of Esculapius!!!!

Is man the most irrational beast of the forest? Never did bullock, or sheep, or snake imagine himself a god. What, then, can all this wild theory mean? Can it be any thing but allegory founded in astrology? Your namilius would inform you as well as Dupuis.

The Hebrew unity of Jehovah, the prohibition of all similitudes, appears to me the greatest wonder of antiquity. How could that nation preserve its creed among the monstrous theologies of all the other nations of the earth? Revelation, you will say, and especial Providence; and I will not contradict you, for I cannot say with Dupuis that a revelation is impossible or improbable.

Christianity, you will say, was a fresh revelation. I will not deny this. As I understand the Christian religion, it was, and is, a revelation. But how has it happened that millions of fables, tales, legends, have been blended with both Jewish and Christian revelation that have made them the most bloody religion that ever existed? How has it happened that all the fine arts, architecture, painting, sculpture, statuary, music, poetry, and oratory, have been prostituted, from the creation of the world, to the sordid and detestable purposes of superstition and fraud?

. . . . Let it once be revealed or demonstrated that there is no future state, and my advice to every man, woman, and child, would be, as our existence would be in our own power, to take opium. For, I am certain, there is nothing in this world worth living for but hope, and every hope will fail us, if the last hope, that of a future state, is extinguished.

In these letters, John Adams refers to himself in the third person. He does so in rebuttal to John Taylor, who had published a book in 1814 which was critical of Adams' ideas on the U.S. Constitution and on government in general. The correspondence between Taylor and Adams ran to thirty-two letters on Adams' side. Adams' first letter was dated April 15, 1814. The others are undated. The following excerpts are drawn from letters 2, 13, 16, 31, and 32.

LETTERS TO JOHN TAYLOR, 1814

NO. 2

It is unnecessary to discuss the nice distinctions, which follow in the first page of your respectable volume, between mind, body, and morals. The essence and substance of mind and body, of soul and body, of spirit and matter, are wholly withheld as yet from our knowledge; from the penetration of our sharpest faculties; from the keenest of our incision knives, the most amplifying of our microscopes. With some of the attributes or qualities of each and of both we are well acquainted. We cannot pretend to improve the essence of either, till we know it. Mr. Adams has never thought of "limiting the improvements or amelioration" of the properties or qualities of either. The definition of matter is,—a dead, inactive, inert substance. That of spirit is,—a living, active substance, sometimes, if not always, intelligent. Morals are no qualities of matter; nor, as far as we know, of simple spirit or simple intelligence. Morals are attributes of spirits *only* when those spirits are *free* as well as intelligent agents, and have consciences or a moral sense, a faculty of discrimination not only between right and wrong, but between good and evil, happiness and misery, pleasure and pain. This freedom of choice and action, united with conscience, necessarily implies a responsibility to a lawgiver and to a law, and has a necessary relation to right and wrong, to happiness and misery.

NO. 13

I know not how, when, or where, you discovered that Mr. Adams "supposed that monarchy, aristocracy, and democracy, or mixtures of them, constituted all the elements of government." This language is not mine. There is but one element of government, and that is, THE PEOPLE. From this element spring all governments. "For a nation to be free, it is only necessary that she wills it." For a nation to be slave, it is only necessary that she wills it. The governments of Hindostan and China, of Caffraria and Kamtschatka, the empires of Alexander the Macedonian, of Zingis Khan and Napoleon, of Tecumseh and Nimrod Hughes, all have grown out of this element,—THE PEOPLE. This fertile element, however, has never yet produced any other government than monarchy, aristocracy, democracy, and mixtures of them. And pray tell me *how* it can produce any other?

You say by "moral liberty." Will you be so good as to give me a logical, mathematical, or moral, or any other definition of this phrase, "moral liberty;" and to tell me who is to exercise this "liberty;" and by what principle or system of morality it is to be exercised? Is not this liberty and morality to reside in the great and universal element, "THE PEOPLE?" Have they not always resided there? And will they not always reside there?

This moral liberty resides in Hindoos and Mahometans, as well as in Christians; in Cappadocian monarchists, as well as in Athenian democrats; in Shaking Quakers, as well as in the General Assembly of the Presbyterian clergy; in Tartars and Arabs, Negroes and Indians, as well as in the people of the United States of America.

NO. 16

In this number I have to hint at some causes which impede the course of investigation in civil and political knowledge. Religion, however, has been so universally associated with government, that it is impossible to separate them in this inquiry.

And where shall I begin, and where end? Shall I begin with the library at Alexandria, and finish with that at Washington, the latter Saracens more ferocious than the former, in proportion as they lived in a more civilized age? Where are the languages of antiquity? all the dialects of the Chaldean tongue? Where is Aristotle's history of eighteen hundred republics, that existed before his time? Where are Cicero's writings upon government? What havoc has been made of books through every century of the Christian era? Where are fifty gospels condemned as spurious by the bull of Pope Gelasius? Where are the forty wagon-loads of Hebrew manuscripts burned in France, by order of another pope, because suspected of heresy? Remember the *index expurgatorius,* the inquisition, the stake, the axe, the halter, and the guillotine; and, oh! horrible, the rack! This is as bad, if not worse, than a slow fire. Nor should the Lion's Mouth be forgotten.

Have you considered that system of holy lies and pious frauds that has raged and triumphed for fifteen hundred years; and which Chateaubriand appears at this day to believe as sincerely as St. Austin did? Upon this system depend the royalty, loyalty, and allegiance of Europe. The vial of holy oil, with which the Kings of France and England are anointed, is one of the most splendid and important events in all the legends. Do you think that Mr. Adams's system "arrests our efforts and appalls our hopes in pursuit of political good?" His maxim is, study government as you do astronomy, by facts, observations, and experiments; not by the dogmas of lying priests and knavish politicians.

The causes that impede political knowledge would fill a hundred volumes. How can I crowd a few hints at them in a single volume, much less, in a single letter?

Give me leave to select one attempt to improve civil, political, and ecclesiastical knowledge; or, at least, to arrest and retard the progress of ignorance, hypocrisy and knavery; and the reception it met in the world, tending to "arrest our efforts and appall our hopes." Can you believe that Jesuits conceived this design? Yet true it is.

About the year 1643, Bollandus, a Jesuit, began the great work, the *"Acta Sanctorum."* Even Jesuits were convinced that impositions upon mankind had gone too far. Henschenius, another Jesuit, assisted him and Papebrock in the labor. The design was to give the lives of the saints, and to distinguish the miracles into the true, the false, and the dubious. They produced forty-seven volumes, in folio, an immense work, which, I believe, has never appeared in America. It was not, I am confident, in the library consumed by Ross, the savage, damned to everlasting fame,[8] and I fear it is not in the noble collection of Mr. Jefferson. I wish it was. This was a great effort in favor of truth, and to arrest imposture, though made by Jesuits. But what was their reward? Among the miracles, pronounced by these able men to be true, there are probably millions which you and I should believe no more than we do those related by Paulinus, Athanasius, Basil, Jerome, or Chrysostom, as of their own knowledge.

Now, let us see how this generous effort in favor of truth was received and rewarded. Libels in abundance were printed against it. The authors were cited before the Inquisition in Spain, and the Pope in Italy, as

---

[8] [Commander of the British troops at the time the public buildings at Washington were burned.—ED.]

authors of gross errors. The Inquisition pronounced its anathema in 1695. All Europe was in anxious suspense. The Pope, himself, was embarrassed by the interminable controversies excited, and, without deciding any thing, had no way to escape but by prohibiting all writings on the subject.

And what were the errors? They were only doubts.

1. Is it certain that the face of Jesus Christ was painted on the handker-chief of Saint Veronica?

2. Had the Carmelites the prophet Elias for their founder?

These questions set Europe in a flame, and might have roasted Papebrock at an *auto-da-fé*, had he been in Spain.

Such dangers as these might "arrest efforts and appall hopes of political good;" but Mr. Adams' system cannot. That gaping, timid animal, man, dares not read or think. The prejudices, passions, habits, associations, and interests of his fellow-creatures surround him on every side; and if his reading or his thoughts interfere with any of these, he dares not acknowledge it. If he is hardly enough to venture even a hint, persecution, in some form or other, is his certain portion. *Party spirit,—l'esprit de corps,—*sects, factions, which threaten our existence in America at this moment, both in church and state, have "arrested all efforts, and appalled all hopes of political good." Have the Protestants accomplished a thorough reformation? Is there a nation in Europe whose government is purified from monkish knavery? Even in England, is not the vial of holy oil still shown to travellers? How long will it be before the head of the Prince Regent, or the head of his daughter, will be anointed with this oil, and the right of impressing seamen from American ships deduced from it.

NO. 31

Turn our thoughts, in the next place, to the characters of learned men. The priesthood have, in all ancient nations, nearly monopolized learning. Read over again all the accounts we have of Hindoos, Chaldeans, Persians, Greeks, Romans, Celts, Teutons, we shall find that priests had all the knowledge, and really governed all mankind. Examine Mahometanism, trace Christianity from its first promulgation; knowledge has been almost exclusively confined to the clergy. And, even since the Reformation, when or where has existed a Protestant or dissenting sect who would tolerate A FREE INQUIRY? The blackest billingsgate, the most ungentlemanly inso-lence, the most yahooish brutality is patiently endured, countenanced, propagated, and applauded. But touch a solemn truth in collision with a dogma of a sect, though capable of the clearest proof, and you will soon find you have disturbed a nest, and the hornets will swarm about your legs and hands and fly into your face and eyes.

NO. 32

A few words more concerning the characters of literary men. What sort of men have had the conduct of the presses in the United States for the last thirty years? In Germany, in England, in France, in Holland, the presses, even the newspapers, have been under the direction of learned men. How has it been in America? How many presses, how many newspapers have been directed by vagabonds, fugitives from a bailiff, a pillory, or a halter in Europe?

You know it is one of the sublimest and profoundest discoveries of the eighteenth century, that knowledge is corruption; that arts, sciences, and taste have deformed the beauty and destroyed the felicity of human nature, which appears only in perfection in the savage state,—the children of nature. One writer gravely tells us that the first man who fenced a tobacco yard, and said, "this is mine," ought instantly to have been put to death; another as solemnly says, the first man who pronounced the word "dieu" ought to have been despatched on the spot; yet these are advocates of toleration and enemies of the Inquisition.[9]

I never had enough of the ethereal spirit to rise to these heights. My humble opinion is, that knowledge, upon the whole, promotes virtue and happiness. I therefore hope that you and all other gentlemen of property, education, and reputation will exert your utmost influence in establishing schools, colleges, academies, and universities, and employ every means and opportunity to spread information, even to the lowest dregs of the people, if any such there are, even among your own domestics and John Randolph's serfs. I fear not the propagation and dissemination of knowledge. The conditions of humanity will be improved and ameliorated by its expansion and diffusion in every direction. May every human being,—man, woman, and child,—be as well informed as possible! But, after all, did you ever see a rose without a briar, a convenience without an inconvenience, a good without an evil, in this mingled world? Knowledge is applied to bad purposes as well as to good ones. Knaves and hypocrites can acquire it, as well as honest, candid, and sincere men. It is employed as an engine and a vehicle to propagate error and falsehood, treason and vice, as well as truth, honor, virtue, and patriotism. It composes and pronounces, both panegyrics and philippics, with exquisite art, to confound all distinctions in society between right and wrong. And if I admit, as I do, that truth generally prevails, and virtue is, or will be triumphant in the end, you must allow that honesty has a hard struggle, and must prevail by many a well-fought

---

[9] *Vide*, Rousseau and Diderot *passim*.

and fortunate battle, and, after all, must often look to another world for justice, if not for pardon.

There is no necessary connection between knowledge and virtue. Simple intelligence has no association with morality. What connection is there between the mechanism of a clock or watch and the feeling of moral good and evil, right or wrong? A faculty or a quality of distinguishing between moral good and evil, as well as physical happiness and misery, that is, pleasure and pain, or, in other words, a CONSCIENCE,—an old word almost out of fashion,—is essential to morality.

Now, how far does simple, theoretical knowledge quicken or sharpen conscience? La Harpe, in some part of his great work, his Course of Literature, has given us an account of a tribe of learned men and elegant writers, who kept a kind of office in Paris for selling at all prices, down to three livres, essays or paragraphs upon any subject, good or evil, for or against any party, any cause, or any person. One of the most conspicuous and popular booksellers in England, both with courtiers and the citizens, who employed many printers and supported many writers, has said to me, "the men of learning in this country are stark mad. There are in this city a hundred men, gentlemen of liberal education, men of science, classical scholars, fine writers, whom I can hire at any time at a guinea a day, to write for me for or against any man, any party, or any cause." Can we wonder, then, at any thing we read in British journals, magazines, newspapers, or reviews?

Where are, and where have been, the greatest masses of science, of literature, or of taste? Shall we look for them in the church or the state, in the universities or the academies? among Greek or Roman philosophers, Hindoos, Brahmins, Chinese mandarins, Chaldean magi, British druids, Indian prophets, or Christian monks? Has it not been the invariable maxim of them all to deceive the people by any lies, however gross? "Bonus populus vult decipi; ergo decipiatur."[10]

And after all that can be done to disseminate knowledge, you never can equalize it. The number of laborers must, and will forever be so much more multitudinous than that of the students, that there will always be giants as well as pygmies, the former of which will have more influence than the latter; man for man, and head for head; and, therefore, the former will be aristocrats, and the latter democrats, if not Jacobins or *sans culottes*.

These morsels, and a million others analogous to them, which will easily occur to you, if you will be pleased to give them a careful mastication and rumination, must, I think, convince you, that no practicable or possible

---

[10] ["The people like to be imposed on; so let them be imposed on."—ED.]

advancement of learning can ever equalize knowledge among men to such a degree, that some will not have more influence in society than others; and, consequently, that some will always be aristocrats, and others democrats. You may read the history of all the universities, academies, monasteries of the world, and see whether learning extinguishes human passions or corrects human vices. You will find in them as many parties and factions, as much jealousy and envy, hatred and malice, revenge and intrigue, as you will in any legislative assembly or executive council, the most ignorant city or village. Are not the men of letters—philosophers, divines, physicians, lawyers, orators, and poets,—all over the world, at perpetual strife with one another? Knowledge, therefore, as well as genius, strength, activity, industry, beauty, and twenty other things, will forever be a natural cause of aristocracy.

At the time Adams wrote this letter, he had the satisfaction of knowing that he was at long last, in a measure, being restored to public favor.

LETTER TO WILLIAM TUDOR, SEPTEMBER 10, 1818

Liberty of conscience to be granted to all Christians, except Papists. Good God! A grant from a king of liberty of conscience! Is it not a grant of the King of kings, which no puppet or *roitelet* upon earth can give or take away?

Samuel Miller, the recipient of the following excerpted letter, was a Presbyterian clergyman, author, and educator. Thinking about his life and thought from the vantage point of his eighty-fifth year, John Adams has something to say about his religious development.

LETTER TO SAMUEL MILLER, JULY 8, 1820

You know not the gratification you have given me by your kind, frank, and candid letter. I must be a very unnatural son to entertain any prejudices against the Calvinists, or Calvinism, according to your confession of faith; for my father and mother, my uncles and aunts, and all my predecessors, from our common ancestor, who landed in this country two hundred years ago, wanting five months, were of that persuasion. Indeed, I have never known any better people than the Calvinists. Nevertheless, I must acknowledge that I cannot class myself under that denomination. My opinions, indeed, on religious subjects ought not to be of any consequence to any but myself. To develop them, and the reasons for them, would require a folio larger than Willard's Body of Divinity, and, after all, I might scatter darkness rather than light.

Before I was twelve years of age, I necessarily became a reader of polemical writings of religion, as well as politics, and for more than seventy years I have indulged myself in that kind of reading, as far as the wandering, anxious, and perplexed kind of life, which Providence has compelled me to pursue, would admit. I have endeavored to obtain as much information as I could of all the religions which have ever existed in the world. Mankind are by nature religious creatures. I have found no nation without a religion, nor any people without the belief of a supreme Being. I have been overwhelmed with sorrow to see the natural love and fear of that Being wrought upon by politicians to produce the most horrid cruelties, superstitions, and hypocrisy, from the sacrifices to Moloch down to those of Juggernaut, and the sacrifies of the kings of Whidah and Ashantee. The great result of all my researches has been a most diffusive and comprehensive charity. I believe with Justin Martyr, that all good men are Christians, and I believe there have been, and are, good men in all nations, sincere and conscientious. That you and I shall meet in a better world, I have no more doubt than I have that we now exist on the same globe. If my natural reason did not convince me of this, Cicero's dream of Scipio, and his essays on friendship and old age, would have been sufficient for the purpose. But Jesus has taught us, that a future state is a social state, when he promised to prepare places in his Father's house of many mansions for his disciples.

By the way, I wonder not at the petition of the pagans to the emperor, that he would call in and destroy all the writings of Cicero, because they tended to prepare the mind of the people, as well as of the philosophers, to receive the Christian religion.

My kind compliments to Mrs. Miller, and thanks for the obliging visit she made me. I interest myself much in her family. Her father was one of my most intimate friends in an earlier part of his life, though we differed in opinion on the French Revolution, in the latter part of his days. I find that differences of opinion in politics, and even in religion, make but little alteration in my feelings and friendships when once contracted.

To an old friend, David Sewall, John Adams looks around at the historical and philosophical landscape.

LETTER TO DAVID SEWALL, MAY 22, 1821

How do you do? As we have been friends for seventy years, and are candidates for promotion to another world, where I hope we shall be better acquainted, I think we ought to inquire now and then after each other's health and welfare, while we stay here. I am not tormented with the fear of death, nor, though suffering under many infirmities, and agitated by many afflictions, weary of life. I have a better opinion of this world and of its Ruler than some people seem to have.

A kind Providence has preserved and supported me for eighty-five years and seven months, through many dangers and difficulties, though in great weakness, and I am not afraid to trust in its goodness to all eternity. I have a numerous posterity, to whom my continuance may be of some importance, and I am willing to await the order of the Supreme Power. We shall leave the world with many consolations. It is better than we found it. Superstition, persecution, and bigotry are somewhat abated; governments are a little ameliorated; science and literature are greatly improved, and more widely spread. Our country has brilliant and exhilarating prospects before it, instead of that solemn gloom in which many of the former parts of our lives have been obscured. The condition of your State, I hope, has improved by its separation from ours, though we scarcely know how to get along without you.

Information of your health and welfare will be a gratification to your sincere friend and humble servant.

4. THOMAS JEFFERSON

"I Never Told My Own Religion, nor Scrutinized That of Another"

IF A man is known by the books he reads and keeps, then the library at Monticello can tell us a great deal about Thomas Jefferson. There are sections on art, architecture, music, history, science, poetry, belles-lettres, religion, and philosophy. Of these, no books were pondered more carefully than the books dealing with the perfectibility of man. He returned time and again to Homer, Euripides, Cicero, Chaucer, Milton, Pope, Dryden, Hume, Adam Smith, Locke, Hobbes, Rousseau, Blackstone, Bolingbroke, Voltaire, Montesquieu, Buffon, and Palladio.

Reading to Jefferson was not a substitute for original thinking but the vital process for generating thought. When he was asked whether there were any sources for the Declaration of Independence, he said there was nothing purely original about the Declaration and that its sources were in history itself. He took pride in his ability to draw the best out of history. And when he specified his own epitaph, as is well known, he did not mention that he was President of the United States. He listed three things:

> Author of the Declaration of American Independence,
> of the Statute of Virginia for Religious Freedom,
> and Father of the University of Virginia

The three achievements are organically related. His quest for the independence of a nation was not separated from the independence of a man. Jefferson thought deeply about education in terms of what was necessary for the growth of the free mind in a free society. Religious freedom to him was a vital prop in the structure of such a free society. He saw how violations of religious freedom led to other violations and oppressions. He knew, too, that one of the surest roads to religious persecution was through religious monopoly.

Jefferson's parents were pioneers of Anglican faith. Much of his early education was under religious auspices. His first schooling was under the

Reverend Douglas A. Scot, who had strong Calvinist convictions. Jefferson's father died when he was fourteen and he became the senior male of the family. His teacher at that time was the Reverend James Maury, a descendant of the Huguenots, who taught him basic science, mathematics, and "other species of polite but useful learning." The object was to "furnish him with the happiest of opportunities, not of making transient visits to, but even fixing his residence within, those sacred recesses, sequestered seats, and classic grounds which are the Muses' favorite haunts."

At seventeen Jefferson entered William and Mary College at Williamsburg, Virginia. Here he met one of the strong influences of his life, Dr. William Small, a young scholar who had come from Scotland, then undergoing an exciting flowering of intellect with reflections and repercussions throughout the western world. The combination of her new incorporation into Great Britain and her successful industrialization resulted in a strong forward thrust for Scotland, in which the universities fully shared. The outpouring in the field of ideas brought with it a reaction against the rigorous Calvinism of recent years. When Benjamin Franklin traveled through Scotland at that time he was excited and impressed, describing his trip as "six weeks of the densest happiness I have met with in any part of my life."

William Small carried this sense of intellectual adventure with him to the new world. He was Jefferson's teacher but still young enough to be his close friend. And it was Small who helped Jefferson to start building a personal library that is still one of the finest of its kind.

Thomas Jefferson graduated from William and Mary with a law degree and entered politics as a member of the Committee of Correspondence and of the House of Burgesses. The Committee of Correspondence was a device by which the states kept in touch with each other. In many ways, it was a seedbed of Union. The House of Burgesses was the name of the representative state legislature in Virginia.

His broad education and wide reading gave Jefferson a strong background for dealing with the major issues of the day. He could make the necessary connections between past, present, and future, and applied his sense of proportion to the whole. When, for example, he wrote his *Summary View of the Rights of British America*, he could draw upon his careful understanding of the legal and historical principles involved. But there was the spur of the moral issue to make his arguments meaningful and compelling with large numbers of people.

No cause in which Jefferson became involved represented more of a challenge to him or called for a greater intellectual and emotional investment than the cause of religious freedom in Virginia. His case was that religion was being stifled by religion itself; that a state that identifies itself with one denomination makes it difficult or impossible for other denominations to exist. Religion had to be protected not so much against the irreligious as against government itself, acting in the name of religion.

In later years, Jefferson said that the fight for religious freedom was perhaps the bitterest of his life. The Anglican Church bore the official seal of Virginia. This resulted in hardships of varying sorts for the other denominations. Jefferson's cause was especially helped by the Presbyterians, the Baptists, and the Methodists, all of whom had good reason to oppose an Established Church. Jefferson reserved to himself the right, however, to criticize the nonestablished denominations whenever he felt their activities were contrary to the full exercise of religious or political freedom. He objected to any preferred status or special privilege which had the effect, in Dumas Malone's words, of creating "artificial aristocracy" or an "unwarranted degree of authority."

The heart of Jefferson's Bill for Religious Freedom in Virginia is contained in the draft of Section II:

> We the General Assembly of Virginia do enact that no man shall be compelled to frequent or support any religious worship, place, or ministry whatsoever, nor shall be enforced, restrained, molested, or burdened in his body or goods, or shall otherwise suffer, on account of his religious opinions or belief; but that all men shall be free to profess, and by argument to maintain, their opinions in matters of religion, and that the same shall in no wise diminish, enlarge, or affect their civil capacities.

The draft proceeded to a broad philosophical and historical statement about the natural rights of man and the place of the free mind in a free society. When the bill was finally enacted, some of Jefferson's eloquent and general statements were deleted, so that the total effect was perhaps less of a declaration or proclamation than he had hoped. But the legal side of it was adequate to accomplish his purpose. After an initial period of disappointment over the final form of the bill, Jefferson regained his pride in it. To James Madison, whose part in leading the fight for the adoption of the bill was critically important, Jefferson could write:

> . . . it is honorable for us to have produced the first legislature who had the courage to declare that the reason of man may be trusted with the formation of his own opinions.

The Act for Establishing Religious Freedom (1786) also had a profound effect on all the American states. It was also the philosophical ancestor of part of the Constitutional Bill of Rights. It was concerned not merely with the toleration of religion, but with workable guarantees that would enable an individual to pursue his own religious bent.

For years, as is apparent in his papers and correspondence, Jefferson tried to persuade Dr. Joseph Priestley, the English scientist-philosopher-minister, to write a version of the New Testament which would contain, in its purest and simplest form, the morals and teachings of Jesus. Jefferson was deeply influenced by the moral and spiritual splendor of Christian idealism as defined by Christ himself. Unable to persuade Priestley to do the work, Jefferson eventually did it himself. Sometime around 1816 Jefferson finished his "Bible"; its title was *The Life and Morals of Jesus*.

Despite this intense interest in and concern for religion, Jefferson was attacked as an unbeliever. The fact that he insisted on the individual's right to seek his spiritual outlet in his own way was mistakenly regarded as an attack on denominational religion. When he ran for the Presidency in 1800 he became the target for groups which expressed their sense of outrage over his religious beliefs. As late as 1830 the Philadelphia Public Library refused him a place on its shelves, calling him an infidel.

Jefferson did not permit himself to become personally involved in controversy over his religious beliefs or affiliation. When the question came up, he would handle it, as did Washington, with complete tact and respect for the views or affiliations of others, but avoid personal debate. In a letter written while in retirement, he said that he had "never told my own religion, nor scrutinized that of another. I never attempted to make a convert, nor wished to change another's creed. I have ever judged of the religion of others by their lives. . . ." To his good friend Benjamin Rush he wrote that his religious beliefs were the "result of a life of inquiry and reflection, and are very different from the Anti-Christian system attributed to me by those who know nothing of my opinions. To the corruptions of Christianity I am indeed opposed, but not to the genuine precepts of Jesus himself. I am a Christian, but I am a Christian in the only sense in which I believe Jesus wished anyone to be, sincerely attached to his doctrine in preference to all others; ascribing to him all human excellence, and believing that he never claimed any other."

In the same letter, Jefferson emphasized his belief in the universalism of Jesus' teachings, uniting all mankind in "one family in the bonds of love, peace, common wants and common aids."

Thomas Jefferson died on the fiftieth anniversary of the Declaration of Independence, as did his friend John Adams. Several days before his death, Jefferson reiterated his hope that "All eyes are opened, or opening, to the rights of man. The general spread of the light of science has already laid open to every view the palpable truth, that the mass of mankind has not been born with saddles on their backs, nor a favored few, booted and spurred, ready to ride them legitimately for the Grace of God. There are grounds of hope for others. For ourselves, let the annual return of this day [July 4] forever refresh our recollections of these rights and an undiminished devotion to them."

Thomas Jefferson put off writing his Autobiography *until he was seventy-eight. When he left the Presidency, he was in debt to the extent of $20,000. He had conducted White House affairs and hospitality without stint; the allowance provided by Congress hardly covered the necessities. Monticello was regarded by foreign visitors and people in government as a sort of honorary White House with a perennially open door. The result was that Jefferson got deeper and deeper into debt, relieved by the sale of 13,000 of his books to Congress and a public subscription. When he was not looking after his guests or attending to affairs at the University of Virginia, which he had established, he read or worked on his* Autobiography *or attended to his correspondence. The following excerpts from the* Autobiography *review some of his positions on religious matters.*

JEFFERSON'S AUTOBIOGRAPHY, BEGUN IN 1821

The first establishment in Virginia which became permanent was made in 1607. I have found no mention of Negroes in the colony until about 1650. The first brought here as slaves were by a Dutch ship; after which the English commenced the trade, and continued it until the revolutionary war. That suspended, *ipso facto*, their further importation for the present, and the business of the war pressing constantly on the legislature, this subject was not acted on finally until the year '78, when I brought in a bill to prevent their further importation. This passed without opposition, and stopped the increase of the evil by importation, leaving to future efforts its final eradication.

The first settlers of this colony were Englishmen, loyal subjects to their king and church, and the grant to Sir Walter Raleigh contained an express proviso that their laws "should not be against the true Christian faith, now professed in the Church of England." As soon as the state of the colony admitted, it was divided into parishes, in each of which was established a minister of the Anglican church, endowed with a fixed salary, in tobacco, a glebe house and land with the other necessary appendages.

To meet these expenses, all the inhabitants of the parishes were assessed, whether they were or not, members of the established church. Towards

Quakers who came here, they were most cruelly intolerant, driving them from the colony by the severest penalties. In process of time, however, other sectarisms were introduced, chiefly of the Presbyterian family; and the established clergy, secure for life in their glebes and salaries, adding to these, generally, the emoluments of a classical school, found employment enough, in their farms and school-rooms, for the rest of the week, and devoted Sunday only to the edification of their flock, by service and a sermon at their parish church. Their other pastoral functions were little attended to. Against this inactivity, the zeal and industry of sectarian preachers had an open and undisputed field; and by the time of the revolution, a majority of the inhabitants had become dissenters from the established church, but were still obliged to pay contributions to support the pastors of the minority.

This unrighteous compulsion, to maintain teachers of what they deemed religious errors, was grievously felt during the regal government, and without a hope of relief. But the first republican legislature, which met in '76, was crowded with petitions to abolish this spiritual tyranny. These brought on the severest contests in which I have ever been engaged. Our great opponents were Mr. Pendleton and Robert Carter Nicholas; honest men, but zealous churchmen. The petitions were referred to the committee of the whole house on the state of the country and, after desperate contests in that committee, almost daily from the 11th of October to the 5th of December, we prevailed so far only, as to repeal the laws which rendered criminal the maintenance of any religious opinions, the forbearance of repairing to church, or the exercise of any mode of worship; and further, to exempt dissenters from contributions to the support of the established church; and to suspend, only until the next session, levies on the members of that church for the salaries of their own incumbents. For although the majority of our citizens were dissenters, as has been observed, a majority of the legislature were churchmen.

Among these, however, were some reasonable and liberal men, who enabled us, on some points, to obtain feeble majorities. But our opponents carried, in the general resolutions of the committee of November 19, a declaration that religious assemblies ought to be regulated, and that provision ought to be made for continuing the succession of the clergy, and superintending their conduct. And, in the bill now passed, was inserted an express reservation of the question, whether a general assessment should not be established by law, on every one, to the support of the pastor of his choice; or whether all should be left to voluntary contributions; and on this question debated at every session, from '76 to '79 (some of our dissenting allies, having now secured their particular object, going over to the advocates of a general assessment), we could only obtain a suspension from session to session until '79, when the question against a general assessment was finally carried, and the establishment of the Anglican church entirely put down. In justice to the two honest but zealous opponents who have been named, I must add, that although, from their natural temperaments, they were more disposed generally to acquiesce in things as they are, than to risk innovations, yet whenever the public will had once decided, none were more faithful or exact in their obedience to it.

*   *   *

I have sometimes asked myself, whether my country is the better for my having lived at all? I do not know that it is. I have been the instrument of doing the following things; but they would have been done by others; some of them, perhaps, a little better.

The Rivanna had never been used for navigation; scarcely an empty canoe had ever passed down it. Soon after I came of age, I examined its obstructions, set on foot a subscription for removing them, got an Act of Assembly passed, and the thing effected, so as to be used completely and fully for carrying down all our produce.

The Declaration of Independence.

I proposed the demolition of the church establishment, and the freedom of religion. It could only be done by degrees; to wit, the Act of 1776, c. 2 exempted dissenters from contributions to the Church, and left the Church clergy to be supported by voluntary contributions of their own sect; was continued from year to year, and made perpetual 1779, c. 36. I prepared the act for religious freedom in 1777, as part of the revisal, which was not reported to the Assembly till 1779, and that particular law not passed till 1785, and then by the efforts of Mr. Madison.

*   *   *

The bill for establishing religious freedom, the principles of which had, to a certain degree, been enacted before, I had drawn in all the latitude of reason and right. It still met with opposition; but, with some mutilations in the preamble, it was finally passed; and a singular proposition proved that its protection of opinion was meant to be universal. Where the preamble declares, that coercion is a departure from the plan of the holy author of our religion, an amendment was proposed, by inserting the word "Jesus Christ" so that it should read, "a departure from the plan of Jesus Christ, the holy author of our religion"; the insertion was rejected by a great majority, in proof that they meant to comprehend, within the mantle of its protection, the Jew and the Gentile, the Christian and the Mohometan, the Hindoo, and Infidel of every denomination.

The Virginia Act for Religious Freedom, which Jefferson had drafted, was passed in 1786, when he was Minister to France. Jefferson, from Paris, sent

copies of the bill to influential people in Europe. His letter to James Madison
in Virginia conveys the reaction.

LETTER TO JAMES MADISON, DECEMBER 16, 1786

The Virginia act for religious freedom has been received with infinite approbation in Europe, and propogated with enthusiasm. I do not mean by the governments, but by the individuals who compose them. It has been translated into French and Italian, has been sent to most of the courts of Europe, and has been the best evidence of the falsehood of those reports which stated us to be in anarchy. It is inserted in the new Encyclopedie, and is appearing in most of the publications respecting America. In fact, it is comfortable to see the standard of reason at length erected after so many ages, during which the human mind has been held in vassalage by kings, priests, and nobles; and it is honorable for us, to have produced the first legislature who had the courage to declare, that the reason of man may be trusted with the formation of his own opinions.

While governor of Virginia (1779-81), Thomas Jefferson received a ques-
tionnaire from François, Marquis de Barbé-Marbois, of the French Legation
in America, asking about the people of the colonies, their customs and cul-
tures and utilities. As often happened, Jefferson's thoroughness in his reply
led to the writing of a detailed statement that had many more uses than
the one originally intended. Out of the reply to the questionnaire grew
Jefferson's famous Notes on Virginia, *the following portion of which is*
concerned with the background of the Act for Religious Freedom which he
fathered.

REPUBLICAN NOTES ON RELIGION AND AN ACT ESTABLISHING RELIGIOUS FREEDOM, PASSED IN THE ASSEMBLY OF VIRGINIA, IN THE YEAR 1786

The first settlers in this country were emigrants from England, of the English church, just at a point of time when it was flushed with complete victory over the religions of all other persuasions. Possessed, as they became, of the powers of making, administering, and executing the laws, they showed equal intolerance in this country with their Presbyterian brethren, who had emigrated to the northern government. The poor Quakers were flying from persecution in England. They cast their eyes on these new countries as asylums of civil and religious freedom; but they found them free only for the reigning sect. Several acts of the Virginia Assembly of 1659, 1662, and 1693, had made it penal in parents to refuse to have their children baptized; had prohibited the unlawful assembling of Quakers; had made it penal for any master of a vessel to bring a Quaker into the state; had ordered those already here, and such as should come hereafter to be imprisoned until they should abjure the country; provided a milder punishment for their first and second return, but death for their third; had inhibited all persons from suffering their meetings in or near their houses, entertaining them individually, or disposing of books which supported their tenets.

If no execution took place here, as did in New England, it was not owing to the moderation of the church, or spirit of the legislature, as may be inferred from the law itself; but to historical circumstances which have not been handed down to us. The Anglicans retained full possession of the country about a century. Other opinions began then to creep in, and the great care of the government to support their own church, having begotten an equal degree of indolence in its clergy, two-thirds of the people had become dissenters at the commencement of the present revolution. The laws, indeed, were still oppressive on them, but the spirit of the one party had subsided into moderation, and of the other had risen to a degree of determination which commanded respect.

The present state of our laws on the subject of religion is this. The convention of May 1776, in their declaration of rights, declared it to be a truth, and a natural right, that the exercise of religion should be free; but when they proceeded to form on that declaration the ordinance of government, instead of taking up every principle declared in the bill of rights, and guarding it by legislative sanction, they passed over that which asserted our religious rights, leaving them as they found them. The same convention, however, when they met as a member of the general assembly in October, 1776, repealed all *acts of Parliament* which had rendered criminal the maintaining any opinions in matters of religion, the forebearing to repair to church, and the exercising any mode of worship; and suspended the laws giving salaries to the clergy, which suspension was made perpetual in October, 1779. Statutory oppressions in religion being thus wiped away, we remain at present under those only imposed by the common law, or by our own acts of assembly. At the common law, *heresy* was a capital offense, punishable by burning. Its definition was left to the ecclesiastical judges, before whom the conviction was, till the statute of the I.El.c.I circumscribed it, by declaring, that nothing should be deemed heresy, but what had been so determined by authority of the canonical scriptures, or by one of the four first general councils, or by other council having for the grounds of their declaration the express and plain words of the scriptures. Heresy, thus circumscribed, being an offense at the common law, our act of assembly of October 1777, c. 17, gives cognizance of it to the general court, by declaring that the jurisdiction of that court shall be general in all matters at the common law. The execution is by the writ *De hœretico comburendo* [On the Burning of a Heretic]. By our own act of assembly of 1705, c. 30, if a person brought up in the Christian religion denies the being of a God, or the Trinity, or asserts there are more gods than one, or denies the Christian religion to be true, or the scriptures to be of divine authority, he is punishable on the first offense by incapacity to hold any office or employment ecclesiastical, civil or military; on the second by disability to sue, to take any gift or legacy, to be guardian, executor, or administrator, and by three years' imprisonment without bail.[1] A father's right to the custody of his own children being founded in law on his right of guardianship, this being taken away, they may of course be severed from him, and put by the authority of the court into more orthodox hands.

This is a summary view of that religious slavery, under which a people have been willing to remain, who have lavished their lives and fortunes for the establishment of their civil freedom.[2] The error seems not sufficiently eradicated, that the operations of the mind, as well as the acts of the body, are subject to the coercion of the laws. But our rulers can have no authority over such natural rights, only as we have submitted to them. The rights of conscience we never submitted, we could not submit. We are answerable for them to our God. The legitimate powers of government extend to such acts only as are injurious to others. But it does me no injury for my neighbor to say there are twenty Gods, or no God. It neither picks my pocket nor breaks my leg. If it be said, his testimony in a court of justice cannot be relied on, reject it then, and be the stigma on him. Constraint may make him worse by making him a hypocrite, but it will never make him a truer man. It may fix him obstinately in his errors, but will not cure them.

Reason and free inquiry are the only effectual agents against terror. Give a loose to them, they will support true religion, by bringing every false one to their tribunal, to the test of their investigation. They are the natural enemies of error, and of error only. Had not the Roman government permitted free inquiry, Christianity could never have been introduced. Had not free inquiry been indulged at the era of reformation, the corruptions of Christianity could not have been purged away. If it be restrained now, the present corruptions will be protected and new ones encouraged. Was the government to prescribe to us our medicine and diet, our bodies would be in such keeping as our souls are now. Thus in France the emetic was once forbidden as a medicine, and the potatoe as an article of food.

---

[1] This pious paragraph is still a Connecticut law.
[2] Furneaux passim.

Government is just as infallible, too, when it fixes systems in physics. Galileo was sent to the inquisition for affirming that the earth was a sphere; the government had declared it to be as flat as a trencher, and Galileo was obliged to abjure his error. This error at length prevailed, the earth became a globe, and Descartes declared it was whirled around its axis by a vortex. The government in which he lived was wise enough to see that this was no question of civil jurisdiction, or we should all have been involved by authority in vortices. In fact, the vortices have been exploded, and the Newtonian principle of gravitation is now more firmly established, on the basis of reason, than it would be were the government to step in, and make it an article of necessary faith. Reason and experiment have been indulged, and error has fled before them. It is error alone which needs the support of government. Truth can stand by itself.

Subject opinion to coercion: whom will you make your inquisitors? Fallible men; men governed by bad passions, by private as well as public reasons. And why subject it to coercion? To produce uniformity. But is uniformity of opinion desirable? No more than of face and stature. Introduce the bed of Procrustes then, and as there is danger that the large men may beat the small, make us all of a size, by lopping the former and stretching the latter.

Difference of opinion is advantageous in religion. The several sects perform the office of a *censor morum* over such other. Is uniformity attainable? Millions of innocent men, women, and children, since the introduction of Christianity, have been burnt, tortured, fined, imprisoned; yet we have not advanced one inch toward uniformity. What has been the effect of coercion? to make one half the world fools and the other half hypocrites. To support roguery and error all over the earth. Let us reflect that it is inhabited by a thousand millions of people. That these profess probably a thousand different systems of religion. That ours is but one of that thousand. That if there be but one right, and ours that one, we should wish to see the nine hundred and ninety-nine wandering sects gathered into the fold of truth. But against such a majority we cannot effect this by force. Reason and persuasion are the only practicable instruments. To make way for these, free inquiry must be indulged; how can we wish others to indulge it while we refuse it ourselves. But every state, says an inquisitor has established some religion. No two, say I, have established the same. Is this a proof of the infallibility of establishments? Our sister states of Pennsylvania and New York, however, have long subsisted without any establishment at all. The experiment was new and doubtful when they made it. It has answered beyond conception. They flourish infinitely. Religion is well supported; of various kinds, indeed, but all good enough; all sufficient to preserve peace and order; or if a sect arises, whose tenets would subvert morals, good sense has fair play, and reasons and laughs it out of doors, without suffering the state to be troubled with it. They do not hang more malefactors than we do. They are not more disturbed with religious dissensions than we are. On the contrary, their harmony is unparalleled, and can be ascribed to nothing but their unbounded tolerance, because there is no other circumstance in which they differ from every nation on earth. They have made the happy discovery, that the way to silence religious disputes, is to take no notice of them.

Let us too give this experiment fair play, and get rid, while we may, of those tyrannical laws. It is true, we are as yet secured against them by the spirit of the times. I doubt whether the people of this country would suffer an execution for heresy, or a three years imprisonment for not comprehending the mysteries of the Trinity. But is the spirit of the people an infallible, a permanent reliance? Is it government? Is this the kind of protection we receive in return for the rights we give up? Besides, the spirit of the times may alter, will alter. Our rulers will become corrupt, our people careless. A single zealot may commence persecutor, and better men be his victims.

It can never be too often repeated, that the time for fixing every essential right on a legal basis is while our rulers are honest, and ourselves united. From the conclusion of this war we shall be going down hill. It will not then be necessary to resort every moment to the people for support. They will be forgotten, therefore, and their rights disregarded. They will forget themselves, but in the sole faculty of making money, and will never think of uniting to effect a due respect for their rights. The shackles, therefore, which shall not be knocked off at the conclusion of this war, will remain on us long, will be made heavier and heavier, till our rights shall revive or expire in a convulsion.

AN ACT FOR ESTABLISHING RELIGIOUS FREEDOM, PASSED IN THE ASSEMBLY OF VIRGINIA IN THE BEGINNING OF THE YEAR 1786

Well aware that Almighty God hath created the mind free; that all attempts to influence it by temporal punishments or burthens, or by civil incapacitations, tend only to beget habits of hypocrisy and meanness, and are a departure from the plan of the Holy Author of our religion, who, being Lord both of body and mind, yet chose not to propagate it by coercions on either, as was in his Almighty power to do;

that the impious presumption of legislators and rulers, civil as well as ecclesiastical, who, being themselves but fallible and uninspired men, have assumed dominion over the faith of others, setting up their own opinions and modes of thinking as the only true and infallible, and as such endeavoring to impose them on others, hath established and maintained false religions over the greatest part of the world, and through all time:

That to compel a man to furnish contributions of money for the propagation of opinions which he disbelieves, is sinful and tyrannical; that even the forcing of him to support this or that teacher of his own religious persuasion, is depriving him of the comfortable liberty of giving his contributions to the particular pastor whose morals he would make his pattern, and whose powers he feels most persuasive to righteousness, and is withdrawing from the ministry those temporal rewards, which, proceeding from an approbation of their personal conduct, are an additional incitement to earnest and unremitting labors for the instruction of mankind; that our civil rights have no dependence on our religious opinions, more than on our opinions in physics or geometry;

that therefore the proscribing any citizen as unworthy the public confidence by laying upon him an incapacity of being called to offices of trust and emolument, unless he profess or renounce this or that religious opinion, is depriving him injuriously of those privileges and advantages to which in common with his fellow citizens he has a natural right;

that it tends also to corrupt the principles of that very religion it is meant to encourage, by bribing, with a monopoly of worldly honors and emoluments, those who will externally profess and conform to it;

that though indeed these are criminal who do not withstand such temptation, yet neither are those innocent who lay the bait in their way;

that to suffer the civil magistrate to intrude his powers into the field of opinion, and to restrain the profession or propagation of principles, on supposition of their ill tendency, is a dangerous fallacy, which at once destroys all religious liberty, because he being of course judge of that tendency, will make his opinions the rule of judgment, and approve or condemn the sentiments of others only as they shall square with or differ from his own;

that it is time enough for the rightful purposes of civil government for its officers to interfere when principles break out into overt acts against peace and good order;

and finally, that truth is great and will prevail if left to herself, that she is the proper and sufficient antagonist to error, and has nothing to fear from the conflict, unless by human interposition disarmed of her natural weapons, free argument and debate, errors ceasing to be dangerous when it is permitted freely to contradict them;

Be it therefore enacted by the General Assembly, That no man shall be compelled to frequent or support any religious worship, place or ministry whatsoever, nor shall be enforced, restrained, molested, or burthened in his body or goods, nor shall otherwise suffer on account of his religious opinions or belief; but that all men shall be free to profess and by argument to maintain their opinions in matters of religion, and that the same shall in no wise diminish, enlarge, or effect their civil capacities.

And though we well know that this assembly, elected by the people for the ordinary purposes of legislation only, have no power to restrain the acts of succeeding assemblies, constituted with powers equal to our own, and that therefore to declare this act irrevocable, would be of no effect in law, yet we are free to declare, and do declare, that the rights hereby asserted are of the natural right of mankind, and that if any act shall be hereafter passed to repeal the present, or to narrow its operation, such act will be an infringement of natural right.

Thomas Jefferson took full responsibility for the care of his nephew, Peter Carr, after the death of the latter's parents. Jefferson's deep interest in education had a productive outlet in young Carr. Jefferson introduced Peter to the worlds he himself knew so well; philosophy, theology, mathematics, astronomy, physics, music, Greek, Latin, English literature, political science. The following letter to Peter is one of the most frequently quoted items in all Jeffersoniana. It was written when Carr was seventeen; Jefferson was in Paris as Minister to France at the time.

LETTER TO PETER CARR, AUGUST 10, 1787

He who made us would have been a pitiful bungler, if he had made the rules of our moral conduct a matter of science. For one man of science, there are thousands who are not. What would have become of them? Man was destined for society. His morality, therefore, was to be formed to this object. He was endowed with a sense of right and wrong, merely relative to this. This sense is as much a part of his nature, as the sense of hearing, seeing, feeling; it is the true foundation of morality, and not the τὸ καλόν truth, &c., as fanciful writers have imagined. The moral sense, or conscience, is as much a part of man as his leg or arm. It is given to all human beings in a stronger or weaker degree, as force of members is given them in a greater or less degree. It may be strengthened by exercise, as may any particular limb of the body. This sense is submitted, indeed, in some degree, to the guidance of reason; but it is a small stock which is required for this; even a less one than what we call common sense.

State a moral case to a ploughman and a professor. The former will decide it as well, and often better than the latter, because he has not been led astray by artificial rules. In this branch, therefore, read good books, because they will encourage, as well as direct your feelings. The writings of Sterne, particularly, form the best course of morality that ever was written. Besides, these, read the books mentioned in the enclosed paper; and above all things, lose no occasion of exercising your dispositions to be grateful, to be generous, to be charitable, to be humane, to be true, just, firm, orderly, courageous, etc. Consider every act of this kind, as an exercise which will strengthen your moral faculties and increase your worth.

Religion. Your reason is now mature enough to examine this object. In the first place, divest yourself of all bias in favor of novelty and singularity of opinion. Indulge them in any other subject rather than that of religion. It is too important, and the consequences of error may be too serious. On the other hand, shake off all the fears and servile prejudices, under which weak minds are servilely crouched. Fix reason firmly in her seat, and call to her tribunal every fact, every opinion. Question with boldness even the existence of a God; because, if there be one, he must more approve of the homage of reason, than that of blindfolded fear.

You will naturally examine first the religion of your own country. Read the Bible, then, as you would read Livy or Tacitus. The facts which are within the ordinary course of nature, you will believe on the authority of the writer, as you do those of the same kind in Livy and Tacitus. The testimony of the writer weighs in their favor, in one scale, and their not being against the laws of nature, does not weigh against them. But those facts in the Bible which contradict the laws of nature, must be examined with more care, and under a variety of faces. Here you must recur to the pretensions of the writer to inspiration from God. Examine upon what evidence his pretensions are founded, and whether that evidence is so strong, as that its falsehood would be more improbable than a change in the laws of nature, in the case he relates. For example, in the book of Joshua, we are told, the sun stood still several hours. Were we to read that fact in Livy or Tacitus, we should class it with their showers of blood, speaking of statues, beasts, etc. But it is said, that the writer of that book was inspired. Examine, therefore, candidly, what evidence there is of his having been inspired. The pretension is entitled to your inquiry, because millions believe it. On the other hand, you are astronomer enough to know how contrary it is to the law of nature that a body revolving on its axis, as the earth does, should have stopped, should not, by that sudden stoppage, have prostrated animals, trees, buildings, and should after a certain time have resumed its revolution, and that without a second general prostration. Is this arrest of the earth's motion, or the evidence which affirms it, most within the law of probabilities?

You will next read the New Testament. It is the history of a personage called Jesus. Keep in your eye the opposite pretensions: 1, of those who say he was begotten by God, born of a virgin, suspended and reversed the laws of nature at will, and ascended bodily into heaven; and 2, of those who say he was a man of illegitimate birth, of a benevolent heart, enthusiastic mind, who set out without pretensions to divinity, ended in believing them, and was punished capitally for sedition, by being gibbeted, according to the Roman law, which punished the first commission of that offense by whipping, and the second by exile, or death, *in furea*. See this law in the Digest, Lib. 48. tit.19. S28.3. and Lipsius Lib. 2 de cruce. cap. 2.

These questions are examined in the books I have mentioned, under the head of Religion, and several others. They will assist you in your inquiries; but keep your reason firmly on the watch in reading them all.

Do not be frightened from this inquiry by any fear of its consequences. If it ends in a belief that there is no God, you will find incitements to virtue in the comfort and pleasantness you feel in its exercise, and the love of others which it will procure you. If you find reason to believe there is a God a consciousness that you are acting under his eye, and that he approves you, will be a vast additional incitement; if that there be a future state, the hope of a happy existence in that increases the appetite to deserve it; if that Jesus was also a God, you will be comforted by a belief of his aid and love.

In fine, I repeat, you must lay aside all prejudice on both sides, and neither believe nor reject anything, because any other persons, or description of persons, have rejected it or believed it. Your own reason is the only oracle given you by heaven, and you are answerable, not for the rightness, but uprightness of the decision.

I forgot to observe, when speaking of the New Testament, that you should read all the histories of Christ, as well as those whom a council of ecclesiastics have decided for us, to be Pseudo-evangelists, as those they named Evangelists. Because these Pseudo-evangelists pretended to inspiration, as much as the others, and you are to judge their pretensions by your own reason, and not by the reason of those ecclesiastics. Most of these are lost. There are some, however, still extant, collected by Fabricius, which I will endeavor to get and send you.

Jefferson tested his ideas against experience, as the excerpt from the following letter, written from Monticello, makes clear. He had helped to bring about important religious reforms in Virginia; but he was careful not to hold to a position long after the reason for it had changed. Here Jefferson argues for the right of clergymen to hold political office. (In discussing various constitutional requirements for the right to vote, he refers to a scheme of constitution which he prepared in 1783 and meant to have proposed when there was in that year a general idea that a convention would be called in "this state" to form a constitution.)

LETTER TO JEREMIAH MOOR, AUGUST 14, 1800

I observe however in the same scheme of a constitution, an abridgment of the right of being elected, which, after 17 years more of experience and reflection, I do not approve. It is the incapacitation of a clergyman from being elected. The clergy, by getting themselves established by law, and ingrafted into the machine of government, have been a very formidable engine against the civil and religious rights of man. They are still so in many countries and even in some of these United States. Even in 1783, we doubted the stability of our recent measures for reducing them to the footing of other useful callings. It now appears that our means were effectual. The clergy here seem to have relinquished all pretension to privilege and to stand on a footing with lawyers, physicians, etc. They ought therefore to possess the same rights.

Ever since the earliest Colonial settlements, the New World had been a haven for people whose ideas or religions had been distasteful to the existing authorities. But then, in the latter half of the 1790's, the hospitality began to wear thin. The Naturalization Act passed by Congress in 1795 was liberal enough, but within a few years all sorts of fears swept through the states— fears that the country was being subverted and that all sorts of conspiracies were being laid against the new nation. France in particular was suspected of meddling in the sovereign affairs of the United States. Meanwhile, accusations of disloyalty were being thrown around and a profound uneasiness settled over the nation. Within a two-month period—June and July, 1798— four acts were passed that were designed to strengthen the internal security of the country but that actually had the effect of adding to the tensions and confusions. Under these acts, visitors or new settlers were under almost constant suspicion and pressure. The President was given arbitrary power of detention or deportation. The image of America suffered abroad. Meanwhile, men like Dr. Joseph Priestley and Dr. Thomas Cooper, who had recently come to the United States to take part in a great adventure of ideas, became uneasy and uncertain. Both were distinguished English scientists and thinkers; their presence here was viewed as an important gain for America by large numbers of men of whom Jefferson and Franklin were in the forefront. But the unorthodox religious opinions of Priestley and Cooper produced a storm of opposition, as Jefferson's letter may indicate.

LETTER TO JOSEPH PRIESTLEY, MARCH 21, 1801

I learnt some time ago that you were in Philadelphia, but that it was only for a fortnight; and supposed you were gone. It was not till yesterday I received information that you were still there, had been very ill, but were on the recovery. I sincerely rejoice that you are so. Yours is one of the few lives precious to mankind, and for the continuance of which every thinking man is solicitous. Bigots may be an exception. What an effort, my dear sir, of bigotry in politics and religion have we gone through! The barbarians really flattered themselves they should be able to bring back the times of vandalism when ignorance put everything into the hands of power and priestcraft. All advances in science were proscribed as innovations. They pretended to praise and encourage education, but it was to be the education of our ancestors. We were to look backwards, not forwards, for improvements; the President himself declaring, in one of his answers to addresses, that we were never to expect to go beyond them in real science. This was the real ground of all the attacks on you.

Those who live by mystery and *charlatanerie*, fearing you would render them useless by simplifying the Christian philosophy,—the most sublime and benevolent, but most perverted system that ever shone on man,—endeavored to crush your well-earnt and well-deserved fame. But it was the Lilliputians upon Gulliver. Our countrymen have recovered from the alarm into which art and industry had thrown them; science and honesty are replaced on their high ground; and you, my dear sir, as their great apostle, are on its pinnacle. It is with heartfelt satisfaction that, in the first moments of my public action, I can hail you with welcome to our land, tender to you the homage of its respect and esteem, cover you under the protection of those laws which were made for the wise and good like you, and disdain the legitimacy of that libel on legislation which, under the form of a law, was for some time placed among them. . . .[3]

The furore over Dr. Priestley died down, but Dr. Cooper was in one controversy after another, from the time he came to the United States in 1793 almost to the date of his death in 1840. Jefferson was instrumental in obtaining an appointment for Cooper at the University of Virginia. Here his radical views of religion and politics created a demand for his ouster, with a resultant debate involving the issue of academic freedom. Cooper left Virginia for Columbia College, South Carolina, to teach geology, law, and chemistry at twice the salary. Jefferson had defended Cooper and was reluctant to have Cooper believe that his "release" from the University of Virginia was given because he was considered undesirable.

LETTER TO THOMAS COOPER, AUGUST 14, 1820

I hope and believe you are mistaken in supposing the reign of fanaticism to be on the advance. I think it certainly declining. It was first excited arti-

---

[3] [Jefferson's note in the margin refers to the "Alien and Sedition Law."—ED.]

ficially by the sovereigns of Europe as an engine of opposition to Bonaparte and to France. It rose to a great height there, and became indeed a powerful engine of loyalism, and of support to their governments. But that loyalism is giving way to very different dispositions, and its prompter fanaticism, is vanishing with it. In the meantime it had been wafted across the Atlantic, and chiefly from England, with their other fashions, but it is here also on the wane. The ambitious sect of Presbyterians indeed, the Loyalists of our country, spare no pains to keep it up. But their views of ascendency over all other sects in the United States seem to excite alarm in all, and to unite them as against a common and threatening enemy. And although the Unitarianism they impute to you is heterodoxy with all of them, I suspect the other sects will admit it to their alliance in order to strengthen the phalanx of opposition against the enterprise of their more aspiring antagonists. Although spiritualism is not most prevalent with all these sects, yet with none of them, I presume, is materialism declared heretical. Mr. Locke, on whose authority they often plume themselves, openly maintained the materialism of the soul; and charged with blasphemy those who denied that it was in the power of an Almighty Creator to endow with the faculty of thought any composition of matter he might think fit. The fathers of the church of the three first centuries generally, if not universally, were materialists, extending it even to the creator himself; nor indeed do I know exactly[4] in what age of the Christian church the heresy of spiritualism was introduced. . . .

In the consultations of the visitors of the university on the subject of releasing you from your engagement with us, although one or two members seemed alarmed at this cry of "fire" from the Presbyterian pulpits, yet the real ground of our decision was that our funds were in fact hypotheticated for five or six years to redeem the loan we had reluctantly made; and although we hoped and trusted that the ensuing legislature would remit the debt and liberate our funds, yet it was not just, on this possibility, to stand in the way of your looking out for a more certain provision. The completing all our buildings for professors and students by the autumn of the ensuing year, is now secured by sufficient contracts, and our confidence is most strong that neither the state nor their legislature will bear to see those buildings shut up for five or six years, when they have the money in hand, and actually appropriated to the object of education, which would open their doors at once for the reception of their sons, now waiting and calling aloud for that institution. The legislature meets on the 1st Monday of December, and before Christmas we shall know what are their intentions.

---

[4] I believe by Athenasius and the council of Nicea.

If such as we expect, we shall then immediately take measures to engage our professors and bring them into place the ensuing autumn or early winter. My hope is that you will be able and willing to keep yourself uncommitted, to take your place among them about that time; and I can assure you there is not a voice among us which will not be cordially given for it. I think, too, I may add, that if the Presbyterian opposition should not die by that time, it will be directed at once against the whole institution, and not amuse itself with nibbling at a single object. It did that only because there was no other, and they might think it politic to mask their designs on the body of the fortress, under the ————— [*sic*] of a battery against a single bastion. I will not despair then of the avail of your services in an establishment which I contemplate as the future bulwark of the human mind in this hemisphere. God bless you and preserve you *multos annos*.

However occupied he may have been with the Presidency his first year in office, Jefferson managed to find time for the kind of correspondence he found so meaningful—philosophical speculation. This excerpt comes from a letter written to the Reverend Issac Story, a minister in Marblehead, Massachusetts, who had written to President Jefferson in an attempt to interest him in a theory concerning the transmigration of souls.

LETTER TO ISAAC STORY, DECEMBER 5, 1801

It is not for me to pronounce on the hypotheses you present of a transmigration of souls from one body to another in certain cases. The laws of nature have withheld from us the means of physical knowledge of the country of spirits, and revelation has, for reasons unknown to us, chosen to leave us in the dark as we were. When I was young, I was fond of the speculations which seemed to promise some insight into that hidden country, but observing at length that they left me in the same ignorance in which they had found me, I have for very many years ceased to read or to think concerning them, and have reposed my head on that pillow of ignorance which a benevolent Creator has made so soft for us, knowing how much we should be forced to use it.

I have thought it better, by nourishing the good passions and controlling the bad, to merit an inheritance in a state of being of which I can know so little, and to trust for the future to Him who has been so good for the past.

I perceive too that these speculations have with you been only the amusement of leisure hours; while your labors have been devoted to the education of your children, making them good members of society, to the instructing men in their duties and performing the other offices of a large parish. I am happy in your approbation of the principles I avowed on entering on the government. Ingenious minds, availing themselves of the imperfection of language, have tortured the expressions out of their plain meaning in order to infer departures from them in practice. If revealed language has not been able to guard itself against misinterpretations, I could not expect it. But if an administration quadrating with the obvious import of my language can conciliate the affections of my opposers, I will merit that conciliation.

At the beginning of his second year in the Presidency, Thomas Jefferson was asked by members of a Connecticut Baptist congregation to designate a day of fasting in connection with the nation's past ordeals. Jefferson had some highly developed ideas on the subject, but thought he would check first with his Attorney General, Levi Lincoln. Following the letter to Attorney General Lincoln are letters to several Baptist Associations.

LETTER TO LEVI LINCOLN, JANUARY 1, 1802

Averse to receiving addresses, yet unable to prevent them, I have generally endeavored to turn them to some account, by making them the occasion, by way of answer, of sowing useful truths and principles among the people, which might germinate and become rooted among their political tenets. The Baptist address, now enclosed, admits of a condemnation of the alliance between Church and State, under the authority of the Constitution. It furnishes an occasion, too, which I have long wished to find, of saying why I do not proclaim fastings and thanksgivings, as my predecessors did. The address, to be sure, does not point at this, and its introduction is awkward. But I foresee no opportunity of doing it more pertinently. I know it will give great offence to the New England clergy; but the advocate of religious freedom is to expect neither peace nor forgiveness from them. Will you be so good as to examine the answer, and suggest any alternations which might prevent an ill effect, or promote a good one, among the people? You understand the temper of those in the North, and can weaken it, therefore, to their stomachs; it is at present seasoned to the Southern taste only. I would ask the favor of you to return it, with the address, in the course of the day or evening.

President Jefferson responds to addresses by Baptist Associations in Danbury, Connecticut, and Baltimore, Maryland.

ADDRESSES TO RELIGIOUS BODIES, 1802, 1808

TO NEHEMIAH DODGE, EPHRAIM ROBBINS, AND STEPHEN S. NELSON: A COM-
MITTEE OF THE DANBURY BAPTIST ASSOCIATION, CONNECTICUT, JANUARY 1,
1802

The affectionate sentiments of esteem and approbation which you are so good as to express towards me, on behalf of the Danbury Baptist Association, give me the highest satisfaction.

My duties dictate a faithful and zealous pursuit of the interests of my constituents, and in proportion as they are persuaded of my fidelity to those duties, the discharge of them becomes more and more pleasing.

Believing with you that religion is a matter which lies solely between man and his God, that he owes account to none other for his faith or his worship, that the legislative powers of government reach actions only, and not opinions, I contemplate with sovereign reverence that act of the whole American people which declared that their legislature should "make no law respecting an establishment of religion, or prohibiting the free exercise thereof," thus building a wall of separation between Church and State. Adhering to this expression of the supreme will of the nation in behalf of the rights of conscience, I shall see with sincere satisfaction the progress of those sentiments which tend to restore to man all his natural rights, convinced he has no natural right in opposition to his social duties.

I reciprocate your kind prayers for the protection and blessing of the common Father and Creator of man, and tender you for yourselves and your religious association, assurances of my high respect and esteem.

TO THE MEMBERS OF THE BALTIMORE BAPTIST ASSOCIATION, OCTOBER 17,
1808

I receive with great pleasure the friendly address of the Baltimore Baptist Association, and am sensible how much I am indebted to the kind dispositions which dictated it.

In our early struggles for liberty, religious freedom could not fail to become a primary object. All men felt the right, and a just animation to obtain it was exhibited by all. I was one only among the many who befriended its establishment, and am entitled but in common with others to a portion of that approbation which follows the fulfillment of a duty.

Excited by wrongs to reject a foreign government which directed our concerns according to its own interests, and not to ours, the principles which justified us were obvious to all understandings, they were imprinted in the breast of every human being; and Providence ever pleases to direct the issue of our contest in favor of that side where justice was. Since this happy separation, our nation has wisely avoided entangling itself in the system of European interests, has taken no side between its rival powers, attached itself to none of its ever-changing confederacies. Their peace is desirable; and you do me justice in saying that to preserve and secure this, has been the constant aim of my administration. The difficulties which involve it, however, are now at their ultimate term, and what will be their issue, time alone will disclose. But be it what it may, a recollection of our former vassalage in religion and civil government, will unite the zeal of every heart, and the energy of every hand, to preserve that independence in both which, under the favor of heaven, a disinterested devotion to the public cause first achieved, and a disinterested sacrifice of private interests will now maintain.

I am happy in your approbation of my reasons for determining to retire from a station, in which the favor of my fellow citizens has so long continued and supported me: I return your kind prayers with supplications to the same almighty Being for your future welfare and that of our beloved country.

TO THE MEMBERS OF THE KETOCTON BAPTIST ASSOCIATION, OCTOBER 18, 1808

In our early struggles for liberty, religious freedom could not fail to become a primary object. All men felt the right, and a just animation to obtain it was excited in all. And although your favor selected me as the organ of your petition to abolish the religious denomination of a privileged church, yet I was but one of the many who befriended its object, and am entitled but in common with them to a portion of that approbation which follows the fulfillment of a duty.

Early in his Presidency, Thomas Jefferson had been asked to proclaim a day with religious significance and replied to it rather circumspectly, denying the request. (See letter to Danbury Baptist Association, January 1, 1802.) Now, toward the end of his Presidency, a similar request came from the Reverend Mr. Samuel Miller. This time, Thomas Jefferson deals with the matter directly.

LETTER TO SAMUEL MILLER, JANUARY 23, 1808

I consider the government of the United States as interdicted by the Constitution from intermeddling with religious institutions, their doctrines, discipline, or exercises. This results not only from the provision that no law shall be made respecting the establishment of free exercise of religion, but from that also which reserves to the States the powers not delegated to the United States. Certainly, no power to prescribe any religious exercise, or to assume authority in religious discipline, has been delegated to the General Government. It must then rest with the States, as far as it can be in any human authority. But it is only proposed that I should *recommend*, not prescribe a day of fasting and prayer. That is, that I should *indirectly* assume to the United States an authority over religious exercises, which the Constitution has directly precluded them from. It must be meant, too, that this recommendation is to carry some authority, and to be sanctioned by some penalty on those who disregard it; not indeed of fine and imprisonment, but of some degree of proscription, perhaps in public opinion. And does the change in the nature of the penalty make the recommendation less a *law* of conduct for those to whom it is directed?

I do not believe it is for the interest of religion to invite the civil magistrate to direct its exercises, its discipline, or its doctrines; nor of the religious societies, that the General Government should be invested with the power of effecting any uniformity of time or matter among them. Fasting and prayer are religious exercises; the enjoining them an act of discipline. Every religious society has a right to determine for itself the times for these exercises, and the objects proper for them, according to their own particular tenets; and this right can never be safer than in their own hands, where the Constitution has deposited it.

I am aware that the practice of my predecessors may be quoted. But I have ever believed, that the example of State executives led to the assumption of that authority by the General Government, without due examination, which would have discovered that what might be a right in a State government, was a violation of that right when assumed by another. Be this as it may, every one must act according to the dictates of his own reason, and mine tells me that civil powers alone have been given to the President of the United States, and no authority to direct the religious exercises of his constituents.

I again express my satisfaction that you have been so good as to give me an opportunity of explaining myself in a private letter, in which I could give my reasons more in detail than might have been done in a public answer; and I pray you to accept the assurances of my high esteem and respect.

In the closing days of his Presidency, Thomas Jefferson wrote to his former Philadelphia landlord, Thomas Leiper, in reply to some question Leiper put to him about his religious and political views. Leiper was an affluent Scottish-born merchant who had liberally supported the revolutionary movement.

LETTER TO THOMAS LEIPER, JANUARY 21, 1809

As to my self, my religious reading has long been confined to the moral branch of religion, which is the same in all religions; while in that branch which consists of dogmas, all differ, all have a different set. The former instructs us how to live well and worthily in society; the latter are made to interest our minds in the support of the teachers who inculcate them. Hence, for one sermon on a moral subject, you hear ten on the dogmas of the sect. However, religion is not the subject for you and me; neither of us know the religious opinions of the other; that is a matter between our Maker and ourselves. We understand each other better in politics, to which therefore I will proceed.

Thomas Jefferson received a pamphlet at Monticello from James Fishback which produced this response.

LETTER TO JAMES FISHBACK, SEPTEMBER 27, 1809

Reading, reflection and time have convinced me that the interests of society require the observation of those moral precepts only in which all religions agree (for all forbid us to murder, steal, plunder, or bear false witness) and that we should not intermeddle with the particular dogmas in which all religions differ, and which are totally unconnected with morality.

In all of them we see good men, and as many in one as another. The varieties in the structure and action of the human mind as in those of the body, are the work of our creator, against which it cannot be a religious duty to erect the standard of uniformity. The practice of morality being necessary for the well-being of society, he has taken care to impress its precepts so indelibly on our hearts that they shall not be effaced by the subtleties of our brain. We all agree in the obligation of the moral precepts of Jesus, and nowhere will they be found delivered in greater purity than in his discourses.

It is, then, a matter of principle with me to avoid disturbing the tranquility of others by the expression of any opinion on the innocent questions on which we schismatize. On the subject of your pamphlet, and the mode of treating it, I permit myself only to observe the candor, moderation and ingenuity with which you appear to have sought truth. This is of good example, and worthy of commendation. If all the writers and preachers on religious questions had been of the same temper, the history of the world would have been of much more pleasing aspect.

Samuel Kercheval, Virginia author, wrote a pamphlet about the administrations of Jefferson and Madison that was designed, apparently, to win favor with the Quakers. Jefferson is not too hopeful on the subject.

LETTER TO SAMUEL KERCHEVAL, JANUARY 19, 1810

Nothing can be more exactly and seriously true than what is there stated; that but a short time elapsed after the death of the great reformer of the Jewish religion, before his principles were departed from by those who professed to be his special servants, and perverted into an engine for enslaving mankind, and aggrandizing their oppressors in Church and state; that the purest system of morals ever before preached to man has been adulterated and sophisticated by artificial constructions, into a mere contrivance to filch wealth and power to themselves; that rational men, not being able to swallow their impious heresies, in order to force them down their throats, they raise the hue and cry of infidelity, while themselves are the greatest obstacles to the advancement of the real doctrine of Jesus, and do, in fact, constitute the real Anti-Christ.

You expect that your book will have some effect on the prejudices which the Society of Friends entertain against the present and late administrations. In this I think you will be disappointed. The Friends are men formed with the same passions, and swayed by the same natural principles and prejudices as others. In cases where the passions are neutral, men will display their respect for the religious *professions* of their sect. But where their passions are enlisted, these *professions* are no obstacle. You observe very truly, that both the late and present administrations conducted the government on principles *professed* by the Friends. Our efforts to preserve peace, our measures as to the Indians, as to slavery, as to religious freedom, were all in consonance with their *profession*. Yet I never expected we should get a vote from them, and in this I was neither deceived nor disappointed. There is no riddle in this to those who do not suffer themselves to be duped by the *professions* of religious sectaries. The theory of American Quakerism is a very obvious one. The mother society is in England. Its members are English by birth and residence, devoted to their own country as good citizens ought to be. The Quakers of these States are colonies or filiations from the mother society, to whom that society sends its yearly lessons. On these, the filiated societies model their opinions, their conduct, their passions and attachments.

A Quaker is essentially an Englishman, in whatever part of the earth he is born or lives. The outrages of Great Britain on our navigation and commerce, have kept us in perpetual bickerings with her. The Quakers here have taken side against their own government, not on their *profession* of peace, for they saw that peace was our object also; but from devotion to the views of the mother society. In 1797-8, when an administration sought war with France, the Quakers were the most clamorous for war. Their principles of peace, as a secondary one, yielded to the primary one of adherence to the Friends in England, and what was patriotism in the original, became treason in the copy. On that occasion, they obliged their good old leader, Mr. Pemberton, to erase his name from a petition to Congress against war, which had been delivered to a Representative of Pennsylvania, a member of the late and present administration; he accordingly permitted the old gentleman to erase his name. You must not therefore expect that your book will have any more effect on the Society of Friends here, than on the English merchants settled among us. I apply this to the Friends in general, not universally. I know individuals among them as good patriots as we have.

A member of the Society of Friends, William Canby, wrote a generous letter to Thomas Jefferson about his life and work, in the course of which he touched upon the compatibility of Jefferson's political acts with Quaker ideas.

LETTER TO WILLIAM CANBY, SEPTEMBER 18, 1813

An eloquent preacher of your religious society, Richard Motte, in a discourse of much emotion and pathos, is said to have exclaimed aloud to his congregation, that he did not believe there was a Quaker, Presbyterian, Methodist, or Baptist in heaven, having paused to give his hearers time to stare and to wonder. He added, that in Heaven, God knew no distinctions, but considered all good men as his children, and as brethren of the same family.

I believe, with the Quaker preacher, that he who steadily observes those moral precepts in which all religions concur, will never be questioned at the gates of heaven, as to the dogmas in which they all differ. That on entering there, all these are left behind us, and the Aristides and Catos, the Penns and Tillotsons, Presbyterians and Baptists, will find themselves united in all principles which are in concert with the reason of the supreme mind.

Of all the systems of morality, ancient or modern, which have come under my observation, none appear to me so pure as that of Jesus. He who follows this steadily need not, I think, be uneasy, although he cannot comprehend the subtleties and mysteries erected on his doctrines by those who, calling themselves his special followers and favorites, would make him come into the world to lay snares for all understandings but theirs.

These metaphysical heads, usurping the judgment seat of God, denounce as his enemies all who cannot perceive the Geometrical logic of Euclid in the demonstrations of St. Athanasius, that three are one, and one is three; and yet that one is not three nor the three one.

In all essential points you and I are of the same religion; and I am too old to go into inquiries and changes as to the unessential. Repeating, therefore, my thankfulness for the kind concern you have been so good as to express, I salute you with friendship and brotherly esteem.

Thomas Law, related to George Washington by marriage, was a somewhat eccentric English writer on economics. At the time this letter was written, Thomas Jefferson was heavily engaged in thinking through and carrying out the design for a great university. This letter, dealing with the foundations of human morality, reflects the depth of Jefferson's concern for the education of the whole man.

LETTER TO THOMAS LAW, JUNE 13, 1814

The copy of your Second Thoughts on Instinctive Impulses, with the letter accompanying it, was received just as I was setting out on a journey to this place, two or there days' distant from Monticello. I brought it with me and read it with great satisfaction, and with the more as it contained exactly my own creed on the foundation of morality in man. It is really curious that on a question so fundamental, such a variety of opinions should have prevailed among men, and those, too, of the most exemplary virtue and first order of understanding. It shows how necessary was the care of the creator in making the moral principle so much a part of our constitution as that no errors of reasoning or of speculation might lead us astray from its observance and practice.

Of all the theories on this question, the most whimsical seems to have been that of Wollaston, who considers *truth* as the foundation of morality. The thief who steals your guinea does wrong only inasmuch as he acts a lie in using your guinea as if it were his own. Truth is certainly a branch of morality, and a very important one to society. But presented as its foundation, it is as if a tree taken up by the roots, had its stem reversed in the air, and one of its branches planted on the ground. Some have made the *love of God* the foundation of morality. This, too, is but a branch of our moral duties, which are generally divided into duties to God and duties to man. If we did a good act merely from the love of God and a belief that it is pleasing to Him, whence arises the morality of the Atheist?

It is idle to say, as some do, that no such being exists. We have the same evidence of the fact as of most of those we act on, to wit: their own affirmations, and their reasonings in support of them. I have observed, indeed, generally, that while in protestant countries the defections from the Platonic Christianity of the priests is to Deism, in catholic countries they are to

Atheism. Diderot, D'Alembert, D'Holbach, Condorcet, are known to have been among the most virtuous of men. Their virtue, then, must have had some other foundation than the love of God.

The τὸ καλόν [virtue] of others is founded in a different faculty, that of taste, which is not even a branch of morality. We have indeed an innate sense of what we call beautiful, but that is exercised chiefly on subjects addressed to the fancy, whether through the eye in visible forms, as landscape, animal figure, dress, drapery, architecture, the composition of colors, etc., or to the imagination directly, as imagery, style, or measure in prose or poetry, or whatever else constitutes the domain of criticism or taste, a faculty entirely distinct from the moral one. Self-interest, or rather self-love, or *egoism* has been more plausibly substituted as the basis of morality. But I consider our relations with others as constituting the boundaries of morality.

With ourselves we stand on the ground of identity, not of relation, which last, requiring two subjects, excludes self-love confined to a single one. To ourselves, in strict language, we can owe no duties, obligation requiring also two parties. Self-love, therefore, is no part of morality. Indeed, it is exactly its counterpart. It is the sole antagonist of virtue, leading us constantly by our propensities to self-gratification in violation of our moral duties to others. Accordingly, it is against this enemy that are erected the batteries of moralists and religionists, as the only obstacle to the practice of morality. Take from man his selfish propensities, and he can have nothing to seduce him from the practice of virtue. Or subdue those propensities by education, instruction or restraint, and virtue remains without a competitor. Egoism, in a broader sense, has been thus presented as the source of moral action.

It has been said that we feed the hungry, clothe the naked, bind up the wounds of the man beaten by thieves, pour oil and wine into them, set him on our own beast and bring him to the inn, because we received ourselves pleasure from these acts. So Helvetius, one of the best men on earth, and the most ingenious advocate of this principle, after defining "interest" to mean not merely that which is pecuniary, but whatever may procure us pleasure or withdraw us from pain [*de l'esprit*, 2, 1,] says, [ib. 2, 2,] "the humane man is he to whom the sight of misfortune is insupportable, and who to rescue himself from this spectacle, is forced to succor the unfortunate object."

This indeed is true. But it is one step short of the ultimate question. These good acts give us pleasure, but how happens it that they give us pleasure? Because nature hath implanted in our breasts a love of others, a sense of duty to them, a moral instinct, in short, which prompts us irresistibly to feel and to succor their distresses, and protests against the language of Helvetius, [ib. 2, 5,] "what other motive than self-interest could determine a man to generous actions? It is as impossible for him to love what is good for the sake of good, as to love evil for the sake of evil." The Creator would indeed have been a bungling artist, had he intended man for a social animal, without planting in him social dispositions. It is true they are not planted in every man, because there is no rule without exceptions; but it is false reasoning which converts exceptions into the general rule. Some men are born without the organs of sight, or of hearing, or without hands. Yet it would be wrong to say that man is born without these faculties, and sight, hearing, and hands may with truth enter into the general definition of man.

The want or imperfection of the moral sense in some men, like the want or imperfection of the senses of sight and hearing in others, is no proof that it is a general characteristic of the species. When it is wanting, we endeavor to supply the defect by education, by appeals to reason and calculation, by presenting to the being so unhappily conformed, other motives to do good and to eschew evil, such as love, or the hatred, or rejection of those among whom he lives, and whose society is necessary to his happiness and even existence; demonstrations by sound calculation that honesty promotes interest in the long run; the rewards and penalties established by the laws; and ultimately the prospects of a future state of retribution for the evil as well as the good done while here. These are the correctives which are supplied by education, and which exercise the functions of the moralist, the preacher, and the legislator; and they lead into a course of correct action all those whose disparity is not too profound to be eradicated. Some have argued against the existence of a moral sense, by saying that if nature had given us such a sense, impelling us to virtuous actions, and warning us against those which are vicious, then nature would also have designated, by some particular earmarks, the two sets of actions which are, in themselves, the one virtuous and the other vicious. Whereas, we find, in fact, that the same actions are deemed virtuous in one country and vicious in another. The answer is that nature has constituted utility to man the standard and best of virtue. Men living in different countries, under different circumstances, different habits and regimens, may have different utilities; the same act, therefore, may be useful, and consequently virtuous in one country which is injurious and vicious in another differently circumstanced. I sincerely, then, believe with you in the general existence of a moral instinct. I think it the brightest gem with which the human character is studded, and the want of it as more degrading than the most hideous of the bodily deformities. I am happy in reviewing the roll of associates in this principle which you present in your second letter, some of which I had not before met with. To these might be added Lord Kaims, one of the ablest of our advocates, who goes so far as to say, in his Principles of Natural Religion, that a man owes no duty to which he is not urged by some impulsive feeling. This is correct, if referred to the standard of general feeling in the given case, and not to the feeling of a single individual. Perhaps I may misquote him, it being fifty years since I read his book.

Miles King, apparently, experienced a revelation and had some communication with ex-President Jefferson on the subject.

LETTER TO MILES KING, SEPTEMBER 26, 1814

I duly received your letter of August 20th, and I thank you for it, because I believe it was written with kind intentions, and a personal concern for my future happiness. Whether the particular revelation which you suppose to have been made to yourself were real or imaginary, your reason alone is the competent judge. For dispute as long as we will on religious tenets, our reason at last must ultimately decide, as it is the only oracle which God has given us to determine between what really comes from him and the phantasms of a disordered or deluded imagination. When he means to make a personal revelation, he carries conviction of its authenticity to the reason he has bestowed as the umpire of truth. You believe you have been favored with such a special communication. Your reason, not mine, is to judge of this; and if it shall be his pleasure to favor me with a like admonition, I shall obey it with the same fidelity with which I would obey his known will in all cases. Hitherto I have been under the guidance of that portion of reason which he has thought proper to deal out to me. I have followed it faithfully in all important cases, to such a degree at least as leaves me without uneasiness; and if on minor occasions I have erred from its dictates, I have trust in him who made us what we are, and know it was not his plan to make us always unerring. He has formed us moral agents. Not that, in the perfection of his state, he can feel pain or pleasure in anything we may do; he is far above our power; but that we may promote the happiness of those with whom he has placed us in society, by acting honestly towards all, benevolently to those who fall within our way, respecting sacredly their rights, bodily and mental, and cherishing especially their freedom of conscience, as we value our own. I must ever believe that religion substantially good which produces an honest life, and we have been authorized by one whom you and I equally respect, to judge of the tree by its fruit. Our particular principles of religion are a subject of accountability to our God alone. I inquire after no man's, and trouble none with mine; nor is

it given to us in this life to know whether yours or mine, our friends or our foes, are exactly the right. Nay, we have heard it said that there is not a Quaker or a Baptist, a Presbyterian or an Episcopalian, a Catholic or a Protestant in heaven; that on entering that gate, we leave those badges of schism behind, and find ourselves united in those principles only in which God has united us all. Let us not be uneasy then about the different roads we may pursue, as believing them the shortest, to that our last abode; but, following the guidance of a good conscience, let us be happy in the hope that by these different paths we shall all meet in the end. And that you and I may there meet and embrace, is my earnest prayer. And with this assurance I salute you with brotherly esteem and respect.

Charles Thomson, Irish-born American revolutionist, served as secretary of the Continental Congress from 1774 to 1789. He was deeply interested in religious studies, science, and natural history. In 1808, he translated the Septuagint and New Testament into English. The intensity of their interests sustained a productive correspondence between Jefferson and Thomson. In the following letter, Jefferson says, "I am a Christian" and proceeds to define the term. This letter somehow served as the basis for rumors that Jefferson had turned against Christianity. (See following letter to Mrs. Harrison Smith.)

LETTER TO CHARLES THOMSON, JANUARY 9, 1816

An acquaintance of fifty-two years, for I think ours dates from 1764, calls for an interchange of notice now and then, that we remain in existence, the monuments of another age, and examples of a friendship unaffected by the jarring elements by which we have been surrounded, or revolutions of government, of party and of opinion. I am reminded of this duty by the receipt, through our friend Dr. Patterson, of your synopsis of the four Evangelists. I had procured it as soon as I saw it advertised, and had become familiar with its use; but this copy is the more valued as it comes from your hand. This work bears the stamp of that accuracy which marks everything from you, and will be useful to those who, not taking things on trust, recur for themselves to the fountain of pure morals. I, too, have made a wee-little book from the same materials, which I call the Philosophy of Jesus; it is a paradigma of his doctrines, made by cutting the texts out of the book, and arranging them on the pages of a blank book, in a certain order of time or subject. A more beautiful or precious morsel of ethics I have never seen; it is a document in proof that *I* am a *real Christian*, that is to say, a disciple of the doctrines of Jesus, very different from the Platonists, who call *me* infidel and *themselves*

Christians and preachers of the gospel, while they draw all their characteristic dogmas from what its author never said nor saw. They have compounded from the heathen mysteries a system beyond the comprehension of man, of which the great reformer of the vicious ethics and deism of the Jews, were he to return on earth, would not recognize one feature. If I had time I would add to my little book the Greek, Latin and French texts, in columns side by side. And I wish I could subjoin a translation of Gosindi's Syntagma of the doctrines of Epicurus, which, nothwithstanding the calumnies of the Stoics and caricatures of Cicero, is the most rational system remaining of the philosophy of the ancients, as frugal of vicious indulgence, and fruitful of virtue as the hyperbolical extravagances of his rival sects.

I retain good health . . .

The sporadic attempts to denounce Jefferson as an unbeliever or an antagonist to Christianity are reflected in the correspondence between Mrs. Harrison Smith and Jefferson. Mrs. Smith, one of the leaders of early Washington society, was the wife of the owner of the National Intelligencer and Washington Advertiser. *She knew the currents and undercurrents of the Capital as well as anyone. Her letter to Jefferson told of the talk supposedly caused by the letters he had written earlier in the year to Charles Thomson. Jefferson once again asserts his principles.*

LETTER TO MRS. HARRISON SMITH, AUGUST 6, 1816

I have received, my dear Madam, your very friendly letter of July 21st, and assure you that I feel with deep sensibility its kind expressions towards myself, and the more as from a person than whom no others could be more in sympathy with my own affections. I often call to mind the occasions of knowing your worth, which the societies of Washington furnished; and none more than those derived from your much valued visit to Monticello.

I recognize the same motives of goodness in the solicitude you express on the rumor supposed to proceed from a letter of mine to Charles Thomson, on the subject of the Christian religion. It is true that, in writing to the translator of the Bible and Testament, that subject was mentioned; but equally so that no adherence to any particular mode of Christianity was there expressed, nor any change of opinions suggested. A change from what? the priests indeed have heretofore thought proper to ascribe to me religious, or rather anti-religious sentiments, of their own fabric, but such as soothed their resentments against the act of Virginia for establishing religious freedom. They wished him to be thought atheist, deist, or devil, who could advocate freedom from their religious dictations. But I have ever thought

religion a concern purely between our God and our consciences, for which we were accountable to him, and not to the priests.

I never told my own religion, nor scrutinized that of another. I never attempted to make a convert, nor wished to change another's creed. I have ever judged of the religion of others by their lives, and by this test, my dear Madam, I have been satisfied yours must be an excellent one, to have produced a life of such exemplary virtue and correctness. For it is in our lives, and not from our words, that our religion must be read.

By the same test the world must judge me. But this does not satisfy the priesthood. They must have a positive, a declared assent to all their interested absurdities. My opinion is that there would never have been an infidel, if there had never been a priest. The artificial structures they have built on the purest of all moral systems, for the purpose of deriving from it pence and power, revolts those who think for themselves, and who read in that system only what is really there. These, therefore, they brand with such nick-names as their enmity chooses gratuitously to impute.

I have left the world, in silence, to judge of causes from their effects; and I am consoled in this course, my dear friend, when I perceive the candor with which I am judged by your justice and discernment; and that, notwithstanding the slanders of the saints, my fellow citizens have thought me worthy of trusts. The imputations of irreligion having spent their force; they think an imputation of change might now be turned to account as a bolster for their duperies. I shall leave them, as heretofore, to grope on the dark.

Thomas Jefferson in retirement had the pleasure or penalty, depending on the individual case, of being asked to comment on numbers of serious books and pamphlets dealing with science, government, philosophy, or religion. In this particular case, Jefferson doubtless found it a pleasure. He had high respect for Ezra Stiles, President of Yale University. Stiles was a scholar of Oriental languages, history, theology, philosophy. He also was an expert on the silkworm. He believed in the abolition of slavery. He carried on a correspondence with the leading men of the time.

LETTER TO EZRA STILES, JUNE 25, 1819

Your favor, Sir, of the 14th, has been duly received, and with it the book you were so kind as to forward to me. For this mark of attention, be pleased to accept my thanks. The science of the human mind is curious, but is one on which I have not indulged myself in much speculation. The times in which I have lived, and the scenes in which I have been engaged, have required me to keep the mind too much in action to have leisure to study minutely its laws of action. I am therefore little qualified to give an opinion on the comparative worth of books on that subject, and little disposed to do it on any book. Yours has brought the science within a small compass, and that is the merit of the first order; and especially with one to whom the drudgery of letter writing often denies the leisure of reading a single page in a week.

On looking over the summary of the contents of your book, it does not seem likely to bring into collision of those sectarian differences which you suppose may exist between us. In that branch of religion which regards the moralities of life, and the duties of a social being, which teaches us to love our neighbors as ourselves, and to do good to all men, I am sure that you and I do not differ. We probably differ on the dogmas of theology, the foundation of all sectarianism, and on which no two sects dream alike; for if they did they would then be of the same. You say you are a Calvinist. I am not. I am of a sect by myself, as far as I know. I am not a Jew, and therefore do not adopt their theology, which supposes the God of infinite justice to punish the sins of the fathers upon their children, unto the third and fourth generations; and the benevolent and sublime reformer of that religion has told us only that God is good and perfect, but has not defined him.

I am, therefore, of his theology, believing that we have neither words nor ideas adequate to that definition. And if we could all, after this example, leave the subject as undefinable, we should all be of one sect, doers of good, and eschewers of evil. No doctrines of his lead to schism. It is the speculations of crazy theologists which have made a Babel of a religion the most moral and sublime ever preached to man, and calculated to heal, and not to create differences. These religious animosities I impute to those who call themselves his ministers, and who engraft their casuistries on the stock of his simple precepts. I am sometimes more angry with them than is authorized by the blessed charities which he preaches. To yourself I pray the acceptance of my great respect.

Thomas and Martha Jefferson had six children, only two of whom (both girls) survived infancy. Jefferson was especially fond of a young boy in the neighborhood, William Short, often referred to as his "foster son." After graduating from William and Mary, Short accompanied Jefferson to France as his secretary.

LETTERS TO WILLIAM SHORT, 1819–20

OCTOBER 31, 1819

As you say of yourself, I too am an Epicurian. I consider the genuine (not the imputed) doctrines of Epicurus as containing everything rational in moral philosophy which Greece and Rome have left us. Epictetus indeed, has given us what was good of the Stoics; all beyond, of their dogmas, being hypocrisy and grimace. Their great crime was in their calumnies of Epicurus and misrepresentations of his doctrines; in which we lament to see the candid character of Cicero engaging as an accomplice. Diffuse, vapid, rhetorical, but enchanting. His prototype Plato, eloquent as himself, dealing out mysticisms incomprehensible to the human mind, has been deified by certain sects usurping the name of Christians; because, in his foggy conceptions, they found a basis of impenetrable darkness whereon to rear fabrications as delirious, of their own invention. These they fathered blasphemously on him whom they claimed as their founder, but who would disclaim them with the indignation which their caricatures of his religion so justly excite. Of Socrates we have nothing genuine but in the Memorabilia of Xenophon; for Plato makes him one of his Collocutors merely to cover his own whimsies under the mantle of his name; a liberty of which we are told Socrates himself complained. Seneca is indeed a fine moralist, disfiguring his work at times with some Stoicisms, and affecting too much of antithesis and point, yet giving us on the whole a great deal of sound and practical morality. But the greatest of all the reformers of the depraved religion of his own country, was Jesus of Nazareth. Abstracting what is really his from the rubbish in which it is buried, easily distinguished by its lustre from the dross of his biographers, and as separable from that as the diamond from the dunghill, we have the outlines of a system of the most sublime morality which has ever fallen from the lips of man; outlines which it is lamentable he did not live to fill up. Epictetus and Epicurus give laws for governing ourselves, Jesus a supplement of the duties and charities we owe to others. The establishment of the innocent and genuine character of this benevolent moralist, and the rescuing it from the imputation of imposture, which has resulted from artificial systems,[5] invented by ultra-Christian sects, unauthorized by a single word ever uttered by him, is a most desirable object, and one to which Priestley has successfully devoted his labors and learning. It would in time, it is to be hoped, effect a quiet euthanasia of the heresies of bigotry and fanaticism which have so long triumphed over human reason, and so generally and deeply afflicted mankind; but this work is to be begun by winnowing the grain from the chaff of the historians of his life. I have sometimes thought of translating Epictetus (for he has never been tolerable translated into English) by adding the genuine doctrines of Epicurus from the Syntagma

---

[5] e.g., The immaculate conception of Jesus, his deification, the creation of the world by him, his miraculous powers, his resurrection and visible ascension, his corporeal presence in the Eucharist, the Trinity, original sin, atonement, regeneration, election, orders of Hierarchy, etc.

of Gassendi, and an abstract from the Evangelists of whatever has the stamp of the eloquence and fine imagination of Jesus. The last I attempted too hastily some twelve or fifteen years ago. It was the work of two or three nights only, at Washington, after getting through the evening task of reading the letters and papers of the day. But with one foot in the grave, these are now idle projects for me. My business is to beguile the wearisomeness of declining life, as I endeavor to do, by the delights of classical reading and of mathematical truths, and by the consolations of a sound philosophy, equally indifferent to hope and fear.

APRIL 13, 1820

Your favor of March the 27th is received, and as you request, a copy of the syllabus is now enclosed. It was originally written to Dr. Rush. On his death, fearing that the inquisition of the public might get hold of it, I asked the return of it from the family, which they kindly complied with. At the request of another friend, I had given him a copy. He lent it to *his* friend to read, who copied it, and in a few months it appeared in the Theological Magazine of London. Happily that repository is scarcely known in this country, and the syllabus, therefore, is still a secret, and in your hands I am sure it will continue so.

But while this syllabus is meant to place the character of Jesus in its true and high light, as no impostor himself, but a great reformer of the Hebrew code of religion, it is not to be understood that I am with him in all his doctrines. I am a Materialist; he takes the side of Spiritualism; he preaches the efficacy of repentance towards forgiveness of sin; I require a counterpoise of good works to redeem it, etc., etc. It is the innocence of his character, the purity and sublimity of his moral precepts, the eloquence of his inculcations, the beauty of the apologues in which he conveys them, that I so much admire; sometimes, indeed, needing indulgence to eastern hyperbolism. My eulogies, too, may be founded on a postulate which all may not be ready to grant. Among the sayings and discourses imputed to him by his biographers, I find many passages of fine imagination, correct morality, and of the most lovely benevolence; and others, again, of so much ignorance, so much absurdity, so much untruth, charlatanism and imposture, as to pronounce it impossible that such contradictions should have proceeded from the same being. I separate, therefore, the gold from the dross; restore to him the former, and leave the latter to the stupidity of some, and roguery of others of his disciples. Of this band of dupes and imposters, Paul was the great Coryphaeus, and first corruptor of the doctrines of Jesus. These palpable interpolations and falsifications of his doctrines, led me to try to sift them apart. I found the work obvious and easy, and that his part composed the most beautiful morsel of morality which has, been given to us by man. The syllabus is therefore of *his* doctrines, not *all* of *mine*. I read them as I do those of other ancient and modern moralists, with a mixture of approbation and dissent. . . .

[In speaking of the plans for building the University of Virginia at Charlottesville, Virginia:] An opposition, in the meantime, has been got up. That of our *alma mater*, William and Mary, is not of much weight. She must descend into the secondary rank of academies of preparation for the University. The serious enemies are the priests of the different religious sects, to whose spells on the human mind its improvement is ominous. Their pulpits are now resounding with denunciations against the appointment of Doctor Cooper, whom they charge as a monotheist in opposition to their tritheism. Hostile as these sects are, in every other point, to one another they unite in maintaining their mystical theogony against those who believe there is one God only. The Presbyterian clergy are loudest; the most intolerant of all sects, the most tyrannical and ambitious; ready at the word of the lawgiver, if such a word could be now obtained, to put the torch to the pile, and to rekindle in this virgin hemisphere, the flames in which their oracle Calvin consumed the poor Servetus, because he could not find in his Euclid the proposition which has demonstrated that three are one and one is three, nor subscribe to that of Calvin, that magistrates have a right to exterminate all heretics to Calvinistic Creed. They pant to re-establish, *by law*, that holy inquisition, which they can now only infuse into *public opinion*. We have most unwisely committed to the hierophants of our particular superstition, the direction of public opinion, that lord of the universe. We have given them stated and privileged days to collect and catechise us, opportunities of delivering their oracles to the people in mass, and of moulding their minds as wax in the hollow of their hands. But in despite of their fulminations against endeavors to enlighten the general mind, to improve the reason of the people, and encourage them in the use of it, the liberality of this State will support this institution, and give fair play to the cultivation of reason. Can you ever find a more eligible occasion of visiting once more your native country, than that of accompanying Mr. Correa, and of seeing with him this beautiful and hopeful institution *in ovo?*

AUGUST 4, 1820

I owe you a letter for your favor of June the 29th, which was received in due time; and there being no subject of the day, of particular interest, I will make this a supplement to mine of April 13th. My aim in that was, to justify the character of Jesus against the fictions of his pseudo-followers.

which have exposed him to the inference of being an impostor. For if we could believe that he really countenanced the follies, the falsehoods, and the charlatanisms which his biographers father on him, and admit the misconstructions, interpolations, and theorizations of the fathers of the early, and fanatics of the latter ages, the conclusion would be irresistible by every sound mind, that he was an impostor. I give no credit to their falsifications of his actions and doctrines, and to rescue his character, the postulate in my letter asked only what is granted in reading every other historian. When Livy and Siculus, for example, tell us things which coincide with our experience of the order of nature, we credit them on their word, and place their narrations among the records of credible history. But when they tell us of calves speaking, of statues sweating blood, and other things against the course of nature, we reject these as fables not belonging to history. In like manner, when an historian, speaking of a character well known and established on satisfactory testimony, imputes to it things incompatible with that character, we reject them without hesitation, and assent to that only of which we have better evidence. Had Plutarch informed us that Caesar and Cicero passed their whole lives in religious exercises, and abstinence from the affairs of the world, we should reject what was so inconsistent with their established characters, still crediting what he relates in conformity with our ideas of them. So again the superlative wisdom of Socrates is testified by all antiquity, and placed on ground not to be questioned. When, therefore, Plato puts into his mouth such paralogisms, such quibbles on words, and sophisms as a school boy would be ashamed of, we conclude they were the whimsies of Plato's own foggy brain, and acquit Socrates of puerilities so unlike his character. (Speaking of Plato, I will add, that no writer, ancient or modern, has bewildered the world with more *ignus fatui*, than this renowned philosopher, in Ethics, in Politics, and Physics. In the latter, to specify a single example, compare his views of the animal economy, in his Timaeus, with those of Mrs. Bryan in her Conversations on Chemistry, and weigh the science of the canonized philosopher against the good sense of the unassuming lady. But Plato's visions have furnished a basis for endless systems of mystical theology, and he is therefore all but adopted as a Christian saint. It is surely time for men to think for themselves, and to throw off the authority of names so artificially magnified. But to return from this parenthesis.) I say, that this free exercise of reason is all I ask for the vindication of the character of Jesus. We find in the writings of his biographers matter of two distinct descriptions. First, a groundwork of vulgar ignorance, of things impossible, of superstitions, fanaticisms, and fabrications. Intermixed with these, again, are sublime ideas of the Supreme Being, aphorisms, and precepts of the purest morality and benevolence, sanctioned by a life of humility, innocence and simplicity of manners, neglect of riches, absence of worldly ambition and honors, with an eloquence and persuasiveness which have not been surpassed. These could not be inventions of the grovelling authors who relate them. They are far beyond the powers of their feeble minds. They show that there was a character, the subject of their history, whose splendid conceptions were above all suspicion of being interpolations from their hands. Can we be at a loss in separating such materials, and ascribing each to its genuine author? The difference is obvious to the eye and to the understanding, and we may read as we run to each his part; and I will venture to affirm, that he who, as I have done, will undertake to winnow this grain from the chaff, will find it not to require a moment's consideration. The parts fall asunder of themselves, as would those of an image of metal and clay.

There are, I acknowledge, passages not free from objection, which we may, with probability, ascribe to Jesus himself; but claiming indulgence from the circumstances under which he acted. His object was the reformation of some articles in the religion of the Jews, as taught by Moses. That sect had presented for the object of their worship, a being of terrific character, cruel, vindictive, capricious, and unjust. Jesus, taking for his type the best qualities of the human head and heart, wisdom, justice, goodness, and adding to them power, ascribed all of these, but in infinite perfection, to the Supreme Being, and formed him really worthy of their adoration. Moses had either not believed in a future state of existence, or had not thought it essential to be explicitly taught to his people. Jesus inculcated that doctrine with emphasis and precision. Moses had bound the Jews to many idle ceremonies, mummeries, and observances of no effect towards producing the social utilities which constitute the essence of virtue; Jesus exposed their futility and insignificance. The one instilled into his people the most anti-social spirit toward other nations; the other preached philanthropy and universal charity and benevolence. The office of reformer of the superstitions of a nation, is ever dangerous. Jesus had to walk on the perilous confines of reason and religion; and a step to right or left might place him within the grasp of the priests of the superstition, a blood-thirsty race, as cruel and remorseless as the being whom they represented as the family God of Abraham, of Isaac and of Jacob, and the local God of Israel. They were constantly laying snares, too, to entangle him in the web of the law. He was justifiable, therefore, in avoiding these by evasions, by sophisms, by misconstructions and misapplications of scraps of the prophets, and in defending himself with these their own weapons, as sufficient, *ad homines*, at least. That Jesus did not mean to impose himself on mankind as the son of God, physically speaking, I have been convinced by the writings of men more learned than myself in that lore. But that he might conscientiously believe himself inspired from above, is very possible. The whole religion of the Jew, inculcated on him from his infancy, was founded in the belief of divine inspiration. The fumes of the most disorded [sic] imaginations were recorded in their religious code, as special communications of the Deity; and as it could not but happen that in the course of ages, events would now and then turn up to which some of these vague rhapsodies might be accommodated by the aid of allegories, figures, types, and other tricks upon words, they have not only preserved their credit with the Jews of all subsequent times, but are the foundation of much of the religions of those who have schismatized from them. Elevated by the enthusiasm of a warm and pure heart, conscious of the high strains of an eloquence which had not been taught him, he might readily mistake the coruscations of his own fine genius for inspirations of an higher order. This belief carried, therefore, no more personal imputation, than the belief of Socrates, that himself was under the care and admonitions of a guardian Daemon. And how many of our wisest men still believe in the reality of these inspirations, while perfectly sane on all other subjects. Excusing, therefore, on these considerations, those passages in the gospels which seem to bear marks of weakness in Jesus, ascribing to him what alone is consistent with the great and pure character of which the same writings furnish proofs, and to their proper authors their own trivialities and imbecilities, I think myself authorized to conclude the purity and distinction of his character, in opposition to the impostures which those authors would fix upon him; and that the postulate of my former letter is no more than is granted in all other historical works.

Colonel John Taylor, despite all his influence in the American Revolutionary period, remains one of the most neglected figures in United States history. He was at the center of the agrarian philosophy that helped shape democratic thinking at the time. He was associated with Thomas Jefferson and James Madison in the work of the Virginia group, especially in the field of religious freedom. Though of aristocratic background, he developed a considerable following among the young radicals of the time. His book, An Inquiry into the Principles and Policy of the Government of the United States, *is credited by Parrington with providing the intellectual foundations of the later Jacksonian movement.*

LETTER TO JOHN TAYLOR, MAY 16, 1820

We regretted much your absence at the late meeting of the Board of Visitors, but did not doubt it was occasioned by uncontrollable circum-

stances. As the matters which came before us were of great importance
to the institution, I think it a duty to inform you of them. . . .

Another subject on this, as on former occasions, gave us embarrassment.
You may have heard of the hue and cry raised from the different pulpits
on our appointment of Doctor Cooper, whom they charge with Unitarianism
as boldly as if they knew the fact, and as presumptuously as if it were a
crime, and one for which, like Servetus, he should be burned; and perhaps you may have seen the particular attack made on him in the Evangelical
magazine. For myself I was not disposed to regard the denunciations of
these satellites of religious inquisition; but our colleagues, better judges
of popular feeling, thought that they were not to be altogether neglected;
and that it might be better to relieve Dr. Cooper, ourselves and the institution from this crusade. I had received a letter from him expressing his
uneasiness, not only for himself, but lest this persecution should become
embarrassing to the visitors, and injurious to the institution; with an offer
to resign, if we had the same apprehensions. The visitors, therefore, desired
the committee of Superintendence to place him at freedom on this subject, and to arrange with him a suitable indemnification. I wrote accordingly
in answer to his, and a meeting of trustees of the college at Columbia happening to take place soon after his receipt of my letter, they resolved
unanimously that it should be proposed to, and urged on their legislature,
to establish a professorship of Geology and Mineralogy, or a professorship of law, with a salary of $1,000 a year to be given him, in addition to
that of chemistry, which is $2,000 a year, and to purchase his collection of
minerals; and they have no doubt of the legislature's compliance. On the
subject of indemnification, he is contented with the balance of the $1,500
we had before agreed to give him, and which he says will not more than
cover his actual losses of time and expense; he adds, "it is right I should
acknowledge the liberality of your board with thanks. I regret the storm
that has been raised on my account; for it has separated me from many
fond hopes and wishes. Whatever my religious creed may be, and perhaps
I do not exactly know it myself, it is a pleasure that my conduct has not
brought, and is not likely to bring, discredit to my friends. Wherever I
have been, it has been my good fortune to meet with, or to make ardent
and affectionate friends. I feel persuaded I should have met with the same
lot in Virginia had it been my chance to have settled there, as I had hoped
and expected, for I think my course of conduct is sufficiently habitual to
count on its effects."

I do sincerely lament that untoward circumstances have brought on us
the irreparable loss of this professor, whom I have looked to as the corner-
stone of our edifice. I know no one who could have aided us so much in

forming the future regulations for our infant institution; and although we may perhaps obtain from Europe equivalents in science, they can never replace the advantages of his experience, his knowledge of the character, habits and manners of our country, his identification with its sentiments and principles, and high reputation he has obtained in it generally.

Jared Sparks, like other leading intellectuals of the time, had varied accomplishments. He is known primarily in history as the editor of George Washington's writings and as his biographer. His main impact on his contemporaries, however, was as president of Harvard from 1849 to 1853. Earlier, he had been a professor of mathematics and natural philosophy at Harvard, and a Unitarian minister in Baltimore. He considered himself an apostle of liberal Christianity. It was in this connection that he had written to Jefferson.

LETTER TO JARED SPARKS, NOVEMBER 4, 1820

Your favor of September 18th is just received, with the book accompanying it. Its delay was owing to that of the box of books from Mr. Guegan, in which it was packed. Being just setting out on a journey I have time only to look over the summary of contents. In this I see nothing in which I am likely to differ materially from you. I hold the precepts of Jesus, as delivered by himself, to be the most pure, benevolent, and sublime which have ever been preached to man. I adhere to the principles of the first age; and consider all subsequent innovations as corruptions of this religion, having no foundation in what came from him. The metaphysical insanities of Athanasius, of Loyola, and of Calvin, are, to my understanding, mere relapses into polytheism, differing from paganism only by being more unintelligible. The religion of Jesus is founded in the unity of God, and this principle, chiefly, gave it triumph over the rabble of heathen gods then acknowledged. Thinking men of all nations rallied readily to the doctrine of one only God, and embraced it with the pure morals which Jesus inculcated. If the freedom of religion, guaranteed to us by law *in theory*, can ever rise *in practice* under the overbearing inquisition of public opinion, truth will prevail over fanaticism, and the genuine doctrines of Jesus, so long perverted by his pseudo-priests, will again be restored to their original purity. This reformation will advance with the other improvements of the human mind, but too late for me to witness it. Accept my thanks for your book, in which I shall read with pleasure your developments of the subject, and with them the assurance of my high respect.

Timothy Pickering was a Revolutionary War general from Massachusetts who served briefly as Secretary of State under President John Adams. General

Pickering was an extreme Federalist and a severe critic of Jefferson. He denounced Jefferson for both his political and religious views. Concerning the latter, he described Jefferson as "one of the learned unbelievers in Revelation" and therefore an unwholesome influence on the youth of the land. On occasion, however, he did manage to express himself in that restrained and polite manner reserved for corresponding with political opponents. It will be observed that Jefferson himself was not unpracticed at this particular art.

LETTER TO TIMOTHY PICKERING, FEBRUARY 27, 1821

I have received, Sir, your favor of the 12th, and I assure you I received it with pleasure. It is true, as you say, that we have differed in political opinions; but I can say with equal truth, that I never suffered a political to become a personal difference. I have been left on this ground by some friends whom I dearly loved, but I was never the first to separate. With some others, of politics different from mine, I have continued in the warmest friendship to this day, and to all, and to yourself particularly, I have ever done moral justice.

I thank you for Mr. Channing's discourse, which you have been so kind as to forward me. It is not yet at hand, but is doubtless on its way. I had received it through another channel and read it with high satisfaction. No one sees with greater pleasure than myself the progress of reason in its advances towards rational Christianity. When we shall have done away the incomprehensible jargon of the Trinitarian arithmetic, that three are one, and one is three; when we shall have knocked down the artificial scaffolding, reared to mask from view the simple structure of Jesus; when, in short, we shall have unlearned everything which has been taught since his day, and got back to the pure and simple doctrines he inculcated, we shall then be truly and worthily his disciples; and my opinion is that if nothing had ever been added to what flowed purely from his lips, the whole world would at this day have been Christian. I know that the case you cite, of Dr. Drake, has been a common one. The religion-builders have so distorted and deformed the doctrines of Jesus, so muffled them in mysticisms, fancies and falsehoods, have caricatured them into forms so monstrous and inconceivable as to shock reasonable thinkers, to revolt them against the whole, and drive them rashly to pronounce its founder an impostor. Had there never been a commentator, there never would have been an infidel. In the present advance of truth, which we both approve, I do not know that you and I may think alike on all points. As the Creator has made no two faces alike, so no two minds, and probably no two creeds. We well know that among Unitarians themselves there are strong shades of difference, as between Doctors Price and Priestley, for example. So there may be peculiarities in your creed and in mine. They are honestly formed without a doubt. I do not wish to trouble the world with mine, nor to be troubled for them. These accounts are to be settled only with him who made us; and to him we leave it, with charity for all others, of whom, also, he is the only rightful and competent judge. I have little doubt that the whole of our country will soon be rallied to the unity of the Creator, and, I hope, to the pure doctrines of Jesus also.

In saying to you so much, and without reserve, on a subject on which I never permit myself to go before the public, I know that I am safe against the infidelities which have so often betrayed my letters to the strictures of those for whom they were not written, and to whom I never meant to commit my peace. To yourself I wish every happiness, and will conclude, as you have done, in the same simple style of antiquity, *da operam ut valeas; hoc mihi gratius facere nihil potes.*[6]

The Reverend Thomas Whittemore, Unitarian clergyman in Massachusetts, was interested in religious periodical literature, some of which he sent Thomas Jefferson from time to time. He also sought confirmation of the fact that Jefferson's religious views coincided with those of the Unitarians. Jefferson, however, held rigidly to his decision to avoid formal identification with any denomination.

LETTER TO THOMAS WHITTEMORE, JUNE 5, 1822

I thank you, Sir, for the pamphlets you have been so kind as to send me, and am happy to learn that the doctrine of Jesus that there is but one God, is advancing prosperously among our fellow citizens. Had his doctrines, pure as they came from himself, been never sophisticated for unworthy purposes, the whole civilized world would at this day have formed but a single sect. You ask my opinion on the items of doctrine in your catechism. I have never permitted myself to meditate a specified creed. These formulas have been the bane and ruin of the Christian church, its own fatal invention, which, through so many ages, made of Christendom a slaughter-house, and at this day divides it into casts of inextinguishable hatred to one another. Witness the present internecine rage of all other sects against the Unitarian. The religions of antiquity had no particular formulas of creed. Those of the modern world none, except those of the religionists calling themselves Christians, and even among these the Quakers have none. And hence, alone, the harmony, the quiet, the brotherly affections, the exemplary and un-schismatising society of the Friends, and I hope the Unitarians, will follow

---

[6] [Give effort in order that you may be strong; you are able to do nothing more pleasing to me than this.—Ed.]

their happy example. With these sentiments of the mischiefs of creeds and confessions of faith, I am sure you will excuse my not giving opinions on the items of any particular one; and that you will accept, at the same time, the assurance of the high respect and consideration which I bear to its author.

James Smith was an Irish-born patriot, one of the signers of the Declaration of Independence and a member of the Continental Congress. Like the Reverend Thomas Whittemore, Mr. Smith sought Thomas Jefferson's confirmation of his Unitarian sympathies. In his reply, Jefferson expressed his oft-quoted prophecy about Unitarianism. Jefferson characteristically ended his letter on a noncontroversial note, expressing equal good will toward Unitarian and Trinitarian alike.

LETTER TO JAMES SMITH, DECEMBER 8, 1822

I have to thank you for pamphlets on the subject of Unitarianism, and to express my gratification with your efforts for the revival of primitive Christianity in your quarter. No historical fact is better established, than that the doctrine of one God, pure and uncompounded, was that of the early ages of Christianity; and was among the efficacious doctrines which gave it triumph over the polytheism of the ancients, sickened with the absurdities of their own theology. Nor was the unity of the Supreme Being ousted from the Christian creed by the force of reason, but by the sword of civil government, wielded at the will of the fanatic Athanasius. The hocus-pocus phantasm of a God like another Cerberus, with one body and three heads, had its birth and growth in the blood of thousands and thousands of martyrs. And a strong proof of the solidity of the primitive faith, is its restoration, as soon as a nation arises which vindicates to itself the freedom of religious opinion, and its external divorce from the civil authority. The pure and simple unity of the Creator of the universe, is now all but ascendant in the eastern States; it is dawning in the West, and advancing towards the South; and I confidently expect that the present generation will see Unitarianism become the general religion of the United States. The Eastern presses are giving us many excellent pieces on the subject, and Priestley's learned writings on it are, or should be, in every hand. In fact, the Athanasian paradox that one is three, and three but one, is so incomprehensible to the human mind, that no candid man can say he has any idea of it, and how can he believe what presents no idea? He who thinks he does, only deceives himself. He proves, also, that man, once surrendering his reason, has no remaining guard against absurdities the most monstrous, and like a ship without rudder is the sport of every wind.

With such persons, gullibility, which they call faith, takes the helm from the hand of reason, and the mind becomes a wreck.

I write with freedom, because, while I claim a right to believe in one God, or so my reason tells me, I yield as freely to others that of believing in three. Both religions, I find, make honest men, and that is the only point society has any right to look to. Although this mutual freedom should produce mutual indulgence, yet I wish not to be brought in question before the public on this or any other subject, and I pray you to consider me as writing under that trust. I take no part in controversies, religious or political. At the age of eighty, tranquility is the greatest good of life, and the strongest of our desires that of dying in the good will of all mankind. And with the assurance of all my good will to Unitarian and Trinitarian, to Whig and Tory, accept for yourself that of my entire respect.

Dr. Benjamin Waterhouse was a substantial and energetic professor of medicine at Harvard who introduced the Jenner method of vaccination against smallpox in the United States. Jefferson saw the value of the vaccination and gave Dr. Waterhouse his full backing. The entire household at Monticello, for example, received inoculations. In addition to his campaign against smallpox, Dr. Waterhouse warred against wine and tobacco. It was in connection with these strictures, and also Dr. Waterhouse's comments on religion, that Thomas Jefferson wrote the following letter.

LETTER TO BENJAMIN WATERHOUSE, JUNE 26, 1822

I have received and read with thankfulness and pleasure your denunciation of the abuses of tobacco and wine. Yet, however sound in its principles, I expect it will be but a sermon to the wind. You will find it as difficult to inculcate these sanative precepts on the sensualities of the present day, as to convince an Athanasian that there is but one God. I wish success to both attempts, and am happy to learn from you that the latter, at least, is making progress, and the more rapidly in proportion as our Platonizing Christians make more stir and noise about it. The doctrines of Jesus are simple, and tend all to the happiness of man.

1. That there is one only God, and he all perfect.

2. That there is a future state of rewards and punishments.

3. That to love God with all thy heart and thy neighbor as thyself is the sum of religion. These are the great points on which he endeavored to reform the religion of the Jews. But compare with these the demoralizing dogmas of Calvin.

1. That there are three Gods.

2. That good works, or the love of our neighbor, are nothing.

3. That faith is everything, and the more incomprehensible the proposition, the more merit in its faith.

4. That reason in religion is of unlawful use.

5. That God, from the beginning, elected certain individuals to be saved, and certain others to be damned; and that no crimes of the former can damn them; no virtues of the latter save.

Now, which of these is the true and charitable Christian? He who believes and acts on the simple doctrines of Jesus? Or the impious dogmatists, as Athanasius and Calvin? Verily I say these are the false shepherds foretold as to enter not by the door into the sheepfold, but to climb up some other way. They are mere usurpers of the Christian name, teaching a counter-religion made up of the *deliria* of crazy imaginations, as foreign from Christianity as is that of Mahomet. Their blasphemies have driven thinking men into infidelity, who have too hastily rejected the supposed author himself, with the horrors so falsely imputed to him. Had the doctrines of Jesus been preached always as pure as they came from his lips, the whole civilized world would now have been Christian. I rejoice that in this blessed country of free inquiry and belief, which has surrendered its creed and conscience to neither Kings nor priests, the genuine doctrine of one only God is reviving, and I trust that there is not a *young man* now living in the United States who will not die an Unitarian.

But much I fear, that when this great truth shall be re-established, its votaries will fall into the fatal error of fabricating formulas of creed and confessions of faith, the engines which so soon destroyed the religion of Jesus, and made of Christendom a mere Aceldama; that they will give up morals for mysteries, and Jesus for Plato. How much wiser are the Quakers, who, agreeing in the fundamental doctrines of the gospel, schismatize about no mysteries, and, keeping within the pale of common sense, suffer no speculative differences of opinion, any more than of feature, to impair the love of their brethren. Be this the wisdom of Unitarians, this the holy mantle which shall cover within its charitable circumference all who believe in one God, and who love their neighbor! I conclude my sermon with sincere assurances of my friendly esteem and respect.

When Dr. Waterhouse received the above letter, he was so delighted with it that he wrote at once to Jefferson, asking for permission to publish. Seldom did Jefferson reply as promptly as he did in this instance. The one thing on which Jefferson was unequivocal and adamant was that he insisted on privacy for his religious views. Besides, as he points out here, he has a proper respect for hornets.

LETTER TO BENJAMIN WATERHOUSE, JULY 19, 1822

An anciently dislocated, and now stiffening wrist, makes writing an operation so slow and painful to me, that I should not so soon have troubled
you with an acknowledgement of your favor of the 8th, but for the
request it contained of my consent to the publication of my letter of June
the 26th. No, my dear Sir, not for the world. Into what a nest of hornets
would it thrust my head! the *genus irritabile vatum*, on whom argument is
lost, and reason is, by themselves, disclaimed in matters of religion. Don
Quixote undertook to redress the bodily wrongs of the world, but the re-
dressment of mental vagaries would be an enterprise more than Quixotic.
I should as soon undertake to bring the crazy skulls of Bedlam to sound
understanding, as inculcate reason into that of an Athanasian. I am old,
and tranquility is now my *summum bonum*. Keep me, therefore, from the
fire and faggots of Calvin and his victim Servetus. Happy in the prospect
of a restoration of primitive Christianity, I must leave to younger athletes
to encounter and lop off the false branches which have been engrafted into
it by the mythologists of the middle and modern ages. I am not aware of
the peculiar resistance to Unitarianism, which you ascribe to Pennsylvania.
When I lived in Philadelphia, there was a respectable congregation of that
sect, with a meeting-house and regular service which I attended, and in
which Doctor Priestley officiated to numerous audiences. Baltimore has one
or two churches, and their pastor, author of an inestimable book on this
subject, was elected chaplain to the late Congress. That doctrine has not yet
been preached to us: but the breeze begins to be felt which precedes the
storm; and fanaticism is all in a bustle, shutting its doors and windows to
keep it out. But it will come, and drive before it the foggy mists of Platonism which have so long obscured our atmosphere. I am in hopes that some
of the disciples of your institution will become missionaries to us, of these
doctrines truly evangelical, and open our eyes to what has been so long
hidden from them. A bold and eloquent preacher would be nowhere listened
to with more freedom than in this State, nor with more firmness of mind.
They might need a preparatory discourse on the text of "prove all things,
hold fast that which is good," in order to unlearn the lesson that reason is
an unlawful guide in religion. They might startle on being first awaked
from the dreams of the night, but they would rub their eyes at once, and
look the spectres boldly in the face. The preacher might be excluded by
our hierophants from their churches and meeting-houses, but would be
attended in the fields by whole acres of hearers and thinkers. Missionaries
from Cambridge would soon be greeted with more welcome, than from the

tritheistical school of Andover. Such are my wishes, such would be my welcomes, warm and cordial as the assurances of my esteem and respect for you.

Two years later, Thomas Cooper wrote to Thomas Jefferson in connection with disturbing developments on the front of religious freedom in the United States. Jefferson presents his own general appraisal of the situation.

LETTER TO THOMAS COOPER, NOVEMBER 2, 1822

Your favor of October the 18th came to hand yesterday. The atmosphere of our country is unquestionably charged with a threatening cloud of fanaticism, lighter in some parts, denser in others, but too heavy in all. I had no idea, however, that in Pennsylvania, the cradle of toleration and freedom of religion, it could have arisen to the height you described. This must be owing to the growth of Presbyterianism. The blasphemy and absurdity of the five points of Calvin, and the impossibility of defending them, render their advocates impatient of reasoning, irritable, and prone to denunciation. In Boston, however, and its neighborhood, Unitarianism has advanced to so great strength as now to humble this haughtiest of all religious sects; insomuch, that they condescend to interchange with them and the other sects, the civilities of preaching freely and frequently in each others' meeting houses. In Rhode Island, on the other hand, no sectarian preacher will permit an Unitarian to pollute his desk. In our Richmond there is much fanaticism, but chiefly among the women. They have their night meetings and praying parties, where, attended by their priests, and sometimes by a hen-pecked husband, they pour forth the effusions of their love to Jesus, in terms as amatory and carnal, as their modesty would permit them to use to a mere earthly lover. In our village of Charlottesville, there is a good degree of religion, with a small spice only of fanaticism. We have four sects, but without either church or meeting-house. The court-house is the common temple, one Sunday in the month to each. Here, Episcopalian and Presbyterian, Methodist and Baptist, meet together, join in hymning their Maker, listen with attention and devotion to each others' preachers, and all mix in society with perfect harmony. It is not so in the districts where Presbyterianism prevails undividedly. Their ambition and tyranny would tolerate no rival if they had power. Systematical in grasping at an ascendency over all other sects, they aim, like the Jesuits, at engrossing the education of the country, are hostile to every institution which they do not direct, and jealous at seeing others begin to attend at all to that object. The diffusion of instruction, to which there is now so growing an attention, will be the remote remedy to this fever of fanaticism; while the more proximate one will be the progress of Unitarianism. That this will, ere long, be the religion of the majority from north to south, I have no doubt.

In our university you know there is no Professorship of Divinity. A handle has been made of this, to disseminate an idea that this is an institution, not merely of no religion, but against all religion. Occasion was taken at the last meeting of the Visitors, to bring forward an idea that might silence this calumny, which weighed on the minds of some honest friends to the institution. In our annual report to the legislature, after stating the constitutional reasons against a public establishment of any religious instruction, we suggest the expediency of encouraging the different religious sects to establish, each for itself, a professorship of their own tenets, on the confines of the university, so near as that their students may attend the lectures there, and have free use of our library, and every other accommodation we can give them; preserving, however, their independence of us and of each other. This fills the chasm objected to ours, as a defect in an institution professing to give instruction in *all* useful sciences. I think the invitation will be accepted, by some sects from candid intentions, and by others from jealousy and rivalship. And by bringing the sects together, and mixing them with the mass of other students, we shall soften their asperities, liberalize and neutralize their prejudices, and make the general religion a religion of peace, reason, and morality.

The following items are taken out of their chronological sequences in order to be presented as a unit. They are concerned with Thomas Jefferson's Bible project—an effort to prepare a version of the New Testament that would give substance to his concept of Christianity.

In a life marked by extraordinary intellectual richness and range of interests, Jefferson gave sustained thought to the idea of a redefinition of Christianity based on the ethics and teachings of Jesus, and completely separated from interpretation, phenomena, and the supernatural. This project matured slowly in his mind over a period of years, growing out of his early theological studies and augmented by his activities in the area of religious freedom. Even under the burden of the Presidency, he continued to give thought to the project; indeed, he started to write it during his second term. For a long time, however, he tried to persuade others whom he thought were more qualified to undertake the work. In particular, Dr. Joseph Priestley of England. A tract written by Dr. Priestley, Socrates and Jesus Compared, deeply impressed Jefferson and stimulated his thinking, particularly on the need for a simplified version of the Old Testament.

If Jefferson, Franklin, and Madison—comprising a philosophical trio among the Founding Fathers—had been asked to name a contemporary who for depth of intellect, moral imagination, and precision of thought most excited their admiration, it is likely they would have agreed on Joseph Priestley. Minister, scientist, philosopher, Priestley was the kind of man who sent up no fireworks calling attention to himself, but whose ideas seemed to tie all the provinces of knowledge together in the cause of human ennoblement. It is also possible that the man whose name would have figured not far behind Priestley's in the estimation of Franklin, Jefferson, and Madison was Dr. Benjamin Rush, physician and philosopher, also a member of the Federal Constitutional Convention.

Jefferson's first choice for the Bible project was Dr. Priestley, but he would have been pleased if Dr. Rush had agreed to do it. Sympathetic as they were, neither Priestley nor Rush was able to undertake the project. In the end, Jefferson wrote the book himself. He made a tentative beginning in the White House and then carried it through to completion at Monticello. He had in front of him when he began 1,189 chapters, or 773,000 words, from the Holy Library. When he was through, he had 25,000 words, extracted textually and limited to the life and morals of Jesus. He made no plans, however, for general publication of the manuscript. An indication of Jefferson's scholarship is that he did the translations himself into Greek, Latin, French, and then put the different texts side by side in a master copy. After his death, the book became part of the family estate. Here it remained until it was placed in the United States National Museum in Washington in 1895. Publication in a limited edition was authorized by the Fifty-seventh Congress for distribution among its members, being printed in 1904. It has since appeared in several editions for general distribution.

"MORALS OF JESUS" LETTERS

TO JOSEPH PRIESTLEY, APRIL 9, 1803

While on a short visit lately to Monticello, I received from you a copy of your comparative view of Socrates and Jesus, and I avail myself of the first moment of leisure after my return to acknowledge the pleasure I had in the perusal of it and the desire it excited to see you take up the subject on a more extended scale.

In consequence of some conversation with Dr. Rush in the year 1798-99, I had promised some day to write him a letter giving him my view of the Christian system. I have reflected often on it since, and even sketched the outlines in my own mind.

I should first take a general view of the moral doctrines of the most remarkable of the ancient philosophers, of whose ethics we have sufficient information to make an estimate, say Pythagoras, Epicurus, Epictetus, Socrates, Cicero, Seneca, Antoninus. I should do justice to the branches of morality they have treated well; but point out the importance of those in which they are deficient.

I should then take a view of the deism and ethics of the Jews, and show in what a degraded state they were, and the necessity they presented of a reformation.

I should proceed to a view of the life, character, and doctrines of Jesus, who, sensible of incorrectness of their ideas of the Deity, and of morality, endeavored to bring them to the principles of a pure deism, and juster notions of the attributes of God, to reform their moral doctrines to the standard of reason, justice and philanthropy, and to inculcate the belief of a future state.

This view would purposely omit the question of his divinity, and even his inspiration. To do him justice, it would be necessary to remark the disadvantages his doctrines had to encounter, not having been committed to writing by himself, but by the most unlettered of men, by memory, long after they had heard them from him; when much was forgotten, much misunderstood, and presented in every paradoxical shape. Yet such are the fragments remaining as to show a master workman, and that his system of morality was the most benevolent and sublime probably that has been ever taught, and consequently more perfect than those of any of the ancient philosophers. His character and doctrines have received still greater injury from those who pretend to be his special disciples, and who have disfigured and sophisticated his actions and precepts, from views of personal interest, so as to induce the unthinking part of mankind to throw off the whole system in disgust, and to pass sentence as in imposter on the most innocent, the most benevolent, the most eloquent and sublime character that ever has been exhibited to man.

This is the outline; but I have not the time, and still less the information which the subject needs. It will therefore rest with me in contemplation only. You are the person of all others would do it best, and most promptly. You have all the materials at hand, and you put together with ease. I wish you could be induced to extend your late work to the whole subject.

TO E. DOWSE, APRIL 19, 1803

There is no act, however virtuous, for which ingenuity may not find some bad motive. I must also add that though I concur with the author in considering the moral precepts of Jesus as more pure, correct, and sublime than those of the ancient philosophers, yet I do not concur with him in the mode of proving it. He thinks it necessary to libel and decry the doctrines of the philosophers; but a man must be blinded indeed by prejudice, who can deny them a great degree of merit. I give them their just due, and yet maintain that the morality of Jesus, as taught by himself, and freed from the corruptions of latter times, is far superior. Their philosophy went chiefly to the government of our passions, so far as respected ourselves, and the procuring our own tranquility. In our duties to others they were short and deficient. They extended their cares scarcely beyond our kindred and friends individually, and our country in the abstract. Jesus embraced with charity and philanthropy our neighbors, our countrymen, and the whole family of mankind. They confined themselves to actions; he pressed his sentiments into the region of our thoughts, and called for purity at the fountain head. In a pamphlet lately published in Philadelphia by Dr. Priestley, he has treated, with more justice and skill than Mr. [Thomas] Bennet, a small portion of this subject. His is a comparative view of Socrates only with Jesus. I have urged him to take up the subject on a broader scale.

Every word which goes from me, whether verbally or in writing, becomes the subject of so much malignant distortion, and perverted construction, that I am obliged to caution my friends against admitting the possibility of my letters getting into the public papers, or a copy of them to be taken under any degree of confidence. The present one is perhaps of a tenor to silence some calumniators, but I never will, by any word or act, bow to the shrine of intolerance, or admit a right of inquiry into the religious opinions of others. On the contrary, we are bound, you, I, and everyone, to make common cause, even with error itself, to maintain the common right of freedom of conscience. We ought with one heart and one hand to hew down the daring and dangerous efforts of those who would seduce the public opinion to substitute itself into that tyranny over religious faith which the laws have so justly abdicated. For this reason, were my opinions up to the standard of those who arrogate the right of questioning them, I would not countenance that arrogance by descending to an explanation. Accept my friendly salutations and high esteem.

In 1803 Jefferson sent Dr. Benjamin Rush the syllabus of his comparison of the moral doctrines of Jesus with those of the other ancient philosophers. In his letter to Dr. Rush, Jefferson emphasized the confidential nature of his study with these words:

"*And in confiding it to you, I know it will not be exposed to the malignant perversions of those who make every word from me a text for new misrepresentations and calumnies. I am, moreover, averse to the communication of my religious tenets to the public, because it would countenance the presumption of those who have endeavored to draw them before that tribunal, and to seduce public opinion to erect itself into that inquest over the rights of conscience, which the laws have so justly proscribed. It behooves every*

*man who values liberty of conscience for himself to resist invasions of it
in the case of others, or their case may, by change of circumstances, become
his own. . . ."*

TO BENJAMIN RUSH, APRIL 21, 1803

In some of the delightful conversations with you, in the evenings of
1798-99, and which served as an anodyne to the afflictions of the crisis
through which our country was then laboring, the Christian religion was
sometimes our topic; and I then promised you, that one day or other, I
would give you my views of it. They are the result of a life of inquiry
and reflection, and very different from that anti-Christian system imputed
to me by those who know nothing of my opinions. To the corruptions of
Christianity I am indeed opposed; but not to the genuine precepts of Jesus
himself. I am a Christian, in the only sense in which he wished any one
to be; sincerely attached to his doctrines, in preference to all others; ascribing to himself every *human* excellence; and believing he never claimed any
other. At the short intervals since these conversations, when I could justifiably
abstract my mind from public affairs, the subject has been under my contemplation. But the more I considered it, the more it expanded beyond the
measure of either my time or information. In the moment of my late
departure from Monticello, I received from Doctor Priestley his little
treatise of "Socrates and Jesus Compared." This being a section of the
general view I had taken of the field, it became a subject of reflection while
on the road, and unoccupied otherwise. The result was, to arrange in my
mind a syllabus, or outline of such an estimate of the comparative merit of
Christianity, as I wished to see executed by some one of more leisure and
information for the task, than myself. This I now send you, as the only
discharge of my promise I can probably ever execute. And in confiding it to
you, I know it will not be exposed to the malignant perversions of those
who make every word from me a text for new misrepresentations and
calumnies. I am moreover averse to the communication of my religious tenets
to the public; because it would countenance the presumption of those
who have endeavored to draw them before that tribunal, and to seduce
public opinion to erect itself into that inquisition over the rights of conscience, which the laws have so justly proscribed. It behooves every man who
values liberty of conscience for himself, to resist invasions of it in the case
of others; or their case may, by change of circumstances, become his own.
It behooves him, too, in his own case, to give no example of concession,
betraying the common right of independent opinion, by answering questions
of faith, which the laws have left between God and himself. Accept my
affectionate salutations.

Syllabus of an Estimate of the Merit of the Doctrines of Jesus, compared with those of others.

In a comparative view of the Ethics of the enlightened nations of antiquity, of the Jews and of Jesus, no notice should be taken of the corruptions of reason among the ancients, to wit, the idolatry and superstition of the vulgar, nor of the corruptions of Christianity by the learned among its professors.

Let a just view be taken of the moral principles inculcated by the most esteemed of the sects of ancient philosophy, or of their individuals; particularly Pythagoras, Socrates, Epicurus, Cicero, Epictetus, Seneca, Antoninus.

I. Philosophers. 1. Their precepts related chiefly to ourselves, and the government of those passions which, unrestrained, would disturb our tranquility of mind.[7] In this branch of philosophy they were really great.

2. In developing our duties to others, they were short and defective. They embraced, indeed, the circles of kindred and friends, and inculcated patriotism, or the love of our country in the aggregate, as a primary obligation; towards our neighbors and countrymen they taught justice, but scarcely viewed them as within the circle of benevolence. Still less have they inculcated peace, charity, and love to our fellow men, or embraced with benevolence the whole family of mankind.

II. Jews. 1. Their system was Deism; that is, the belief in one only God. But their ideas of him and his attributes were degrading and injurious.

2. Their Ethics were not only imperfect, but often irreconcilable with the sound dictates of reason and morality, as they respect intercourse with those around us; and repulsive and anti-social, as respecting other nations. They needed reformation, therefore, in an eminent degree.

III. Jesus. In this state of things among the Jews, Jesus appeared. His parentage was obscure; his condition poor; his education null; his natural endowments great; his life correct and innocent; he was meek, benevolent, patient, firm, disinterested, and of the sublimest eloquence.

The disadvantages under which his doctrines appear are remarkable.

---

[7] To explain, I will exhibit the heads of Seneca's and Cicero's philosophical works, the most extensive of any we have received from the ancients. Of ten heads in Seneca, seven relate to ourselves, viz. *de ira, consolatio, de tranquilitate, de constantia sapientis, de otio sapientis, de vita beata, de brevitate vitae;* two relate to others, *de clementia de beneficiis;* and one relates to the government of the world, *de providentia.* Of eleven tracts of Cicero, five respect ourselves, viz. *de finibus, Tusculana, academica, paradoxa, de Senectute;* one, *de officiis,* relates partly to ourselves, partly to others; one, *de amicitia,* relates to others; and four are on different subjects, to wit, *de natura deorum, de divinatione, de fato,* and *somnium Scipionis.*

1. Like Socrates and Epictetus, he wrote nothing himself.

2. But he had not, like them, a Xenophon or an Arrian to write for him. I name not Plato, who only used the name of Socrates to cover the whimsies of his own brain. On the contrary, all the learned of his country, entrenched in its power and riches, were opposed to him, lest his labors should undermine their advantages; and the committing to writing his life and doctrines fell on unlettered and ignorant men; who wrote, too, from memory, and not till long after the transactions had passed.

3. According to the ordinary fate of those who attempt to enlighten and reform mankind, he fell an early victim to the jealousy and combination of the altar and the throne, at about thirty-three years of age, his reason having not yet attained the *maximum* of its energy, nor the course of his preaching, which was but of three years at most, presented occasions for developing a complete system of morals.

4. Hence, the doctrines which he really delivered were defective as a whole, and fragments only of what he did deliver have come to us mutilated, misstated, and often unintelligible.

5. They have been still more disfigured by the corruptions of schismatising followers, who have found an interest in sophisticating and perverting the simple doctrines he taught, by engrafting on them the mysticisms of a Grecian sophist, frittering them into subtleties, and obscuring them with jargon, until they have caused good men to reject the whole in disgust and to view Jesus himself as an imposter.

Notwithstanding these disadvantages, a system of morals is presented to us which, if filled up in the style and spirit of the rich fragments he left us, would be the most perfect and sublime that has ever been taught by man.

The question of his being a member of the Godhead, or in direct communication with it, claimed for him by some of his followers, and denied by others, is foreign to the present view, which is merely an estimate of the intrinsic merits of his doctrines.

1. He corrected the Deism of the Jews, confirming them in their belief of one only God, and giving them juster notions of his attributes and government.

2. His moral doctrines, relating to kindred and friends, were more pure and perfect than those of the most correct of the philosophers, and greatly more so than those of the Jews; and they went far beyond both in inculcating universal philanthropy, not only to kindred and friends, to neighbors and countrymen, but to all mankind, gathering all into one family, under the bonds of love, charity, peace, common wants, and common aids. A development of this head will evince the peculiar superiority of the system of Jesus over all others.

3. The precepts of philosophy, and of the Hebrew code, laid hold of actions only. He pushed his scrutinies into the heart of man; erected his tribunal in the region of his thoughts, and purified the waters at the fountain head.

4. He taught, emphatically, the doctrines of a future state, which was either doubted, or disbelieved by the Jews; and wielded it with efficacy, as an important incentive, supplementary to the other motives to moral conduct.

TO JOSEPH PRIESTLEY, JANUARY 29, 1804

I rejoice that you have undertaken the task of comparing the moral doctrines of Jesus with those of the ancient Philosophers. You are so much in possession of the whole subject, that you will do it easier and better than any other person living. I think you cannot avoid giving, as preliminary to the comparison, a digest of his moral doctrines, extracted in his own words from the Evangelists, and leaving out everything relative to his personal history and character. It would be short and precious. With a view to do this for my own satisfaction, I had sent to Philadelphia to get two testaments (Greek) of the same edition, and two English, with a design to cut out the morsels of morality and paste them on the leaves of a book, in the manner you describe as having been pursued in forming your Harmony. But I shall now get the thing done by better hands.

The Reverend Charles Clay was rector of St. Anne's Parish in Albemarle County, Virginia, where Thomas Jefferson was once nominally a vestryman. He had long conversations with Jefferson on theological subjects; in fact, as Jefferson indicates, he probably heard more of and about Jefferson's religious views than anyone else.

TO CHARLES CLAY, JANUARY 29, 1815

Your letter of December 20th was four weeks on its way to me. I thank you for it; for although founded on a misconception, it is evidence of that friendly concern for my peace and welfare, which I have ever believed you to feel. Of publishing a book on religion, my dear Sir, I never had an idea. I should as soon think of writing for the reformation of Bedlam, as of the world of religious sects. Of these there must be, at least, ten thousand, every individual of every one of which believes all wrong but his own. To undertake to bring them all right, would be like undertaking, single-handed, to fell the forests of America. Probably you have heard me say I had taken the four Evangelists, had cut out from them every text they had recorded of the moral precepts of Jesus, and arranged them in a certain order, and although they appeared but as fragments, yet fragments of the most sublime edifice of morality which had ever been exhibited to man. This I have probably mentioned to you, because it is true; and the idea of its publication may have suggested itself as an inference of your own mind. I not only write nothing on religion, but rarely permit myself to speak on it, and never but in a reasonable society. I have probably said more to you than any other person, because we have had more hours of conversation in *duetto* in our meetings at the Forest. I abuse the priests, indeed, who have so much abused the pure and holy doctrines of their master, and who have laid me under no obligations of reticence as to the tricks of their trade. The genuine system of Jesus, and the artificial structures they have erected, to make them the instruments of wealth, power, and preeminence to themselves, are as distinct things in my view as light and darkness; and while I have classed them with soothsayers and necromancers, I place him among the greatest reformers of morals, and scourges of priestcraft that have ever existed. They felt him as such, and never rested until they had silenced him by death. But his heresies against Judaism prevailing in the long run, the priests have tacked about, and rebuilt upon them the temple which he destroyed, as splendid, as profitable, and as imposing as that.

Government, as well as religion, has furnished its schisms, its persecutions, and its devices for flattering idleness on the earnings of the people. It has its hierarchy of emperors, kings, princes, and nobles, as that has of popes, cardinals, archbishops, bishops, and priests. In short, cannibals are not to be found in the wilds of America only, but are revelling on the blood of every living people. Turning, then, from this loathsome combination of Church and State, and weeping over the follies of our fellow men, who yield themselves the willing dupes and drudges of these mountebanks, I consider reformation and redress as desperate, and abandon them to the Quixotism of more enthusiastic minds.

TO F. A. VAN DER KEMP, APRIL 25, 1816

Pursuing the same ideas after writing the Syllabus, I made, for my own satisfaction, an extract from the Evangelists of his morals, selecting those only whose style and spirit proved them genuine, and his own; and they are as distinguishable from the matter in which they are imbedded as diamonds in dunghills. A more precious morsel in ethics was never seen. It was too hastily done, however, being the work of one or two evenings only, while I lived at Washington, overwhelmed with other business, and it is my intention to go over it again at more leisure. This shall be the work of the ensuing winter. I gave it the title of "the Philosophy of Jesus extracted from the text of the Evangelists." To this Syllabus and extract, if a history of his life can be added, written with the same view of the subject, the world will see, after the fogs shall be dispelled, in which for fourteen centuries he has been enveloped by jugglers to make money of him, when the genuine character shall be exhibited, which they have dressed up in the rags of an imposter, the world, I say, will at length see the immortal merit of this first of human sages. I rejoice that you think of undertaking this work. It is one I have long wished to see written of the scale of a Laertius or a Nepos. Nor can it be a work of labor, or of volume, for his journeyings from Judea to Samaria, and Samaria to Galilee, do not cover much country; and the incidents of his life require little research. They are all at hand, and need only to be put into human dress; noticing such only as are within the physical laws of nature, and offending none by a denial or even a mention of what is not. If the Syllabus and extract (which are short) either in substance, or at large, are worth a place under the same cover with your biography, they are at your service. I ask one only condition, that no possibility shall be admitted of my name being even intimated with the publication. If done in England, as you seem to contemplate, there will be the less likelihood of my being thought of. I shall be much gratified to learn that you pursue your intention of writing the life of Jesus, and pray you to accept the assurances of my great respect and esteem.

Jefferson completed his version of The Life and Morals of Jesus of Nazareth. *The following passages are drawn from that book.*

THE LIFE AND MORALS OF JESUS OF NAZARETH

ONE

And it came to pass in those days that there went out a decree from Cesar Augustus, that all the world should be taxed. (And this taxing was first made when Cyrenius was governor of Syria.) And all went to be taxed, every one into his own city. And Joseph also went up from Galilee, out of the city of Nazareth, into Judea, unto the city of David, which is called Bethlehem (because he was of the house and lineage of David): to be taxed with Mary his espoused wife, being great with child. And so it was, that, while they were there, the days were accomplished that she should be delivered. And she brought forth her firstborn son, and wrapped him in swaddling clothes, and laid him in a manger; because there was no room for them in the inn.

And when eight days were accomplished for the circumcising of the child, his name was called Jesus.

And when they had performed all things according to the law of the Lord, they returned into Galilee, to their own city Nazareth. And the child grew, and waxed strong in spirit, filled with wisdom.

And when he was twelve years old, they went up to Jerusalem after the custom of the feast. And when they had fulfilled the days, as they returned, the child Jesus tarried behind in Jerusalem; and Joseph and his mother knew not of it. But they, supposing him to have been in the company, went a day's journey; and they sought him among their kinsfolk and acquaintance. And when they found him not, they turned back again to Jerusalem, seeking him. And it came to pass that after three days they found him in the temple, sitting in the midst of the doctors, both hearing them, and asking them questions. And all that heard him were astonished at his understanding and answers.

And when they saw him, they were amazed: and his mother said unto him, "Son, why hast thou thus dealt with us? behold, thy father and I have sought thee sorrowing."

And he went down with them, and came to Nazareth, and was subject unto them. And Jesus increased in wisdom and stature.

* * *

Now in the fifteenth years of the reign of Tiberius Cesar, Pontius Pilate being governor of Judea, and Herod being tetrarch of Galilee, and his brother Philip tetrarch of Iturea and of the region of Trachonitis, and Lysanias the tetrarch of Abilene, Annas and Caiaphas being the high priests, John did baptize in the wilderness.

And the same John had his raiment of camels' hair, and a leathern girdle about his loins; and his meat was locusts and wild honey.

Then went out to him Jerusalem, and all Judea, and all the region round about Jordan, and were baptized of him in Jordan. Then cometh Jesus from Galilee to Jordan unto John, to be baptized of him.

And Jesus himself began to be about thirty years of age.

After this he went down to Capernaum, he, and his mother, and his brethren, and his disciples; and they continued there not many days.

And the Jews' passover was at hand; and Jesus went up to Jerusalem, and found in the temple those that sold oxen, and sheep, and doves, and the changers of money, sitting: And, when he had made a scourge of small cords, he drove them all out of the temple, and the sheep, and the oxen; and poured out the changers' money, and overthrew the tables; and said unto them that sold doves, "Take these things hence; make not my Father's house an house of merchandise."

* * *

After these things came Jesus and his disciples into the land of Judea; and there he tarried with them, and baptized.

Now, when Jesus had heard that John was cast into prison, he departed into Galilee: for Herod himself had sent forth, and laid hold upon John, and bound him in prison for Herodias' sake, his brother Philip's wife: for he had married her. For John had said unto Herod, "It is not lawful for thee to have thy brother's wife."

Therefore Herodias had a quarrel against him, and would have killed him; but she could not: for Herod feared John, knowing that he was a just man, and an holy, and observed him; and when he heard him, he did many things, and heard him gladly.

And when a convenient day was come, that Herod on his birthday made a supper to his lords, high captains, and chief estates of Galilee; and when the daughter of the said Herodias came in and danced, and pleased Herod and them that sat with him, the king said unto the damsel, "Ask of me whatsoever thou wilt, and I will give it thee." And he sware unto her, "Whatsoever thou shalt ask of me, I will give it thee, unto the half of my kingdom."

And she went forth, and said unto her mother, "What shall I ask?"

And she said, "The head of John the Baptist."

And she came in straightway with haste unto the king, and asked, saying, "I will that thou give me, by and by in a charger, the head of John the Baptist."

And the king was exceeding sorry; yet for his oath's sake, and for their sakes which sat with him, he would not reject her. And immediately the king sent an executioner, and commanded his head to be brought: and he went and beheaded him in the prison, and brought his head in a charger, and gave it to the damsel: and the damsel gave it to her mother.

* * *

And they went into Capernaum; and straightway on the sabbath-day, he entered into the synagogue, and taught. And they were astonished at his doctrine: for he taught them as one that had authority, and not as the scribes.

At that time Jesus went on the sabbath-day through the corn; and his disciples were an hungered, and began to pluck the ears of corn, and to eat. But when the Pharisees saw it, they said unto him, "Behold, thy disciples do that which is not lawful to do upon the sabbath-day."

But he said unto them, "Have ye not read what David did when he was an hungered, and they that were with him: how he entered into the house of God, and did eat the shewbread, which was not lawful for him to eat, neither for them which were with him, but only for the priests? Or, have ye not read in the law, how that on the sabbath-days, the priests in the temple profane the sabbath, and are blameless?"

And when he was departed thence, he went into their synagogue: and, behold, there was a man which had his hand withered. And they asked him, saying, "Is it lawful to heal on the sabbath-days?" that they might accuse him.

And he said unto them, "What man shall there be among you, that shall have one sheep and if it fall into a pit on the sabbath-day, will he not lay hold on it, and lift it out? How much then is a man better than a sheep? Wherefore it is lawful to do well on the sabbath-days." And he said unto them, "The sabbath was made for man, and not man for the sabbath."

Then the Pharisees went out, and held a council against him, how they might destroy him. But when Jesus knew it, he withdrew himself from thence: and great multitudes followed him.

*   *   *

And it came to pass in those days, that he went up into a mountain to pray, and continued all night in prayer to God. And when it was day, he called unto him his disciples; and of them he chose twelve, whom also he named Apostles: Simon, (whom he also named Peter), and Andrew his brother, James and John, Philip and Bartholomew, Matthew and Thomas, James the son of Alpheus, and Simon called Zelotes, and Judas the brother of James, and Judas Iscariot, which also was the traitor.

And he came down with them, and stood in the plain; and the company of his disciples, and a great multitude of people out of all Judea and Jerusalem, and from the sea-coast of Tyre and Sidon, which came to hear him.

And seeing the multitudes, he went up into a mountain: and when he was set, his disciples came unto him: and he opened his mouth, and taught them, saying,

> *"Blessed are the poor in spirit:*
> *For theirs is the Kingdom of heaven.*
>
> *Blessed are they that mourn:*
> *For they shall be comforted.*
>
> *Blessed are the meek:*
> *For they shall inherit the earth.*
>
> *Blessed are they which do hunger and thirst*
> *   after righteousness:*
> *For they shall be filled.*
>
> *Blessed are the merciful:*
> *For they shall obtain mercy.*
>
> *Blessed are the pure in heart:*
> *For they shall see God.*
>
> *Blessed are the peace-makers:*
> *For they shall be called the children of God.*

*Blessed are they which are persecuted for right-
eousness' sake:*
For theirs is the kingdom of heaven.

*Blessed are ye when men shall revile you, and
persecute you, and shall say all manner of
evil against you falsely, for my sake.*

*Rejoice, and be exceeding glad: for great is
your reward in heaven: for so persecuted
they the prophets which were before you.*

But woe unto you that are rich!
For ye have received your consolation.

Woe unto you that are full!
For ye shall hunger.

Woe unto you that laugh now!
For ye shall mourn and weep.

*Woe unto you when all men shall speak well
of you!*
For so did their fathers to the false prophets.

"Ye are the salt of the earth: but if the salt have lost his savour, wherewith shall it be salted? it is thenceforth good for nothing, but to be cast out,
and to be trodden under foot of men.

"Ye are the light of the world. A city that is set on an hill cannot be
hid. Neither do men light a candle, and put it under a bushel, but on a
candlestick, and it giveth light unto all that are in the house. Let your
light so shine before men, that they may see your good works, and glorify
your Father which is in heaven.

"Think not that I am come to destroy the law, or the prophets: I am
not come to destroy, but to fulfil. For verily I say unto you, 'Till heaven
and earth pass, one jot or one tittle shall in no wise pass from the law, till
all be fulfilled.' Whosoever, therefore, shall break one of these least commandments, and shall teach men so, he shall be called the least in the
kingdom of heaven: but whosoever shall do, and teach them, the same shall
be called great in the kingdom of heaven. For I say unto you that, except
your righteousness shall exceed the righteousness of the scribes and Pharisees,
ye shall in no case enter into the kingdom of heaven.

"Ye have heard that it was said by them of old time, 'Thou shalt not
kill'; and whosoever shall kill shall be in danger of the judgment. But I
say unto you that, whosoever is angry with his brother without cause, shall
be in danger of the judgment: and whosoever shall say to his brother, 'Raca,'
shall be in danger of the council: but whosoever shall say, 'Thou fool,' shall

be in danger of hellfire. Therefore, if thou bring thy gift to the altar, and there rememberest that thy brother hath aught against thee; leave there thy gift before the altar, and go thy way; first be reconciled to thy brother, and then come and offer thy gift. Agree with thine adversary quickly, whilst thou art in the way with him; lest at any time the adversary deliver thee to the judge and the judge deliver thee to the officer, and thou be cast into prison. Verily I say unto thee, 'Thou shalt by no means come out thence, till thou hast paid the uttermost farthing.'

"Ye have heard that it was said by them of old time, 'Thou shalt not commit adultery.' But I say unto you that whosoever looketh on a woman to lust after her hath committed adultery with her already in his heart. And if thy right eye offend thee, pluck it out, and cast it from thee: for it is profitable for thee that one of thy members should perish, and not that thy whole body should be cast into hell and if thy right hand offend thee, cut it off, and cast it from thee: for it is profitable for thee, that one of thy members should perish, and not that thy whole body should be cast into hell. It hath been said, 'Whosoever shall put away his wife, let him give her a writing of divorcement.' But I say unto you, that whosoever shall put away his wife, saving for the cause of fornication, causeth her to commit adultery: and whosoever shall marry her that is divorced committeth adultery.

"Again, ye have heard that it hath been said by them of old time, 'Thou shalt not forswear thyself, but shalt perform unto the Lord thine oaths.' But I say unto you, 'Swear not at all: neither by heaven: for it is God's throne: nor by the earth: for it is his footstool: neither by Jerusalem: for it is the city of the great King. Neither shalt thou swear by thy head, because thou canst not make one hair white or black. But let your communication be, "Yea, yea"; "Nay, nay": for whatsoever is more than these cometh of evil.'

"Ye have heard that it hath been said, 'An eye for an eye, and a tooth for a tooth.' But I say unto you, that ye resist not evil: but whosoever shall smite thee on thy right cheek, turn to him the other also. And if any man will sue thee at the law, and take away thy coat, let him have thy cloak also. And whosoever shall compel thee to go a mile, go with him twain. Give to him that asketh thee, and from him that would borrow of thee, turn not thou away.

"Ye have heard that it hath been said, 'Thou shalt love thy neighbour, and hate thine enemy.' But I say unto you, 'Love your enemies, bless them that curse you, do good to them that hate you, and pray for them which despitefully use you, and persecute you; that ye may be the children of your Father which is in heaven: for he maketh his sun to rise on the evil and on the good, and sendeth rain on the just and on the unjust.' For if ye love them which love you, what reward have ye? do not even the publicans the same? And if ye salute your brethren only, what do ye more than others? do not even the publicans so?

"And if ye lend to them of whom ye hope to receive, what thanks have ye? for sinners also lend to sinners to receive as much again. But love ye your enemies, and do good, and lend, hoping for nothing again: and your reward shall be great, and ye shall be the children of the Highest: for he is kind unto the unthankful, and to the evil. Be ye, therefore, merciful, as your Father also is merciful.

"Take heed that ye do not your alms before men, to be seen of them: otherwise ye have no reward of your Father which is in heaven. Therefore, when thou doest thine alms, do not sound a trumpet before thee, as the hypocrites do in the synagogues, and in the streets, that they may have glory of men. Verily I say unto you, 'They have their reward.' But when thou doest alms, let not thy left hand know what thy right hand doeth: that thine alms may be in secret: and thy Father, which seeth in secret, himself shall reward thee openly.

"And when thou prayest, thou shalt not be as the hypocrites are: for they love to pray standing in the synagogues, and in the corners of the streets, that they may be seen of men. Verily I say unto you, 'They have their reward.' But thou, when thou prayest, enter into thy closet; and, when thou hast shut thy door, pray to thy Father which is in secret; and thy Father which seeth in secret, shall reward thee openly. But when ye pray, use not vain repetitions, as the heathen do: for they think that they shall be heard for their much speaking. Be not ye, therefore, like unto them: for your Father knoweth what things ye have need of, before ye ask him. After this manner, therefore pray ye:

'*Our Father which art in heaven,*
Hallowed be thy name.
Thy kingdom come.
Thy will be done
In earth, as it is in heaven.

Give us this day
Our daily bread.
And forgive us our debts,
As we forgive our debtors.
And lead us not into temptation,
But deliver us from evil:

For thine is the kingdom,
And the power,
And the glory,
For ever. Amen.'

"For if ye forgive men their trespasses, your heavenly Father will also forgive you: but if ye forgive not men their trespasses, neither will your Father forgive your trespasses.

"Moreover, when ye fast, be not as the hypocrites, of a sad countenance: for they disfigure their faces, that they may appear unto men to fast. Verily I say unto you, 'They have their reward.' But thou, when thou fastest, anoint thine head, and wash thy face; that thou appear not unto men to fast, but unto thy Father which is in secret: and thy Father, which seeth in secret shall reward thee openly.

"Lay not up for yourselves treasures upon
  earth,
Where moth and rust doth corrupt,
And where thieves break through and steal:

But lay up for yourselves treasures in heaven,
Where neither moth nor rust doth corrupt,
And where thieves do not break through nor
  steal.

For where your treasure is, there will your heart be also.

"The light of the body is the eye: if, therefore, thine eye be single, thy whole body shall be full of light. But if thine eye be evil, thy whole body shall be full of darkness. If, therefore, the light that is in thee be darkness, how great is that darkness?

"No man can serve two masters: for either he will hate the one, and love the other; or else he will hold to the one, and despise the other. Ye cannot serve God and mammon.

"Therefore I say unto you, 'Take no thought for your life, what ye shall eat or what ye shall drink; nor yet for your body, what ye shall put on.' Is not the life more than meat, and the body than raiment? Behold the fowls of the air: for they sow not, neither do they reap, nor gather into barns; yet your heavenly Father feedeth them. Are ye not much better than they? Which of you, by taking thought, can add one cubit unto his stature? And why take ye thought for raiment? Consider the lilies of the field how they grow: they toil not, neither do they spin: and yet I say unto you, that even Solomon in all his glory was not arrayed like one of these.

"Wherefore, if God so clothe the grass of the field, which today is, and tomorrow is cast into the oven, shall he not much more clothe you? O ye of little faith? Therefore take no thought, saying, 'What shall we eat?' or, 'What shall we drink?' or, 'Wherewithal shall we be clothed?' (For after all these things do the Gentiles seek): for your heavenly Father knoweth that ye have need of all these things. But seek ye first the kingdom of God, and his righteousness; and all these things shall be added unto you. Take therefore no thought for the morrow: for the morrow shall take thought for the things of itself. Sufficient unto the day is the evil thereof.

"Judge not, that ye be not judged. For with what judgment ye judge, ye shall be judged: and with what measure ye mete, it shall be measured to you again. Give, and it shall be given unto you: good measure, pressed down, and shaken together, and running over, shall men give into your bosom. And why beholdest thou the mote that is in thy brother's eye, but considered not the beam that is in thine own eye? Or how wilt thou say to thy brother, 'Let me pull out the mote out of thine eye'; and, behold, a beam is in thine own eye? Thou hypocrite! First cast out the beam out of thine own eye; and then shalt thou see clearly to cast out the mote out of thy brother's eye.

"Give not that which is holy unto the dogs,
Neither cast ye your pearls before swine,
Lest they trample them under their feet,
And turn again and rend you.

Ask, and it shall be given you:
Seek, and ye shall find:
Knock, and it shall be opened unto you:

For every one that asketh receiveth;
And he that seeketh findeth;
And to him that knocketh it shall be opened.

Or what man is there of you whom if his son ask bread, will he give him a stone? Or if he ask a fish, will he give him a serpent? If ye then, being evil, know how to give good gifts unto your children, how much more shall your Father which is in heaven give good things to them that ask him? Therefore all things whatsoever ye would that men should do to you, do ye even so to them: for this is the law and the prophets.

"Enter ye in at the strait gate: for wide is the gate, and broad is the way, that leadeth to destruction, and many there be which go in thereat: because strait is the gate, and narrow is the way, which leadeth unto life, and few there be that find it.

"Beware of false prophets, which come to you in sheep's clothing, but inwardly they are ravening wolves. Ye shall know them by their fruits. Do men gather grapes of thorns, or figs of thistles? Even so, every good tree bringeth forth good fruit; but a corrupt tree bringeth forth evil fruit. A good tree cannot bring forth evil fruit, neither can a corrupt tree bring forth good fruit. Every tree that bringeth not forth good fruit is hewn down, and cast into the fire. Wherefore by their fruits ye shall know them.

"A good man, out of the good treasure of the heart, bringeth forth good things: and an evil man, out of the evil treasure, bringeth forth evil things. But I say unto you, that every idle word that men shall speak, they shall give account thereof in the day of judgment. For by thy words thou shalt be justified, and by thy words thou shalt be condemned.

"Therefore whosoever heareth these sayings of mine, and doeth them, I will liken him unto a wise man, which built his house upon a rock: and the rain descended, and the floods came, and the winds blew, and beat upon that house; and it fell not: for it was founded upon a rock. And every one that heareth these sayings of mine, and doeth them not, shall be likened unto a foolish man, which built his house upon the sand: and the rain descended, and the floods came, and the winds blew, and beat upon that house; and it fell, and great was the fall of it."

And it came to pass when Jesus had ended these sayings, the people were astonished at his doctrine: for he taught them as one having authority, and not as the scribes.

*   *   *

When he was come down from the mountain, great multitudes followed him. And he went round about the villages, teaching:

"Come unto me, all ye that labour and are heavy laden, and I will give you rest. Take my yoke upon you and learn of me; for I am meek and lowly in heart: and ye shall find rest unto your souls. For my yoke is easy, and my burden is light."

And one of the Pharisees desired him that he would eat with him. And he went into the Pharisee's house, and sat down to meat. And, behold, a woman in the city, which was a sinner, when she knew that Jesus sat at meat in the Pharisee's house, brought an alabaster box of ointment, and stood at his feet behind him weeping, and began to wash his feet with tears, and did wipe them with the hairs of her head, and kissed his feet, and anointed them with the ointment.

Now, when the Pharisee which had bidden him saw it, he spake within himself, saying, "This man, if he were a prophet, would have known who and what manner of woman this is that toucheth him; for she is a sinner."

And Jesus, answering, said unto him, "Simon, I have somewhat to say unto thee."

And he saith, "Master, say on."

"There was a certain creditor, which had two debtors: the one owed five hundred pence, and the other fifty. And when they had nothing to pay, he frankly forgave them both. Tell me, therefore, which of them will love him most?"

Simon answered, and said, "I suppose that he to whom he forgave most."

And he said unto him, "Thou hast rightly judged."

And he turned to the woman and said unto Simon, "Seest thou this woman? I entered into thine house, thou gavest me no water for my feet: but she hath washed my feet with tears, and wiped them with the hairs of her head. Thou gavest me no kiss: but this woman, since the time I came in, hath not ceased to kiss my feet. My head with oil thou didst not anoint: but this woman hath anointed my feet with ointment."

There came then his brethren and his mother, and, standing without, sent unto him, calling him. And the multitude sat about him, and they said unto him, "Behold, thy mother and thy brethren without seek for thee."

And he answered them, saying, "Who is my mother, or my brethren?"

And he looked round about on them which sat about him, and said, "Behold my mother and my brethren! For whosoever shall do the will of God, the same is my brother, and my sister, and mother."

*   *   *

In the mean time, when there were gathered together an innumerable multitude of people, insomuch that they trode one upon another, he began to say unto his disciples first of all,

"Beware ye of the leaven of the Pharisees, which is hypocrisy. For there is nothing covered, that shall not be revealed; neither hid, that shall not be known. Therefore whatsoever ye have spoken in darkness, shall be heard in the light; and that which ye have spoken in the ear in closets shall be proclaimed upon the housetops.

"And I say unto you, my friends, 'Be not afraid of them that kill the body, and after that have no more that they can do.' But I will forewarn you whom ye shall fear: 'Fear him, which, after he hath killed, hath power to cast into hell'; yea, I say unto you, 'Fear him.' Are not five sparrows sold for two farthings? And not one of them is forgotten before God. But even the very hairs of your head are numbered. Fear not, therefore: ye are of more value than many sparrows."

And one of the company said unto him, "Master, speak to my brother, that he divide the inheritance with me."

And he said unto him, "Man, who made me a judge, or a divider over you?"

And he said unto them, "Take heed, and beware of covetousness; for a man's life consisteth not in the abundance of the things which he possesseth."

And he spake a parable unto them, saying,

"The ground of a certain rich man brought forth plentifully: And he thought within himself, saying, 'What shall I do, because I have no room where to bestow my fruits?' And he said, 'This will I do: I will pull down my barns, and build greater; and there will I bestow all my fruits and my goods. And I will say to my soul, "Soul, thou hast much goods laid up for many years: take thine ease, eat, drink, and be merry." ' But God said unto him, 'Thou fool! this night thy soul shall be required of thee; then whose shall those things be, which thou hast provided?' So is he that layeth up treasure for himself, and is not rich toward God."

And he said unto his disciples,

"Therefore I say unto you, 'Take no thought for your life, what ye shall eat; neither for the body, what ye shall put on.' The life is more than meat and the body is more than raiment. Consider the ravens: for they neither sow nor reap; which neither have storehouse nor barn, and God feedeth them. How much more are ye better than the fowls? And which of you, with taking thought, can add to his stature one cubit? If ye then be not able to do that thing which is least, why take ye thought for the rest? Consider the lilies how they grow: they toil not, they spin not, and yet I say unto you, that Solomon, in all his glory, was not arrayed like one of these.

"If then God so clothe the grass, which is today in the field, and tomorrow is cast into the oven; how much more will he clothe you? O ye of little faith! And seek not ye what ye shall eat, or what ye shall drink; neither be ye of doubtful mind. For all these things do the nations of the world seek after: and your Father knoweth that ye have need of these things. But rather seek ye the kingdom of God; and all these things shall be added unto you.

"Fear not, little flock; for it is your Father's good pleasure to give you the kingdom. Sell that ye have, and give alms; provide yourselves bags which wax not old, a treasure in the heavens that faileth not, where no thief approacheth, neither moth corrupteth. For where your treasure is, there will your heart be also.

"Let your loins be girded about, and your lights burning: and ye yourselves like unto men that wait for their lord, when he will return from the wedding; that when he cometh and knocketh, they may open unto him immediately. Blessed are those servants, whom the lord, when he cometh, shall find watching: verily I say unto you that he shall gird himself, and make them to sit down to meat, and will come forth and serve them. And if he shall come in the second watch, or come in the third watch, and find them so, blessed are those servants. And this know, that if the good man of the house had known what hour the thief would come, he would have watched, and not have suffered his house to be broken through. Be ye, therefore, ready also: for the Son of Man cometh at an hour when ye think not."

Then Peter said unto him, "Lord, speakest thou this parable unto us, or even to all?"

And the Lord said, "Who then is that faithful and wise steward, whom his lord shall make ruler over his household, to give them their portion of meat in due season? Blessed is that servant, whom his lord, when he cometh, shall find so doing. Of a truth I say unto you, that he will make him ruler over all that he hath. But, and if that servant say in his heart, 'My lord delayeth his coming'; and shall begin to beat the men-servants, and maidens, and to eat and drink, and to be drunken; the lord of that servant will come in a day when he looketh not for him, and at an hour when he is not aware, and will cut him in sunder. And that servant, which knew his lord's will, and prepared not himself, neither did according to his will, shall be beaten with many stripes. But he that knew not, and did commit things worthy of stripes shall be beaten with few stripes: for unto whomsoever much is given, of him shall be much required: and to whom men have committed much, of him they will ask the more."

And he said also to the people,

"When ye see a cloud rise out of the west, straightway ye say, 'There cometh a shower,' and so it is. And when ye see the south wind blow, ye say, 'There will be heat'; and it cometh to pass. Ye hypocrites! ye can discern the face of the sky and of the earth; but how is it, that ye do not discern this time? Yea, and why even of yourselves judge ye not what is right?

"When thou goest with thine adversary to the magistrate, as thou art in the way, give diligence that thou mayest be delivered from him; lest he hale thee to the judge, and the judge deliver thee to the officer, and the officer cast thee into prison. I tell thee, 'Thou shalt not depart thence, till thou hast paid the very last mite.' "

* * *

There were present at that season some that told him of the Galileans, whose blood Pilate had mingled with their sacrifices. And Jesus, answering, said unto them, "Suppose ye that these Galileans were sinners above all the Galileans, because they suffered such things? I tell you, 'Nay; but, except ye repent, ye shall all likewise perish.' Or those eighteen upon whom the tower in Siloam fell, and slew them; think ye that they were sinners above all men that dwelt in Jerusalem? I tell you, 'Nay, but except ye repent, ye shall all likewise perish.' "

He spake also this parable:

"A certain man had a fig-tree planted in his vineyard; and he came and sought fruit thereon, and found none. Then he said unto the dresser of his vineyard, 'Behold, these three years I come seeking fruit on this fig-tree, and find none: cut it down, why cumbereth it the ground?' And he, answering, said unto him, 'Lord, let it alone this year also, till I shall dig about it, and dung it: and if it bear fruit, well: and if not, then after that thou shalt cut it down.' "

And as he spake, a certain Pharisee besought him to dine with him: and he went in, and sat down to meat. And when the Pharisee saw it, he marvelled that he had not first washed before dinner. And the Lord said unto him,

"Now do ye Pharisees make clean the outside of the cup and the platter; but your inward part is full of ravening and wickedness. Ye fools! did not he that made that which is without, make that which is within also? But rather give alms of such things as ye have; and, behold, all things are clean unto you. But woe unto you, Pharisees! for ye tithe mint, and rue, and all manner of herbs, and pass over judgment and the love of God: these ought ye to have done, and not to leave the other undone. Woe unto you, Pharisees! for ye love the uppermost seats in the synagogues, and greetings in the markets. Woe unto you, scribes and Pharisees, hypocrites! for ye are as graves which appear not, and the men that walk over them are not aware of them."

Then answered one of the lawyers, and said unto him, "Master, thus saying, thou reproachest us also."

And he said, "Woe unto you also, ye lawyers! for ye lade men with burdens grievous to be borne, and ye yourselves touch not the burdens with one of your fingers. Woe unto you, Lawyers! for ye have taken away the key of knowledge: ye entered not in yourselves, and them that were entering in ye hindered."

And as he said these things unto them, the scribes and the Pharisees began to urge him vehemently, and to provoke him to speak of many things: laying wait for him, and seeking to catch something out of his mouth, that they might accuse him.

*   *   *

The same day went Jesus out of the house, and sat by the sea side. And great multitudes were gathered together unto him, so that he went into a ship and sat; and the whole multitude stood on the shore. And he spake many things unto them in parables, saying,

"Behold, a sower went forth to sow; and, when he sowed some seeds fell by the wayside and the fowls came and devoured them. Some fell upon stony places, where they had not much earth: and forthwith they sprung up, because they had no deepness of earth: and when the sun was up, they were scorched: and, because they had not root, they withered away. And some fell among thorns; and the thorns sprung up and choked them. But other fell into good ground and brought forth fruit, some an hundred-fold, some sixty-fold, some thirty-fold. Who hath ears to hear, let him hear."

And when he was alone, they that were about him, with the twelve, asked of him the parable.

"Hear ye, therefore, the parable of the sower. When any one heareth the word of the kingdom, and understandeth it not, then cometh the wicked one, and catcheth away that which was sown in his heart. This is he which received seed by the wayside. But he that received the seed in the stony places, the same is he that heareth the word, and anon with joy receiveth it; yet hath he not root in himself, but dureth for a while; for when tribulation or persecution ariseth because of the word, by and by he is offended. He also that received seed among the thorns is he that heareth the word; and the care of this world, and the deceitfulness of riches, choke the word, and he becometh unfruitful. But he that received seed into the good ground, is he that heareth the word and understandeth it; which also beareth fruit, and bringeth forth, some an hundred-fold, some sixty, some thirty."

And he said unto them, "Is a candle brought to be put under a bushel, or under a bed, and not to be set on a candlestick? For there is nothing hid which shall not be manifested; neither was any thing kept secret, but that it should come abroad. If any man have ears to hear, let him hear."

Another parable put he forth unto them, saying,

"The kingdom of heaven is likened unto a man which sowed good seed in his field: but, while men slept, his enemy came and sowed tares among the wheat, and went his way. But when the blade was sprung up, and brought forth fruit, then appeared the tares also. So the servants of the house-holder came and said unto him, 'Sir, didst not thou sow good seed in thy field? from whence then hath it tares?' He said unto them, 'An enemy hath done this.' The servants said unto him, 'Wilt thou then that we go and gather them up?' But he said, 'Nay, lest, while ye gather up the tares, ye root up also the wheat with them. Let both grow together until the harvest; and in the time of harvest I will say to the reapers, "Gather ye together first the tares, and bind them in bundles to burn them: but gather the wheat into my barn." ' "

Then Jesus sent the multitude away, and went into the house: and his disciples came unto him, saying, "Declare unto us the parable of the tares of the field."

He answered and said unto them, "He that soweth the good seed is the Son of Man; the field is the world; the good seed are the children of the kingdom; but the tares are the children of the wicked one; the enemy that sowed them is the devil; the harvest is the end of the world: and the reapers are the angels. As, therefore, the tares are gathered and burned in the fire; so shall it be in the end of this world. The Son of Man shall send forth his angels, and they shall gather out of his kingdom all things that offend, and them which do iniquity; and shall cast them into a furnace of fire: there shall be wailing and gnashing of teeth. Then shall the righteous shine forth as the sun in the kingdom of their Father. Who hath ears to hear, let him hear.

"Again, the kingdom of heaven is like unto treasure hid in a field; the which when a man hath found he hideth, and, for joy thereof, goeth and selleth all that he hath, and buyeth that field.

"Again, the kingdom of heaven is like unto a merchantman, seeking goodly pearls, who, when he had found one pearl of great price, went and sold all that he had, and bought it.

"Again, the kingdom of heaven is like unto a net, that was cast into the sea, and gathered of every kind: which, when it was full, they drew to shore, and sat down, and gathered the good into vessels, but cast the bad away. So shall it be at the end of the world: the angels shall come forth, and sever the wicked from among the just, and shall cast them into the furnace of fire: there shall be wailing and gnashing of teeth."

Jesus saith unto them, "Have ye understood all these things?"

They say unto him, "Yea, Lord."

Then said he unto them,

"Therefore every scribe which is instructed unto the kingdom of heaven is like unto a man that is an householder, which bringeth forth out of his treasure things new and old."

And he said, "So is the kingdom of God, as if a man should cast seed into the ground; and should sleep and rise night and day, and the seed should spring and grow up, he knoweth not how: for the earth bringeth forth fruit of herself; first the blade, then the ear, after that the full corn in the ear. But when the fruit is brought forth, immediately he putteth in the sickle, because the harvest is come."

And he said, "Whereunto shall we liken the kingdom of God? or with what comparison shall we compare it? It is like a grain of mustard seed, which, when it is sown in the earth, is less than all the seeds that be in the earth: But when it is sown, it groweth up, and becometh greater than all herbs, and shooteth out great branches; so that the fowls of the air may lodge under the shadow of it."

And with many such parables spake he the word unto them, as they were able to hear it. But without a parable spake he not unto them: and when they were alone, he expounded all things to his disciples.

And it came to pass, that, as they went in the way, a certain man said unto him, "Lord, I will follow thee whithersoever thou goest."

And Jesus said unto him, "Foxes have holes, and birds of the air have nests; but the Son of Man hath not where to lay his head."

And he said unto another, "Follow me."

But he said, "Lord, suffer me first to go and bury my father."

Jesus said unto him, "Let the dead bury their dead: but go thou and preach the kingdom of God."

And another also said, "Lord, I will follow thee: but let me first go bid them farewell, which are at home at my house."

And Jesus said unto him, "No man having put his hand to the plough, and looking back, is fit for the kingdom of God."

And after these things, he went forth, and saw a publican named Levi, sitting at the receipt of custom: and he said unto him, "follow me." And he left all, rose up, and followed him. And Levi made him a great feast in his own house; and many publicans and sinners sat also together with Jesus and his disciples: for there were many and they followed him. And when the scribes and Pharisees saw him eat with publicans and sinners, they said unto his disciples, "How is it that he eateth and drinketh with publicans and sinners?" When Jesus heard it, he saith unto them, "They that are whole have no need of the physician, but they that are sick. I came not to call the righteous, but sinners to repentance."

And he spake also a parable unto them, "No man putteth a piece of a new garment upon an old; if otherwise, then both the new maketh a rent, and the piece that was taken out of the new agreeth not with the old. And no man putteth new wine into old bottles; else the new wine will burst the bottles, and be spilled, and the bottles shall perish. But new wine must be put into new bottles; and both are preserved." And it came to pass, that when Jesus had finished these parables, he departed thence.

And when he was come into his own country, he taught them in their synagogue, insomuch that they were astonished, and said, "Whence hath this man this wisdom, and these mighty works? Is not this the carpenter's son? is not his mother called Mary? and his brethren, James, and Joses, and Simon, and Judas? And his sisters, are they not all with us? Whence then hath this man all these things?" And they were offended in him.

But Jesus said unto them, "A prophet is not without honour, save in his own country, and in his own house."

But when he saw the multitudes, he was moved with compassion on them, because they fainted, and were scattered abroad, as sheep having no shepherd.

And he calleth unto him the twelve, and began to send them forth by two and two; and commanded them, saying, "Go not into the way of the Gentiles, and into any city of the Samaritans enter ye not: but go rather to the lost sheep of the house of Israel. Provide neither gold, nor silver, nor brass in your purses; nor script for your journey, neither two coats, neither shoes, nor yet staves: for the workman is worthy of his meat. And into whatsoever city or town ye shall enter, enquire who in it is worthy; and there abide till ye go thence. And when ye come into an house, salute it; and if the house be worthy, let your peace come upon it: but if it be not worthy, let your peace return to you. And whosoever shall not receive you, nor hear your words, when ye depart out of that house, or city, shake off the dust of your feet. Verily I say unto you, 'It shall be more tolerable for the land of Sodom and Gomorrah, in the day of judgment, than for that city.'

"Behold, I send you forth as sheep in the midst of wolves: be ye, therefore, wise as serpents, and harmless as doves. But beware of men: for they will deliver you up to the councils, and they will scourge you in their synagogues: and ye shall be brought before governors and kings for my sake, for a testimony against them and the Gentiles. But when they persecute you in this city, flee ye into another: Fear them not, therefore: for there is nothing covered that shall not be revealed; and hid, that shall not be known.

"What I tell you in darkness, that speak ye in light: and what ye hear in the ear, that preach ye upon the housetops. And fear not them which kill the body, but are not able to kill the soul: but rather fear him which is able to destroy both soul and body in hell. Are not two sparrows sold for a farthing? and one of them shall not fall on the ground without your Father. But the very hairs of your head are all numbered. Fear ye not, therefore, ye are of more value than many sparrows." And they went out, and preached that men should repent.

And the apostles gathered themselves together unto Jesus, and told him all things, both what they had done, and what they had taught. . . .

TWO

"I am the good shepherd: the good shepherd giveth his life for the sheep. But he that is an hireling, and not the shepherd, whose own the sheep are not, seeth the wolf coming, and leaveth the sheep, and fleeth: and the wolf catcheth them, and scattereth the sheep. The hireling fleeth, because he is an hireling, and careth not for the sheep.

"I am the good shepherd, and know my sheep, and am known of mine. And other sheep I have, which are not of this fold: them also I must bring, and they shall hear my voice; and there shall be one fold, and one shepherd."

And, behold, a certain lawyer stood up, and tempted him, saying, "Master, what shall I do to inherit eternal life?"

He said unto him, "What is written in the law? how readest thou?"

And he answering said, "Thou shalt love the Lord thy God with all thy heart, and with all thy soul, and with all thy strength, and with all thy mind: and thy neighbour as thyself."

And he said unto him, "Thou hast answered right: this do, and thou shalt live."

But he, willing to justify himself, said unto Jesus, "And who is my neighbour?"

And Jesus, answering, said,

"A certain man went down from Jerusalem to Jericho, and fell among thieves, which stripped him of his raiment, and wounded him, and departed, leaving him half dead. And, by chance, there came down a certain priest that way; and when he saw him, he passed by on the other side. And likewise a Levite, when he was at the place, came and looked on him, and passed by on the other side. But a certain Samaritan, as he journeyed, came where he was: and when he saw him, he had compassion on him. And went to him, and bound up his wounds, pouring in oil and wine, and set him on his own beast, and brought him to an inn, and took care of him. And on the morrow, when he departed, he took out two pence, and gave them to the host, and said unto him, 'Take care of him: and whatsoever you spendest more, when I come again, I will repay thee.' Which now of these three thinkest thou was a neighbour unto him that fell among the thieves?"

And he said, "He that shewed mercy on him."

Then said Jesus unto him, "Go, and do thou likewise."

*　　*　　*

And it came to pass, that as he was praying in a certain place, when he ceased, one of his disciples said unto him, "Lord, teach us to pray, as John also taught his disciples."

And he said unto them, "When ye pray, say,

> *"Our Father which art in heaven,*
> *Hallowed be thy name.*
> *Thy kingdom come.*
> *Thy will be done,*
> *As in heaven,*
> *So in earth.*
>
> *Give us day by day*
> *Our daily bread.*
> *And forgive us our sins;*
> *For we also forgive every one that is indebted*
> *   to us.*
> *And lead us not into temptation,*
> *But deliver us from evil."*

And he said unto them,

"Which of you shall have a friend, and shall go unto him at midnight, and say unto him, 'Friend, lend me three loaves: for a friend of mine in his journey is come to me, and I have nothing to set before him'? And he from within shall answer, and say, 'Trouble me not: the door is now shut, and my children are with me in bed; I cannot rise and give thee.'

"I say unto you, 'Though he will not rise and give him, because he is his friend; yet because of his importunity he will rise and give him as many as he needeth.'

"And I say unto you, 'Ask, and it shall be given you, seek, and ye shall find: knock, and it shall be opened unto you. For every one that asketh, receiveth; and he that seeketh, findeth; and to him that knocketh, it shall be opened. If a son shall ask bread of any of you that is a father, will he give him a stone? or, if he ask a fish, will he for a fish give him a serpent? Or, if he shall ask an egg, will be offer him a scorpion? If ye then, being evil know how to give good gifts unto your children; how much more shall your heavenly Father give the Holy Spirit to them that ask him?' "

*   *   *

And it came to pass, as he went into the house of one of the chief Pharisees to eat bread on the sabbath-day, that they watched him. And, behold, there was a certain man before him, which had the dropsy. And Jesus, answering, spake unto the lawyers and Pharisees, saying, "Is it lawful to heal on the sabbath-day?" And they held their peace.

And he saith unto them, "Which of you shall have an ass or an ox fallen into a pit, and will not straightway pull him out on the sabbath-day?" And they could not answer him again to these things.

And he put forth a parable to those which were bidden, when he marked how they chose out the chief rooms; saying unto them,

"When thou are bidden of any man to a wedding, sit not down in the highest room; lest a more honourable man than thou be bidden of him, and he that bade thee and him come and say to thee, 'Give this man place,' and thou begin with shame to take the lowest room. But when thou art bidden, go and sit down in the lowest room; that when he that bade thee cometh, he may say unto thee, 'Friend, go up higher': then shalt thou have worship in the presence of them that sit at meat with thee: for whosoever exalteth himself shall be abased; and he that humbleth himself shall be exalted."

Then said he also to him that bade him,

"When thou makest a dinner or a supper, call not thy friends, nor thy brethren, neither thy kinsmen, nor thy rich neighbours; lest they also bid thee again, and a recompense be made thee. But when thou makest a feast, call the poor, the maimed, the lame, the blind: and thou shalt be blessed; for they cannot recompense thee: for thou shall be recompensed at the resurrection of the just."

Then said he unto him,

"A certain man made a great supper, and bade many: and sent his servant at supper-time to say to them that were bidden, 'Come, for all things are now ready.' And they all with one consent began to make excuse. The first said unto him, 'I have bought a piece of ground, and I must needs go and see it: I pray thee have me excused.' And another said, 'I have bought five yoke of oxen, and I go to prove them: I pray thee have me excused.' And another said, 'I have married a wife; and therefore I cannot come.' So that servant came, and shewed his lord these things. Then the master of the house, being angry, said to his servant, 'Go out quickly into the streets and lanes of the city, and bring in hither the poor, and the maimed, and the halt, and the blind.' And the servant said, 'Lord, it is done as thou hast commanded, and yet there is room.' And the lord said unto the servant, 'Go out into the highways and hedges, and compel them to come in, that my house may be filled. For I say unto you that none of those men which were bidden shall taste of my supper.'

"For which of you, intending to build a tower, sitteth not down first, and counteth the cost, whether he have sufficient to finish it? lest haply, after he hath laid the foundation, and is not able to finish it, all that behold it begin to mock him, saying, 'This man began to build, and was not able to finish.' Or what king, going to make war against another king, sitteth not down first, and consulteth whether he be able with ten thousand to meet him that cometh against him with twenty thousand? Or else, while the other is yet a great way off, he sendeth an ambassage, and desireth conditions of peace."

*   *   *

Then drew near unto him all the publicans and sinners for to hear him. And the Pharisees and scribes murmured, saying, "This man receiveth sinners, and eateth with them."

And he spake this parable unto them, saying,

"What man of you, having an hundred sheep, if he lose one of them, doth not leave the ninety and nine in the wilderness, and go after that which is lost, until he find it? And when he hath found it, he layeth it on his shoulders, rejoicing. And when he cometh home, he calleth together his friends and neighbours, saying unto them, 'Rejoice with me; for I have found my sheep which was lost.' I say unto you, that likewise joy shall be in heaven over one sinner that repenteth, more than over ninety and nine just persons, which need no repentance.

"Either what woman, having ten pieces of silver, if she lost one piece, doth not light a candle, and sweep the house, and seek diligently till she find it? And when she hath found it, she calleth her friends and her neighbours together, saying, 'Rejoice with me; for I have found the piece which I had lost.' Likewise, I say unto you, there is joy in the presence of the angels of God, over one sinner that repenteth."

And he said,

"A certain man had two sons: and the younger of them said to his father, 'Father, give me the portion of goods that falleth to me.' And he divided unto them his living. And not many days after the younger son gathered all together, and took his journey into a far country, and there wasted his substance with riotous living. And when he had spent all, there arose a mighty famine in that land; and he began to be in want. And he went and joined himself to a citizen of that country; and he sent him into his fields to feed swine. And he would fain have filled his belly with the husks that the swine did eat: and no man gave unto him.

"And when he came to himself, he said, 'How many hired servants of my father's have bread enough, and to spare, and I perish with hunger! I will arise, and go to my father, and will say unto him, "Father, I have sinned against heaven, and before thee, and am no more worthy to be called thy son: make me as one of thy hired servants." '

"And he arose, and came to his father. But, when he was yet a great way off, his father saw him, and had compassion, and ran, and fell on his neck, and kissed him. And the son said unto him, 'Father, I have sinned against heaven, and in thy sight, and am no more worthy to be called thy son.' But the father said to his servants, 'Bring forth the best robe, and put it on him; and put a ring on his hand, and shoes on his feet: and bring hither the fatted calf, and kill it; and let us eat, and be merry: for this my son was dead, and is alive again; he was lost, and is found.' And they began to be merry.

"Now, his elder son was in the field: and as he came and drew nigh to the house, he heard music and dancing. And he called one of the servants, and asked what these things meant. And he said unto him, 'Thy brother is come; and thy father hath killed the fatted calf, because he hath received him safe and sound.' And he was angry, and would not go in: therefore came his father out, and entreated him. And he, answering, said to his father, 'Lo, these many years do I serve thee, neither transgressed I at any time thy commandment; and yet thou never gavest me a kid, that I might make merry with my friends: but as soon as this thy son was come, which hath devoured thy living with harlots, thou has killed for him the fatted calf.' And he said unto him, 'Son, thou art ever with me, and all that I have is thine. It was meet that we should make merry, and be glad: for this thy brother was dead, and is alive again; and was lost, and is found.'"

Of the unjust steward.

And he said also unto his disciples,

"There was a certain rich man, which had a steward; and the same was accused unto him that he had wasted his goods. And he called him, and said unto him, 'How is it that I hear this of thee? give an account of thy stewardship; for thou mayest be no longer steward.' Then the steward said within himself, 'What shall I do, for my lord taketh away from me the stewardship? I cannot dig; to beg I am ashamed. I am resolved what to do, that, when I am put out of the stewardship, they may receive me into their houses.' So he called every one of his lord's debtors unto him, and said unto the first, 'How much owest thou unto my lord?' And he said, 'An hundred measures of oil.' And he said unto him, 'Take thy bill, and sit down quickly, and write fifty.' Then said he to another, 'And how much owest thou?' And he said, 'An hundred measures of wheat.' And he said unto him, 'Take thy bill, and write fourscore.' And the lord commended the unjust steward, because he had done wisely: for the children of this world are in their generation wiser than the children of light. And I say unto you, 'Make to yourselves friends of the mammon of unrighteousness; that, when ye fail, they may receive you into everlasting habitations. He that is faithful in that which is least, is faithful also in much; and he that is unjust in the least, is unjust also in much. If, therefore, ye have not been faithful in the unrighteous mammon, who will commit to your trust the true riches? And if ye have not been faithful in that which is another man's, who shall give you that which is your own?'

"No servant can serve two masters: for either he will hate the one, and love the other; or else he will hold to the one, and despise the other. Ye cannot serve God and mammon."

And the Pharisees also, who were covetous, heard all these things: and they derided him. And he said unto them,

"Ye are they which justify yourselves before men; but God knoweth your hearts: for that which is highly esteemed among men is abomination in the sight of God."

* * *

"Whosoever putteth away his wife, and marrieth another, committeth adultery: and whosoever marrieth her that is put away from her husband, committeth adultery.

"There was a certain rich man, which was clothed in purple and fine linen, and fared sumptuously every day: and there was a certain beggar, named Lazarus, which was laid at his gate full of sores, and desiring to be fed with the crumbs which fell from the rich man's table: moreover, the dogs came and licked his sores. And it came to pass, that the beggar died, and was carried by the angels into Abraham's bosom: the rich man also died, and was buried; and in hell he lifted up his eyes, being in torments, and seeth Abraham afar off, and Lazarus in his bosom.

"And he cried, and said, 'Father Abraham, have mercy on me; and send Lazarus, that he may dip the tip of his finger in water, and cool my tongue; for I am tormented in this flame.' But Abraham said, 'Son, remember that thou in thy life time receivedst thy good things, and likewise Lazarus evil things: but now he is comforted, and thou art tormented. And, besides all this, between us and you there is a great gulf fixed: so that they which would pass from hence to you cannot; neither can they pass to us, that would come from thence.'

"Then he said, 'I pray thee, therefore, father, that thou wouldest send him to my father's house: for I have five brethren; that he may testify unto them, lest they also come into this place of torment.' Abraham saith unto him, 'They have Moses and the prophets: let them hear them.'

"And he said, 'Nay, Father Abraham: but if one went unto them from the dead, they will repent.' And he said unto him, 'If they hear not Moses and the prophets, neither will they be persuaded though one rose from the dead.' "

To avoid giving offence.

Then said he unto the disciples,

"It is impossible but that offences will come: but woe unto him through whom they come. It were better for him that a mill-stone were hanged about his neck, and he cast into the sea, than that he should offend one of these little ones. Take heed to yourselves: if thy brother trespass against thee, rebuke him; and if he repent, forgive him. And if he trespass against thee seven times in a day, and seven times in a day turn again to thee, saying, 'I repent'; thou shalt forgive him.

"But which of you having a servant plowing, or feeding cattle, will say unto him by and by, when he is come from the field, 'Go and sit down to meat'? and will not rather say unto him, 'Make ready wherewith I may sup, and gird thyself, and serve me, till I have eaten and drunken; and afterward thou shalt eat and drink'? Doth he thank that servant because he did the things that were commanded him? I trow not. So likewise ye, when ye shall have done all those things which are commanded you, say, 'We are unprofitable servants: we have done that which was our duty to do.' "

And when he was demanded of the Pharisees, when the kingdom of

God should come, he answered them, and said, "The kingdom of God cometh not with observation."

"And as it was in the days of Noe, so shall it be also in the days of the Son of Man: they did eat, they drank, they married wives, they were given in marriage, until the day that Noe entered into the ark; and the flood came, and destroyed them all. Likewise also, as it was in the days of Lot, they did eat, they drank, they bought, they sold, they planted, they builded: but the same day that Lot went out of Sodom, it rained fire and brimstone from heaven, and destroyed them all. Even thus shall it be in the day when the Son of Man is revealed. In that day, he which shall be upon the house-top, and his stuff in the house, let him not come down to take it away: and he that is in the field, let him likewise not return back. Remember Lot's wife.

"Whosoever shall seek to save his life shall lose it; and whosoever shall lose his life shall preserve it. I tell you, in that night there shall be two men in one bed; the one shall be taken, and the other shall be left. Two women shall be grinding together; the one shall be taken, and the other left. Two men shall be in the field; the one shall be taken, and the other left."

The importunate widow.

And he spake a parable unto them, to this end, that men ought always to pray, and not to faint, saying,

"There was in a city a judge, which feared not God, neither regarded man: And there was a widow in that city; and she came unto him, saying, 'Avenge me of mine adversary.' And he would not for a while: but afterward he said within himself, 'Though I fear not God, nor regard man; yet, because this widow troubleth me, I will avenge her, lest by her continual coming she weary me.' And the Lord said, 'Hear what the unjust judge saith.' And shall not God avenge his own elect, which cry day and night unto him, though he bear long with them? I tell you, that he will avenge them speedily. Nevertheless, when the Son of Man cometh, shall he find faith on the earth?"

And he spake this parable unto certain which trusted in themselves, that they were righteous, and despised others:

"Two men went up into the temple to pray; the one a Pharisee, and the other a publican. The Pharisee stood and prayed thus with himself, 'God, I thank thee, that I am not as other men are, extortioners, unjust, adulterers, or even as this publican. I fast twice in the week, I give tithes of all that I possess.' And the publican, standing afar off, would not lift up so much as his eyes unto heaven, but smote upon his breast, saying, 'God be merciful to me a sinner.' I tell you, this man went down to his house justified rather than the other: for every one that exalteth himself shall be abased: and he that humbleth himself shall be exalted."

*   *   *

Now it came to pass, as they went, that he entered into a certain village: and a certain woman, named Martha, received him into her house. And she had a sister called Mary, which also sat at Jesus' feet, and heard his word. But Martha was cumbered about much serving, and came to him and said, "Lord, dost thou not care that my sister hath left me to serve alone? Bid her, therefore, that she help me."

And Jesus, answered, and said unto her, "Martha, Martha, thou art careful, and troubled about many things: but one thing is needful: and Mary hath chosen that good part which shall not be taken away from her." . . .

THREE

The labourers in the vineyard.

"For the kingdom of heaven is like unto a man that is an householder, which went out early in the morning to hire labourers into his vineyard. And when he had agreed with the labourers for a penny a day, he sent them into his vineyard. And he went out about the third hour, and saw others standing idle in the market-place, and said unto them, 'Go ye also into the vineyard: and whatsoever is right I will give you.' And they went their way. Again he went out about the sixth and ninth hour, and did likewise. And about the eleventh hour he went out, and found others standing idle, and saith unto them, 'Why stand ye here all the day idle?'

"They say unto him, 'Because no man hath hired us.'

"He saith unto them, 'Go ye also into the vineyard; and whatsoever is right, that shall ye receive.'

"So when even was come, the Lord of the vineyard saith unto his steward, 'Call the labourers, and give them their hire, beginning from the last unto the first.' And when they came that were hired about the eleventh hour, they received every man a penny. But when the first came, they supposed that they should have received more; and they likewise received every man a penny. And when they had received it, they murmured against the good man of the house, saying,

" 'These last have wrought but one hour, and thou hast made them equal unto us, which have borne the burden and heat of the day.'

"But he answered one of them, and said,

" 'Friend, I do thee no wrong: didst not thou agree with me for a penny? Take that thine is, and go thy way: I will give unto this last, even as unto thee. Is it not lawful for me to do what I will with mine own? is thine eye evil because I am good?' So the last shall be first, and the first last: for many be called, but few chosen."

The publican Zaccheus.

And Jesus entered and passed through Jericho. And, behold, there was a man named Zaccheus, which was the chief among the publicans, and he was rich. And he sought to see Jesus who he was: and could not for the press, because he was little of stature. And he ran before, and climbed up into a sycamore-tree to see him; for he was to pass that way. And, when Jesus came to the place, he looked up, and saw him, and said unto him,

"Zaccheus, make haste, and come down; for today I must abide at thy house." And he made haste, and came down, and received him joyfully. And when they saw it, they all murmured, saying, that he was gone to be guest with a man that is a sinner.

And Zaccheus stood, and said unto the Lord,

"Behold, Lord, the half of my goods I give to the poor; and if I have taken any thing from any man by false accusation, I restore him fourfold."

And Jesus said unto him,

"This day is salvation come to this house, forasmuch as he also is a son of Abraham. For the Son of Man is come to seek and to save that which was lost."

And, as they heard these things, he added, and spake a parable, because he was nigh to Jerusalem, and because they thought that the kingdom of God should immediately appear. He said, therefore,

"A certain nobleman went into a far country to receive for himself a kingdom, and to return. And he called his ten servants, and delivered them ten pounds, and said unto them, 'Occupy till I come.' But his citizens hated him and sent a message after him, saying, 'We will not have this man to reign over us.'

"And it came to pass, that when he was returned, having received the kingdom, then he commanded these servants to be called unto him, to whom he had given the money, that he might know how much every man had gained by trading.

"Then came the first, saying, 'Lord, thy pound hath gained ten pounds.'

"And he said unto him, 'Well, thou good servant; because thou hast been faithful in a very little, have thou authority over ten cities.'

"And the second came, saying, 'Lord, thy pound hath gained five pounds.'

"And he said likewise to him, 'Be thou also over five cities.'

"And another came, saying, 'Lord, behold, here is thy pound which I have kept laid up in a napkin: for I feared thee, because thou art an austere man; thou takest up that thou layedst not down, and reapest that thou didst not sow.'

"And he saith unto him, 'Out of thine own mouth will I judge thee, thou wicked servant. Thou knewest that I was an austere man, taking up that I laid not down, and reaping that I did not sow: Wherefore then gavest not thou my money into the bank, that at my coming I might have required mine own with usury?'

"And he said unto them that stood by, 'Take from him the pound, and give it to him that hath ten pounds.' "

(And they said unto him, "Lord, he hath ten pounds.")

"For I say unto you that unto every one which hath, shall be given; and from him that hath not, even that he hath, shall be taken away from him. But those mine enemies, which would not that I should reign over them, bring hither, and slay them before me."

And when he had thus spoken, he went before, ascending up to Jerusalem.

*   *   *

And when they drew nigh unto Jerusalem, and were come to Bethpage, unto the mount of Olives, then sent Jesus two disciples, saying unto them,

"Go into the village over against you, and straightway ye shall find an ass tied, and a colt with her: loose them, and bring them unto me. And if any man say aught unto you, ye shall say, 'The Lord hath need of them'; and straightway he will send them." And the disciples went, and did as Jesus commanded them, and brought the ass, and the colt, and put on them their clothes and they set him thereon.

And a very great multitude spread their garments in the way, others cut down branches from the trees, and strewed them in the way. And when he was come into Jerusalem, all the city was moved, saying, "Who is this?"

The Pharisees, therefore, said among themselves, "Perceive ye how ye prevail nothing? behold, the world is gone after him."

And there were certain Greeks among them, that came up to worship at the feast: the same came, therefore, to Philip, which was of Bethsaida of Galilee, and desired him, saying, "Sir, we would see Jesus." Philip cometh and telleth Andrew; and again, Andrew and Philip tell Jesus.

And Jesus answered them, saying,

"Verily, verily, I say unto you, except a corn of wheat fall into the ground and die, it abideth alone: but if it die, it bringeth forth much fruit."

And he left them, and went out of the city into Bethany; and he lodged there.

And on the morrow, when they were come from Bethany, Jesus went into the temple, and began to cast out them that sold and bought in the temple, and overthrew the tables of the money-changers, and the seats of them that sold doves; and would not suffer that any man should carry any vessel through the temple. And he taught, saying unto them,

"Is it not written, 'My house shall be called of all nations the house of prayer'? but ye have made it a den of thieves." And the scribes and chief priests heard it, and sought how they might destroy him: for they feared him, because all the people was astonished at his doctrine.

And when even was come he went out of the city.

And they come again to Jerusalem: and as he was walking in the temple, there came to him the chief priests, and the scribes, and the elders.

And he said unto them,

"But what think ye, A certain man had two sons; and he came to the first, and said, 'Son, go work today in my vineyard.' He answered and said, 'I will not': but afterward he repented, and went. And he came to the second, and said likewise. And he answered and said, 'I go, sir': and went not. Whether of them twain did the will of his father?"

They say unto him, "The first."

Jesus saith unto them, "Verily I say unto you that, the publicans and the harlots go into the kingdom of God before you."

* * *

Hear another parable:

"A certain man planted a vineyard, and set an hedge about it, and digged a place for the wine-fat, and built a tower, and let it out to husbandmen, and went into a far country. And at the season he sent to the husbandmen a servant, that he might receive from the husbandmen of the fruit of the vineyard. And they caught him, and beat him, and sent him away empty. And again he sent unto them another servant; and at him they cast stones, and wounded him in the head, and sent him away shamefully handled. And again he sent another; and him they killed, and many others; beating some, and killing some.

"Having yet, therefore, one son, his well-beloved, he sent him also last unto them, saying, 'They will reverence my son.' But those husbandmen said among themselves, 'This is the heir; come, let us kill him, and the inheritance shall be ours.' And they took him, and killed him, and cast him out of the vineyard.

"What shall, therefore, the lord of the vineyard do? He will come and destroy the husbandmen, and will give the vineyard unto others."

And when the chief priests and Pharisees had heard his parables, they perceived that he spake of them. But when they sought to lay hands on him, they feared the multitude, because they took him for a prophet.

And Jesus answered, and spake unto them again by parables, and said,

"The kingdom of heaven is like unto a certain king, which made a marriage for his son, and sent forth his servants to call them that were bidden to the wedding; and they would not come. Again, he sent forth other servants, saying, 'Tell them which are bidden, "Behold, I have prepared my dinner: my oxen and my fatlings are killed, and all things are ready: come unto the marriage." ' But they made light of it, and went their ways, one to his farm, another to his merchandise: and the remnant took his servants, and intreated them spitefully, and slew them. But when the king heard thereof, he was wroth: and he sent forth his armies, and destroyed those murderers, and burnt up their city.

"Then saith he to his servants, 'The wedding is ready, but they which were bidden were not worthy. Go ye therefore into the highways, and, as many as ye shall find, bid to the marriage.' So those servants went out into the highways, and gathered together all as many as they found, both bad and good: and the wedding was furnished with guests.

"And when the king came in to see the guests, he saw there a man which had not on a wedding garment: and he saith unto him, 'Friend, how camest thou in hither, not having a wedding garment?' And he was speechless. Then saith the king to the servants, 'Bind him hand and foot, and take him away, and cast him into outer darkness; there shall be weeping and gnashing of teeth: for many are called, but few are chosen.'"

Then went the Pharisees, and took counsel how they might entangle him in his talk. And they sent out unto him their disciples, with the Herodians, saying,

"Master, we know that thou are true, and teachest the way of God in truth, neither carest thou for any man: for thou regardest not the person of men. Tell us, therefore, what thinkest thou? Is it lawful to give tribute unto Cesar, or not?"

But Jesus perceived their wickedness, and said, "Why tempt ye me, ye hypocrites? Shew me the tribute-money."

And they brought unto him a penny. And he saith unto them, "Whose is this image and superscription?"

They say unto him, "Cesar's."

Then saith he unto them, "Render, therefore, unto Cesar the things which are Cesar's; and unto God the things that are God's."

When they heard these words, they marvelled, and left him, and went their way.

The same day came to him the Sadducees, which say that there is no resurrection, and asked him, saying, "Master, Moses said, 'If a man die, having no children, his brother shall marry his wife, and raise up seed unto his brother.' Now, there were with us seven brethren: and the first when he had married a wife, deceased; and having no issue, left his wife unto his brother: likewise the second also, and the third, unto the seventh. And last of all the woman died also. Therefore, in the resurrection, whose wife shall she be of the seven? for they all had her."

Jesus answered, and said unto them,

"Ye do err, not knowing the scriptures, nor the power of God. For in the resurrection they neither marry, nor are given in marriage: but are as the angels of God in heaven. But as touching the resurrection of the dead, have ye not read that which was spoken unto you by God, saying, 'I am the God of Abraham, and the God of Isaac, and the God of Jacob'? God is not the God of the dead, but of the living."

And when the multitude heard this, they were astonished at his doctrine.

And one of the scribes came, and having heard them reasoning together, and perceiving that he had answered them well, asked him, "Which is the first commandment of all?"

And Jesus answered him,

"The first of all the commandments is, 'Hear, O Israel: The Lord our God is one Lord: and thou shalt love the Lord thy God with all thy heart, and with all thy soul, and with all thy mind, and with all thy strength.' This is the first commandment.

"And the second is like, namely this: 'Thou shalt love thy neighbour as thyself.'

"There is none other commandment greater than these.

"On these two commandments hang all the law and the prophets."

And the scribe said unto him, "Well, Master, thou hast said the truth: for there is one God; and there is none other but he: and to love him with all the heart, and with all the understanding, and with all the soul, and with all the strength, and to love his neighbour as himself, is more than all whole burnt-offerings and sacrifices."

The Pharisees exposed.

Then spake Jesus to the multitude, and to his disciples saying,

"The scribes and the Pharisees sit in Moses' seat: all therefore whatsoever they bid you observe, that observe and do; but do not ye after their works: for they say and do not. For they bind heavy burdens and grievous to be borne, and lay them on men's shoulders; but they themselves will not move them with one of their fingers. But all their works they do for to be seen of men: they make broad their phylacteries, and enlarge the borders of their garments, and love the uppermost rooms at feasts, and the chief seats in the synagogues, and greetings in the markets, and to be called of men, Rabbi, Rabbi.

"But be not ye called Rabbi; for one is your Master, even Christ; and all ye are brethren. And call no man your Father upon the earth: for one is your Father, which is in heaven. Neither be ye called masters: for one is your master, even Christ. But he that is greatest among you shall be your servant. And whosoever shall exalt himself shall be abased; and he that shall humble himself shall be exalted.

"But woe unto you, scribes and Pharisees, hypocrites; for ye shut up the kingdom of heaven against men: for ye neither go in your selves; neither suffer ye them that are entering, to go in.

"Woe unto you, scribes and Pharisees, hypocrites! for ye devour widows' houses, and for a pretence make long prayer: therefore ye shall receive the greater damnation.

"Woe unto you, scribes and Pharisees, hypocrites! for ye compass sea and land to make one proselyte; and when he is made, ye make him twofold more the child of hell than yourselves.

"Woe unto you, ye blind guides! which say, 'Whosoever shall swear by the temple, it is nothing; but whosoever shall swear by the gold of the temple, he is a debtor.' Ye fools and blind! for whether is greater, the gold, or the temple that sanctifieth the gold? And, 'whosoever shall swear by the altar, it is nothing; but whosoever sweareth by the gift that is upon it, he is guilty.' Ye fools, and blind! for whether is greater, the gift, or the altar that sanctifieth the gift? Whoso, therefore, shall swear by the altar, sweareth by it, and by all things thereon. And whoso shall swear by the temple, sweareth by it, and by him that dwelleth therein. And he that shall swear by heaven, sweareth by the throne of God, and by him that sitteth thereon.

"Woe unto you, scribes and Pharisees, hypocrites! for ye pay tithe of mint, and anise, and cummin, and have omitted the weightier matters of the law, judgment, mercy, and faith: these ought ye to have done, and not to leave the other undone. Ye blind guides! which strain at a gnat, and swallow a camel.

"Woe unto you, scribes and Pharisees, hypocrites! for ye make clean the outside of the cup and of the platter, but within they are full of extortion and excess. Thou blind Pharisee, cleanse first that which is within the cup and platter, that the outside of them may be clean also.

"Woe unto you, scribes and Pharisees, hypocrites! for ye are like unto whited sepulchres, which indeed appear beautiful outward, but are within full of dead men's bones, and of all uncleanness. Even so ye also outwardly appear righteous unto men, but within ye are full of hypocrisy and iniquity.

"Woe unto you, scribes and Pharisees, hypocrites! because ye build the tombs of the prophets, and garnish the sepulchres of the righteous. And say, 'If we had been in the days of our fathers, we would not have been partakers with them in the blood of the prophets.' Wherefore ye be witnesses unto yourselves, that ye are the children of them which killed the prophets. Fill ye up then the measure of your fathers. Ye serpents, ye generation of vipers! how can ye escape the damnation of hell?"

* * *

And Jesus sat over against the treasury, and beheld how the people cast money into the treasury; and many that were rich cast in much: And there came a certain poor widow and she threw in two mites, which make a farthing. And he called unto him his disciples, and saith unto them,

"Verily, I say unto you that this poor widow hath cast more in than all they which have cast into the treasury: for all they did cast in of their abundance; but she of her want did cast in all that she had, even all her living."

FOUR

Jerusalem's destruction foretold.

And Jesus went out, and departed from the temple; and his disciples came to him, for to shew him the buildings of the temple. And Jesus said unto them,

"See ye not all these things? Verily I say unto you, 'There shall not be left here one stone upon another, that shall not be thrown down.'

"Then let them which be in Judea flee into the mountains: let him which is on the house-top not come down to take anything out of his house: neither let him which is in the field return back to take his clothes. And woe unto them that are with child, and to them that give suck in those days! But pray ye that your flight be not in the winter, neither on the sabbath-day: for then shall be great tribulations, such as was not since the beginning of the world to this time, no, nor ever shall be.

"Immediately after the tribulation of those days shall the sun be darkened, and the moon shall not give her light, and the stars shall fall from heaven, and the powers of the heavens shall be shaken.

"Now learn a parable of the fig-tree; when his branch is yet tender, and putteth forth leaves, ye know that summer is nigh: so likewise ye, when ye shall see all these things, know that it is near, even at the doors.

"But of that day and hour knoweth no man, no, not the angels of heaven, but my Father only. But as the days of Noe were, so shall also the coming of the Son of Man be. For in the days that were before the flood they were eating and drinking, marrying and giving in marriage, until the day that Noe entered into the ark, and knew not until the flood came, and took them all away; then shall two be in the field; the one shall be taken, and the other left. Two women shall be grinding at the mill; the one shall be taken, and the other left.

"Watch, therefore: for ye know not what hour your Lord doth come. But know this, that if the good man of the house had known in what watch the thief would come, he would have watched, and would not have suffered his house to be broken up. Therefore be ye also ready. Who then is a faithful and wise servant, whom his lord hath made ruler over his household, to give them meat in due season? Blessed is that servant, whom his lord, when he cometh, shall find so doing. Verily I say unto you that he shall make him ruler over all his goods. But and if that evil servant shall say in his heart, 'My lord delayeth his coming'; and shall begin to smite his fellow-servants, and to eat and drink with the drunken, the lord of that servant shall come in a day when he looketh not for him, and in an hour that he is not aware of, and shall cut him asunder and appoint him his portion with the hypocrites: there shall be weeping and gnashing of teeth."

Parable of the ten virgins.

"Then shall the kingdom of heaven be likened unto ten virgins, which took their lamps and went forth to meet the bridegroom. And five of them were wise, and five were foolish. They that were foolish took their lamps, and took no oil with them: but the wise took oil in their vessels with their lamps. While the bridegroom tarried, they all slumbered and slept. And at midnight there was a cry made, 'Behold, the bridegroom cometh: go ye out to meet him.' Then all those virgins arose, and trimmed their lamps. And the foolish said unto the wise, 'Give us of your oil; for our lamps are gone out.' But the wise answered, saying, 'Not so: lest there be not enough for us and you: but go ye rather to them that sell, and buy for yourselves.' And while they went to buy, the bridegroom came: and they that were ready went in with him to the marriage; and the door was shut. Afterward came also the other virgins, saying, 'Lord, Lord, open to us.' But he answered and said, 'Verily I say unto you, "I know you not." ' Watch therefore.

"For the kingdom of heaven is as a man traveling into a far country, who called his own servants, and delivered unto them his goods. And unto one he gave five talents, to another two, and to another one; to every man according to his several ability; and straightway took his journey. Then he that had received the five talents went and traded with the same, and made them other five talents. And likewise he that had received two, he also gained other two. But he that had received one, went and digged in the earth, and hid his lord's money. After a long time the lord of those servants cometh, and reckoneth with them.

"And so he that had received five talents came, and brought other five talents, saying, 'Lord, thou deliveredst unto me five talents: Behold, I have gained beside them five talents more.' His lord said unto him, 'Well done, thou good and faithful servant: thou hast been faithful over a few things, I will make thee ruler over many things: enter thou into the joy of thy lord.'

"He also that had received two talents came, and said, 'Lord, thou deliveredst unto me two talents: behold, I have gained two other talents beside them.' His lord said unto him, 'Well done, good and faithful servant: thou hast been faithful over a few things, I will make thee ruler over many things: enter thou into the joy of thy lord.'

"Then he which had received the one talent came, and said, 'Lord, I knew thee, that thou art an hard man, reaping where thou hast not sown, and gathering where thou hast not strawed: and I was afraid, and went and hid thy talent in the earth: lo, there thou hast that is thine.'

"His lord answered, and said unto him, 'Thou wicked and slothful servant, thou knewest that I reap where I sowed not, and gather where I have not strawed: thou oughtest, therefore, to have put my money to the exchangers, and then at my coming I should have received mine own with usury.'

" 'Take therefore the talent from him, and give it unto him which hath ten talents. For unto every one that hath shall be given, and he shall have abundance: but from him that hath not, shall be taken away even that which he hath. And cast ye the unprofitable servant into outer darkness: there shall be weeping and gnashing of teeth.'

"And take heed to yourselves, lest at any time your hearts be overcharged with surfeiting, and drunkenness, and cares of this life, and so that day come upon you unawares. For as a snare shall it come on all them that dwell on the face of the whole earth. Watch ye, therefore, and pray always, that ye may be accounted worthy to escape all these things that shall come to pass, and to stand before the Son of Man. . . ."

Conspiracy against Christ.

After two days was the feast of the passover, and of unleavened bread: and the chief priests and the scribes sought how they might take him by craft, and put him to death. But they said, "Not on the feast day, lest there be an uproar of the people."

And being in Bethany, in the house of Simon the leper, as he sat at meat, there came a woman having an alabaster-box of ointment of spikenard, very precious; and she brake the box, and poured it on his head. And there were some that had indignation within themselves, and said, "Why was this waste of the ointment made? For it might have been sold for more than three hundred pence, and have been given to the poor."

And they murmured against her. And Jesus said,

"Let her alone, why trouble ye her? she hath wrought a good work on me. For ye have the poor with you always, and whensoever ye will, ye may do them good; but me ye have not always. She hath done what she could; she is come aforehand to anoint my body to the burying."

Then one of the twelve called Judas Iscariot, went unto the chief priests, and said unto them, "What will ye give me, and I will deliver him unto you?" And they covenanted with him for thirty pieces of silver. And from that time he sought opportunity to betray him.

Now, the first day of the feast of unleavened bread, the disciples came to Jesus, saying unto him, "Where wilt thou that we prepare for thee to eat the passover?"

And he said, "Go into the city to such a man, and say unto him, 'The Master saith, "My time is at hand, I will keep the passover at thy house with my disciples." ' "

And the disciples did as Jesus had appointed them; and they made ready the passover.

Now, when the even was come, he sat down with the twelve.

And there was also a strife among them, which of them should be accounted the greatest. And he said unto them,

"The kings of the Gentiles exercise lordship over them; and they that exercise authority upon them are called benefactors. But ye shall not be so: but he that is greatest among you, let him be as the younger; and he that is chief, as he that doth serve. For whether is greater, he that sitteth at meat, or he that serveth? is not he that sitteth at meat? but I am among you as he that serveth."

And supper being ended he riseth from supper, and laid aside his garments; and took a towel, and girded himself. After that he poureth water into a basin, and began to wash the disciples' feet, and to wipe them with the towel wherewith he was girded. Then cometh he to Simon Peter: and Peter saith unto him, "Lord, dost thou wash my feet?" Jesus answered, and said unto him, "What I do, thou knowest not now; but thou shalt know hereafter." Peter saith unto him, "Thou shalt never wash my feet." Jesus answered him, "If I wash thee not, thou hast no part with me." Simon Peter saith unto him, "Lord, not my feet only, but also my hands and my head." Jesus saith to him, "He that is washed, needeth not, save to wash his feet, but is clean every whit: and ye are clean, but not all." For he knew who should betray him; therefore said he, "Ye are not all clean." So, after he had washed their feet, and had taken his garments, and was set down again, he said unto them, "Know ye what I have done unto you? Ye call me Master and Lord: and ye say well; for so I am. If I then, your Lord and Master, have washed your feet, ye also ought to wash one another's feet. For I have given you an example, that ye should do as I have done to you. Verily, verily, I say unto you, 'The servant is not greater than his lord: neither he that is sent, greater than he that sent him.' If ye know these things, happy are ye if ye do them."

When Jesus had thus said, he was troubled in spirit, and testified, and said, "Verily, verily, I say unto you that one of you shall betray me."

Then the disciples looked one on another, doubting of whom he spake. Now there was leaning on Jesus' bosom one of his disciples, whom Jesus loved. Simon Peter, therefore, beckoned to him, that he should ask who it should be of whom he spake. He then, lying on Jesus' breast, saith unto him, "Lord, who is it?"

Jesus answered, "He it is, to whom I shall give a sop, when I have dipped it." And when he had dipped the sop, he gave it to Judas Iscariot, the son of Simon.

*   *   *

Therefore, when he was gone out, Jesus said,

"A new commandment I give unto you: that ye love one another; as I have loved you, that ye also love one another.

"By this shall all men know that ye are my disciples, if ye have love one to another."

Then saith Jesus unto them, "All ye shall be offended because of me this night."

Peter answered, and said unto him, "Though all men shall be offended because of thee, yet will I never be offended. I am ready to go with thee, both into prison, and to death."

And he said, "I tell thee, Peter, 'The cock shall not crow this day, before that thou shalt thrice deny that thou knowest me.'"

Peter said unto him, "Though I should die with thee, yet will I not deny thee." Likewise also said all the disciples.

Then cometh Jesus with them unto a place called Gethsemane, and saith unto the disciples, "Sit ye here, while I go and pray yonder." And he took with him Peter and the two sons of Zebedee, and began to be sorrowful and very heavy. Then saith he unto them, "My soul is exceeding sorrowful, even unto death: tarry ye here, and watch with me." And he went a little farther, and fell on his face, and prayed saying, "Oh my Father, if it be possible, let this cup pass from me: nevertheless, not as I will, but as thou wilt." And he cometh unto the disciples, and findeth them asleep, and saith unto Peter, "What! could ye not watch with me one hour? Watch and pray, that ye enter not into temptation: the spirit indeed is willing, but the flesh is weak." He went away again the second time, and prayed, saying, "O my Father, if this cup may not pass away from me, except I drink it, thy will be done." And he came and found them asleep again: for their eyes were heavy. And he left them, and went away again, and prayed the third time, saying the same words. Then cometh he to his disciples, and saith unto them, "Sleep on now, and take your rest."

Judas betrayeth Jesus.

When Jesus had spoken these words, he went forth with his disciples over the brook Cedron, where was a garden, into the which he entered, and his disciples. And Judas also, which betrayed him, knew the place: for Jesus oft-times resorted thither with his disciples. Judas then, having received a band of men and officers from the chief priests and Pharisees, cometh thither with lanterns, and torches, and weapons.

Now he that betrayeth him gave them a sign, saying, "Whomsoever I shall kiss, that same is he: hold him fast." And forthwith he came to Jesus, and said, "Hail, Master," and kissed him.

And Jesus said unto him, "Friend, wherefore art thou come?"

Jesus, therefore, knowing all things that should come upon him, went forth, and said unto them, "Whom seek ye?"

They answered him, "Jesus of Nazareth."

Jesus saith unto them, "I am he." (And Judas also, which betrayed him, stood with them.) As soon then as he had said unto them, "I am he," they went backward, and fell to the ground. Then asked he them again, "Whom seek ye?" And they said, "Jesus of Nazareth." Jesus answered, "I have told you, that I am he: if, therefore, ye seek me, let these go their way."

Then came they and laid hands on Jesus, and took him. And, behold, one of them, which were with Jesus, stretched out his hand, and drew his sword, and struck a servant of the high priest, and smote off his ear. Then said Jesus unto him, "Put up again thy sword into his place: for all they that take the sword shall perish with the sword."

In that same hour said Jesus to the multitudes, "Are ye come out as against a thief, with swords, and staves for to take me? I sat daily with you teaching in the temple, and ye laid no hold on me." Then all the disciples forsook him and fled.

And there followed him a certain young man, having a linen cloth cast about his naked body; and the young man laid hold on him: and he left the linen cloth, and fled from them naked. And they that had laid hold on Jesus, led him away to Caiaphas the high priest, where the scribes and the elders were assembled.

And Simon Peter followed Jesus, and so did another disciple. That disciple was known unto the high priest, and went in with Jesus into the palace of the high priest. But Peter stood at the door without. Then went out that other disciple, which was known unto the high priest, and spake unto her that kept the door, and brought in Peter. And the servants and officers stood there, who had made a fire of coals, (for it was cold,) and they warmed themselves: and Peter stood with them, and warmed himself. Then saith the damsel, that kept the door, unto Peter, "Art not thou also one of this man's disciples?" He saith, "I am not." And Simon Peter stood and warmed himself: they said, therefore, unto him, "Art not thou also one of his disciples?" He denied it, and said, "I am not." One of the servants of the high priest, (being his kinsman whose ear Peter cut off,) saith, "Did not I see thee in the garden with him?" Peter then denied again: and immediately the cock crew.

And Peter remembered the words of Jesus, which said unto him, "Before the cock crow, thou shalt deny me thrice." And he went out and wept bitterly.

The high priest then asked Jesus of his disciples, and of his doctrine. Jesus answered him,

"I spake openly to the world; I ever taught in the synagogue, and in the temple, whither the Jews always resort; and in secret have I said nothing. Why asketh thou me? ask them which heard me, what I have said unto them: behold, they know what I said."

And, when he had thus spoken, one of the officers which stood by struck Jesus with the palm of his hand, saying, "Answerest thou the high priest so?"

Jesus answered him,

"If I have spoken evil, bear witness of the evil; but if well, why smitest thou me?"

And they led Jesus away to the high priest; and with him were assembled all the chief priests, and the elders, and the scribes. And the chief priests, and all the council sought for witness against Jesus to put him to death; and found none: for many bare false witness against him, but their witness agreed not together. And there arose certain, and bare false witness against him, saying, "We heard him say, 'I will destroy this temple that is made with hands, and within three days I will build another made without hands.'" But neither so did their witness agree together. And the high priest stood up in the midst, and asked Jesus, saying, "Answerest thou nothing? what is it which these witness against thee?" But he held his peace, and answered nothing. Again the high priest asked him, and said unto him, "Art thou the Christ, the Son of the Blessed?"

And he said unto them, "If I tell you, ye will not believe: and if I also ask you, ye will not answer me, nor let me go."

Then said they all, "Art thou then the Son of God?" And he said unto them, "Ye say that I am."

Then the high priest rent his clothes, and saith, "What need we any further witnesses? Ye have heard the blasphemy: what think ye?" And they all condemned him to be guilty of death. And some began to spit on him, and to cover his face, and to buffet him, and to say unto him, "Prophesy"; and the servants did strike him with the palms of their hands.

Then led they Jesus from Caiaphas unto the hall of judgment, and it was early; and they themselves went not into the judgment-hall, lest they should be defiled; but that they might eat the passover.

Pilate then went out unto them, and said, "What accusation bring ye against this man?"

They answered, and said unto him, "If he were not a malefactor, we would not have delivered him up unto thee."

Then said Pilate unto them, "Take ye him, and judge him according to your law."

The Jews therefore said unto him, "It is not lawful for us to put any man to death."

Then Pilate entered into the judgment-hall again, and called Jesus, and said unto him, "Art thou the King of the Jews?"

Jesus answered him,

"Sayest thou this thing of thyself, or did others tell it thee of me?"

Pilate answered,

"Am I a Jew? Thine own nation and the chief priests have delivered thee unto me. What hast thou done?"

Jesus answered,

"My kingdom is not of this world. If my kingdom were of this world, then would my servants fight, that I should not be delivered to the Jews: but now is my kingdom not from hence."

Pilate therefore said unto him,

"Art thou a King then?"

Jesus answered,

"Thou sayest that I am a king. To this end was I born, and for this cause came I into the world, that I should bear witness unto the truth. Every one that is of the truth heareth my voice."

Pilate saith unto him, "What is truth?"

And when he had said this, he went out again unto the Jews, and saith unto them, "I find in him no fault at all."

And they were the more fierce saying, "He stirreth up the people, teaching throughout all Jewry, beginning from Galilee to this place."

Then said Pilate unto him,

"Hearest thou not how many things they witness against thee?"

When Pilate heard of Galilee, he asked whether the man were a Galilean. And as soon as he knew that he belonged unto Herod's jurisdiction, he sent him to Herod, who himself also was at Jerusalem at that time. And when Herod saw Jesus he was exceeding glad: for he was desirous to see him of a long season, because he had heard many things of him; and he hoped to have seen some miracle done by him. Then he questioned with him in many words; but he answered him nothing. And the chief priests and scribes stood, and vehemently accused him. And Herod, with his men of war, set him at nought, and mocked him, and arrayed him in a gorgeous robe, and sent him again to Pilate.

And the same day Pilate and Herod were made friends together: for before they were at enmity between themselves. And Pilate, when he had called together the chief priests, and the rulers, and the people, said unto them,

"Ye have brought this man unto me, as one that perverteth the people: and, behold, I, having examined him before you, have found no fault in this man, touching those things whereof ye accuse him: no, nor yet Herod: for I sent you to him: and lo, nothing worthy of death is done unto him. I will therefore chastise him, and release him."

Now at that feast the governor was wont to release unto the people a prisoner, whom they would. And they had then a notable prisoner, called Barabbas. Therefore, when they were gathered together, Pilate said unto them, "Whom will ye that I release unto you? Barabbas, or Jesus, which is called Christ?" for he knew that for envy they had delivered him.

When he was set down on the judgment-seat, his wife sent unto him, saying, "Have thou nothing to do with that just man: for I have suffered many things this day in a dream because of him." But the chief priests and elders persuaded the multitude that they should ask Barabbas, and destory Jesus.

The governor answered and said unto them, "Whether of the twain will ye that I release unto you?"

They said, "Barabbas."

Pilate saith unto them, "What shall I do then with Jesus, which is called Christ?"

They all say unto him, "Let him be crucified." And the governor said, "Why, what evil hath he done?" But they cried out the more, saying, "Let him be crucified."

Then released he Barabbas, unto them; and when he had scourged Jesus, he delivered him to be crucified. Then the soldiers of the governor took Jesus into the common hall, and gathered unto him the whole band of soldiers. And when they had plaited a crown of thorns, they put it upon his head, and a reed in his right hand; and they bowed the knee before him, and mocked him, saying, "Hail, King of the Jews!" And they spit upon him, and took the reed, and smote him on the head. And after they had mocked him, they took the robe off from him, and put his own raiment on him, and led him away to crucify him.

Then Judas which had betrayed him when he saw that he was condemned, repented himself, and brought again the thirty pieces of silver to the chief priests and elders, saying, "I have sinned, in that I have betrayed the innocent blood." And they said, "What is that to us? see thou to that." And he cast down the pieces of silver in the temple, and departed, and went and hanged himself. And the chief priest took the silver pieces, and said, "It is not lawful for to put them into the treasury, because it is the price of blood." And they took counsel, and bought with them the potter's field, to bury strangers in. Wherefore that field was called, "The field of blood," unto this day.

And, as they led him away they laid hold upon one Simon, a Cyrenian, coming out of the country, and on him they laid the cross, that he might bear it after Jesus. And there followed him a great company of people, and of women, which also bewailed and lamented him. But Jesus, turning unto them, said,

"Daughters of Jerusalem, weep not for me, but weep for yourselves, and for your children. For, behold, the days are coming, in the which they shall say, 'Blessed are the barren, and the wombs that never bare, and the paps which never gave suck.' Then shall they begin to say to the mountains, 'Fall on us'; and to the hills, 'Cover us.' For if they do these things in a green tree, what shall be done in the dry?"

And there were also two others, malefactors, led with him to be put to death.

And he, bearing his cross, went forth into a place called the place of a skull, which is called in the Hebrew, Golgotha; where they crucified him, and two others with him, on either side one, and Jesus in the midst.

And Pilate wrote a title, and put it on the cross, and the writing was,

JESUS OF NAZARETH,
THE KING OF THE JEWS.

This title then read many of the Jews: for the place where Jesus was crucified was nigh to the city: and it was written in Hebrew, and Greek, and Latin. Then said the chief priests of the Jews to Pilate, "Write not, 'The King of the Jews,' but that he said, 'I am King of the Jews.' " Pilate answered, "What I have written, I have written."

Then the soldiers, when they had crucified Jesus, took his garments, and made four parts, to every soldier a part, and also his coat: now the coat was without seam, woven from the top throughout. They said, therefore, among themselves, "Let us not rend it, but cast lots for it, whose it shall be."

And they that passed by reviled him, wagging their heads, and saying, "Thou that destroyest the temple, and buildest it in three days, save thyself. If thou be the Son of God, come down from the cross."

Likewise also the chief priests mocking him, with the scribes and elders, said, "He saved others; himself he cannot save. If he be the King of Israel, let him now come down from the cross, and we will believe him. He trusted in God; let him deliver him now, if he will have him: for he said, 'I am the Son of God.' "

And one of the malefactors, which were hanged, railed on him, saying, "If thou be Christ, save thyself and us." But the other, answering, rebuked him, saying, "Dost not thou fear God, seeing thou art in the same condemnation? And we indeed justly; for we receive the due rewards of our deeds: but this man hath done nothing amiss."

Then said Jesus,

"Father forgive them, For they know not what they do."

Now there stood by the cross of Jesus, his mother, and his mother's sister, Mary the wife of Cleophas, and Mary Magdalene. When Jesus, therefore, saw his mother, and the disciple standing by whom he loved, he saith unto his mother, "Woman, behold thy Son!"

Then saith he to the disciple, "Behold thy mother!" And from that hour that disciple took her unto his own home.

And about the ninth hour, Jesus cried with a loud voice, saying, "Eli, Eli, lama sabachthani?" that is to say, "My God, my God, why hast thou forsaken me?"

Some of them that stood there, when they heard that, said, "This man calleth for Elias." And straightway one of them ran, and took a sponge, and filled it with vinegar, and put it on a reed, and gave him to drink. The rest said, "Let be, let us see whether Elias will come to save him."

Jesus, when he had cried again with a loud voice, yielded up the ghost.

And many women were there, beholding afar off, which followed Jesus from Galilee, ministering unto him: among which was Mary Magdalene, and Mary the mother of James and Joses, and the mother of Zebedee's children.

The Jews, therefore, because it was the preparation, that the bodies should not remain upon the cross on the sabbath-day, (for that sabbath-day was an high day,) besought Pilate that their legs might be broken, and that they might be taken away. Then came the soldiers, and brake the legs of the first, and of the other which was crucified with him. But when they came to Jesus, and saw that he was dead already, they brake not his legs: but one of the soldiers with a spear pierced his side, and forthwith came thereout blood and water.

And after this, Joseph of Arimathea, (being a disciple of Jesus but secretly for fear of the Jews,) besought Pilate that he might take away the body of Jesus: and Pilate gave him leave. He came therefore, and took the body of Jesus. And there came also Nicodemus (which at the first came to Jesus by night and brought a mixture of myrrh and aloes, about an hundred pound weight). Then took they the body of Jesus, and wound it in linen clothes with the spices, as the manner of the Jews is to bury. Now, in the place where he was crucified, there was a garden; and in the garden a new sepulchre, wherein was never man yet laid. There laid they Jesus, and rolled a great stone to the door of the sepulchre, and departed.

5. THE JEFFERSON-ADAMS LETTERS

"Sentiments of Respect and Affectionate Attachment"

"THE public and the papers have been much occupied lately in placing us in a point of opposition to each other," Thomas Jefferson wrote to John Adams on December 28, 1796. "I trust with confidence that less of it has been felt by ourselves personally . . . I leave to others the sublime delights of riding in the storm, better pleased with sound sleep and a warm berth below, with the society of neighbors, friends and fellow-laborers of the earth, than of spies and sycophants. No one then will congratulate you with purer disinterestedness than myself."

John Adams had just been elected President of the United States. His opponent, over whom he won in the electoral college by only three votes, was Thomas Jefferson. In accordance with the laws of the United States at that time, Jefferson thus became Vice-President of the United States, a position which, he anticipated, was not apt to interfere with his digestion or his slumbers. In concluding his letter to John Adams, Jefferson expressed the hope that Adams's administration "may be filled with glory, and happiness to yourself and advantage to us," and identified himself as "one who tho' in the course of our own voyage through life, various little incidents have happened or been contrived to separate us, retain still for you the solid esteem of the moments when we were working for our independence, and sentiments of respect and affectionate attachment."

In the early days of America's struggle for freedom and independence, young John Adams was caught up in the emotional and intellectual excitement of the Revolution. He not only understood what Thomas Jefferson and Thomas Paine were talking about; he had words of his own to contribute. The words might not have been as impassioned as those of his Revolutionary colleagues, but they were measured, cogent, compelling. He was the ideal man to second a resolution, and nothing that he ever seconded stood higher historically than the Declaration of Independence, written by Jefferson.

With the passing of the years, however, his ideas became less and less revolutionary. Where at one time he had fought for human rights, in later years he thought and wrote about natural aristocracy among men, about the inevitability of social and economic distinctions, about the importance of precedent and gradual conditioning. He was impatient with all the talk about natural rights, especially in connection with the French Revolution, which made him apprehensive about the "turbulent passions of men" and the difficulty of bringing these passions under control.

James Madison, appalled at the anti-revolutionary turn that John Adams had taken, expressed the belief that Adams was secretly a monarchist. But John Adams had not gone that far, as his letter to cousin Samuel Adams may indicate: "It is a fixed principle with me that all good government is and must be republican." This was another way of saying that John Adams believed in a free society, but he insisted on believing it in his own inimitable and inimical way. This often unpredictable and always independent manner brought him into open conflict with most of the principal figures of the Revolutionary and constitutional period of American history. He was in opposition to Jefferson, and vice versa, during much of the period from 1789 through 1808, though he voted for Jefferson in 1804. While he was one of Hamilton's most powerful supporters through some of the early ordeals of the Federalist party, he eventually broke with Hamilton, too.

As for Thomas Jefferson, though he may have mellowed in his later years, he never lost his revolutionary flame; his philosophy was consistent and moved forward in a straight line. But in manner Jefferson was the most gracious of men. He was a delight to know, expressed his opinions in a way to arouse no resentment, and was a genius in drawing other men out. Adams no doubt viewed Jefferson as proof of his theory of the natural aristocrat; Jefferson was propertied, he was esteemed for his judgments, he was a born leader, he could read Greek and Latin and quote passages from memory, he could give or take a poetical allusion, he could work with blueprints, he knew Blackstone, and he could play the violin. What more could anyone ask, especially a man who had as much respect for natural and acquired endowments as John Adams? And when the political struggle receded, and the issues that once separated them could be viewed with relief if not with total detachment, the two men were drawn to each other again. Their reconciliation is one of the pleasanter episodes in American history, for it produced a sustained exchange of correspondence that is on a plane by itself. The exchange lasted for more than fifteen years; its range of subjects was as universal as their own interests. It is difficult to say exactly how the correspondence began; but even in the earliest letters of which there are records, there are philosophical and historical references which served to stimulate and challenge both men. That they enjoyed writing long tracts to each other there can be no doubt. Indeed, the scope and depth of their letters make clear that they were writing not merely to achieve catharsis, but to develop a point of view.

John Adams was easily the more conscientious correspondent. Thomas Jefferson might allow months to go by before he felt able to write the kind of thoughtful, detailed letter his exchange with Adams required. Adams, on the other hand, was both prompt and diligent. The excerpts selected for inclusion here deal mainly with philosophical or religious matters.

Whatever the circumstances of their origin, the Jefferson-Adams letters restored and reinforced the old friendship between the two. They were young men—very young—when they helped to found a new nation. And now, in their declining years, they could assess the results of their work and give their minds unobstructed access to each other and to the world of ideas. John Adams and Thomas Jefferson died within a few hours of each other. Their deaths came on July 4, 1826. It was the fiftieth anniversary of the Declaration of Independence.

The reader is reminded that the following letters are excerpted.

JEFFERSON TO ADAMS, JANUARY 21, 1812

A letter from you calls up recollections very dear to my mind. It carries me back to the times when, beset with difficulties and dangers, we were fellow-laborers in the same cause, struggling for what is most valuable to man, his right of self-government. Laboring always at the same oar, with some wave ever ahead, threatening to overwhelm us, and yet passing harmless under our bark, we knew not how we rode through the storm with heart and hand, and made a happy port. Still we did not expect to be without rubs and difficulties; and we have had them. First, the detention of the western posts, then the coalition of Pillnitz, outlawing our commerce with France, and the British enforcement of the outlawry. In your day, French depredations; in mine, English, and the Berlin and Milan decrees; now the English orders of council, and the piracies they authorize. When these shall be over, it will be the impressment of our seamen or something else; and so we have gone on, and so we shall go on, puzzled and prospering beyond example in the history of man. And I do believe we shall continue to grow, to multiply and prosper until we exhibit an association, powerful, wise and happy, beyond what has yet been seen by men. As for France and England, with all their preëminence in science, the one is a den of robbers, and the other of pirates. And if science produces no better fruits than tyranny, murder, rapine and destitution of national morality, I would rather wish our country to be ignorant, honest and estimable, as our neighboring savages are. But whither is senile garrulity leading me? Into politics, of which I have taken final leave. I think little of them and say less.

I have given up newspapers in exchange for Tacitus and Thucydides, for Newton and Euclid, and I find myself much the happier. Sometimes, indeed, I look back to former occurrences, in remembrance of our old friends and fellow-laborers, who have fallen before us. Of the signers of the Declaration of Independence, I see now living not more than half a dozen on your side of the Potomac, and on this side, myself alone. You and I have been wonderfully spared, and myself with remarkable health, and a considerable activity of body and mind. I am on horseback three or four hours of every day; visit three or four times a year a possession I have ninety miles distant, performing the winter journey on horseback. I walk little, however, a single mile being too much for me, and I live in the midst of my grandchildren, one of whom has lately promoted me to be a great grandfather. I have heard with pleasure that you also retain good health, and a greater power of exercise in walking than I do. But I would rather have heard this from yourself, and that, writing a letter like mine, full of egotisms, and of details of your health, your habits, occupations and enjoyments, I should have the pleasure of knowing that in the race of life, you do not keep, in its physical decline, the same distance ahead of me which you have done in political honors and achievements. No circumstances have lessened the interest I feel in these particulars respecting yourself; none have suspended for one moment my sincere esteem for you, and I now salute you with unchanged affection and respect.

JEFFERSON TO ADAMS, JUNE 11, 1812

You ask if there is any book that pretends to give any account of the traditions of the Indians, or how one can acquire an idea of them? Some scanty accounts of their traditions, but fuller of their customs and characters, are given us by most of the early travellers among them; these you know were mostly French. Lafitan, among them, and Adair an Englishman, have written on this subject; the former two volumes, the latter one, all in quarto. But unluckily Lafitan had in his head a preconceived theory on the mythology, manners, institutions and government of the ancient nations of Europe, Asia and Africa, and seems to have entered on those of America only to fit them into the same frame, and to draw from them a confirmation of his general theory. He keeps up a perpetual parallel, in all those articles, between the Indians of America and the ancients of the other quarters of the globe. He selects, therefore, all the facts and adopts all the falsehoods which favor his theory, and very gravely retails such absurdities as zeal for a theory could alone swallow. He was a man of much classical and scriptural reading, and has rendered his book not unentertaining. He resided five years among the Northern Indians, as a Missionary, but collects his matter much more from the writings of others, than from his own observations.

Adair too had his kinks. He believed all the Indians of America to be descended from the Jews; the same laws, usages, rites and ceremonies, the same sacrifices, priests, prophets, fasts and festivals, almost the same religion, and that they all spoke Hebrew. For, although he writes particularly of the Southern Indians only, the Catawbas, Creeks, Cherokees, Chickasaws and Chocktaws, with whom alone he was personally acquainted, yet he generalizes whatever he found among them, and brings himself to believe that the hundred languages of America, differing fundamentally every one from every other, as much as Greek from Gothic, yet have all one common prototype. He was a trader, a man of learning, a self-taught Hebraist, a strong religionist, and of as sound a mind as Don Quixote in whatever did not touch his religious chivalry. His book contains a great deal of real instruction on its subject, only requiring the reader to be constantly on his guard against the wonderful obliquities of his theory.

The scope of your inquiry would scarcely, I suppose, take in the three folio volumes of Latin of De Bry. In these, facts and fable are mingled together, without regard to any favorite system. They are less suspicious, therefore, in their complexion, more original and authentic, than those of Lafitan and Adair. This is a work of great curiosity, extremely rare, so as never to be bought in Europe, but on the breaking up and selling some ancient library. On one of these occasions a bookseller procured me a copy, which, unless you have one, is probably the only one in America.

You ask further, if the Indians have any order of priesthood among them, like the Druids, Bards or Minstrels of the Celtic nations? Adair alone, determined to see what he wished to see in every object, metamorphoses their conjurers into an order of priests, and describes their sorceries as if they were the great religious ceremonies of the nation. Lafitan called them by their proper names. Jongleurs, Devins, Sortileges; De Bry praestigiatores; Adair himself sometimes Magi, Archimagi, cunning men, Seers, rain makers; and the modern Indian interpreters call them conjurers and witches. They are persons pretending to have comunications with the devil and other evil spirits, to foretell future events, bring down rain, find stolen goods, raise the dead, destroy some and heal others by enchantment, lay spells, etc. And Adair, without departing from his parallel of the Jews and Indians, might have found their counterpart much more aptly, among the soothsayers, sorcerers and wizards of the Jews, their Gannes and Gambres, their Simon Magus, Witch of Endor, and the young damsel whose sorceries disturbed Paul so much; instead of placing them in a line with their high-priest, their chief priests, and their magnificent hierarchy generally.

In the solemn ceremonies of the Indians, the persons who direct or officiate, are their chiefs, elders and warriors, in civil ceremonies or in those of war; it is the head of the cabin in their private or particular feasts or ceremonies; and sometimes the matrons, as in their corn feasts. And even here, Adair might have kept up his parallel, with ennobling his conjurers. For the ancient patriarchs, the Noahs, the Abrahams, Isaacs and Jacobs, and even after the consecration of Aaron, the Samuels and Elijahs, and we may say further, every one for himself offered sacrifices on the altars. The true line of distinction seems to be, that solemn ceremonies, whether public or private, addressed to the Great Spirit, are conducted by the worthies of the nation, men or matrons, while conjurers are resorted to only for the invocation of evil spirits. The present state of the several Indian tribes, without any public order of priests, is proof sufficient that they never had such an order. Their steady habits permit no innovations, not even those which the progress of science offers to increase the comforts, enlarge the understanding, and improve the morality of mankind. Indeed, so little idea have they of a regular order of priests, that they mistake ours for conjurers, and call them by that name.

JEFFERSON TO ADAMS, MAY 27, 1813

Another of our friends of seventy-six is gone, my dear Sir, another of the co-signers of the Independence of our country. And a better man than Rush could not have left us, more benevolent, more learned, or finer genius, or more honest. We too must go, and that ere long. I believe we are under half a dozen at present; I mean the signers of the Declaration. Yourself, Gerry, Carroll, and myself, are all I know to be living. I am the only one south of the Potomac. Is Robert Treat Payne, or [William] Floyd living? It is long since I heard of them, and yet I do not recollect to have heard of their deaths.

JEFFERSON TO ADAMS, JUNE 15, 1813

I wrote you a letter on the 27th of May, which probably would reach you about the 3rd instant, and on the 9th I received yours of the 29th of May. Of Lindsay's Memoirs I had never before heard, and scarcely indeed of himself. It could not, therefore, but be unexpected, that two letters of mine should have anything to do with his life. The name of his editor was new to me, and certainly presents itself for the first time under unfavorable circumstances. Religion, I suppose, is the scope of his book; and that a writer on that subject should usher himself to the world in the very act of the grossest abuse of confidence, by publishing private letters which passed between two friends, with no views to their ever being made public, is an instance of inconsistency as well as of infidelity, of which I would rather be the victim than the author.

By your kind quotation of the dates of my two letters, I have been enabled to turn to them. They had completely vanished from my memory. The last is on the subject of religion, and by its publication will gratify the priesthood with new occasion of repeating their comminations against me. They wish it to be believed that he can have no religion who advocates its freedom. This was not the doctrine of Priestley; and I honored him for the example of liberality he set to his order.

JEFFERSON TO ADAMS, JUNE 27, 1813

> Ἴδαν ἐς πολύδενδρον ἀνὴρ ὑλατόμος ἐλθὼν
> παπταίνει, παρεόντος ἄδην, πόθεν ἄρξεται ἔργου·
> τί πρῶτον καταλέξω; ἐπεὶ πάρα μυρία εἰπεῖν.[1]

And I, too, my dear Sir, like the wood-cutter of Ida, should doubt where to begin, were I to enter the forest of opinion, discussions, and contentions which have occurred in our day. I should say with Theocritus,

> τί πρῶτον καταλέξω; ἐπεὶ πάρα μυρία εἰπεῖν.[2]

But I shall not do it. The *summum bonum* with me is now truly epicurian, ease of body and tranquility of mind; and to these I wish to consign my remaining days. Men have differed in opinion, and been divided into parties by these opinions, from the first origin of societies, and in all governments where they have been permitted freely to think and to speak. The same political parties which now agitate the United States, have existed through all time. Whether the power of the people or that of the αριστοι [aristocracy] should prevail, were questions which kept the States of Greece and Rome in eternal convulsions, as they now schismatize every people whose minds and mouths are not shut up by the gag of a despot. . . .

When our present government was in the new, passing from Confederation to Union, how bitter was the schism between the Feds and Antis. Here you and I were together again. For although, for a moment, separated by the Atlantic from the scene of action, I favored the opinion that nine States should confirm the constitution, in order to secure it, and the others hold off until certain amendments, deemed favorable to freedom, should be

---

[1] [Now when the fellow goes up to a thick Ida (wooded area) he looks about him where to begin in all that plenty. And so I, where now shall I take up my tale when I might speak in ten thousand ways.—ED.]

[2] [And so I, where now shall I take up my tale when I might speak in ten thousand ways.—ED.]

made. I rallied in the first instant to the wiser proposition of Massachusetts, that all should confirm, and then all instruct their delegates to urge those amendments. The amendments were made, and all were reconciled to the government. But as soon as it was put into motion, the line of division was again drawn. We broke into two parties, each wishing to give the government a different direction; the one to strengthen the most popular branch, the other the more permanent branches, and to extend their permanence. Here you and I separated for the first time, and as we had been longer than most others on the public theatre, and our names therefore were more familiar to our countrymen, the party which considered you as thinking with them, placed your name at their head; the other, for the same reason, selected mine. But neither decency nor inclination permitted us to become the advocates of ourselves, or to take part personally in the violent contests which followed.

We suffered ourselves, as you so well expressed it, to be passive subjects of public discussion. And these discussions, whether relating to men, measures or opinions, were conducted by the parties with an animosity, a bitterness and an indecency which had never been exceeded. All the resources of reason and of wrath were exhausted by each party in support of its own, and to prostrate the adversary opinions; one was upbraided with receiving the anti-federalists, the other the old tories and refugees, into their bosom. Of this acrimony, the public papers of the day exhibit ample testimony, in the debates of Congress, of State Legislatures, of stump-orators, in addresses, answers, and newspaper essays; and to these, without question, may be added the private correspondences of individuals; and the less guarded in these, because not meant for the public eye, not restrained by the respect due to that, but poured forth from the overflowings of the heart into the bosom of a friend, as a momentary easement of our feelings.

In this way, and in answers to addresses, you and I could indulge ourselves. We have probably done it, sometimes with warmth, often with prejudice, but always, as we believed, adhering to truth. I have not examined my letters of that day. I have no stomach to revive the memory of its feelings. But one of these letters, it seems, has got before the public, by accident and infidelity, by the death of one friend to whom it was written, and of his friend to whom it had been communicated, and by the malice and treachery of a third person, of whom I had never before heard, merely to make mischief, and in the same satanic spirit in which the same enemy had intercepted and published, in 1776, your letter animadverting on Dickinson's character. How it happened that I quoted you in my letter to Doctor Priestley, and for whom, and not for yourself, the strictures were meant, has been explained to you in my letter of the 15th, which had been committed to the post eight days before I received yours of the 10th, 11th and 14th. That gave you the reference which these asked to the particular answer alluded to in the one to Priestley. The renewal of these old discussions, my friend, would be equally useless and irksome. To the volumes then written on these subjects, human ingenuity can add nothing new, and the rather, as lapse of time has obliterated many of the facts. And shall you and I, my dear Sir, at our age, like Priam of old, gird on the *"arma, diu desueta, trementibus, aevo humeris?"*[3] Shall we, at our age, become the Athletae of party, and exhibit ourselves as gladiators in the arena of the newspapers? Nothing in the universe could induce me to it. My mind has been long fixed to bow to the judgment of the world, who will judge my acts, and will never take counsel from me as to what that judgment shall be. If your objects and opinions have been misunderstood, if the measures and principles of others have been wrongfully imputed to you, as I believe they have been, that you should leave an explanation of them, would be an act of justice to yourself. I will add, that it has been hoped that you would leave such explanations as would place every saddle on its right horse, and replace on the shoulders of others the burthens they shifted on yours.

But all this, my friend, is offered, merely for your consideration and judgment, without presuming to anticipate what you alone are qualified to decide for yourself. I mean to express my own purpose only, and the reflections which have led to it. To me, then, it appears, that there have been differences of opinion and party differences, from the first establishment of governments to the present day, and on the same questions which now divides our own country; that these will continue through all future time, that every one takes his side in favor of the many, or of the few, according to his constitution, and the circumstances in which he is placed; that opinions, which are equally honest on both sides, should not affect personal esteem or social intercourse; that as we judge between the Claudii and the Gracchi, the Wentworths and the Hampdens of past ages, so of those among us whose names may happen to be remembered for awhile, the next generations will judge, favorably or unfavorably, according to the complexion of individual minds, and the side they shall themselves have taken; that nothing new can be added by you or me to what has been said by others, and will be said in every age in support of the conflicting opinions on government; and that wisdom and duty dictate an humble resignation to the verdict of our future peers. In doing this myself, I shall certainly not suffer moot questions to affect the sentiments of sincere friendship and respect, consecrated to you by so long a course of time, and of which I now repeat sincere assurances.

---

[3] [armor, disused for a long time, upon trembling shoulders.—ED.]

ADAMS TO JEFFERSON, JUNE 28, 1813

I know not what, unless it were the prophet of Tippecanoe, had turned my curiosity to inquiries after the metaphysical science of the Indians, their ecclesiastical establishments, and theological theories; but your letter, written with all the accuracy, perpiscuity, and elegance of your youth and middle age, as it has given me great satisfaction, deserves my best thanks.

It has given me satisfaction, because, while it has furnished me with information *where* all the knowledge is to be obtained that books afford, it has convinced me that I shall never know much more of the subject than I do now. As I have never aimed at making my collection of books upon this subject, I have none of those you abridged in so concise a manner. Lafitan Adair, and De Bry, were known to me only by name.

The various ingenuity which has been displayed in inventions of hypothesis, to account for the original population of America, and the immensity of learning profusely extended to support them, have appeared to me for a longer time than I can precisely recollect, what the physicans call the *Literae nihil Sanantes.*[4] Whether serpents teeth were sown here and sprang up men; whether men and women dropped from the clouds upon this Atlantic Island; whether the Almighty created them here, or whether they emigrated from Europe, are questions of no moment to the present or future happiness of man. Neither agriculture, commerce, manufactures, fisheries, science, literature, taste, religion, morals, nor any other good will be promoted, or any evil averted, by any discoveries that can be made in answer to these questions.

The opinions of the Indians and their usages, as they are represented in your obliging letter of the 11th of June, appear to me to resemble the Platonizing Philo, or the Philonizing Plato, more than the genuine system of Indianism.

The philosophy both of Philo and Plato are at least as absurd. It is indeed less intelligible.

Plato borrowed his doctrines from Oriental and Egyptian philosophers, for he had travelled both in India and Egypt.

The oriental philosophy, imitated and adopted, in part, if not the whole, by Plato and Philo, was

1. One God the good.
2. The ideas, the thoughts, the reason, the intellect, the logos, the ratio of God.
3. Matter, the universe, the production of the logos, or contemplations of God. This matter was the source of evil.

---

[4] [mere learning which cures nothing.—Ed.]

Perhaps the three powers of Plato, Philo, the Egyptians, and Indians, cannot be distinctly made out, from your account of the Indians, but—

1. The great spirit, the good, who is worshipped by the kings, sachems, and all the great men, in their solemn festivals, as the Author, the Parent of good.

2. The Devil, or the source of evil. They are not metaphysicians enough as yet to suppose it, or at least to call it matter, like the wiscains of Antiquity, and like Frederick the Great, who has written a very silly essay on the origin of evil, in which he ascribes it all to matter, as if this was an original discovery of his own.

The watchmaker has in his head an idea of the system of a watch before he makes it. The mechanician of the universe had a complete idea of the universe before he made it; and this idea, this logos, was almighty, or at least powerful enough to produce the world, but it must be made of matter which was eternal; for creation out of nothing was impossible. And matter was unmanageable. It would not, and could not be fashioned into any system, without a large mixture of evil in it; for matter was essentially evil.

The Indians are not metaphysicians enough to have discovered this *idea*, this logos, this intermediate power between good and evil, God and matter. But of the two powers, the good and the evil, they seem to have a full conviction; and what son or daughter of Adam and Eve has not?

This logos of Plato seems to resemble, if it was not the prototype of, the *Ratio and its Progress* of Manilious, the astrologer; of the *Progress of the Mind* of Condorcet, and the *Age of Reason* of Tom Paine.

I could make a system too. The seven hundred thousand soldiers of Zingis, when the whole, or any part of them went to battle, they sent up a howl, which resembled nothing that human imagination has conceived, unless it be the supposition that all the devils in hell were let loose at once to set up an infernal scream, which terrified their enemies, and never failed to obtain them victory. The Indian yell resembles this; and, therefore, America was peopled from Asia.

Another system. The armies of Zingis, sometimes two or three or four hundred thousand of them, surrounded a province in a circle, and marched towards the centre, driving all the wild beasts before them, lions, tigers, wolves, bears, and every living thing, terrifying them with their howls and yells, their drums, trumpets, &c., till they terrified and tamed enough of them to victual the whole army. Therefore, the Scotch Highlanders, who practice the same thing in miniature, are emigrants from Asia. Therefore, the American Indians, who, for anything I know, practice the same custom, are emigrants from Asia or Scotland.

I am weary of contemplating nations from the lowest and most beastly degradations of human life, to the highest refinement of civilization. I am weary of Philosophers, Theologians, Politicians, and Historians. They are an immense mass of absurdities, vices, and lies. Montesquieu had sense enough to say in jest, that all our knowledge might be comprehended in twelve pages of duodecimo, and I believe him in earnest. I could express my faith in shorter terms. He who loves the workman and his work, and does what he can to preserve and improve it, shall be accepted of him.

I have also felt an interest in the Indians, and a commiseration for them from my childhood. Aaron Pomham the priest, and Moses Pomham the king of the Punkapang and Neponset tribes, were frequent visitors at my father's house, at least seventy years ago. I have a distinct remembrance of their forms and figures. They were very aged, and the tallest and stoutest Indians I have ever seen. The titles of king and priest, and the names of Moses and Aaron, were given them no doubt by our Massachusetts divines and statesmen. There was a numerous family in this town, whose wigwam was within a mile of this house. This family were frequently at my father's house, and I, in my boyish rambles, used to call at their wigwam, where I never failed to be treated with whortleberries, blackberries, strawberries or apples, plums, peaches, &c., for they had planted a variety of fruit trees about them. But the girls went out to service, and the boys to sea, till not a soul is left. We scarcely see an Indian in a year. I remember the time when Indian murder, scalpings, depredations and conflagrations, were as frequent on the Eastern and Northern frontier of Massachusetts, as they are now in Indiana, and spread as much terror. But since the conquest of Canada, all has ceased; and I believe with you that another conquest of Canada will quiet the Indians forever, and be as great a blessing to them as to us.

The instance of Aaron Pomham made me suspect that there was an order of priesthood among them. But, according to your account, the worship of the good spirit was performed by the kings, sachems, and warriors, as among the ancient Germans whose highest rank of nobility were priests. The worship of the evil spirit, 'Αθανάτους μὲν πρῶτα θέους νόμῳ ὡς διάκειται τίμα.[5]

We have war now in earnest. I lament the contumacious spirit that appears about me. But I lament the cause that has given too much apology for it; the total neglect and absolute refusal of all maritime protection and defence. Money, mariners, and soldiers, would be at the public service, if only a few frigates had been ordered to be built. Without this, our Union will be a brittle china vase, a house of ice, or a palace of glass.

---

[5] [Above all things honor the immortal gods established by law.—Ed.]

It is very true that the denunciations of the priesthood are fulminated against every advocate for a complete freedom of religion. Comminations, I believe, would be plenteously pronounced by even the most liberal of them, against atheism, deism,—against every man who disbelieved or doubted the resurrection of Jesus, or the miracles of the New Testament. Priestley himself would denounce the man who should deny the Apocalypse, or the prophecies of Daniel. Priestley and Lindsey have both denounced as idolaters and blashphemers all the Trinitarians and even the Arians. Poor weak man! when will thy perfection arrive? Thy perfectibility I shall not deny, for a greater character than Priestley or Godwin has said, "Be ye perfect," &c. For my part, I cannot "deal damnation round the land" on all I judge the foes of God or man. But I did not intend to say a word on this subject in this letter. As much of it as you please, hereafter; but let me now return to politics.

With some difficulty I have hunted up or down the "address of the young men of the city of Philadelphia, the district of Southwark, and the northern liberties," and the answer.

The addressers say, "actuated by the *same principles* on which our forefathers achieved their independence, the recent attempts of a foreign power to derogate from the rights and dignity of our country, awaken our liveliest sensibility and our strongest indignation." Huzza, my brave boys! Could Thomas Jefferson or John Adams hear these words with insensibility and without emotion? These boys afterwards add, "we regard our liberty and independence as the richest portion given us by our ancestors." And who were these ancestors? Among them were Thomas Jefferson and John Adams; and I very coolly believe that no two men among these ancestors did more towards it than those two. Could either hear this like a statue? If, one hundred years hence, your letters and mine should see the light, I hope the reader will hunt up this address, and read it all, and remember that we were then engaged, or on the point of engaging, in a war with France. I shall not repeat the answer till we come to the paragraph upon which you criticized to Dr. Priestley, though every word of it is true; and I now rejoice to see it recorded though I had wholly forgotten it.

The paragraph is, "Science and morals are the great pillars on which this country has been raised to its present population, opulence, and prosperity; and these alone can advance, support, and preserve it. Without wishing to damp the ardor of curiosity, or influence the freedom of inquiry, I will hazard a prediction, that after the most industrious and impartial researches, the longest liver of you all will find no principles, institutions, or systems of education more fit, *in general*, to be transmitted to your posterity than those you have received from your ancestors."

Now, compare the paragraph in the answer with the paragraph in the address, as both are quoted above, and see if we can find the extent and the limits of the meaning of both.

Who composed that army of fine young fellows that was then before my eyes? There were among them Roman Catholics, English Episcopalians, Scotch and American Presbyterians, Methodists, Moravians, Anabaptists, German Lutherans, German Calvinists, Universalists, Arians, Priestleyans, Socinians, Independents, Congregationalists, Horse Protestants, and House Protestants,[6] Deists and Atheists, and Protestants *"qui ne croyent rien"* [who believe nothing]. Very few, however, of several of these species; nevertheless, all educated in the *general principles* of Christianity, and the general principles of English and American liberty.

Could my answer be understood by any candid reader or hearer, to recommend to all the others the general principles, institutions, or systems of education of the Roman Catholics, or those of the Quakers, or those of the Presbyterians, or those of the Methodists, or those of the Moravians, or those of the Universalists, or those of the Philosophers? No. The *general principles* on which the fathers achieved independence, were the only principles in which that beautiful assembly of young men could unite, and these principles only could be intended by them in their address, or by me in my answer. And what were these *general principles?* I answer, the general principles of Christianity, in which all those sects were united, and the *general principles* of English and American liberty, in which all those young men united, and which had united all parties in America, in majorities sufficient to assert and maintain her independence. Now I will avow, that I then believed and now believe that those general principles of Christianity are as eternal and immutable as the existence and attributes of God; and that those principles of liberty are as unalterable as human nature and our terrestrial, mundane system. I could, therefore, safely say, consistently with all my then and present information, that I believed they would never make discoveries in contradiction to these *general principles*. In favor of these *general principles*, in philosophy, religion, and government, I could fill sheets of quotations from Frederic of Prussia, from Hume, Gibbon, Bolingbroke, Rousseau, and Voltaire, as well as Newton and Locke; not to mention thousands of divines and philosophers of inferior fame.

I might have flattered myself that my settlements were sufficiently known to have protected me against suspicions of narrow thoughts, contracted

---

[6] [The words "Horse" and "House" are approximate renditions of Adams' handwriting.—Ed.]

sentiments, bigoted, enthusiastic, or superstitious principles, civil, political, philosophical, or ecclesiastical. The first sentence of the preface to my Defence of the Constitution, vol. i, printed in 1787, is in these words: "The arts and sciences, in general, during the three or four last centuries, have had a regular course of progressive improvement. The inventions in mechanic arts, the discoveries in natural philosophy, navigation, and commerce, and the advancement of civilization and humanity, have occasioned changes in the condition of the world, and the human character, which would have astonished the most refined nations of antiquity," &c. I will quote no farther, but request you to read again that whole page, and then say whether the writer of it could be suspected of recommending to youth "to look backward instead of forward," for instruction and improvement. This letter is already too long. In my next I shall consider "the terrorism of the day."

ADAMS TO JEFFERSON, JULY 9, 1813

Whenever I set down to write to you, I am precisely in the situation of the wood-cutter on Mount Ida. I cannot see wood for trees. So many subjects crowd upon me, that I know not with which to begin. But I will begin, at random, with Belsham; who is, as I have no doubt, a man of merit. He had no malice against you, nor any thought of doing mischief; nor has he done any, though he has been imprudent. The truth is, the dissenters of all denominations in England, and especially the Unitarians, are cowed, as we used to say at College. They are ridiculed, insulted, persecuted. They can scarcely hold their heads above water. They catch at straws and shadows to avoid drowning. Priestley sent your letter to Lindsay, and Belsham printed it from the same motive, *i.e.*, to derive some countenance from the name of Jefferson. Nor has it done harm here. Priestley says to Lindsay, "You see he is almost one of us, and he hopes will soon be altogether such as we are." Even in our New England, I have heard a high Federal Divine say, your letters had increased his respect for you.

"The same political parties which now agitate the United States, have existed through all time;" precisely. And this is precisely the complaint in the preface to the first volume of my defence. While all other sciences have advanced, that of government is at a stand; little better understood; little better practiced now, than three or four thousand years ago. What is the reason? I say, parties and factions will not suffer, or permit improvements to be made. As soon as one man hints at an improvement, his rival opposes it. No sooner has one party discovered or invented an amelioration of the condition of man, or the order of society, than the opposite party belies it, misconstrues, misrepresents it, ridicules it, insults it, and persecutes it. Records are destroyed. Histories are annihilated, or interpolated, or prohibited: sometimes by popes, sometimes by emperors, sometimes by aristocratical, and sometimes by democratical assemblies, and sometimes by mobs.

Aristotle wrote the history of eighteen hundred republics which existed before his time. Cicero wrote two volumes of discourses on government, which, perhaps, were worth all the rest of his works. The works of Livy and Tacitus, &c., that are lost, would be more interesting than all that remain. Fifty gospels have been destroyed, and where are St. Luke's world of books that have been written? If you ask my opinion who has committed all the havoc, I will answer you candidly,—Ecclesiastical and Imperial despotism has done it, to conceal their frauds.

Why are the histories of all nations, more ancient than the Christian era, lost? Who destroyed the Alexandrian library? I believe that Christian priests, Jewish rabbis, Grecian sages, and emperors, had as great a hand in it as Turks and Mahometans.

Democrats, Rebels and Jacobins, when they possessed a momentary power, have shown a disposition both to destroy and forge records as vandalical as priests and despots. Such has been and such is the world we live in.

I recollect, near some thirty years ago, to have said carelessly to you that I wished I could find time and means to write something upon aristocracy. You seized upon the idea, and encouraged me to do it with all that friendly warmth that is natural and habitual to you. I soon began, and have been writing upon that subject ever since. I have been so unfortunate as never to be able to make myself understood.

Your "ἄριστοί" [aristocracy] are the most difficult animals to manage of anything in the whole theory and practice of government. They will not suffer themselves to be governed. They not only exert all their own subtlety, industry, and courage, but they employ the commonalty to knock to pieces every plan and model that the most honest architects in legislation can invent to keep them within bounds. Both patricians and plebeians are as furious as the workmen in England, to demolish labor-saving machinery.

But who are these "ἄριστοί"? Who shall judge? Who shall select these choice spirits from the rest of the congregation? Themselves? We must first find out and determine who themselves are. Shall the congregation choose? Ask Xenophon; perhaps hereafter I may quote you Greek. Too much in a hurry at present, English must suffice, Xenophon says that the ecclesia always chooses the worst men they can find, because none others will do their dirty work. This wicked motive is worse than birth or wealth. Here I want to quote Greek again. But the day before I received your letter of June 27th, I gave the book to George Washington Adams, going to the academy at Hingham. The title is ΗΘΙΚΗ ΠΟΙΗΣΙΣ,[7] a collection of moral

---

[7] [Moral Poetry,—ED.]

sentences from all the most ancient Greek poets. In one of the oldest of them, I read in Greek, that I cannot repeat, a couplet, the sense of which was: "Nobility in men is worth as much as it is in horses, asses, or rams; but the meanest blooded puppy in the world, if he gets a little money, is as good a man as the best of them." Yet birth and wealth together have prevailed over virtue and talents in all ages. The many will acknowledge no other "ἄριστοί."

Your experience of this truth will not much differ from that of your best friend.

ADAMS TO JEFFERSON, JULY 17, 1813

In your letter to Priestley, of March 21st, 1801, dated at Washington, you call the Christian philosophy, "the most sublime and benevolent, but most perverted system, that ever shone on man." That it is the most sublime and benevolent, I agree; but whether it has been more perverted than that of Moses, of Confucius, of Zoroaster, of Sanchoniathon, of Numa, of Mahomet, of the Druids, of the Hindoos, &c, &c., &c., I can not as yet determine, because I am not sufficiently acquainted with these systems, or the history of their effects, to form a decisive opinion of the result of the comparison.

In your letter, dated Washington, April 9, 1803, you say, "in consequence of some conversation with Dr. Rush, in the year 1798-99, I had promised him, some day, to write him a letter, giving him my view of the Christian system. I have reflected upon it since, and even sketched the outlines in my own mind. . . .

"Sancte Socrate! Ora pro nobis!"[8] Erasmus. Priestley, in his letter to Lindsay, inclosing a copy of your letter to him, says, "he is generally considered as an unbeliever. If so, however, he cannot be far from us, and I hope in the way to be not only almost, but altogether what we are. He now attends public worship very regularly, and his moral conduct was never impeached."

Now, I see not but you are as good a Christian as Priestley and Lindsay. Piety and morality were the end and object of the Christian system, according to them and according to you. They believed in the resurrection of Jesus, in his miracles and inspirations. But what inspirations? Not all that is recorded in the New Testament or the Old. They have not yet told us how much they believe or disbelieve. They have not told us how much allegory, how much parable they find, nor how they explained them all in the New Testament or Old.

John Quincy Adams has written, for years, to his sons, boys of ten and

---

[8] [O holy Socrates! Pray for us.!—ED.]

twelve, a series of letters, in which he pursues a plan more extensive than yours, but agreeing in most of the essential points. I wish these letters could be preserved in the bosoms of his boys. But women and priests will get them; and I expect, if he makes a peace, he will have to retire, like Jay, to study prophecies to the end of his life.

I have more to say upon this subject of religion.

ADAMS TO JEFFERSON, JULY 18, 1813

I have more to say on religion. For more than sixty years I have been attentive to this great subject. Controversies between Calvinists and Arminians, Trinitarians and Unitarians, Deists and Christians, Atheists and both, have attracted my attention, whenever the singular life I have led would admit, to all these questions. The history of this little village of Quincy, if it were worth recording, would explain to you how this happened. I think I can now say I have read away bigotry, if not enthusiasm.

What does Priestley mean by an unbeliever, when he applies it to you? How much did he unbelieve himself? Gibbon had him right when he denominated his creed "scanty." We are to understand, no doubt, that he believed the resurrection of Jesus, some of his miracles, his inspiration; but in what degree? He did not believe in the inspiration of the writings that contain his history. Yet he believed in the Apocalyptic beast, and he believed as much as he pleased in the writings of Daniel and John. This great and extraordinary man, whom I sincerely loved, esteemed, and respected, was really a phenomenon; a comet in the system, like Voltaire, Bolingbroke, and Hume. Had Bolingbroke or Voltaire taken him in hand, what would they have made of him and his creed?

I do not believe you have read much of Priestley's "Corruptions of Christianity," his History of early opinions concerning Jesus Christ, his predestination, his no soul system, or his controversy with Horsley. I have been a diligent student for many years in books whose titles you have never seen. In Priestley's and Lindsay's writings, in Farmer, Cappe, in Tucker, or Edward Search's Light of Nature Pursued, in Edwards and Hopkins, and, lately in Ezra Stiles Ely, his reverend and learned panegyrists, and his elegant and spirited opponents. I am not wholly uninformed of the controversies in Germany, and the learned researches of universities and professors, in which the sanctity of the Bible and the inspiration of its authors are taken for granted or waived, or admitted or not denied. I have also read Condorcet's Progress of the Human Mind. Now, what is all this to you? No more than if I should tell you that I read Dr. Clarke, and Dr. Waterland, and Emlyn, and Leland's View or Review of the Deistical writers, more than fifty years ago, which is a literal truth.

I blame you not for reading Euclid and Newton, Thucydides and Theocritus, for I believe you will find as much entertainment and instruction in them as I have found in my theological and ecclesiastical instructors, or even, as I have found, in a profound investigation of the life, writings, and doctrines of Erastus, whose disciples were Milton, Harington, Selden, St. John, the Chief Justice, father of Bolingbroke, and others, the choicest spirits of their age; or in La Harpe's history of the philosophy of the eighteenth century; or in Van der Kemp's vast map of the causes of the revolutionary spirit, in the same preceding centuries. These things are to me the marbles and nine-pins of old age; I will not say the beads and prayer-books. I agree with you as far as you go, most cordially, and, I think, solidly. How much farther I go, how much more I believe than you, I may explain in a future letter. Thus much I will say at present. I have found so many difficulties that I am not astonished at your stopping where you are; and, so far from sentencing you to perdition, I hope soon to meet you in another country.

ADAMS TO JEFFERSON, JULY 22, 1813

Dr. Priestley, in a letter to Mr. Lindsay, Northumberland, November 4, 1803, says:

"As you were pleased with my comparison of Socrates and Jesus, I have begun to carry the same comparison to all the heathen moralists, and I have all the books that I want for the purpose except Simplicius and Arrian on Epictetus, and them I hope to get from a library in Philadelphia; lest, however, I should fail there, I wish you or Mr. Belsham would procure and send them from London. While I am capable of anything I cannot be idle, and I do not know that I can do anything better. This, too, is an undertaking that Mr. Jefferson recommends to me."

In another letter, dated Northumberland, January 16th, 1804, Dr. Priestley says to Mr. Lindsay:

"I have now finished and transcribed for the press, my comparison of the Grecian philosophers with those of Revelation, and with more ease and more to my own satisfaction than I expected. They who liked my pamphlet entitled, 'Socrates and Jesus compared,' will not, I flatter myself, dislike this work. It has the same object and completes the scheme. It has increased my own sense of the unspeakable value of revelation, and must, I think, that of every person who will give due attention to the subject."

I have now given you all that relates to yourself in Priestley's letters.

This was possibly and not improbably, the last letter this great, this learned, indefatigable, most excellent and extraordinary man ever wrote, for on the 4th of February, 1804, he was released from his labors and sufferings. Peace, rest, joy and glory to his soul! For I believe he had one, and one of the greatest.

I regret, oh how I lament that he did not live to publish this work! It must exist in manuscript. Cooper must know something of it. Can you learn from him where it is, and get it printed?

I hope you will still perform your promise to Dr. Rush.

If Priestley had lived, I should certainly have corresponded with him. His friend Cooper, who, unfortunately for him and me and you, had as fatal an influence over him as Hamilton had over Washington, and whose rash hot head led Priestley into all his misfortunes and most of his errors in conduct, could not have prevented explanations between Priestley and me.

I should propose to him a thousand, a million questions. And no man was more capable or better disposed to answer them candidly than Dr. Priestley.

Scarcely anything that has hapened to me in my curious life, has made a deeper impression upon me than that such a learned, ingenious, scientific and talented madcap as Cooper, could have influence enough to make Priestley my enemy.

I will not yet communicate to you more than a specimen of the questions I would have asked Priestley.

One is; Learned and scientific, Sir!—You have written largely about matter and spirit, and have concluded there is no human soul. Will you please to inform me what matter is? and what spirit is? Unless we know the meaning of words, we cannot reason in or about words.

I shall never send you all my questions that I would put to Priestley, because they are innumerable; but I may hereafter send you two or three.

I am, in perfect charity, your old friend.

ADAMS TO JEFFERSON, AUGUST 9, 1813

I believe I told you in my last that I had given you all in Lindsay's memorial that interested you, but I was mistaken. In Priestley's letter to Lindsay, December 19th, 1803, I find this paragraph:

"With the work I am now composing, I go on much faster and better than I expected, so that in two or three months, if my health continues as it now is, I hope to have it ready for the press, though I shall hardly proceed to print it till we have dispatched the notes.

"It is upon the same plan with that of Socrates and Jesus compared, considering all the more distinguished of the Grecian sects of philosophy, till the establishment of Christianity in the Roman empire. If you liked that pamphlet, I flatter myself you will like this.

"I hope it is calculated to show, in a peculiarly striking light, the great advantage of revelation, and that it will make an impression on candid unbelievers if they will read.

"But I find few that will trouble themselves to read anything on the subject, which, considering the great magnitude and interesting nature of the subject, is a proof of a very improper state of mind, unworthy of a rational being."

I send you this extract for several reasons. First, because you set him upon this work. Secondly, because I wish you to endeavor to bring it to light and get it printed. Thirdly, because I wish it may stimulate you to pursue your own plan which you promised to Dr. Rush.

I have not seen any work which expressly compares the morality of the Old Testament with that of the New, in all their branches, nor either with that of the ancient philosophers. Comparisons with the Chinese, the East Indians, the Africans, the West Indians, &c., would be more difficult; with more ancient nations impossible. The documents are destroyed.

JEFFERSON TO ADAMS, AUGUST 22, 1813

I very much suspect that if thinking men would have the courage to think for themselves, and to speak what they think, it would be found they do not differ in religious opinions as much as is supposed. I remember to have heard Dr. Priestley say, that if all England would candidly examine themselves, and confess, they would find that Unitarianism was really the religion of all; and I observe a bill is now depending in parliament for the relief of Anti-Trinitarians. It is too late in the day for men of sincerity to pretend they believe in the Platonic mysticisms that three are one and one is three; and yet that the one is not three, and the three are not one; to divide mankind by a single letter into ὁμοούσιον and ὁμοιούσιον.[9] But this constitutes the craft, the power and the profit of the priests. Sweep away their gossamer fabrics of factitious religion, and they would catch no more flies. We should all then, like the Quakers, live without an order of priests, moralize for ourselves, follow the oracle of conscience, and say nothing about what no man can understand, nor therefore believe; for I suppose belief to be the assent of the mind to an intelligible proposition.

It is with great pleasure I can inform you that Priestley finished the comparative view of the doctrines of the philosophers of antiquity, and of Jesus, before his death; and that it was printed soon after. And, with still greater pleasure, that I can have a copy of his work forwarded from Philadelphia, by a correspondent there, and presented for your acceptance, by the same mail which carries you this, or very soon after. The branch of the work which the title announces, is executed with learning and candor, as was everything Priestley wrote, but perhaps a little hastily; for he felt himself pressed by the hand of death. The Abbé Batteux had, in fact, laid the foundation of this part in his Causes Premières, with which he has given us

---

[9] [of the same substance and of similar substance.—ED.]

the originals of Ocellus and Timaeus, who first committed the doctrines of Pythagoras to writing, and Enfield, to whom the Doctor refers, had done it more copiously. But he has omitted the important branch, which, in your letter of August 9, you say you have never seen executed, a comparison of the morality of the Old Testament with that of the New. And yet, no two things were ever more unlike. I ought not to have asked him to give it. He dared not. He would have been eaten alive by his intolerant brethren, the Cannibal priests. And yet, this was really the most interesting branch of the work.

Very soon after my letter to Doctor Priestley, the subject being still in my mind, I had leisure during an abstraction from busines for a day or two, while on the road, to think a little more on it, and to sketch more fully than I had done to him, a syllabus of the matter which I thought should enter into the work. I wrote it to Doctor Rush, and there ended all my labor on the subject; himself and Doctor Priestley being the only two depositories of my secret. The fate of my letter to Priestley, after his death, was a warning to me on that of Doctor Rush; and at my request, his family were so kind as to quiet me by returning my original letter and syllabus. By this, you will be sensible how much interest I take in keeping myself clear of religious disputes before the public, and especially of seeing my syllabus disembowelled by the Aruspices of the modern Paganism. Yet I enclose it *to you* with entire confidence, free to be perused by yourself and Mrs. Adams, but by no one else, and to be returned to me.

You are right in supposing, in one of yours, that I had not read much of Priestley's Predestination, his no-soul system, or his controversy with Horsley. But I have read his Corruptions of Christianity, and Early Opinions of Jesus, over and over again; and I rest on them, and on Middleton's writings, especially his letters from Rome, and to Waterland, as the basis of my own faith. These writings have never been answered, nor can be answered by quoting historical proofs, as they have done. For these facts, therefore, I cling to their learning, so much superior to my own.

ADAMS TO JEFFERSON, SEPTEMBER 14, 1813

I owe you a thousand thanks for your favor of August 22nd and its enclosures, and for Doctor Priestley's doctrines of Heathen Philosophy compared with those of Revelation. Your letter to Dr. Rush and the syllabus, I return inclosed with this, according to your injunction, though with great reluctance. May I beg a copy of both? They will do you no harm; me and others much good. I hope you will pursue your plan, for I am confident you will produce a work much more valuable than Priestley's, though that is curious, and considering the expiring powers with which is was written, admirable.

The bill in parliament for the relief of Anti-Trinitarians, is a great event, and will form an epoch in ecclesiastical history. The motion was made by my friend Smith, of Clapham, a friend of the Belshams. I should be very happy to hear that the bill is passed.

The human understanding is a revelation from its Maker, which can never be disputed or doubted. There can be no scepticism, Pyrrhonism, or incredulity or infidelity, here. No prophecies, no miracles are necessary to prove this celestial communication. This revelation has made it certain that two and one make three, and that one is not three nor can three be one. We can never be so certain of any prophecy, or the fulfilment of any prophecy, or of any miracle, or the design of any miracle, as we are from the revelation of nature, that is, Nature's God, that two and two are equal to four. Miracles or prophecies might frighten us out of our wits; might scare us to death; might induce us to lie, to say that we believe that two and two make five. But we should not believe it. We should know the contrary.

Had you and I been forty days with Moses on Mount Sinai, and admitted to behold the divine Shekinah, and there told that one was three and three one, we might not have had courage to deny it, but we could not have believed it. The thunders and lightnings, and earthquakes, and the transcendent splendors and glories might have overwhelmed us with terror and amazement, but we could not have believed the doctrine. We should be more likely to say in our hearts—whatever we might say with our lips—, This is chance. There is no God, no truth. This is all delusion, fiction, and a lie, or it is all chance. But what is chance? It is motion, it is action, it is event, it is phenomenon without cause. Chance is no cause at all, it is nothing. And nothing has produced all this pomp and splendor. And nothing may produce our eternal damnation in the flames of hell-fire and brimstone, for what we know, as well as this tremendous exhibition of terror and falsehood.

God has infinite wisdom, goodness and power. He created the universe. His duration is eternal, *a parte ante* and *a parte post*. His presence is as extensive as space. What is space? An infinite spherical *vacuum*. He created this speck of dirt and the human species for his glory, and with the deliberate design of making nine-tenths of our species miserable forever, for his glory. This is the doctrine of Christian theologians, in general, ten to one. Now, my friend, can prophecies or miracles convince you or me that infinite benevolence, wisdom and power, created, and preserved for a time, innumerable millions, to make them miserable forever, for his own glory? Wretch! What is his glory? Is he ambitious? Does he want promotion? Is he vain, tickled with adulation, exulting and triumphing in his power and the sweetness of his vengeance? Pardon me, my Maker, for these awful questions. My answer to them is always ready. I believe no such things. My adoration of the Author of the Universe is too profound and too sincere. The love of God and his creation—delight, joy, triumph, exultation in my own existence—though but an atom, a molecule *organique* in the universe—are my religion.

Howl, snarl, bite, ye Calvinistic, ye Athanasian divines, if you will. Ye will say I am no Christian. I say ye are no Christians, and there the account is balanced. Yet I believe all the honest men among you are Christians, in my sense of the word.

When I was at college, I was a mighty metaphysician, at least thought myself such. And such men as Locke, Hemenway and West thought me so too, for we were forever disputing, though in great good humor.

When I was sworn as an attorney in, 1758, in Boston, though I lived in Braintree, I was in a low state of health; thought in danger of a consumption; living on milk, vegetable pudding, and water. Not an atom of meat, or a drop of spirit; my next neighbor, my cousin, my friend, Dr. Savil, was my physician. He was anxious about me, and did not like to take upon himself the sole responsibility of my recovery. He invited me on a visit to Dr. Ezekiel Hersey, a physician of great fame, who felt my pulse, looked in my eyes, heard Savil describe my regimen and course of medicine, and then pronounced his oracle: "Persevere, and as sure as there is a God in Heaven you will recover." He was an everlasting talker, and ran out into history, philosophy, metaphysics, &c., and frequently put questions to me as if he wanted to sound me, and see if there was anything in me besides hectic fever. I was young, and then very bashful, however saucy I may have sometimes been since. I gave him very modest and very diffident answers. But when he got upon metaphysics, I seemed to feel a little bolder, and ventured into something like argument with him. I drove him up, as I thought, into a corner, from which he could not escape. "Sir, it will follow, from what you have now advanced, that the universe, as distinct from God, is both infinite and eternal." "Very true," said Dr. Hersey, "your inference is just; the consequence is inevitable, and I believe the universe to be both eternal and infinite." Here I was brought up. I was defeated. I was not prepared for this answer. This was fifty-five years ago. When I was in England, from 1785 to 1788, I may say I was intimate with Dr. Price. I had much conversation with him at his own house, at my house, and at the houses and tables of many friends. In some of our most unreserved conversations, when we have been alone, he has repeatedly said to me: "I am inclined to believe that the universe is eternal and infinite. It seems to me that an eternal and infinite effect must necessarily flow from an eternal and infinite cause; and an infinite wisdom, goodness, and power, that could have been induced to produce a universe in time, must have produced it from eternity. It seems to me, the effect must flow from the cause."

Now, my friend, Jefferson, suppose an eternal, self-existent being, existing from eternity, possessed of infinite wisdom, goodness and power, in absolute, total solitude, six thousand years ago, conceiving the benevolent project of creating a universe! I have no more to say at present. It has been long, very long, a settled opinion in my mind, that there is now, ever will be, and never was, but one being who can understand the universe. And that it is not only vain but wicked, for insects to pretend to comprehend it.

JEFFERSON TO ADAMS, OCTOBER 13, 1813

I now send you, according to your request, a copy of the syllabus. To fill up this skeleton with arteries, with veins, with nerves, muscles and flesh, is really beyond my time and information. Whoever could undertake it would find great aid in [William] Enfield's judicious abridgement of [Johann Jakob] Brucker's History of Philosophy, in which he has reduced five or six quarto volumes, of one thousand pages each of Latin closely printed, to two moderate octavos of English open type.

To compare the morals of the Old, with those of the New Testament, would require an attentive study of the former, a search through all its books for its precepts, and through all its history for its practices, and the principles they prove. As commentaries, too, on these, the philosophy of the Hebrews must be inquired into, their Mishna, their Gemara, Cabbala, Jezirah, Sohar, Cosri, and their Talmud, must be examined and understood, in order to do them full justice. Brucker, it would seem, has gone deeply into these repositories of their ethics, and Enfield, his epitomizer, concludes in these words: "Ethics were so little understood among the Jews, that in their whole compilation called the Talmud, there is only one treatise on moral subjects. Their books of morals chiefly consisted in a minute enumeration of duties. From the law of Moses were deduced six hundred and thirteen precepts, which were divided into two classes, affirmative and negative, two hundred and forty-eight in the former and three hundred and sixty-five in the latter. It may serve to give the reader some idea of the low state of moral philosophy among the Jews in the middle age, to add that of the two hundred and forty-eight affirmative precepts, only three were considered as obligatory upon women, and that in order to obtain salvation, it was judged sufficient to fulfil any one single law in the hour of death; the observance of the rest being deemed necessary, only to increase the felicity of the future life. What a wretched depravity of sentiment and manners must have prevailed, before such corrupt maxims could have obtained credit! It is impossible to collect from these writings a consistent series of moral doctrine." Enfield, B. 4, Chap. 3.

It was the reformation of this "wretched depravity" of morals which Jesus undertook. In extracting the pure principles which he taught, we should have to strip off the artificial vestments in which they have been muffled by priests, who have travestied them into various forms, as instruments of riches and power to themselves. We must dismiss the Platonists and Plotinists, the Stagyrites and Gamalielites, the Eclectics, the Gnostics and Scholastics, their essences and emanations, their Logos and Demiurgos, Aeons and Daemons, male and female, with a long train of etc., etc., etc., or, shall I say at once, of nonsense. We must reduce our volume to the simple evangelists, select, even from them, the very words only of Jesus, paring off the amphiboligisms into which they have been led, by forgetting often, or not understanding, what had fallen from him, by giving their own misconceptions as his dicta, and expressing unintelligibly for others what they had not understood themselves. There will be found remaining the most sublime and benevolent code of morals which has ever been offered to man.

I have performed this operation for my own use, by cutting verse by verse out of the printed book, and arranging the matter which is evidently his, and which is as easily distinguishable as diamonds in a dunghill. The result is an octavo of forty-six pages, of pure and unsophisticated doctrines, such as were professed and acted on by the *unlettered* Apostles, the Apostolic Fathers, and the Christians of the first century. Their Platonising successors, indeed, in after times, in order to legitimate the corruptions which they had incorporated into the doctrines of Jesus, found it necessary to disavow the primitive Christians, who had taken their principles from the mouth of Jesus himself, of his Apostles, and the Fathers contemporary with them. They excommunicated their followers as heretics, branding them with the opprobrious name of Ebionites or Beggars.

For a comparison of the Grecian philosophy with that of Jesus, materials might be largely drawn from the same source. Enfield gives a history and detailed account of the opinions and principles of the different sects. These relate to the Gods, their natures, grades, places, and powers; the demi-Gods and Daemons, and their agency with man; the universe, its structure, extent and duration; the origin of things from the elements of fire, water, air and earth; the human soul, its essence and derivation; the *summum bonum* and *finis bonorum*; with a thousand idle dreams and fancies on these and other subjects, the knowledge of which is withheld from man; leaving but a short chapter for his moral duties, and the principal section of that given to what he owes himself, to precepts for rendering him impassible, and unassailable by the evils of life, and for preserving his mind in a state of constant serenity.

Such a canvas is too broad for the age of seventy, and especially of one whose chief occupations have been in the practical business of life. We must leave, therefore, to others, younger, and more learned than we are, to prepare this euthanasia for Platonic Christianity, and its restoration to the primitive simplicity of its founder. I think you give a just outline of the theism of the three religions, when you say that the principle of the Hebrew was the fear, of the Gentile the honor, and of the Christian the love of God.

An expression in your letter of September the 14th, that "the human understanding is a revelation from its maker," gives the best solution that I believe can be given of the question, "what did Socrates mean by his Daemon?" He was too wise to believe, and too honest to pretend, that he had real and familiar converse with a superior and invisible being. He probably considered the suggestions of his conscience, or reason, as revelations or inspirations from the Supreme mind, bestowed, on important occasions, by a special superintending Providence.

I acknowledge all the merit of the hymn of Cleanthes to Jupiter, which you ascribe to it. It is as highly sublime as a chaste and correct imagination can permit itself to go. Yet in the contemplation of a being so superlative, the hyperbolic flights of the Psalmist may often be followed with approbation, even with rapture; and I have no hesitation in giving him the palm over all the hymnists of every language and of every time. Turn to the 148th psalm, in Brady and Tate's version. Have such conceptions been ever before expressed? Their version of the 15th psalm is more to be esteemed for its pithiness than its poetry. Even Sternhold, the leaden Sternhold, kindles, in a single instance, with the sublimity of his original, and expresses the majesty of God descending on the earth, in terms not unworthy of the subject:

> The Lord descended from above,
> And underneath his feet he cast
> On Cherubim and Seraphim
> And on the wings of mighty winds
> And bowed the heav'ns most high;
> The darkness of the sky.
> Full royally he rode;
> Came flying all abroad.   Psalm xviii. 9, 10.

JEFFERSON TO ADAMS, OCTOBER 28, 1813

I agree with you that there is a natural aristocracy among men. The grounds of this are virtue and talents. Formerly, bodily powers gave place among the aristoi. But since the invention of gunpowder has armed the weak as well as the strong with missile death, bodily strength, like beauty, good humor, politeness and other accomplishments, has become but an auxiliary ground of distinction. There is also an artificial aristocracy, founded on wealth and birth, without either virtue or talents; for with these it would belong to the first class. The natural aristocracy I consider as the most precious gift of nature, for the instruction, the trusts, and government of society. And indeed, it would have been inconsistent in creation to have formed man for the social state, and not to have provided virtue and wisdom enough to manage the concerns of the society. May we not even say, that that form of government is the best, which provides the most effectually for a pure selection of these natural aristoi into the offices of government? The artificial aristocracy is a mischievous ingredient in government, and provision should be made to prevent its ascendency. On the question, what is the best provision, you and I differ; but we differ as rational friends, using the free exercise of our own reason, and mutually indulging its errors. You think it best to put the pseudo-aristoi into a separate chamber of legislation, where they may be hindered from doing mischief by their co-ordinate branches, and where, also, they may be a protection to wealth against the Agrarian and plundering enterprises of the majority of the people. I think that to give them power in order to prevent them from doing mischief, is arming them for it, and increasing instead of remedying the evil. For if the co-ordinate branches can arrest their action, so may they that of the co-ordinates. Mischief may be done negatively as well as positively. Of this, a cabal in the Senate of the United States has furnished many proofs. Nor do I believe them necessary to protect the wealthy; because enough of these will find their way into every branch of the legislation, to protect themselves. From fifteen to twenty legislatures of our own, in action for thirty years past, have proved that no fears of an equalization of property are to be apprehended from them. I think the best remedy is exactly that provided by all our constitutions, to leave to the citizens the free election and separation of the aristoi from the pseudo-aristoi, of the wheat from the chaff. In general they will elect the really good and wise. In some instances, wealth may corrupt, and birth blind them; but not in sufficient degree to endanger the society.

It is probable that our difference of opinion may, in some measure, be produced by a difference of character in those among whom we live. From what I have seen of Massachusetts and Connecticut myself, and still more from what I have heard, and the character given of the former by yourself, who know them so much better, there seems to be in those two states a traditionary reverence for certain families, which has rendered the offices of the government nearly hereditary in those families. I presume that from an early period of your history, members of those families happening to possess virtue and talents, have honestly exercised them for the good of the people, and by their services have endeared their names to them. In coupling Connecticut with you, I mean it politically only, not morally.

For having made the Bible the common law of their land, they seem to have modeled their morality on the story of Jacob and Laban. But although this hereditary succession to office with you, may, in some degree, be founded in real family merit, yet in a much higher degree, it has proceeded from your strict alliance of Church and State. These families are canonized in the eyes of the people on common principles, "you tickle me, and I will tickle you." In Virginia we have nothing of this. Our clergy, before the revolution, having been secured against rivalship by fixed salaries, did not give themselves the trouble of acquiring influence over the people. Of wealth, they were great accumulations in particular families, handed down from generation to generation, under the English law of entails. But the only object of ambition for the wealthy was a seat in the King's Council. All their court then was paid to the crown and its creatures; and they Philipised in all collisions between the King and the people. Hence they were unpopular; and that unpopularity continues attached to their names. . . .

The law for religious freedom, having put down the aristocracy of the clergy, and restored to the citizen the freedom of the mind, and those of entails and descents nurturing an equality of condition among them, this on education would have raised the mass of the people to the high ground of moral respectability necessary to their own safety, and to orderly government; and would have completed the great object of qualifying them to select the veritable aristoi, for the trusts of government, to the exclusion of the pseudalists; and the same Theognis who has furnished the epigraphs of your two letters, assures us that

Οὐδεμίαν πω, Κυρν᾽, ἀγαθοὶ πόλιν ὤλεσαν ἄνδρες.[10]

Although this law has not yet been acted on but in a small and inefficient degree, it is still considered as before the legislature, with other bills of the revised code, not yet taken up, and I have great hope that some patriotic spirit will, at a favorable moment, call it up, and make it the key-stone of the arch of our government. . . .

Even in Europe a change has sensibly taken place in the mind of man. Science had liberated the ideas of those who read and reflect, and the American example had kindled feelings of right in the people. An insurrection has consequently begun, of science, talents, and courage, against rank and birth, which have fallen into contempt. It has failed in its first effort, because the mobs of the cities, the instrument used for its accomplishment, debased by ignorance, poverty, and vice, could not be restrained to rational action. But the world will recover from the panic of this first catastrophe. Science is progressive, and talents and enterprise on the alert. Resort may

---

[10] [Up to this time, Kurn, good men have destroyed not even one city.—ED.]

be had to the people of the country, a more governable power from their principles and subordination; and rank, and birth, and tinsel-aristocracy will finally shrink into insignificance, even there. This, however, we have no right to meddle with. It suffices for us, if the moral and physical condition of our own citizens qualifies them to select the able and good for the direction of their government, with a recurrance of elections at such short periods as will enable them to displace an unfaithful servant, before the mischief he meditates may be irremediable.

I have thus stated my opinion on a point on which we differ, not with a view to controversy, for we are both too old to change opinions which are the result of a long life of inquiry and reflection; but on the suggestions of a former letter of yours, that we ought not to die before we have explained ourselves to each other. We acted in perfect harmony, through a long and perilous contest for our liberty and independence. A constitution has been acquired, which, though neither of us thinks perfect, yet both consider as competent to render our fellow citizens the happiest and the securest on whom the sun has ever shone. If we do not think exactly alike as to its imperfections, it matters little to our country, which, after devoting to it long lives of disinterested labor, we have delivered over to our successors in life, who will be able to take care of it and of themselves.

Of the pamphlet on aristocracy which has been sent to you, or who may be its author, I have heard nothing but through your letter. If the person you suspect, it may be known from the quaint, mystical, and hyperbolical ideas, involved in affected, new-fangled and pedantic terms which stamp his writings. Whatever it be, I hope your quiet is not to be affected at this day by the rudeness or intemperance of scribblers; but that you may continue in tranquility to live and to rejoice in the prosperity of our country; until it shall be your own wish to take your seat among the aristoi who have gone before you.

ADAMS TO JEFFERSON, NOVEMBER 15, 1813

Accept my thanks for the comprehensive syllabus in your favor of October 12th.

The Psalms of David, in sublimity, beauty, pathos, and originality, or, in one word, in poetry, are superior to all the odes, hymns and songs in our language. But I had rather read them in our prose translation than in any version I have seen. His morality, however, often shocks me, like Tristram Shandy's execrations.

Blacklock's translation of Horace's "Justum" is admirable; superior to Addison's. Could David be translated as well, his superiority would be universally acknowledged. We cannot compare the sublime poetry. By Virgil's

"Pollio," we may conjecture there was prophecy as well as sublimity. Why have those verses been annihilated? I suspect Platonic Christianity, Pharisaical Judaism or Machiavilian politics, in this case, as in all other cases, of the destruction of records and literary monuments.

The auri sacra fames, et dominandi saeva cupido.[11]

Among all your researches in Hebrew history and controversy, have you ever met a book the design of which is to prove that the ten commandments, as we have them in our Catechisms and hung up in our churches, were not the ten commandments written by the finger of God upon tables delivered to Moses on Mount Sinai, and broken by him in a passion with Aaron for his golden calf, nor those afterwards engraved by him on tables of stone; but a very different set of commandments?

There is such a book, by J. W. Goethe's Schriften, Berlin, 1775-1779. I wish to see this book. You will perceive the question in Exodus, 20: 1, 17, 22, 28; chapter 24: 3, &c; chapter 24: 12; chapter 25: 31; chapter 31: 18; chapter 31: 19; chapter 34: 1; chapter 34: 10, &c.

I will make a covenant with all this people. Observe that which I command this day:

1. Thou shalt not adore any other God. Therefore take heed not to enter into covenant with the inhabitants of the country; neither take for your sons their daughters in marriage. They would allure thee to the worship of false Gods. Much less shall you in any place erect images.

2. The feast of unleavened bread shalt thou keep. Seven days shalt thou eat unleavened bread, at the time of the month Abib; to remember that about that time, I delivered thee from Egypt.

3. Every first born of the mother is mine; the male of thine herd, be it stock or flock. But you shall replace the first born of an ass with a sheep. The first born of your sons shall you redeem. No man shall appear before me with empty hands.

4. Six days shalt thou labor. The seventh day thou shalt rest from ploughing and gathering.

5. The feast of weeks shalt thou keep with the firstlings of the wheat harvest; and the feast of harvesting at the end of the year.

6. Thrice in every year all male persons shall appear before the Lord. Nobody shall invade your country, as long as you obey this command.

7. Thou shalt not sacrifice the blood of a sacrifice of mine, upon leavened bread.

8. The sacrifice of the Passover shall not remain till the next day.

---

[11] [The holy hunger for gold and the raging desire for ruling.—ED.]

9. The firstlings of the produce of your land, thou shalt bring to the house of the Lord.

10. Thou shalt not boil the kid, while it is yet sucking.

And the Lord spake to Moses: Write these words, as after these words I made with you and with Israel a covenant.

I know not whether Goethe translated or abridged from the Hebrew, or whether he used any translation, Greek, Latin, or German. But he differs in form and words somewhat from our version, Exodus 34: 10 to 28. The sense seems to be the same. The tables were the evidence of the covenant, by which the Almighty attached the people of Israel to himself. By these laws they were separated from all other nations, and were reminded of the principal epochs of their history.

When and where originated our ten commandments? The tables and the ark were lost. Authentic copies in few, of any hands; the ten Precepts could not be observed, and were little remembered.

If the book of Deuteronomy was compiled, during or after the Babylonian captivity, from traditions, the error or amendment might come in those.

But you must be weary, as I am at present of problems, conjectures, and paradoxes, concerning Hebrew, Grecian and Christian and all other antiquities; but while we believe that the *finis bonorum* will be happy, we may have learned men to their disquisitions and criticisms.

I admire your employment in selecting the philosophy and divinity and separating it from all mixtures. If I had eyes and nerves I would go through both Testaments and mark all that I understand. To examine the Mishna, Gemara, Cabbala, Jezirah, Sohar, Cosri and Talmud of the Hebrews would require the life of Methuselah, and, after all his 969 years would be wasted to very little purpose. The daemon of hierarchical despotism has been at work both with the Mishna and Gemara. In 1238 a French Jew made a discovery to the Pope (Gregory the 9th) of the heresies of the Talmud. The Pope sent thirty-five articles of error to the Archbishops of France, requiring them to seize the books of the Jews and burn all that contained any errors. He wrote in the same terms to the kings of France, England, Arragon, Castile, Leon, Navarre, and Portugal. In consequence of this order, twenty cartloads of Hebrew books were burnt in France; and how many times twenty cartloads were destroyed in other kingdoms? The Talmud of Babylon and that of Jerusalem were composed from 120 to 500 years after the destruction of Jerusalem.

If Lightfoot derived light from what escaped from Gregory's fury, in explaining many passages in the New Testament, by comparing the expressions of the Mishna with those of the Apostles and Evangelists, how many proofs of the corruptions of Christianity might we find in the passages burnt?

ADAMS TO JEFFERSON, NOVEMBER 15, 1813

The proverbs of Theognis, like those of Solomon, are observations on human nature, ordinary life, and civil society, with moral reflections on the facts. I quoted him as a witness of the fact, that there was as much difference in the races of men as in the breeds of sheep, and as a sharp reprover and censurer of the sordid, mercenary practice of disgracing birth by preferring gold to it. Surely no authority can be more expressly in point to prove the existence of inequalities, not of rights, but of moral, intellectual, and physical inequalities in families, descents and generations. If a descent from pious, virtuous, wealthy, literary, or scientific ancestors, is a letter or recommendation, or introduction in a man's favor, and enables him to influence only one vote in addition to his own, he is an aristocrat; for a democrat can have but one vote. Aaron Burr has 100,000 votes from the single circumstance of his descent from President Burr and President Edwards.

Your commentary on the proverbs of Theognis, reminded me of two solemn characters; the one resembling John Bunyan, the other Scarron. The one John Torrey, the other Ben Franklin. Torrey, a poet, an enthusiast, a superstitious bigot, once very gravely asked my brother, whether it would not be better for mankind if children were always begotten by religious motives only? Would not religion in this sad case have as little efficacy in encouraging procreation, as it has now in discouraging it? I should apprehend a decrease of population, even in our country where it increases so rapidly.

ADAMS TO JEFFERSON, DECEMBER 3, 1813

The proverbs of the old Greek poets are as short and pithy as any of Solomon or Franklin. Hesiod has several. His Ἀθανάτους μὲν πρῶτα θέους νόμῳ ὡς διάκειται τίμα. Honor the gods established by law. I know not how we can escape martyrdom without a discreet attention to this precept. You have suffered, and I have suffered more than you, for want of a strict observance of this rule.

There is another oracle of this Hesiod, which requires a kind of dance upon a tight rope and a slack rope too, in philosophy and theology: πίστις δ' ἀρῦ ὅμως καὶ ἀπιστία ὤλεσαν ἄνδρας. If believing too little or too much is so fatal to mankind, what will become of us all?

In studying the perfectability of human nature and its progress towards perfection in this world, on this earth, remember that I have met many curious and interesting characters.

About three hundred years ago, there appeared a number of men of letters, who appeared to endeavor to believe neither too little nor too much. They labored to imitate the Hebrew archers, who could shoot to an hair's breadth. The Pope and his church believed too much. Luther and his church believed too little. This little band was headed by three great scholars: Erasmus, Vives and Budaeus. This triumvirate is said to have been at the head of the republic of letters in that age. Had Condorcet been master of his subject, I fancy he would have taken more notice, in his History of the Progress of Mind, of these characters. Have you their writings? I wish I had. I shall confine myself at present to Vives. He wrote commentaries on the City of God of St. Augustine, some parts of which were censured by the Doctors of the Louvain, as too bold and too free. I know not whether the following passage of the learned Spaniard was among the sentiments condemned or not:

"I have been much afflicted," says Vives, "when I have seriously considered how diligently, and with what exact care, the actions of Alexander, Hannibal, Scipio, Pompey, Caesar and other commanders, and the lives of Socrates, Plato, Aristotle, and other philosophers, have been written and fixed in an everlasting remembrance, so that there is not the least danger they can ever be lost; but then the acts of the Apostles and marytrs and saints of our religion, and of the affairs of the rising and established church, being involved in much darkness, are almost totally unknown, though they are of so much greater advantage than the lives of the philosophers or great generals, both as to the improvement of our knowledge and practice. For what is written of these holy men, except a very few things, is very much corrupted and defaced with the mixture of many fables, while the writer, indulging his own humor, doth not tell us what the saint did, but what the historian would have had him do. And the fancy of the writer dictates the life and not the truth of things." And again Vives says: "There have been men who have thought it a great piece of piety, to invent lies for the sake of religion."

The great Cardinal Barronius, too, confesses: "There is nothing which seems so much neglected to this day, as a true and certain account of the affairs of the church, collected with an exact diligence. And that I may speak of the more ancient, it is very difficult to find any of them who have published commentaries on this subject, which have hit the truth in all points."

Canus, too, another Spanish prelate of great name, says: "I speak it with grief, and not by way of reproach, Laertius has written the lives of the philosophers with more ease and industry than the Christians have those of the saints. Suetonius has represented the lives of the Caesars with much more truth and sincerity than the Catholics have the affairs (I will not say of the emperors) but even those of the martyrs, holy virgins and confessors. For they have not concealed the vice nor the very suspicions of vice, in good and commendable philosophers or princes, and in the worst of them they discover the very colors or appearances of virtue. But the greatest part of our writers either follow the conduct of their affections, or industriously feign many things; so that I, for my part, am very often both weary and ashamed of them, because I know that they have thereby brought nothing of advantage to the church of Christ, but very much inconvenience." Vives and Canus are moderns, but Arnobius, the converter of Lactantius, was ancient. He says: "But neither could all that was done be written, or arrive at the knowledge of all men—many of our great actions being done by obscure men and those who had no knowledge of letters. And if some of them are committed to letters and writings, yet even here, by the malice of the devils and men like them, whose great design and study is to intercept and ruin this truth, by interpolating or adding some things to them, or by changing or taking out words, syllables or letters, they have put a stop to the faith of wise men, and corrupted the truth of things."

Indeed, Mr. Jefferson, what could be invented to debase the ancient Christianism, which Greeks, Romans, Hebrews and Christian factions, above all the Catholics, have not fraudulently imposed upon the public? Miracles after miracles have rolled down in torrents, wave succeeding wave in the Catholic church, from the Council of Nice, and long before, to this day.

Aristotle, no doubt, thought his Οὔτε πάσα πιστεύοντες, οὔτε πάσιν ἀπιστεύοντες,[12] very wise and very profound; but what is its worth? What man, woman or child ever believed everything or nothing? Oh! that Priestley could live again, and have leisure and means! An inquirer after truth, who had neither time nor means, might request him to search and re-search for answers to a few questions:

1. Have we more than two witnesses of the life of Jesus—Matthew and John?

2. Have we one witness to the existence of Matthew's gospel in the first century?

3. Have we one witness of the existence of John's gospel in the first century?

4. Have we one witness to the existence of Mark's gospel in the first century?

5. Have we one witness of the existence of Luke's gospel in the first century?

6. Have we any witness of the existence of St. Thomas' gospel, that is the gospel of the infancy in the first century?

7. Have we any evidence of the existence of the Acts of the Apostles in the first century?

8. Have we any evidence of the existence of the supplement to the Acts of

---

[12] [Woe to those who believe all men; woe to those who disbelieve all men.—ED.]

the Apostles, Peter and Paul, or Paul and Tecle, in the first century?

Here I was interrupted by a new book, Chateaubriand's Travels in Greece, and Palestine and Egypt, and by a lung fever with which the amiable companion of my life has been violently and dangerously attacked.

December 13th. I have fifty more questions to put to Priestley, but must adjourn them to a future opportunity.

I have read Chateaubriand with as much delight as I ever read Bunyan's Pilgrims' Progress, Robinson Crusoe's Travels, or Gulliver's, or Whitefield's, or Wesley's Life, or the Life of St. Francis, St. Anthony, or St. Ignatius Loyola. A work of infinite learning, perfectly well written, a magazine of information, but enthusiastic, bigoted, superstitious, Roman Catholic throughout. If I were to indulge in jealous criticisms and conjecture, I should suspect that there had been an (Ecuemenical counsel of Popes, Cardinals and Bishops, and that this traveller has been employed at their expense to make this tour, to lay a foundation for the resurrection of the Catholic Hierarchy in Europe.

Have you read La Harpe's Course de Literature, in fifteen volumes? Have you read St. Pierre's Studies of Nature?

I am now reading the controversy between Voltaire and Manotte.

Our friend Rush has given us for his last legacy, an analysis of some of the diseases of the mind.

Johnson said, "We are all more or less mad;" and who is or has been more mad than Johnson?

I know of no philosopher, or theologian, or moralist, ancient or modern, more profound, more infallible than Whitefield, if the anecdote I heard be true.

He began: "Father Abraham," with his hands and eyes gracefully directed to the heavens, as I have more than once seen him; "Father Abraham, who have you there with you? Have you Catholics?"

"No."

"Have you Protestants?"

"No."

"Have you Churchmen?"

"No."

"Have you Dissenters?"

"No."

"Have you Presbyterians?"

"No."

"Quakers?"

"No."

"Anabaptists?"

"No."

"Who have you there? Are you alone?"

"No."

"My brethren, you have the answer to all these questions in the words of my text: 'He who feareth God and worketh righteousness, shall be accepted of Him.'"

Allegiance to the Creator and Governor of the Milky-Way, and the Nebulae, and benevolence to all his creatures, is my Religion.

Si quid novisti rectius istis, candidus imperti.[13]

I am as ever.

ADAMS TO JEFFERSON, DECEMBER 25, 1813

Answer my letter at your leisure. Give yourself no concern. I write as a refuge and protection against *ennui*.

The fundamental principle of all philosophy and all Christianity is, "*Rejoice always in all things.*" "Be thankful at all times for all good, and all that we call evil." Will it not follow, that I ought to rejoice and be thankful that Priestley has lived? Aye, that Voltaire has lived? I should have given my reason for rejoicing in Voltaire, &c. It is because I believe they have done more than even Luther or Calvin to lower the tone of that proud hierarchy that shot itself up above the clouds, and more to propagate religious liberty than Calvin, or Luther, or even Locke. That Gibbon has lived? That Hume has lived, though a conceited Scotchman? That Bolingbroke has lived, though a haughty, arrogant, supercilious dogmatist? That Burke and Johnson have lived, though superstitious slaves, or self-deceiving hypocrites both? Is it not laughable to hear Burke call Bolingbroke a superficial writer; to hear him ask, "who ever read him through!" Had I been present, I should have answered him: "I, I myself! I have read him through, more than fifty years ago, and more than five times in my life, and once within five years past. And, in my opinion, the epithet 'superficial' belongs to you and your friend Johnson more than to him." I might say much more; but I believe Burke and Johnson to have been as political Christians as Leo X.

I return to Priestley, though I have great complaints against him for personal injuries and persecution, at the same time that I forgive it all, and hope and pray that he may be pardoned for it all above. Dr. Brocklesby, an intimate friend and convivial companion of Johnson, told me, that Johnson died in agonies of horror of annihilation; and all the accounts we

---

[13] [Horace, "If you know anything better than these maxims of mine, tell me candidly."—ED.]

have of his death corroborate this account of Brocklesby. Dread of annihilation! Dread of nothing! A dread of nothing, I should think, would be no dread at all. Can there be any real, substantial, rational fear of nothing? Were you on your deathbed, and in your last moments informed by demonstration or revelation that you would cease to think and to feel at your dissolution, should you be terrified? You might be ashamed of yourself for having lived so long, to bear the proud man's contumely; you might be ashamed of your Maker, and compare Him to a little girl amusing herself, her brothers, and sisters by blowing bubbles in soapsuds; you might compare Him to boys, sporting with crackers and rockets, or to men employed in making more artificial fireworks, or to men and women at fairs and operas, or Sadler's Wells exploits; or to politicians, in their intrigues; or to heroes, in their butcheries; or to Popes, in their devilisms. But what should you fear? Nothing. *Emori nolo; sed me mortuum esse nihil aestimo.*[14]

To return to Priestley—you could make a more luminous book than his upon the "Doctrines of Heathen Philosophers, compared with those of Revelation." Why has he not given us a more satisfactory account of the Pythagorean philosophy and theology? He barely names Ocellus, who lived long before Plato. His treatise of kings and monarchy has been destroyed, I conjecture, by Platonic philosophers, Platonic Jews or Christians, or by fraudulent republicans or despots. His treatise of the universe has been preserved. He labors to prove the eternity of the world. The Marquis D'Argens translated it in all its noble simplicity. The Abbé Batteux has given another translation. D'Argens not only explains the text, but sheds more light upon the ancient systems. His remarks are so many treatises, which develop the concatenation of ancient opinions. The most essential ideas of the theology, of the physics, and of the morality of the ancients are clearly explained, and their different doctrines compared with one another, and with modern discoveries. I wish I owned this book, and one hundred thousand more that I want every day, now when I am almost incapable of making any use of them. No doubt, he informs us that Pythagoras was a great traveller.

Priestley barely mentions Timaeus; but it does not appear that he had read him. Why has he not given us an account of him and his book? He was before Plato, and gave him the idea of his Timaeus, and much more of his philosophy. After his master, he maintained the existence of matter; that matter was capable of receiving all sorts of forms; that a moving power agitates all the parts of it, and that an intelligence directed the moving power; that this intelligence produced a regular and harmonious world.

---

[14] [I do not wish to die, but I won't care when I am dead.—ED.]

The intelligence had seen a plan, an IDEA (logos), in conformity to which it wrought, and without which it would not have known what it was about, nor what it wanted to do. This plan was the idea, image, or model, which had represented to the Supreme Intelligence the world before it existed, which had directed it in its action upon the moving power, and which it contemplated in forming the elements, the bodies, and the world. This model was distinguished from the intelligence which produced the world, as the architect is from his plans. He divided the production cause of the world into a spirit, which directed the moving force, and into an image, which determined it in the choice of the directions which it gave to the moving force, and the forms which it gave to matter.

I wonder that Priestley has overlooked this, because it is the same philosophy with Plato's, and would have shown that the Pythagorean, as well as the Platonic philosophers, probably concurred in the fabrication of the Christian Trinity. Priestley mentions the name of Archytas, but does not appear to have read him, though he was a successor of Pythagoras, and a great mathematician, a great statesman, and a great general. John Gram, a learned and honorable Dane, has given a handsome edition of his works, with a Latin translation, and an ample account of his life and writings. Zaleucus, the legislator of Locris, and Charondas of Sybaris, were disciples of Pythagoras, and both celebrated to immortality for the wisdom of their laws, five hundred years before Christ. Why are those laws lost? I say, the spirit of party has destroyed them; civil, political, and ecclesiastical bigotry. Despotical, monarchical, aristocratical, and democratical fury, have all been employed in this work of destruction of everything that could give us true light, and a clear insight of antiquity. For every one of these parties, when possessed of power, or when they have been undermost, and struggling to get uppermost, has been equally prone to every species of fraud and violence and usurpation. Why has not Priestley mentioned these legislators? The preamble to the laws of Zaleucus, which is all that remains, is as orthodox as Christian theology as Priestley's, and Christian benevolence and forgiveness of injuries almost as clearly expressed.

Priestley ought to have done impartial justice to philosophy and philosophers. Philosophy, which is the result of reason, is the first, the original revelation of the Creator to his creature, man. When this revelation is clear and certain, by intuition or necessary inductions, no subsequent revelation, supported by prophecies or miracles, can supersede it. Philosophy is not only the love of wisdom, but the science of the universe and its cause. There is, there was, and there will be but one master of philosophy in the universe. Portions of it, in different degrees, are revealed to creatures. Philosophy looks with an impartial eye on all terrestrial religions. I have examined all, as well as my narrow sphere, my straitened means, and my busy life would allow me; and the result is, that the Bible is the best book in the world. It contains more of my little philosophy than all the libraries I have seen; and such parts of it as I cannot reconcile to my little philosophy, I postpone for future investigation. Priestley ought to have given us a sketch of the religion and morals of Zoroaster, of Sanchoniathon, of Confucius, and all the founders of religions before Christ, whose superiority would, from such comparison, have appeared the more transcendent. Priestley ought to have told us that Pythagoras passed twenty years in his travels in India, in Egypt, in Chaldea, perhaps in Sodom and Gomorrah, Tyre and Sidon. He ought to have told us, that in India he conversed with the Brahmins, and read the Shasta, five thousand years old, written in the language of the sacred Sanscrit, with the elegance and sentiments of Plato. Where is to be found theology more orthodox, or philosophy more profound, than in the introduction to the Shasta?

"God is one, creator of all, universal sphere, without beginning, without end. God governs all the creation by a general providence, resulting from his eternal designs. Search not the essence and the nature of the Eternal, who is one; your research will be vain and presumptuous. It is enough, that, day by day and night by night, you adore his power, his wisdom, and his goodness, in his works. The Eternal willed, in the fulness of time, to communicate of his essence and of his splendor, to beings capable of perceiving it. They as yet existed not. The Eternal willed, and they were. He created Birma, Vitsnow, and Sib."

These doctrines, sublime, if ever there were any sublime, Pythagoras learned in India, and taught them to Zaleucus and his other disciples. He there learned also his metempsychosis; but this never was popular, never made much progress in Greece or Italy, or any other country besides India and Tartary, the religion of the grand immortal Lama. And how does this differ from the possessions of demons in Greece and Rome, from the demon of Socrates, from the worship of cows and crocodiles in Egypt and elsewhere? After migrating through various animals, from elephants to serpents, according to their behaviour, souls that, at last, behaved well, became men and women, and then, if they were good, they went to Heaven. All ended in Heaven, if they became virtuous. Who can wonder at the widow of Malabar? Where is the lady who, if her faith were without doubt that she should go to Heaven with her husband on the one hand, or migrate into a toad or a wasp on the other, would not lie down on the pile, and set fire to the fuel? Modifications and disguises of the metempsychosis had crept into Egypt, and Greece, and Rome, and other countries. Have you read Farmer on the demons and possessions of The New Testament?

According to the Shasta, Moisayer, with his companions, rebelled against the Eternal, and were precipitated down to Ondero, the region of darkness.

Do you know anything of the prophecy of Enoch? Can you give me a comment on the 6th, the 9th, and the 14th verses of the epistle of Jude?

If I am not weary of writing, I am sure you must be of reading such incoherent rattle. I will not persecute you so severely in future, if I can help it, so farewell.

JEFFERSON TO ADAMS, JANUARY 24, 1814

You ask me if I have ever seen the work of J. W. Goethe's Schriften? Never; nor did the question ever occur to me before where get we the Ten Commandments. The book indeed gives them to us verbatim, but where did it get them? For itself tells us they were written by the finger of God on tables of stone, which were destroyed by Moses; it specifies those on the second set of tables in different form and substance, but still without saying how the others were recovered. But the whole history of these books is so defective and doubtful, that it seems vain to attempt minute inquiry into it; and such tricks have been played with their text, and with the texts of other books relating to them, that we have a right from that cause to entertain much doubt what parts of them are genuine. In the New Testament there is internal evidence that parts of it have proceeded from an extraordinary man; and that other parts are of the fabric of very inferior minds. It is as easy to separate those parts, as to pick out diamonds from dunghills. The matter of the first was such as would be preserved in the memory of the hearers, and handed on by tradition for a long time; the latter such stuff as might be gathered up, for imbedding it, anywhere, at any time. I have nothing of Vives, or Budaeus and very little of Erasmus. If the familiar histories of the Saints, the want of which they regret, would have given us the histories of those tricks which these writers acknowledge to have been practised, and of the lies they agree have been invented for the sake of religion, I join them in their regrets. These would be the only parts of their histories worth reading. It is not only the sacred volumes they have thus interpolated, gutted, and falsified, but the works of others relating to them and even the laws of the land. We have a curious instance of one of these pious frauds in the laws of Alfred. He composed, you know, from the laws of the Heptarchy, a digest for the government of the United Kingdom, and in his preface to that work he tells us expressly the sources from which he drew it, to wit, the laws of Ina, of Offa, and Aethelbert (not naming the Pentateuch). But his pious interpolator, very awkwardly, *premises* to his work four chapters of Exodus (from the 20th to the 23rd) as a part of the laws of the land; so that Alfred's *preface* is made to stand in the body of the work. Our judges too have lent a ready hand to further these frauds, and have been willing to lay the yoke of their own opinions on the necks of others; to extend the coercions of municipal law to the dogmas of their religion, by declaring that these make a part of the law of the land. In the Year-Book 34, H.6, p. 38, in Quare impedit, where the question was how far the common law takes notice of the ecclesiastical law, Prisot, Chief Justice, in the course of his argument, says, "a tiels leis que ils de seint eglise ont, en *ancien scripture,* covient a nous a donner credence; car ces common luy sur quels touts manners leis sont fondes; et auxy, siv, nous sumus obliges de canustre lour esy de saint eglise," etc. Finch begins the business of falsification by mistranslating and misstating the words of Prisot thus: "to such laws of the church as have warrant in *holy scripture* our law giveth credence." Citing the above case and the words of Prisot in the margin, Finch's law, B. 1, c. 3, here then we find *ancien scripture,* ancient writing, translated "holy scripture." This, Wingate, in 1658, erects into a maxim of law in the very words of Finch, but citing Prisot and not Finch. And Sheppard, tit. Religion, in 1675 laying it down in the same words of Finch, quotes the Year-Book, Finch and Wingate. Then comes Sir Matthew Hale, in the case of the King v. Taylor, 1 Ventr. 293, 3. Keb. 607, and declares that "Christianity is part and parcel of the laws of England." Citing nobody, and resting it, with his judgment against the witches, on his own authority, which indeed was sound and good in all cases into which no superstition or bigotry could enter. Thus strengthened, the court in 1728, in the King v. Woolston, would not suffer it to be questioned whether to write against Christianity was punishable at common law, saying it had been so settled by Hale in Taylor's case, 2 Stra. 834. Wood, therefore, 409, without scruple, lays down as a principle, that all blaspheming and profaneness are offences at the common law, and cites Strange. Blackstone, in 1763, repeats, in the words of Sir Matthew Hale, that "Christianity is part of the laws of England," citing Ventris and Strange, *ubi supra.* And Lord Mansfield, in the case of the Chamberlain of London v. Evans, in 1767, qualifying somewhat the position, says that "the essential principles of revealed religion are part of the common law." Thus we find this string of authorities all handing by one another on a single hook, a mistranslation by Finch of the words of Prisot, or on nothing. For all quote Prisot, or one another, or nobody. Thus Finch misquotes, Prisot; Wingate also, but using Finch's words; Sheppard quotes Prisot, Finch and Wingate; Hale cites nobody; the court in Woolston's case cite Hale; Wood cites Woolston's case Blackstone that and Hale, and Lord Mansfield volunteers his own *ispe dixit.* And who now can question but that the whole Bible and Testament are a part of the common law? And that Connecticut, in her blue laws, laying it down as a principle that the laws of God should be the laws of their land, except where their own contradicted them, did anything more than express, with a salvo, what the English judges had less cautiously declared without any restriction? And what, I dare say, our cunning Chief Justice would swear to, and find as many sophisms to twist it out of the general terms of our declarations of rights, and even the stricter text of the Virginia "act for the freedom of religion," as he did to twist Burr's neck out of the halter of treason. May we not say then with him who was all candor and benevolence, "woe unto you, ye lawyers, for ye lade men with burthens grievous to bear."

I think with you, that Priestley, in his comparison of the doctrines of philosophy and revelation, did not do justice to the undertaking. But he felt himself pressed by the hand of death. Enfield has given us a more distinct account of the ethics of the ancient philosophers; but the great work of which Enfield's is an abridgment, Brucker's History of Philosophy, is the treasure which I would wish to possess, as a book of reference or of special research only, for who could read six volumes quarto, of one thousand pages each, closely printed, of modern Latin? Your account of D'Argens' Ocellus makes me wish for him also. Ocellus furnishes a fruitful text for a sensible and learned commentator. The Abbé Batteux, which I have, is a meagre thing.

ADAMS TO JEFFERSON, FEBRUARY, 1814

Your researches in the laws of England establishing Christianity as the law of the land, and part of the common law, are curious and very important. Questions without number will arise in this country. Religious controversies, and ecclesiastical contests are as common, and will be as sharp as any in civil politics, foreign and domestic. In what sense, and to what extent the Bible is law, may give rise to as many doubts and quarrels as any of our civil, political, military, or maritime laws, and will intermix with them all, to irritate factions of every sort. I dare not look beyond my nose into futurity. Our money, our commerce, our religion, our National and State Constitutions, even our arts and sciences, are so many seed plots, of division, faction, sedition and rebellion. Everything is transmuted into an instrument of electioneering. Election is the grand Brahma, the immortal Lama, I had almost said, the Juggernaut; for wives are almost ready to burn upon the pile, and children to be thrown under the wheel. You will perceive, by these figures, that I have been looking into oriental history, and Hindoo religion. I have read voyages, and travels, and everything I could collect, and the last is Priestley's "Comparison of the Institutions of Moses with those of the Hindoos, and other Ancient Nations," a work of great labor, and not less haste. I thank him for the labor, and forgive, though I lament the hurry. You would be fatigued to read, and I, just recruiting from a little longer confinement and indisposition than I have had for thirty years, have not strength to write many observations. But I have been disappointed in the principal points of my curiosity:

1st. I am disappointed by finding that no just comparison can be made, because of the original Shasta, and the original Vedams are not obtained, or if obtained, not yet translated into any European language.

2nd. In not finding such morsels of the sacred books as have been translated and published, which are more honorable to the original Hindoo religion than anything he has quoted.

3rd. In not finding a full development of the history of the doctrine of the Metempsichosis which originated—

4th. In the history of the rebellion of innumerable hosts of angels in Heaven against the Supreme Being, who after some thousands of years of war, conquered them, and hurled them down to the regions of total darkness, where they have suffered a part of the punishment of their crime, and then were mercifully released from prison, permitted to ascend to earth, and migrate into all sorts of animals, reptiles, birds, beasts, and men, according to their rank and character, and even into vegetables, and minerals, there to serve on probation. If they passed without reproach their several graduations, they were permitted to become cows and men. If as men they behaved well, i.e., to the satisfaction of the priests, they were restored to their original rank and bliss in Heaven.

5th. In not finding the Trinity of Pythagoras and Plato, their contempt of matter, flesh, and blood, their almost adoration of fire and water, their metempsichosis, and even the prohibition of beans, so evidently derived from India.

6th. In not finding the prophecy of Enoch deduced from India, in which the fallen angels make such a figure. But you are weary. Priestley has proved the superiority of the Hebrews, to the Hindoos, as they appear in the Gentoo laws, and institutes of Menu; but the comparison remains to be made with the Shasta.

In his remarks on Mr. Dupuis, page 342, Priestley says: "The history of the fallen angels is another circumstance, on which Mr. Dupuis lays much stress. According to the Christians he says, Vol. I, page 336, there was from the beginning a division among the angels: some remaining faithful to the light, and others taking the part of darkness, &c.; but this supposed history is not found in the Scriptures. It has only been inferred, from a wrong interpretation of one passage in the 2nd epistle of Peter, and a corresponding one in that of Jude, as has been shown by judicious writers. That there is such a person as the Devil, is not a part of my faith, nor that of many other Christians, nor am I sure that it was the belief of any of the Christian writers. Neither do I believe the doctrine of demoniacal possessions, whether it was believed by the sacred writers or not; and yet my unbelief in these articles does not affect my faith in the great facts of which the Evangelists were eye and ear witnesses. They might not be competent judges in the one case, though perfectly so with respect to the other."

I will ask Priestley, when I see him, do you believe those passages in Peter and Jude to be interpolations? If so, by whom made? And when? And where? And for what end? Was it to support, or found, the doctrine of the fall of man, original sin, the universal corruption, depravation and guilt of human nature and mankind; and the subsequent incarnation of God to make atonement and redemption? Or do you think that Peter and Jude believed the book of Enoch to have been written by the seventh from Adam, and one of the sacred canonical books of the Hebrew Prophets? Peter, 2nd epistle, c. 2d, v. 4th, says "For if God spared not the angels that sinned, but cast them down to *hell* and delivered them into chains of *darkness* to be reserved unto Judgment." Jude, v. 6th, says, "and the angels which kept their first estate, but left their own habitations, he hath reserved in everlasting chains under darkness, unto the judgment of the great day." Verse 14th, "And Enoch, also, the seventh from Adam, prophesied of these sayings, behold the Lord cometh with ten thousands of his saints, to execute judgment upon all," &c., Priestley says, "a wrong interpretation" has been given to these texts. I wish he had favored us with his right interpretation of them. In another place, page 326, Priestley says, "There is no circumstance of which Mr. Dupuis avails himself so much, or repeats so often, both with respect to the Jewish and Christian religions, as the history of the *Fall of Man*, in the book of Genesis." I believe with him, and have maintained in my writings, that this history is either an allegory, or founded on uncertain tradition, that it is an hypothesis to account for the origin of evil, adopted by Moses, which by no means accounts for the facts.

March 3rd. So far was written almost a month ago; but sickness has prevented progress. I had much more to say about this work. I shall never be a disciple of Priestley. He is as absurd, inconsistent, credulous, and incomprehensible, as Athanasius. Read his letter to the Jews in this volume. Could a rational creature write it? Aye! such rational creatures as Rochefoucauld, and Condorcet, and John Taylor, in politics, and Towers' Jurious, and French Prophets in Theology. Priestley's account of the philosophy and religion of India, appears to me to be such a work as a man of busy research would produce—who should undertake to describe Christianity from the sixth to the twelfth century, when a deluge of wonders overflowed the world; when miracles were performed and proclaimed from every convent, and monastery, hospital, churchyard, mountain, valley, cave and cupola.

There is a book which I wish I possessed. It has never crossed the Atlantic. It is entitled Acta Sanctorum, in forty-seven volumes in folio. It contains the lives of the saints. It was compiled in the beginning of the sixteenth century by Bollandus, Henschenius and Papebrock. What would I give to possess in one immense mass, one stupendous draught, all the legends, true, doubtful, and false.

These Bollandists dared to discuss some of the facts, and hint that some of them were doubtful. E. G. Papebrock doubted the antiquity of the Carmellites from Elias; and whether the face of Jesus Christ was painted on the handkerchief of St. Veronique; and whether the prepuce of the Saviour of the world, which was shown in the church of Antwerp, could be proved to be genuine? For these bold skepticisms he was libelled in pamphlets, and denounced by the Pope, and the Inquisition in Spain. The Inquisition condemned him; but the Pope not daring to acquit or condemn him, prohibited all writings pro. and con. But as the physicians cure one disease by exciting another, as a fever by a salivation, this Bull was produced by a new claim. The brothers of the Order of Charity asserted a descent from Abraham, nine hundred years anterior to the Carmellites.

A philosopher who should write a description of Christianism from the Bollandistic Saints of the sixth and tenth century would probably produce a work tolerably parallel to Priestley's upon the Hindoos.

JEFFERSON TO ADAMS, JULY 5, 1814

I am just returned from one of my long absences, having been at my other home for five weeks past. Having more leisure there than here for reading, I amused myself with reading seriously Plato's Republic. I am wrong, however, in calling it amusement, for it was the heaviest task-work I ever went through. I had occasionally before taken up some of his other works, but scarcely ever had patience to go through a whole dialogue. While wading through the whimsies, the puerilities, and unintelligible jargon of this work, I laid it down often to ask myself how it could have been, that the world should have so long consented to give reputation to such nonsense as this? How the soi-disant Christian world, indeed, should have done it, is a piece of historical curiosity. But how could the Roman good sense do it? And particularly, how could Cicero bestow such eulogies on Plato? Although Cicero did not wield the dense logic of Demosthenes, yet he was able, learned, laborious, practised in the business of the world, and honest. He could not be the dupe of mere style of which he was himself the first master in the world.

With the moderns, I think, it is rather a matter of fashion and authority. Education is chiefly in the hands of persons who, from their profession, have an interest in the reputation and dreams of Plato. They give the tone while at school, and few in their after years have occasion to revise their college opinions. But fashion and authority apart, and bringing Plato to the test of reason, take from him his sophisms, futilities and incomprehensibilities, and what remains? In truth, he is one of the race of genuine sophists, who has escaped the oblivion of his brethren, first by the elegance of his diction, but chiefly, by the adoption and incorporation of his whimsies into the body of artificial Christianity. His foggy mind is forever presenting the semblances of objects which, half seen through a mist, can be defined neither in form nor dimensions. Yet this, which should have consigned him to early oblivion, really procured him immortality of fame and reverence.

The Christian priesthood, finding the doctrines of Christ levelled to every understanding, and too plain to need explanation, saw in the mysticism of Plato materials with which they might build up an artificial system, which might, from its indistinctness, admit everlasting controversy, give employment for their order, and introduce it to profit, power and pre-eminence. The doctrines which flowed from the lips of Jesus himself are within the comprehension of a child; but thousands of volumes have not yet explained the Platonisms engrafted on them; and for this obvious reason, that nonsense can never be explained. Their purposes, however, are answered. Plato is canonized; and it is now deemed as impious to question his merits as those of an Apostle of Jesus. He is peculiarly appealed to as an advocate of the immortality of the soul; and yet I will venture to say, that were there no better arguments than his in proof of it, not a man in the world would believe it.

It is fortunate for us, that Platonic republicanism has not obtained the same favor as Platonic Christianity; or we should now have been all living, men, women and children, pell mell together, like beasts of the field or forest. Yet "Plato is a great philosopher," said La Fontaine. But, says Fontenelle, "do you find his ideas very clear?" "Oh no! he is of an obscurity impenetrable." "Do you not find him full of contradictions?" "Certainly," replied La Fontaine, "he is but a sophist." Yet immediately after, he exclaims again, "Oh, Plato was a great philosopher." Socrates had reason, indeed, to complain of the misrepresentations of Plato; for in truth, his dialogues are libels on Socrates.

ADAMS TO JEFFERSON, JULY 16, 1814

I am bold to say, that neither you nor I will live to see the course which the "wonders of the times" will take. Many years, and perhaps centuries must pass before the current will acquire a settled direction. If the Christian religion, as I understand it, or as you understand it, should maintain its ground, as I believe it will, yet Platonic, Pythagoric, Hindoo, and cabalistical Christianity, which is Catholic Christianity, and which has prevailed for fifteen hundred years, has received a mortal wound, of which the monster must finally die. Yet so strong is his constitution, that he may endure for centuries before he expires. Government has never been much studied by mankind; but their attention has been drawn to it in the latter part of the last century and the beginning of this, more than at any former period, and the vast variety of experiments which have been made of constitutions in America, in France, in Holland, in Geneva, in Switzerland, and even in Spain and South America, can never be forgotten. They will be studied, and their immediate and remote effects and final catastrophes noted.

The result in the time will be improvements; and I have no doubt that the horrors we have experienced for the last forty years will ultimately terminate in the advancement of civil and religious liberty, and amelioration in the condition of mankind. For I am a believer in the probable improvability and improvement, the ameliorability and amelioration in human affairs; though I could never understand the doctrine of the perfectibility of the human mind. This has always appeared to me like the philosophy of theology of the Gentoos, namely, that a Brahmin, by certain studies for a certain time pursued, and by certain ceremonies a certain number of times repeated, becomes omniscient and almighty.

Our hopes, however, of sudden tranquility ought not to be too sanguine. Fanaticism and superstition will still be selfish, subtle, intriguing, and, at times, furious. Despotism will still struggle for domination; monarchy will still study to rival nobility in popularity; aristocracy will continue to envy all above it, and despise and oppress all below it; democracy will envy all, contend with all, endeavor to pull down all, and when by chance it happens to get the upper hand for a short time, it will be revengeful, bloody, and cruel. These and other elements of fanaticism and anarchy will yet for a long time continue a fermentation, which will excite alarms and require vigilance.

ADAMS TO JEFFERSON, JUNE 20, 1815

The fit of recollection came upon both of us so nearly at the same time, that I may, some time or other, begin to think there is something in Priestley's and Hartley's vibrations. The day before yesterday I sent to the post-office a letter to you, and last night I received your kind favor of the 10th.

The question before the human race is, whether the God of Nature shall govern the world by his own laws, or whether priests and kings shall rule it by fictitious miracles? Or, in other words, whether authority is originally in the people? or whether it has descended for 1800 years in a succession of popes and bishops, or brought down from heaven by the Holy Ghost in the form of a dove, in a phial of holy oil?

Who shall take the side of God and Nature? Brachmans? Mandarins? Druids? Or Tecumseh and his brother the prophet? Or shall we become disciples of the Philosophers? And who are the Philosophers? Frederic? Voltaire? Rousseau? Buffon? Diderot? or Condorcet? These philosophers have shown themselves as incapable of governing mankind, as the Bourbons or the Guelphs. Condorcet has let the cat out of the bag. He has made precious confessions. I regret that I have only an English translation of his "Outlines of an Historical View of the Progress of the Human mind." But in pages 247, 248, and 249, you will find it frankly acknowledged, that the philosophers of the eighteenth century, adopted all the maxims, and practiced all the arts of the Pharisees, the ancient priests of all countries, the Jesuits, the Machiavillians, etc., etc., to overthrow the institutions that such arts had established. This new philosophy was, by his own account, as insidious, fraudulent, hypocritical, and cruel, as the old policy of the priests, nobles, and kings. When and where were ever found, or will be found, sincerity, honesty, or veracity, in any sect or party in religion, government or philosophy? Johnson and Burke were more of Catholics than Protestants at heart, and Gibbon became an advocate for the inquisition.

There is no act of uniformity in the Church, or State, philosophic. As many sects and systems among them, as among Quakers and Baptists. Bonaparte will not revive inquisitions, Jesuits, or slave trade, for which habitudes the Bourbons have been driven again into exile.

We shall get along with, or without war. I have at last procured the Marquis D'Argens' Ocellus, Timaeus, and Julian. Three such volumes I never read. They are a most perfect exemplification of Condorcet's precious confessions. It is astonishing they have not made more noise in the world. Our Athanasians have printed in a pamphlet in Boston, your letters and Priestley's from Belsham's Lindsey. It will do you no harm. Our correspondence shall not again be so long interrupted.

ADAMS TO JEFFERSON, NOVEMBER 13, 1815

. . . Nevertheless, according to the few lights that remain to us, we may say that the eighteenth century, notwithstanding all its errors and vices, has been, of all that are past, the most honorable to human nature. Knowledge and virtue were increased and diffused; arts, sciences, useful to men, ameliorating their condition, were improved more than in any former equal period.

But what are we to say now? Is the nineteenth century to be a contrast to the eighteenth? Is it to extinguish all the lights of its predecessor? Are the Sorbonne, the Inquisition, the Index expurgatorius, and the Knights-errant of St. Ignatius Loyola to be revived and restored to all their salutary powers of supporting and propagating the mild spirit of Christianity? The proceedings of the allies and their Congress at Vienna, the accounts from Spain and France, and the Chateaubriands, and the Genlis, indicate which way the wind blows. The priests are at their old work again; the Protestants are denounced, and another St. Bartholomew's day threatened. This, how-ever, will probably, twenty-five years hence, be honored with the character of *"the effusions of a splenetic mind, rather than as the sober reflections of an unbiased understanding."*

JEFFERSON TO ADAMS, JANUARY 11, 1816

Of the last five months I have passed four at my other domicil, for such it is in a considerable degree. No letters are forwarded to me there, because the cross post to that place is circuitous and uncertain; during my absence, therefore, they are accumulating here, and awaiting acknowledgments. This has been the fate of your favor of November 13.

I agree with you in all its eulogies on the eighteenth century. It certainly witnessed the sciences and arts, manners and morals, advanced to a higher degree than the world had ever before seen. And might we not go back to the era of the Borgias, by which time the barbarous ages had reduced national morality to its lowest point of depravity, and observe that the arts and sciences, rising from that point, advanced gradually through all the sixteenth, seventeenth and eighteenth centuries, softening and correcting the manners and morals of man? I think, too, we may add to the great honor of science and the arts, that their natural effect is, by illuminating public opinion, to erect it into a censor, before which the most exalted tremble for their future, as well as present fame.

With some exceptions only, through the seventeenth and eighteenth centuries, morality occupied an honorable chapter in the political code of nations. You must have observed while in Europe, as I thought I did, that those who administered the governments of the greater powers at least, had a respect to faith, and considered the dignity of their government as involved in its integrity. A wound indeed was inflicted on this character of honor in the eighteenth century by the partition of Poland. But this was the atrocity of a barbarous government chiefly, in conjunction with a smaller one still scrambling to become great, while one only of those already great, and having character to lose, descended to the baseness of an accomplice in the crime. France, England, Spain, shared in it only inasmuch as they stood aloof and permitted its perpetration. . . .

I know not what to think of your letter of the 11th of January, but that it is one of the most consolatory I ever received.

To trace the commencement of the Reformation, I suspect we must go farther back than Borgia, or even Huss or Wickliff, and I want the *Acta Sanctorum* to assist me in this research. That stupendous monument of human hypocrisy and fanaticism, the church of St. Peter at Rome, which was a century and a half in building, excited the ambition of Leo the Xth, who believed no more of the Christian religion than Diderot, to finish it; and finding St. Peter's pence insufficient, he deluged all Europe with indulgences for sale, and excited Luther to controvert his authority to grant them. Luther, and his associates and followers, went less than half way in detecting the corruptions of Christianity, but they acquired reverence and authority among their followers almost as absolute as that of the Popes had been.

To enter into details would be endless; but I agree with you, that the natural effect of science and arts is to erect public opinion into a censor, which must in some degree be respected by all.

There is no difference of opinion or feeling between us, concerning the partition of Poland, the intended partitions of Pillnitz, or the more daring partitions of Vienna.

Your question "How the apostasy from national rectitude can be accounted for?"—is too deep and wide for my capacity to answer. I leave Fisher Ames to dogmatize up the affairs of Europe and mankind. I have done too much in this way. A burned child dreads the fire. I can only say at present, that it should seem that human reason, and human conscience, though I believe there are such things, are not a match for human passions, human imaginations, and human enthusiasm. You, however, I believe, have hit one. Mark, "the fires the governments of Europe felt kindling under their seats;" and I will hazard a shot at another, the priests of all nations imagined they felt approaching such flames, as they had so often kindled about the bodies of honest men. Priests and politicians, never before, so suddenly and so unanimously concurred in re-establishing darkness and ignorance, superstition and despotism. The morality of Tacitus is the morality of patriotism, and Britain and France have adopted his creed; i.e., that all things were made for Rome. "*Jura negat sibi lata, nihil non arrogat armis,*"[15] said Achilles. "Laws were not made for me," said the Regent of France, and his cardinal minister Du Bois. The universe was made for me,

---

[15] [Horace, "He says that laws were not made for him, but that he claims for himself all he can get in war."—ED.]

says man. Jesus despised and condemned such patriotism; but what nation, or what christian, has adopted his system? He was, as you say, "the most benevolent Being that ever appeared on earth." France and England, Bourbons and Bonaparte, and all the sovereigns of Vienna, have acted on the same principle. "All things were made for my use. So man for mine, replies a pampered goose." The philosophers of the eighteenth century have acted on the same principles. When it is to combat evil, 'tis lawful to employ the devil. *Bonus populus vult decipi, decipiatur.*[16] They have employed the same falsehood, the same deceit, which philosophers and priests of all ages have employed for their own selfish purposes. We now know how their efforts have succeeded. The old deceivers have triumphed over the new. Truth must be more respected than it has ever been, before any great improvement can be expected in the condition of mankind. As Rochfaucauld his maxims drew "from history and from practice," I believe them true. From the whole nature of man, moral, intellectual, and physical, he did not draw them.

We must come to the principles of Jesus. But when will all men and all nations do as they would be done by? Forgive all injuries, and love their enemies as themselves? I leave those profound philosophers, whose sagacity perceives the perfectibility of human nature; and those illuminated theologians, who expect the Apocalyptic reign;—to enjoy their transporting hopes, provided always that they will not engage us in crusades and French Revolutions, nor burn us for doubting. My spirit of prophecy reaches no farther than, New England GUESSES.

You ask, how it has happened that all Europe has acted on the principle, "that Power was Right." I know not what answer to give you, but this, that Power always sincerely, conscientiously, *de tres bon [ne] foi,*[17] believes itself right. Power always thinks it has a great soul, and vast views, beyond the comprehension of the weak; and that it is doing God service, when it is violating all his laws. Our passions, ambition, avarice, love, resentment, etc., possess so much metaphysical subtlety, and so much overpowering eloquence, that they insinuate themselves into the understanding and the conscience, and convert both to their party; and I may be deceived as much as any of them, when I say, that Power must never be trusted without a check.

ADAMS TO JEFFERSON, MARCH 2, 1816

I cannot be serious! I am about to write you the most frivolous letter you ever read. Would you go back to your cradle, and live over again your

---

[16] ["The people like to be imposed on; so let them be imposed on.—ED.]
[17] ["In good faith."—ED.]

seventy years? I believe you would return me a New England answer, by asking me another question, "Would you live your eighty years over again?" If I am prepared to give you an explicit answer, the question involves so many considerations of metaphysics and physics, of theology and ethics, of philosophy and history, of experience and romance, of tragedy, comedy, and farce, that I would not give my opinion without writing a volume to justify it. I have lately lived over again in part, from 1753, when I was junior sophister at college, till 1769, when I was digging in the mines as a barrister at law for silver and gold in the town of Boston, and got as much of the shining dross for my labor, as my utmost avarice at that time craved. At the hazard of the little vision that is left me, I have read the history of that period of sixteen years, in the six first volumes of the Baron de Grimm. In a late letter to you, I expressed a wish to see a history of quarrels, and calamities of authors in France, like that of D'Israeli in England; I did not expect it so soon, but now I have it in a manner more masterly than I ever hoped to see it. It is not only a narrative of the incessant great wars between the ecclesiastics and the philosophers, but of the little skirmishes and squabbles of poets, musicians, architects, painters, tragedians, comedians, opera singers, and dancers, chansons, vaudevilles, epigrams, madrigals, epitaphs, sonnets, etc.

No man is more sensible than I am of the service to science and letters, humanity, fraternity, and liberty, that would have been rendered by the encyclopedists and economists, by Voltaire, D'Alembert, Buffon, Diderot, Rousseau, La Lande, Frederic and Catherine, if they had possessed common sense. But they were all totally destitute of it. They seemed to think that all Christendom was convinced, as they were, that all religion was *"visions judaiques,"* and that their effulgent lights had illuminated all the world; they seemed to believe that whole nations and continents had been changed in their principles, opinions, habits, and feelings, by the sovereign grace of their almighty philosophy, almost as suddenly as Catholics and Calvinists believe in instantaneous conversion. They had not considered the force of early education on the minds of millions, who had never heard of their philosophy.

And what was their philosophy? Atheism—pure, unadulterated atheism. Diderot, D'Alembert, Frederic, De La Lande, and Grimm, were indubitable atheists. The universe was master only, and eternal. Spirit was a word without a meaning. Liberty was a word without a meaning. There was no liberty in the universe; liberty was a word void of sense. Every thought, word, passion, sentiment, feeling, all motion and action was necessary. All beings and attributes were of eternal necessity; conscience, morality, were all nothing but fate. This was their creed, and this was to perfect human nature, and convert the earth into a paradise of pleasure.

Who and what is this fate? He must be a sensible fellow. He must be a master of science; he must be a master of spherical trigonometry, and great circle sailing; he must calculate eclipses in his head by intuition; he must be master of the science of infinitesimals, *"la science des infiniment petits."* He must involve and extract all the roots by intuition, and be familiar with all possible or imaginable sections of the cone. He must be a master of the arts, mechanical and imitative; he must have more eloquence than Demosthenes, more wit than Swift or Voltaire, more humor than Butler or Trumbull; and what is more comfortable than all the rest, he must be good-natured; for this is upon the whole a good world. There is ten times as much pleasure as pain in it.

Why, then, should we abhor the word *God,* and fall in love with the word *fate?* We know there exists energy and intellect enough to produce such a world as this, which is a sublime and beautiful one, and a very benevolent one, notwithstanding all our snarling; and a happy one, if it is not made otherwise by our own fault.

Ask a mite in the centre of your mammoth cheese, what he thinks of the *"τὸ πᾶν."*[18] I should prefer the philosophy of Timaeus of Locris, before that of Grimm, Diderot, Frederic, and D'Alembert. I should even prefer the Shaster of Indostan, or the Chaldean, Egyptian, Indian, Greek, Christian, Mahometan, Teutonic, or Celtic theology. Timaeus and Ocellus taught that three principles were eternal: God, matter, and form. God was good and had ideas; matter was necessity, fate, dead, without form, without feeling, perverse, untractable, capable, however, of being cut into forms of spheres, circles, triangles, squares, cubes, cones, etc. The ideas of the good God labored upon matter to bring it into form; but matter was fate, necessity, dullness, obstinacy, and would not always conform to the ideas of the good God, who desired to make the best of all possible worlds, but matter, fate, necessity, resisted, and would not let him complete his idea. Hence all the evil and disorder, pain, misery, and imperfection of the universe.

We all curse Robespierre and Bonaparte; but were they not both such restless, vain, extravagant animals as Diderot and Voltaire? Voltaire was the greatest literary character and Bona the greatest military character of the eighteenth century; there is all the difference between them; both equally heroes and equally cowards.

When you asked my opinion of a university, it would have been easy to advise mathematics, experimental philosophy, natural history, chemistry, and astronomy, geography, and the fine arts, to the exclusion of ontology,

---

[18] [Universe]

metaphysics and theology. But knowing the eager impatience of the human mind to search into eternity and infinity, the first cause and the last end of all things, I thought best to leave its liberty to inquire, till it is convinced, as I have been these fifty years, that there is but one being in the universe who comprehends it, and our last resource is resignation.

This Grimm must have been in Paris when you were there. Did you know him or hear of him?

I have this moment received two volumes more; but these are from 1777 to 1782, leaving the chain broken from 1769 to 1777. I hope hereafter to get the two intervening volumes.

JEFFERSON TO ADAMS, APRIL 8, 1816

I have to acknowledge your two favors of February the 16th and March the 2nd, and to join sincerely in the sentiment of Mrs. Adams, and regret that distance that separates us so widely. An hour of conversation would be worth a volume of letters. But we must take things as they come.

You ask, if I would agree to live my seventy or rather seventy-three years over again? To which I say, yea. I think with you, that it is a good world on the whole; that it has been framed on a principle of benevolence, and more pleasure than pain dealt out to us. There are, indeed, (who might say nay) gloomy and hypochondriac minds, inhabitants of diseased bodies, disgusted with the present, and despairing of the future; always counting that the worst will happen, because it may happen. To these I say, how much pain have cost us the evils which have never happened! My temperament is sanguine. I steer my bark with Hope in the head, leaving Fear astern. My hopes, indeed, sometimes fail; but not oftener than the forebodings of the gloomy. There are, I acknowledge, even in the happiest life, some terrible convulsions, heavy set-offs against the opposite page of the account. I have often wondered for what good end the sensations of grief could be intended. All our other passions, within proper bounds, have an useful opposite. And the perfection of the moral character is, not in stoical apathy, so hypocritically vaunted, and so untruly too, because impossible, but in a just equilibrium of all the passions. I wish the pathologists then would tell us what is the use of grief in the economy, and of what good it is in the cause, proximate or remote.

Did I know Baron Grimm while at Paris? Yes, most intimately. He was the pleasantest and most conversable member of the diplomatic corps while I was there; a man of good fancy, acuteness, irony, cunning and egoism. No heart, not much of any science, yet enough of every one to speak its language; his forte was Belles-lettres, painting and sculpture. In these he was the oracle of society, and as such, was the Empress Catharine's private correspondent and factor in all things not diplomatic. It was through him I got her permission for poor Ledyard to go to Kamschatka, and cross over thence to the Western coast of America, in order to penetrate across our continent in the opposite direction to that afterwards adopted for Lewis and Clarke; which permission she withdrew after he had got within two hundred miles of Kamschatka, had him seized, brought back, and set down in Poland. Although I never heard Grimm express the opinion directly, yet I always supposed him to be of the school of Diderot, D'Alembert, D'Holbach; the first of whom committed his system of atheism to writing in "*Le bon sens,*" and the last in his "*Systeme de la Nature.*" It was a numerous school in the Catholic countries, while the infidelity of the Protestant took generally the form of theism. The former always insisted that it was a mere question of definition between them, the hypostasis of which, on both sides, was "*Nature,*" or "*the Universe;*" that both agreed in the order of the existing system, but the one supposed it from eternity, the other as having begun in time. And when the atheist descanted on the uneasing motion and circulation of matter through the animal, vegetable and mineral kingdoms, never resting, never annihilated, always changing form, and under all forms gifted with the power of reproduction; the theist pointing "to the heavens above, and to the earth beneath, and to the waters under the earth," asked, if these did not proclaim a first cause, possessing intelligence and power; power in the production, and intelligence in the design and constant preservation of the system; urged the palpable existence of final causes; that the eye was made to see, and the ear to hear, and not that we see because we have eyes, and hear because we have ears; an answer obvious to the senses, as that of walking across the room, was to the philosopher; demonstrated the nonexistence of motion. It was in D'Holbach's conventicles that Rousseau imagined all the machinations against him were contrived; and he left, in his Confessions, the most biting anecdotes of Grimm. These appeared after I left France; but I have heard that poor Grimm was so much afflicted by them, that he kept his bed several weeks. I have never seen the Memoirs of Grimm. Their volume has kept them out of our market.

I have lately been amusing myself with Levi's Book, in answer to Dr. Priestley. It is a curious and tough work. His style is inelegant and incorrect, harsh and petulent to his adversary, and his reasoning flimsy enough. Some of his doctrines were new to me, particularly that of his two resurrections; the first, a particular one of all the dead, in body as well as soul, who are to live over again, the Jews in a state of perfect obedience to God, the other nations in a state of corporeal punishment for the sufferings they have inflicted on the Jews. And he explains this resurrection of the bodies to be only of the original stamen of Leibnitz, or the human *calculus* in *semine mas-*

culino [masculine seed], considering that as a mathematical point, insusceptible of separation or division. The second resurrection, a general one of souls and bodies, eternally to enjoy divine glory in the presence of the Supreme Being. He alleges that the Jews alone preserve the doctrine of the unity of God. Yet their God would be deemed a very indifferent man with us; and it was to correct their anamorphosis of the Deity, that Jesus preached, as well as to establish the doctrine of a future state. However, Levi insists, that that was taught in the Old Testament, and even by Moses himself and the prophets. He agrees that an anointed prince was prophesied and promised; but denies that the character and history of Jesus had any analogy with that of the one person promised. He must be fearfully embarrassing to the Hierophants of fabricated Christianity; because it is their own armor in which he clothes himself for the attack. For example, he takes passages of scripture from their context, (which would give them a very different meaning) strings them together, and makes them point towards what object he pleases; he interprets them figuratively, typically, analogically, hyperbolically; he calls in the aid of emendation, transposition, ellipse, metonymy, and every other figure of rhetoric; the name of one man is taken for another, one place for another, days and weeks for months and years; and finally, he avails himself all his advantage over his adversaries by his superior knowledge of the Hebrew, speaking in the very language of the divine communication, while they can only fumble on with conflicting and disputed translations.

Such is this war of giants. And how can such pigmies as you and I decide between them? For myself, I confess that my head is not formed *tantas componere lites.*[19] And as you began yours of March the 2nd, with a declaration that you were about to write me the most frivolous letter I had ever read, so I will close mine by saying, I have written you a full match for it, and by adding my affectionate respects for Mrs. Adams, and the assurance of my constant attachment and consideration for yourself.

ADAMS TO JEFFERSON, MAY 3, 1816

Yours of April 8th has long since been received.

J.   "Would you agree to live your eighty years over again forever?"

A.   I once heard our acquaintance, Chew, of Philadelphia, say, "He should like to go back to twenty-five, to all eternity;" but I own my soul would start and shrink back on itself at the prospect of an endless succession of *Boules* [sic] *de Savon* [soap bubbles] almost as much as the certainty of annihilation. For what is human life? I can speak only for one. I have had more comfort than distress, more pleasure than pain ten to one, nay, if you

---

[19] [Virgil, "To adjust such grave disputes."—ED.]

please, an hundred to one. A pretty large dose, however, of distress and pain. But after all, what is human life? A vapor, a fog, a dew, a cloud, a blossom, a flower, a rose, a blade of grass, a glass bubble, a tale told by an idiot, a *Boule de Savon*, vanity of vanities, an eternal succession of which would terrify me almost as much as annihilation."

J.   "Would you prefer to live over again, rather than accept the offer of a better life in a future state?"

A.   Certainly not.

J.   "Would you live again rather than change for the worse in a future state, for the sake of trying something new?"

A.   Certainly yes.

J.   "Would you live over again once or forever, rather than run the risk of annihilation, or of a better or a worse state at or after death?"

A.   Most certainly I would not.

J.   "How valiant you are!"

A.   Aye, at this moment, and at all other moments of my life that I can recollect; but who can tell what will become of his bravery when his flesh and his heart shall fail him? Bolingbroke said "his philosophy was not sufficient to support him in his last hours." D'Alembert said: "Happy are they who have courage, but I have none." Voltaire, the greatest genius of them all, behaved like the greatest coward of them all at his death, as he had like the wisest fool of them all in his lifetime. Hume awkwardly affected to sport away all sober thoughts. Who can answer for his last feelings and reflections, especially as the priests are in possession of the custom of making them the greatest engines of their craft. *Procul est prophani!*"[20]

J.   "How shall we, how can we estimate the real value of human life?"

A.   I know not; I cannot weigh sensations and reflections, pleasures and pains, hopes and fears, in money-scales. But I can tell you how I have heard it estimated by philosophers. One of my old friends and clients, a mandamus counsellor against his will, a man of letters and virtues, without one vice that I ever knew or suspected, except garrulity, William Vassall, asserted to me, and strenuously maintained, that *"pleasure is no compensation for pain."* "An hundred years of the keenest delights of human life could not atone for one hour of bilious cholic that he had felt." The sublimity of this philosophy my dull genius could not reach. I was willing to state a fair account between pleasure and pain, and give credit for the balance, which I found very great in my favor.

Another philosopher, who, as we say, believed nothing, ridiculed the notion of a future state. One of the company asked, "Why are you an enemy

---

[20] [Virgil, "Keep off, ye profane!"—Ed.]

to a future state? Are you weary of life? Do you detest existence?" "Weary of life? Detest existence?" said the philosopher. "No! I love life so well, and am so attached to existence, that to be sure of immortality, I would consent to be pitched about with forks by the devils, among flames of fire and brimstone, to all eternity."

I find no resources in my courage for this exalted philosophy. I had rather be blotted out.

Il faut trancher cet mot![21] What is there in life to attach us to it but the hope of a future and a better? It is a cracker, a rocket, a fire-work at best.

I admire your navigation, and should like to sail with you, either in your bark, or in my own along side of yours. Hope with her gay ensigns displayed at the prow, fear with her hobgoblins behind the stern. Hope springs eternal, and hope is all that endures. Take away hope and what remains? What pleasure, I mean? Take away fear and what pain remains? Ninety-nine one hundredths of the pleasures and pains of life are nothing but hopes and fears.

All nations known in history or in travels, have hoped, believed and expected a future and a better state. The Maker of the Universe, the cause of all things, whether we call it *fate*, or *chance*, or GOD, has inspired this hope. If it is a *fraud*, we shall never know it. We shall never resent the imposition, be grateful for the illusion, nor grieve for the disappointment. We shall be no more. Credit Grimm, Diderot, Buffon, La Lande, Condorcet, d'Holbach, Frederic, Catherine; *non ego*. Arrogant as it may be, I shall take the liberty to pronounce them all *Idiologians*. Yet I would not persecute a hair of their heads. The world is wide enough for them and me.

Suppose the cause of the universe should reveal to all mankind at once a *certainty* that they all must die within a century and that death is an eternal extinction of all living powers, of all sensation and reflection. What would be the effect? Would there be one man, woman or child existing on this globe, twenty years hence? Would not every human being be a Madame Deffand, Voltaire's "Aveugle clairvoyante," [clear-sighted blind woman] all her lifetime regretting her existence, bewailing that she had ever been born, grieving that she had ever been dragged, without her consent, into being. Who would bear the gout, the stone, the cholic, for the sake of a *Boule de Savon*, when a pistol, a cord, a pond, or a phial of laudanum was at hand? What would men say to their Maker? Would they thank him? No; they would reproach him; they would curse him to his face. Voilà!

A sillier letter than my last. For a wonder, I have filled a sheet, and a greater wonder, I have read fifteen volumes of Grimm. *Digito comesse*

---

[21] ["We must not mince matters!"—ED.]

labellum.[22] I hope to write you more upon this and other topics of your letter. I have read also a History of the Jesuits, in four volumes. Can you tell me the author, or anything of this work?

ADAMS TO JEFFERSON, MAY 6, 1816

Grief drives men into habits of serious reflection, sharpens the understanding, and softens the heart; it compels them to arouse their reason, to assert its empire over their passions, propensities and prejudices; to elevate them to a superiority over all human events; to give them the *felicis animi immotam tranquillitatem;*[23] in short, to make them Stoics and Christians. After all, as grief is a pain, it stands in the predicament of all other evil, and the great question occurs, what is the origin, and what is the final cause of evil? This perhaps is known only to Omniscience. We poor mortals have nothing to do with it—but to fabricate all the good we can out of all inevitable evils—and to avoid all that are avoidable, and many such there are, among which are our own unnecessary apprehensions and imaginary fears. Though stoical apathy is impossible, yet patience, and resignation, and tranquillity may be acquired by consideration, in a great degree, very much for the happiness of life.

I have read Grimm, in fifteen volumes, of more than five hundred pages each. I will not say like Uncle Toby, "you shall not die till you have read him." But you ought to read him, if possible. It is the most entertaining work I ever read. He appears exactly as you represent him. What is most remarkable of all is his impartiality. He spares no characters but Necker and Diderot. Voltaire, Buffon, D'Alembert, Helvetius, Rousseau, Marmontel, Condorcet, La Harpe, Beaumarchais, and all others, are lashed without ceremony. Their portraits as faithfully drawn as possible. It is a complete review of French literature and fine arts from 1753 to 1790. No politics. Criticisms very just. Anecdotes without number, and very merry. One ineffably ridiculous, I wish I could send you, but it is immeasurably long. D'Argens, a little out of health and shivering with the cold in Berlin, asked leave of the King to take a ride to Gascony, his native province. He was absent so long that Frederic concluded the air of the south of France was like to detain his friend; and as he wanted his society and services, he contrived a trick to bring him back. He fabricated a mandement in the name of the Archbishop of Aix, commanding all the faithful to seize the Marquis D'Argens, author of Ocellus, Timaus and Julian, works atheistical, deistical, heretical and impious in the highest degree. This mandement, composed in a style of ecclesiastical eloquence that never was exceeded by

---

[22] [To consume a book with the finger, i.e., to thumb through it quickly.—ED.]
[23] [imperturbable serenity of a happy mind.—ED.]

Pope, Jesuit, Inquisitor, or Sorbonite, he sent in print by a courier to D'Argens, who, frightened out of his wit, fled by cross roads out of France, and back to Berlin, to the greater joy of the philosophical court; for the laugh of Europe, which they had raised at the expense of the learned Marquis.

JEFFERSON TO ADAMS, AUGUST 1, 1816

Your two philosophical letters of May 4th and 6th have been too long in my carton of "letters to be answered." To the question, indeed, on the utility of grief, no answer remains to be given. You have exhausted the subject. I see that, with the other evils of life, it is destined to temper the cup we are to drink.

> Two urns by Jove's high throne have ever stood,
> The source of evil one, and one of good;
> From thence the cup of mortal man he fills,
> Blessings to these, to those distributes ills;
> To most he mingles both.

Putting to myself your question, would I agree to live my seventy-three years over again forever? I hesitate to say. With Chew's limitations from twenty-five to sixty, I would say yes; and I might go further back, but not come lower down. For, at the latter period, with most of us, the powers of life are sensibly on the wane, sight becomes dim, hearing dull, memory constantly enlarging its frightful blank and parting with all we have ever seen or known, spirits evaporate, bodily debility creeps on palsying every limb, and so faculty after faculty quits us, and where then is life? If, in its full vigor, of good as well as evil, your friend Vassall could doubt its value, it must be purely a negative quantity when its evils alone remain. Yet I do not go into his opinion entirely. I do not agree that an age of pleasure is no compensation for a moment of pain. I think, with you, that life is a fair matter of account, and the balance often, nay generally, in its favor. It is not indeed easy, by calculation of intensity and time, to apply a common measure, or to fix the par between pleasure and pain; yet it exists, and is measurable. On the question, for example, whether to be cut for the stone? The young, with a longer prospect of years, think these overbalance the pain of the operation. Dr. Franklin, at the age of eighty, thought his residuum of life not worth that price. I should have thought with him, even taking the stone out of the scale. There is a ripeness of time for death, regarding others as well as ourselves, when it is reasonable we should drop off, and make room for another growth. When we have lived our generation out, we should not wish to encroach on another. I enjoy good health; I am happy in what is around me, yet I assure you, I am ripe for leaving all, this year, this day, this hour. If it could be doubted whether we would go back to twenty-five, how can it be whether we would go forward from seventy-three? Bodily decay is gloomy in prospect, but of all human contemplations the most abhorrent is body without mind. Perhaps, however, I might accept of time to read Grimm before I go. Fifteen volumes of anecdotes and incidents, within the compass of my own time and cognizance, written by a man of genius, of taste, of point, an acquaintance, the measure and traverses of whose mind I know, could not fail to turn the scale in favor of life during their perusal. . . . Bigotry is the disease of ignorance, of morbid minds; enthusiasm of the free and buoyant. Education and free discussion are the antidotes of both. We are destined to be a barrier against the returns of ignorance and barbarism. Old Europe will have to lean on our shoulders, and to hobble along by our side, under the monkish trammels of priests and kings, as she can. What a colossus shall we be when the southern continent comes up to our mark! What a stand will it secure as a ralliance for the reason and freedom of the globe! I like the dreams of the future better than the history of the past,—so good night! I will dream on, always fancying that Mrs. Adams and yourself are by my side marking the progress and obliquities of ages and countries.

ADAMS TO JEFFERSON, AUGUST 9, 1816

Your poet, the Ionian I suppose, ought to have told us whether Jove, in the distribution of good and evil from his two urns, observes any rule of equity or not; whether he thunders out flames of eternal fire on the many, and power, and glory, and felicity on the few, without any consideration of justice?

Let us state a few questions *sub rosâ*.

1. Would you accept a life, if offered you, of equal pleasure and pain? For example. One million of moments of pleasure, and one million of moments of pain! (1,000,00 moments of pleasure = 1,000,000 moments of pain.) Suppose the pleasure as exquisite as any in life, and the pain as exquisite as any; for example, stone-gravel, gout, headache, earache, toothache, colic, etc. I would not. I would rather be blotted out.

2. Would you accept a life of one year of incessant gout, headache, etc., for seventy-two years of such life as you have enjoyed? I would not. (One year of colic = seventy-two of *Boules de Savon*; pretty, but unsubstantial.) I had rather be extinguished. You may vary these Algebraical equations at pleasure and without end. All this ratiocination, calculation, call it what you will, is founded on the supposition of no future state. Promise me eternal life free from pain, although in all other respects no better than

our present terrestrial existence, I know not how many thousand years of Smithfield fevers I would not endure to obtain it. In fine, without the supposition of a future state, mankind and this globe appear to me the most sublime and beautiful bubble, and bauble, that imagination can conceive.

Let us then wish for immortality at all hazards, and trust the Ruler with his skies. I do; and earnestly wish for his commands, which to the utmost of my power shall be implicitly and piously obeyed.

It is worth while to live to read Grimm, whom I have read; and La Harpe and Mademoiselle D'Espinasse the fair friend of D'Alembert, both of whom Grimm characterizes very distinguished, and are, I am told, in print. I have not seen them, but hope soon to have them. . . .

May we be "a barrier against the returns of ignorance and barbarism"! "What a colossus shall we be"! But will it not be of brass, iron and clay? Your taste is judicious in liking better the dreams of the future, than the history of the past. Upon this principle I prophecy that you and I shall soon meet, and be better friends than ever.

ADAMS TO JEFFERSON, SEPTEMBER 3, 1816

Dr. James Freeman is a learned, ingenious, honest and benevolent man, who wishes to see President Jefferson, and requests me to introduce him. If you would introduce some of your friends to me, I could, with more confidence, introduce mine to you. He is a Christian, but not a Pythagorian, a Platonic, or a Philonic Christian. You will ken him, and he will ken you; but you may depend he will never betray, deceive or injure you.

Without hinting to him anything which had passed between you and me, I asked him your question, "What are the uses of grief?" He stared and said, "The Question was new to him." All he could say at present was, that he had known, in his own parish, more than one instance of ladies who had been thoughtless, modish, extravagant in a high degree, who, upon the death of a child, had become thoughtful, modest, humble; as prudent, amiable women as any he had known. Upon this I read to him your letters and mine upon this subject of grief, with which he seemed to be pleased. You see, I was not afraid to trust him, and you need not be.

JEFFERSON TO ADAMS, OCTOBER 14, 1816

Destutt Tracy, is, in my judgment, the ablest writer living on intellectual subjects, or the operations of the understanding. . . . This work, which is on Ethics, I have not seen, but suspect I shall differ from it in its foundation, although not in its deductions. I gather from his other works that he adopts the principle of Hobbes, that justice is founded in contact solely, and does not result from the construction of man. I believe, on the contrary, that it is instinct and innate, that the moral sense is as much a part of our constitution as that of feeling, seeing, or hearing; as a wise creator must have seen to be necessary in an animal destined to live in society; that every human mind feels pleasure in doing good to another; that the non-existence of justice is not to be inferred from the fact that the same act is deemed virtuous and right in one society which is held vicious and wrong in another; because, as the circumstances and opinions of different societies vary, so the acts which may do them right or wrong must vary also; for virtue does not consist in the act we do, but in the end it is to effect. If it is to effect the happiness of him to whom it is directed, it is virtuous, while in a society under different circumstances and opinions, the same act might produce pain, and would be vicious. The essence of virtue is in doing good to others, while what is good may be one thing in one society and its contrary in another. Yet, however we may differ as to the foundations of morals (and as many foundations have been assumed as there are writers on the subject nearly) so correct a thinker as Tracy will give us a sound system of morals. And, indeed, it is remarkable, that so many writers, setting out from so many different premises yet meet all in the same conclusions. This looks as if they were guided, unconsciously, by the unerring hand of instinct.

ADAMS TO JEFFERSON, NOVEMBER 4, 1816

I have read not only the Analysis [Tracy's] but eight volumes out of twelve of the "*Origine de tous les Cultes*," and, if life lasts, will read the other four. But, my dear Sir, I have been often obliged to stop and talk to myself, like the reverend, allegorical, hieroglyphical, and apocalyptical Mr. John Bunyan, and say, "*sobrius esto*, John, be not carried away by sudden blasts of wind, by unexpected flashes of lightning, nor terrified by the sharpest crashes of thunder."

We have now, it seems, a national Bible Society, to propagate King James's Bible through all nations. Would it not be better to apply these pious subscriptions to purify Christendom from the corruptions of Christianity than to propagate those corruptions in Europe, in Asia, Africa, and America? Suppose we should project a society to translate Dupuis into all languages and offer a reward in medals of diamonds to any man or body of men who would produce the best answer to it. . . .

Conclude not from all this that I have renounced the Christian religion, or that I agree with Dupuis in all his sentiments. Far from it. I see in every page something to recommend Christianity in its purity, and something to discredit its corruptions. If I had strength, I would give you my opinion of it in a fable of the bees. The Ten Commandments and the Sermon on the Mount contain my religion.

I agree perfectly with you that "the moral sense is as much a part of our condition as that of feeling," and in all that you say upon this subject.

JEFFERSON TO ADAMS, JANUARY 11, 1817

Forty-three volumes read in one year, and twelve of them quarto! Dear Sir, how I envy you! Half a dozen octavos in that space of time, are as much as I am allowed. I can read by candlelight only, and stealing long hours from my rest; nor would that time be indulged to me, could I, by that light see to write. From sunrise to one or two o'clock, and often from dinner to dark, I am drudging at the writing table. And all this to answer letters into which neither interest nor inclination on my part enters; and often from persons whose names I have never before heard. Yet, writing civilly, it is hard to refuse them civil answers. This is the burthen of my life, a very grievous one indeed, and one which I must get rid of. Delaplaine lately requested me to give him a line on the subject of his book; meaning, as I well knew, to publish it. This I constantly refuse; but in this instance yielded, that in saying a word for him, I might say two for myself. I expressed in it freely my sufferings from this source; hoping it would have the effect of an indirect appeal to the discretion of those, strangers and others, who, in the most friendly dispositions, oppress me with their concerns, their pursuits, their projects, inventions and speculations, political, moral, religious, mechanical, mathematical, historical, etc., etc., etc. I hope the appeal will bring me relief, and that I shall be left to exercise and enjoy correspondence with the friends I love, and on subjects which they, or my own inclinations present. In that case, your letters shall not be so long on my files unanswered, as sometimes they have been, to my great mortification. . . .

The result of your fifty or sixty years of religious reading, in the four words, "Be just and good," is that in which all our inquiries must end; as the riddles of all the priesthoods end in four more, "*ubi panis, ibi deus.*"[24] What all agree in, is probably right. What no two agree in, most probably wrong. One of our fan-coloring biographers, who paints small men as very great, inquired of me lately, with real affection too, whether he might consider as authentic, the change in my religion much spoken of in some circles. Now this supposed that they knew what had been my religion before, taking for it the word of their priests, whom I certainly never made the confidants of my creed. My answer was, "say nothing of my religion. It is known to my God and myself alone. Its evidence before the world is to be

---

[24] [where there is bread, there is god.—ED.]

sought in my life; if that has been *honest and dutiful* to society, the religion which has regulated it cannot be a bad one."

ADAMS TO JEFFERSON, APRIL 19, 1817

I verily believe I was as wise and good seventy years ago, as I am now. At that period Lemuel Bryant was my parish priest, and Joseph Cleverly my Latin schoolmaster. Lemuel was a jocular and liberal scholar and divine, Joseph a scholar and a gentleman but a bigoted Episcopalian of the school of Bishop Saunders and Dr. Hicks; a downright, conscientious, passive obedience man in church and state. The parson and the pedagogue lived much together, but were eternally disputing about government and religion!

One day, when the schoolmaster had been more than commonly fanatical, and declared, "if he were a monarch, he would have but one religion in his dominions," the parson coolly replied, "Cleverly! you would be the best man in the world, if you had no religion."

Twenty times, in the course of my late reading, have I been on the point of breaking out, "this would be the best of all possible worlds, if there was no religion in it! ! !"

But in this exclamation, I should have been as fanatical as Bryant or Cleverly. Without religion, this world would be as something not fit to be mentioned in polite company—I mean hell. So far from believing in the total and universal depravity of human nature, I believe there is no individual totally depraved. The most abandoned scoundrel that ever existed, never yet wholly extinguished his conscience, and, while conscience remains, there is some religion. Popes, Jesuits, and Sorbonnists, and Inquisitors, have some conscience and some religion. So had Marius and Sylla. Caesar, Catiline and Antony, and Augustus, had not much more, let Virgil and Horace say what they will. What shall we think of Virgil and Horace, Sallust, Quintilian, Pliny, and even Tacitus? And even Cicero, Brutus, and Seneca? Pompey I leave out of the question, as a mere politician and soldier. Every one of these great creatures has left indelible marks on conscience, and, consequently, of religion, though every one of them has left abundant proofs of profligate violations of their conscience, by their little and great passions and paltry interests.

The vast prospect of mankind, which these books have passed in review before me, from the most ancient records, histories, traditions, and fables that remain to us, to the present day, has sickened my very soul, and almost reconciled me to Swift's travels among the Yahoos. Yet I never can be a misanthrope. *Homo sum.* I must hate myself before I can hate my fellow-men, and that I cannot and will not do. No, I will not hate any of them, base, brutal, and devilish as some of them have been to me. From the bottom of my soul I pity my fellow-men. Fears and terrors appear to have produced a universal credulity. Fears of calamities in life, and punishments after death, seem to have possessed the souls of all men. But fears of pain and death here do not seem to have been so unconquerable as fears of what is to come hereafter. Priests, hierophants, popes, despots, emperors, kings, princes, nobles, have been as credulous as shoe-blacks, boots, and kitchen-scullions. The former seem to have believed in their divine rights as sincerely as the latter. *Auto-da-fés* in Spain and Portugal, have been celebrated with as good faith as excommunications have been refused[25] in Philadelphia. How is it possible that mankind should submit to be governed as they have been, is to me an inscrutable mystery. How they could bear to be taxed to build the temple of Diana at Ephesus, the pyramids of Egypt, Saint Peter's at Rome, Notre Dame at Paris, St. Paul's in London, with a million *et ceteras*, when my navy yards and my *quasi* army made such a popular clamor, I know not. Yet my peccadilloes never excited such a rage as the late compensation law! ! !

JEFFERSON TO ADAMS, MAY 5, 1817

If by *religion* we are to understand *sectarian dogmas*, in which no two of them agree, then your exclamation on that hypothesis is just, "that this would be the best of all possible worlds, if there were no religion in it." But if the moral precepts, innate in man, and made a part of his physical constitution, as necessary for a social being, if the sublime doctrines of philanthropism and deism taught us by Jesus of Nazareth, in which all agree, constitute a true religion, then, without it, this would be, as you again say, "something not fit to be named, even indeed, a hell."

JEFFERSON TO ADAMS, NOVEMBER 13, 1818

The public papers, my dear friend, announce the fatal event of which your letter of October the 20th had given me ominous foreboding.[26] Tried myself in the school of affliction, by the loss of every form of connection which can rive the human heart, I know well, and feel what you have lost, what you have suffered, are suffering, and have yet to endure. The same trials have taught me that for ills so immeasurable, time and silence are the only medicine. I will not, therefore, by useless condolences, open afresh the sluices of your grief, nor, although mingling sincerely my tears with yours, will I say a word more where words are vain, but that it is of some comfort to us both, that the term is not very distant, at which we are to deposit in the

---

[25] [Adams' handwriting was here indistinct.—ED.]
[26] [The death of Adams' wife Abigail on October 28.—ED.]

same cerement, our sorrows and suffering bodies, and to ascend in essence to an ecstatic meeting with the friends we have loved and lost, and whom we shall still love and never lose again. God bless you and support you under your heavy affliction.

ADAMS TO JEFFERSON, DECEMBER 18, 1819

I must answer your great question of the 10th in the words of D'Alembert to his correspondent, who asked him what is matter, *"Je vous avoue que je n'en sais rien."*[27] In some part of my life, I read a great work of a Scotchman on the court of Augustus, in which, with much learning, hard study, and fatiguing labor, he undertook to prove that—had Brutus and Cassius been conquerors, they would have restored virtue and liberty to Rome. *Mais je n'en crois rien.*[28] Have you ever found in history one single example of a nation, thoroughly corrupted, that was afterwards restored to virtue? And without virtue, there can be no political liberty.

If I were a Calvinist, I might pray that God, by a miracle of divine grace, would instantaneously convert a whole contaminated nation from turpitude to purity; but even in this I should be inconsistent, for the fatalism of Mahometans, Materialists, Atheists, Pantheists, and Calvinists, and Church of England articles, appear to me to render all prayer futile and absurd. The French and the Dutch, in our day, have attempted reforms and revolutions. We know the results, and I fear the English reformers will have no better success.

ADAMS TO JEFFERSON, JANUARY 17, 1820

When we say God is a spirit, we know what we mean, as well as we do when we say that the pyramids of Egypt are matter. Let us be content, therefore, to believe him to be a spirit, that is, an essence that we know nothing of, in which originally and necessarily reside all energy, all power, all capacity, all activity, all wisdom, all goodness.

Behold the creed and confession of faith of your ever affectionate friend.

JEFFERSON TO ADAMS, MARCH 14, 1820

I consider him [Dugald Stuart] and Tracy as the ablest metaphysicians living; by which I mean investigators of the thinking faculty of man. Stuart seems to have given its natural history from facts and observations; Tracy its modes of action and deduction, which he calls Logic, and Idealogy; and Cabanis, in his Physique et Morale de l'Homme, has investigated anatomi-cally and most ingeniously, the particular organs in the human structure which may most probably exercise that faculty. And they ask why may not the mode of action called thought have been given to a material organ of

---

[27] [I vow to you that I know nothing about it.—ED.]
[28] [But I don't believe it.—ED.]

peculiar structure, as that of magnetism to the needle, or of elasticity to the spring by a particular manipulation of the steel. They observe that on ignition of the needle or spring, their magnetism and elasticity cease. So on dissolution of the material organ by death, its action of thought may cease also, and that nobody supposes that the magnetism or elasticity retire to hold a substantive and distinct existence. These were qualities only of particular conformations of matter; change the conformation, and its qualities change also. Mr. Locke, you know, and other materialists, have charged with blasphemy the spiritualists who have denied the Creator the power of endowing certain forms of matter with the faculty of thought. These, however, are speculations and subtleties in which, for my own part, I have little indulged myself.

When I meet with a proposition beyond finite comprehension, I abandon it as I do a weight which human strength cannot lift, and I think ignorance, in these cases, is truly the softest pillow on which I can lay my head. Were it necessary, however, to form an opinion, I confess I should, with Mr. Locke, prefer swallowing one incomprehensibility rather than two. It requires one effort only to admit the single incomprehensibility of matter endowed with thought, and two to believe, first that of an existence called spirit, of which we have neither evidence nor idea, and then secondly how that spirit, which has neither extension nor solidity, can put material organs into motion.

These are things which you and I may perhaps know ere long. We have so lived as to fear neither horn of the dilemma. We have, willingly, done injury to no man; and have done for our country the good which has fallen in our way, so far as commensurate with the faculties given us. That we have not done more than we could, cannot be imputed to us as a crime before any tribunal. I look, therefore, to the crisis, as I am sure you also do, as one *"qui summum nec metuit diem nec optat."*[29] In the meantime be our last as cordial as were our first affections.

JEFFERSON TO ADAMS, AUGUST 15, 1820

But enough of criticism: let me turn to your puzzling letter of May the 12th, on matter, spirit, motion, etc. Its crowd of scepticisms kept me from sleep. I read it, and laid it down; read it, and laid it down, again and again; and to give rest to my mind, I was obliged to recur ultimately to my habitual anodyne, "I feel, therefore I exist." I feel bodies which are not myself: there other existences then. I call them *matter*. I feel them changing place. This gives me *motion*. Where there is an absence of matter, I call it *void*, or *nothing*, or *immaterial space*.

---

[29] [who neither fears nor desires the last day.—ED.]

On the basis of sensation, of matter and motion, we may erect the fabric of all the certainties we can have or need; I cannot conceive *thought* to be an action of a particular organization of matter, formed for that purpose by its creator, as well as that *attraction* is an action of matter, or *magnetism* of loadstone. When he who denies to the Creator the power of endowing matter with the mode of action called *thinking*, shall show how he could endow the sun with the mode of action called *attraction*, which reins the planets in the track of their orbits, or how an absence of matter can have a will, and by that will put matter into motion, then the Materialist may be lawfully required to explain the process by which matter exercises the faculty of thinking. When once we quit the basis of sensation, all is in the wind. To talk of *immaterial* existences is to talk of *nothings*. To say that the human souls, angels, God, are immaterial, is to say, they are *nothings*, or that there is no God, no angels, no soul. I cannot reason otherwise: but I believe I am supported in my creed of materialism by the Lockes, the Tracys, and the Stuarts. At what age[30] of the Christian church this heresy of *immaterialism* or masked atheism, crept in, I do not exactly know. But a heresy it certainly is. Jesus taught nothing of it. He told us, indeed, that "God is a spirit." But he has not defined what a spirit is, nor said that it is not *matter*. And the ancient fathers generally, of the three first centuries, held it to be matter, light and thin indeed, an etherial gas; but still matter . . . All heresies being now done away with us, these schismatists are merely atheists, differing from the material atheist only in their belief, that "nothing made something," and from the material deist, who believes that matter alone can operate on matter.

Rejecting all organs of information, therefore, but my senses, I rid myself of the pyrrhonisms with which an indulgence in speculations hyperphysical and antiphysical, so uselessly occupy and disquiet the mind. A single sense may indeed be sometimes deceived, but rarely; and never all our senses together, with their faculty of reasoning. They evidence realities, and there are enough of these for all the purposes of life, without plunging into the fathomless abyss of dreams and phantasms. I am satisfied, and sufficiently occupied with the things which are, without tormenting or troubling myself about those which may indeed be, but of which I have no evidence.

I am sure that I really know many, many things, and none more surely than that I love you with all my heart, and pray for the continuance of your life until you shall be tired of it yourself.

ADAMS TO JEFFERSON, MAY 19, 1821

Must we, before we take our departure from this grand and beautiful world, surrender all our pleasing hopes of the progress of society, of the

---

[30] [Athanasius and the Council of Nicaea, A.D. 325.—ED.]

improvement of the intellect and moral condition of the world, of the reformation of mankind?

The Piedmontese revolution scarcely assumed a form, and the Neapolitan bubble burst. And what should hinder the Spanish and Portuguese constitutions from running to the same ruin? The Cortes is in one assembly vested with the legislative power. The king and his priests, armies, navies, and all other officers, are vested with the executive authority of government. Are not here two authorities up, neither supreme? And they not necessarily rivals, constantly contending, like law, physic, and divinity, for superiority? just ready for civil war? . . .

The art of lawgiving is not so easy as that of architecture or painting. New York and Rhode Island, are struggling for conventions to reform their constitutions, and I am told that there is danger of making them worse. Massachusetts has had her convention; but our sovereign lords, the people, think themselves wiser than their representatives, and in several articles I agree with their lordships. Yet there never was a cooler, a more patient, candid, or a wiser deliberative body than that convention.

I may refine too much, I may be an enthusiast, but I think a free government is a complicated piece of machinery, the nice and exact adjustment of whose springs, wheels, and weights, is not yet well comprehended by the the artists of the age, and still less by the people.

I began this letter principally to inquire after your health, and to repeat assurances of the affection of your friend.

JEFFERSON TO ADAMS, SEPTEMBER 12, 1821

I am just returned from my other home, and shall within a week go back to it for the rest of the autumn. I find here your favor of August 20th, and was before in arrear for that of May 19th. I cannot answer, but join in, your question of May 19th. Are we to surrender the pleasing hopes of seeing improvement in the moral and intellectual condition of man? The events of Naples and Piedmont cast a gloomy cloud over that hope, and Spain and Portugal are not beyond jeopardy. And what are we to think of this northern triumvirate, arming their nations to dictate despotisms to the rest of the world? And the evident connivance of England, as the price of secret stipulations for continental armies, if her own should take side with her malcontent and pulverized people? And what of the poor Greeks, and their small chance of amelioration even if the hypocritical Autocrat should take them under the iron cover of his Ukazes. Would this be lighter or safer than that of the Turk?

These, my dear friend, are speculations for the new generation, as, before they will be resolved, you and I must join our deceased brother Floyd. Yet I will not believe our labors are lost. I shall not die without a hope that light and liberty are on steady advance. We have seen, indeed, once within the records of history, a complete eclipse of the human mind continuing for centuries. And this, too, by swarms of the same northern barbarians, conquering and taking possession of the countries and governments of the civilized world. Should this be again attempted, should the same northern hordes, allured again by the corn, wine, and oil of the south, be able again to settle their swarms in the countries of their growth, the art of printing alone, and the vast dissemination of books, will maintain the mind where it is, and raise the conquering ruffians to the level of the conquered, instead of degrading these to that of their conquerors.

And even should the cloud of barbarism and despotism again obscure the science and liberties of Europe, this country remains to preserve and restore light and liberty to them. In short, the flames kindled on the 4th of July, 1776, have spread over too much of the globe to be extinguished by the feeble engines of despotism; on the contrary, they will consume these engines and all who work them. . . .

ADAMS TO JEFFERSON, SEPTEMBER 24, 1821

I thank you for your favor of the 12th instant. Hope springs eternal. Eight millions of Jews hope for a Messiah more powerful and glorious than Moses, David, or Solomon; who is to make them as powerful as he pleases. Some hundreds of millions of Musslemen expect another prophet more powerful than Mahomet, who is to spread Islamism over the whole earth. Hundreds of millions of Christians expect and hope for a millennium in which Jesus is to reign for a thousand years over the whole world before it is burnt up. The Hindoos expect another and final incarnation of Vishnu, who is to do great and wonderful things, I know not what. All these hopes are founded on real or pretended revelation. The modern Greeks, too, it seems, hope for a deliverer who is to produce them—the Themistocleses and Demostheneses—the Platos and Aristotles—the Solons and Lycurguses. On what prophecies they found their belief, I know not. You and I hope for splendid improvements in human society, and vast amelioration in the condition of mankind. Our faith may be supposed by more rational arguments than any of the former, I own that I am very sanguine in the belief of them, as I hope and believe you are, and your reasoning in your letter confirmed me in them.

JEFFERSON TO ADAMS, JUNE 1, 1822

It is very long, my dear Sir, since I have written to you. . . .

To turn to the news of the day, it seems that the Cannibals of Europe are going to eating one another again . . . I hope we shall prove how much happier for man the Quaker policy is, and that the life of the feeder is better than that of the fighter; and it is some consolation that the desolation by these maniacs of one part of the earth is the means of improving it in other parts. Let the latter be our office, and let us milk the cow, while the Russian holds her by the horns, and the Turk by the tail. God bless you, and give you health, strength, and good spirits, and as much of life as you think worth having.

ADAMS TO JEFFERSON, MARCH 10, 1823

The sight of your well known hand writing in your favor of 25th February last, gave me great pleasure, as it proved your arm to be restored, and your pen still manageable. May it continue till you shall become as perfect a Calvinist as I am in one particular. Poor Calvin's infirmities, his rheumatism, his gouts and sciatics, made him frequently cry out, *"Mon Dieu! jusqu'à quand!"* Lord, how long! Prat, once chief justice of New York, always tormented with infirmities, dreamt that he was situated on a single rock in the midst of the Atlantic Ocean. He heard a voice:

"Why mourns the bard, Apollo bids thee rise,
Renounce the dust, and claim thy native skies."

JEFFERSON TO ADAMS, APRIL 11, 1823

The wishes expressed in your last favor, that I may continue in life and health until I become a Calvinist, at least in his exclamation of, *"Mon Dieu! jusqu'à quand!"* would make me immortal. I can never join Calvin in addressing *his* God. He was indeed an atheist, which I can never be; or rather his religion was daemonism. If ever man worshipped a false God, he did. The being described in his five points, is not the God whom you and I acknowledge and adore, the creator and benevolent governor of the world; but a daemon of malignant spirit. It would be more pardonable to believe in no God at all, then to blaspheme him by the atrocious attributes of Calvin. Indeed, I think that every Christian sect gives a great handle to atheism by their general dogma, that, without a revelation, there would not be sufficient proof of the being of a God.

Now one-sixth of mankind only are supposed to be Christians; the other five-sixths, then, who do not believe in the Jewish and Christian revelation, are without a knowledge of the existence of a God! This gives completely a *gain de cause* to the disciples of Ocellus, Timaeus, Spinosa, Diderot, and D'Holbach. The argument which they rest on as triumphant and unanswerable, is, that in every hypotheses of cosmogony, you must admit an eternal pre-existence of something; and according to the rule of sound philosophy, you are never to employ two principles to solve a difficulty when one will suffice. They say then, that it is more simple to believe at once in the eternal pre-existence of the world, as it is now going on, and may forever go on by the principle of reproduction which we see and witness, than to believe in the external pre-existence of an ulterior cause, or creator of the world, a being whom we see not and know not, of whose form, substance and mode, or place of existence, or of action, no sense informs us, no power of the mind enables us to delineate or comprehend.

On the contrary, I hold (without appeal to revelation) that when we take a view of the universe, in its parts, general or particular, it is impossible for the human mind not to perceive and feel a conviction of design, consummate skill, and indefinite power in every atom of its composition. The movements of the heavenly bodies, so exactly held in their course by the balance of centrifugal and centripetal forces; the structure of our earth itself, with its distribution of lands, waters and atmosphere; animal and vegetable bodies, examined in all their minutest particles; insects, mere atoms of life, yet as perfectly organized as man or mammoth; the mineral substances, their generation and uses; it is impossible, I say, for the human mind not to believe, that there is in all this, design, cause and effect, up to an ultimate cause, a fabricator of all things from matter and motion, their preserver and regulator while permitted to exist in their present forms, and their regeneration into new and other forms.

We see, too, evident proofs of the necessity of a superintending power, to maintain the universe in its course and order. Stars, well known, have disappeared, new ones have come into view; comets, in their incalculable courses, may run foul of suns and planets, and require renovation under other laws; certain races of animals are become extinct; and were there no restoring power, all existences might extinguish successively, one by one, until all should be reduced to a shapeless chaos. So irresistible are these evidences of an intelligent and powerful agent, that, of the infinite numbers of men who have existed through all time, they have believed, in the proportion of a million at least to unit, in the hypothesis of an eternal pre-existence of a creator, rather than in that of a self-existent universe. Surely this unanimous sentiment renders this more probable, than that of the few in the other hypothesis. Some early Christians, indeed, have believed in the co-eternal pre-existence of both the creator and the world, without changing their relation of cause and effect. . . .

Of the nature of this being we know nothing. Jesus tells us, that "God is a spirit." John 4:24. But without defining what a spirit is: "πνεῦμα ὁ θέος."[31] Down to the third century, we know it was still deemed material; but of a

---

[31] [God is (a) spirit.—ED.]

lighter, subtler matter than our gross bodies. So says Origen. . . . So also Tertullian. . . . These two fathers were of the third century. Calvin's character of this Supreme Being seems chiefly copied from that of the Jews. But the reformation of these blasphemous attributes, and substitution of those more worthy, pure and sublime, seems to have been the chief object of Jesus in his discourses to the Jews; and his doctrine of the cosmogony of the world is very clearly laid down in the first three verses of the first chapter of John. . . . Which truly translated means, "In the beginning God existed, and reason [or mind] was with God, and that mind was God. This was in the beginning with God. All things were created by it, and without it was made not one thing which was made."

Yet this text, so plainly declaring the doctrine of Jesus, that the world was created by the supreme, intelligent being, has been perverted by modern Christians to build up a second person of their tritheism, by a mistranslation of the word λόγος. One of its legitimate meanings, indeed, is "a word." But in that sense it makes an unmeaning jargon; while the other meaning "reason," equally legitimate, explains rationally the eternal pre-existence of God, and his creation of the world.

Knowing how incomprehensible it was that "a word," the mere action or articulation of the organs of speech could create a world, they undertook to make of this articulation a second pre-existing being, and ascribe to him, and not to God, the creation of the universe. The atheist here plumes himself on the uselessness of such a God, and the simpler hypothesis of a self-existent universe.

The truth is, that the greatest enemies to the doctrines of Jesus are those, calling themselves the expositors of them, who have perverted them for the structure of a system of fancy absolutely incomprehensible, and without any foundation in his genuine words. And the day will come, when the mystical generation of Jesus, by the Supreme Being as his father, in the womb of a virgin, will be classed with the fable of the generation of Minerva in the brain of Jupiter. But we may hope that the dawn of reason and freedom of thought in these United States, will do away all this artificial scaffolding and restore to us the primitive and genuine doctrines of this the most venerated reformer of human errors.

So much for your quotation of Calvin's "Mon Dieu! jusqu'a quand!" in which, when addressed to the God of Jesus, and our God, I join you cordially, and await his time and will with more readiness than reluctance. May we meet there again, in Congress, with our ancient colleagues, and receive with them the seal of approbation, "well done, good and faithful servants."

ADAMS TO JEFFERSON, AUGUST 15, 1823

I am no king killer, merely because they are kings. Poor creatures! they know no better; they sincerely conscientiously believe that God made them to rule the world. I would not, therefore, behead them, or send them to St. Helena, to be treated as Bonaparte was; but I would shut them up like the man in the iron mask, feed them well, and give them as much finery as they please, until they could be converted to right reason and common sense.

JEFFERSON TO ADAMS, JANUARY 8, 1825

I have lately been reading the most extraordinary of all books, and at the same time the most demonstrative by numerous and unequivocal facts. It is Flouren's experiments on the functions of the nervous system, in vertebrated animals. He takes out the cerebrum completely, leaving the cerebellum and other parts of the system uninjured. The animal loses all its senses of hearing, seeing, feeling, smelling, tasting, is totally deprived of will, intelligence, memory, perception, etc. Yet lives for months in perfect health, with all its powers of motion, but without moving but on external excitement, starving even on a pile of grain, unless crammed down its throat; in short, in a state of the most absolute stupidity. He takes the cerebellum out of others, leaving the cerebrum untouched. The animal retains all its senses, faculties and understanding, but loses the power of regulated motion, and exhibits all the symptoms of drunkenness. While he makes incisions in the cerebrum and cerebellum, lengthwise and crosswise, which heal and get well, a puncture in the medulla elongata is instant death; and many other most interesting things too long for a letter.

Cabanis had proved by the anatomical structure of certain portions of the human frame, that they might be capable of receiving from the hand of the Creator the faculty of thinking; Flourens proves that they have received it; that the cerebrum is the thinking organ; and that life and health may continue, and the animal be entirely without thought, if deprived of that organ.

I wish to see what the spiritualists will say to this. Whether in this state the soul remains in the body, deprived of its essence of thought? or whether it leaves it, as in death, and where it goes?

His memoirs and experiments have been reported on with approbation by a committee of the institute, composed of Cuvier, Bertholet, Dumaril, Portal and Pinel. But all this, you and I shall know better when we meet again, in another place, and at no distant period. In the meantime, that the revived powers of your frame, and the anodyne of philosophy may preserve you from all suffering is my sincere and affectionate prayer.

ADAMS TO JEFFERSON, JANUARY 23, 1825

We think ourselves possessed, or, at least, we boast that we are so, of liberty of conscience on all subjects, and of the right of free inquiry and private judgment in all cases, and yet how far are we from these exalted privileges in fact. There exists, I believe, throughout the whole Christian world, a law which makes it blasphemy to deny, or to doubt the divine inspiration of all the books of the Old and New Testaments, from Genesis to Revelations. In most countries of Europe it is punished by fire at the stake, or the rack, or the wheel. In England itself, it is punished by boring through the tongue with a red-hot poker.

In America it is not much better; even in our own Massachusetts, which I believe, upon the whole, is as temperate and moderate in religious zeal as most of the States, a law was made in the latter end of the last century, repealing the cruel punishments of the former laws, but substituting fine and imprisonment upon all those blasphemers upon any book of the Old Testament or New.

Now, what free inquiry, when a writer must surely encounter the risk of fine or imprisonment for adducing any argument for investigation into the divine authority of those books? Who would run the risk of translating Dupuis? I cannot enlarge upon this subject, though I have it much at heart. I think such laws a great embarrassment, great obstructions to the improvement of the human mind. Books that cannot bear examination, certainly ought not to be established as divine inspiration by penal laws.

It is true, few persons appear desirous to put such laws in execution, and it is also true that some few persons are hardy enough to venture to depart from them. But as long as they continue in force as laws, the human mind must make an awkward and clumsy progress in its investigations. I wish they were repealed. The substance and essence of Christianity, as I understand it, is eternal and unchangeable, and will bear examination forever, but it has been mixed with extraneous ingredients, which I think will not bear examination, they ought to be separated.

JEFFERSON TO ADAMS, MARCH 25, 1826

My grandson, Thomas J. Randolph, the bearer of this letter, being on a visit to Boston, would think he had seen nothing were he to leave without seeing you. Although I truly sympathize with you in the trouble these interruptions give, yet I must ask for him permission to pay to you his personal respects. Like other young people, he wishes to be able in the winter nights of old age, to recount to those around him, what he has heard and learnt of the heroic age preceding his birth, and which of the Argonauts individually he was in time to have seen.

It was the lot of our early years to witness nothing but the dull monotony of a colonial subservience; and of our riper years, to breast the labors and perils of working out of it. Theirs are the Halcyon calms succeeding the storm which our Argosy had so stoutly weathered. Gratify his ambition, then, by receiving his best bow; and my solicitude for your health, by enabling him to bring me a favorable account of it. Mine is but indifferent, but not so my friendship and respect for you.

6. JAMES MADISON

"What Is Here a Right Towards Men Is a Duty Towards the Creator"

IT is difficult to write a biography of James Madison without at the same time writing an intimate account of the constitutional period of American history. For if Franklin and Jefferson were the philosophers of the period, and Washington its overseer, then Madison was the chief engineer and foreman. For it was Madison who kept most of the parts in moving order. He had the kind of knowledge and temperament that could work from the blueprints of others or make his own, and then put both into execution. He had a precise, analytical mind; Henry Clay once described him as "cool, dispassionate, practical, and safe." No man was better prepared for the American Constitutional Convention; no man knew more about political science or worked harder to prepare a draft acceptable to the states. It is natural that historians should regard him as "Father of the Constitution."

Madison was also a master chronicler, observer, and commentator. His notes on the Philadelphia Constitutional Convention represent the only full account of the one major event in history that proves it is possible for governments to be carefully designed and created by the human intelligence, rather than to be the product of accident, ebb and flow, or brute will. Madison was one of the authors of *The Federalist* papers, which served the purpose of educating the American people on the great issues and principles involved in transforming a group of sovereign states into a balanced federation. In such a federation, authority was balanced with responsibility. The central government did that which the states could not do, namely, to govern in those matters of common danger and common needs to all the people. The state governments were given full and protected jurisdiction in all other matters, namely, the conduct of government as it intimately affected the individual. Most importantly, the principle was established that federally enacted law was to apply directly to the individual, who in turn would have clearly defined rights. The big transition, therefore, from the confederation to federation was one from voluntary agreement to binding law, establishing a direct connection between the central government and the individual.

The Constitutional Convention and the Presidency of the United States (1808-16) are two of Madison's three principal areas of service to the American people. The third is his activity in behalf of religious freedom. He was primarily responsible for obtaining the acceptance in Virginia of Jefferson's historic Statute of Religious Freedom. He was the principal sponsor of the Bill of Rights embodied in the first ten amendments to the Constitution, the first article of which guaranteed freedom of religion and prohibited the establishment of a national church.

James Madison, like some of his eminent contemporaries, studied for the ministry. His theological studies at Princeton University (then the College of New Jersey) were under John Witherspoon, who gave Madison an awareness of the broad base necessary for serious religious studies. Even after Madison returned to Virginia he continued his theological interests. He also developed strong concern over the situation in Virginia as it concerned freedom of worship.

The early settlers who came to Virginia had continued the Anglican Church tradition. The discriminations against other religions followed almost as a matter of course. Congregational ministers who came to the Virginia colony in 1642 were made to leave. The Assembly passed a Law of Uniformity with the result that even the Puritan section of the State Church could not operate. The discriminations continued in one form or another for more than a century. At the time of Madison's return from Princeton, several "well-meaning men," as he described them, were put in prison for their religious views. Baptists were being fined or imprisoned for holding unauthorized meetings. Dissenters were taxed for the support of the State Church. Preachers had to be licensed. Madison saw at first hand the repetition of the main evils of the Old Country. But he also saw deep dissatisfaction among the people—the kind of dissatisfaction that would grow and that would serve as a mighty battering ram for religious freedom.

Madison referred only rarely to his personal religious beliefs. It was an article of faith with him that a man's relation to the Creator was in itself a sacred matter, to be protected if necessary by the government. His own theological knowledge was as wide as that possessed by any of the other Founding Fathers. His knowledge buttressed his own religious convictions. At the same time, it reinforced his determination to prevent any denomination from getting the kind of authority that would enable it to dominate the others. Freedom to believe or not believe must be a basic right in a democratic society.

In 1776, at the age of twenty-five, he was chosen a delegate to the new Virginia Convention called to draft a new constitution for the state. He proposed an amendment declaring that all men were entitled to the free exercise of religion. The amendment was defeated, but Madison had defined his cause. He was elected to the Continental Congress. After completing his term he returned to Virginia, where he became a member of the house of delegates and served on the Committee on Religion. Here he led the fight against special privileges for the Episcopal clergy and against a general assessment for the Church. Support grew for his position and he won his fight against the assessment. He then took up the battle in behalf of Jefferson's Bill for Religious Freedom. It was a difficult but exciting challenge; he knew that the bill would have meaning for all the states. It was an historic issue in American history. Thanks largely to his stewardship, the bill was passed.

His analytical abilities were recognized and respected by his contemporaries. When Madison argued a point he generally scored it. Like Washington, he was close to both Jefferson and Hamilton. He agreed with Hamilton at the Constitutional Convention about the need for a strong central government. In later years, he felt that there was some danger, as did Jefferson, of too much power being concentrated in the Federal government. When Jefferson became President, his natural choice for Secretary of State was James Madison. They made what many historians consider to be the best two-man foreign policy team, in terms of harmony of views and effectiveness of operation, in American history. When Jefferson approached the end of his second term, his personal choice as successor was Madison. Madison received the nomination and won the election, becoming the fourth United States President. At the completion of his term in 1817, he retired to his estate in Virginia, occupying himself in service to education and with his correspondence. In 1829, he emerged from retirement to participate in the Virginia Constitutional Convention, which afforded him an opportunity to work in the area of minority rights, one of his favorite concerns.

All his life he had been in frail health. He was a small man physically; when he took the oath of office for the Presidency, he looked so wan and wizened that some feared he might not last out the ceremony. But he lived to the age of eighty-five, following the affairs of the nation with the same careful, analytical interest that had marked all his public activities. He never speculated on his own place in eternity; he did, however, say that a "well-founded commonwealth may be immortal."

James Madison was a student of theology when he wrote this letter to William Bradford, Jr., a close friend, later to become U.S. Attorney General. Madison had only recently graduated from the college in New Jersey that was to become Princeton University, where he returned as a graduate student, excelling in his religious studies, especially Hebrew. In this letter, written at the age of twenty-two, he shows the beginning of a strong consistency in his own articles of faith and in his convictions concerning the relationship of government to religion. Happily for the United States, James Madison's doubts concerning his health, expressed so vividly in this letter, turned out to be without substance.

LETTER TO WILLIAM BRADFORD, JR., NOVEMBER 9, 1772

However nice and cautious we may be in detecting the follies of mankind, and framing our economy according to the precepts of Wisdom and Religion, I fancy there will commonly remain with us some latent expectation of obtaining more than ordinary happiness and prosperity till we feel the convincing argument of actual disappointment. Though I will not determine whether we shall be much the worse for it if we do not allow it to intercept our views towards a future state, because strong desires and great hopes instigate us to arduous enterprises, fortitude, and perseverance. Nevertheless, a watchful eye must be kept on ourselves, lest while we are building ideal monuments of renown and bliss here, we neglect to have our names enrolled in the annals of Heaven.

These thoughts come into my mind because I am writing to you, and thinking of you. As to myself, I am too dull and infirm now to look out for any extraordinary things in this world, for I think my sensations for many months past have intimated to me not to expect a long or healthy life; though it may be better with me after some time, [but] I hardly dare expect it, and therefore have little spirit and alacrity to set about anything that is difficult in acquiring and useless in possessing after one has exchanged time for eternity. But you have health, youth, fire, and genius, to bear you along through the high track of public life, and so may be more interested and delighted in improving on hints that respect the temporal though momentous concerns of man.

Writing again to Bradford, the young Madison shows his awareness of the big groundswells of revolution then building up, and the significance of the changes then impending to religious institutions. The beliefs put down here were to serve as a working basis for many official actions in years to come.

LETTER TO WILLIAM BRADFORD, JR., JANUARY 24, 1774

I congratulate you on your heroic proceedings in Philadelphia with regard to the tea. I wish Boston may conduct matters with as much discretion as they seem to do with boldness. They seem to have great trials and difficulties by reason of the obduracy and ministerialism of their Governor. However, political contests are necessary sometimes, as well as military, to afford exercise and practice, and to instruct in the art of defending liberty and property. I verily believe the frequent assaults that have been made on America (Boston especially) will in the end prove of real advantage.

If the Church of England had been the established and general religion in all the northern colonies as it has been among us here, and uninterrupted tranquility had prevailed throughout the continent, it is clear to me that slavery and subjection might and would have been gradually insinuated among us. Union of religious sentiments begets a surprising confidence, and ecclesiastical establishments tend to great ignorance and corruption; all of which facilitate the execution of mischievous projects.

I want again to breathe your free air. I expect it will mend my constitution and confirm my principles. I have indeed as good an atmosphere at home as the climate will allow; but have nothing to brag of as to the state and liberty of my country. Poverty and luxury prevail among all sorts; pride, ignorance, and knavery among the priesthood, and vice and wickedness among the laity. This is bad enough, but it is not the worst I have to tell you. That diabolical, hell-conceived principle of persecution rages among some; and to their eternal infamy, the clergy can furnish their quota of imps for such business. This vexes me the worst of anything whatever. There are at this time in the adjacent country not less than five or six well-meaning men in close jail for publishing their religious sentiments, which in the main are very orthodox. I have neither patience to hear, talk, or think of anything relative to this matter; for I have squabbled and scolded, abused and ridiculed, so long about it to little purpose, that I am without common patience. So I must beg you to pity me, and pray for liberty of conscience to all.

At the time the following letter was written, Madison was not yet engaged in public work, but was pursuing his reading on philosophical and theological subjects, and helping as a tutor with younger members of the family. But he was becoming increasingly drawn to the political life. A few months later, he became chairman of the Committee for Public Safety in Orange County,

Virginia. Meanwhile, as is apparent in the following communication, he followed closely developments bearing on religious matters in the colony.

LETTER TO WILLIAM BRADFORD, JR., APRIL 1, 1774

Our Assembly is to meet the first of May, when it is expected something will be done in behalf of the dissenters. Petitions, I hear, are already forming among the persecuted Baptists, and I fancy it is in the thoughts of the Presbyterians also, to intercede for greater liberty in matters of religion. For my own part, I cannot help being very doubtful of their succeeding in the attempt. The affair was on the carpet during the last session; but such incredible and extravagant stories were told in the House of the monstrous effects of the enthusiasm prevalent among the sectaries, and so greedily swallowed by their enemies, that I believe they lost footing by it. And the bad name they still have with those who pretend too much contempt to examine into their principles and conduct, and are too much devoted to the ecclesiastical establishment to hear of the toleration of dissentients, I am apprehensive, will be again made a pretext for rejecting their request.

The sentiments of our people of fortune and fashion on this subject are vastly different from what you have been used to. That liberal, Catholic, and equitable way of thinking, as to the rights of conscience, which is one of the characteristics of a free people, and so strongly marks the people of your province, is but little known among the zealous adherents to our hierarchy. We have, it is true, some persons in the Legislature of generous principles both in Religion and Politics; but number, not merit, you know, is necessary to carry points there. Besides, the clergy are a numerous and powerful body, have great influence at home by reason of their connection with and dependence on the Bishops and Crown, and will naturally employ all their art and interest to depress their rising adversaries; for such they must consider dissenters who rob them of the good will of the people, and may, in time, endanger their livings and security.

You are happy in dwelling in a land where those inestimable privileges are fully enjoyed; and the public has long felt the good effects of this religious as well as civil liberty. Foreigners have been encouraged to settle among you. Industry and virtue have been promoted by mutual emulation and mutual inspection; commerce and the arts have flourished; and I cannot help attributing those continual exertions of genius which appear among you to the inspiration of liberty, and that love of fame and knowledge which always accompany it. Religious bondage shackles and debilitates the mind, and unfits it for every noble enterprise, every expanded prospect.

How far this is the case with Virginia will more clearly appear when the ensuing trial is made.

James Madison took an active part as delegate, shaping the historic Constitution of Virginia, with its clear statement on human rights that was to serve as an inspiration eleven years later at the Constitutional Convention in Philadelphia. The first draft of the article dealing with religious freedom at the Virginia Convention was drawn up by Madison. The quotation is from the Journal of the Virginia Convention.

VIRGINIA JOURNAL, 1776

That Religion, or the duty which we owe to our CREATOR, and the manner of discharging it, can be directed only by reason and conviction, not by force or violence: and therefore, that all men should enjoy the fullest toleration in the exercise of religion, according to the dictates of conscience, unpunished, and unrestrained by the magistrate, unless under colour of religion, any man disturb the peace, the happiness, or safety of Society. And that it is the mutual duty of all to practice Christian forbearance, love, and charity, towards each other.

A *manuscript variation of this passage reads:* "That Religion or the duty we owe our Creator, and the manner of discharging it, being under the direction of reason and conviction only, not of violence or compulsion, all men are equally entitled to the full and free exercise of it, according to the dictates of conscience; and therefore that no man or class of men, ought, on account of religion to be invested with peculiar emoluments or privileges, nor subjected to any penalties or disabilities, unless under colour of religion, the preservation of equal liberty and the existence of the State be manifestly endangered."

That Religion, or the duty we owe to our CREATOR, and the manner of discharging it can be directed only by reason and conviction, not by force or violence, and therefore all men are equally entitled to the free exercise of religion, according to the dictates of conscience; and that it is the mutual duty of all to practice Christian forbearance love and charity towards each other.

In the late spring of 1784, a resolution was introduced in the Virginia Assembly seeking official state recognition for the Episcopal Church. The resolution was debated for two days, with notable opposition from Baptists and Presbyterians. John B. Smith, president of Hampden-Sydney College, wrote to Madison on June 21, 1784, that the bill was insulting to non-Episcopalians. Any measure, he said, to enable the Episcopal clergy to reg-

ulate all spiritual concerns of that church was an express attempt "to draw the State into an elicit connection and commerce with them," and to put the legislature in the position of being at the head of the church. He regretted that Christian ministers should virtually declare their church to be a mere political machine. Madison discusses the outcome of this bill in a letter to Thomas Jefferson.

LETTER TO T. JEFFERSON, JULY 3, 1784

Several Petitions came forward in behalf of a general Assessment which was reported by the Committee of Religion to be reasonable. The friends of the measure did not choose to try their strength in the House. The Episcopal Clergy introduced a notable project for re-establishing their independence of the laity. The foundation of it was that the whole body should be legally incorporated, invested with the present property of the Church, made capable of acquiring indefinitely—empowered to make canons and bye-laws not contrary to the laws of the land, and incumbents when once chosen by vestries, to be immovable otherwise than by sentence of the Convocation. Extraordinary as such a project was, it was preserved from a dishonorable death by the talents of Mr. [*Patrick*] Henry. It lies over for another Session.

In November, 1784, James Madison wrote some notes for a speech he planned to give in the Virginia Assembly on the subject of assessments for support of religion. The resolution, introduced by Patrick Henry, declared that the "people of the Commonwealth ought to pay a moderate tax or contribution for the support of the Christian religion, or of some Christian church, denomination, or communion of Christians, or of some form of Christian worship." The notes were set down in a very small hand on the back of a letter. Few materials on Madison show so clearly the working of his mind, his ability to see far into his subject without ever losing his sense of the whole.

MADISON NOTES, 1784

    I. Rel. not within purview of civil authority. Tendency of estab'g Xnty—
        1. to project of Uniformity.
        2. to penal laws for support'g it.
        Progress of Gen. Asses't proves this tendency.
        Difference between estab'g and tolerating errour.
        "True question—not Is Rel. necessary,—but
    II. are Relig's Esta'bts necessary for Religion? No.
        1. Propensity of man to Religion.

2. Experience shews Relig. corrupted by Estab'ts.

3. Downfall of States mentioned by Mr. H.—happened where there was estab't.

4. Experience gives no model of Gen'l Ass't.

5. Case of Pa. explained—not solitary. N.J. See const. of it. R.I., N.Y., D. factions greater in S.C.

6. Case of primitive Xnty.
    of Reformation.
    of Dissenters formerly.

7. Progress of Religious liberty.

III. Policy—

1. promote emigrations from State.

2. prevent immig. into it, as *asylum*.

IV. Necessity of Estab't inferred from state of co'y.
    True causes of disease.

1. War

2. bad laws $\begin{cases} \text{common to other States \& produce same} \\ \text{compl'ts in N.E.} \end{cases}$

3. pretext from taxes.

4. state of administration of Justice.

5. transition from old to new plan.

6. policy and hopes of friends to G. Ass't.

True remedies not Estab't—but, being out of war,

1. laws to cherish virtue.

2. administration of justice.

3. personal example—associations for R.

4. By present vote, cut off hope of G. ass't.

5. Education of youth.

V. Probable effects of Bill,

1. limited.

2. in particular.

3. What is Xnty? Courts of law to Judge.

4. What edition: Hebrew, Septuagint, or Vulgate? What copy, what translation?

5. What books canonical, what apocryphal? the papists holding to be the former what protestants the latter, the Lutherans the latter what the protestants & papists ye former.

6. In what light are they to be viewed, as dictated every letter by inspiration, or the essential parts only? Or the matter in general not the words?

7. What sense the true one for if some doctrines be essential to Xnty those who reject these, whatever name they take are no Xn Society?

8. Is it Trinitarianism, Arianism, Socinianism? Is it salvation by faith or works also, by free grace or by will, &c., &c.

9. What clue is to guide (a) Judge thro' this labyrinth when ye question comes before them whether any particular society is a Xn society?

10. Ends in what is orthodoxy, what heresy. Dishonors christianity. panegyric on it, on our side.
Decl. Rights.

Shortly after making these notes, Madison wrote to James Monroe on the same subject.

LETTER TO JAMES MONROE, NOVEMBER 14, 1784

But their principal attention has been and is still occupied with a scheme proposed for a General Assessment; 47 have carried it against 32. In its present form it excludes all but Christian Sects.

The Presbyterian Clergy have remonstrated against any narrow principles, but indirectly favor a more comprehensive establishment. I think the bottom will be enlarged and that a trial will be made of the practicability of the project. The Successor to Mr. H[arrison] is not yet appointed or nominated. It is in the option of Mr. H[enry], and I fancy he will not decline the service.

The status of the Henry resolution was pithily reported by Madison in a letter to Monroe:

LETTER TO JAMES MONROE, DECEMBER 24, 1784

The General Assessment on the question for engrossing it, was yesterday carried by 44 against 42. Today its third reading was put off till November next, by 45 against 37 or thereabouts, and it is to be printed for consideration of the people.

Madison wrote a long letter to Thomas Jefferson on various political, philosophical, and religious matters. The section quoted here concerns an act for incorporating the Protestant Episcopal Church under consideration by the Virginia Assembly.

LETTER TO THOMAS JEFFERSON, JANUARY 9, 1785

This act declares the Ministers & vestries who are to be triennially chosen in each parish a body corporate, enables them to hold property not exceeding the value of £800 per annum, and gives sanction to a Convention which is to be composed of the Clergy and a lay deputy from each parish, and is to regulate the affairs of the Church. It was understood by the House of Delegates that the Convention was to consist of two laymen for each clergyman, and an amendment was received for that express purpose. It so happened that the insertion of the amendment did not produce that effect, and the mistake was never discovered till the bill had passed and was in print.

Another circumstance still more singular is that the act is so construed as to deprive the Vestries of the uncontrolled right of electing Clergymen, unless it be referred to them by the canons of the Convention, and that this usurpation actually escaped the eye both of the friends and adversaries of the measure, both parties taking the contrary for granted throughout the whole progress of it. The former as well as the latter appear now to be dissatisfied with what has been done, and will probably concur in a revision if not a repeal of the law.

Independently of these oversights the law is in various points of view exceptionable. But the necessity of some sort of incorporation for the purpose of holding and managing the property of the Church could not well be denied, nor a more harmless modification of it now obtained. A negative of the bill too would have doubled the eagerness and the pretexts for a much greater evil, a general Assessment, which, there is good ground to believe was parried by this partial gratification of its warmest votaries.

A Resolution for a legal provision for the "teachers of the Christian Religion" had early in the Session been proposed by Mr. [Patrick] Henry, and in spite of all the opposition that could be mustered, carried by 47 against 32 votes. Many Petitions from below the blue ridge had prayed for such a law; and though several from the Presbyterian laity beyond it were in a contrary stile, the Clergy of that Sect favored it. The other Sects seemed to be passive.

The Resolution lay some weeks before a bill was brought in, and the bill some weeks before it was called for, after the passage of the incorporating act it was taken up, and on the third reading, ordered by a small majority to be printed for consideration. The bill, in its present dress, proposes a tax of blank per C't on all taxable property for support of Teachers of the Christian Religion. Each person when he pays his tax is to name the society to which he dedicates it, and in case of refusal to do so, the tax is to be applied to the maintenance of a school in the County. As the bill stood for some time, the application in such cases was to be made by the Legislature to pious uses.

In a committee of the whole it was determined by a majority of 7 or 8 that the word "Christian" should be changed for the word "Religious." On the report to the House the *pathetic zeal of the late Governor Harrison* gained a like majority for reinstating discrimination.

Should the bill pass into a law in its present form it may and will be easily eluded. It is chiefly obnoxious on account of its dishonorable principle and dangerous tendency.

In a letter to James Monroe, Madison returns to the matter of the assessment for religious support.

LETTER TO JAMES MONROE, APRIL 12, 1785

The only proceeding of the late Session of Assembly which makes a noise through the Country is that which relates to a General Assessment. The Episcopal people are generally for it, though I think the zeal of some of them has cooled. The laity of the other sects are equally unanimous on the other side. So are all the Clergy except the Presbyterian who seem as ready to set up an establishment which is to take them in as they were to pull down that which shut them out. I do not know a more shameful contrast than might be found between their memorials on the latter and former occasion.

Another running report to Thomas Jefferson on the General Assessment Bill.

LETTER TO THOMAS JEFFERSON, APRIL 27, 1785

The Bill for a General Assessment has produced some fermention below the Mountains and a violent one beyond them. The contest at the next Session on this question will be a warm and precarious one.

Some clear indications of the direction being taken by public opinion on the various measures having to do with public support of religion are found in a letter by Madison to Monroe.

LETTER TO JAMES MONROE, MAY 29, 1785

It gives me much pleasure to observe by 2 printed reports sent me by Col. Grayson that, in the latter Congress had expunged a clause contained in the first for setting apart a district of land in each Township for supporting the Religion of the majority of inhabitants. How a regulation so unjust in itself, so foreign to the Authority of Congress, so hurtful to the sale of the public land, and smelling so strongly of an antiquated Bigotry, could have received the countenance of a Committee is truly a matter of astonishment. In one view it might have been no disadvantage to this State in case the General Assessment should take place, as it would have given a repellent quality to the new Country in the estimation of those whom our own encroachments of Religious Liberty would be calculated to banish to it. But the adversaries to the assessment begin to think the prospect here flattering to their wishes.

The printed Bill has excited great discussion and is likely to prove the sense of the Community to be in favor of the liberty now enjoyed. I have heard of several Countries where the late representatives have been laid aside for voting for the Bill, and not of a single one where the reverse has happened. The Presbyterian Clergy too who were in general friends to the scheme, are already in another tone, either compelled by the laity of that sect, or alarmed at the probability of further interferences of the Legislature, if they once begin to dictate in matters of Religion.

Less than two months later, Madison reports to Monroe again on the highly controversial situation in Virginia relating to the relationship of government to religion.

LETTER TO JAMES MONROE, JUNE 21, 1785

Finding from a letter of Mr. Mazzei that you have never been furnished with a copy of the Bill for establishing the Christian Religion in this State, I now enclose one, regretting that I had taken it for granted that you must have been supplied through some other channel. A very warm opposition will be made to this innovation by the people of the middle and back Counties, particularly the latter. They do not scruple to declare it an alarming usurpation on their fundamental rights and that though the General Assembly should give it the form, they will not give it the validity of a law. If there be any limitation to the power of the Legislature, particularly if this limitation is to be sought in our Declaration of Rights or Form of Government, I own the Bill appears to me to warrant this language of the people.

The issue in the state is a major one. Madison is glad to supply arguments for debate, but does not wish his name to be used.

LETTER TO EDMUND RANDOLPH, JULY 26, 1785

Your favor of the 17th instant inclosing a letter from Mr. Jones and a copy of the ecclesiastical Journal, came safe to hand. If I do not dislike the contents of the letter, it is because they furnish as I conceive fresh and forcible arguments against the General Assessment. It may be of little consequence, what tribunal is to judge of Clerical misdemeanors or how firmly the incumbent may be fastened on the parish, whilst the Vestry and people may hear and pay him or not as they like. But should a legal salary be annexed to the title, this phantom of power would be substantiated into a real monster of oppression. . . .

At the instance of Col. Nicholas of Albemarle, I undertook the draught of the inclosed remonstrance against the General Assessment. Subscriptions to it are on foot I believe in sundry Counties, and will be extended to others. My choice is that my name may not be associated with it. I am not sure that I know precisely your ideas on this subject; but were they more variant from mine than I take them to be I should not be restrained from a confidential communication.

More than a year after the General Assessment Bill was introduced in the Virginia Assembly, the issue approached its final test. Madison has decided the time is right to identify himself openly and actively against the measure. He sends a copy of his "Remonstrance" to Thomas Jefferson.

LETTER TO THOMAS JEFFERSON, AUGUST 20, 1785

The opposition to the General Assessment gains ground. At the instance of some of its adversaries I drew up the remonstrance herewith inclosed. It has been sent through the medium of confidential persons in a number of the upper Counties, and I am told will be pretty extensively signed. The Presbyterian clergy have at length espoused the side of the opposition, being moved either by a fear of their laity or a jealousy of the Episcopalians. The mutual hatred of these sects has been much inflamed by the late Act incorporating the latter. I am far from being sorry for it, as a coalition between them could alone endanger our religious rights, and a tendency to such an event had been suspected.

The text of Madison's "Memorial and Remonstrance" against Religious Assessments, as presented to the General Assembly of Virginia in the fall of 1785. It is interesting to compare this statement with the notes he jotted down a year earlier in terms of the basic principles he defined. This statement is one of the clearest and most important public documents relating to the relationship of government to religion in a free society.

MEMORIAL AND REMONSTRANCE, 1785

We, the subscribers, citizens of the said Commonwealth, having taken into serious consideration, a Bill printed by order of the last Session of General Assembly, entitled "A Bill establishing a provision for Teachers of the Christian Religion," and conceiving that the same, if finally armed with the sanctions of a law, will be a dangerous abuse of power, are bound as faithful members of a Free State, to remonstrate against it, and to declare the reasons by which we are determined. We remonstrate against the said Bill.

1. Because we hold it for a fundamental and undeniable truth, "that Religion or the duty which we owe to our Creator and the Manner of discharging it, can be directed only by reason and conviction, not by force or violence." The Religion then of every man must be left to the conviction and conscience of every man; and it is the right of every man to exercise it as these may dictate. This right is in its nature an unalienable right. It is unalienable; because the opinions of men, depending only on the evidence contemplated by their own minds, cannot follow the dictates of other men: It is unalienable also; because what is here a right towards men, is a duty towards the Creator. It is the duty of every man to render to the Creator such homage, and such only, as he believes to be acceptable to him. This duty is precedent both in order of time and degree of obligation, to the claims of Civil Society. Before any man can be considered as a member of Civil Society, he must be considered as a subject of the Governor of the Universe: And if a member of Civil Society, who enters into any subordinate Association, must always do it with a reservation of his duty to the general authority; much more must every man who becomes a member of any particular Civil Society, do it with a saving of his allegiance to the Universal Sovereign. We maintain therefore that in matters of Religion, no man's right is abridged by the institution of Civil Society, and that Religion is wholly exempt from its cognizance. True it is, that no other rule exists, by which any question which may divide a Society, can be ultimately determined, but the will of the majority; but it is also true, that the majority may trespass on the rights of the minority.

2. Because if religion be exempt from the authority of the Society at large, still less can it be subject to that of the Legislative Body. The latter are but the creatures and vicegerents [sic] of the former. Their jurisdiction is both derivative and limited: it is limited with regard to the coordinate departments, more necessarily is it limited with regard to the constituents. The preservation of a free government requires not merely, that the metes and bounds which separate each department of power may be invariably maintained; but more especially, that neither of them be suffered to overleap the great Barrier which defends the rights of the people. The Rulers who are guilty of such an encroachment, exceed the commission from which they derive their authority, and are Tyrants. The People who submit to it

are governed by laws made neither by themselves, nor by an authority derived from them, and are slaves.

3. Because, it is proper to take alarm at the first experiment on our liberties. We hold this prudent jealousy to be the first duty of citizens, and one of [the] noblest characteristics of the late Revolution. The freemen of America did not wait till usurped power had strengthened itself by exercise, and entangled the question in precedents. They saw all the consequences in the principle, and they avoided the consequences by denying the principle. We revere this lesson too much, soon to forget it. Who does not see that the same authority which can establish Christianity, in exclusion of all other Religions, may establish with the same ease any particular sect of Christians, in exclusion of all other Sects? That the same authority which can force a citizen to contribute three pence only of his property for the support of any one establishment, may force him to conform to any other establishment in all cases whatsoever?

4. Because, the bill violates that equality which ought to be the basis of every law, and which is more indispensible, in proportion as the validity or expediency of any law is more liable to be impeached. If "all men are by nature equally free and independent," all men are to be considered as entering into Society on equal conditions; as relinquishing no more, and therefore retaining no less, one than another, of their natural rights. Above all are they to be considered as retaining an "*equal* title to the free exercise of Religion according to the dictates of conscience". Whilst we assert for ourselves a freedom to embrace, to profess, and to observe the Religion which we believe to be of divine origin, we cannot deny an equal freedom to those whose minds have not yet yielded to the evidence which has convinced us. If this freedom be abused, it is an offence against God, not against man: To God, therefore, not to man, must an account of it be rendered. As the Bill violates equality by subjecting some to peculiar burdens; so it violates the same principle, by granting to others peculiar exemptions. Are the Quakers and Menonists the only sects who think a compulsive support of their religions unnecessary and unwarrantable? Can their piety alone be intrusted with the care of public worship? Ought their Religions to be endowed above all others, with extraordinary privileges, by which proselytes may be enticed from all others? We think too favorably of the justice and good sense of these denominations, to believe that they either covet pre-eminencies over their fellow citizens, or that they will be seduced by them, from the common opposition to the measure.

5. Because the bill implies either that the Civil Magistrate is a competent Judge of Religious truth; or that he may employ Religion as an engine of Civil policy. The first is an arrogant pretension falsified by the contra-

dictory opinions of Rulers in all ages, and throughout the world: The second an unhallowed perversion of the means of salvation.

6. Because the establishment proposed by the Bill is not requisite for the support of the Christian Religion. To say that it is, is a contradiction to the Christian Religion itself; for every page of it disavows a dependence on the powers of this world: it is a contradiction to fact; for it is known that this Religion both existed and flourished, not only without the support of human laws, but in spite of every opposition from them; and not only during the period of miraculous aid, but long after it had been left to its own evidence, and the ordinary care of Providence: Nay, it is a contradiction in terms; for a Religion not invented by human policy, must have pre-existed and been supported, before it was established by human policy. It is moreover to weaken in those who profess this Religion a pious confidence in its innate excellence, and the patronage of its Author; and to foster in those who still reject it, a suspicion that its friends are too conscious of its fallacies, to trust it to its own merits.

7. Because experience witnesseth that ecclesiastical establishments, instead of maintaining the purity and efficacy of Religion, have had a contrary operation. During almost fifteen centuries, has the legal establishment of Christianity been on trial. What have been its fruits? More or less in all places, pride and indolence in the Clergy; ignorance and servility in the laity; in both, superstition, bigotry and persecution. Enquire of the Teachers of Christianity for the ages in which it appeared in its greatest lustre; those of every sect, point to the ages prior to its incorporation with Civil policy. Propose a restoration of this primitive state in which its Teachers depended on the voluntary rewards of their flocks; many of them predict its downfall. On which side ought their testimony to have greatest weight, when for or when against their interests?

8. Because the establishment in question is not necessary for the support of Civil Government. If it be urged as necessary for the support of Civil Government only as it is a means of supporting Religion, and it be not necessary for the latter purpose, it cannot be necessary for the former. If Religion be not within [the] cognizance of Civil Government, how can its legal establishment be said to be necessary to civil Government? What influence in fact have ecclesiastical establishments had on Civil Society? In some instances they have been seen to erect a spiritual tyranny on the ruins of Civil authority; in many instances they have been seen upholding the thrones of political tyranny; in no instance have they been seen the guardians of the liberties of the people. Rulers who wished to subvert the public liberty, may have found an established clergy convenient auxiliaries. A just government, instituted to secure and perpetuate it, needs them not. Such a

government will be best supported by protecting every citizen in the enjoyment of his Religion with the same equal hand which protects his person and his property; by neither invading the equal rights of any Sect, nor suffering any Sect to invade those of another.

9. Because the proposed establishment is a departure from that generous policy, which, offering an asylum to the persecuted and oppressed of every Nation and Religion, promised a lustre to our country, and an accession to the number of its citizens. What a melancholy mark is the Bill of sudden degeneracy? Instead of holding forth an asylum to the persecuted, it is itself a signal of persecution. It degrades from the equal rank of Citizens all those whose opinions in Religion do not bend to those of the Legislative authority. Distant as it may be, in its present form, from the Inquisition it differs from it only in degree. The one is the first step, the other the last in the career of intolerance. The magnanimous sufferer under this cruel scourge in foreign Regions, must view the Bill as a Beacon on our Coast, warning him to seek some other haven, where liberty and philanthropy in their due extent may offer a more certain repose from his troubles.

10. Because, it will have a like tendency to banish our Citizens. The allurements presented by other situations are every day thinning their number. To superadd a fresh motive to emigration, by revoking the liberty which they now enjoy, would be the same species of folly which has dishonored and depopulated flourishing kingdoms.

11. Because, it will destroy that moderation and harmony which the forbearance of our laws to intermeddle with Religion, has produced amongst its several sects. Torrents of blood have been spilt in the old world, by vain attempts of the secular arm to extinguish Religious discord, by proscribing all difference in Religious opinions. Time has at length revealed the true remedy. Every relaxation of narrow and rigorous policy, wherever it has been tried, has been found to assuage the disease. The American Theatre has exhibited proofs, that equal and complete liberty, if it does not wholly eradicate it, sufficiently destroys its malignant influence on the health and prosperity of the State. If with the salutary effects of this system under our own eyes, we begin to contract the bonds of Religious freedom, we know no name that will too severely reproach our folly. At least let warning be taken at the first fruits of the threatened innovation. The very appearance of the Bill has transformed that "Christian forbearance, love and charity," which of late mutually prevailed, into animosities and jealousies, which may not soon be appeased. What mischiefs may not be dreaded should this enemy to the public quiet be armed with the force of a law?

12. Because, the policy of the Bill is adverse to the diffusion of the light of Christianity. The first wish of those who enjoy this precious gift, ought to be that it may be imparted to the whole race of mankind. Compare the

number of those who have as yet received it with the number still remaining under the dominion of false Religions; and how small is the former! Does the policy of the Bill tend to lessen the disproportion? No; it at once discourages those who are strangers to the light of [revelation] from coming into the Region of it; and countenances, by example the nations who continue in darkness, in shutting out those who might convey it to them. Instead of levelling as far as possible, every obstacle to the victorious progress of truth, the Bill with an ignoble and unchristian timidity would circumscribe it, with a wall of defence, against the encroachments of error.

13. Because attempts to enforce by legal sanctions, acts obnoxious to so great a proportion of Citizens, tend to enervate the laws in general, and to slacken the bands of Society. If it be difficult to execute any law which is not generally deemed necessary or salutary, what must be the case where it is deemed invalid and dangerous? And what may be the effect of so striking an example of impotency in the Government, on its general authority.

14. Because a measure of such singular magnitude and delicacy ought not to be imposed, without the clearest evidence that it is called for by a majority of citizens: and no satisfactory method is yet proposed by which the voice of the majority in this case may be determined, or its influence secured. "The people of the respective counties are indeed requested to signify their opinion respecting the adoption of the Bill to the next Session of Assembly." But the representation must be made equal, before the voice either of the Representatives or of the Counties, will be that of the people. Our hope is that neither of the former will, after due consideration, espouse the dangerous principle of the Bill. Should the event disappoint us, it will still leave us in full confidence, that a fair appeal to the latter will reverse the sentence against our liberties.

15. Because, finally, "the equal right of every citizen to the free exercise of his Religion according to the dictates of conscience" is held by the same tenure with all our other rights. If we recur to its origin, it is equally the gift of nature; if we weigh its importance, it cannot be less dear to us; if we consult the Declaration of those rights which pertain to the good people of Virginia, as the "basis and foundation of Government," it is enumerated with equal solemnity, or rather studied emphasis. Either then, we must say, that the will of the Legislature is the only measure of their authority; and that in the plenitude of this authority, they may sweep away all our fundamental rights; or, that they are bound to leave this particular right untouched and sacred: Either we must say, that they may control the freedom of the press, may abolish the trial by jury, may swallow up the Executive and Judiciary Powers of the State; nay that they may despoil us of our very right of suffrage, and erect themselves into an independent and hereditary

assembly: or we must say, that they have no authority to enact into law the Bill under consideration. We the subscribers say, that the General Assembly of this Commonwealth have no such authority: And that no effort may be omitted on our part against so dangerous an usurpation, we oppose to it, this remonstrance; earnestly praying, as we are in duty bound, that the Supreme Lawgiver of the Universe, by illuminating those to whom it is addressed, may on the one hand, turn their councils from every act which would affront his holy prerogative, or violate the trust committed to them: and on the other, guide them into every measure which may be worthy of his [blessing may re]dound to their own praise, and may establish more firmly the liberties, the prosperity, and the Happiness of the Commonwealth.

Madison won his fight in Virginia. Two years later, he was at Philadelphia representing his state at the Constitutional Convention which had been called for the purpose of reviewing and revising the Articles of Confederation. The states were neither secure nor happy in their relations to one another under the Articles of Confederation. Instead of benefiting from the large degree of sovereignty provided under the Confederation, the states were tying themselves up in knots in their dealings with one another. The dominant theme at the Federal Convention envisioned the creation of a central government with sovereign powers of its own adequate to safeguard the common security and advance the general welfare of the people of the member states.

The relationship of the Federal Government to religion was not a major issue at the Convention. By this time, the relationship had clarified itself in most of the states, as in the case of Virginia. Hence the paucity of comment by Madison relating to this subject.

MADISON JOURNALS, JUNE 12, 1788

The honorable member has introduced the subject of religion. Religion is not guarded—there is no bill of rights declaring that religion should be secure. Is a bill of rights a security for Religion? Would the bill of rights, in this state, exempt the people from paying for the support of one particular sect, if such sect were exclusively established by law? If there were a majority of one sect, a bill of rights would be a poor protection for liberty. Happily for the states, they enjoy the utmost freedom of religion. This freedom arises from that multiplicity of sects, which pervades America, and which is the best and only security for religious liberty in any society. For where there is such a variety of sects, there cannot be a majority of any one sect to oppress and persecute the rest. Fortunately for this common-

wealth, a majority of the people are decidedly against any exclusive establishment—I believe it to be so in the other states. There is not a shadow of right
in the general government to intermeddle with religion. Its least interference
with it, would be a most flagrant usurpation. I can appeal to my uniform
conduct on this subject, that I have warmly supported religious freedom.
It is better that this security should be depended upon from the general
legislature, than from one particular state. A particular state might concur
in one religious project. But the United States abound in such a variety of
sects, that it is a strong security against religious persecution, and it is
sufficient to authorize a conclusion, that no one sect will ever be able to out-
number or depress the rest.

*During the debates over the new Constitution, Madison kept up a corre-
spondence with Jefferson, then in Paris. A not inconsiderable part of the
exchange concerned the possible need for a Bill of Rights. Madison, as is
apparent in the following letter, refused to be drawn into a strongly partisan
position. When the U.S. Congress was convened at its first session in New
York City, a Bill of Rights was passed and submitted to the states. It is
significant that the first clause of the First Amendment is concerned with
religious freedom: "Congress shall make no law respecting an establishment
of religion, or prohibiting the free exercise thereof. . . ." Jefferson's reply to
the following letter from Madison strongly endorsed the need for an explicit
enumeration of human rights.*

LETTER TO THOMAS JEFFERSON, OCTOBER 17, 1788

The little pamphlet herewith inclosed will give you a collective view
of the alterations which have been proposed for the new Constitution.
Various and numerous as they appear they certainly omit many of the
true grounds of opposition. The articles relating to Treaties, to paper money,
and to contracts, created more enemies than all the errors in the System
positive and negative put together. It is true nevertheless that not a few,
particularly in Virginia have contended for the proposed alterations from
the most honorable & patriotic motives; and that among the advocates for
the Constitution there are some who wish for further guards to public
liberty & individual rights.

As far as these may consist of a constitutional declaration of the most
essential rights, it is probable they will be added; though there are many
who think such addition unnecessary, and not a few who think it misplaced
in such a Constitution. There is scarce any point on which the party in
opposition is so much divided as to its importance and its propriety.

My own opinion has always been in favor of a bill of rights; provided it be so framed as not to imply powers not meant to be included in the enumeration. At the same time I have never thought the omission a material defect, nor been anxious to supply it even by *subsequent* amendment, for any other reason than *that is anxiously* desired by others. I have favored it because I supposed it might be of use, and if properly executed could not be of disservice. I have not viewed it in an important light:

1. Because I conceive that in a certain degree, though not in the extent argued by Mr. Wilson, the rights in question are reserved by the manner in which the federal powers are granted.

2. Because there is great reason to fear that a positive declaration of some of the most essential rights could not be obtained in the requisite latitude. I am sure that the rights of conscience in particular, if submitted to public definition would be narrowed much more than they are likely ever to be by an assumed power. One of the objections in New England was that the Constitution by prohibiting religious tests, opened a door for Jews, Turks & infidels.

3. Because the limited powers of the federal Government and the jealousy of the subordinate Governments, afford a security which has not existed in the case of the State Governments, and exists in no other.

4. Because experience proves the inefficacy of a bill of rights on those occasions when its control is most needed. Repeated violations of these parchment barriers have been committed by overbearing majorities in every State. In Virginia I have seen the bill of rights violated in every instance where it has been opposed to a popular current. Notwithstanding the explicit provision contained in that instrument for the rights of Conscience, it is well known that a religious establishment would have taken place in that State, if the Legislative majority had found as they expected, a majority of the people in favor of the measure; and I am persuaded that if a majority of the people were now of one sect, the measure would still take place and on narrower ground than was then proposed, notwithstanding the additional obstacle which the law has since created.

While amendments to the Constitution were being considered in the First Session of the new U.S. Congress, James Madison urged a change in Article I, Section 9. The change was not accepted—at least in that particular form. Instead, the appropriate guarantees were provided in the First Amendment to the Constitution.

CONSTITUTIONAL NOTES, JUNE 8, 1789

. . . . That in article 1st, section 9, between clauses 3 and 4, be inserted these clauses, to wit: The civil rights of none shall be abridged on account of religious belief or worship, nor shall any national religion be established, nor shall the full and equal rights of conscience be in any manner, or in any pretext, infringed.

In his letter to William Bradford, at the highly advanced age of twenty-one, Madison had confided that he did not think he would live very long. But here he is, President of the United States at the age of fifty-seven with another generation of activity ahead of him. In his third year of the Presidency, he vetoed a bill that would give corporate identity to the Protestant Episcopal Church. The reader will observe many resemblances between Madison's reasons for the veto and his earlier positions, so carefully thought through, when somewhat similar issues faced the Virginia Assembly. Thus experience in the state helped serve the nation.

LEGISLATIVE VETO, FEBRUARY 21, 1811

To the House of Representatives of the United States:

Having examined and considered the bill entitled "An Act incorporating the Protestant Episcopal Church in the town of Alexandria, in the District of Columbia," I now return the bill to the House of Representatives, in which it originated, with the following objections:

Because the bill exceeds the rightful authority to which governments are limited by the essential distinction between civil and religious functions, and violates in particular the article of the Constitution of the United States which declares that "Congress shall make no law respecting a religious establishment."

The bill enacts into and establishes by law sundry rules and proceedings relative purely to the organization and polity of the church incorporated, and comprehending even the election and removal of the minister of the same, so that no change could be made therein by the particular society or by the general church of which it is a member, and whose authority it recognizes.

This particular church, therefore, would so far be a religious establishment by law, a legal force and sanction being given to certain articles in its constitution and administration. Nor can it be considered that the articles thus established are to be taken as the descriptive criteria only of the corporate identity of the society, inasmuch as this identity must depend on other characteristics, as the regulations established are generally unessential and alterable according to the principles and canons by which churches of that denomination govern themselves, and as the injunctions and prohibitions contained in the regulations would be enforced by the penal consequences applicable to a violation of them according to the local law.

Because the bill vests in the said incorporated church an authority to provide for the support of the poor and the education of poor children of the same, an authority which, being altogether superfluous if the provision is to be the result of pious charity, would be a precedent for giving to religious societies as such a legal agency in carrying into effect a public and civil duty.

In 1811, President Madison offered Mordecai M. Noah the post of consul at Riga, Russia, but Mr. Noah declined. Mr. Noah was a lawyer, playwright, and journalist. Two years later, the President again offered Mr. Noah a post in the Foreign Service, this time as consul in Tunis. Mr. Noah accepted. Some years later (during the Administration of James Monroe) a minor controversy developed over the recall of Mr. Noah from the Foreign Service. The official reports said there was some irregularity in the handling of accounts. But an undercurrent persisted in the belief that there might be some element of religious discrimination in the recall. Mr. Noah wrote in 1818 to Madison, then in retirement in Montpelier, Vermont, calling his attention to new evidence indicating no wrongdoing. The following is Madison's reply.

LETTER TO MORDECAI M. NOAH, MAY 15, 1818

I have received your letter of the 6th, with the eloquent discourse delivered at the Consecration of the Jewish Synagogue. Having ever regarded the freedom of religious opinions and worship as equally belonging to every sect, and the secure enjoyment of it as the best human provision for bringing all either into the same way of thinking, or into that mutual charity which is the only substitute, I observe with pleasure the view you give of the spirit in which your Sect partake of the blessings offered by our Government and Laws.

As your foreign Mission took place whilst I was in the Administration, it cannot but be agreeable to me to learn that your accounts have been closed in a manner so favorable to you. And I know too well the justice and candor of the present Executive to doubt, that an official [*illegible*] will be readily allowed to explanations necessary to protect your character against the effect of any impressions whatever ascertained to be erroneous. It is certain that your religious profession was well known at the time you received your Commission; and that in itself could not be a motive for your recall.

I thank you Sir for your friendly wishes and tender you mine.

Madison's earliest thoughts on the relationship between government and religion led him to the conviction that the standard theory on this relationship was incorrect. This theory was that government could not function with-

out the support of the Church, and that the Church required government
backing for its own existence. Madison successfully led the fight against this
proposition in Virginia, the implications and benefits of which substantially
carried over to the Union as a whole. Now, in retirement at his estate in
Virginia, in a mansion the portico of which had been designed by his good
friend Thomas Jefferson, Madison could reflect on the practical operation
of the new theories that were woven into the texture of the American govern-
ment. His letter to Robert Walsh is something of a summing up of the story
of government and religion in the early days of the Republic.

LETTER TO ROBERT WALSH, MARCH 2, 1819

I received some days ago your letter of February 15, in which you intimate
your intention to vindicate our Country against misrepresentations propagated
abroad, and your desire of information on the subject of Negro slavery, of
moral character, of religion, and of education in Virginia, as affected by
the Revolution, and our public Institutions. . . .

That there has been an increase of religious instruction since the revolution can admit of no question. The English church was originally the established religion; the character of the clergy that above described. Of other
sects there were but few adherents, except the Presbyterians who pre-
dominated on the west side of the Blue Mountains. A little time previous to
the Revolutionary struggle the Baptists sprang up, and made a very rapid
progress.

Among the early acts of the Republican Legislature, were those abolishing the Religious establishment, and putting all Sects at full liberty and on a
perfect level.

At present the population is divided, with small exceptions, among the
Protestant Episcopalians, the Presbyterians, the Baptists and the Methodists. Of their comparative numbers I can command no sources of information. I conjecture the Presbyterians and Baptists to form each about a third,
and the two other sects together of which the Methodists are much the
smallest, to make up the remaining third.

The Old churches, built under the establishment at the public expense,
have in many instances gone to ruin, or are in a very dilapidated state,
owing chiefly to a transition desertion of the flocks to other worships.
A few new ones have latterly been built particularly in the towns.

Among the other sects, Meeting Houses have multiplied and continue
to multiply; though in general they are of the plainest and cheapest sort.
But neither the number nor the style of the Religious edifices is a true
measure of the state of religion.

Religious instruction is now diffused throughout the Community by preachers of every sect with almost equal zeal, though with very unequal acquirements; and at private houses and open stations and occasionally in such as are appropriated to Civil use, as well as buildings appropriated to that use. The qualifications of the Preachers, too among the new sects where there was the greatest deficiency, are understood to be improving.

On a general comparison of the present and former times, the balance is certainly and vastly on the side of the present, as to the number of religious teachers the zeal which actuates them, the purity of their lives, and the attendance of the people on their instructions.

It was the Universal opinion of the Century preceding the last, that Civil Government could not stand without the prop of a Religious establishment, and that the Christian religion itself, would perish if not supported by a legal provision for its Clergy. The experience of Virginia conspicuously corroborates the disproof of both opinions. The Civil Government, tho' bereft of everything like an associated hierarchy, possesses the requisite stability and performs its functions with complete success; whilst the number, the industry, and the morality of the Priesthood, and the devotion of the people have been manifestly increased by the total separation of the Church from the State.

As Madison had anticipated many years earlier, religions, like man himself, would flourish so long as the conditions of growth were right. He received many letters in his retirement from representatives of minority religious groups, almost all of them expressing admiration and gratitude for Madison's contribution to religious freedom in America. The following reply was sent to Jacob de la Motta, about whom our research has not been productive.

LETTER TO JACOB DE LA MOTTA, AUGUST, 1820

I have received your letter of the 7th inst. with the Discourse delivered at the Consecration of the Hebrew Synagogue at Savannah, for which you will please to accept my thanks.

The history of the Jews must forever be interesting. The modern part of it is, at the same time so little generally known, that every ray of light on the subject has its value.

Among the features peculiar to the Political system of the United States, is the perfect equality of rights which it secures to every religious Sect. And it is particularly pleasing to observe in the good citizenship of such as have been most distrusted and oppressed elsewhere, a happy illustration of the safety and success of this experiment of a just and benignant policy. Equal laws protecting equal rights, are found as they ought to be presumed, the best guarantee of loyalty and love of country; as well as best calculated to cherish that mutual respect and good will among Citizens of every religious denomination which are necessary to social harmony and most favorable to the advancement of truth. The account you give of the Jews of your Congregation brings them fully within the scope of these observations.

In the twilight of his life, Madison could turn from the political problems affecting and growing out of religion to the deeper and more consequential aspects of spiritual belief. In his youth he had studied theology. His systematic thinking on the subject is in abundant evidence in the following letter to Frederick Beasley, an author on religious tracts who sent Madison a copy of his new book.

LETTER TO FREDERICK BEASLEY, NOVEMBER 20, 1825

I have duly received the copy of your little tract on the proofs of the Being and Attributes of God. To do full justice to it, would require not only a more critical attention than I have been able to bestow on it, but a resort to the celebrated work of Dr. Clarke, which I read fifty years ago only, and to that of Dr. Waterland also which I never read.

The reasoning that could satisfy such a mind as that of Clarke, ought certainly not to be slighted in the discussion. And the belief in a God All Powerful wise and good, is so essential to the moral order of the World and to the happiness of man, that arguments which enforce it cannot be drawn from too many sources nor adapted with too much solicitude to the different characters and capacities to be impressed with it.

But whatever effect may be produced on some minds by the more abstract train of ideas which you so strongly support, it will probably always be found that the course of reasoning from the effect to the cause, "from Nature to Nature's God," Will be the more universal and persuasive application.

The finiteness of the human understanding betrays itself on all subjects, but more especially when it contemplates such as involve infinity. What may safely be said seems to be, that the infinity of time and space forces itself on our conception, a limitation of either being inconceivable; that the mind prefers at once the idea of a self-existing cause to that of an infinite series of cause and effect, which augments, instead of avoiding the difficulty; and that it finds more facility in assenting to the self-existence of an invisible cause possessing infinite power, wisdom and goodness, than to the self-existence of the universe, visibly destitute of those attributes, and which may be the effect of them. In this comparative facility of conception and belief, all philosophical Reasoning on the subject must perhaps terminate. But that I may not get farther beyond my depth, and without the resources which bear you up in fathoming efforts, I hasten to thank you for the favour which has made me your debtor, and to assure you of my esteem and my respectful regards.

An ex-President is often called upon by writers and historians for data or viewpoints useful for new accounts or interpretations. The historical importance of Madison's role in helping to defeat the bill calling for public support of religious instruction in the pre-Federal Virginia Assembly was recognized in a query from George Mason. In his reply, Madison enclosed a copy of the "Memorial and Remonstrance Against Religious Assessments."

LETTER TO GEORGE MASON, JULY 14, 1826

During the session of the General Assembly 1784-5 a bill was introduced into the House of Delegates providing for the legal support of Teachers of the Christian Religion, and being patronized by the most popular talents in the House, seemed likely to obtain a majority of votes. In order to arrest its progress it was insisted with success that the bill should be postponed till the evening session, and in the meantime be printed for public consideration. That the sense of the people might be the better called forth, your highly distinguished ancestor Colonel George Mason, Colonel George Nicholas also possessing public weight and some others thought it advisable that a remonstrance against the bill should be prepared for general circulation and signature and imposed on me the task of drawing up such a paper. The draft having received their sanction, a large number of printed copies were distributed, and so extensively signed by the people of every religious denomination that at the ensuing session the projected measure was entirely frustrated; and under the influence of the public sentiment thus manifested the celebrated bill "Establishing Religious Freedom" enacted into a permanent barrier against Future attempts on the rights of conscience as declared in the Great Charter prefixed to the Constitution of the State. Be pleased to accept my friendly respects.

At the age of eighty-one, Madison continues to state with clarity and vigor his convictions concerning the place of religion in a free society. This letter was sent to "the Reverend Adams" in 1832. In many ways, it is a summing up both of Madison's own experiences in dealing with this subject and his personal philosophy.

LETTER TO THE REVEREND ADAMS, 1832

I received in due time the printed copy of your Convention sermon on the relation of Christianity to Civil Government with a manuscript request of my opinion on the subject.

There appears to be in the nature of man what insures his belief in an invisible cause of his present existence, and anticipation of his future existence. Hence the propensities and susceptibilities in that case of religion which with a few doubtful or individual exceptions have prevailed throughout the world.

Waiving the rights of Conscience, not included in the surrender implied by the social State, and more or less invaded by all religious Establishments, the simple question to be decided is whether a support of the best and purest religion, the Christian religion itself ought not so far at least as pecuniary means are involved, to be provided for by the Government rather than be left to the voluntary provisions of those who profess it. And on this question experience will be an admitted Umpire the more adequate as the connection between Governments and Religion have existed in such various degrees and forms, and now can be compared with examples where connection has been entirely dissolved.

In the Papal System, Government and Religion are in a manner consolidated, and that is found to be the worst of Government.

In most of the Governments of the old world, the legal establishment of a particular religion and without or with very little toleration of others makes a part of the Political and Civil organization and there are few of the most enlightened judges who will maintain that the system has been favorable either to Religion or to Government.

Until Holland ventured on the experiment of combining a liberal toleration with the establishment of a particular creed, it was taken for granted, that an exclusive and intolerant establishment was essential, and notwithstanding the light thrown on the subject by that experiment, the prevailing opinion in Europe, England not excepted, has been that Religion could not be preserved without the support of Government nor Government be supported without an established religion that there must be at least an alliance of some sort between them.

It remained for North America to bring the great and interesting subject to a fair, and finally to a decisive test.

In the Colonial State of the Country, there were four examples, Rhode Island, New Jersey, Pennsylvania and Delaware, and the greater part of New York where there were no religious Establishments; the support of Religion being left to the voluntary associations and contributions of individuals; and certainly the religious condition of those Colonies, will well bear a comparison with that where establishments existed.

As it may be suggested that experiments made in Colonies more or less under the Control of a foreign Government, had not the full scope necessary to display their tendency, it is fortunate that the appeal can now be made to their effects under a complete exemption from any such control.

It is true that the New England States have not discontinued establishments of Religion formed under very peculiar circumstances; but they have by successive relaxations advanced towards the prevailing example; and without any evidence of disadvantage either to Religion or good Government.

And if we turn to the Southern States where there was, previous to the Declaration of Independence, a legal provision for the support of Religion; and since that event a surrender of it to a spontaneous support by the people, it may be said that the difference amounts nearly to a contrast in the greater purity and industry of the Pastors and in the greater devotion of their flocks, in the latter period than in the former. In Virginia the contrast is particularly striking, to those whose memories can make the comparison. It will not be denied that causes other than the abolition of the legal establishment of Religion are to be taken into view in accounting for the change in the Religious character of the community. But the existing character, distinguished as it is by its religious features, and the lapse of time now more than 50 years since the legal support of Religion was withdrawn sufficiently prove that it does not need the support of Government and it will scarcely be contended that Government has suffered by the exemption of Religion from its cognizance, or its pecuniary aid.

The apprehension of some seems to be that Religion left entirely to itself may run into extravagances injurious both to Religion and to social order; but besides the question whether the interference of Government *in any form* would not be more likely to increase than control the tendency, it is a safe calculation that in this as in other cases of excessive excitement, Reason will gradually regain its ascendancy. Great excitements are less apt to be permanent than to vibrate to the opposite extreme.

Under another aspect of the subject, there may be less danger that Religion, if left to itself, will suffer from a failure of the pecuniary support applicable to it than that an omission of the public authorities to limit the duration of their Charters to Religious Corporations, and the amount of property acquirable by them, may lead to an injurious accumulation of wealth from the lavish donations and bequests prompted by a pious zeal or by an atoning remorse. Some monitary examples have already appeared.

Whilst I thus frankly express my view of the subject presented in your sermon, I must do you the justice to observe that you very ably maintained yours. I must admit moreover that it may not be easy, in every possible case, to trace the line of separation between the rights of religion and the Civil authority with such distinctness as to avoid collisions and doubts on unessential points. The tendency to a usurpation on one side or the other, or to a corrupting coalition or alliance between them, will be best guarded against by an entire abstinence of the Government from interference in any way whatever, beyond the necessity of preserving public order, and protecting each sect against trespasses on its legal rights by others.

I owe you Sir an apology for the delay in complying with the request of my opinion on the subject discussed in your sermon; if not also for the brevity and it may be thought crudeness of the opinion itself. I must rest the apology on my great age now in its 83rd year, with more than the ordinary infirmities, and especially on the effect of a chronic Rheumatism, combined with both, which makes my hand and fingers as averse to the pen as they are awkward in the use of it.

7. ALEXANDER HAMILTON

"Fly to the Bosom of Your God, and Be Comforted"

"I AM inviolably attached to the essential rights of mankind, and the true interests of society. I consider liberty in a genuine unadulterated sense, as the greatest of terrestrial blessings. I am convinced that the whole human race is entitled to it, and that it can be wrested from no part of them, without the blackest and most aggravated guilt."

These were important words in the years immediately preceding the American Revolution. They appeared in pamphlet form in reply to the "Westchester Farmer," whose writings advocated loyalty to Great Britain. The "Westchester Farmer" had issued powerful tracts calling for sober and responsible thought instead of impulsive and dangerous insurrectionist talk and action. The fever blisters caused by anti-British feeling began to cool off here and there. Revolution in 1774 was still an ugly word and some people welcomed the reasons that might justify a calmer outlook.

But the reasoning of the "Westchester Farmer" was shattered by two unsigned pamphlets that had wide distribution. Every argument of the Farmer was carefully examined and refuted. There was a wealth of historical allusion. Unlike some of the flamboyant pre-Revolutionary materials, these unsigned pamphlets were written without temper or abuse. There was an elegance of thought and expression that won wide acclaim, even though the author was unidentified. Another excerpt from the pamphlets refuting the Farmer:

"The Sacred Rights of Mankind are not to be rummaged for among old parchments or musty records. They are written, as with a sunbeam, in the whole volume of human nature, by the Hand of the Divinity itself, and can never be erased or obscured by moral power."

It turned out that the author was not William Livingston or John Jay or one of the leading clergymen of the period, as some had supposed. The author was a young undergraduate from King's College who, to make matters even more incredible, had come to America only two years earlier. His name was Alexander Hamilton. He had been born in the West Indies of a Scottish father and a mother of English and French origin.

Others may have been appalled by the fact of his youth; Hamilton was too busy to give it much thought. At an age when most boys are concerned about their right to stay out until midnight, Alexander Hamilton was worried about the natural rights of mankind. He may have been precocious, but the articles he produced were absolutely genuine, as the impact of his writings at the time may attest. "There are displayed in these papers a power of reasoning and sarcasm, a knowledge of the principles of government and of the English constitution, and a grasp of the merits of the whole controversy that would have done honor to any man at any age," George Ticknor Curtis wrote in his *Constitutional History of the United States.* Hamilton's pamphlets, said Curtis, showed "a more remarkable maturity than has ever been exhibited by any other person, at so early an age, in the same department of thought."

Hamilton's brilliance, however, was not confined to the issues involved in the struggle for justice against the Crown. When the Revolution began, he wrote an analysis of the military problems facing the colonists and outlined a basic military strategy. Whether or not Washington happened to see this particular account, the fact remains that the plan of battle actually put into effect is substantially the same as that recommended by Hamilton. It is also a fact that General Washington appointed young Hamilton, then just turned twenty, as his aide-de-camp with the rank of lieutenant colonel. Thus began a collaboration which was to last many years and affect the course of American history. Washington, as commander in chief, had important messages and papers to write—to Congress, to foreign governments, to leaders in the states. He found in Hamilton a cool, resourceful mind in which historical experience was neatly balanced by insight into the contemporary situation. Hamilton, moreover, had as lucid and persuasive a pen as any man of the period possessed, not excluding Thomas Jefferson or James Madison. Hamilton also had a full view of his ultimate objective and was in an excellent position to help move other men in that direction.

When victory over Great Britain was threatened by the inability of the American states to get along with one another, the ultimate objective became increasingly clear in Hamilton's mind. And at the Philadelphia Constitutional Convention, called for the purpose of rescuing the states from virtual anarchy, Hamilton was ready for the major contribution of his life. He defined and espoused the principles of federalism, that is, the creation of government with powers strictly limited in scope but fully adequate to the needs of the states, which retained sovereignty and jurisdiction in all other matters. The need for a direct connection between the central Federal Government and the individual citizen was another basic principle. Hamilton also served as advocate and commentator. With James Madison and

John Jay, he issued *The Federalist* papers, perhaps the most brilliant and incisive examination into the nature and function of popular government that has appeared in any language at any time, Hamilton was thirty-two when the first issue of *The Federalist* appeared.

Hamilton's intimate association with Washington continued throughout the Convention. And when Washington became the first President, he brought Hamilton with him as Secretary of the Treasury. Hamilton's sole experience with financial matters up to this point had been as helper in a storekeeper's office in a West Indian sugar island when he was not quite fifteen. In a number of respects, Hamilton filled a role not unlike that of a prime minister in Washington's cabinet. Thomas Jefferson became Secretary of State.

A substantial number of books have been written about the conflicts within Washington's administration, and about the disruptive effects of the rivalry between Jefferson and Hamilton. Ever since that first administration, students of American history have kept the debate going, siding with one or the other. Indeed, the controversy through the years has been so animated as to make it seem almost miraculous that the early American Republic could have survived such a conflict of basic philosophies. Yet it is entirely possible that the United States was able to find its footing in those early years not despite the differences between Jefferson and Hamilton but because of them. The combination of the two—even though they did not work as a team—gave the country what it most needed, both the form and substance of representative government. Jefferson was strong on the spirit of a free society; Hamilton was strong on the structure of a free society. Hamilton was a constitutional architect. Jefferson breathed life into the Constitution. Hamilton was inclined toward aristocracy in some aspects of his political thought. Jefferson helped to furnish the necessary correctives and gave people confidence in the new government. Jefferson was inclined to lean heavily on states' rights. There might not have been a Constitutional Convention if it had not been for men like Hamilton.

Whatever the rivalry between the two, we can recall that Hamilton supported Jefferson for the Presidency when the latter was tied with Aaron Burr in the electoral count. True, Hamilton would probably have voted for the devil himself rather than see Burr in the Presidency; even so, the act softens the final image of his relationship with Jefferson.

Whatever Hamilton's aristocratic coloration, it is significant that the principal philosophical influences in his formative years were substantially the same as those which enriched the thinking of men like Jefferson and Adams. Hamilton argued vigorously, for example, in behalf of the natural rights of man. In so doing, he leaned heavily on the ideas of John Locke and David Hume, who were among the invisible Founding Fathers.

Natural rights to Hamilton were part of man's relationship to God. "The Supreme Being gave existence to man, together with the means of preserving and beautifying that existence. He endowed him with rational faculties, by the help of which to discern and pursue such things as were consistent with his duty and interest; and invested him with an inviolable right to personal liberty and personal safety. Hence, in a state of nature, no man had any moral power to deprive another of his life, limbs, property, or liberty; nor the least authority to command or exact obedience from him, except that which arose from the ties of consanguinity."

At one time, Hamilton had some ideas about a "Christian Constitutional Society," based on ethical values and the clearly defined framework of representative government.

Almost everything Hamilton wrote on the subject of religion was connected to his philosophical views on man in relation to the state and to his fellows. He did, however, in a letter to his wife, written in anticipation of his possible death in the duel with Aaron Burr, make it clear that religion to him transcended impersonal matters. "I need not tell you of the pangs I feel from the idea of quitting you and exposing you to the anguish I know you would feel," he said. "The consolations of religion, my beloved, can alone support you; and these you have a right to enjoy. Fly to the bosom of your God, and be comforted."

A few hours later, it became necessary for Elizabeth Hamilton to live with this advice instead of a husband. For Alexander Hamilton, age forty-seven, had been mortally wounded. His life was a product of the Enlightenment, his death an echo of the Dark Ages. Despite his soaring brilliance and his confidence in great designs, he was a victim of pride, temper, and the grotesquely irrational.

In the Royal Danish-American Gazette of October 3, 1772, there appeared an account of a hurricane. It was written by a boy in his early teens and came to the attention of a Presbyterian clergyman named James Knox, who had come to Danish St. Croix, where he met young Hamilton. Knox took a deep interest in Hamilton and arranged for the publication of the letter, remarkable both for the precocious literary talent it displays and the religious turn of young Hamilton's mind.

THE ROYAL DANISH-AMERICAN GAZETTE, OCTOBER 3, 1772

I take up my pen just to give you an imperfect account of one of the most dreadful Hurricanes that memory or any records whatever can trace, which happened here on the 31st ultimo at night.

It began about dusk, at North, and raged very violently till ten o'clock. Then ensued a sudden and unexpected interval, which lasted about an hour. Meanwhile the wind was shifting round to the South West point, from whence it returned with redoubled fury and continued to 'till near three o'clock in the morning. Good God! what horror and destruction—it's impossible for me to describe—or you to form any idea of it. It seemed as if a total dissolution of nature was taking place. The roaring of the sea and wind—fiery meteors flying about it in the air—the prodigious glare of almost perpetual lightning—the crash of the falling houses—and the ear-piercing shrieks of the distressed, were sufficient to strike astonishment into Angels. A great part of the buildings throughout the Island are leveled to the ground—almost all the rest very much shattered—several persons killed and numbers utterly ruined—whole families running about the streets, unknowing where to find a place of shelter—the sick exposed to the keeness of water and air—without a bed to lie upon—or a dry covering to their bodies—and our harbours entirely bare. In a word, misery, in all its most hideous shapes, spread over the whole face of the country.—A strong smell of gunpowder added somewhat to the terrors of the night; and it was observed that the rain was surprizingly salt. Indeed the water is so brackish and full of sulphur that there is hardly any drinking it.

My reflections and feelings on this frightful and melancholy occasion, are set forth in the following self-discourse.

Where now, oh! vile worm, is all thy boasted fortitude and resolution? what is become of thy arrogance and self-sufficiency?—why dost thou tremble and stand aghast? how humble—how helpless—how contemptible you now appear. And for why? the jarring elements—the discords of clouds? Oh, impotent presumptuous fool! how durst thou offend that Omnipotence whose nod alone were sufficient to quell the destruction that hovers over thee, or crush thee into atoms? see thy wretched helpless state, and learn to know thyself. Learn to know the best support. Despise thyself, and adore thy God. How sweet—how unutterably sweet were now, the voice of an approving conscience. Then couldst thou say—hence ye idle alarms, why do I shrink? what have I to fear? a pleasing calm suspense! a short repose from calamity to end in eternal bliss? Let the Earth rend—let the planets forsake their course—let the Sun be extinguished and the Heavens burst asunder— yet what have I to dread? my staff can never be broken—in Omnipotence I trusted. . . .

Thus did I reflect, and thus at every gust of the wind, did I conclude,— till it pleased the Almighty to allay it.—Nor did my emotions proceed either from the suggestions of too much natural fear, or a conscience overburthened with crimes of an uncommon cast.—I thank God, this was not the case.

The scenes of horror exhibited around us, naturally awakened such ideas in every thinking breast, and aggravated the deformity of every failing of our lives. It were a lamentable insensibility indeed, not to have had such feelings —and I think inconsistent with human nature.

Our distressed, helpless condition taught us humility and contempt of ourselves—The horrors of the night—the prospect of an immediate, cruel death—or, as one may say, of being crushed by the Almighty in his anger— filled us with terror. And every thing that had tended to weaken our interest with him, upbraided us in the strongest colours, with our baseness and folly.—That which, in a calm unruffled temper, we call a natural cause, seemed then like the correction of the Deity.—Our imagination represented him as an incensed master, executing vengeance on the crimes of his servants. —The father and benefactor were forgot, and in that view, a consciousness of our guilt filled us with despair.

But see, the Lord relents—he hears our prayer—the Lightning ceases— the winds are appeased—the warring elements are reconciled and all things promise peace.—The darkness is dispell'd—and drooping nature revives at the approaching dawn. Look back Oh! my soul—look back and tremble.— Rejoice at thy deliverance, and humble thyself in the presence of thy deliverer.

Yet, hold, Oh vain mortal!—check thy ill timed joy. Art thou so selfish to exult because thy lot is happy in a season of universal woe? Hast thou no feeling for the miseries of thy fellow-creatures? and art thou incapable of the soft pangs of sympathetic sorrow?—Look around thee and shudder at the view. See desolation and ruin where'er thou turnest thine eye? . . . Hark the bitter groans of distress . . . Oh distress unspeakable! my heart bleeds—but I have no power to solace!—O ye, who revel in affluance, see the afflictions of humanity and bestow your superfluity to ease them.—Say not, we have suffered also, and thence withhold your compassion. What are your sufferings compared to those?—ye have still more than enough left. Act wisely—succour the miserable and lay up a treasure in Heaven.

I am afraid, Sir, you will think this description more the effort of imagination than a true picture of realities. But I can affirm with the greatest truth, that there is not a single circumstance touched upon, which I have no absolutely been an eye witness to.

Our General has issued several very salutary and humane regulations, and both in his publick and private measures, has shewn himself *the Man*.

Ideas such as the following served as the basis for Alexander Hamilton's fast-growing influence among New York radicals. Whatever his later political affiliations, young Hamilton made his initial reputation as a foe of conservatives. At the time this pamphlet, called The Farmer Refuted, *appeared in February, 1775, Alexander Hamilton was eighteen and an undergraduate at King's College (now Columbia University). The pamphlet appeared over the signature "A Sincere Friend to America."*

THE FARMER REFUTED, 1775

I shall, for the present, pass over that part of your pamphlet in which you endeavor to establish the supremacy of the British Parliament over America. After a proper *éclaircissement* of this point, I shall draw such inferences as will sap the foundation of everything you have offered.

The first thing that presents itself is a wish, that "I had, explicitly, declared to the public my ideas of the *natural rights* of mankind. Man, in a state of nature (you say), may be considered as perfectly free from all restraint of *law* and *government*; and then, the weak must submit to the strong."

I shall, henceforth, begin to make some allowance for that enmity you have discovered to the *natural rights* of mankind. For, though ignorance of them, in this enlightened age, cannot be admitted as a sufficient excuse for you, yet it ought, in some measure, to extenuate your guilt. If you will follow my advice, there still may be hopes of your reformation. Apply yourself, without delay, to the study of the law of nature. I would recommend to your perusal, Grotius, Puffendorf, Locke, Montesquieu, and Burlemaqui. I might mention other excellent writers on this subject; but if you attend diligently to these, you will not require any others.

There is so strong a similitude between your political principles and those maintained by Mr. Hobbes, that, in judging from them, a person might very easily *mistake* you for a disciple of his. His opinion was exactly coincident with yours, relative to man in a state of nature. He held, as you do, that he was then perfectly free from all restraint of *law* and *government*. Moral obligation, according to him, is derived from the introduction of civil society; and there is no virtue but what is purely artificial, the mere contrivance of politicians for the maintenance of social intercourse. But the reason he ran into this absurd and impious doctrine was, that he disbelieved the existence of an intelligent, superintending principle, who is the governor, and will be the final judge, of the universe.

As you sometimes swear *by Him that made you,* I conclude your sentiments do not correspond with his in that which is the basis of the doctrine you both agree in; and this makes it possible to imagine whence this congruity between you arises. To grant that there is a Supreme Intelligence who rules the world and has established laws to regulate the actions of

His creatures, and still to assert that man, in a state of nature, may be considered as perfectly free from all restraints of *law* and *government*, appears, to a common understanding, altogether irreconcilable.

Good and wise men, in all ages, have embraced a very dissimilar theory. They have supposed that the Deity, from the relations we stand in to Himself and to each other, has constituted an eternal and immutable law, which is indispensably obligatory upon all mankind, prior to any human institution whatever.

This is what is called the law of nature, "which, being coeval with mankind, and dictated by God himself, is, of course, superior in obligations to any other. It is binding over all the globe, in all countries, and at all times. No human laws are of any validity, if contrary to this; and such of them as are valid derive all their authority, mediately or immediately, from this original."—Blackstone.

Upon this law depend the natural rights of mankind: the Supreme Being gave existence to man, together with the means of preserving and beautifying that existence. He endowed him with rational faculties, by the help of which to discern and pursue such things as were consistent with his duty and interest; and invested him with an inviolable right to personal liberty and personal safety.

Hence, in a state of nature, no man had any *moral* power to deprive another of his life, limbs, property, or liberty; nor the least authority to command or exact obedience from him, except that which arose from the ties of consanguinity.

Hence, also, the origin of all civil government. . . .

Few items of British legislation in the years immediately preceding the American Revolution were as controversial as the Quebec Act, passed in May, 1774. This act was widely interpreted by the American colonists as an attempt by the British to drive a wedge between Canada and the states. Under the act, old French laws were revived and the Catholic Church was given various benefits. Hamilton sought to inflame the colonists against Great Britain by holding up the Quebec Act as a warning of what to expect. It is difficult to say whether this appeal to religious prejudice had any effectiveness. Certain it is that it did not bring Canadians any closer to the colonists. The following material is excerpted from Holt's Journal and was titled "Remarks on the 'Quebec Bill.' "

REMARKS ON THE "QUEBEC BILL," 1775—No. 2

The characteristic difference between a tolerated and established religion consists in this: With respect to the support of the former, the law is passive and improvident, leaving it to those who profess it to make as much, or as little, provision as they shall judge expedient; and to vary and alter that provision, as their circumstances may require. In this manner the Presbyterians and other sects are tolerated in England. They are allowed to exercise their religion without molestation, and to maintain their clergy as they think proper. These are wholly dependent upon their congregations, and can exact no more than they stipulate and are satisfied to contribute.

But with respect to the support of the latter, the law is active and provident. Certain precise dues (tithes, etc.) are legally annexed to the clerical office, independent on the liberal contributions of the people; which is exactly the case with the Canadian priests; and, therefore, no reasonable, impartial man will doubt that the religion of the Church of Rome is established in Canada. While tithes were the free, though customary, gift of the people, as was the case before the passing of the act in question, the Roman Church was only in a state of toleration; but when the law came to take cognizance of them, and, by determining their permanent existence, destroyed the free agency of the people, it then resumed the nature of an establishment, which it had been divested of at the time of the capitulation.

As to the Protestant religion, it is often asserted that sample provision has been made by the act for its future establishment; to prove which the writer before-mentioned has quoted a clause in the following mutilated manner: "It is provided," says he, "that his Majesty, his heirs or successors, may make such provision out of the accustomed dues, or rights, for the encouragement of the Protestant religion, and for the maintenance of a Protestant clergy within the said province, as he or they shall, from time to time, think necessary and expedient."

It must excite a mixture of anger and disdain to observe the wretched arts to which a designing administration and its abettors are driven in order to conceal the enormity of their measures. This whole clause, in its true and original construction, is destitute of meaning; and was evidently inserted for no other end than to *deceive* by the *appearance* of a provident regard for the Protestant religion. The act first declares: "That his Majesty's subjects professing the religion of the Church of Rome may have and enjoy the free exercise of their religion; and that the clergy of the said church may hold, receive, and enjoy their accustomed dues and rights." Then follows this clause: "Provided, nevertheless, that it shall be lawful for his Majesty, his heirs and successors, to make such provision, out of the rest of the said accustomed dues and rights, for the encouragement of the Protestant religion, for the maintenance and support of a Protestant clergy within the said province, as he or they shall, from time to time, think necessary and expedient."

Thus we see the Romish clergy are to have, hold, and enjoy their accustomed dues and rights, and the *rest* and remainder of them is to be applied toward the encouragement of the Protestant religion; but when they have had their wonted dues, I fancy it will puzzle the administration, by any effort of political chemistry, to produce the *rest*, or remainder. Suppose, for instance, A made an actual settlement of a hundred pounds on B; and, by a subsequent act, should declare that B should continue to hold and enjoy his accustomed and annual bounty; and that the *rest* of the said bounty should be given to C: it is evident that C would have nothing, because there would be no *rest* whatever.

Exactly parallel and analogous is the case in hand. The Romish priests are to have their accustomed dues and rights; and the *rest* of the said dues and rights is to be dedicated to the encouragement of the Protestant religion. In the above-recited quotation there is a chasm, the words "the *rest* of" being artfully omitted, to give the passage some meaning which it has not in itself. With this amendment, the sense must be that his Majesty might appropriate what portion of the customary revenues of the Romish clergy he should think proper to the support and maintenance of Protestant churches. But, according to the real words of the act, he can only devote "the rest," or remainder, of such revenues to that purpose, which, as I have already shown, is nothing.

So that the seeming provision in favor of the Protestant religion is entirely verbal and delusory. Excellent must be the encouragement it will derive from this source. But this is not all. Had there been really provision made, to be applied at the discretion of his Majesty, I should still consider this act as an atrocious infraction on the rights of Englishmen, in a point of the most delicate and momentous concern. No Protestant Englishman would consent to let the free exercise of his religion depend upon the mere pleasure of any man, however great or exalted. The privilege of worshipping the Deity in the manner his conscience dictates, which is one of the dearest he enjoys, must in that case be rendered insecure and precarious. Yet this is the unhappy situation to which the Protestant inhabitants of Canada are now reduced.

The will of the king must give law to their consciences. It is in his power to keep them for ever dispossessed of all religious immunities, and there is too much reason to apprehend that the same motives which instigated the act would induce him to give them as little future encouragement as possible.

I imagine it will clearly appear, from what has been offered, that the Roman Catholic religion, instead of being tolerated, as stipulated by the treaty of peace, is established by the late act, and that the Protestant religion has been left entirely destitute and unbefriended in Canada. But if

there should be any who think that the indulgence granted does not extend
to a perfect establishment, and that it may be justified by the terms of the
treaty and the subsequent conduct of the Canadians, and if they should also
be at a loss to perceive the dangerous nature of the act, with respect to the
other colonies, I would beg their further attention to the following considerations.

However justifiable this act may be in relation to the province of
Quebec, with its ancient limits, it cannot be defended by the least plausible
pretext, when it is considered as annexing such a boundless extent of new
territory to the old.

If a free form of government had "been found by experience to be
inapplicable to the state and circumstances of the province," and if "a
toleration less generous—although it might have fulfilled the letter of the
articles of the treaty—would not have answered the expectations of the
Canadians, nor have left upon their minds favorable impressions of British
justice and honor,"—if these reasons be admitted as true, and allowed their
greatest weight, they only prove that it might be just and politic to place
the province of Quebec, alone, with its former boundaries, in the circumstances of civil and religious government which are established by this act.
But when it is demanded, why it has also added the immense tract of country
that surrounds all these colonies to that province, and has placed the whole
under the same exceptionable institutions, both civil and religious, the
advocates for administration must be confounded and silenced.

This act develops the dark designs of the ministry more fully than any
thing they have done, and shows that they have formed a systematic project
of absolute power.

The present policy of it is evidently this: By giving a legal sanction to
the accustomed dues of the priests, it was intended to interest them in
behalf of the administration; and by means of the dominion they possessed
over the minds of the laity, together with the appearance of good-will
toward their religion, to prevent any dissatisfaction which might arise from
the loss of civil rights, and to propitiate them to the great purpose in contemplation—first, the subjugation of the colonies, and afterward that of
Great Britain itself. It was necessary to throw out some such lure to reconcile them to the exactions of that power which has been communicated to
the king, and which the emergency of the times may require in a very
extensive degree.

The future policy of it demands particular attention. The nature of its
civil government will hereafter put a stop to emigrations from other parts
of the British dominions thither, and from all other free countries. The
preeminent advantages secured to the Roman Catholic religion will dis-

courage all Protestant settlers, of whatever nation; and on these accounts, the province will be settled and inhabited by none but Papists. If lenity and moderation are observed in administering the laws, the natural advantages of this fertile infant country, united to the indulgence given to their religion, will attract droves of emigrants from all the Roman Catholic States in Europe, and these colonies, in time, will find themselves encompassed with innumerable hosts of neighbors, disaffected to them, both because of difference in religion and government. How dangerous their situation would be, let every man of common sense judge.

What can speak in plainer language the corruption of the British Parliament than this act, which invests the king with absolute power over a little world (if I may be allowed the expression), and makes such ample provision for the Popish religion, and leaves the Protestant in such a dependent, disadvantageous situation, that he is like to have no other subjects in this part of his domain, than Roman Catholics, who, by reason of their implicit devotion to their priests, and the superlative reverence they bear those who countenance and favor their religion, will be the voluntary instruments of ambition, and will be ready, at all times, to second the oppressive designs of the administration against the other parts of the empire.

Hence, while our ears are stunned with the dismal sounds of New England's republicanism, bigotry, and intolerance, it behooves us to be upon our guard against the deceitful wiles of those who would persuade us that we have nothing to fear from the operation of the Quebec Act. We should consider it as being replete with danger to ourselves, and as threatening ruin to our posterity. Let us not, therefore, suffer ourselves to be terrified at the prospect of an imaginary and fictitious Scylla; and, by that means, be led blindfold into a real and destructive Charybdis.

Whatever the basis for Hamilton's reputation as a cool, contriving political strategist who never forgave an opponent, there is considerable evidence to indicate that he was not without charity in political matters. His belief in civil liberties was neither ornamental nor expendable, as the following two statements may indicate.

A LETTER FROM PHOCION TO THE CONSIDERATE CITIZENS OF NEW-YORK, 1784

Viewing the subject in every possible light, there is not a single interest of the community but dictates moderation rather than violence. That honesty is still the best policy; that justice and moderation are the surest supports of every government, are maxims which, however they may be called trite, are at all times true; though too seldom regarded, but rarely neglected with impunity.

Were the people of America with one voice to ask: "What shall we do to perpetuate our liberties and secure our happiness?" the answer would be: "GOVERN WELL," and you have nothing to fear either from internal disaffection or external hostility. Abuse not the power you possess, and you need never apprehend its diminution or loss. But if you make a wanton use of it; if you furnish another example that despotism may debase the government of the many as well as the few, you, like all others that have acted the same part, will experience that licentiousness is the forerunner to slavery. . . .

A SECOND LETTER FROM PHOCION TO THE CONSIDERATE CITIZENS OF NEW-YORK CONTAINING REMARKS ON MENTOR'S REPLY, 1784

If we set out with justice, moderation, liberality, and a scrupulous regard to the Constitution, the government will acquire a spirit and tone productive of permanent blessings to the community. If, on the contrary, the public councils are guided by humor, passion, and prejudice; if from resentment to individuals, or a dread of partial inconveniences, the Constitution is slighted, or explained away, upon every frivolous pretext, the future spirit of government will be feeble, distracted, and arbitrary. The rights of the subjects will be the sport of every party vicissitude. There will be no settled rule of conduct, but every thing will fluctuate with the alternate prevalency of contending factions.

The world has its eye upon America. The noble struggle we have made in the cause of liberty has occasioned a kind of revolution in human sentiment. The influence of our example has penetrated the gloomy regions of despotism, and has pointed the way to enquiries which may shake it to its deepest foundations. Men begin to ask, every where: Who is this tyrant that dares to build his greatness on our misery and degradation? What commission has he to sacrifice millions to the wanton appetites of himself and a few minions that surround his throne?

To ripen enquiry into action, it remains for us to justify the revolution by its fruits.

If the consequences prove that we really have asserted the cause of human happiness, what may not be expected from so illustrious an example? In a greater or less degree the world will bless and imitate.

But if experience, in this instance, verifies the lesson long taught by the enemies of liberty, that the bulk of mankind are not fit to govern themselves; that they must have a master, and were only made for the rein and the spur; we shall then see the final triumph of despotism over liberty; the advocates of the latter must acknowledge it to be an *ignis fatuus*, and abandon the pursuit. With the greatest advantages for promoting it that ever a people had, we shall have betrayed the cause of human nature.

Between the time he accepted Aaron Burr's challenge to a duel (June 27, 1804) and the time the duel was held (July 11), Alexander Hamilton did considerable thinking and writing. He knew as well as anyone—then or later—that a duel was an insane and barbarous business. But he also knew that public opinion, whatever the law might say against dueling, would have condemned him if he failed to accept the challenge. As he makes clear in this public statement just before the duel, Hamilton knew his political career would be wrecked if he backed down. He had one resolve which was known to his intimates. He did not believe he had a right to kill Burr, no matter what the provocation—not even in a duel. He would satisfy the requirements of his honor by appearing at the duel, but he would not shoot to kill; there was even some doubt in his mind that he would shoot. Burr was burdened by no such resolves or hesitations.

PERSONAL NOTES, 1804

On my expected interview with Col. Burr, I think it proper to make some remarks explanatory of my conduct, motives, and views. I was certainly desirous of avoiding this interview for the most cogent reasons:

(1) My religious and moral principles are strongly opposed to the practice of dueling, and it would ever give me pain to be obliged to shed the blood of a fellow-creature in a private combat forbidden by the laws.

(2) My wife and children are extremely dear to me, and my life is of the utmost importance to them in various views.

(3) I feel a sense of obligation towards my creditors; who, in case of accident to me by the forced sale of my property, may be in some degree sufferers. I did not think myself at liberty as a man of probity lightly to expose them to this hazard.

(4) I am conscious of no ill-will to Col. Burr, distinct from political opposition, which, as I trust, has proceeded from pure and upright motives.

Lastly, I shall hazard much and can possibly gain nothing by the issue of the interview.

But it was, as I conceive, impossible for me to avoid it. There were intrinsic difficulties in the thing and artificial embarrassments, from the manner of proceeding on the part of Col. Burr.

Intrinsic, because it is not to be denied that my animadversions on the political principles, character, and views of Col. Burr have been extremely severe; and on different occasions I, in common with many others, have made very unfavorable criticisms on particular instances of the private conduct of this gentleman. In proportion as these impressions were entertained with sincerity and uttered with motives and for purposes which might appear to me commendable, would be the difficulty (until they could be removed by evidence of their being erroneous) of explanation or apology.

The disavowal required of me by Col. Burr in a general and indefinite form was out of my power, if it had really been proper for me to submit to be questioned, but I was sincerely of opinion that this could not be, and in this opinion I was confirmed by that of a very moderate and judicious friend whom I consulted. Besides that, Col. Burr appeared to me to assume, in the first instance, a tone unnecessarily peremptory and menacing, and, in the second, positively offensive.

Yet I wished, as far as might be practicable, to leave a door open to accommodation. This, I think, will be inferred from the written communication made by me and by my directions, and would be confirmed by the conversations between Mr. Van Ness and myself which arose out of the subject. I am not sure whether, under all the circumstances, I did not go further in the attempt to accommodate than a punctilious delicacy will justify. If so, I hope the motives I have stated will excuse me.

It is not my design, by what I have said, to affix any odium on the conduct of Col. Burr in this case. He doubtless has heard of animadversions of mine which bore very hard upon him, and it is probable that as usual they were accompanied with some falsehoods. He may have supposed himself under a necessity of acting as he has done. I hope the grounds of his proceeding have been such as ought to satisfy his own conscience.

I trust, at the same time, that the world will do me the justice to believe that I have not censured him on light grounds nor from unworthy inducements. I certainly have had strong reasons for what I have said, though it is possible that in some particulars I may have been influenced by misconstruction or misinformation. It is also my ardent wish that I may have been more mistaken than I think I have been; and that he, by his future conduct, may show himself worthy of all confidence and esteem and prove an ornament and a blessing to the country. As well, because it is possible that I may have injured Col. Burr, however convinced myself that my opinions and declarations have been well-founded, as from my general principles and temper in relation to similar affairs, I have resolved, if our interview is conducted in the usual manner and if pleases God to give me the opportunity to reserve and throw away my first fire, and I have thoughts even of reserving my second fire, and thus giving a double opportunity to Col. Burr to pause and reflect.

It is not, however, my intention to enter into any explanations on the ground. Apology from principle, I hope, rather than pride, is out of the question. To those who, with me, abhorring the practice of duelling, may think that I ought on no account to have added to the number of bad examples, I answer that my relative situation, as well in public as private, enforcing all the considerations which constitute what men of the world denominate honor, imposed on me (as I thought) a peculiar necessity not to decline the call. The ability to be in future useful, whether in resisting mischief or in effecting good, in those crises of our public affairs which seem likely to happen, would probably be inseparable from a conformity with public prejudice in this particular.

The following day, July 10, 1804, Hamilton wrote two letters to his wife, both fairly short. The first:

LETTER TO MRS. HAMILTON, JULY 10, 1804

This letter, my dear Eliza, will not be delivered to you, unless I shall first have terminated my earthly career, to begin, as I humbly hope, from redeeming grace and divine mercy, a happy immortality. If it had been possible for me to have avoided the interview, my love for you and my precious children would have been alone a decisive motive. But it was not possible, without sacrifices which would have rendered me unworthy of your esteem. I need not tell you of the pangs I feel from the idea of quitting you, and exposing you to the anguish I know you would feel. Nor could I dwell on the topic, lest it should unman me. The consolations of religion, my beloved, can alone support you; and these you have a right to enjoy. Fly to the bosom of your God, and be comforted. With my last idea I shall cherish the sweet hope of meeting you in a better world. Adieu, best of wives—best of women. Embrace all my darling children for me.

The second was written the same evening, at 10 P.M.

LETTER TO MRS. HAMILTON, JULY 10, 1804

My Beloved Eliza:

Mrs. Mitchell[1] is the person in the world to whom, as a friend, I am under the greatest obligation. I have not hitherto done my duty to her. But resolved to repair my omission to her as much as possible, I have encouraged her to come to this country, and intend, if it shall be in my power, to render the evening of her days comfortable. But if it shall please God to put this out of my power, and to enable you hereafter to be of service to her, I entreat you to do it, and to treat her with the tenderness of a sister. This is my second letter. The scruples of a Christian have determined me to expose my own life to any extent, rather than subject myself to the guilt of taking the life of another. This much increases my hazards and redoubles my pangs for you. But you had rather I should die innocent than live guilty. Heaven can preserve me, and I humbly hope will; but, in the con-

---

[1] [Sister of Peter Lytton and of Hamilton's mother, according to the statements in J. C. Hamilton's unfinished life of his father.—Ed.]

trary event, I charge you to remember that you are a Christian. God's will be done! The will of a merciful God must be good. Once more,

Adieu, my darling, darling wife.

Two days before the duel, Hamilton, with characteristic thoroughness, attended to some contingencies.

LAST WILL AND TESTAMENT OF ALEXANDER HAMILTON, JULY 9, 1804

In the name of God, Amen.

I, Alexander Hamilton, of the city of New York, counsellor at law, do make this my last will and testament, as follows: First, I appoint John B. Church, Nicholas Fish, and Nathaniel Pendleton, of the city aforesaid, esquires, to be executors and trustees of this my will; and I devise to them, their heirs and assigns, as joint tenants, and not as tenants in common, all my estate, real and personal, whatsoever and wheresoever upon trust, at their discretion to sell and dispose of the same at such time and times, in such manner, and upon such terms as they the survivors and survivor shall think fit; and out of the proceeds to pay all the debts which I shall owe at the time of my decease; in whole, if the fund shall be sufficient; proportionally, if it shall be insufficient; and the residue, if any there shall be, to pay and deliver to my excellent and dear wife, Elizabeth Hamilton.

Though, if it should please God to spare my life, I may look for a considerable surplus out of my present property; yet if he should speedily call me to the eternal world, a forced sale, as is usual, may possibly render it insufficient to satisfy my debts. I pray God that something may remain for the maintenance and education of my dear wife and children. But should it on the contrary happen that there is not enough for the payment of my debts, I entreat my dear children, if they or any of them shall ever be able, to make up the deficiency. I without hesitation commit to their delicacy a wish which is dictated by my own.—Though conscious that I have too far sacrificed the interests of my family to public avocations, and on this account have the less to claim to burthen my children, yet I trust in their magnanimity to appreciate, as they ought, this my request. In so unfavorable an event of things, the support of their dear mother, with the most respectful and tender attention, is a duty all the sacredness of which they will feel. Probably her own patrimonial resources will preserve her from indigence. But in all situations they are charged to bear in mind that she has been to them the most devoted and best of mothers.

In testimony whereof, I have hereunto subscribed my hand, the ninth day of July, in the year of our Lord one thousand eight hundred and four.

ALEXANDER HAMILTON

Signed, sealed, published, and declared, as and for his last will and testament in our presence, who have subscribed the same in his presence, the words *John B. Church* being above interlined.

Dominick F. Blake
Graham Newell
Theo. B. Valleau

8. SAMUEL ADAMS

"Revelation Assures Us That Righteousness Exalteth a Nation"

IT is doubtful whether any American ever stood higher on a soapbox or used it to greater advantage than Samuel Adams. His cause was independence and he aimed to make it known. In Massachusetts, at least, no man had more to say or said it in a more involved style. But his meaning always came through; he had even less ambiguity than subtlety. His speeches and writings were compounded in equal parts of blistering indignation and righteousness. He was a political agitator and a good one. Boston might have had its Tea Party without him, but it would not have been the same. For it was Adams who seized upon the moral issue involved in Lord North's Tea Act and used it as a prod both to create a Continental Congress and to bring about open insurrection. Governor Thomas Hutchinson was all for law and order; but Samuel Adams stood up and declared that the "meeting can do nothing more to save the country." This was the magic word and the "Mohawks" proceeded to the wharf and undertook the most celebrated dumping operation in history.

Samuel Adams's liberal use of Biblical authority for his nontheological opinions is to some extent a reflection of his stern Calvinist family background. His father helped to establish the New South Church. He also owned a brewery. Later, Samuel maintained connections with both. Young Adams went to Harvard College, and, like his second cousin John, had some inclinations toward the ministry. Also like John, however, he soon persuaded himself that his abilities lay more in the direction of the law. In this he had the encouragement of his father but the disapprobation of his mother. He gave up the law. Business came next. It developed that he had no spectacular gifts in this direction; money management is an art, but his approach was grimly inartistic. He confessed to cousin John that he "never looked forward in his life; never planned, laid a scheme, or formed a design for laying up anything for himself or others after him" (John Adams' paraphrase). Viewing the totality of Samuel Adams, John Adams

344

could observe that he was a "universal good character unless it should be admitted that he is too attentive to the public, and not enough to himself and his family."

This latter was a reference to the fact that Samuel Adams had found public affairs more attractive than business and presumably less costly. Whatever the consequent family problem, it could not be denied that Samuel Adams was now in a field that responded to his eruptive zeal. He threw himself into political organization and crusading journalism, and developed a wide following for his flat stands against aristocracy, social injustice, and British rule. His targets were large and difficult to miss. Economic and political conservatives felt increasingly uneasy when he was near. Radical support won him a series of elective positions. When he turned his full energies into the fight for the natural rights of the colonists, he was in a zone of impressive public interest and response.

The Boston Tea Party thrust him into the popular leadership of the independence movement in New England. He had little finesse and even less generosity toward his opponents; but any history of the Revolutionary period of American history must acknowledge the importance of his role. Revolutions are not made or fought only by theorists or patient people; and Adams was a revolutionist, first and foremost.

Samuel Adams's religious views are characteristically severe and uncompromising. He had an orthodox, Puritanical outlook, the correctness of which he did not hesitate to pronounce. He was crudely intolerant of Quakers, Catholics, and other sects which were juxtaposed against his own set of certainties. He denounced Catholicism as the "idolatry of Christians." As for the Quakers, he wrote that "Nothing can equal the barefaced falsehood of the Quakers and Tories in this city, unless perhaps their folly . . ." he declared in a letter. "These Quakers are in general a sly artful people, not altogether destitute, as I conceive, of worldly views in their religious professions."

Not all his views were this churlish or negative. In writing to his daughter in his declining years, he could be pious without being ungenerous. "If you carefully fulfill the various duties of life, from a principle of obedience to your heavenly Father, you shall enjoy that peace which the world cannot give nor take away. You know you cannot gratify me so much as by seeking most earnestly the favor of Him who made and supports you—who will supply you with whatever his infinite wisdom sees best for you in this world, and above all, who has given us his Son to purchase for us the reward of eternal life."

His highly conservative religious beliefs and his attitudes toward the religious beliefs of others were in marked contrast to those of most of the other leading men of the American Revolutionary and constitutional period. He serves as a reminder, therefore, that there was no uniformity of spiritual outlook among the Founding Fathers.

Samuel Adams was largely inactive in the years following the American Revolution. He was a delegate to the Philadelphia Constitutional Convention, found very little there to his liking, but in the end voted to adopt the United States Constitution that finally created a workable form of central government for the colonies he had labored mightily to help set free. He died in 1803. A Unitarian clergyman, William Bentley, entered this note in his diary shortly after Adams's death: "He was feared by his enemies, but too secret to be loved by his friends." He was a radical who made himself the champion of the working class but who suffered the fate of most agitators: he had little or no influence beyond his own time.

The Boston Gazette was a fighting newspaper in the most literal sense. It was written and edited by revolutionaries. Some of the fever heat was supplied by Samuel Adams, who wanted national freedom and wanted it fast. His energies and his radical views were not confined to purely political matters. After the manner of the period, he wrote under a pseudonym. The fact that he signed himself "Puritan" is especially interesting in view of some of the words he employs.

"PURITAN PAPERS," 1768

APRIL 4, 1768

Messieurs Edes & Gill:

While the generous Farmer has been employing his shining talents, in awakening a continent to a sense of the danger their civil rights are in from incroaching power: While it is grown fashionable, for men of ingenuity and public spirit, with a noble ardour, to warn us against a tame submission to the iron rods; and LIBERTY, LIBERTY, is the cry: I confess I am surprised to find, that so little attention is given to the danger we are in, of the utter loss of those religious rights, the enjoyment of which our good forefathers had more especially in their intention, when they explored and settled this new world.

To say the truth, I have from long observation been apprehensive, that what we have above everything else to fear, is POPERY: And I now bespeak the solemn attention of my beloved countrymen, to a course of letters which I am preparing, and propose to publish in your paper upon the momentous and melancholy subject. I expect to be treated with sneer and ridicule by those *artful* men who have come into our country *to spy out our liberties*; and who are restless to bring us into *bondage*, and can be successful only when the people are in a sound sleep: from this consideration I hope my readers will not be offended, if I now, and then, cry aloud to them with a great degree of warmth and pathos: This I shall most certainly do, whether they will hear or whether they will forbear; for I cannot even now think on the subject without feeling my zeal enkindle. I know full well that it is farthest from the imagination of some of our solid men and *pious* Divines, whom I intend particularly to address on the occasion, that ever this *enlightened* continent should become the *worshippers* of the *beast*: But who would have thought that the obliged and instructed Israelites would so soon after they were delivered from the Egyptian *task-masters* have fallen down before a *golden* calf! There is a variety of ways in which Popery, the idolatry of Christians, may be introduced into America; which at present I shall not so much as hint at, but shall point them out hereafter in their proper order. Yet, my dear countrymen—suffer me at this time, in the bowels of my compassion, to warn you all, as you value your precious *civil* liberty, and everything you can call dear to you, to be upon your guard against Popery. My fears of Popery have induced me to travel through this great continent as a spectator, to satisfy myself: And the more I know of the circumstances of America, I am sorry to say it, the more reason I find to be apprehensive of Popery. Bless me! Could our ancestors look out of their graves and see so many of *their own* sons, decked with the worst of *foreign superfluities*, the ornaments of the *whore of Babylon*, how would it break their sacred Repose! But amidst my gloomy apprehensions, it is a consolation to me to observe, that some of our towns, maintain their integrity, and show a laudable zeal against Popery. To do honor to those towns as much as in my power, I intend to publish a list of them. And as I am not particularly attached to any town in the province, but that which gave me birth, I am determined that if any others shall be roused by my future lucubrations to oppose Popery, as I trust and hope they will, they shall have the same notice taken of them in another paper.

Yours,
A PURITAN

APRIL 11, 1768

Messieurs Edes & Gill:

As the love of fame operates more or less in every human breast, I must acknowledge I have had some feelings of it in my own mind, since you were so courteous as to publish to the world my last letter: I had a consciousness that I was influenced by no motives in writing it, but what appeared to me to be justifiable and praise-worthy; and indeed I was under a sort of constraint to mention my fears; for I did verily believe, and I do so still, that much more is to be dreaded from the growth of Popery in America, than from Stamp-Acts or *any other* Acts destructive of men's *civil* rights: Nay, I could not help fancying that the Stamp-Act itself was contrived with a design only to inure the people to the habit of contemplating themselves as the slaves of men; and the transition from thence to a subjection to Satan, is mighty easy.

As soon as I received your paper, and had read my letter, I took my horse and journeyed *Eastward*—to be sure not from any *superstitious* notion I had of paying *homage* to that quarter of the heavens, but purely to make a visit to a few old friends, whom I know to be inspired with a zeal against Popery.

In crossing the ferry, well known by the name of Charles, I lit of a well-dressed man, who observing an uncommon silence among the passengers, and being desirous, as I thought to raise a little innocent chat in a circle of folks, who in all likelihood will never meet again, he started a question. Whether the river had its name in honor to the first or second Charles? A difference of sentiments immediately arose, perhaps rather to enliven the conversation, than from an ignorance of so simple a matter in any of the company; but the question was soon decided, or rather *overset*, by one of the ferrymen, who with a certain warmth, *put in his oar*, and said that it was not a groat's matter which of them had the honor of it, for they were both *Papists*; and he wished such a trifling circumstance as it might seem to be, would not tend to bring in Popery some time or other on both sides the river, especially into that town which bears the same name.— I bethought myself of my list of protestant towns, and recollected that Charlestown was one: Surely, thought I, there can be no danger of Charlestown; and yet if there be anything in this man's shrewd observation, there is some reason to fear that Charlestown is not so much on its guard against Popery as I imagined. I began to be inquisitive with myself what could be the meaning of this *back-stroke* of Mr. Ferryman; and my great anxiety and impatience to know the worst of it, led me to whisper in his ear, when I paid him my ferriage, that if he would step into the neighboring tavern, I had something of importance to say to him: No sooner were we seated, but I unburthened my mind to him—Honest Friend, said I, what reason have you to fear the growth of Popery in Charlestown? I should not have expected that any one would have *represented* Charlestown as Papists— When I made use of the word *represented*, which was purely accidental, and without any *particular* meaning in me, I observed in his looks a certain promptitude to utter himself, which induced me to give way to him—I find, said he, that your mind runs upon Representatives; why truly the time of election draws near. You mistake me, friend, said I, my mind runs upon nothing but the danger of Popery. Very well, he replied, and are we not to choose sound Protestants for our representatives, as we would avoid the danger of Popery?—That's true, said I, you are very right; but did ever a papist represent the town of Charlestown? No, no, said he, no, no, I have nothing to charge on any of our good gentlemen, as papists; they come to our meeting every sabbath; and so he went on to speak very handsomely, etc.—But what do *you* mean by Popery? said he: and before I had time even to attempt to answer a question of so great moment, he explained it himself, and with looks full of meaning, said, that *Popery* was the *worshipping of graven images*. That's the very thing said I, but do any of our representatives worship graven images? Here he was called to his duty, and I had only time to tell him, that I was upon a little excursion into the country, to inquire of some friends about Popery—that the hint he had given in the ferry-boat had shocked me greatly, and when I returned I should hope he would explain to me his mind more fully.

I then pursued my journey to Medford, where I dined, and conversed upon the danger of Popery with a traveller from the western parts of this province, who alarmed me very much with a story he related, which I shall open to my readers in some of my future letters.—I communicated to him my design, and my list of protestant towns—he told me they were many of them very stanch, but that some of them he feared were not so apprehensive of Popery as they should be; and particularly mentioned them, which I noted in my memorandum book, and so we parted.—I mounted my horse and proceeded to Salem, which town I had heard, (whether true or not I cannot tell) had formerly been visited by a *romish* priest, who had used all his arts and tricks to draw them from their adherence to the protestant cause; and it was said that he had in some measure prevailed, so that they began to wonder after the beast: But I have reason to believe that their eyes are now open, and that they will soon convince the world, that they have repented, and *will do their first works.*—From Marblehead I started away for Haverhill—a town once marked by the French and Indian *papists* for ruin—There I settled a correspondence with a very sensible and honest man, well spirited against Popery, who assured me that some fears I had suggested to him should be removed; and that he would in less than six weeks give me a convincing proof that the town of Haverhill, at least a very great majority, were enemies to Popery, or he should much wonder. I intended to have travelled as far east as York.—This town I have a very great affection for, on account of the intimacy I once had with their late very venerable and aged pastor, who while he lived was greatly instrumental in keeping out Popery there. The influence of this good old puritan among his people, lasted many years after his death; and I am told that the most of them speak of him to this day with great reverence: Some, it is said, have lately set up *the Image,* and have been seen in *public* company with the *crucifixes* at their breasts; but I do not avouch for the truth of it. If it be a fact, I hope the town of York, which has always been remarkable for stanch *puritanism,* will take the most effectual method to discountenance such glaring appearances of Popery.

I shall at present give you no further account of this journey, only that on my return to Charlestown I tarried there a night for the sake of further conversation with the ferryman, from whom I received great light, but little comfort.—A few anecdotes worthy of notice I shall send you at another time.

Yours,
A Puritan

Arthur Lee, a native Virginian, was educated in Edinburgh and London and espoused the American cause in England. Samuel Adams was pleased to have a correspondent who could say sharp things to the Lion. At the time this letter was written—1771—the Revolutionary movement in America was confined largely to radicals. Even Benjamin Franklin counseled caution against those who advocated an open break with England. Lee, like Adams, was not burdened by a cautious spirit.

LETTER TO ARTHUR LEE, SEPTEMBER 27, 1771

. . . . Inclosed you have a copy of the protests of diverse patriotic clergymen in Virginia against an Episcopate in America. It is part of the plan the design of which is to secure a ministerial influence in America, which in all reason is full strong enough without the aid of the clergy. The junction of the Cannon and the feudal law you know has been fatal to the liberties of mankind. The design of the first settlers of New England in particular was to settle a plan of government upon the true principles of liberty in which the clergy should have no authority. It is no wonder then that we should be alarmed at the designs of establishing such a power. It is a singular pleasure to us that the colony of Virginia though Episcopalian should appear against it as you will see by the vote of thanks of the House of Burgesses to the protesting gentlemen; they declare their protest to be a "wise and well timed opposition." I wish it could be published in London. I had the pleasure of knowing Mr. Hewet who was in this town about two years ago in company with Mr. Eyre of Northampton County, in Virginia, who is a member of the House of Burgesses. I did not then know that Mr. Hewet was a clergyman.

I fear I have tired your patience and conclude by assuring you that I am in strict truth

Sir your friend and humble servant

John Scollay, of Boston, was a patriot and a selectman. Adams was careful to keep in touch with his fellow revolutionists of Boston.

LETTER TO JOHN SCOLLAY, APRIL 30, 1776

While I was sitting down to write you a friendly letter I had the pleasure of receiving your favor of the 22 instant by the post. My intention was to congratulate you and your brethren the Selectmen, upon the precipitate flight of the British Army and its adherents from the town of Boston, and to urge on you the necessity of fortifying the harbour so as that the enemies ships might never approach it hereafter. Our grateful acknowledgments are due to the Supreme Being who has not been regardless of the multiplied oppressions which the inhabitants of that city have suffered under the hand of an execrable tyrant. Their magnanimity and perseverance during the severe conflict has afforded a great example to the world, and will be recorded by the impartial historian to their immortal honor. They are now restored to their habitations and privileges; and as they are purged of those wretches a part of whose policy has been to corrupt the morals of the people, I am persuaded they will improve the happy opportunity of re-establishing ancient principles and purity of manners—I mention this in the first place because I fully agree in opinion with a very celebrated author, that "freedom or slavery will prevail in a (city or) country according as the disposition and manners of the people render them fit for the one or the other"; and I have long been convinced that our enemies have made it an object, to eradicate from the minds of the people in general a sense of true religion and virtue, in hopes thereby the more easily to carry their point of enslaving them. Indeed, my friend, this is a subject so important in my mind, that I know not how to leave it. Revelation assures us that "Righteousness exalteth a nation"—Communities are dealt with in this world by the wise and just Ruler of the Universe. He rewards or punishes them according to their general character. The diminution of public virtue is usually attended with that of public happiness, and the public liberty will not long survive the total extinction of morals. "The Roman Empire, says the historian, *must* have sunk, though the Goths had not invaded it. Why? Because the Roman virtue was sunk." Could I be assured that America would remain virtuous, I would venture to defy the utmost efforts of enemies to subjugate her. You will allow me to remind you, that the morals of that city which has borne so great a share in the American contest, depend much upon the vigilance of the respectable body of Magistrates, of which you are a member.

The Reverend Peter Thacher preached a sermon commemorating the Boston Massacre that achieved some fame. Samuel Adams was serving in the Continental Congress at the time this letter was written. His hostility towards Quakers, Tories, and Catholics is extreme; but the extreme is where Sam Adams made his home.

LETTER TO PETER THACHER, AUGUST 11, 1778

. . . . Nothing can equal the barefaced falsehood of the Quakers and Tories in this city, unless perhaps their folly, in giving out that M. Gerard does not come in the character of a public minister, but only to obtain pay for the stores we have received from that country. These Quakers are in general a sly artful people, not altogether destitute, as I conceive, of worldly views in their religious profession. They carefully educate their children in their own contracted opinions and manners, and I dare say they have in their hearts as perfect a system of uniformity of worship in their way, and are busily employed about spiritual domination as ever Laud himself was, but having upon professed principles renounced the use of the carnal weapon, they cannot consistently practice the too common method made use of in former times, of dragooning men into sound beliefs. One might submit to their own inward feelings, whether they do not now and then secretly wish for fire from Heaven in support of their cause, in order to bring them upon a footing with those whose consciences dictate the kindling fires on Earth for the pious purpose of convincing gainsayers, and who keep the sword in their hands to enforce it. He who in the spirit of the Apostle professes to wish peace to all those who love the Lord Jesus Christ in sincerity, must discover an unmortified pride and a want of Christian charity to destroy the peace of others who profess to have that sincere affection to the common Master, because they differ from him in matters of mere opinion.

Samuel Adams writes two fatherly notes, one to his daughter Hannah, the other to the young man who is marrying her. Adams was in his last year as member of the Continental Congress at the time he wrote these letters.

LETTER TO HANNAH ADAMS, AUGUST 17, 1780

Nothing I assure you, but want of leisure, has prevented my acknowledging the receipt of your very obliging letter of the 12th of July. You cannot imagine with how much pleasure I received it. I have no reason to doubt your sincerity when you express the warmest affection for your mother and me, because I have had the most convincing proof of it in the whole course of your life. Be equally attentive to every relation into which all-wise Providence may lead you, and I will venture to predict for my dear daughter, an unfailing source of happiness in the reflections of her own mind. If you carefully fulfill the various duties of life, from a principle of obedience to your heavenly Father, you shall enjoy that peace which the world cannot give nor take away. In steadily pursuing the path of wisdom and virtue I am sometimes inclined to think you have been influenced with a view of pleasing me. This is indeed endearing, and I owe you the debt of gratitude. But the pleasing an earthly parent, I am persuaded, has not been your principal motive to be religious. If this has any influence on your mind, you know you cannot gratify me so much, as by seeking most earnestly, the favor of Him who made and supports you—who will supply you with whatever his infinite wisdom sees best for you in this world, and above all, who has given us his Son to purchase for us the reward of eternal life—Adieu, and believe that I have all the feelings of a father.

LETTER TO T. WELLS, NOVEMBER 22, 1780

Although I have not yet acknowledged the obliging letter you wrote to me some time ago, I would not have you entertain a doubt of my sincere respect and the confidence I place in you. I think I gave you the strongest proof of this when I was last in Boston. From that moment I have considered myself particularly interested in your welfare. It cannot indeed be otherwise, since I then consented that you should form the most intimate connection with the dear girl whom I pride myself in calling my daughter. I did this with caution and deliberation; and having done it, I am now led to contemplate the relation in which I am myself to stand with you, and I can (hardly) forbear the same style in this letter, which I should take the liberty to use if I was writing to her.

The marriage state was designed to complete the sum of human happiness in this life. It sometimes proves otherwise; but this is owing to the parties themselves, who either rush into it without due consideration, or fail in point of discretion in their conduct towards each other afterwards. It requires judgment on both sides, to conduct with exact propriety; for though it is acknowledged, that the superiority is and ought to be in the man, yet as the management of a family in many instances necessarily devolves on the woman, it is difficult always to determine the line between the authority of the one and the subordination of the other. Perhaps the advice of the good bishop of St. Asaph on another occasion, might be adopted on this, and that is, not to govern too much.

When the married couple strictly observe the great rules of honor and justice towards each other, differences, if any happen, between them, must proceed from small and trifling circumstances. Of what consequence is it whether a turkey is brought on the table boiled or roasted? And yet, how often are the passions suffered to interfere in such mighty disputes, till the tempers of both become so soured that they can scarcely look upon each other with any tolerable degree of good humor.

I am not led to this particular mode of treating the subject from an apprehension of more than common danger, that such kind of fracas will frequently take place in that connection, upon which, much of my future comfort in life will depend. I am too well acquainted with the liberality of your way of thinking to harbor such a jealousy; and I think I can trust to my daughter's discretion if she will only promise to exercise it.

I feel myself at this moment so domestically disposed that I could say a thousand things to you, if I had leisure. I could dwell on the importance of piety and religion, of industry and frugality, of prudence, economy, regularity and an even government, all which are essential to the well being of a family. But I have not time. I cannot however help repeating piety, because I think it indispensible. Religion in a family is at once its brightest ornament and its best security. The first point of justice, says a writer I have met with, consists in piety; nothing certainly being so great a debt upon us, as to render to the Creator and Preserver those acknowledgments which are due to Him for our being, and the hourly protection he affords us.

As governor of Massachusetts, Samuel Adams had many things to say to the legislature of a sovereign state that belonged to the free, independent, and sovereign United States. His concern here is for the "virtuous education" of youth.

LETTER TO THE MASSACHUSETTS LEGISLATURE, JANUARY 17, 1794

I fear I have dwelt too long upon this subject. Another presents itself to my mind, which I think is indeed great and important; I mean the education of our children and youth. Perhaps the minds even of infants may receive impressions, good or bad, at an earlier period than many imagine. It has been observed, that "education has a greater influence on manners, than human laws can have." Human laws excite fears and apprehensions, lest crimes committed may be detected and punished: But a virtuous education is calculated to reach and influence the heart, and to prevent crimes.

A very judicious writer, has quoted Plato, who in showing what care of the security of states ought to be taken of the education of youth, speaks of it as almost sufficient to supply the place both of legislation and administration. Such an education, which leads the youth beyond mere outside show, will impress their minds with a profound reverence of the Deity, universal benevolence, and a warm attachment and affection towards their country. It will excite in them a just regard to Divine Revelation, which informs them of the original character and dignity of man; and it will inspire them with a sense of true honor, which consists in conforming as much as possible, their principles, habits, and manners to that original character. It will enlarge their powers of mind, and prompt them impartially to search for truth in the consideration of every subject that may employ their thoughts; and among other branches of knowledge, it will instruct them in the skill of political architecture and jurisprudence; and qualify them to discover any error, if there should be such, in the forms and administration of Governments, and point out the method of correcting them. But I need not press this subject, being persuaded, that this Legislature from the inclination of their minds, as well as in regard to the duty enjoined by the Constitution, will cherish "the interest of literature, the sciences and all their seminaries."

Thanksgiving Day proclamations by governors have become a firm part of New England tradition. As governor of Massachusetts, Samuel Adams issues a declaration that seems considerably more mellowed than earlier pronouncements.

PROCLAMATION, OCTOBER 14, 1795

Published by Authority (Seal) Commonwealth of Massachusetts

BY THE GOVERNOR

A PROCLAMATION FOR A DAY OF PUBLIC THANKSGIVING AND PRAISE

Forasmuch as the occasional meeting of a people for the exercise of piety and devotion towards God, more especially of those who enjoy the light of divine revelation, has a strong tendency to impress their minds with a sense of dependence upon Him and their obligations to Him.

I have thought fit, according to the ancient and laudable practice of our renowned ancestors, to appoint a day of public thanksgiving to God, for the great benefits which He has been pleased to bestow upon us, in the year past. And I do by advice and consent of the Council, appoint Thursday, the nineteenth day of November next, to be observed as a day of public thanksgiving and praise throughout this commonweath: calling upon the ministers of the Gospel of all denominations, with their respective congregations to assemble on that day to offer to God, their unfained gratitude, for his great goodness to the people of the United States in general, and of this commonwealth in particular.

More especially in that He hath in His good providence united the several states under a national compact formed by themselves, whereby they may defend themselves against external enemies, and maintain peace and harmony with each other.

That internal tranquility has been continued within this commonwealth; and that the voice of health is so generally heard in the habitations of the people.

That the earth has yielded her increase, so that the labors of our industrious husbandmen have been abundantly crowned with plenty.

That our fisheries have been so far prospered.—Our trade notwithstanding obstructions it has met with, has yet been profitable to us, and the works of our hands have been established.

That while other nations have been involved in war, attended with an uncommon profusion of human blood, we in the course of Divine Providence, have been preserved from so grievous a calamity, and have enjoyed so great a measure of the blessing of peace.

And I do recommend that together with our thanksgiving, humble prayer may be offered to God, that we may be enabled, by the subsequent obedience of our hearts and manners, to testify the sincerity of our professions of gratitude, in the sight of God and man; and thus be prepared for the reception of future divine blessings.

That God would be pleased to guide and direct the administration of the Federal government, and those of the several states, in union, so that the whole people may continue to be safe and happy in the constitutional enjoyment of their rights, liberties and privileges, and our governments be greatly respected at home and abroad.

And while we rejoice in the blessing of health bestowed upon us, we would sympathize with those of our sister states, who are visited with a contagious and mortal disease; and fervently supplicate the Father of mercies that they may speedily be restored to a state of health and prosperity.

That He would in His abundant mercy regard our fellow citizens and others, who are groaning under abject slavery, in Algiers, and direct the most effectual measures for their speedy relief.

That He would graciously be pleased to put an end to all tyranny and usurpation, that the people who are under the yoke of oppression may be made free; and that the nations who are contending for freedom may still be secured by His almighty aid, and enabled under His influence to complete wise systems of civil government, founded in the equal rights of men and calculated to establish their permanent security and welfare.

And finally, that the peaceful and glorious reign of our Divine Redeemer may be known and enjoyed throughout the whole family of mankind.

And I do recommend to the people of this commonwealth, to abstain from all such labor and recreation as may not be consistent with the solemnity of the said day.

Given at the Council-Chamber, in Boston, the fourteenth day of October in the year of our Lord, One Thousand Seven Hundred and Ninety-Five, and in the Twentieth Year of the independence of the United States of America.

SAMUEL ADAMS

True Copy—Attest

John Avery, jun. Sec'ry
God Save the Commonwealth of Massachusetts!

9. JOHN JAY

"We Differ in Opinion; and, I Am Persuaded, with Equal Sincerity"

IF a *New York Social Register* had been drawn up in the year 1776, one of the names that would have been included almost automatically was that of John Jay. He was young—only thirty-one—but he had already acquired the kind of name that was most eagerly sought after by organizations or causes eager to put on their very best face before the public. John Jay was conservative, intelligent, well-mannered, and effective. No one could ever accuse him of radicalism or unsavory ties. In fact, to be connected in any way with John Jay was to practice a form of innocence by association. He was the son of a wealthy businessman; he had graduated from King's College; he was a successful lawyer, a member of one of the most prominent firms in New York; he had married into one of the most influential families in New York. He had every qualification for his role as the father of American conservatism.

At the age of twenty-nine he had become a delegate to the Continental Congress at Philadelphia. He was its youngest member, but he created a reputation for judiciousness and sagacity and was selected to prepare the draft address to the people of Great Britain relating to the grievances of the American states. Some American loyalists, no doubt, were shocked at the fact that John Jay should support the Revolutionary cause, but he did it out of conviction, maintaining his position with the conservative branch of the Whig Party. "Loyalism was strongest in the upper classes," Morison and Commager wrote in *The Growth of the American Republic*. "The merchants in the North, except in Boston and the smaller New England seaports, were pretty evenly divided; and many lawyers remained faithful to the King. . . . When the conservatives realized that liberty could be won only by opening the floodgates to 'dirty democrats,' many drew back in alarm; others, like John Jay, held their noses and carried on. . . ."

No one could ever doubt John Jay's sincerity or his adherence to the

Revolutionary cause; even so, he was something of a contrast to radicals like Samuel Adams or Thomas Paine, or even to Jefferson and Washington, for that matter. This disparity did not prevent him from making major contributions to American independence and the United States Constitution. For John Jay was the balance wheel of the Revolution, the man who moved serenely forward from one distinguished position to another in helping to create a new free nation. He was chief justice of the State of New York during the Revolution. He became president of the Revolutionary Continental Congress. He was a roving ambassador and troubleshooter abroad; he had to rely on his own judgment to make important commitments for the United States in foreign capitals, whether with respect to peace treaties or trade agreements. For the most part, his judgments were proved to be correct, but now and then there would be angry repercussions in the United States; on one occasion he was burned in effigy. It is said that the British had been confidentially advised that John Jay could "bear any opposition to what he advances, provided that regard is shown his abilities," and that "John Jay's weak side is Mr. Jay." Be that as it may, he invariably achieved the object of his assignment. When he returned from Europe in 1784, after a prolonged absence, Congress appointed him to the post of Secretary of Foreign Affairs.

John Jay was not present at the Constitutional Convention, but he was a powerful advocate of the Constitution, writing five *Federalist* letters, under the pseudonym "Publius," and the acclaimed "Address to the People of the State of New-York on the subject of the Constitution . . . ," signed "A Citizen of New-York." At the New York State ratifying convention, he threw his full prestige behind Hamilton in the successful fight for adopting the Constitution.

President George Washington, in creating his first administration, gave John Jay his choice of positions. Jay thus became the first Chief Justice of the United States under the new Constitution. He was forty-four at the time.

When Chief Justice Jay led his fellow jurists to the bench for the first time, one could observe a break from the English custom of judicial dress. For the first U.S. Supreme Court had taken Jefferson's advice to abandon the "monstrous wig which makes the English judges look like rats peeping through bunches of oakum."

Jay served on the High Court for six years. His judicial service was disrupted, however, when President Washington found it necessary to send the best envoy we could find to represent us in London in order to get the British to abandon policies that infringed on our sovereignty. Even before John Jay returned from London, the citizens of New York—despite some bitter opposition to his work abroad—elected him governor. He was re-elected for a full term and retired from public life in 1801 at the age of fifty-seven.

In religion, as in all other things, John Jay was conservative. But his own orthodox beliefs did not cause him to lose sight of what he considered to be a fundamental principle of a free society: the religious rights of all must not be prejudiced or jeopardized. When, for example, the Continental Congress met for the first time on September 5, 1774, it was moved that the daily sessions should be opened with prayer. John Jay, deeply devout, objected to this on the ground that there was too much diversity of belief and custom to make such a prayer feasible or practicable. He cited the fact that among the members were Presbyterians, Congregationalists, Anabaptists, Episcopalians, Quakers, etc. Up rose Samuel Adams in full puritanical voice and splendor and demanded the right, though a Congregationalist, to hear an Episcopal clergyman. "I am no bigot," he declared. John Jay did not consider himself a bigot, either; he had stated what he considered a fundamental principle that had validity whether one held liberal or orthodox religious views. The Congress decided in favor of Samuel Adams and appointed a chaplain.

It would be a mistake to conclude from Jay's opposition to a chaplain in Congress that he was opposed to denominational religion. He was a consistent churchgoer and an opponent of Deism, particularly of the Thomas Paine variety. He questioned Paine's good faith, quite literally, and consistently opposed his Deistic views. He was one of the early presidents of the American Bible Society, of which his son, William, was a founder. William Jay was also a prominent abolitionist. In retirement John Jay became active in church and religious affairs. His last papers are concerned with church policy, in which he argues against the assumption of any authority by the church in civil affairs. He was also apprehensive about "the gradual introduction and industrious propagation of high church doctrine. . . . There never was a time when these doctrines promoted peace on earth or good-will among men." He reminded his associates that their church had been formed after the Revolution with the "truth and simplicity of the Gospel" uppermost in mind; and he urged them to return to this basic concept.

In this sense, though he was considerably apart from Jefferson, Madison, and John Adams in his personal religious beliefs, accepting the literal truth of the Bible and worshipping accordingly, John Jay was at one with them in his concern for the religious liberties of all. He died in 1829 at the age of eighty-four.

John Jay's sense of history and his confidence in the emergence of a grand American design are reflected in this passage from his "Charge to the Grand Jury" of Ulster County, New York.

CHARGE TO JURY, 1777

The Americans are the first people whom Heaven has favoured with an opportunity of deliberating upon, and choosing the forms of government under which they should live. All other constitutions have derived their existence from violence or accidental circumstances, and are therefore probably more distant from their perfection, which, though beyond our reach, may nevertheless be approached under the guidance of reason and experience.

Jay's antagonism to the ideas of Thomas Paine, especially in the field of religion, is abundantly evident in the following letter to the Reverend Uzal Ogden.

LETTER TO UZAL OGDEN, FEBRUARY 14, 1796

As to "The Age of Reason," it never appeared to me to have been written from a disinterested love of truth or of mankind, nor am I persuaded that either of those motives induced certain characters to take such singular pains to distribute and give it reputation and currency in this country. Religion, morality, and a virtuous and enlightened clergy will always be impediments to the progress and success of certain systems and designs, and therefore will not cease to experience both direct and indirect hostilities from those who meditate or embark in them.

The Mr. Rittenhouse referred to in this letter from John Jay to Dr. Benjamin Rush was the late president of the American Philosophical Society, having succeeded Benjamin Franklin in that post. Rittenhouse died the year before this letter was written. He was the inventor of the collimating telescope, i.e., one that had a slit at the principal focal length from the lens. He also pioneered with spider webs in the eyepiece of the telescope.

LETTER TO BENJAMIN RUSH, MARCH 22, 1797

I have received and read with pleasure your elegant eulogium on the late Mr. Rittenhouse. Such attention to worthy characters cherish and encourage modest merit. As a man and a philosopher, his title to esteem and praise is, I believe, universally acknowledged.

The "Illustrations of the Prophecies," which you mention, I have not seen. On my return to New York I will inquire for it. The author's applying certain of the prophecies to certain recent events renders his work the more interesting. I have frequently known this to be done with more imagination than judgment, but from your account of the book I presume it is not liable to that remark. The subject naturally excites attention, and the present extraordinary state of things permits an idea to slide into the mind that even additional events, admitting of a like application, may precede a general peace.

We live, my dear sir, in times that furnish abundant matter for serious and profound reflections. It is a consolatory one that every scourge of every kind by which nations are punished or corrected is under the control of a wise and benevolent Sovereign.

Jedidiah Morse, recipient of the following three letters from John Jay, was a Congregational clergyman who, after the manner of the period, attained excellence in varied fields. He was one of the leaders of Christian orthodox theology; he engaged in arduous historical studies, of which the Annals of the American Revolution *was one; he is regarded as the father of American geography, for his books and textbooks in this field were for many years the standard works. His correspondence with John Jay reflects his multiple interests. The excerpts from John Jay's replies deal mainly with religious matters.*

LETTERS TO JEDIDIAH MORSE, 1797–1813

FEBRUARY 28, 1797

. . . . It is to be regretted, but so I believe the fact to be, that except the Bible there is not a true history in the world. Whatever may be the virtue, discernment, and industry of the writers, I am persuaded that truth and error (though in different degrees) will imperceptibly become and remain mixed and blended until they shall be separated forever by the great and last refining fire.

JANUARY 30, 1799

You will herewith receive copies of the acts of our two last sessions. A variety of official and other affairs, which, although in numerous instances of little importance, yet required to be dispatched with punctuality, induced me, from time to time, to postpone replying to your obliging letter of the 19th November, and to thank you for the interesting pamphlets you were so kind as to send with it.

We see many things, my dear sir, which might be altered for the better, and that, I believe, has been the case at all times. But at this period, there certainly are an uncommon number and series of events and circumstances which assume an aspect unusually portentous. The seeds of trouble are sowing and germinating in our country as well as in many others; they are cultivated with a zeal so singularly blind as not, in many instances, to be easily accounted for. Infidelity has become a political engine, alarming both by the force and the extent of its operations. It is doubtless permitted to be used for wise ends, though we do not clearly discern them; when those ends shall be accomplished, it will be laid aside.

Much ill-use has been and will yet be made of secret societies. I think with you that they should not be encouraged, and that the most virtuous and innocent of them would do well to concur in suspending them for the present.

What precisely is to be understood of the death and resurrection of the witnesses, will probably be explained only by the *event*. I have an idea, that either the Old and New Testaments, or the moral and revealed law, are the two witnesses: witnesses to the existence, attributes, promises, and denunciations of the Supreme Being. Atheism is now killing these witnesses. That all true and pious apostles or believers are everywhere or generally to be slain, seems hardly credible. Whatever or whoever the witnesses may be, it is certain that the slaughter is not yet perfected. I much doubt whether, in any view of the subject, the clergy of the Church of Rome are of the number.

The Pope has lost his triple crown, and his spiritual dominion is rapidly declining. The Turk is now a party to the war; whether any or what consequences will result from it to Mahomet, is yet to be seen. Wide is the field open for *conjectures*.

That our country is to drink very deep of the cup of tribulation, I am not apprehensive; but that we shall entirely escape, does not appear to me very probable. I suspect that the Jacobins are still more numerous, more desperate, and more active in this country than is generally supposed. It is true, they are less indecorous and less clamorous than they have been. How few of their *leaders* have abandoned their errors, their associations, their opposition to their own government, and their devotion to a foreign one! Why, and by whom, were the Kentucky and Virginia resolutions contrived, and for what purposes? I often think of Pandora's box; although it contained every kind of evil, yet is it said that *hope* was placed at the bottom. This is a singular fable, and it admits of many, and some of them very extensive, applications.

JANUARY 1, 1813

Accept my thanks for your friendly letter of the 17th ult., and for the sermon and report which accompanied it.

Whether our religion permits *Christians* to vote for *infidel* rulers, is a question which merits more consideration than it seems yet to have generally received, either from the clergy or the laity. It appears to me, that what the prophet said to Jehoshaphat about his attachment to Ahab,[1] affords a salutary lesson on another interesting topic.

Although the mere *expediency* of public measures may not be a proper subject for the pulpit, yet, in my opinion, it is the right and duty of our pastors to press the observance of all moral and religious duties, and to animadvert on every course of conduct which may be repugnant to them. . . .

As may have been apparent at various times in these pages, it was necessary for men in public position to engage in a considerable correspondence for the purpose of silencing rumors or reports which reflected adversely on their religious positions. Thomas Jefferson, writing to Mrs. Harrison Smith, for example, had to cope with loose talk because someone had seen something in a letter he had written to someone else. In this case, John Jay, governor of New York, tries to correct an impression that some of his best French friends were atheists. The statements about him had appeared in a book on British resources.

LETTER TO JOHN BRISTED, APRIL 23, 1811

Accept my thanks for the book on the "Resources of Britain", which you were so obliging as to send me. It abounds in interesting matter, and if the facts and calculations stated in it are correct, there appears to be reason to conclude that Britain has less danger to apprehend from a long-continued war than from a premature peace.

In the twelfth page there is an anecdote which seems to refer to me; if it does, it is proper for me to observe that your information on that head is not entirely accurate. While in France I was neither present at the death nor at the funeral of any French philosopher. During my residence there, I do not recollect to have had more than two conversations with atheists about their tenets.

I was at a large party, of which were several of that description. They spoke freely and contemptuously of religion. I took no part in the conversation. In the course of it, one of them asked me if I believed in Christ. I answered that I did, and that I thanked God that I did. Nothing further passed between me and them or any of them on that subject.

Some time afterward, one of my family being dangerously ill, I was advised to send for an English physician, who had resided many years at Paris. He was said to be very skilful, but, it was added, he is an atheist.

---

[1] "Shouldst thou help the ungodly, and love them that hate the Lord?"

I sent for him, and had reason to think very highly of his skill.

For several weeks the patient required numerous visits, so that I saw the doctor often. He was a sedate, decent man. I frequently observed him drawing the conversation towards religion, and I constantly gave it another direction. He, nevertheless, during one of his visits, very abruptly remarked that there was no God, and he hoped the time would come when there would be no religion in the world.

I very concisely remarked that if there was no God there could be no moral obligations, and I did not see how society could subsist without them.

He did not hesitate to admit that, if there was no God, there could be no moral obligations, but insisted that they were not necessary, for that society would find a substitute for them in enlightened self-interest.

I soon turned the conversation to another topic, and he, probably perceiving that his sentiments met with a cold reception, did not afterwards resume the subject.

The Reverend John M. Mason was a frequent visitor at the home of the Jays. The book he sent to John Jay elicited a response, part of which had a Jeffersonian ring to it.

LETTER TO JOHN M. MASON, MAY 22, 1816

Accept my thanks for the friendly letter, and for the book[2] which you were so obliging as to send me by my son.

I have made some progress in reading it. The *principle* I approve, and am glad it has employed a pen very able to do it justice.

Had all uninspired expositors been content with the simplicity of the gospel, and not been wise above what is written, the Church would probably have suffered less than it has from worldly wisdom and scholastic subtleties.

John Jay's religious beliefs were at polar opposites from those of Paine, and in considerable contrast to those of Jefferson or Franklin or John Adams. But he was completely at one with Jefferson in his respect for the rights of others to hold convictions different from his own. He was severely reluctant to be drawn into religious discussion or debate.

LETTER TO JOHN MURRAY, APRIL 15, 1818

In my letter to you of the 16th October last, I hinted that I might perhaps write and send you a few more lines on the question, whether war of every description is forbidden by the gospel.

---

[2] [*A Plea for Catholic Communion.*—ED.]

I will now add some remarks to those which were inserted in my answer to your first letter. In that answer, the lawfulness of war, in certain cases, was inferred from those Divine *positive* institutions which authorized and regulated it. For although those institutions were not dictated by the moral law, yet they cannot be understood to authorize what the moral law forbids.

The moral or natural law was given by the Sovereign of the universe to all mankind; with them it was co-eval, and with them it will be co-existent. Being founded by infinite wisdom and goodness on essential right, which never varies, it can require no amendment or alteration.

Divine positive ordinances and institutions, on the other hand, being founded on expediency, which is not always perpetual or immutable, admit of, and have received, alteration and limitation in sundry instances.

There were several Divine *positive* ordinances and institutions at very early periods. Some of them were of limited obligation, as circumcision; others of them were of universal obligation, as the Sabbath, marriage, sacrifices, the particular punishment for murder.

The Lord of the *Sabbath* caused the day to be changed. The ordinances of Moses suffered the Israelites to exercise more than the original liberty allowed to marriage, but our Saviour repealed that indulgence. When sacrifices had answered their purpose as types of the great Sacrifice, etc., they ceased. The punishment for murder has undergone no alteration, either by Moses or by Christ.

I advert to this distinction between the moral law and positive institutions, because it enables us to distinguish the reasonings which apply to the one, from those which apply *only* to the other—ordinances being mutable, but the moral law always the same.

To this you observe, by way of objection, that the law was given by Moses, but that grace and truth came by Jesus Christ; and hence that, even as it relates to the *moral law*, a more *perfect* system is enjoined by the gospel than was required under the law, which admitted of an eye for an eye, and a tooth for a tooth, tolerating a spirit of retaliation. And further, that, if the moral law was the same now that it was before the flood, we must call in question those precepts of the gospel which prohibit some things *allowed* of and practised by the patriarchs.

It is true that the law was given by Moses, not however in his individual or private capacity, but as the agent or instrument, and by the authority of the Almighty. The law demanded exact obedience, and proclaimed: "Cursed is every one that continueth not in all things which are written in the book of the law to do them." The law was inexorable, and by requiring *perfect* obedience, under a penalty so inevitable and dreadful, operated as a schoolmaster to bring us to Christ for *mercy*.

Mercy, and grace, and favour did come by Jesus Christ; and also that truth which verified the promises and predictions concerning him, and which exposed and corrected the various errors which had been imbibed respecting the Supreme Being, his attributes, laws, and dispensations. Uninspired commentators have dishonored the law, by ascribing to it, in certain cases, a sense and meaning which it did not authorize, and which our Saviour rejected and reproved.

The inspired prophets, on the contrary, express the most exalted ideas of the law. They declare that the law of the Lord is *perfect*; that the statutes of the Lord are *right*; and that the commandment of the Lord is *pure*; that God would *magnify* the law and make it honorable, etc.

Our Saviour himself assures us that he came not to destroy the law and the prophets, but to fulfil; that whoever shall do and teach the commandments, shall be called great in the kingdom of heaven; that it is easier for heaven and earth to pass, than title of the law to fail. This certainly amounts to a full approbation of it. Even after the resurrection of our Lord, and after the descent of the Holy Spirit, and after the miraculous conversion of Paul, and after the direct revelation of the Christian dispensation to him, he pronounced this memorable encomium on the law, viz.: "The law is *holy*, and the commandments *holy*, *just*, and *good*."

It is true that one of the *positive* ordinances of Moses, to which you allude, did ordain retaliation or, in other words, a tooth for a tooth. But we are to recollect that it was ordained, not as a rule to regulate the conduct of private individuals towards each other, but as a legal penalty or punishment for certain offences. Retaliation is also manifest in the punishment prescribed for murder—life for life. Legal punishments are adjusted and inflicted by the law and magistrate, and not by unauthorized individuals. These and all other positive laws or ordinances established by Divine direction, must of necessity be consistent with the moral law. It certainly was not the design of the law or ordinance in question, to encourage a spirit of personal or private revenge. On the contrary, there are express injunctions in the law of Moses which inculcate a very different spirit; such as these: "Thou shalt not avenge, nor bear any grudge against the children of thy people; but thou shalt love thy neighbor as thyself." "Love the stranger, for ye were strangers in Egypt." "If thou meet thy enemy's ox or his ass going astray, thou shalt surely bring it back to him," etc., etc.

There is reason to believe that Solomon understood the law in its true sense, and we have his opinion as to retaliation of injuries, viz.: "Say not, I will recompense evil; but wait upon the Lord, and He will save thee." Again: "Say not, I will do to him as he hath done to me. I will render to the man according to his work." And again: "If thine enemy be hungry, give him bread to eat; and if he be thirsty, give him water to drink; for thou shalt heap coals of fire upon his head, and the Lord shall reward thee."

But a greater than Solomon has removed all doubts on this point. On being asked by a Jewish lawyer which was the great commandment in the law, our Saviour answered: "Thou shalt love the Lord thy God with all thy heart, and with all thy soul, and with all thy mind. This is the *first* and the great commandment, and the *second* is like unto it: Thou shalt love thy neighbor as thy self. On *these* two commandments hang all the law and the prophets." It is manifest, therefore, that the love of God and the love of man are enjoined by the law; and as the genuine love of the one comprehends that of the other, the apostle assures us that "Love is the fulfilling of the *law*."

It is, nevertheless, certain, that erroneous opinions respecting retaliation, and who were to be regarded as *neighbors*, had long prevailed, and that our Saviour blamed and corrected those and many other unfounded doctrines.

That the patriarchs sometimes violated the moral law, is a position not to be disputed. They were men, and subject to the frailties of our fallen nature. But I do not know nor believe, that any of them violated the moral law by the authority or with the approbation of the Almighty. I can find no instance of it in the Bible. Nor do I know of any action done according to the moral law, that is censured or forbidden by the gospel. On the contrary, it appears to me that the gospel strongly enforces the whole moral law, and clears it from the vain traditions and absurd comments which had obscured and misapplied certain parts of it.

As, therefore, Divine ordinances did authorize just war, as those ordinances were necessarily consistent with the moral law, and as the moral law is incorporated in the Christian dispensation, I think it follows that the right to wage *just* and *necessary* war is admitted, and not abolished, by the gospel.

You seem to doubt whether there ever was a *just* war, and that it would puzzle even Solomon to find one.

Had such a doubt been proposed to Solomon an answer to it would probably have been suggested to him by a very memorable and interesting war which occurred in his day. I allude to the war in which his brother Absalom on the one side, and his father David on the other, were the belligerent parties. That war was caused by, and proceeded from, "the lusts" of Absalom, and was horribly wicked. But the war waged against him by David was not caused by, nor did proceed from, "the lusts" of David, but was right, just, and necessary. Had David submitted to be dethroned by his detestable son, he would, in my opinion, have violated his moral duty and betrayed his official trust.

vokcd, atrocious, and unredressed injuries.

Thus two kinds of justifiable warfare arose; one against domestic male-factors; the other against foreign aggressors. The first being regulated by the law of the land; the second by the law of nations; and both consistently with the moral law.

As to the *first* species of warfare, in every state or kingdom, the government or executive ruler has, throughout all ages, pursued, and often at the expense of blood, attacked, captured, and subdued murderers, robbers, and other offenders; by force confining them in chains and in prisons, and by force inflicting on them punishment; never rendering to them good for evil, for that duty attaches to individuals in their personal or private capacities, but not to rulers or magistrates in their official capacities. This species of war has constantly and universally been deemed just and indispensable. On this topic the gospel is explicit. It commands us to obey the higher powers or ruler. It reminds us that "he beareth not the sword in vain"; that "he is the minister of God, and a revenger to execute wrath upon him that doeth evil." Now, if he is not to bear the *sword* in *vain*, it follows that he is to *use* it to execute wrath on evil-doers, and consequently to draw blood and to kill on proper occasions.

As to the *second* species of warfare, it certainly is as reasonable and as right that a nation be secure against injustice, disorder, and rapine from without as from within; and therefore it is the right and duty of the government or ruler to use force and the sword to protect and maintain the rights of his people against evil-doers of another nation. The reason and necessity of using force and the sword being the same in both cases, the right or the law must be the same also.

We are commanded to render to our government, or to our Caesar, "the things that are Caesar's," that is, the things which belong to him, and not the things which do not belong to him. And surely this command cannot be construed to intend or imply that we ought to render to the Caesar of another nation more than belongs to him.

In case some powerful Caesar should demand of us to receive and obey a king of his nomination, and unite with him in all his wars, or that he would commence hostilities against us, what answer would it be proper for us to give such a demand? In my opinion, we ought to refuse, and vigorously defend our independence by arms. To what other expedient could we have recourse? I cannot think that the gospel authorizes or encourages us, on such an occasion, to abstain from resistance, and to expect miracles to deliver us.

A very feeble unprepared nation, on receiving such a demand, might hesitate and find it expedient to adopt the policy intimated in the gospel, viz.: "What king, going to war against another king, sitteth not down first and consulteth whether he be able with ten thousand to meet him that cometh against him with twenty thousand; or else he sendeth an ambassage, and desireth conditions of peace"—that is, makes the best bargain he can.

If the United States should unanimously RESOLVE never more to use the sword, would a certified copy of it prove to be an effectual Mediterranean passport? Would it reform the predatory rulers of Africa, or persuade the successive potentates of Europe to observe towards us the conduct of *real* Christians? On the contrary, would it not present new facilities, and consequently produce new excitements, to the gratification of avarice and ambition?

It is true that even just war is attended with evils, and so likewise is the administration of government and of justice; but is that a good reason for abolishing either of them? They are means by which greater evils are averted. Among the various means necessary to obviate or remove, or repress, or to mitigate the various calamities, dangers, and exigencies, to which in this life we are exposed, how few are to be found which do not subject us to troubles, privations, and inconveniences of one kind or other. To prevent the incursion or continuance of evils, we must submit to the use of those means, whether agreeable or otherwise, which reason and experience prescribe. . . .

I nevertheless believe, and have perfect faith in the prophecy, that the time will come when "the nations will beat their swords into plough-shares, and their spears into pruning-hooks; when nation shall not lift up sword against nation, neither shall they learn war any more." But does not this prophecy clearly imply, and give us plainly to understand, that in the *meanwhile*, and *until* the arrival of that blessed period, the nations will not beat their swords into plough-shares, nor their spears into pruning-hooks; that nation will not forbear to lift up sword against nation, nor cease to learn war?

It may be asked, Are we to do nothing to hasten the arrival of that happy period? Literally no created being can either accelerate or retard its arrival. It will not arrive sooner nor later than the appointed time. . . .

But whatever may be the time or the means adopted by Providence for the abolition of war, I think we may, without presumption, conclude that mankind must be prepared and fitted for the reception, enjoyment, and preservation of universal permanent peace, before they will be blessed with it. Are they as yet fitted for it? Certainly not. Even if it was practicable, would it be wise to disarm the good before "the wicked cease from troubling?" By what other means than arms and military force can unoffending rulers and nations protect their rights against unprovoked aggressions from within and from without? Are there any other means to which they could recur, and on the efficacy of which they could rely? To this question I have not as yet heard, nor seen, a direct and precise answer.

These remarks would have been written and sent sooner had my health been better. Expedition not being requisite, I attended to them only at intervals which allowed and invited me to do so.

We differ in opinion, and, I am persuaded, with equal sincerity.

John Jay's son, William, was one of the organizers of the American Bible Society and also a prominent advocate of the abolition of slavery. Various attempts were made by William and other officers of the Bible Society to have Jay accept its presidency. Jay did not like the idea of being a nominal president; but he accepted on condition that the members understand his limitations. To a large extent, his activity in the Society took the form of his annual address.

ANNUAL ADDRESSES TO THE AMERICAN BIBLE SOCIETY

MAY 9, 1822

There is reason to believe that the original, and the subsequent fallen, state of man, his promised redemption from the latter, and the institution of sacrifices having reference to it, were well known to many of every antediluvian generation. That these great truths were known to Noah, appears from the Divine favor he experienced; from his being a preacher of righteousness; and from the time and the description of the sacrifices which he offered. That he carefully and correctly communicated this knowledge to his children, is to be presumed from his character and longevity.

After the astonishing catastrophe at Babel, men naturally divided into different associations, according to their languages; and migrating into various regions, multiplied into distinct nations. Tradition, doubtless, still continued to transmit these great truths from generation to generation; but the diminution of longevity, together with the defects and casualties incident to tradition, gradually rendered it less and less accurate. These important truths thus became, in process of time, disfigured, obscure, and disregarded. Custom and usage continued the practice of sacrifices, but the design of their institution ceased to be remembered. Men "sought out many inventions" and true religion was supplanted by fables and idolatrous rites. Their mythology manifests the inability of *mere* human reason, even when combined with the learning of Egypt, and the philosophy of Greece and Rome, to acquire the knowledge of our actual state and future destiny, and of the conduct proper to be observed in relation to both.

By the merciful interposition of Providence, early provision was made for preserving these great truths from universal oblivion; and for their being ultimately diffused throughout the world. They were communicated to Abraham. He was also favored with additional information relative to the expected redemption, and with a promise that the Redeemer should be of his family. That family was thenceforth separated and distinguished from others, and on becoming a nation, was placed under theocratic government. To that family and nation, the Divine oracles and revelations were committed; and such of them as Infinite Wisdom deemed proper for the future instruction of every nation, were recorded and carefully preserved. By those revelations, the promise and expectation of redemption were from time to time renewed, and sundry distinctive marks and characteristic circumstances of the Redeemer predicted. The same merciful Providence has also been pleased to cause every material event and occurrence respecting our Redeemer, together with the gospel he proclaimed, and the miracles and predictions to which it gave occasion, to be faithfully recorded and preserved for the information and benefit of all mankind.

All these records are set forth in the Bible which we are distributing; and from them it derives an incalculable degree of importance; for as every man must soon pass through his short term of existence there, into a state of life of endless duration, the knowledge necessary to enable him to prepare for *such* a chance cannot be too highly estimated.

The Gospel was no sooner published than it proceeded to triumph over obstacles which its enemies thought insurmountable, and numerous heathen nations rendered joyful "obedience to the faith." Well-known events afterward occurred, which impeded its progress, and even contracted the limits of its sway. Why those events were permitted, and why the conversion of the great residue of the Gentiles was postponed, has not been revealed to us. The Scriptures inform us, that the coming in of the fulness of the Gentiles will not be accomplished while Jerusalem shall continue to be trodden down by them. As a distant future period appears to have been allotted for its accomplishment, so a distant future season was doubtless assigned for its effectual commencement. Although the time appointed for the arrival of that season cannot be foreseen, yet we have reason to presume that its approach, like the approach of most other seasons, will be preceded and denoted by appropriate and significant indications. As the conversion of the Gentiles is doubtless to be effected by the instrumentality of Christian nations, so these will doubtless be previously prepared and qualified for that great work; and their labor in it be facilitated by the removal or mitigation of obstructions and difficulties. The tendency, which certain recent events have to promote *both* these purposes, gives them the aspect of such indications.

Great and multifarious were the calamities inflicted on the nations of Europe by their late extensive war; a war of longer duration, and in the course of which more blood and tears were shed, more rapacity and desolation committed, more cruelty and perfidy exercised, and more national and individual distress experienced, than in any of those which are recorded in modern history. During the continuance, and on the conclusion of such a war, it was natural to expect, that the pressure of public and personal dangers and necessities would have directed and limited the thoughts, cares, and efforts of rulers and people to their existing exigencies; and to the means necessary to acquire security, to repair waste, and terminate privations.

Yet, strange as it may appear, desires, designs, and exertions of a very different kind, mingled with these urgent temporal cares. The people of Great Britain formed, and have nobly supported their memorable Bible Society. Their example has been followed not only by the people of this country, but also by nations who had not yet obliterated the vestiges of war and conflagration. At no former period have the people of Europe and America instituted so many associations for diffusing and impressing the knowledge and influence of the Gospel, and for various other charitable and generous purposes, as since the beginning of the present century. These associations comprehend persons of every class; and their exemplary zeal and philanthropy continue to incite feelings and meditations well calculated to prepare us all for the great work before mentioned. We have also lived to see some of the *obstructions* to it removed, and some of its *difficulties* mitigated.

Throughout many generations there have been professing Christians, who, under the countenance and authority of their respective governments, treated the heathen inhabitants of certain countries in Africa as articles of commerce; taking and transporting multitudes of them, like beasts of burden, to distant regions; to be sold, and to toil and die in slavery. During the continuance of such a traffic, with what consistence, grace, or prospect of success, could such Christians send missionaries to present the Bible, or preach the Christian doctrines of brotherly kindness and charity to the people of those countries?

So far as respects Great Britain and the United States, that obstacle has been removed; and other Christian nations have partially followed their example. Although similar circumstances expose some of them to an opposition like that which Great Britain experienced, it is to be hoped that an overruling Providence will render it equally unsuccessful. I allude to the territorial and personal concerns which prompted the opposition with which the advocates for the act of abolition had to contend. It will be recollected that many influential individuals deeply interested in the slave-trade, together with others who believed its continuance to be indispensable to the prosperity of the British West India Islands, made strenuous opposition to its abolition, even in the British parliament. Delays were caused by it, but considerations of a higher class than those which excited the opposition finally prevailed, and the parliament abolished that detestable trade. Well-merited honor was thereby reflected on the Legislature; and particularly on that excellent and celebrated member of it, whose pious zeal and unwearied perseverance were greatly and conspicuously instrumental to the removal of that obstacle. Their example, doubtless, has weighed with those other nations who are in a similar predicament, and must tend to encourage them to proceed and act in like manner. . . .

Let us therefore persevere steadfastly in distributing the Scriptures far and near, and without note or comment. We are assured that they "are profitable for doctrine, for reproof, for correction, for instruction in righteousness." They comprise the inestimable writings by which the inspired apostles, who were commanded to preach the *Gospel* to *all* people, have transmitted it, through many ages, down to our days. The apostles were opposed in preaching the Gospel, but they nevertheless persisted. We are opposed in dispensing the Scriptures which convey the knowledge of it; and let us follow their example. An eminent ancient counsellor gave excellent advice to *their* adversaries; and his reasoning affords salutary admonition to *our* opponents. That advice merits attention, and was concluded in the following memorable words:

"Refrain from these men, and let them alone; for if this counsel or this work be of men, it will come to naught; but if it be of God, ye cannot overthrow it; lest haply ye be found even to fight against God."

MAY 8, 1823

That all men, throughout all ages, have violated their allegiance to their great Sovereign, is a fact to which experience and revelation bear ample and concurrent testimony. The Divine attributes forbid us to suppose that the Almighty Sovereign of the universe will permit any province of His empire to remain forever in a state of revolt. On the contrary, the sacred Scriptures assure us, that it shall not only be reduced to obedience, but also be so purified and improved as that righteousness and felicity shall dwell and abide in it.

Had it not been the purpose of God, that His will should be done on earth as it is done in Heaven, He would not have commanded us to pray for it. That command implies a prediction and a promise that in due season it shall be accomplished. If therefore the will of God is to be done on earth as it is done in Heaven, it must undoubtedly be known throughout the earth, before it can be done throughout the earth; and consequently, He who has decreed that it shall be so done, will provide that it shall be so known.

Our Redeemer having directed that the Gospel should be preached throughout the world, it was preached accordingly; and being witnessed from on high, "with signs and wonders, and with divers miracles and gifts of the Holy Ghost," it became preponderant, and triumphant, and effulgent. But this state of exaltation, for reasons unknown to us, was suffered to undergo a temporary depression. A subsequent period arrived, when the pure doctrines of the Gospel were so alloyed by admixtures, and obscured by appendages, that its lustre gradually diminished, and like the fine gold mentioned by the prophet, it became dim.

Since the Reformation, artifice and error have been losing their influence on ignorance and credulity, and the Gospel has been resuming its purity. We now see Christians, in different countries, and of different denominations, spontaneously and cordially engaged in conveying the Scriptures, and the knowledge of salvation, to the heathen inhabitants of distant regions. So singular, impressive, and efficient is the impulse which actuates them, that without the least prospect of earthly retribution, they cheerfully submit to such pecuniary contributions, such appropriations of time and industry, and, in many instances, to such hazards and privations, and such derelictions of personal comfort and convenience, as are in direct opposition to the propensities of human nature.

Can such extraordinary and unexampled undertakings possibly belong to that class of enterprises, which we are at liberty to adopt or decline as we please; enterprises which no duty either commands or forbids? This is more than a mere speculative question; and therefore the evidence respecting the character and origin of these undertakings cannot be too carefully examined, and maturely weighed; especially as this evidence is accumulating, and thereby acquiring additional claims to serious attention. . . .

Nor are these the only events and changes which are facilitating the distribution, and extending the knowledge of the Scriptures. For a long course of years, many European nations were induced to regard toleration as pernicious, and to believe that the people had no right to think and judge for themselves respecting religious tenets and modes of worship. Hence it was deemed advisable to prohibit their reading the Bible, and to grant that privilege only to persons of a certain description. Intolerance is passing away, and in France, where it formerly prevailed, Bible Societies have been established by permission of the government, and are proceeding prosperously, under the auspices of men high in rank, in character, and in station.

From the nature, the tendency, and the results of these recent and singular changes, events, and institutions; from their coincidence and admirable adjustment, as means for making known the Holy Scriptures, and inculcating the will of their Divine and merciful Author, throughout the world; and from the devotedness with which they are carrying into operation, there is reason to conclude that they have been produced by Him in whose hands are the hearts of all men.

If so, we are engaged in His service; and that consideration forbids us to permit our ardour or exertions to be relaxed or discouraged by attempts to depreciate our motives, to impede or discredit our proceedings, or to diminish our temporal resources. The Scriptures represent Christians as being engaged in a spiritual warfare, and, therefore, both in their associated and individual capacities, they are to expect and prepare for opposition. On the various inducements which prompt this opposition, much might be said; though very little, if any thing, that would be new. The present occasion admits only of general and brief remarks, and not of particular and protracted disquisitions.

Whatever may be the characters, the prejudices, the views, or the arts of our opponents, we have only to be faithful to our Great Leader. They who march under the banners of EMMANUEL have God with them; and consequently have nothing to fear.

MAY 13, 1824

We have the satisfaction of again observing, that by the blessing of Providence on the zeal of our fellow-citizens, and on the fidelity, diligence, and prudence with which our affairs are conducted, they continue in a state of progressive improvement. The pleasure we derive from it is not a little increased by the consideration that we are transmitting essential benefits to multitudes in various regions, and that the value and important consequences of these benefits extend and will endure beyond the limits of time. By so doing, we render obedience to the commandment by which He who "made of one blood all nations of men," and established a fraternal relation between the individuals of the human race, hath made it their duty to love and be kind to one another.

We know that a great proportion of mankind are ignorant of the revealed will of God, and that they have strong claims to the sympathy and compassion which we, who are favored with it, feel and are manifesting for them. To the most sagacious among the heathen it must appear wonderful and inexplicable that such a vicious, suffering being as man should have proceeded in such a condition from the hands of his Creator. Having obscure and confused ideas of a future state, and unable to ascertain how far justice may yield to mercy or mercy to justice, they live and die (as our heathen ancestors did) involved in darkness and perplexities.

By conveying the Bible to people thus circumstanced we certainly do them a most interesting act of kindness. We thereby enable them to learn, that man was originally created and placed in a state of happiness, but, becoming disobedient, was subjected to the degradation and evils which he and his posterity have since experienced. The Bible will also inform them, that our gracious Creator has provided for us a Redeemer, in whom all the nations of the earth should be blessed—that this Redeemer has made atonement "for the sins of the whole world," and thereby reconciling the Divine justice with the Divine mercy, has opened a way for our redemption and salvation; and that these inestimable benefits are of the free gift and grace of God, not of our deserving, nor in our power to deserve. The Bible will also animate them with many explicit and consoling assurances of the Divine mercy to our fallen race, and with repeated invitations to accept the offers of pardon and reconciliation. The truth of these facts and the sincerity of these assurances being unquestionable, they cannot fail to promote the happiness of those by whom they are gratefully received, and of those by whom they are benevolently communicated.

We have also the satisfaction of observing that the condition of the Church continues to improve. When at certain periods subsequent to the Reformation, discordant opinions on ecclesiastical subjects began to prevail, they produced disputes and asperities which prompted those who embraced the same peculiar opinions to form themselves into distinct associations or sects. Those sects not only permitted Christian fraternity with each other to be impaired by coldness, reserve, and distrust, but also, on the occurrence of certain occasions, proceeded to alternate and culpable acts of oppression. Even their endeavors to increase the number of Christians were often too intimately connected with a desire to increase the number of their adherents; and hence they became more solicitous to repress competition than to encourage reciprocal respect and good-will.

These prejudices, however, have gradually been giving way to more laudable feelings. By the progress of civilization and useful knowledge many individuals became better qualified to distinguish truth from error, and the diffusion of their reasonings among the people enabled them to judge and to act with less risk of committing mistakes. Since the rights of man and the just limits of authority in Church and State have been more generally and clearly understood, the Church has been less disturbed by that zeal which "is not according to knowledge"; and liberal sentiments and tolerant principles are constantly enlarging the sphere of their influence.

To the advantages which the Church has derived from the improved state of society, may be added those which are resulting from the institution of Bible societies. With whatever degree of tenacity any of the sects may adhere to their respective peculiarities, they all concur in opinion respecting the Bible, and the propriety of extensively distributing it without note or comment. They therefore readily become members of Bible societies, and in that capacity freely cooperate. Their frequent meetings and consultations produce an intercourse which affords them numerous opportunities of forming just estimates of one another, and of perceiving that prepossessions are not always well founded. This intercourse is rendered the more efficient by the great and increasing number of clerical members from dissimilar denominations. Convinced by observation and experience that persons of great worth and piety are attached to sects different from their own, the duties of their vocation, and their respectable characters, naturally incline them to recommend and encourage Christian friendliness.

It is well known, that both cathedrals and meeting-houses have heretofore exhibited individuals who have been universally and justly celebrated as real and useful Christians; and it is also well known, that at present not a few, under similar circumstances and of similar characters, deserve the like esteem and commendation. As *real* Christians are made so by Him without whom we "can do nothing," it is equally certain that He receives them into His family, and that in *His* family mutual love and uninterrupted concord never cease to prevail. There is no reason to believe or suppose that this family will be divided into separate classes, and that separate apartments in the mansions of bliss will be allotted to them according to the different sects from which they had proceeded.

These truths and considerations direct our attention to the *new* commandment of our Saviour, that his disciples "do love one another": although an anterior commandment required, that, "as we had opportunity" we should "do good unto all men"; yet this *new* one makes it our duty to do so "especially to the household of faith". In the early ages of the Church, Christians were highly distinguished by their obedience to it; and it is to be regretted that the conduct of too many of their successors has in this respect been less worthy of imitation.

Our days are becoming more and more favored and distinguished by new and unexpected accessions of strength to the cause of Christianity. A zeal unknown to many preceding ages has recently pervaded almost every Christian country, and occasioned the establishment of institutions well calculated to diffuse the knowledge and impress the precepts of the Gospel both at home and abroad. The number and diversity of these institutions, their concurrent tendency to promote these purposes, and the multitudes who are cordially giving them aid and support, are so extraordinary, and so little analogous to the dictates of human propensities and passions, that no adequate cause can be assigned for them but the goodness, wisdom, and will of HIM who made and governs the world.

We have reason to rejoice that such institutions have been so greatly multiplied and cherished in the United States; especially as a kind Providence has blessed us, not only with peace and plenty, but also with the full and secure enjoyment of our civil and religious rights and privileges. Let us, therefore, persevere in our endeavors to promote the operation of these institutions, and to accelerate the attainment of their objects. Their unexampled rise, progress and success in giving light to the heathen, and in rendering Christians more and more "obedient to the faith", apprise us that the great Captain of our salvation is going forth, "conquering and to conquer" and is directing and employing these means and measures for that important purpose. They, therefore, who enlist in His service, have the highest encouragement to fulfill the duties assigned to their respective stations; for most certain it is, that those of His followers who steadfastly and vigorously contribute to the furtherance and completion of His conquests, will also participate in the transcendent glories and blessings of HIS TRIUMPH.

MAY 12, 1825

You have the satisfaction of perceiving, from the report of the board of managers, that the prosperous and promising state of our affairs continues to evince the laudable and beneficial manner in which they have been constantly conducted.

We have to regret that the pleasing reflections and anticipations suggested by these auspicious circumstances are mingled with the sorrow which the recent death of our late worthy and beloved Vice-president has caused, and widely diffused. Our feelings are the more affected by it, as the benefits we have derived from his meritorious and incessant attention to all our concerns have constantly excited both our admiration and our gratitude.

As the course of his life was uniformly under the direction of true religion and genuine philanthropy, it forbids us to doubt of his being in a state of bliss, and associated with "the spirits of just men made perfect." Notwithstanding this consoling consideration, his departure will not cease to be lamented by this society, nor by those of his other fellow-citizens on whom his patriotic services, his exemplary conduct, and his disinterested benevolence have made correspondent impressions.

But the loss we have sustained by this afflicting event should not divert our thoughts from subjects which bear a relation to the design of our institution, and consequently to the purpose for which we annually assemble.

It may not therefore be unseasonable to remark that the great objects of the Bible, and the distribution of it, *without note or comment*, suggest sundry considerations which have claims to attention.

Christians know that man was destined for two worlds—the one of transient, and the other of perpetual duration; and that his welfare in both depends on his acceptance and use of the means for obtaining it, which his merciful Creator has for that purpose appointed and ordained. Of these inestimable and unmerited blessings the greater proportion of the human race are yet to be informed; and, to that end, we are communicating the same to them exactly in that state in which, by the direction and inspiration of their Divine Author, they were specified and recorded in the Bible, which we are distributing without note or comment.

As these gracious dispensations provide for our consolation under the troubles incident to a state of probation in this life, and for our perfect and endless felicity in the next, no communications can be of higher or more general interest. Wherever these dispensations become known and observed, they not only prepare men for a better world, but also diminish the number and pressure of those sufferings which the corrupt propensities and vicious passions of men prompt them to inflict on each other; and which sufferings are of greater frequency and amount than those which result from other causes.

Time and experience will decide whether the distribution of the Bible, without note or comment, will have any, and what effect, on the progress of the Gospel. Hitherto nothing unfavorable to this course of proceeding has occurred; and the expedience of it continues to derive a strong argument from its tendency to decrease the inconveniences which usually attend the circulation of discordant comments. Whenever any questionable opinions relative to any Scripture doctrine meet with zealous advocates, and with zealous opponents, they seldom fail to excite the passions as well as the mental exertions of the disputants. Controversies like these are not always conducted with moderation and delicacy, nor have they been uniformly consistent with candor and charity. On the contrary, the ardor with which the parties contend for victory frequently generates prejudices; and insensibly renders them more anxious to reconcile the Scriptures to their reasonings, than their reasonings to the Scriptures. The doubts and perplexities thereby disseminated are not favorable to those whose faith is not yet steadfast, nor to those who from temperament or imbecility are liable to such impressions.

These remarks, however, are far from being applicable to those excellent and instructive comments which have been written by authors of eminent talent, piety, and prudence; and which have been received with general and well-merited approbation.

It is to be regretted that comments of a very different character and description have caused errors to germinate and take root in Christian countries. Some of these were fabricated by individuals, who, finding that they could not carry their favorite propensities and habits with them through the "narrow way" prescribed by the Gospel, endeavored to discredit Christianity by objections which exhibit stronger marks of disingenuous, than of correct and candid reasoning. By artfully and diligently encouraging defection from Scripture, and from Scripture doctrines, they gradually introduced and spread that contempt for both, which in the last century was publicly displayed in impious acts of profaneness, and in dreadful deeds of ferocity. These atrocities repressed the career of infidelity, and infidels thereupon became less assuming, but not less adverse.

Even among professing Christians, and of distinct denominations, there are not a few of distinguished attainments and stations who have sedulously endeavored so to interpret and paraphrase certain passages in the Bible, as to render them congruous with peculiar opinions, and auxiliary to particular purposes.

Certain other commentators, doubtless from a sincere desire to increase Christian knowledge by luminous expositions of abstruse subjects, have attempted to penetrate into the recesses of profound mysteries, and to dispel their obscurity by the light of reason. It seems they did not recollect that *no man can explain what no man can understand*. Those mysteries were revealed to our faith, to be believed on the credit of Divine testimony; and were not addressed to our mental abilities for explication. Numerous objects which include mysteries daily occur to our senses. We are convinced of their existence and reality, but of the means and processes by which they become what they are, and operate as they do, we all continue ignorant. Hence it may rationally be concluded, that the mysteries of the *spiritual* world are still farther remote from the limited sphere of human perspicacity.

Among the biblical critics, there are some who have incautiously intermingled their learned and judicious investigations with enigmatical subtleties and hypothetical speculations, which tend more to engender doubts and disputes than to produce real edification.

Additional animadversions on this subject would be superfluous; nor can it be necessary to examine, whether an indiscrimate circulation of comments would merit or meet with general approbation. They who think it advisable that comments should accompany the Bible, doubtless prefer and intend what in their opinion would be a judicious, limited, and exclusive selection of them. It is well known that, composed as this and other Bible societies are, such a selection could not be formed by them with requisite unanimity. They therefore wisely declined disturbing their union by attempting it, and very prudently concluded to distribute the Bible without any other comments than those which result from the illustrations which different parts of it afford to each other. Of this no individuals have reason to complain, especially as they are perfectly at liberty to circulate their favorite authors as copiously and extensively as they desire or think proper.

Our Redeemer commanded his apostles to preach the Gospel to every creature: to that end it was necessary that they should be enabled to understand and to preach it correctly, and to demonstrate its Divine origin and institution by incontestible proofs. The Old Testament, which contained the promises and prophesies respecting the Messiah, was finished at a period antecedent to the coming of our Saviour, and therefore afforded no information nor proof of his advent and subsequent proceedings. To qualify the apostles for their important task, they were blessed with the direction and guidance of the Holy Spirit, and by him were enabled to preach the Gospel with concordant accuracy, and in divers languages: they were also enbued with power to prove the truth of their doctrine, and of their authority to preach it, by wonderful and supernatural signs and miracles.

A merciful Providence also provided that some of these inspired men should commit to writing such accounts of the Gospel, and of their acts and proceedings in preaching it, as would constitute and establish a *standard* whereby future preachers and generations might ascertain what they ought to believe and to do; and be thereby secured against the danger of being misled by the mistakes and corruptions incident to tradition. The Bible contains these writings, and exhibits such a connected series of the Divine revelations and dispensations respecting the present and future state of mankind, and so amply attested by internal and external evidence, that we have no reason to desire or expect that further miracles will be wrought to confirm the belief and confidence which they invite and require.

On viewing the Bible in this light, it appears that an extensive and increasing distribution of it has a direct tendency to facilitate the progress of the Gospel throughout the world. That it will proceed, and in due time be accomplished, there can be no doubt; let us therefore continue to promote it with unabated zeal, and in full assurance that the omnipotent Author and Protector of the Gospel will not suffer his gracious purposes to be frustrated by the arts and devices, either of malignant "principalities and powers," or of "spiritual wickedness in high places."

When John Jay moved to Bedford, New York, he attended Presbyterian church services, there being no Episcopal church in the vicinity. He joined with others of similar persuasion in building an Episcopal church. He declined any church office, but consulted frequently with church representatives. He was asked, and agreed, to communicate with the large and influential Trinity Church Corporation on behalf of his Bedford church. The following excerpt is from a statement he prepared for that purpose.

LETTER TO THE CORPORATION OF TRINITY CHURCH

The office of induction ought not, in our opinion, to be permitted to glide silently into operation, and acquire claims to obedience from successive instances of unguarded acquiscence. Whether that instrument is with or without precedent in the Christian Church, or by whom or for what purposes it was devised, are questions on which we make no remarks. Amid the prayers and piety by which it is decorated, are to be found unconstitutional assumptions of power, accompanied with a degree of parade and pageantry which, however conducive to other objects, have no natural connection with the mere business of induction. We believe that episcopacy was of apostolic institution, but we do not believe in the various high-church doctrines and prerogatives which art and ambition, triumphing over credulity and weakness, have annexed to it.

By the office of induction, the bishop is to give a formal commission, under his episcopal seal and signature, to the minister whom the corporation had called and engaged to be their rector; giving and granting to him the bishop's license and *authority* to perform the office of a priest of that parish.

We believe that every Episcopalian priest, ordained according to the rules of our Church, has, in virtue of that ordination, good right and authority to preach the Gospel and perform divine service in any parish; but we admit the propriety of being restrained by the bishop from calling and settling any other than an Episcopalian minister so ordained and of fair character. We therefore think it fit that the bishop's approbation on these two points should precede a call. We believe that we have a right to contract with and employ any such minister to be our rector; and that such contract is the only valid and proper commission which he can have to be our particular minister or rector. . . .

As to the bishop's being the arbiter and judge of disputes between a congregation and their rector, we observe, that all such of their disputes as turn on questions of a civil nature belong to the jurisdiction of the courts of law; and that no canon can either deprive those courts of that jurisdiction, nor divest any freeman of his right to have those disputes determined by the laws and by a jury of the country; and consequently, that no canon can or ought to constitute the bishop to be the arbiter or judge of them. But where the disputes turn on points of doctrine, we admit the fitness of their being decided by the bishop, so far as to settle the dispute; but not in all cases so far as to settle the doctrine; for there has been a time when, if the people had continued to believe and adhere to all the decisions and doctrines of their bishops, we should not have heard of, nor have been blessed with the reformed Protestant religion.

We cannot consider it as being altogether consistent with decorum, that the office of induction should order the senior warden, who is the first officer of the corporation, to stand at an appointed place, on the day of induction, during Divine service, holding the keys of the church in his hand in open view, as a mere pageant. We cannot approve of his being directed then to deliver the keys to the new incumbent, as a *token* that the parish did *acknowledge* him to be, what they had already made him to be, *their* rector. We can as little approve of what the new incumbent is thereupon to say to the senior warden, viz., "I receive these keys as pledges of the bishop's *episcopal induction,* and of your *recognition.*"

Recognition of what? That they, the church-wardens, vestry, and congregation, are all ciphers in the business. It is not easy to observe and examine these things without feeling some degree of indignation. We cannot dismiss the office of induction without expressing our disapprobation of introducing an opinion on a disputed point into one of the prayers directed to be used on the day of induction; it is this:

"O holy Jesus, who has purchased to thyself an universal church, and has promised to be with the ministers of *apostolic succession* to the end of the world."

This is not the promise literally, but the promise paraphrased and expounded. The promise of our Saviour is, "And lo, I am with you alway, even unto the end of the world."

As the apostles were all to die in a few years, this promise could not be understood as limited to them personally, but as extending to a certain description of persons throughout all ages of the world. To what description of persons does the promise extend? To this question, they who made the above paraphrase answer, that it intends and extends to *"the ministers of apostolic succession."* If it be asked, whether the ministers of the Calvinistic and of certain other churches are of apostolic succession, it is answered by all our bishops and clergy that they are not. It follows, therefore, of necessary consequence, that our bishops and clergy, and their congregation, when they offer up their prayer to Almighty God, must offer it with the meaning and understanding that the gracious promise mentioned in it is confined to Episcopalian ministers, and therefore excludes the ministers of all other denominations of Christians.

Who is there among us that can be prepared to declare, in solemn prayer, and in such positive and unqualified terms, that none but Episcopalian ministers have any part or lot in this important promise? Who is there that can be certain that the apostles, as to that promise, were not considered as the representatives of all who should become sincere and pious converts to, and believers in, the doctrines which they were sent to publish and to teach? What good reason can be assigned for our being called upon by the office of induction to adopt thus solemnly in prayer a doubtful exposition and construction of the promise; for doubtful it most certainly is, having from the reformation to this day been a subject of controversy and dispute between the ablest and best Christian divines. Great, indeed, must be the confidence and hardihood of those advocates for this construction of the promise who can, without hesitation, deny that our blessed Redeemer was with those non-Episcopalian ministers and congregations amounting to several hundred thousands, who for his sake endured all the varieties and rigors of persecution. If the great Captain of our Salvation was not with them, how and by whom were they enabled to meet and sustain such trials so firmly, to resist the adversary so resolutely, and to fight the good fight of faith so triumphantly?

It may not be unworthy of remark, that as a prophecy is best understood from its completion, so the manner in which a Divine promise is performed, affords the best exposition of its true and original meaning.

Lastly. Let it be remembered, and corporations should recollect their charters, that in the year 1795 the Protestant-Episcopal church in this State did apply for and did obtain an act of the Legislature in this State, passed the seventeenth day of March in that year, which contains the following clause:

"And be it further enacted, that the churchwardens and vestry for the time being, shall be, and hereby are vested with full power to call and induct a rector to the church, when and so often as there shall be a vacancy therein."

We submit to your consideration whether measures should not be taken to do away the office of induction; and if there must be such a thing introduced into the church, that it may be such a one as will leave both clergy and laity in quiet possession of their respective rights.

It is with sincere regret and reluctance that we find ourselves urged, by obvious considerations, to proceed to remarks on another interesting topic, which cannot be agreeable to many whose affections and good-will we are solicitous to cultivate by every becoming mark of respect. We know how much the welfare of our infant church depends on their friendly disposition towards us, and it certainly is as little our inclination as it is our interest to incur their displeasure. But painful as it may be, we must maintain our right, even at the risk of losing their good-will.

For a considerable time past, we have observed a variety of circumstances connected with church affairs which, on being combined and compared one with the other, justify inferences which, in our opinion, are exceedingly interesting, not only to the rights of the laity, but also to our churches in general, and to yours in particular. We allude to the gradual introduction and industrious propagation of high church doctrines. Of late years, they have frequently been seen lifting up their heads and appearing in places where their presence was neither necessary nor expected. There never was a time when those doctrines promoted peace on earth or good-will among men. Originating under the auspices and in the days of darkness and despotism, they patronized darkness and despotism down to the Reformation. Ever encroaching on the rights of governments and people, they have constantly found it convenient to incorporate, as far as possible, the claims of the clergy with the principles and practice of religion; and their advocates have not ceased to preach for Christian doctrines the commandments and devices of men.

To you it cannot be necessary to observe, that high church doctrine are not accommodated to the state of society, nor to the tolerant principles, nor to the ardent love of liberty which prevail in our country. It is well known that our church was formed after the Revolution with an eye to what was then believed to be the truth and simplicity of the Gospel; and there appears to be some reason to regret that the motives which then governed have since been less operative.

We know that our obscure and unimportant corporation can do but little. Providence has placed you under different circumstances. You have stronger inducements to watchfulness, more means to do good, and more power to avert evil.

Permit us to hope that the subjects of this letter will engage your serious consideration. Whatever may be the result, we shall have the satisfaction of reflecting that we have done our duty, in thus explicitly protesting against measures and proceedings which, if persevered in, must and will, sooner or later, materially affect the tranquillity and welfare of the Church.

10. THOMAS PAINE

"I Consider Myself in the Hands of My Creator"

A MAN who was willing to travel anywhere in the world to combat atheism and to establish the proof of the existence of God can hardly be denounced as an atheist himself, but this is what happened to Thomas Paine. His crusade was based on the love of God and man, yet he was flayed as an infidel and enemy of religion.

The answer perhaps is that Paine, for all his skill in the art of persuasion, did not recognize that most people could accept blunt and rough tactics in political argument but were considerably more sensitive in the field of religion. The very qualities that made him so effective in arguing for American independence or the rights of man—his hammerlike use of words, his smashing directness, his ability to find the soft spots in an opposing argument—these qualities aroused fierce antagonism in theological debate, even among those who accepted much of Paine's basic position.

No man likes to be called a fool; and Thomas Paine argued his position in a way that made his opponents appear to be the grossest simpletons. He pitted himself against religious literalism, certainly so far as the Bible was concerned; but he was something of a literalist himself. He analyzed it in the most precise terms. He allowed not at all for the symbolic meaning and appeal of the Bible. He ignored the fact that people do not expend their energies in searching for flaws in the fabric of belief. They neither expect nor demand religious concepts to be tidy, tight, and rigorously proved. There is an essential poetry in things of the spirit that is more basic to many people than demonstrable fact. There is also a certain continuity, some of the strands of which involve family and upbringing. Even when people are aware of the logical imperfections of some aspects of their creeds, they do not always view them as liabilities. Very little of this was taken into account by Paine in his sharply analytical and belligerent approach to those who disagreed with him. He juxtaposed the world of reason against the world of formal belief; but many people saw no conflict between the two.

The paradox of Thomas Paine, of course, is that his war against credal belief was carried on in the cause of the spiritual nature of man and not against it. The heart of religion to him was belief in God rather than prescribed approaches to God. Therefore, belief in God was the most sacred and personal thing in the world. He felt that no proof of God was necessary beyond that which was readily apparent to the God-given senses of man. No one need look for a text beyond the "Bible of Creation." In such a book, "every part of science, whether connected with the geometry of the universe, with the systems of animal and vegetable life, or with the properties of inanimate matter, is a text for devotion as well as for philosophy—for gratitude as for human improvement. It will perhaps be said, that, if such a revolution in the system of religion takes place, every preacher ought to be a philosopher. Most certainly. And every house of devotion a school of science."

Ideas such as these led him late in his career to found the "Theophilanthropy" movement in France. Paine was particularly disturbed about the widespread atheism in France and set out to combat it. Theophilanthropy, explained Paine, was based on the "existence of God and the immortality of the soul." The term is compounded of three Greek words—God, Love, Man. The Theophilanthropists, he said, sought to rescue religion from its two principal enemies—religious fanatics and atheists. Their weapon against the fanatics was to be reason and morality; against the atheists, natural philosophy.

Before considering the outcome of the Theophilanthropic movement in France, it might be useful to consider the larger phenomenon of Thomas Paine. No man's words had a greater impact on the people of the American colonies in arousing them to the call of national independence. But his words were directed against his native country. Thomas Paine was an Englishman. He had not come to America until he was thirty-seven, in 1774—only two years before the Declaration of Independence. He was born in Norfolk, in 1737. His father was a Quaker. His formal education was meager. He attended some science lectures; he read books, not too widely but intensively. He was profoundly affected by both discrimination against Quakers and by the gloom of the meetinghouse. He later wrote that he could not help thinking—and smiling at the thought—"that if the taste of a Quaker had been consulted at the creation, what a silent and drab-coloured creation it would have been!" It was also as a young boy that he happened to read a book about Virginia, and his "inclination from that day of seeing the western side of the Atlantic never left me."

He had some modest training as a mechanic and had various jobs connected with boats. This failed to sustain his interest and he became a tax examiner and investigator. All the while he studied and dreamed at home over maps and globes **and** scientific books. His work was judged unsatisfactory and he found himself back again as a staymaker. It is believed that he also turned to the ministry for a brief time. Meanwhile he was writing and arguing and attracting attention.

The turning point in the life of Thomas Paine came in his mid-thirties when he met the American Benjamin Franklin in London. Franklin was a man to capture the imagination, and Paine had imagination to burn. Paine saw in Franklin the complete man—thoroughly self-educated, a philosopher, scientist, statesman, man of letters. He was fascinated by Franklin's electrical experiments. It seems likely that Franklin's interest in the human situation apart from national boundaries added to Paine's admiration. Paine was opposed to monarchy as a matter of principle—whether in America, England, or anywhere else. He had certain abilities: a flair for eloquent, persuasive writing, a blistering zeal for human rights, a talent for fitting people and causes together. Benjamin Franklin spoke to Paine about America. In 1774, he sailed from England with letters of introduction from Franklin. Thus begins the first public career of Thomas Paine.

It didn't take Paine very long in America to make his impact. The cause of independence was a thing of fits and starts at the time he arrived. But the open, concerted movement for national independence dates from the publication of Paine's *Common Sense* in January 1776. George Washington credited it with working "a powerful change in the minds of many men." *Common Sense* was only a pamphlet, but it made the arguments for separation and for the establishment of a republic come alive and inspired people to meet a dramatic challenge. And then, during the War for Independence, when the battle was not going too well, Paine started his series of *Crisis* papers, beginning with the words: "These are the times that try men's souls." Once again, he galvanized a people into attempting the seemingly impossible.

For his service to the cause of the American Revolution, Thomas Paine won the admiration and gratitude of the American Congress and the people. But he had also demonstrated a lack of discretion that was to cost him his official position as secretary for the Committee for Foreign Affairs of Congress. He had revealed some information which France thought prejudicial to its good relations with the American people, and Paine was forced to resign. There were other incidents; Paine had made many friends but there were more than a few persons who, having felt his sting, would have been pleased to see him fry in hell.

Thomas Paine did not limit his energies to the cause of independence. He enlisted his passions in the fight to abolish slavery. It is not known for sure whether he wrote the preamble to the act renouncing slavery in

Pennsylvania; but his part in agitating for such an act, and his ideas on the subject, are clearly reflected in the statement:

"It is not for us to enquire why, in the creation of mankind, the inhabitants of the several parts of the earth were distinguished by a difference in feature or complexion. It is sufficient to know that all are the work of the Almighty Hand. . . . We esteem it a peculiar blessing granted to us, that we are enabled this day to add one more step to universal civilization, by removing, as much as possible, the sorrows of those, who have lived in undeserved bondage, and from which, by the assumed authority of the Kings of Great Britain, no longer effectual legal relief could be obtained. . . . We find our hearts enlarged with kindness and benevolence towards men of all conditions and nations; and we conceive ourselves at this particular period called upon by the blessings which we have received, to manifest the sincerity of our profession, and to give a substantial proof of our gratitude."

In 1781 Thomas Paine sailed secretly for France on a money-raising expedition; the American Revolution was running out of fuel. Paine joined Franklin, and a more persuasive pair the French Government had seldom seen; supplies in abundance were sent to America. This was exactly what Washington needed to mount an offensive against Cornwallis.

Meanwhile, Paine's own fortunes had not gone well. He had given everything he had to the cause of the American Revolution; he accepted no royalties for the countless copies of his pamphlets. When the war ended in victory for the United States of America, Paine was almost penniless. He wanted to return to England to see his aged parents, but he lacked the means for passage. New York led the way in giving him a house and land (in New Rochelle), and Pennsylvania followed by giving him some cash (£500). Congress also voted him $3,000. In 1787, he returned to England. Thus begins the second major phase in the life of Paine.

One of his major reasons for going to Europe in 1787 was to advance some of his scientific and mechanical ideas. He had devised a planing machine; built a wheel with a concentric rim; made a smokeless candle; developed theories on the use of gunpowder for a motor; and had invented an iron bridge. This latter he considered his most important work in the field of science and mechanics. A model of the bridge was exhibited in London and Paris and attracted large crowds. Patents were granted and the revolution in bridges began.

Thomas Paine, inventor, soon found it necessary to return to his dominant interest, human freedom. He became caught up in the political situation in France and England and soon was back at his pamphlets. He opposed Pitt's policies and worked for friendly relations with France. In reply to

Burke he wrote one of the most effective political tracts ever to appear in any language, *The Rights of Man*. Burke had some conservative views on the French Revolution which seemed to Paine to be totally at odds with what was happening in France, had already happened in America, and what seemed to be in the making in England.

The core of *The Rights of Man* was that man is of divine origin and therefore has natural rights. To secure these rights is the function of government, which must act in man's behalf. The Deity did not create nobles and lords. "It is by distortedly exalting some men, that others are distortedly disbased." Pressure was brought against *The Rights of Man*. Printers and distributors were harassed or punished. Despite this, some 200,000 copies were distributed. The Crown was most uneasy, to say the least. Paine was indicted for treason. Even before the trial took place, however, he received word that he had been elected to the French Convention. He fled to France. He had always regarded himself as a citizen of the world; now people engaged in a struggle for freedom of human rights were taking him at his word.

In France, Paine was to have even more tumultuous revolutionary experiences than any he had had in America. He was against royalty, but he could not stomach the extremist group. The rights of man so far as Paine was concerned did not cease being important when they were violated by revolutionaries. He stood against the public hysteria and random brutality. He believed in deposing the king, not decapitating him. He opposed the Jacobins and incurred the wrath of Robespierre. He was fortunate to escape the guillotine, but he did not escape jail. In jail, he worked on a statement of his religious beliefs, *The Age of Reason*. Thus begins the third phase in the life of Thomas Paine.

Robespierre's downfall was also marked by a return of Thomas Paine to the Convention. It was also marked by Paine's prominence in the field of religious thought. He intended *The Age of Reason* to reawaken faith in God, especially in France where one of the aftermaths of revolution was skepticism and negation. He called for a return to simplicity of worship. He related the political rights of man to the religious rights of man. He believed that the Bible had been used as a sanction for witchcraft, violence, suppression of minority religious views, and the justification for poverty. It was against all these things that he now wrote with all the force of logic and incisiveness that he had mustered in his political pamphlets. "In my publications on religious subjects," he later wrote, "my endeavors have been directed to bring man to a right use of the reason that God has given him; to impress on him the great principles of divine morality, justice, and mercy, and a benevolent disposition to all men, and to all creatures;

and to inspire in him a spirit of trust, confidence and consolation, in his Creator, unshackled by the fables of books pretending to be the word of God."

In this mood Paine and some friends founded a branch of the Theophilanthropists in Paris in 1797. The group attempted to find the best in the religions of mankind and bring them together in a harmonic whole. The aim was morality based on the spiritual nature of man and the existence of God. The Theophilanthropists created considerable controversy but eventually became absorbed in various liberal movements within the church itself.

Thomas Paine returned to New York in 1802. He was no longer a hero. His *Age of Reason* had been interpreted as a vulgar attack on Christianity. Besides, he had written a harsh and tactless letter while in jail, criticizing his old friend George Washington. When he died, on June 8, 1809, no monument was erected to his memory. Later, Andrew Jackson told a friend: "Thomas Paine needs no monument made by hands; he has erected a monument in the hearts of all lovers of liberty."

Paine also left some words, among them:

> The world is my country,
> All mankind are my brethren,
> To do good is my religion,
> I believe in one God and no more.

Thomas Paine addressed The Age of Reason *to "my fellow-citizens of the United States of America." He wrote the book in Paris, completing it in January, 1794. He expressed the hope in a dedication note that his fellow Americans would do him "the justice to remember that I have always strenuously supported the right of every man to his own opinion, however different that opinion might be to mine. He who denies to another this right, makes a slave of himself to his present opinion, because he precludes himself the right of changing it. The most formidable weapon against errors of every kind is reason. I have never used any other, and I trust I never shall."*

Both in England and the United States, the publication of The Age of Reason *produced an explosive reaction. It appears that the book was more reviled than read, judging from some of the things said about it. Paine was repeatedly denounced as an infidel and atheist, despite the fact that his work was directed as much against atheism as it was against orthodoxy. In England, the publisher was imprisoned, the book suppressed, and the author hanged in effigy. In America, the denunciation was severe but it was offset to some extent by its widespread distribution in the United States*

by deist societies. It was widely discussed on a popular level and became
the basis for a general movement of Deism.

Thomas Paine hoped his ideas in religion would be regarded as the
logical extension of the revolution in politics. It was presented in this light
by his followers, but after a while the book fell out of circulation and the
old conception of Paine as an atheist became fairly general. The material
that follows is a relatively short excerpt from The Age of Reason. *The full*
text is imperative for anyone who wishes to understand the foundations of
his religious beliefs.

THE AGE OF REASON

It has been my intention, for several years past, to publish my thoughts
upon religion. I am well aware of the difficulties that attend the subject,
and from that consideration, had reserved it to a more advanced period of
life. I intended it to be the last offering I should make to my fellow-citizens
of all nations, and that at a time when the purity of the motive that induced me to it could not admit of a question, even by those who might
disapprove the work. The circumstance that has now taken place in France
of the total abolition of the whole national order of priesthood, and of
everything appertaining to compulsive systems of religion, and compulsive
articles of faith, has not only precipitated my intention, but rendered a work
of this kind exceedingly necessary, lest in the general wreck of superstition, of
false systems of government and false theology, we lose sight of morality,
of humanity and of the theology that is true.

As several of my colleagues, and others of my fellow-citizens of France,
have given me the example of making their voluntary and individual profession of faith, I also will make mine; and I do this with all that sincerity
and frankness with which the mind of man communicates with itself.

I believe in one God, and no more; and I hope for happiness beyond this
life.

I believe in the equality of man; and I believe that religious duties consist
in doing justice, loving mercy, and endeavoring to make our fellow-creatures
happy.

But, lest it should be supposed that I believe many other things in addition to these, I shall, in the progress of this work, declare the things I do
not believe, and my reasons for not believing them.

I do not believe in the creed professed by the Jewish Church, by the
Roman Church, by the Greek Church, by the Turkish Church, by the Protestant Church, nor by any church that I know of. My own mind is my own
church.

All national institutions of churches, whether Jewish, Christian or Turkish, appear to me no other than human inventions, set up to terrify and enslave mankind, and monopolize power and profit.

I do not mean by this declaration to condemn those who believe otherwise; they have the same right to their belief as I have to mine. But it is necessary to the happiness of man that he be mentally faithful to himself. Infidelity does not consist in believing, or in disbelieving; it consists in professing to believe what he does not believe.

It is impossible to calculate the moral mischief, if I may so express it, that mental lying has produced in society. When a man has so far corrupted and prostituted the chastity of his mind as to subscribe his professional belief to things he does not believe he has prepared himself for the commission of every other crime.

He takes up the trade of a priest for the sake of gain, and in order to qualify himself for that trade he begins with a perjury. Can we conceive any thing more destructive to morality than this?

Soon after I had published the pamphlet "Common Sense," in America, I saw the exceeding probability that a revolution in the system of government would be followed by a revolution in the system of religion. The adulterous connection of church and state, wherever it has taken place, whether Jewish, Christian or Turkish, had so effectually prohibited by pains and penalties every discussion upon established creeds, and upon first principles of religion, that until the system of government should be changed, those subjects could not be brought fairly and openly before the world; but that whenever this should be done, a revolution in the system of religion would follow. Human inventions and priestcraft would be detected; and man would return to the pure, unmixed and unadulterated belief of one God, and no more.

*   *   *

The true deist has but one Deity; and his religion consists in contemplating the power, wisdom, and benignity of the Deity in his works, and in endeavoring to imitate him in every thing moral, scientifical, and mechanical.

The religion that approaches the nearest of all others to true Deism, in the moral and benign part thereof, is that professed by the Quakers; but they have contracted themselves too much by leaving the works of God out of their system. Though I reverence their philanthropy, I can not help smiling at the conceit, that if the taste of a Quaker could have been consulted at the creation, what a silent and drab-colored creation it would have been! Not a flower would have blossomed its gaities, nor a bird been permitted to sing.

I proceed to other matters. After I had made myself master of the use of the globes, and of the orrery,[1] and conceived an idea of the infinity of space, and of the eternal divisibility of matter, and obtained, at least, a general knowledge of what was called natural philosophy, I began to compare, or, as I have before said, to confront, the internal evidence those things afford with the Christian system of faith.

Though it is not a direct article of the Christian system that this world that we inhabit is the whole of inhabitable creation, yet it is so worked up there-with, from what is called the Mosaic account of the creation, the story of Eve and the apple, and the counterpart of that story, the death of the Son of God, that to believe otherwise, that is, to believe that God created a plurality of worlds, at least as numerous as what we call stars, renders the Christian system of faith at once little and ridiculous; and scatters it in the mind like feathers in the air. The two beliefs can not be held together in the same mind; and he who thinks that he believes both, has thought but little of either.

Though the belief of a plurality of worlds was familiar to the ancients, it is only within the last three centuries that the extent and dimensions of this globe that we inhabit have been ascertained. Several vessels, following the tract of the ocean, have sailed entirely round the world, as a man may march in a circle, and come round by the contrary side of the circle to the spot he set out from. The circular dimensions of our world, in the widest part, as a man would measure the widest round of an apple, or a ball, is only twenty-five thousand and twenty English miles, reckoning sixty-nine miles and an half to an equatorial degree, and may be sailed round in the space of about three years.

A world of this extent may, at first thought, appear to us to be great; but if we compare it with the immensity of space in which it is suspended, like a bubble or a balloon in the air, it is infinitely less in proportion than the smallest grain of sand is to the size of the world, or the finest particle of dew to the whole ocean, and is therefore but small; and, as will be here-after shewn, is only one of a system of worlds, of which the universal creation is composed.

It is not difficult to gain some faint idea of the immensity of space in which this and all the other worlds are suspended, if we follow a progres-sion of ideas. When we think of the size or dimensions of a room, our

---

[1] The orrery has its name from the person who invented it. It is a machinery of clock-work, representing the universe in miniature: and in which the revolution of the earth round itself and round the sun, the revolution of the moon round the earth, the revolution of the planets round the sun, their relative distances from the sun, as the center of the whole system, their relative distances from each other, and their different magnitudes, are represented as they really exist in what we call the heavens.

ideas limit themselves to the walls, and there they stop. But when our eye, or our imagination darts into space, that is, when it looks upward into what we call the open air, we cannot conceive any walls or boundaries it can have; and if for the sake of resting our ideas we suppose a boundary, the question immediately renews itself, and asks, what is beyond that boundary? and in the same manner, what beyond the next boundary? and so on until the fatigued imagination returns and says, *there is no end*. Certainly, then, the Creator was not pent for room when he made this world no larger than it is; and we have to seek the reason in something else.

If we take a survey of our own world, or rather of this, of which the Creator has given us the use as our portion in the immense system of creation, we find every part of it, the earth, the waters, and the air that surround it, filled, and as it were crowded with life, down from the largest animals that we know of to the smallest insects the naked eye can behold, and from thence to others still smaller, and totally invisible without the assistance of the microscope. Every tree, every plant, every leaf, serves not only as an habitation, but as a world to some numerous race, till animal existence becomes so exceedingly refined, that the effluvia of a blade of grass would be food for thousands.

Since then no part of our earth is left unoccupied, why is it to be supposed that the immensity of space is a naked void, lying in eternal waste? There is room for millions of worlds as large or larger than ours, and each of them millions of miles apart from each other.

*   *   *

As therefore the Creator made nothing in vain, so also must it be believed that he organized the structure of the universe in the most advantageous manner for the benefit of man; and as we see, and from experience feel, the benefits we derive from the structure of the universe, formed as it is, which benefits we should not have had the opportunity of enjoying if the structure, so far as relates to our system, had been a solitary globe, we can discover at least one reason why a *plurality* of worlds has been made, and that reason calls forth the devotional gratitude of man, as well as his admiration.

But it is not to us, the inhabitants of this globe, only, that the benefits arising from a plurality of worlds are limited. The inhabitants of each of the worlds of which our system is composed, enjoy the same opportunities of knowledge as we do. They behold the revolutionary motions of our earth, as we behold theirs. All the planets revolve in sight of each other; and, therefore, the same universal school of science presents itself to all.

Neither does the knowledge stop here. The system of worlds next to us exhibits, in its revolutions, the same principles and school of science, to the inhabitants of their system, as our system does to us, and in like manner throughout the immensity of space.

Our ideas, not only of the almightiness of the Creator, but of his wisdom and his beneficence, become enlarged in proportion as we contemplate the extent and the structure of the universe. The solitary idea of a solitary world, rolling or at rest in the immense ocean of space, gives place to the cheerful idea of a society of worlds, so happily contrived as to administer, even by their motion, instruction to man. We see our own earth filled with abundance; but we forget to consider how much of that abundance is owing to the scientific knowledge the vast machinery of the universe has unfolded.

* * *

It has been by rejecting the evidence, that the word or works of God in the creation, affords to our senses, and the action of our reason upon that evidence, that so many wild and whimsical systems of faith, and of religion, have been fabricated and set up. There may be many systems of religion that so far from being morally bad are in many respects morally good: but there can be but ONE that is true; and that one necessarily must, as it ever will, be in all things consistent with the ever existing word of God that we behold in his works.

* * *

With respect to Mystery, every thing we behold is, in one sense, a mystery to us. Our own existence is a mystery: the whole vegetable world is a mystery. We cannot account how it is that an acorn, when put into the ground, is made to develop itself and become an oak. We know not how it is that the seed we sow unfolds and multiplies itself, and returns to us such an abundant interest for so small a capital.

The fact, however, as distinct from the operating cause, is not a mystery, because we see it; and we know also the means we are to use, which is no other than putting the seed in the ground. We know, therefore, as much as is necessary for us to know; and that part of the operation that we do not know, and which if we did, we could not perform, the Creator takes upon himself and performs it for us. We are, therefore, better off than if we had been let into the secret, and left to do it for ourselves.

But though every created thing is, in this sense, a mystery, the word mystery cannot be applied to *moral truth*, any more than obscurity can be applied to light. The God in whom we believe is a God of moral truth, and not a God of mystery or obscurity. Mystery is the antagonist of truth. It is a fog of human invention that obscures truth, and represents it in distortion. Truth never envelops *itself* in mystery; and the mystery in which it is at any time enveloped, is the work of its antagonist, and never of itself.

Religion, therefore, being the belief of a God, and the practice of moral truth, cannot have connection with mystery. The belief of a God, so far from having any thing of mystery in it, is of all beliefs the most easy, because it arises to us, as is before observed, out of necessity. And the practice of moral truth, or, in other words, a practical imitation of the moral goodness of God, is no other than our acting towards each other as he acts benignly towards all. We cannot *serve* God in the manner we serve those who cannot do without such service; and, therefore, the only idea we can have of serving God, is that of contributing to the happiness of the living creation that God has made. This cannot be done by retiring ourselves from the society of the world, and spending a recluse life in selfish devotion.

*   *   *

In the same sense that every thing may be said to be a mystery, so also may it be said that every thing is a miracle, and that no one thing is a greater miracle than another. The elephant, though larger, is not a greater miracle than a mite; nor a mountain a greater miracle than an atom. To an almighty power it is no more difficult to make the one than the other, and no more difficult to make a million of worlds than to make one. Every thing, therefore, is a miracle, in one sense; whilst, in the other sense, there is no such thing as a miracle. It is a miracle when compared to our power, and to our comprehension. It is not a miracle compared to the power that performs it. But as nothing in this description conveys the idea that is affixed to the word miracle, it is necessary to carry the inquiry further.

Mankind have conceived to themselves certain laws, by which what they call nature is supposed to act; and that a miracle is something contrary to the operation and effect of those laws. But unless we know the whole extent of those laws, and of what are commonly called the powers of nature, we are not able to judge whether any thing that may appear to us wonderful or miraculous, be within, or be beyond, or be contrary to, her natural power of acting.

The ascension of a man several miles high into the air, would have everything in it that constitutes the idea of a miracle, if it were not known that a species of air can be generated several times lighter than the common atmospheric air, and yet possess elasticity enough to prevent the balloon, in which that light air is inclosed, from being compressed into as many times less bulk, by the common air that surrounds it. In like manner, extracting flashes or sparks of fire from the human body, as visibly as from a steel struck with a flint, and causing iron or steel to move without any visible agent, would also give the idea of a miracle, if we were not acquainted with electricity and magnetism; so also would many other experiments in natural philosophy, to those who are not acquainted with the subject. The restoring persons to life who are to appearance dead, as is practised upon drowned persons, would also be a miracle, if it were not known that animation is capable of being suspended without being extinct.

* * *

Though, speaking for myself, I admit the possibility of revelation, I totally disbelieve that the Almighty ever did communicate any thing to man, by any mode of speech, in any language, or by any kind of vision, or appearance, or by any means which our senses are capable of receiving, otherwise than by the universal display of himself in the works of the creation, and by that repugnance we feel in ourselves to bad actions, and disposition to good ones.

The most detestable wickedness, the most horrid cruelties, and the greatest miseries, that have afflicted the human race, have had their origin in this thing called revelation, or revealed religion. It has been the most dishonorable belief against the character of the divinity, the most destructive to morality, and the peace and happiness of man, that ever was propagated since man began to exist.

* * *

What is it we want to know? Does not the creation, the universe we behold, preach to us the existence of an Almighty power, that governs and regulates the whole? And is not the evidence that this creation holds out to our senses infinitely stronger than any thing we can read in a book that any imposter might make and call the word of God? As for morality, the knowledge of it exists in every man's conscience.

Here we are. The existence of an Almighty power is sufficiently demonstrated to us, though we cannot conceive, as it is impossible we should, the nature and manner of its existence. We cannot conceive how we came here ourselves, and yet we know for a fact that we are here. We must know also, that the power that called us into being, can if he please, and when he pleases, call us to account for the manner in which we have lived here; and therefore without seeking any other motive for the belief, it is rational to believe that he will, for we know beforehand that he can. The probability or even possibility of the thing is all that we ought to know; for if we knew it as a fact, we should be the mere slaves of terror; our belief would have no merit, and our best actions no virtue.

Deism then teaches us, without the possibility of being deceived, all that is necessary or proper to be known. The creation is the Bible of the Deist. He there reads, in the hand-writing of the Creator himself, the certainty of his existence, and the immutability of his power; and all other Bibles and Testaments are to him forgeries. The probability that we may be called to account hereafter, will, to reflecting minds, have the influence of belief; for it is not our belief or disbelief that can make or unmake the fact. As this is the state we are in, and which it is proper we should be in, as free agents, it is the fool only, and not the philosopher, nor even the prudent man, that will live as if there were no God . . .

Were a man impressed as fully and strongly as he ought to be with the belief of a God, his moral life would be regulated by the force of belief; he would stand in awe of God and of himself, and would not do the thing that could not be concealed from either. To give this belief the full opportunity of force, it is necessary that it acts alone. This is Deism.

* * *

We can know God only through his works. We cannot have a conception of any one attribute, but by following some principle that leads to it. We have only a confused idea of his power, if we have not the means of comprehending something of its immensity. We can have no idea of his wisdom, but by knowing the order and manner in which it acts. The principles of science lead to this knowledge; for the Creator of man is the Creator of science, and it is through that medium that man can see God, as it were, face to face.

Could a man be placed in a situation, and endowed with power of vision to behold at one view, and to contemplate deliberately, the structure of the universe, to mark the movements of the several planets, the cause of their varying appearances, the unerring order in which they revolve, even to the remotest comet, their connection and dependence on each other, and to know the system of laws established by the Creator, that governs and regulates the whole; he would then conceive, far beyond what any church theology can teach him, the power, the wisdom, the vastness, the munificence of the Creator.

He would then see that all the knowledge man has of science, and that all the mechanical arts by which he renders his situation comfortable here are derived from that source: his mind, exalted by the scene, and convinced by the fact, would increase in gratitude as it increased in knowledge: his religion or his worship would become united with his improvement as a man: any employment he followed that had connection with the principles of the creation,—as everything of agriculture, of science, and of the mechanical arts, has,—would teach him more of God, and of the gratitude he owes to him, than any theological Christian sermon he now hears. Great objects inspire great thoughts; great munificence excites great gratitude; but the grovelling tales and doctrines of the Bible and the Testament are fit only to excite contempt.

Though man cannot arrive, at least in this life, at the actual scene I have described, he can demonstrate it, because he has knowledge of the principles upon which the creation is constructed. We know that the greatest works can be represented in model, and that the universe can be represented by the same means. The same principles by which we measure an inch or an acre of ground will measure to millions in extent. A circle of an inch in diameter has the same geometrical properties as a circle that would circumscribe the universe. The same properties of a triangle that will demonstrate upon paper the course of a ship, will do it on the ocean; and, when applied to what are called the heavenly bodies, will ascertain to a minute the time of an eclipse, though those bodies are millions of miles distant from us.

* * *

Had we, at this day, no knowledge of machinery, and were it possible that man could have a view, as I have before described, of the structure and machinery of the universe he would soon conceive the idea of constructing some at least of the mechanical works we now have; and the idea so conceived would progressively advance in practice. Or could a model of the universe, such as is called an orrery, be presented before him and put in motion, his mind would arrive at the same idea. Such an object and such a subject would, whilst it improved him in knowledge useful to himself as a man and a member of society, as well as entertaining, afford far better matter for impressing him with a knowledge of, and a belief in the Creator, and of the reverence and gratitude that man owes to him, than the stupid texts of the Bible and the Testament, from which, be the talents of the preacher what they may, only stupid sermons can be preached. If man must preach, let him preach something that is edifying, and from the texts that are known to be true.

The Bible of the creation is inexhaustible in texts. Every part of science, whether connected with the geometry of the universe, with the systems of animal and vegetable life, or with the properties of inanimate matter, is a text as well for devotion as for philosophy—for gratitude as for human improvement. It will perhaps be said, that if such a revolution in the system of religion takes place, every preacher ought to be a philosopher. *Most certainly*, and every house of devotion a school of science.

* * *

I leave the ideas that are suggested in the conclusion of the work to rest on the mind of the reader; certain as I am that when opinions are free, either in matters of government or religion, truth will finally and powerfully prevail.

Thomas Paine was seldom out of legal difficulty because of his writings. And the men who helped him and believed in him did so at considerable risk and penalty. A London printer by the name of Daniel I. Eaton published Paine's Examination of the Prophecies. *Eaton's punishment was eighteen months' imprisonment, plus standing in the pillory for one hour each month. Richard Carlile, another English publisher, was fined £1,500 and sentenced to three years imprisonment. In 1797, a suit was brought by the Society for the Suppression of Vice and Immorality against Thomas Williams, a London publisher, for having printed* The Age of Reason. *The prosecutor was Thomas Erskine, articulate and powerful—the same Thomas Erskine who only five years earlier had unsuccessfully defended Paine against the attempt of the English government to suppress* The Rights of Man. *Erskine contended that the king had taken a solemn oath to maintain the Christian religion and that no man had the right not only "to deny its very existence, but to pour forth a shocking and insulting invective." When the judge charged the jury, he used the phrase "malignant purposes" to describe the publication of the book. The jury did not take much time to find Williams guilty. He spent one year in jail.*

Paine wrote an open letter to Thomas Erskine defending his position. The letter was published in Paris. Excerpts follow.

LETTER TO THOMAS ERSKINE, SEPTEMBER, 1797

A bookseller of the name of Williams has been prosecuted in London on a charge of blasphemy for publishing a book entitled "The Age of Reason." Blasphemy is a word of vast sound, but of equivocal and almost of indefinite signification, unless we confine it to the simple idea of hurting or injuring the reputation of any one, which was its original meaning. As a word, it existed before Christianity existed, being a Greek word, or Greek anglicized, as all the etymological dictionaries will show.

But behold how various and contradictory has been the signification and application of this equivocal word: Socrates, who lived more than four hundred years before the Christian era, was convicted of blasphemy for preaching against the belief of a plurality of gods, and for preaching the belief of one god, and was condemned to suffer death by poison: Jesus Christ was convicted of blasphemy under the Jewish law, and was crucified.

Calling Mahomet an imposter would be blasphemy in Turkey; and denying the infallibility of the Pope and the Church would be blasphemy at Rome. What then is to be understood by this word blasphemy? We see that in the case of Socrates truth was condemned as blasphemy. Are we sure that truth is not blasphemy in the present day? Woe however be to those who make it so, whoever they may be.

A book called the Bible has been voted by men, and decreed by human laws, to be the Word of God, and the disbelief of this is called blasphemy.

But if the Bible be not the Word of God, it is the laws and the execution of them that is blasphemy, and not the disbelief. Strange stories are told of the Creator in that book. He is represented as acting under the influence of every human passion, even of the most malignant kind.

If these stories are false we err in believing them to be true, and ought not to believe them. It is therefore a duty which every man owes to himself, and reverentially to his Maker, to ascertain by every possible inquiry whether there be a sufficient evidence to believe them or not.

My own opinion is, decidedly, that the evidence does not warrant the belief, and that we sin in forcing that belief upon ourselves and upon others. In saying this I have no other object in view than truth. But that I may not be accused of resting upon bare assertion, with respect to the equivocal state of the Bible, I will produce an example, and I will not pick and cull the Bible for the purpose.

I will go fairly to the case. I will take the first two chapters of Genesis as they stand, and show from thence the truth of what I say, that is, that the evidence does not warrant the belief that the Bible is the Word of God.

[*In the original pamphlet the first two chapters of Genesis are here quoted in full.*]

These two chapters are called the Mosaic account of the Creation; and we are told, nobody knows by whom, that Moses was instructed by God to write that account.

It has happened that every nation of people has been world-makers; and each makes the world to begin his own way, as if they had all been brought up, as Hudibras says, to the trade. There are hundreds of different opinions and traditions how the world began. My business, however, in this place, is only with those two chapters.

I begin then by saying, that those two chapters, instead of containing, as has been believed, one continued account of the Creation, written by Moses, contain two different and contradictory stories of a creation, made by two different persons, and written in two different styles of expression. The evidence that shows this is so clear, when attended to without prejudice, that did we meet with the same evidence in any Arabic or Chinese account of a creation, we should not hesitate in pronouncing it a forgery.

I proceed to distinguish the two stories from each other.

The first story begins at the first verse of the first chapter and ends at the end of the third verse of the second chapter; for the adverbial conjunction, THUS, with which the second chapter begins (as the reader will see) connects itself to the last verses of the first chapter, and those three verses belong to, and make the conclusion of, the first story.

The second story begins at the fourth verse of the second chapter, and ends with that chapter. Those two stories have been confused into one, by cutting off the last three verses of the first story, and throwing them to the second chapter.

I go now to show that those stories have been written by two different persons.

From the first verse of the first chapter to the end of the third verse of the second chapter, which makes the whole of the first story, the word God is used without any epithet or additional word conjoined with it, as the reader will see: and this style of expression is invariably used throughout the whole of this story, and is repeated no less than thirty-five times, viz: "In the beginning God created the heavens and the earth, and the spirit of God moved on the face of the waters, and God said, let there be light, and God saw the light," etc.

But immediately from the beginning of the fourth verse of the second chapter, where the second story begins, the style of expression is always the *Lord God*, and this style of expression is invariably used to the end of the chapter, and is repeated eleven times; in the one it is always God, and never the *Lord God*, in the other it is always the *Lord God* and never God. The first story contains thirty-four verses, and repeats the single word God thirty-five times.

The second story contains twenty-two verses, and repeats the compound word *Lord God* eleven times; this difference of style, so often repeated, and so uniformly continued, shows that those two chapters, containing two different stories, are written by different persons; it is the same in all the different editions of the Bible, in all the languages I have seen.

Having thus shown, from the difference of style, that those two chapters, divided, as they properly divide themselves, at the end of the third verse of the second chapter, are the work of two different persons, I come to show you, from the contradictory matters they contain, that they cannot be the work of one person, and are two different stories.

It is impossible, unless the writer was a lunatic, without memory, that one and the same person could say, as is said in i. 27, 28, "So God created man in His Own image, in the image of God created He him; male and female created He them; and God blessed them, and God said unto them, be fruitful and multiply, and replenish the earth, and subdue it, and have dominion over the fish of the sea, and over the fowl of the air, and every living thing that moveth on the face of the earth."

It is, I say, impossible that the same person who said this, could afterwards say, as is said in ii. 5, "and there was not a man to till the ground"; and then proceed in verse seven to give another account of the making a man for the first time, and afterwards of the making a woman out of his rib.

Again, one and the same person could not write, as is written in i. 29: "Behold I (God) have given you every herb bearing seed, which is on the face of all the earth; and every tree, in which is the fruit of a tree bearing seed, to you it shall be for meat"; and afterwards say, as is said in the second chapter, that the Lord God planted a tree in the midst of a garden, and forbade man to eat thereof.

Again, one and the same person could not say, "Thus the heavens and the earth were finished, and all the host of them, and on the seventh day God ended all His work which He had made", and immediately after set the Creator to work again, to plant a garden, to make a man and a woman, etc., as done in the second chapter.

Here are evidently two different stories contradicting each other. According to the first, the two sexes, the male and the female, were made at the same time. According to the second, they were made at different times; the man first, and the woman afterwards.

According to the first story, they were to have dominion over all the earth. According to the second, their dominion was limited to a garden. How large a garden it could be that one man and one woman could dress and keep in order, I leave to the prosecutor, the judge, the jury, and Mr. Erskine to determine.

The story of the talking serpent and its tête-à-tête with Eve; the doleful adventure called the *Fall of Man*; and how he was turned out of this fine garden, and how the garden was afterwards locked up and guarded by a flaming sword (if any one can tell what a flaming sword is), belong altogether to the second story. They have no connection with the first story. According to the first there was no garden of Eden; no forbidden tree: the scene was the whole earth, and the fruit of all trees were allowed to be eaten.

In giving this example of the strange state of the Bible, it cannot be said I have gone out of my way to seek it, for I have taken the beginning of the book; nor can it be said I have made more of it than it makes of itself. That there are two stories is as visible to the eye, when attended to, as that there are two chapters, and that they have been written by different persons, nobody knows by whom.

If this then is the strange condition the beginning of the Bible is in it leads to a just suspicion that the other parts are no better, and consequently it becomes every man's duty to examine the case. I have done it for myself, and am satisfied that the Bible is *fabulous*.

Perhaps I shall be told in the cant language of the day, as I have often been told by the Bishop of Llandaff and others, of the great and laudable pains that many pious and learned men have taken to explain the obscure and reconcile the contradictory, or as they say the *seemingly contradictory*, passages of the Bible. It is because the Bible needs such an undertaking, that is one of the first causes to suspect it is *not* the Word of God: this single reflection, when carried home to the mind, is in itself a volume.

What! does not the Creator of the Universe, the Fountain of all Wisdom, the Origin of all Science, the Author of all Knowledge, the God of Order and of Harmony, know how to write? When we contemplate the vast economy of the creation, when we behold the unerring regularity of the visible solar system, the perfection with which all its several parts revolve, and by corresponding assemblage form a whole;—when we launch our eye into the boundless ocean of space, and see ourselves surrounded by innumerable words, not one of which varies from its appointed place—when we trace the power of a creator, from a mite to an elephant, from an atom to an universe—can we suppose that the mind that could conceive such a design, and the power that executed it with incomparable perfection, cannot write without the inconsistence, or that a book so written can be the work of such a power?

The writings of Thomas Paine, even of Thomas Paine, need no commentator to explain, compound, derange and rearrange their several parts, to render them intelligible; he can relate a fact, or write an essay, without forgetting in one page what he has written in another: certainly then, did the God of all perfection condescend to write or dictate a book, that book would be as perfect as Himself is perfect. The Bible is not so, and it is confessedly not so, by the attempts to amend it.

Perhaps I shall be told that though I have produced one instance I cannot produce another of equal force. One is sufficient to call in question the genuineness or authenticity of any book that pretends to be the Word of God; for such a book would, as before said, be as perfect as its author is perfect.

I will, however, advance only four chapters further into the book of Genesis, and produce another example that is sufficient to invalidate the story to which it belongs.

We have all heard of Noah's Flood; and it is impossible to think of the whole human race—men, women, children, and infants, except one family —deliberately drowning, without feeling a painful sensation. That heart must be a heart of flint that can contemplate such a scene with tranquility.

There is nothing of the ancient mythology, nor in the religion of any people we know of upon the globe, that records a sentence of their God, or of their gods, so tremendously severe and merciless. If the story be not true, we blasphemously dishonor God by believing it, and still more so in forcing, by laws and penalties, that belief upon others. I go now to show from the face of the story that it carries the evidence of not being true.

I know not if the judge, the jury, and Mr. Erskine, who tried and convicted Williams, ever read the Bible or know anything of its contents, and therefore I will state the case precisely.

There was no such people as Jews or Israelites in the time that Noah is said to have lived, and consequently there was no such law as that which is called the Jewish or Mosaic law. It is, according to the Bible, more than six hundred years from the time the flood is said to have happened, to the time of Moses, and consequently the time the Flood is said to have happened was more than six hundred years prior to the law, called the Law of Moses, even admitting Moses to have been the giver of that law, of which there is great cause to doubt.

We have here two different epochs, or points of time—that of the Flood, and that of the Law of Moses—the former more than six hundred years prior to the latter. But the maker of the story of the Flood, whoever he was, has betrayed himself by blundering, for he has reversed the order of the times. He has told the story, as if the Law of Moses was prior to the Flood; for he has made God to say to Noah (Gen. vii. 2), "Of every clean beast, thou shalt take unto thee by sevens, a male and his female, and of beasts that are *not clean* by two, the male and his female."

This is the Mosaic law, and could only be said after that law was given, not before. There was no such thing as beasts clean and unclean in the time of Noah. It is nowhere said they were created so. They were only *declared* to be so, *as meats*, by the Mosaic law, and that to the Jews only, and there were no such people as Jews in the time of Noah. This is the blundering condition in which this strange story stands.

When we reflect on a sentence so tremendously severe as that of consigning the whole human race, eight persons excepted, to deliberate drowning; a sentence, which represents the Creator in a more merciless character than any of those whom we call Pagans ever represented the Creator to be, under the figure of any of their deities, we ought at least to suspend our belief of it, on a comparison of the beneficent character of the Creator with the tremendous severity of the sentence; but when we see the story told with such evident contradiction of circumstances, we ought to set it down for nothing better than a Jewish fable told by nobody knows whom and nobody knows when.

It is a relief to the genuine and sensible soul of man to find the story unfounded. It frees us from two painful sensations at once; that of having hard thoughts of the Creator, on account of the severity of the sentence; and that of sympathizing in the horrid tragedy of a drowning world. He who cannot feel the force of what I mean is not, in my estimation, of character worthy the name of a human being. . . .

I am not going in the course of this letter to write a commentary on the Bible. The two instances I have produced, and which are taken from the beginning of the Bible, show the necessity of examining it. It is a book that has been read more, and examined less, than any book that ever existed.

Had it come to us as an Arabic or Chinese book, and said to have been a sacred book by the people from whom it came, no apology would have been made for the confused and disorderly state it is in. The tales it relates of the Creator would have been censured, and our pity excited for those who believed them. We should have vindicated the goodness of God against such a book, and preached up the disbelief of it out of reverence to Him. . . .

For my own part, my belief in the perfection of the Deity will not permit me to believe that a book so manifestly obscure, disorderly, and contradictory can be His work. I can write a better book myself. This belief in me proceeds from my belief in the Creator. I cannot pin my faith upon the *say so* of Hilkiah the priest, who said he found it, or any part of it, nor upon Shaphan the scribe, nor upon any priest nor any scribe, or man of the law of the present day.

As to acts of Parliament, there are some that say there are witches and wizards; and the persons who made those acts (it was in the time of James I) made also some acts which call the Bible the Holy Scriptures, or Word of God. But acts of Parliament decide nothing with respect to God; and as these acts of Parliament makers were wrong with respect to witches and wizards, they may also be wrong with respect to the book in question.

It is therefore necessary that the book be examined; it is our duty to examine it; and to suppress the right of examination is sinful in any government, or in any judge or jury. The Bible makes God to say to Moses, Deut. vii. 2, "And when the Lord thy God shall deliver them before thee, thou shalt smite them, and utterly destroy them, thou shalt make no covenant with them, *nor show mercy unto them.*"

Not all the priests, nor scribes, nor tribunals in the world, nor all the authority of man, shall make me believe that God ever gave such a *Robespierrian precept* as that of showing *no mercy*; and consequently it is impossible that I, or any person who believes as reverentially of the Creator as I do, can believe such a book to be the Word of God.

There have been, and still are, those, who while they *profess* to believe the Bible to be the Word of God, affect to turn it into ridicule. Taking their profession and conduct together, they act blasphemously; because they act as if *God Himself* was not to be believed. The case is exceedingly different with respect to "The Age of Reason." That book is written to show, from the Bible itself, that there is abundant matter to suspect it is not the Word of God, and that we have been imposed upon, first by Jews, and afterwards by priests and commentators.

Not one of those who have attempted to write answers to "The Age of Reason," have taken the ground upon which only an answer could be written. The case in question is not upon any point of doctrine, but altogether upon a matter of fact. Is the book called the Bible the Word of God, or is it not? If it can be proved to be so, it ought to be believed as such; if not, it ought not to be believed as such. This is the true state of the case. "The Age of Reason" produces evidence to show, and I have in this letter produced additional evidence, that it is *not* the Word of God. Those who take the contrary side, should prove that it is. But this they have not done, nor attempted to do, and consequently they have done nothing to the purpose. . . .

The prosecution against Williams charges him with publishing a book, entitled "The Age of Reason," which, it says, is an impious, blasphemous pamphlet, tending to ridicule and bring into contempt the Holy Scriptures. Nothing is more easy than to find abusive words, and English prosecutions are famous for this species of vulgarity.

The charge however is sophistical; for the charge, as growing out of the pamphlet should have stated, not as it now states, to ridicule and bring into contempt the Holy Scriptures, but to show that the book called the Holy Scriptures are not the Holy Scriptures. It is one thing if I ridicule a work as being written by a certain person; but it is quite a different thing if I write to prove that such work was not written by such person.

In the first case, I attack the person through the work; in the other case, I defend the honor of the person against the work. That is what "The Age of Reason" does, and consequently the charge in the indictment is sophistically stated. Every one will admit, that if the Bible be *not* the Word of God we err in believing it to be His word, and ought not to believe it. Certainly then, the ground the prosecution should take would be to prove that the Bible is in fact what it is called. But this the prosecution has not done, and cannot do.

In all cases the prior fact must be proved before the subsequent facts can be admitted in evidence. In a prosecution for adultery, the fact of marriage, which is the prior fact, must be proved, before the facts to prove adultery can be received. If the fact of marriage cannot be proved, adultery cannot be proved; and if the prosecution cannot prove the Bible to be the Word of God, the charge of blasphemy is visionary and groundless.

In Turkey they might prove, if the case happened, that a certain book was bought of a certain bookseller, and that the said book was written against the Koran. In Spain and Portugal they might prove that a certain book was bought of a certain bookseller, and that the said book was written against the infallibility of the Pope.

Under the ancient mythology they might have proved that a certain writing was bought of a certain person, and that the said writing was written against the belief of a plurality of gods, and in the support of the belief of one god: Socrates was condemned for a work of this kind.

All these are but subsequent facts, and amount to nothing, unless the prior facts be proved. The prior fact, with respect to the first case is, Is the *Koran* the Word of God? With respect to the second, Is the infallibility of the Pope a truth? With respect to the third, Is the belief of a plurality of gods a true belief? And in like manner with respect to the present prosecution, Is the book called the *Bible* the Word of God?

If the present prosecution prove no more than could be proved in any or all of these cases, it proves only as they do, or as an inquisition would prove; and in this view of the case, the prosecutors ought to at least leave off reviling that infernal institution, the Inquisition.

The prosecution, however, though it may injure the individual, may promote the cause of truth; because the manner in which it has been conducted appears a confession to the world that there is no evidence to prove that the *Bible* is the Word of God. On what authority then do we believe the many strange stories that the Bible tells of God? . . .

The law that instituted special juries, makes it necessary that the jurors be *merchants*, or of the degree of *squires*. A special jury in London is generally composed of merchants; and in the country, of men called country squires, that is, fox-hunters, or men qualified to hunt foxes. The one may decide very well upon a case of pounds, shillings and pence, or of the counting-house: and the other of the jockey-club or the chase. But who would not laugh, that because such men can decide such cases they can also be jurors upon theology.

Talk with some London merchants about Scripture, and they will understand you mean *scrip*, and tell you how much it is worth at the Stock Exchange. Ask them about theology and they will say they know of no such gentleman upon 'Change. Tell some country squires of the sun and moon standing still, the one on the top of a hill, the other in a valley, and they will swear it is a lie of one's own making.

Tell them that God Almighty ordered a man to make a cake and bake it with a t—d and eat it, and they will say it is one of Dean Swift's blackguard stories. Tell them it is in the Bible and they will lay a bowl of punch it is not, and leave it to the parson of the parish to decide. Ask *them* also about theology and they will say they know of no such a one on the turf.

An appeal to such juries serves to bring the Bible into more ridicule than anything the author of "The Age of Reason" has written; and the manner in which the trial has been conducted shows that the prosecutor dares not come to the point, nor meet the defense of the defendant. But all other cases apart, on what grounds of right, otherwise than on the right assumed by an inquisition, do such prosecutions stand?

Religion is a private affair between every man and his Maker, and no tribunal or third party has a right to interfere between them. It is not properly a thing of this world; it is only practised in this world; but its object is in a future world; and it is not otherwise an object of just laws than for the purpose of protecting the equal rights of all, however various their belief may be.

If one man choose to believe the book called the Bible to be the Word of God, and another, from the convinced idea of the purity and perfection of God compared with the contradictions the book contains—from the lasciviousness of some of its stories, like that of Lot getting drunk and debauching his two daughters, which is not spoken of as a crime, and for which the most absurd apologies are made—from the immorality of some of its precepts, like that of showing no mercy—and from the total want of evidence on the case—thinks he ought not to believe it to be the Word of God, each of them has an equal right; and if the one has a right to give his reasons for believing it to be so, the other has an equal right to give his reasons for believing the *contrary*.

Anything that goes beyond this rule is an inquisition. Mr. Erskine talks of his moral education: Mr. Erskine is very little acquainted with theological subjects, if he does not know there is such a thing as a *sincere* and *religious* belief that the Bible is not the Word of God. This is my belief; it is the belief of thousands far more learned than Mr. Erskine; and it is a belief that is every day increasing. It is not infidelity, as Mr. Erskine profanely and abusively calls it; it is the direct reverse of infidelity. It is a pure religious belief, founded on the idea of the perfection of the Creator.

If the Bible be the Word of God it needs not the wretched aid of prosecutions to support it, and you might with as much propriety make a law to protect the sunshine as to protect the Bible. Is the Bible like the sun, or the work of God? We see that God takes good care of the creation He has made. He suffers no part of it to be extinguished: and He will take the same care of His word, if he ever gave *one*.

But men ought to be reverentially careful and suspicious how they ascribe books to Him as His *word*, which from this confused condition would dishonor a common scribbler, and against which there is abundant evidence, and every cause to suspect imposition. Leave the Bible to itself. God will take care of it if He has anything to do with it, as He takes care of the sun and the moon, which need not your laws for their better protection. . . .

I shall not add more upon that subject; but in order to show Mr. Erskine that there are religious establishments for public worship which make no profession of faith of the books called Holy Scriptures, nor admit of priests, I will conclude with an account of a society lately begun in Paris, and which is very rapidly extending itself.

The society takes the name of Théophilantropes, which would be rendered in English by the word Theophilanthropists, a word compounded of three Greek words, signifying God, Love, and Man. The explanation given to this word is lovers of God and man, or adorers of God and friends of man, *adorateurs de Dieu et amis des hommes*. The society proposes to publish each year a volume, entitled *Année Religieuse des Théophilantropes*, Year Religious of the Theophilanthropists. The first volume is just published, entitled: Religious Year of the Theophilanthropists: or Adorers of God and Friends of Man.

Being a collection of the discourses, lectures, hymns and canticles, for all the religious and moral festivals of the Theophilanthropists during the course of the year, whether in their public temples or in their private families, published by the author of the "Manual of the Theophilanthropists."

The volume of this year, which is the first, contains two hundred and fourteen pages of *duodecimo*. The following is the table of contents:

1. Precise history of the Theophilanthropists.
2. Exercises common to all the festivals.
3. Hymn, No. 1, God of whom the universe speaks.
4. Discourse upon the existence of God.
5. Ode, II. The heavens instruct the earth.
6. Precepts of wisdom, extracted from the book of the Adorateurs.
7. Canticle, No. III. God Creator, soul of nature.
8. Extracts from divers moralists, upon the nature of God, and upon the physical proofs of His existence.
9. Canticle, No. IV. Let us bless at our waking the God who gave us light.
10. Moral thoughts extracted from the Bible.
11. Hymn, No. V. Father of the universe.
12. Contemplation of nature on the first days of the spring.
13. Ode, No. VI. Lord in Thy glory adorable.
14. Extracts from the moral thoughts of Confucius.
15. Canticle in praise of actions, and thanks for the works of the creation.

16. Continuation from the moral thoughts of Confucius.
17. Hymn, No. VII. All the universe is full of Thy magnificance.
18. Extracts from the ancient sage of India upon the duties of families.
19. Upon the spring.
20. Thoughts moral of divers Chinese authors.
21. Canticle, No. VIII. Everything celebrates the glory of the Eternal.
22. Continuation of the moral thoughts of Chinese authors.
23. Invocation for the country.
24. Extracts from the moral thoughts of Theognis.
25. Invocation Creator of man.
26. Ode, No. IX. Upon death.
27. Extracts from the book of the Moral Universal, upon happiness.
28. Ode, No. X. Supreme Author of nature..

INTRODUCTION

ENTITLED

PRECISE HISTORY OF THE THEOPHILANTHROPISTS

"Toward the month of Véndemiaire, of the year 5 (September, 1796) there appeared at Paris, a small work entitled 'Manual of the Théoantropophiles,' since called, for the sake of easier pronounciation, Théophilantropes (Theophilanthropists), published by C_____.

"The worship set forth in this manual, of which the origin is from the beginning of the world, was then professed by some families in the silence of domestic life. But no sooner was the manual published than some persons, respectable for their knowledge and their manners, saw in the formation of a society open to the public an easy method of spreading moral religion and of leading by degrees great numbers to the knowledge thereof, who appear to have forgotten it. This consideration ought of itself not to leave indifferent those persons who know that morality and religion, which is the most solid support thereof, are necessary to the maintenance of society, as well as to the happiness of the individual. These considerations determined the families of the Theophilanthropists to unite publicly for the exercise of their worship.

"The first society of this kind opened in the month of Nivose, year 5 (January, 1797), in the Street Denis, No. 34, corner of Lombard Street. The care of conducting this society was undertaken by five fathers of families. They adopted the manual of the Theophilanthropists.

"They agreed to hold their days of public worship on the days corresponding to Sundays, but without making this a hindrance to other societies to choose such other day as they thought more convenient. Soon after this, more societies were opened, of which some celebrate on the *decadi* (tenth day), and others on the Sunday.

"It was also resolved that the committee should meet one hour each week for the purpose of preparing or examining the discourses and lectures proposed for the next general assembly; that the general assemblies should be called fêtes (festivals) religious and moral; that those festivals should be conducted in principle and form, in a manner as not to be considered as the festivals of an exclusive worship; and that in recalling those who might not be attached to any particular worship, those festivals might also be attended as moral exercises by disciples of every sect, and consequently avoid, by scrupulous care, everything that might make the society appear under the name of a sect.

"The Society adopts neither *rites* nor *priesthood*, and it will never lose sight of the resolution not to advance anything, as a society, inconvenient to any sect or sects, in any time or country, and under any government.

"It will be seen, that it is so much the more easy for the Society to keep within this circle, because that the dogmas of the Theophilanthropists are those upon which all the sects have agreed, that their moral is that upon which there has never been the least dissent; and that the name they have taken expresses the double end of all the sects, that of leading to the *adoration of God and love of man.*

"The Theophilanthropists do not call themselves the disciples of such or such a man. They avail themselves of the wise precepts that have been transmitted by writers of all countries and in all ages.

"The reader will find in the discourses, lectures, hymns and canticles, which the Theophilanthropists have adopted for their religious and moral festivals, and which they present under the title of *Année Religieuse*, extracts from moralists, ancient and modern, divested of maxims too severe or too loosely conceived, or contrary to piety, whether toward God or toward man."

*   *   *

Next follow the dogmas of the Theophilanthropists, or things they profess to believe. These are but two, and are thus expressed, *les Théophilantropes croient à l'existence de Dieu, et à l'immortalité de l'âme*: the Theophilanthropists believe in the existence of God, and the immortality of the soul.

The manual of the Theophilanthropists, a small volume of sixty pages, *duodecimo*, is published separately, as is also their catechism, which is of the same size. The principles of the Theophilanthropists are the same as those published in the first part of "The Age of Reason" in 1793, and in the second part, in 1795. The Theophilanthropists, as a society, are silent upon all the things they do not profess to believe, as the *sacredness* of the books called the Bible. etc.

They profess the immortality of the soul, but they are silent on the immortality of the body, or that which the Church of England calls the resurrection. The author of "The Age of Reason" gives reasons for everything he *disbelieves*, as well as those he *believes*; and where this cannot be done with safety, the government is a despotism and the Church an inquisition.

It is more than three years since the first part of "The Age of Reason" was published, and more than a year and a half since the publication of the second part: the Bishop of Llandaff undertook to write an answer to the second part; and it was not until after it was known that the author of "The Age of Reason" would reply to the Bishop, that the prosecution against the book was set on foot; and which is said to be carried on by some clergy of the English Church.

If the Bishop is one of them, and the object be to prevent an exposure of the numerous and gross errors he has committed in his work (and which he wrote when report said that Thomas Paine was dead), it is a confession that he feels the weakness of his cause, and finds himself unable to maintain it. In this case he has given me a triumph I did not seek, and Mr. Erskine, the herald of the prosecution, has proclaimed it.

The same year in which Thomas Williams was sent to prison for printing The Age of Reason, *which the prosecutor denounced as blasphemous, Thomas Paine started a movement in Paris to combat atheism. In the following address to the Paris Society of Theophilanthropists, of which he was one of the founders, Paine argued with the same intense feelings against the atheistic concept of the universe as he did against revelation. He felt that atheism was the product of a severe reaction to orthodoxy.*

THE EXISTENCE OF GOD, 1797

Religion has two principal enemies, fanaticism and infidelity, or that which is called atheism. The first requires to be combated by reason and morality, the other by natural philosophy.

The existence of a God is the first dogma of the Theophilanthropists. It is upon this subject that I solicit your attention; for though it has been often treated of, and that most sublimely, the subject is inexhaustible; and there will always remain something to be said that has not been before advanced. I go therefore to open the subject, and to crave your attention to the end.

The universe is the bible of a true Theophilanthropist. It is there that he reads of God. It is there that the proofs of His existence are to be sought and to be found. As to written or printed books, by whatever name they are called, they are the works of man's hands, and carry no evidence in themselves that God is the Author of any of them. It must be in something that man could not make that we must seek evidence for our belief, and that something is the universe, the true Bible—the inimitable work of God.

Contemplating the universe, the whole system of Creation, in this point of light, we shall discover, that all that which is called natural philosophy is properly a divine study. It is the study of God through His works. It is the best study, by which we can arrive at a knowledge of His existence, and the only one by which we can gain a glimpse of His perfection.

Do we want to contemplate His power? We see it in the immensity of the creation. Do we want to contemplate His wisdom? We see it in the unchangeable order by which the incomprehensible WHOLE is governed. Do we want to contemplate His munificence? We see it in the abundance with which He fills the earth. Do we want to contemplate His mercy? We see it in His not withholding that abundance even from the unthankful. In fine, do we want to know what GOD is? Search not written or printed books, but the Scripture called the *creation*.

It has been the error of the schools to teach astronomy and all the other sciences and subjects of natural philosophy as accomplishments only; whereas they should be taught theologically, or with reference to the *Being* who is the Author of them: for all the principles of science are of divine origin. Man cannot make, or invent, or contrive principles; he can only discover them, and he ought to look through the discovery to the Author.

When we examine an extraordinary piece of machinery, an astonishing pile of architecture, a well executed statue, or a highly finished painting where life and action are imitated, and habit only prevents our mistaking a surface of light and shade for cubical solidity, our ideas are naturally led to think of the extensive genius and talents of the artist.

When we study the elements of geometry, we think of Euclid. When we speak of gravitation, we think of Newton. How then is it that when we study the works of God in the creation we stop short, and do not think of GOD? It is from the error of the schools in having taught those subjects as accomplishments only, and thereby separated the study of them from the *Being* who is the Author of them.

The schools have made the study of theology to consist in the study of opinions in written or printed books; whereas theology should be studied in the works or books of the Creation. The study of theology in books of opinions has often produced fanaticism, rancor and cruelty of temper; and from hence have proceeded the numerous persecutions, the fanatical quarrels, the religious burnings and massacres, that have desolated Europe.

But the study of theology in the works of the creation produces a direct contrary effect. The mind becomes at once enlightened and serene, a copy of the scene it beholds: information and adoration go hand in hand; and all the social faculties become enlarged.

The evil that has resulted from the error of the schools in teaching natural philosophy as an accomplishment only has been that of generating in the pupils a species of atheism. Instead of looking through the works of creation to the Creator himself, they stop short and employ the knowledge they acquire to create doubts of His existence. They labor with studied ingenuity to ascribe everything they behold to innate properties of matter, and jump over all the rest by saying that matter is eternal.

Let us examine this subject; it is worth examining; for if we examine it through all its cases, the result will be that the existence of a SUPERIOR CAUSE, or that which man calls GOD, will be discoverable by philosophical principles.

In the first place, admitting matter to have properties, as we see it has, the question still remains, how came matter by those properties? To this they will answer that matter possessed those properties eternally. This is not solution, but assertion; and to deny it is equally as impossible of proof as to assert it.

It is then necessary to go further; and therefore I say—if there exist a circumstance that is *not* a property of matter, and without which the universe, or to speak in a limited degree, the solar system composed of planets and a sun, could not exist a moment, all the arguments of atheism, drawn from properties of matter, and applied to account for the universe, will be overthrown, and the existence of a superior cause, or that which man calls God, becomes discoverable, as is before said, by natural philosophy.

I go now to show that such a circumstance exists, and what it is.

The universe is composed of matter, and, as a system, is sustained by motion. Motion is *not a property* of matter, and without this motion the solar system could not exist. Were motion a property of matter, that undiscovered and undiscoverable thing called perpetual motion would establish itself.

It is because motion is not a property of matter, that perpetual motion is an impossibility in the hand of every being but that of the Creator of motion. When the pretenders to atheism can produce perpetual motion, and not till then, they may expect to be credited.

The natural state of matter, as to place, is a state or rest. Motion, or change of place, is the effect of an external cause acting upon matter. As to that faculty of matter that is called gravitation, it is the influence which two or more bodies have reciprocally on each other to unite and be at rest. Everything which has hitherto been discovered, with respect to the motion of the planets in the system, relates only to the laws by which motion acts, and not to the cause of motion.

Gravitation, so far from being the cause of motion to the planets that compose the solar system, would be the destruction of the solar system, were revolutionary motion to cease; for as the action of spinning upholds a top, the revolutionary motion upholds the planets in their orbits, and prevents them from gravitating and forming one mass with the sun. In one sense of the word, philosophy knows, and atheism says, that matter is in perpetual motion.

But the motion here meant refers to the *state* of matter, and that only on the surface of the earth. It is either decomposition, which is continually destroying the form of bodies of matter, or recomposition, which renews that matter in the same or another form, as the decomposition of animal or vegetable substances enters into the composition of other bodies.

But the motion that upholds the solar system is of an entire different kind, and is not a property of matter. It operates also to an entire different effect. It operates to *perpetual preservation*, and to prevent any change in the state of the system.

Giving then to matter all the properties which philosophy knows it has, or all that atheism ascribes to it, and can prove, and even supposing matter to be eternal, it will not account for the system of the universe, or of the solar system, because it will not account for motion, and it is motion that preserves it.

When, therefore, we discover a circumstance of such immense importance that without it the universe could not exist, and for which neither matter, nor any nor all the properties can account, we are by necessity forced into the rational conformable belief of the existence of a cause superior to matter, and that cause man calls GOD.

As to that which is called nature, it is no other than the laws by which motion and action of every kind, with respect to unintelligible matter, are regulated. And when we speak of looking through nature up to nature's God, we speak philosophically the same rational language as when we speak of looking through human laws up to the Power that ordained them.

God is the power of first cause, nature is the law, and matter is the subject acted upon.

But infidelity, by ascribing every phenomenon to properties of matter, conceives a system for which it cannot account, and yet it pretends to demonstration. It reasons from what it sees on the surface of the earth, but it does not carry itself on the solar system existing by motion.

It sees upon the surface a perpetual decomposition and recomposition of matter. It sees that an oak produces an acorn, an acorn an oak, a bird an egg, an egg a bird, and so on. In things of this kind it sees something which it calls a natural cause, but none of the causes it sees is the cause of that motion which preserves the solar system.

Let us contemplate this wonderful and stupendous system consisting of matter, and existing by motion. It is not matter in a state of rest, nor in a state of decomposition or recomposition. It is matter systemized in perpetual orbicular or circular motion. As a system that motion is the life of it: as animation is life to an animal body, deprive the system of motion and, as a system, it must expire.

Who then breathed into the system the life of motion? What power impelled the planets to move, since motion is not a property of the matter of which they are composed? If we contemplate the immense velocity of this motion, our wonder becomes increased, and our adoration enlarges itself in the same proportion.

To instance only one of the planets, that of the earth we inhabit, its distance from the sun, the center of the orbits of all the planets, is, according to observations of the transit of the planet Venus, about one hundred million miles; consequently, the diameter of the orbit, or circle in which the earth moves round the sun, is double that distance; and the measure of the circumference of the orbit, taken as three times its diameter, is six hundred million miles. The earth performs this voyage in three hundred and sixty-five days and some hours, and consequently moves at the rate of more than one million six hundred thousand miles every twenty-four hours.

Where will infidelity, where will atheism, find cause for this astonishing velocity of motion, never ceasing, never varying, and which is the preservation of the earth in its orbit? It is not by reasoning from an acorn to an oak, from an egg to a bird, or from any change in the state of matter on the surface of the earth, that this can be accounted for.

Its cause it not to be found in matter, nor in anything we call nature. The atheist who affects to reason, and the fanatic who rejects reason, plunge themselves alike into inextricable difficulties.

The one perverts the sublime and enlightening study of natural philosophy into a deformity of absurdities by not reasoning to the end. The other loses himself in the obscurity of metaphysical theories, and dishonors the Creator by treating the study of His works with contempt. The one is a half-rational of whom there is some hope, the other a visionary to whom we must be charitable.

When at first thought we think of a Creator, our ideas appear to us undefined and confused; but if we reason philosophically, those ideas can be easily arranged and simplified. *It is a Being whose power is equal to His will.*

Observe the nature of the will of man. It is of an infinite quality. We cannot conceive the possibility of limits to the will. Observe, on the other hand, how exceedingly limited is his power of acting compared with the nature of his will. Suppose the power equal to the will, and man would be a God. He would will himself eternal, and be so. He could will a creation, and could make it.

In this progressive reasoning, we see in the nature of the will of man half of that which we conceive in thinking of God; add the other half, and we have the whole idea of a Being who could make the universe, and sustain it by perpetual motion; because He could create that motion.

We know nothing of the capacity of the will of animals, but we know a great deal of the difference of their powers. For example, how numerous are the degrees, and how immense is the difference of power, from a mite to a man.

Since then everything we see below us shows a progression of power, where is the difficulty in supposing that there is, at the *summit of all things*, a Being in whom an infinity of power unites with the infinity of the will? When this simple idea presents itself to our mind, we have the idea of a perfect Being that man calls God.

It is comfortable to live under the belief of the existence of an infinite protecting power; and it is an addition to that comfort to know that such a belief is not a mere conceit of the imagination, as many of the theories that are called religious are; nor a belief founded only on tradition or received opinion; but is a belief deducible by the action of reason upon the things that compose the system of the universe; a belief arising out of visible facts. So demonstrable is the truth of this belief that if no such belief had existed, the persons who now controvert it would have been the persons who would have produced and propagated it; because by beginning to reason they would have been led to reason progressively to the end, and thereby have discovered that matter and the properties it has will not account for the system of the universe, and that there must necessarily be a superior cause.

It was the excess to which imaginary systems of religion had been carried, and the intolerance, persecutions, burnings and massacres they occasioned, that first induced certain persons to propagate infidelity; thinking, that upon the whole it was better not to believe at all than to believe a multitude of things and complicated creeds that occasioned so much mischief in the world.

But those days are past, persecution has ceased, and the antidote then set up against it has no longer even the shadow of apology. We profess, and we proclaim in peace, the pure, unmixed, comfortable and rational belief of a God as manifested to us in the universe. We do this without any apprehension of that belief being made a cause of persecution as other beliefs have been, or of suffering persecution ourselves. To God, and not to man, are all men to account for their belief.

It has been well observed, at the first institution of this Society, that the dogmas it professes to believe are from the commencement of the world; that they are not novelties, but are confessedly the basis of all systems of religion, however numerous and contradictory they may be.

All men in the outset of the religion they profess are Theophilanthropists. It is impossible to form any system of religion without building upon those principles, and therefore they are not sectarian principles, unless we suppose a sect composed of all the world.

I have said in the course of this discourse that the study of natural philosophy is a divine study, because it is the study of the works of God in the creation. If we consider theology upon this ground, what an extensive field of improvement in things both divine and human opens itself before us!

All the principles of science are of divine origin. It was not man that invented the principles on which astronomy, and every branch of mathematics, are founded and studied. It was not man that gave properties to the circle and the triangle. Those principles are eternal and immutable.

We see in them the unchangeable nature of the Divinity. We see in them immortality, an immortality existing after the material figures that express those properties are dissolved in dust.

The Society is at present in its infancy, and its means are small; but I wish to hold in view the subject I allude to, and instead of teaching the philosophical branches of learning as ornamental accomplishments only, as they have hitherto been taught, to teach them in a manner that shall combine theological knowledge with scientific instruction.

To do this to the best advantage some instruments will be necessary, for the purpose of explanation, of which the Society is not yet possessed. But as the views of this Society extend to public good as well as to that of the individual, and as its principles can have no enemies, means may be devised to procure them.

If we unite to the present instruction a series of lectures on the ground I have mentioned, we shall, in the first place, render theology the most delightful and entertaining of all studies. In the next place we shall give scientific instruction to those who could not otherwise obtain it. The mechanic of every profession will there be taught the mathematical principles necessary to render him a proficient in his art; the cultivator will there see developed the principles of vegetation; while, at the same time, they will be led to see the hand of God in all these things.

Before Thomas Paine left for America in 1802, he wrote an article called "Dream." It was drawn or adapted from part of The Age of Reason. *The first publication was in Paris in 1803, later being incorporated in his* Examination of the Prophecies. *Herewith an excerpt from "Dream."*

AN ESSAY ON DREAM, 1802

As a great deal is said in the New Testament about dreams, it is first necessary to explain the nature of Dream, and to show by what operation of the mind a dream is produced during sleep. . . .

In order to understand the nature of Dream, or of that which passes in ideal vision during a state of sleep, it is first necessary to understand the composition and decomposition of the human mind.

The three great faculties of the mind are IMAGINATION, JUDGMENT and MEMORY. Every action of the mind comes under one or the other of these faculties. In a state of wakefulness, as in the day-time, these three faculties are all active; but that is seldom the case in sleep, and never perfectly: and this is the cause that our dreams are not so regular and rational as our waking thoughts.

The seat of that collection of powers or faculties that constitute what is called the mind is in the brain. There is not, and cannot be, any visible demonstration of this anatomically, but accidents happening to living persons show it to be so. An injury done to the brain by a fracture of the skull will sometimes change a wise man into a childish idiot—a being without a mind. But so careful has nature been of that *sanctum sanctorum* of man, the brain, that of all the external accidents to which humanity is subject, this occurs the most seldom. But we often see it happening by long and habitual intemperance.

Whether those three faculties occupy distinct apartments of the brain, is known only to that ALMIGHTY POWER that formed and organized it. We can see the external effects of muscular motion in all the members of the body, though its *primum mobile*, or first moving cause, is unknown to man.

Our external motions are sometimes the effect of intention, sometimes not. If we are sitting and intend to rise, or standing and intend to sit or to walk, the limbs obey that intention as if they heard the order given. But we make a thousand motions every day, and that as well waking as sleeping, that have no prior intention to direct them. Each member acts as if it had a will or mind of its own.

Man governs the whole when he pleases to govern, but in the interim the several parts, like little suburbs, govern themselves without consulting the sovereign.

And all these motions, whatever be the generating cause, are external and visible. But with respect to the brain, no ocular observation can be made upon it. All is mystery; all is darkness in that womb of thought.

Whether the brain is a mass of matter in continual rest; whether it has a vibrating, pulsative motion, or a heaving and falling motion like matter in fermentation; whether different parts of the brain have different motions according to the faculty that is employed, be it the imagination, the judgment, or the memory, man knows nothing of. He knows not the cause of his own wit. His own brain conceals it from him.

Comparing invisible by visible things, as metaphysical can sometimes be compared to physical things, the operations of these distinct and several faculties have some resemblance to a watch. The main spring which puts all in motion corresponds to the imagination; the pendulum which corrects and regulates that motion corresponds to the judgment; and the hand and dial, like the memory, record the operation.

Now in proportion as these several faculties sleep, slumber, or keep awake, during the continuance of a dream, in that proportion the dream will be reasonable or frantic, remembered or forgotten.

If there is any faculty in mental man that never sleeps it is that volatile thing the imagination. The case is different with the judgment and memory. The sedate and sober constitution of the judgment easily disposes it to rest; and as to the memory, it records in silence and is active only when it is called upon.

That the judgment soon goes to sleep may be perceived by our sometimes beginning to dream before we are fully asleep ourselves. Some random thought runs in the mind and we start, as it were, into recollection that we are dreaming between sleeping and waking.

If a pendulum of a watch by any accident becomes so displaced that it can no longer control and regulate the elastic force of the spring, the works are instantly thrown into confusion, and continue so as long as the spring continues to have force.

In like manner if the judgment sleeps while the imagination keeps awake, the dream will be a riotous assemblage of misshapen images and ranting ideas, and the more active the imagination is the wilder the dream will be. The most inconsistent and the most impossible things will appear right; because that faculty whose province it is to keep order is in a state of absence. The master of the school is gone out and the boys are in an uproar.

If the memory sleeps, we shall have no other knowledge of the dream than that we have dreamt, without knowing what it was about. In this case it is sensation rather than recollection that acts. The dream has given us some sense of pain or trouble, and we feel it as a hurt, rather than remember it as vision.

If the memory slumbers we shall have a faint remembrance of the dream, and after a few minutes it will sometimes happen that the principal passages of the dream will occur to us more fully. The cause of this is that the memory will sometimes continue slumbering or sleeping after we are awake ourselves, and so fully that it may and sometimes does happen that we do not immediately recollect where we are, nor what we have been about, or have to do. But when the memory starts into wakefulness it brings the knowledge of these things back upon us like a flood of light, and sometimes the dream with it.

But the most curious circumstance of the mind in a state of dream is the power it has to become the agent of every person, character and thing of which it dreams. It carries on conversation with several, asks questions, hears answers, gives and receives information, and it acts all these parts itself.

Yet however various and eccentric the imagination may be in the creating of images and ideas, it cannot supply the place of memory with respect to things that are forgotten when we are awake. For example, if we have forgotten the name of a person, and dream of seeing him and asking him his name, he cannot tell it; for it is ourselves asking ourselves the question.

But though the imagination cannot supply the place of real memory, it has the wild faculty of counterfeiting memory. It dreams of persons it never knew, and talks to them as if it remembered them as old acquaintances. It relates circumstances that never happened, and tells them as if they had happened. It goes to places that never existed, and knows where all the streets and houses are, as if we had been there before. The scenes it creates are often as scenes remembered. It will sometimes act a dream within a dream, and, in the delusion of dreaming, tell a dream it never dreamed, and tell it as if it was from memory.

It may also be remarked, that the imagination in a dream has no idea of time, *as time*. It counts only by circumstances; and if a succession of circumstances pass in a dream that would require a great length of time to accomplish them, it will appear to the dreamer that a length of time equal thereto has passed also.

As this is the state of the mind in a dream, it may rationally be said that every person is mad once in twenty-four hours, for were he to act in the day as he dreams in the night, he would be confined for a lunatic. In a state of wakefulness, those three faculties being all active, and acting in unison, constitute the rational man.

In dream it is otherwise, and, therefore, that state which is called insanity appears to be no other than a dismission of those faculties, and a cessation of the judgment during wakefulness that we so often experience during sleep; and idiocy, into which some persons have fallen, is that cessation of all the faculties of which we can be sensible when we happen to wake before our memory. . . .

Every new religion, like a new play, requires a new apparatus of dresses and machinery, to fit the new characters it creates. The story of Christ in the New Testament brings a new being upon the stage, which it calls the Holy Ghost; and the story of Abraham, the father of the Jews, in the Old Testament, gives existence to a new order of beings it calls angels. There was no Holy Ghost before the time of Christ, nor angels before the time of Abraham.

We hear nothing of these winged gentlemen, till more than two thousand years, according to the Bible chronology, from the time they say the heavens, the earth and all therein were made. After this, they hop about as thick as birds in a grove. The first we hear of pays his addresses to Hagar in the wilderness; then three of them visit Sarah; another wrestles a fall with Jacob; and these birds of passage having found their way to earth and back, are continually coming and going. They eat and drink, and up again to heaven.

What they do with the food they carry away in their bellies, the Bible does not tell us. Perhaps they do as the birds do, discharge it as they fly; for neither the Scripture nor the Church hath told us there are necessary houses for them in heaven. One would think that a system loaded with such gross and vulgar absurdities as Scripture religion is could never have obtained credit; yet we have seen what priestcraft and fanaticism could do, and credulity believe.

From angels in the Old Testament we get to prophets, to witches, to seers of visions, and dreamers of dreams; and sometimes we are told, as in I Samuel ix, 15, that God whispers in the ear. At other times we are not told, how the impulse was given, or whether sleeping or waking. In II Samuel xxiv, I, it is said, "*And again the anger of the Lord was kindled against Israel, and he moved David against them to say, Go number Israel and Judah.*" And in I Chronicles xxi, I, when the same story is again related, it is said, "*And Satan stood up against Israel, and moved David to number Israel.*"

Whether this was done sleeping or waking, we are not told, but it seems that David, whom they call "a man after God's own heart," did not know by what spirit he was moved; and as to the men called inspired penmen, they agree so well about the matter that in one book they say it was God, and in the other that it was the devil. . . .

The God of eternity and of all that is real, is not the god of passing dreams and shadows of man's imagination. The God of truth is not the god of fable; the belief of a god begotten and a god crucified, is a god blasphemed. It is making a profane use of reason.

I shall conclude this Essay on Dream with the first two verses of Ecclesiasticus xxxiv, one of the books of the Aprocrypha. "*The hopes of a man void of understanding are vain and false; and dreams lift up fools. Whoso regardeth dreams is like him that catcheth at a shadow and followeth after the wind."*

New York City has always had its intellectual circles. At the turn of the nineteenth century it went by the name of the "Columbian Illuminati." The leader of the group at this time was Elihu Palmer, a former divinity student who became a rationalist lecturer and writer. Palmer began a new journal in 1804 called The Prospect, which ran severely analytical examinations of established religion. Paine contributed several papers to The Prospect, excerpts from which follow.

PROSPECT PAPERS, 1804

OF THE WORD "RELIGION," AND OTHER WORDS OF UNCERTAIN SIGNIFICATION

The word *religion* is a word of forced application when used with respect to the worship of God. The root of the word is the Latin verb *ligo*, to tie or bind. From *ligo*, comes *religo*, to tie or bind over again, to make more fast— from *religo*, comes the substantive *religio*, which, with the addition of *n* makes the English substantive *religion*.

The French use the word properly: when a woman enters a convent she is called a *novitiate*, that is, she is upon trial or probation. When she takes the oath, she is called a *religieuse*, that is, she is tied or bound by that oath to the performance of it. We use the word in the same kind of sense when we say we will religiously perform the promise that we make.

But the word, without referring to its etymology, has, in the manner it is used, no definite meaning, because it does not designate what religion a man is of. There is the religion of the Chinese, of the Tartars, of the Brahmins, of the Persians, of the Jews, of the Turks, etc.

The word Christianity is equally as vague as the word religion. No two sectaries can agree what it is. It is *lo here* and *lo there*. The two principal sectaries, Papists and Protestants, have often cut each other's throats about it.

The Papists call the Protestants heretics, and the Protestants call the Papists idolators. The minor sectaries have shown the same spirit of rancor, but as the civil law restrains them from blood, they content themselves with preaching damnation against each other.

The word *protestant* has a positive signification in the sense it is used. It means protesting against the authority of the Pope, and this is the only article in which the Protestants agree. In every other sense, with respect to religion, the word protestant is as vague as the word Christian.

When we say an Episcopalian, a Presbyterian, a Baptist, a Quaker, we know what those persons are, and what tenets they hold; but when we say a "Christian," we know he is not a Jew nor a Mahometan, but we know not if he be a trinitarian or an anti-trinitarian, a believer in what is called the immaculate conception, or a disbeliever, a man of seven sacraments, or of two sacraments, or of none. The word "Christian" describes what a man is not, but not what he is.

The word *theology*, from *Theos*, the Greek word for God, and meaning the study and knowledge of God, is a word that strictly speaking belongs to Theists or Deists, and not to the Christians. The head of the Christian Church is the person called Christ, but the head of the Church of the Theists, or Deists, as they are more commonly called (from *Deus*, the Latin word for God), is God Himself; and therefore the word "Theology" belongs to that Church which has Theos or God for its head, and not to the Christian Church which has the person called Christ for its head. Their technical word is *Christianity*, and they cannot agree on what Christianity is.

The words *revealed religion* and *natural religion* also require explanation. They are both invented terms, contrived by the Church for the support of its priestcraft. With respect to the first, there is no evidence of any such thing, except in the universal revelation that God has made of His power, His wisdom, His goodness, in the structure of the universe, and in all the works of creation.

We have no cause for ground from anything we behold in those works to suppose God would deal partially by mankind, and reveal knowledge to one nation and withhold it from another, and then damn them for not knowing it. The sun shines an equal quantity of light all over the world— and mankind in all ages and countries are endued with reason, and blessed with sight, to read the visible works of God in the creation, and so intelligent is the book that *he that runs may read*.

We admire the wisdom of the ancients, yet they had no Bibles nor books called "revelation." They cultivated the reason that God gave them, studied Him in His works, and arose to eminence.

As to the Bible, whether true or fabulous, it is a history, and history is not a revelation. If Solomon had seven hundred wives, and three hundred concubines, and if Samson slept in Delilah's lap, and she cut his hair off, the relation of those things is mere history that needed no revelation from heaven to tell it; neither does it need any revelation to tell us that Samson was a fool for his pains, and Solomon too.

As to the expressions so often used in the Bible, that *the word of the Lord* came to such an one, or such an one, it was the fashion of speaking in those times, like the expression used by a Quaker, that the *spirit moveth him*, or that used by priests, that they *have a call*. We ought not to be deceived by phrases because they are ancient. But if we admit the supposition that God would condescend to reveal Himself in words, we ought not to believe it would be in such idle and profligate stories as are in the Bible; and it is for this reason, among others which our reverence to God inspires, that the Deists deny that the book called the Bible is the Word of God, or that it is revealed religion.

With respect to the term *natural religion*, it is upon the face of it, the opposite of artificial religion, and it is impossible for any man to be certain that what is called *revealed religion* is not artificial.

Man has the power of making books, inventing stories of God, and calling them revelation, or the Word of God. The Koran exists as an instance that this can be done, and we must be credulous indeed to suppose that this is the only instance and Mahomet the only imposter. The Jews could match him, and the Church of Rome could overmatch the Jews. The Mahometans believe the Koran, the Christians believe the Bible, and it is education makes all the difference.

Books, whether Bibles or Korans, carry no evidence of being the work of any other power than man. It is only that which man cannot do that carries the evidence of being the work of a superior power. Man could not invent and make a universe—he could not invent nature, for nature is of divine origin. It is the laws by which the universe is governed.

When, therefore, we look through nature up to nature's God, we are in the right road of happiness, but when we trust to books as the Word of God, and confide in them as revealed religion, we are afloat on the ocean of uncertainty, and shatter into contending factions. The term, therefore, *natural religion*, explains itself to be *divine religion*, and the term *revealed religion* involves in it the suspicion of being *artificial*.

To show the necessity of understanding the meaning of words, I will mention an instance of a minister, I believe of the Episcopalian Church of Newark, in [New] Jersey. He wrote and published a book, and entitled it "An Antidote to Deism." An antidote to *Deism* must be *Atheism*. It has no other antidote—for what can be an antidote to the belief of a God, but the disbelief of God? Under the tuition of such pastors, what but ignorance and false information can be expected?

OF THE RELIGION OF DEISM COMPARED WITH THE CHRISTIAN RELIGION, AND THE SUPERIORITY OF THE FORMER OVER THE LATTER

Every person, of whatever religious denomination he may be, is a Deist in the first article of his Creed. Deism, from the Latin word *Deus*, God, is the belief of a God, and this belief is the first article of every man's creed.

It is on this article, universally consented to by all mankind, that the Deist builds his church, and here he rests. Whenever we step aside from this article, by mixing it with articles of human invention, we wander into a labyrinth of uncertainty and fable, and become exposed to every kind of imposition by pretenders to revelation.

The Persian shows the Zend-Avesta of Zoroaster, the lawgiver of Persia, and calls it the divine law; the Brahmin shows the *Shaster*, revealed, he says, by God to Brahma, and given to him out of a cloud; the Jew shows what he calls the Law of Moses, given, he says, by God, on the Mount Sinai; the Christian shows a collection of books and epistles, written by nobody knows who, and called the New Testament; and the Mahometan shows the Koran, given, he says, by God to Mahomet: each of these calls itself *revealed religion*, and the *only* true Word of God, and this the followers of each profess to believe from the habit of education, and each believes the others are imposed upon.

But when the divine gift of reason begins to expand itself in the mind and calls man to reflection, he then reads and contemplates God and His works, and not in the books pretending to be revelation. The creation is the Bible of the true believer in God. Everything in this vast volume inspires him with sublime ideas of the Creator. The little and paltry, and often obscene, tales of the Bible sink into wretchedness when put in comparison with this mighty work.

The Deist needs none of those tricks and shows called miracles to confirm his faith, for what can be a greater miracle than the creation itself and his own existence?

There is a happiness in Deism, when rightly understood, that is not to be found in any other system of religion. All other systems have something in them that either shock our reason, or are repugnant to it, and man, if he thinks at all, must stifle his reason in order to force himself to believe them.

But in Deism our reason and our belief become happily united. The wonderful structure of the universe, and everything we behold in the system of creation, prove to us, far better than books can do, the existence of a God, and at the same time proclaim His attributes.

It is by the exercise of our reason that we are enabled to contemplate God in His works, and imitate Him in His way. When we see His care and goodness extended over all His creatures, it teaches us our duty toward each other, while it calls forth our gratitude to Him. It is by forgetting God in His works, and running after the books of pretended revelation, that man has wandered from the straight path of duty and happiness, and become by turns the victim of doubt and the dupe of delusion.

OF THE SABBATH-DAY IN CONNECTICUT

The word Sabbath, means REST; that is, cessation from labor, but the stupid Blue Laws[2] of Connecticut make a labor of rest, for they oblige a person to sit still from sunrise to sunset on a Sabbath-day, which is hard work. Fanaticism made those laws, and hypocrisy pretends to reverence them, for where such laws prevail hypocrisy will prevail also.

One of those laws says, "No person shall run on a Sabbath-day, nor walk in his garden, nor elsewhere; but reverently to and from meeting." These fanatical hypocrites forgot that God dwells not in temples made with hands, and that the earth is full of His glory.

One of the finest scenes and subjects of religious contemplation is to walk into the woods and fields, and survey the works of the God of the Creation. The wide expanse of heaven, the earth covered with verdure, the lofty forest, the waving corn, the magnificent roll of mighty rivers, and the murmuring melody of the cheerful brooks, are scenes that inspire the mind with gratitude and delight.

But this the gloomy Calvinist of Connecticut must not behold on a Sabbath-day. Entombed within the walls of his dwelling, he shuts from his view the Temple of Creation. The sun shines no joy to him. The gladdening voice of nature calls on him in vain. He is deaf, dumb and blind to everything around that God has made. Such is the Sabbath-day in Connecticut.

From whence could come this miserable notion of devotion? It comes from the gloominess of the Calvinistic creed. If men love darkness rather than light, because their works are evil, the ulcerated mind of a Calvinist, who sees God only in terror, and sits brooding over the scenes of hell and damnation, can have no joy in beholding the glories of the creation. Nothing in that mighty and wondrous system accords with his principles or his devotion.

He sees nothing there that tells him that God created millions on purpose to be damned, and that the children of a span long are born to burn forever in hell. The creation preaches a different doctrine to this. We there see that the care and goodness of God is extended impartially over all the creatures He has made. The worm of the earth shares His protection equally with the elephant of the desert. The grass that springs beneath our feet grows by His bounty as well as the cedars of Lebanon.

Everything in the creation reproaches the Calvinist with unjust ideas of God, and disowns the hardness and ingratitude of his principles. Therefore he shuns the sight of them on a Sabbath-day.

---

[2] Called Blue Laws because they were originally printed on blue paper.

HINTS TOWARD FORMING A SOCIETY FOR INQUIRING INTO THE TRUTH OR
FALSEHOOD OF ANCIENT HISTORY, SO FAR AS HISTORY IS CONNECTED WITH
SYSTEMS OF RELIGION ANCIENT AND MODERN

It has been customary to class history into three divisions, distinguished by
the names of Sacred, Profane and Ecclesiastical. By the first is meant the
Bible; by the second, the history of nations, of men and things; and by the
third, the history of the church and its priesthood.

Nothing is more easy than to give names, and, therefore, mere names
signify nothing unless they lead to the discovery of some cause for which
that name was given. For example, *Sunday* is the name given to the first day
of the week, in the English language, and it is the same in the Latin, that is,
it has the same meaning (*Dies solis*), and also in the German and also
in several other languages.

Why then was this name given to that day? Because it was the day dedicated by the ancient world to the luminary which in the English we call the
Sun, and therefore the day *Sun-day*, or the day of the Sun; as in the like
manner we call the second day Monday, the day dedicated to the Moon.

Here the name *Sunday* leads to the cause of its being called so, and we
have visible evidence of the fact, because we behold the Sun from whence
the name comes; but this is not the case when we distinguish one part of
history from another by the name of *Sacred*.

All histories have been written by men. We have no evidence, nor any
cause to believe, that any have been written by God. That part of the Bible
called the Old Testament, is the history of the Jewish nation, from the time
of Abraham, which begins in Genesis xi, to the downfall of that nation by
Nebuchadnezzar, and is no more entitled to be called sacred than any other
history. It is altogether the contrivance of priestcraft that has given it that
name. So far from its being *sacred*, it has not the appearance of being true
in many of the things it relates.

It must be better authority than a book which any imposter might make, as
Mahomet made the Koran, to make a thoughtful man believe that the sun
and moon stood still, or that Moses and Aaron turned the Nile, which is
larger than the Delaware, into blood; and that the Egyptian magicians did
the same. These things have too much the appearance of romance to be
believed for fact.

It would be of use to inquire, and ascertain the time, when that part of the
Bible called the Old Testament first appeared. From all that can be collected
there was no such book till after the Jews returned from captivity in Babylon,
and that is the work of the Pharisees of the Second Temple. How they came
to make Kings xix and Isaiah xxxvii word for word alike, can only be ac-

counted for by their having no plan to go by, and not knowing what they were about.

The same is the case with respect to the last verses in II Chronicles, and the first verses in Ezra; they also are word for word alike, which shows that the Bible has been put together at random.

But besides these things there is great reason to believe we have been imposed upon with respect to the antiquity of the Bible, and especially with respect to the books ascribed to Moses. Herodotus, who is called the father of history, and is the most ancient historian whose works have reached to our time, and who traveled into Egypt, conversed with the priests, historians, astronomers and learned men of that country, for the purpose of obtaining all the information of it he could, and who gives an account of the ancient state of it, makes no mention of such a man as Moses, though the Bible makes him to have been the greatest hero there, nor of any one circumstance mentioned in the book of Exodus respecting Egypt, such as turning the rivers into blood, the dust into lice, the death of the first born throughout all the land of Egypt, the passage of the Red Sea, the drowning of Pharaoh and all his host, things which could not have been a secret in Egypt, and must have been generally known, had they been facts; and, therefore, as no such things were known in Egypt, nor any such man as Moses at the time Herodotus was there, which is about 2,200 years ago, it shows that the account of these things in the books ascribed to Moses is a made story of later times; that is, after the return of the Jews from the Babylonian captivity, and that Moses is not the author of the books ascribed to him.

With respect to the cosmogony, or account of the Creation, in Genesis i, of the Garden of Eden in chapter ii, and of what is called the Fall of Man in chapter iii, there is something concerning them we are not historically acquainted with. In none of the books of the Bible, after Genesis, are any of these things mentioned or even alluded to.

How is this to be accounted for? The obvious inference is that either they were not known, or not believed to be facts, by the writers of the other books of the Bible, and that Moses is not the author of the chapters where these accounts are given.

The next question on the case is how did the Jews come by these notions, and at what time were they written? To answer this question we must first consider what the state of the world was at the time the Jews began to be a people, for the Jews are but a modern race compared with the antiquity of other nations.

At the time there were, even by their own account, but thirteen Jews or Israelites in the world, *Jacob and his twelve sons*, and four of these were bastards, the nations of Egypt, Chaldea, Persia and India, were great and populous, abounding in learning and science, particularly in the knowledge of astronomy, of which the Jews were always ignorant.

The chronological tables mention that eclipses were observed at Babylon above two thousand years before the Christian era, which was before there was a single Jew or Israelite in the world.

All those ancient nations had their cosmogonies, that is, their accounts how the creation was made, before there was such people as Jews or Israelites. An account of these cosmogonies of India and Persia is given by Henry Lord, chaplain to the East India Company at Surat, and published in London in 1630. The writer of this has seen a copy of the edition of 1630, and made extracts from it. The work, which is now scarce, was dedicated by Lord to the Archbishop of Canterbury.

We know that the Jews were carried captive into Babylon by Nebuchadnezzar, and remained in captivity several years, when they were liberated by Cyrus, King of Persia. During their captivity they would have had an opportunity of acquiring some knowledge of the cosmogony of the Persians, or at least of getting some ideas how to fabricate one to put at the head of their own history after their return from captivity. This will account for the cause, for some cause there must have been, that no mention nor reference is made to the cosmogony in Genesis in any of the books of the Bible supposed to have been written before the captivity, nor is the name of Adam to be found in any of those books.

The books of Chronicles were written after the return of the Jews from captivity, for the third chapter of the first book gives a list of all the Jewish kings from David to Zedekiah, who was carried captive into Babylon, and to four generations beyond the time of Zedekiah. In Chron. i, I, the name of Adam is mentioned, but not in any book in the Bible written before that time, nor could it be, for Adam and Eve are names taken from the cosmogony of the Persians.

Henry Lord, in his book, written from Surat and dedicated, as I have already said, to the Archbishop of Canterbury, says that in the Persian cosmogony the name of the first man was *Adamoh*, and of the woman *Hevah*.[3] From hence comes the Adam and Eve of the book of Genesis. In the cosmogony of India, of which I shall speak in a future number, the name of the first man was *Pourous*, and of the woman *Parcoutee*. We want a knowledge of the Sanscrit language of India to understand the meaning of the names, and I mention it in this place, only to show that it is from the cosmogony of Persia, rather than that of India, that the cosmogony in

---

[3] In an English edition of the Bible, in 1583, the first woman is called Hevah.

Genesis has been fabricated by the Jews, who returned from captivity by the liberality of Cyrus, King of Persia.

There is, however, reason to conclude, on the authority of Sir William Jones, who resided several years in India, that these names were very expressive in the language to which they belonged, for in speaking of this language, he says (see the Asiatic Researches), "The Sanscrit language, whatever be its antiquity, is of wonderful structure; it is more perfect than the Greek, more copious than the Latin, and more exquisitely refined than either."

These hints, which are intended to be continued, will serve to show that a society for inquiring into the ancient state of the world, and the state of ancient history, so far as history is connected with systems of religion, ancient and modern, may become a useful and instructive institution.

There is good reason to believe we have been in great error with respect to the antiquity of the Bible, as well as imposed upon by its contents. Truth ought to be the object of every man; for without truth there can be no real happiness to a thoughtful mind, or any assurance of happiness hereafter. It is the duty of man to obtain all the knowledge he can, and then make the best use of it.

TO MR. MOORE, OF NEW YORK, COMMONLY CALLED BISHOP MOORE

I have read in the newspapers your account of the visit you made to the unfortunate General Hamilton, and of administering to him a ceremony of your church which you call the *Holy Communion*.

I regret the fate of General Hamilton, and I so far hope with you that it will be a warning to thoughtless man not to sport away the life that God has given him; but with respect to other parts of your letter I think it very reprehensible, and betrays great ignorance of what true religion is. But you are a priest, you get your living by it, and it is not your worldly interest to undeceive yourself.

After giving an account of your administering to the deceased what you call the Holy Communion, you add, "By reflecting on this melancholy event let the humble believer be encouraged ever to hold fast that precious faith which is the *only source of true consolation* in the last extremity of nature. Let the infidel be persuaded to abandon his opposition to the Gospel."

To show you, Sir, that your promise of consolation from Scripture has no foundation to stand upon, I will cite to you one of the greatest falsehoods upon record, and which was given, as the record says, for the purpose, and as a promise, of consolation.

In the epistle called the First Epistle of Paul to the Thessalonians, iv, the writer consoles the Thessalonians as to the case of their friends who were already dead.

He does this by informing them, and he does it he says, by the word of the Lord (a most notorious falsehood), that the general resurrection of the dead and the ascension of the living will be in his and their days; that their friends will then come to life again; that the dead in Christ will rise first.— "Then WE (says he, ver. 17, 18) which *are alive and remain* shall be *caught up* together with THEM *in the clouds, to meet the Lord in the air,* and so shall we ever be with the Lord. Wherefore *comfort* one another with these words."

Delusion and falsehood cannot be carried higher than they are in this passage. You, Sir, are but a novice in the art. The words admit of no equivocation. The whole passage is in the first person and the present tense, "We which *are alive.*"

Had the writer meant a future time, and a distant generation, it must have been in the third person and the future tense. "*They* who *shall then* be alive." I am thus particular for the purpose of nailing you down to the text, that you may not ramble from it, nor put other constructions upon the words than they will bear, which priests are very apt to do.

Now, Sir, it is impossible for serious man, to whom God has given the divine gift of reason, and who employs that reason to reverence and adore the God that gave it, it is, I say, impossible for such a man to put confidence in a book that abounds with fable and falsehood as the New Testament does. This passage is but a sample of what I could give you.

You call on those whom you style "*infidels*" (and they in return might call you an idolator, a worshiper of false gods, a preacher of false doctrines), "to abandon their opposition to the Gospel." Prove, Sir, the Gospel to be true, and the opposition will cease of itself; but until you do this (which we know you cannot do) you have no right to expect they will notice your call. If by *infidels* you mean *Deists* (and you must be exceedingly ignorant of the origin of the word Deist, and know but little of *Deus*, to put that construction upon it), you will find yourself overmatched if you begin to engage in a controversy with them.

Priests may dispute with priests, and sectaries with sectaries, about the meaning of what they *agree* to call Scripture, and end as they began; but when you engage with a Deist you must keep to fact. Now, Sir, you cannot prove a single article of your religion to be true, and we tell you so publicly. Do it *if you can.* The Deistical article, *the belief of a God,* with which your creed begins, has been borrowed by your church from the ancient Deists, and even this article you dishonor by putting a *dream-begotten* phantom[4]

---

[4] The first chapter of Matthew, relates that Joseph, the betrothed husband of Mary, dreamed that the angel told him that his intended bride was with child by the Holy Ghost. It is not every husband, whether carpenter or priest, that can be so easily satisfied, for lo! it was a dream. Whether Mary was in a dream when this

which you call His son, over His head, and treating God as if he was super-annuated.

Deism is the only profession of religion that admits of worshiping and reverencing God in purity, and the only one on which the thoughtful mind can repose with undisturbed tranquility. God is almost forgotten in the Christian religion. Everything, even the creation, is ascribed to the son of Mary.

In religion, as in everything else, perfection consists in simplicity. The Christian religion of Gods within Gods, like wheels within wheels, is like a complicated machine that never goes right, and every projector in the art of Christianity is trying to mend it. It is its defects that have caused such a number and variety of tinkers to be hammering at it, and still it goes wrong.

In the visible world no time-keeper can go equally true with the sun; and in like manner, no complicated religion can be equally true with the pure and unmixed religion of Deism.

Had you not offensively glanced at a description of men whom you call by a false name, you would not have been troubled nor honored with this address; neither has the writer of it any desire or intention to enter into controversy with you. He thinks the temporal establishment of your church politically unjust and offensively unfair; but with respect to religion itself; distinct from temporal establishments; he is happy in the enjoyment of his own, and he leaves you to make the best you can of yours.

ON DEISM, AND THE WRITINGS OF THOMAS PAINE

"*Great is Diana of the Ephesians,*" was the cry of the people of Ephesus (Acts xix, 28); and the cry of "*our holy religion*" has been the cry of superstition in some instances, and of hypocrisy in others, from that day to this.

The Brahmin, the follower of Zoroaster, the Jew, the Mahometan, the Church of Rome, the Greek Church, the Protestant Church, split into several hundred contradictory sectaries, preaching in some instances damnation against each other, all cry out, "*our holy religion.*"

The Calvinist, who damns children of a span long to hell to burn forever for the glory of God (and this is called Christianity), and the Universalist who preaches that all shall be saved and none shall be damned (and this is also called Christianity), boast alike of their *holy religion* and their Christian faith.

Something more therefore is necessary than mere *cry* and wholesale assertion, and that something is *truth*; and as inquiry is the road to truth, he that is opposed to inquiry is not a friend to truth.

was done we are not told. It is, however, a comical story. There is no woman living can understand it.—T. P.

The God of truth is not the God of fable; when, therefore, any book is introduced into the world as the Word of God, and made a groundwork for religion, it ought to be scrutinized more than other books to see if it bear evidence of being what it is called. Our reverence to God demands that we do this, lest we ascribe to God what is not His and our duty to ourselves demands it lest we take fable for fact, and rest our hope of salvation on a false foundation.

It is not our calling a book *holy* that makes it so, any more than our calling a religion holy that entitles it to the name. Inquiry therefore is necessary in order to arrive at truth. But inquiry must have some principle to proceed on, some standard to judge by, superior to human authority.

When we survey the works of creation, the revolutions of the planetary system, and the whole economy of what is called nature, which is no other than the laws the Creator has prescribed to matter, we see unerring order and universal harmony reigning throughout the whole. No one part contradicts another. The sun does not run against the moon, nor the moon against the sun, nor the planets against each other. Everything keeps its appointed time and place.

This harmony in the works of God is so obvious, that the farmer of the field, though he cannot calculate eclipses, is as sensible of it as the philosophical astronomer. He sees the God of order in every part of the visible universe.

Here, then, is the standard to which everything must be brought that pretends to be the work or Word of God, and by this standard it must be judged, independently of anything and everything that man can say or do. His opinion is like a feather in the scale compared with the standard that God Himself has set up.

It is, therefore, by this standard that the Bible and all other books pretending to be the Word of God (and there are many of them in the world) must be judged, and not by the opinions of men or the decrees of ecclesiastical councils. These have been so contradictory that they have often rejected in one council what they had voted to be the Word of God in another; and admitted what had been before rejected.

In this state of uncertainty in which we are, and which is rendered still more uncertain by the numerous contradictory sectaries that have sprung up since the time of Luther and Calvin, what is man to do? The answer is easy. Begin at the root—begin with the Bible itself. Examine it with the utmost strictness. It is our duty so to do.

Compare the parts with each other, and the whole with the harmonious, magnificent order that reigns throughout the visible universe, and the result will be, that if the same Almighty wisdom that created the universe dictated also the Bible, the Bible will be as harmonious and as magnificent in all its parts and in the whole as the universe is.

But, if instead of this, the parts are found to be discordant, contradicting in one place what is said in another (as in II Sam. xxiv, I, and I Chron. xxi, I, where the same action is ascribed to God in one book and to Satan in the other), abounding also in idle and obscene stories, and representing the Almighty as a passionate, whimsical Being, continually changing His mind, making and unmaking His own works as if He did not know what He was about, we may take it for certainty that the Creator of the universe is not the author of such a book, that it is not the Word of God, and that to call it so is to dishonor His name.

The Quakers, who are a people more moral and regular in their conduct than the people of other sectaries, and generally allowed so to be, do not hold the Bible to be the Word of God. They call it *a history of the times*, and a bad history it is, and also a history of bad men and of bad actions, and abounding with bad examples.

For several centuries past the dispute has been about doctrines. It is now about fact. Is the Bible the Word of God, or is it not? For until this point is established, no doctrine drawn from the Bible can afford real consolation to man, and he ought to be careful he does not mistake delusion for truth. This is a case that concerns all men alike.

There has always existed in Europe, and also in America, since its establishment, a numerous description of men (I do not here mean the Quakers) who did not, and do not believe the Bible to be the Word of God. These men never formed themselves into an established society, but are to be found in all the sectaries that exist, and are more numerous than any, perhaps equal to all, and are daily increasing. From *Deus*, the Latin word for God, they have been denominated *Deists*, that is, believers in God. It is the most honorable appellation that can be given to man, because it is derived immediately from the Deity. It is not an artificial name like Episcopalian, Presbyterian, etc., but is a name of sacred signification, and to revile it is to revile the name of God.

Since then there is so much doubt and uncertainty about the Bible, some asserting and others denying it to be the Word of God, it is best that the whole matter come out. It is necessary for the information of the world that it should.

A better time cannot offer than while the Government,[5] patronizing no one sect or opinion in preference to another, protects equally the rights of all; and certainly every man must spurn the idea of an ecclesiastical tyranny,

---

[5] [Administration of President Jefferson.—ED.]

engrossing the rights of the press, and holding it free only for itself.

While the terrors of the Church, and the tyranny of the State, hung like a pointed sword over Europe, men were commanded to believe what the Church told them, or go to the stake. All inquiries into the authenticity of the Bible were shut out by the Inquisition. We ought therefore to suspect that a great mass of information respecting the Bible, and the introduction of it into the world, has been suppressed by the united tyranny of Church and State, for the purpose of keeping people in ignorance, and which ought to be known.

The Bible has been received by the Protestants on the authority of the Church of Rome, and on no other authority. It is she that has said it is the Word of God. We do not admit the authority of that Church with respect to its pretended *infallibility*, its manufactured miracles, its setting itself up to forgive sins, its amphibious doctrine of transubstantiation, etc.; and we ought to be watchful with respect to any book introduced by her, or her ecclesiastical councils, and called by her the Word of God: and the more so, because it was by propagating that belief and supporting it by fire and faggot that she kept up her temporal power.

That the belief of the Bible does no good in the world, may be seen by the irregular lives of those, as well priests as laymen, who profess to believe it to be the Word of God, and the moral lives of the Quakers who do not. It abounds with too many ill examples to be made a rule for moral life, and were a man to copy after the lives of some of its most celebrated characters he would come to the gallows.

Thomas Paine has written[6] to show that the Bible is not the Word of God, that the books it contains were not written by the persons to whom they are ascribed, that it is an anonymous book, and that we have no authority for calling it the Word of God, or for saying it was written by inspired penmen, since we do not know who the writers were.

This is the opinion not only of Thomas Paine, but of thousands and tens of thousands of the most respectable characters in the United States and in Europe. These men have the same right to their opinions as others have to contrary opinions, and the same right to publish them. Ecclesiastical tyranny is not admissible in the United States.

With respect to morality, the writings of Thomas Paine are remarkable for purity and benevolence; and though he often enlivens them with touches of wit and humor, he never loses sight of the real solemnity of his subject. No man's morals, either with respect to his Maker, himself, or his neighbor,

---

[6] [Thomas Paine referred to himself in the third person in this unsigned *Prospect* paper.—ED.]

can suffer by the writings of Thomas Paine.

It is now too late to abuse Deism, especially in a country where the press is free, *or where free presses can be established.* It is a religion that has God for its patron and derives its name from Him. The thoughtful mind of man, wearied with the endless contents of sectaries against sectaries, doctrines against doctrines, and priests against priests, finds its repose at last in the contemplative belief and worship of one God and the practice of morality; for as Pope wisely says—"He can't be wrong whose life is in the right."

Thomas Paine did not consider his Age of Reason to be complete. He wrote an extensive new section, but Thomas Jefferson prevailed on him not to publish if for fear that it would supply fresh ammunition to his enemies. In 1807, however, Paine published most of the new section in a series of pamphlets, now generally known as The Examination of the Prophecies. *Included in the pamphlets was the following short passage, called "My Private Thoughts on a Future State."*

MY PRIVATE THOUGHTS ON A FUTURE STATE, 1807

I have said, in the first part of "The Age of Reason," that "*I hope for happiness after this life.*" This hope is comfortable to me, and I presume not to go beyond the comfortable idea of hope, with respect to a future state.

I consider myself in the hands of my Creator, and that He will dispose of me after this life consistently with His justice and goodness. I leave all these matters to Him, as my Creator and friend, and I hold it to be presumption in man to make an article of faith as to what the Creator will do with us hereafter. I do not believe because a man and a woman make a child that it imposes on the Creator the unavoidable obligation of keeping the being so made in eternal existence hereafter. It is in His power to do so, or not to do so, and it is not in our power to decide which He will do.

The book called the New Testament, which I hold to be fabulous and have shown to be false, gives an account in Matthew xxv of what is there called the last day, or the day of judgment.

The whole world, according to that account, is divided into two parts, the righteous and the unrighteous, figuratively called the sheep and the goats. They are then to receive their sentence. To the one, figuratively called the sheep, it says, "*Come ye blessed of my Father, inherit the kingdom prepared for you from the foundation of the world.*" To the other, figuratively called the goats, it says, "*Depart from me, ye cursed, into everlasting fire, prepared for the devil and his angels.*"

Now the case is, the world cannot be thus divided: the moral world, like the physical world, is composed of numerous degrees of character, running imperceptibly one into the other, in such a manner that no fixed point of division can be found in either. That point is nowhere, or is everywhere.

The whole world might be divided into two parts numerically, but not as to moral character; and therefore the metaphor of dividing them, as sheep and goats can be divided, whose difference is marked by their external figure, is absurd. All sheep are still sheep; all goats are still goats; it is their physical nature to be so. But one part of the world are not all good alike, nor the other part all wicked alike. There are some exceedingly good; others exceedingly wicked.

There is another description of men who cannot be ranked with either the one or the other—they belong neither to the sheep nor the goats; and there is still another description of them who are so very insignificant, both in character and conduct, as not to be worth the trouble of damning or saving, or of raising from the dead.

My own opinion is, that those whose lives have been spent in doing good, and endeavoring to make their fellow-mortals happy, for this is the only way in which we can serve God, *will be happy hereafter*; and that the very wicked will meet with some punishment. But those who are neither good nor bad, or are too insignificant for notice, will be dropped entirely.

This is my opinion. It is consistent with my idea of God's justice, and with the reason that God has given me, and I gratefully know that He has given me a large share of that divine gift.

Editor's Notes

Often, in reading a book based substantially on research, it has occurred to me that it might be of some interest to have the author's ideas concerning other books that ought to be written in the same general field. In connection with the present book, several areas of potential usefulness came to mind. For example, I could find no up-to-date, full-length biography of Dr. Joseph Priestley. Yet everything said about him by Jefferson, Franklin, and Adams indicates that, intellectually at least, he was perhaps one of the most commanding figures of the period—certainly in terms of his influence on many of the leading thinkers of the time. Some American or English biographer may feel justified in assigning himself to this task.

Another subject awaiting a modern biographer is Ezra Stiles, the president of what was Yale College during part of the American Revolution. His interests and influence in the fields of education, law, theology, philosophy, and public affairs give ample justification for further study. His daughter's husband, Abiel Holmes (father of Oliver Wendell Holmes), wrote a biography in 1798. One by J. L. Kingsley was published in 1845. So far as I know, there has been nothing since.

No material examined by the editor gave him greater pleasure than was afforded by the correspondence between Thomas Jefferson and John Adams. However, these letters were not to be found in any single definitive edition; they had to be assembled from the collected writings or papers of each man. Clearly, this exchange deserves a book of its own. If there is a richer and more stimulating dialogue between two great American statesmen in our history I do not know of it.

Over the years, I have searched in vain for a fully annotated and carefully indexed edition of *The Federalist Papers*, suitable for detailed reference work. Perhaps some publisher might feel justified in bringing out such an edition.

Finally, an author might find rich material for a book dealing with the experience of America under the Alien and Sedition Laws shortly after the turn of the nineteenth century. In several places in the preceding pages, especially in the Jefferson section, there is some indication of the importance of this experience and its relevance in the situation today. Apart from the subject itself, there is perhaps no more rewarding or exciting period of American history in which to work. No more exciting period, that is, with the exception of the present.

Guide to Further Reading and Research

WRITINGS BY AND ABOUT THE FOUNDING FATHERS

JOHN ADAMS

ADAMS, JOHN. *John Adams, Diary and Autobiography.* Edited by Lyman H. Butterfield, et al. 4 vols. Cambridge: Belknap Press, 1961.

EAST, ROBERT A. *John Adams.* Boston: Twayne, 1979.

HANDLER, EDWARD. *America and Europe in Political Thought of John Adams.* Cambridge: Harvard University Press, 1964.

HOWE, JOHN R., JR. *Changing Political Thought of John Adams.* New Jersey: Princeton University Press, 1966.

SHAW, PETER. *The Character of John Adams.* Chapel Hill: University of North Carolina Press, 1976.

BENJAMIN FRANKLIN

CONNER, PAUL W. *Poor Richard's Politics: Benjamin Franklin and His New American Order.* New York: Oxford University Press, 1965.

FRANKLIN, BENJAMIN. *The Autobiography of Benjamin Franklin.* Edited by Henry Steele Commager. New York: Random House, 1944.

———. *Benjamin Franklin: A Biography in His Own Words.* Edited by Thomas Fleming. New York: Newsweek, The Founding Fathers Series, 1972.

———. *Papers.* Edited by Leonard V. Labaree. 19 vols. New Haven: Yale University Press, 1960–1975.

———. *Benjamin Franklin: Writings.* Edited by J. A. Leo Lemay. New York: The Library of America, 1987.

HAWKE, DAVID FREEMAN. *Franklin.* New York: Harper & Row, 1976.

WRIGHT, EDMOND. *Franklin of Philadelphia.* Cambridge: Belknap Press, 1986.

ALEXANDER HAMILTON

COOKE, JACOB E., ed. *Alexander Hamilton.* Series: American Profiles. New York: Scribners, 1982.

HAMILTON, ALEXANDER. *Papers.* Edited by Harold C. Syrett and Jacob E. Cooke. 27 vols. New York: Columbia University Press, 1961–1987.

MORRIS, RICHARD B., ed. *Alexander Hamilton and the Founding of the Nation.* New York: Dial Press, 1957.

ROSSITER, CLINTON. *Alexander Hamilton and the Constitution.* New York: Harcourt, Brace & World, 1964.

445

STOURZH, GERALD. *Alexander Hamilton and Idea of Republican Government.* Stanford: Stanford University Press, 1970.

THOMAS JEFFERSON

DUMBAULD, EDWARD. *Thomas Jefferson and the Law.* Norman: University of Oklahoma Press, 1978.

JEFFERSON, THOMAS. *Adams-Jefferson Letters.* Edited by Lester J. Cappon. 2 vols. Chapel Hill: University of North Carolina Press, 1959.

LEVY, LEONARD W. *Jefferson and Civil Liberties: The Darker Side.* New York: Quadrangle Books, 1973.

MALONE, DUMAS. *Jefferson and His Times.* 5 vols. Boston: Little, Brown, 1948–1975.

PEDEN, WILLIAM. *Thomas Jefferson: Notes on the State of Virginia.* New York: W. W. Norton, 1982.

PETERSON, MERRILL D. *Thomas Jefferson and the New Nation: A Biography.* New York: Oxford University Press, 1970.

———. *Thomas Jefferson.* Boston: Little, Brown, 1974.

RANDOLPH, SARAH N. *The Domestic Life of Thomas Jefferson.* Charlottesville: University of Virginia Press, 1985.

STUART, REGINALD CHARLES. *The Half-Way Pacifist: Thomas Jefferson's View of the War.* Toronto: University of Toronto Press, 1978.

JAMES MADISON

BURNS, EDWARD M. *James Madison: Philosopher of the Constitution.* New York: Octagon Books, 1968.

KETCHAM, RALPH. *James Madison: A Biography.* New York: MacMillan, 1971.

MADISON, JAMES. *Papers.* Edited by William T. Hutchinson and William M. Rachal. 6 vols. Chicago: University of Chicago Press, 1962–1969.

———. *The Papers of James Madison.* Edited by Robert A. Rutland. Charlottesville: University of Virginia Press, 1979.

MEYERS, MARVIN, ed. *The Mind of the Founder: Sources of the Political Thought of James Madison.* Hanover, NH: University Press of New England, 1981.

MOORE, VIRGINIA. *The Madisons.* New York: McGraw Hill Co., 1979.

SHULTZ, HAROLD S. *James Madison.* New York: Twayne, 1970.

STAGG, J. C. A. *Mr. Madison's War.* New Jersey: Princeton University Press, 1983.

THOMAS PAINE

ALDRIDGE, ALFRED O. *Thomas Paine's American Ideology.* Newark: University of Delaware Press, 1984.

HAWKE, DAVID F. *Paine.* New York: Harper & Row, 1974.

FONER, ERIC. *Tom Paine and Revolutionary America.* New York: Oxford University Press, 1976.

PAINE, THOMAS. *The Complete Writings of Thomas Paine.* New York: The Citadel Press, 1945.

———. *The Writings of Thomas Paine.* New York: G. P. Putnam's Sons, 1894–1896.

GEORGE WASHINGTON

FLEXNER, JAMES T. *George Washington.* 3 vols. London: Little, Brown, 1967–1970.

————. *George Washington and the New Nation (1783–1793).* Boston: Little, Brown, 1969.

————. *George Washington: Anguish and Farewell (1793–1799).* Boston: Little, Brown, 1972.

————. *Washington the Indispensable Man.* New York: New American Library, 1974.

MORGAN, EDMUND S. *The Genius of George Washington.* New York: W. W. Norton, 1980.

WASHINGTON, GEORGE. *The Diaries of George Washington.* Edited by Donald Jackson. Charlottesville: University of Virginia Press, 1976.

————. *The Papers of George Washington.* Edited by W. W. Abbot. Charlottesville: University of Virginia Press, 1983.

GENERAL BACKGROUND

APTHEKER, HERBERT. *A History of the American People: The American Revolution 1763–1783.* New York: International Publishers, 1985.

————. *Early Years of the Republic.* New York: International Publishers, 1976.

BANCROFT, GEORGE. *History of the American Revolution.* London: R. Bentley, 1854.

————. *History of the United States of America.* 6 vols. Boston: Little, Brown, 1876.

COMMAGER, HENRY STEELE, ed. *Documents of American History.* New York: F. S. Crofts & Co., 1940.

COMMAGER, HENRY STEELE, and ALLAN NEVANS. *The Heritage of America.* Boston: Little, Brown, 1939.

COUNTRYMAN, EDWARD. *The American Revolution.* New York: Hill & Wang, 1985.

DANN, JOHN C. *The Revolution Remembered: Eyewitness Accounts of the War for Independence.* Chicago: The University of Chicago Press, 1980.

FISKE, JOHN. *The American Revolution.* Boston: Houghton Mifflin Co., 1897.

————. *The Beginnings of New England.* Boston: Houghton Mifflin Co., 1889.

FREIDMAN, LAWRENCE M. *A History of American Law.* New York: Simon & Schuster, 1973.

HOLT, WYTHE, ed. *Essays in Nineteenth-Century American Legal History.* Westport, CT: Greenwood Press, 1976.

MIDDLEKAUFF, ROBERT. *The Glorious Cause: The American Revolution, 1763–1789.* New York: Oxford University Press, 1982.

MORRIS, RICHARD B., ed. *Encyclopedia of American History.* New York: Harper & Row, 1970.

MORRISON, SAMUEL ELIOT, and HENRY STEELE COMMAGER. *The Growth of the American Republic.* New York: Oxford University Press, 1950.

POLITICS AND THE FOUNDING FATHERS

ADAIR, DOUGLAS. *Fame and the Founding Fathers.* New York: W. W. Norton, 1974.

BECKER, CARL L. *The Declaration of Independence; a Study in the History of Political Ideas.* New York: Knopf, 1942.

BILLIAS, GEORGE ATHAN. *Elbridge Gerry: Founding Father and Republican Statesman*. New York: McGraw Hill, 1976.

BURNS, JAMES MCGREGOR. *The Vineyard of Liberty*. New York: Vintage Books, 1982.

COMMAGER, HENRY STEELE. *The Empire of Reason*. New York: Oxford University Press, 1977.

DABNEY, VIRGINIUS, ed. *The Patriots: The American Revolution Generation of Genius*. New York: Atheneum, 1975.

KETCHAM, RALPH. *Presidents Above Party: The First American Presidency, 1789–1829*. Chapel Hill: University of North Carolina Press, 1984.

LEDER, LAWRENCE H. *Liberty and Authority: Early American Political Ideology, 1689-1763*. New York: W. W. Norton, 1976.

MAIER, PAULINI. *The Old Revolutionaries: Political Lives in the Age of Samuel Adams*. New York: Vintage, 1980.

MEYERS, MARVIN. *The Jacksonian Persuasion: Politics and Belief*. Stanford: Stanford University Press, 1984.

———. *The Workshop of Democracy*. New York: Vintage Books, 1985.

MORRIS, RICHARD B. *Seven Who Shaped Our Destiny: The Founding Fathers as Revolutionaries*. New York: Harper & Row, 1973.

RAKOVE, JACK N. *The Beginnings of National Politics: An Interpretive History of the Continental Congress*. New York: Knopf, 1979.

SCHLESINGER, ARTHUR M. *The Politics of Upheaval*. Boston: Houghton Mifflin, 1960.

TOCQUEVILLE, ALEXIS DE. *Democracy in America*. New York: Knopf, 1945.

WOOD, GORDON S. *The Creation of the American Republic (1776–1787)*. New York: W. W. Norton, 1972.

THE CONSTITUTION

BEARD, CHARLES A. *An Economic Interpretation of the Constitution of the United States*. New York: The Free Press, 1986.

BERNSTEIN, RICHARD B. *Are We to be a Nation? The Making of the Constitution*. Cambridge: Harvard University Press, 1987.

COLLIER, CHRISTOPHER and JAMES LINCOLN COLLIER. *Decision in Philadelphia*. New York: Ballantine Books, 1986.

DOREN, CARL VAN. *The Great Rehearsal*. New York: Penguin Books, 1986.

HYMAN, HAROLD M. *A More Perfect Union: The Impact of the Civil War and Reconstruction on the Constitution*. The Impact of the Civil War Series. New York: Knopf, 1973.

KAMMEN, MICHAEL. *A Machine that Would Go of Itself: The Constitution in American Culture*. New York: Vintage, 1986.

KELLY, ALFRED H., and WINFRED A. HARBISON. *The American Constitution: Its Origins and Development*. New York: W. W. Norton, 1976.

KENYON, CECELIA M., ed. *The Antifederalists*. Boston: Northeastern University Press, 1985.

LEVY, LEONARD. *Judgements: Essays on American Constitutional History*. Chicago: Quadrangle Books, 1972.

MORRIS, RICHARD B. *Witnesses at the Creation: Hamilton, Madison, Jay and the Constitution*. New York: New American Library, 1985.

POLE, J. R. *The American Constitution For and Against.* New York: Hill & Wang, 1987.

STORING, HERBERT J., ed. *The Antifederalists: Writings by the Opponents of the Constitution.* Chicago: University of Chicago Press, 1985.

EARLY AMERICAN LIFE AND ITS INFLUENCES

AHLSTROM, SYDNEY E. *A Religious History of the American People.* New Haven: Yale University Press, 1972.

BARKER, CHARLES A. *American Convictions: Cycles of Public Thought, 1600–1850.* Philadelphia: Lippincott, 1970.

BERTHOFF, ROWLAND T. *An Unsettled People: Social Order and Disorder in American History.* New York: Harper & Row, 1976.

CONKIN, PAUL K. *Puritans & Pragmatists: Eight Eminent American Thinkers.* Bloomington: Indiana University Press, 1976.

CRONON, WILLIAM. *Changes in the New Land: Indians, Colonists, and the Ecology of New England.* New York: Hill & Wang, 1983.

DAVIS, JOSEPH L. *Sectionalism in America, 1774–1787.* Madison: University of Wisconsin Press, 1976.

DAVIS, S. RUFUS. *The Federal Principal: A Journey Through Time in Quest of a Meaning.* Berkeley: University of California Press, 1978.

GRAYMONT, BARBARA. *The Iroquois in the American Revolution.* Syracuse: Syracuse University Press, 1972.

HEIMERT, ALAN. *Religion and the American Mind.* Cambridge: Harvard University Press, 1966.

HOFSTADTER, RICHARD. *America at 1750: A Social Portrait.* New York: Knopf, 1972.

JENSEN, MERRILL. *The American Revolution within America.* New York: New York University Press, 1974.

KERBER, LINDA K. *Women of the Republic: Intellect and Ideology in Revolutionary America.* Chapel Hill: University of North Carolina Press, 1980.

MILLER, PERRY. *The Life of the Mind in America, from the Revolution to the Civil War.* New York: Harcourt, Brace & World, 1965.

———. *The New England Mind from Colony to Province.* Cambridge: Belknap Press, 1953.

MILLER, PERRY, and THOMAS H. JOHNSON, eds. *The Puritans.* New York: Harper & Row, 1963.

MILLS, FREDERICK V. *Bishops by Ballot: An Eighteenth-Century Ecclesiastical Revolution.* New York: Oxford University Press, 1978.

MORGAN, EDMUND S. *The Gentle Puritan: A Life of Ezra Stiles, 1727–1795.* New Haven: Yale University Press, 1962.

NYE, RUSSEL BLAINE. *The Cultural Life of the New Nation, 1776–1830.* New York: Harper & Row, 1960.

O'DONNELL, JAMES H. *Southern Indians in the American Revolution.* Knoxville: University of Tennessee Press, 1973.

SCHLESINGER, ARTHUR M. *The Birth of a Nation: A Portrait of the American People on the Eve of Independence.* New York: Knopf, 1968.

SCHNEIDER, HERBERT W. *History of American Philosophy.* New York: Columbia University Press, 1946.

VAUGHAN, ALDEN T., and EDWARD W. CLARK, eds. *Puritans Among the Indians*. Cambridge: Belknap Press, 1981.

WILLS, GARY. *Explaining America: The Federalist*. Garden City: Doubleday, 1981.

AMERICAN PREJUDICE

BERLIN, IRA, and RONALD HOFFMAN, eds. *Slavery and Freedom in the Age of the American Revolution*. Urbana: The University of Illinois Press, 1983.

MACLEOD, DUNCAN. *Slavery, Race and the American Revolution*. London: Cambridge University Press, 1974.

POLE, J. R. *The Pursuit of Equality in American History*. Berkeley: University of California Press, 1978.

RINGER, BENJAMIN B. *We the People and Others: Duality and America's Treatment of Racial Minorities*. New York: Tavistock Publications, 1983.

WIECEK, WILLIAM M. *The Sources of Antislavery Constitutionalism in America, 1760–1848*. Ithaca: Cornell University Press, 1977.

INDEX

Wherever possible, correct spellings are given here, since from one author to another names are rendered differently. In some cases the correct spelling is followed, in parentheses, by that given in the text.

Aaron, 222, 247, 433

Abraham, 153, 222, 252, 262, 374, 427, 433

Absalom, 368

Acts of the Apostles, 251–52

Adair, James, 220, 221–22, 226

Adam, 261, 435

Adams, Abigail, 91, 271, 278, 283 n.

Adams, George Washington, 232

Adams, Hannah, 352–53

Adams, Henry, 76

Adams, John, 6, 15, 156, 329, 344–45, 360, 365, 444; on alliances, 96; *Autobiography*, 77–79; biography of, 74–77; on Christianity, 99–100, 101, 104–5; *Defence of the Constitutions . . .*, 97; diary of, 79–84, 86–89, 99–100; *Discourses on Davila*, 97–99; "Dissertation on the Canon and Feudal Law," 84–86; on economic disparity, 97–99; on genius and eternal life, 93–94
—letters to: Richard Cranch, 91–93; M. Genêt, 96; Grand Jurors of Hampshire County, 100; (and from) Thomas Jefferson. *See* Jefferson-Adams letters; Robert R. Livingston, 94–95; Samuel Miller, 111–12; Richard Price, 95; Samuel Quincy, 93–94; Ben-

jamin Rush, 101–2; David Sewall, 112–13; John Taylor, 105–11; William Tudor, 111; F. A. Van der Kemp, 102–5
—"Novanglus" paper, 89–90; religious development of, 111–12; religious influences on, 77–79; on Supreme Being, 91–93, 113

Adams, John Quincy, 76, 233–34

Adams, Rev., 322–25

Adams, Samuel, 5, 12, 46, 88, 218, 359, 360; biography of, 344–46; on education, 354–55; on Episcopate in America, 350; on evacuation of Boston, 351–52
—letters to: Hannah Adams, 352–53; Arthur Lee, 350–51; Massachusetts legislature, 354–55; John Scollay, 351–52; Peter Thacher, 352; T. Wells, 353–54
—on marriage, 353–54; on Popery, 346–50; "Puritan Papers," 346–50; on Quakers and Tories, 352; Thanksgiving Day Proclamation, 355–57

Addison, Joseph, 30, 246

Aethelbert, 257

Ahab, 364

Aitken (Aikin), Robert, 56

Alembert, Jean d', 142, 269, 270, 272, 274, 276, 279, 284

Alexander the Great, 250

Alfred, King, 257
Alien and Sedition Acts, 101, 131 n.
American Bible Society, 360, 373–84
American Revolution, x
Ames, Fisher, 267
Anabaptists, 9, 87, 360
Anderson, James, 67
Angels, Thomas Paine on, 427
Anglican Church. See Church of England; Protestant Episcopal Church
Anthony, St., 252
Antoninus, 165, 169
Antony, 282
Archytas, 255
Argens, Marquis d', 254, 259, 265, 276–77
Arianism, 229, 230
Aristotle, 106, 250, 251, 288
Arminianism, 77, 82, 234
Arnobius, 251
Arnold, Benedict, 46, 49–50
Arrian, 170, 235
Articles of Confederation, 314
Ashfield, 87
Athanasius, St., 107, 132n, 140, 156, 159, 160–61, 162, 240, 261, 286 n.
Atheism, 14, 18, 102–3, 142, 229, 234, 269, 272, 286, 289, 291, 363; John Adams on, 269–70; Jay on, 364–65; and Paine, 389–90, 394–95, 417, 420
Augustine, St., 250
Augustus, 282, 284
Avery, John, Jr., 357

Babeuf, François Noel (Lalande, pseud.), 269, 275
Babylon, 433, 434, 435
Backus, Rev. Isaac, 87
Bacon, Francis, 10, 79
Balch, Mr., 82
Baltimore, Lord, 2
Baltimore Baptist Association, 135–36
Baptist Church, 58
Baptists, 9, 24, 102, 116, 163, 265, 301, 319, 428; discrimination against, 296, 300; Jefferson's addresses to, 134–36
Barbe-Marbois, François, Marquis de, 121
Baronius, Caesar, Cardinal, 250
Basil, St., 107
Bass, Mr., 77
Batteux, Charles, 237, 254, 259
Beasley, Frederick, 321–22
Beaumarchais, Pierre de, 276
Becker, Carl, 11
Belsham, Thomas, 231, 235, 239, 265
Benezet, Anthony, 39
Bennet, Thomas, 167
Bentham, Jeremy, 10
Bentley, William, 346
Bérenger, René, 101
Berlin Decree, 219
Bertholet, Comte Claude Louis, 292
Bible, 22, 23, 56, 360, 362; Adams on, 256, 293; as "common law," 245; facts in, and the laws of nature, 128–29; and human conduct, 80–81; Jay on, 363; King James', 280; New Testament of. See Jefferson, Thomas, Life and Morals of Jesus; Paine on, 389, 393, 403, 404–14, 424, 427, 429–30, 431, 433–37, 439, 440, 441; as the source of religious belief, 8; Ten Commandments of, 247–48, 257, 281; and war, 365–71. See also American Bible Society
Bill of Rights. See Constitution
Blacklock, Thomas, 246
Blackstone, Sir William, 114, 258, 333
Blake, Dominick F., 343
Blount, Charles, 101
Blue laws, 432
Bolingbroke, Lord, 79, 94, 101, 102, 114, 230, 234, 253, 274
Bolland, Jean de, 107, 262
Book of Common Prayer, 20
Borgia, Cesare, 267
Boston Massacre, 352
Boston Tea Party, 344, 345
Boyle's Lectures, 24

Bradford, William, 71
Bradford, William, Jr., 298–301, 317
Brady, Nicholas, 243
Bridgen, Edward, 40
Brocklesby, Dr., 253–54
Brucker, Johann Jakob, 241, 259
Brutus, 282, 284
Bry, Théodore de, 221, 226
Bryan, Mrs., 152
Bryant (Briant), Rev. Lemuel, 77, 282
Budaeus, 250, 257
Buffon, Comte de, 114, 265, 269, 275, 276
Bunyan, John, 249, 252, 280
Burke, Edmund, 79, 101, 253, 265, 393
Burlamaqui, Jean Jacques, 332
Burr, Aaron, 249, 259, 328, 329, 339–41
Butler, Samuel, 270

Cabanis, Pierre, 284, 293
Cabbala, 241, 248
Caesar, Julius, 4, 152, 250, 282
Calonne, Charles Alexandre de, 71
Calvin, John, 253, 291, 439
Calvinism, 8, 12, 115, 289, 344; Adams on, 75, 82, 111, 234, 240, 269; divergent groups in, 5; Jefferson on, 148, 151, 156, 160–61, 162, 163; Paine on, 432, 438
Canada, 40, 46, 48–49, 333–37
Canby, William, 140–41
Canterbury, Archbishop of, 435
Canus, Melchior, 250–51
Cappe, 234
Carlile, Richard, 404
Carmelites, 108, 262
Carr, Peter, 127–29
Carroll, Charles, 222
Carroll, John, 40
Cassius, 284
Catawba Indians, 221
Catherine the Great, 269, 271–72, 275
Catholic Church, Roman. See Roman Catholic Church
Catiline, 282

Channing, William Ellery, 157
Charles II, 23, 348
Charles River, 348
Charlestown, 348–49, 350
Charondas, 255
Chase, Samuel, 87
Chateaubriand, François René de, 107, 252, 266
Chaucer, Geoffrey, 114
Cheetham, J., 101
Cherokee Indians, 221
Chew, Benjamin, 273, 277
Cheyne, John, 78, 94
Chickasaw Indians, 221
China, 415
Choctaw Indians, 221
Chovet, Dr., 86
Christianity, 1, 8, 47, 74, 82, 123; John Adams on, 99–100, 229–31, 259–60; and Deism, 430–31; Jefferson on, 145–47, 157–58, 160–62
Chronicles, 434, 435, 440
Chrysostom, St., 107
Church, John B., 342, 343
Church of England, viii, ix, 23, 47, 114, 116, 120, 121–22, 296, 299, 417. See also Protestant Episcopal Church
Cicero, 30, 106, 112, 114, 146, 149, 152, 165, 169, 232, 262, 282
Clarke, Samuel, 234, 321
Clay, Charles, 171–72
Clay, Henry, 295
Cleverly, Joseph, 282
Collins, John, 24
Collins, Peasley, 82 n.
Columbia College, S.C., 131, 155
Columbian Illuminati, 428
Comenius, John Amos, 11
Commager, Henry Steele, 358
Condorcet, Marquis de, 10, 142, 227, 234, 250, 261, 265, 275, 276
Confucius, 233, 256, 414, 415
Congregationalism, 5, 296, 360
Congress, 56, 65, 71, 86, 101, 118, 244, 297, 315, 344, 358, 359, 360, 391, 392
Congress of Vienna, 266, 267

Connecticut, 3, 244–45, 258–59; Sabbath day, 432
Constitution, 3, 4, 7, 13–15, 45, 64, 70, 105, 134, 136–37, 223–24, 246, 259, 315, 328, 338, 346, 355, 359, 361; Bill of Rights, xii, 64, 117, 296, 315–17
Constitutional Convention, 3–4, 17–18, 44–45, 295, 301, 314, 327–28, 346, 359
Conway, Henry Seymour, 96
Cook, James, 40
Cooper, Dr. Thomas, 102, 130, 131–33, 151, 155–56, 163–64, 236
Copernicus, Nicolaus, 10
Cornwallis, Charles, 392
Correa da Serra, José Francisco, 151
Cosri, 241, 248
Cranch, Richard, 91–93
Creationists, vii
Creek Indians, 221
Curran, John Philpot, 7
Curtis, George Ticknor, 327
Cushing, Thomas, 88
Custis, John Parke, 52
Cuvier, Baron Georges, 292
Cyrus, King of Persia, 435, 436

Danbury Baptist Association, 135
David, 246, 288, 368, 370, 427, 435
Declaration of Independence, 4, 10, 76, 114, 117, 120, 217, 219, 220, 222
Deffand, Marquise du, 275
Deism, 12, 24, 47, 74–75, 78, 101, 141, 166, 169, 170, 229, 234, 283; and Thomas Paine, 360, 395, 396, 401–2, 429, 430–31, 437–42
De la Motta, Jacob, 320–321
Delaplaine, Joseph, 281
Delaware, 323
Delaware Indians, 54–55
Delilah, 429
Demosthenes, 262, 270, 288
Descartes, René, 124
Deuteronomy, Book of, 248

Diana of the Ephesians, 438
Dickinson, John, 5, 224
Diderot, Denis, 10, 142, 265, 267, 269, 270, 272, 275, 276, 289
Diodorus Siculus, 152
Diogenes Laërtius, 250
D'Israeli, Isaac, 269
Dodge, Nehemiah, 135
Dowse, E., 166–67
Drake, Dr., 157
Dreams, Thomas Paine on, 424–48
Dryden, John, 25, 114
Dubois, Guillaume, 267
Dudley, Joseph, 86
Dumaril, 292
Dunkers, 5
Dupuis, Charles Francçis, 104, 260–61, 280, 293
Dutch Reformed Church, 57, 60

Eaton, Daniel I., 404
Ecclesiasticus, 427–28
Edes & Gill (publishers, Boston Gazette), 346, 347
Edwards, Jonathan, 249
Eisenhower, David, xiii
Elias, 108, 262
Elijah, 222
Ely, Ezra Stiles, 234
Emerson, Ralph Waldo, 17
Emlyn, Thomas, 234
Enfield, William, 238, 241, 242, 259
England, 3, 4, 19, 293, 364, 375; and the American states, 4, 10, 96, 327, 358–59, 392–93; dissenters in, 231; Jefferson on, 219, 237; and the Quakers, 121, 139–40; religious diversity in, 334
Enlightenment, 9–10, 329
Enoch, 257, 260, 261
Ephesus, 438
Epictetus, 149, 165, 169, 170, 235
Epicurus, 146, 148–49, 165, 169
Erasmus, Desiderius, 233, 250, 257
Erastus, Thomas, 235
Erskine, Thomas, 404–17
Euclid, 140, 151, 220, 234, 418
Euripides, 114
Eve, 397, 407
Exodus, Book of, 247–48, 434

Eyre, Mr., 350
Ezra, Book of, 434

Fabricius, Johann Albert, 129
Fairfax, Bryan, 52–53
Farmer, Hugh, 234, 256
Federalist, The, 295, 328, 359
Federalist party, 76, 100–101, 157, 218, 223, 359
Finch, Sir Henry, 258
Fish, Nicholas, 342
Fishback, James, 138
Flourens, Pierre Jean Marie, 292
Floyd, William, 222, 287
Folger, Abiah, 23
Folger, Peter, 23–24
Fontenelle, Bernard de, 263
Foster, John, 36
Founding Fathers, vii–viii, xiii, 1–8, 11–15
France, 10, 96, 123, 130, 132, 139, 219, 249, 364–65, 390, 392–94, 395, 414, 415, 417
Francis St., 252
Franklin, Benjamin, 5, 6–7, 15, 47, 75, 95, 115, 130, 164–65, 277, 295, 350, 361, 365, 391, 392; *Autobiography,* 23–39; biography of, 16–19; on churchgoing, 19–20; diary of, 40–41; hope for mankind, 43
    —letters to: his daughter Sarah, 19–20; Ezra Stiles, 41–43; Benjamin Vaughan, 20–21
    —Lord's Prayer, version of, 20–23; religious development and ideas of, 23–39
Franklin, Benjamin (uncle of B. Franklin), 23, 24
Franklin, Josiah, 23
Franklin, Sarah, 19
Frederick the Great, 227, 230, 265, 269, 270, 275, 276
Freeman, Dr. James, 279
Freneau, Philip, 5

Galileo, 2, 124
Gardiner, Major, 79, 80
Gassendi, Pierre, 146, 150
Gaustad, Edwin Scott, 9

Gelasius, Pope, 106
Germara, 241, 248
Genesis, Book of, 405–9, 433, 434, 435–36
Genêt, Edmé Jacques, 96
Genêt, Edmond ("Citizen"), 95
Georgia, 37–38
Gérard, Conrad, 352
Germany, 10, 234
Gerry, Elbridge, 222
Gibbon, Edward, 230, 234, 253, 265
Gideon, 370
Godwin, William, 7, 229
Goethe, J. W. von, 7, 247, 248, 257
Gram, John, 255
Grattan, Henry, 10
Grayson, William, 306
Great Awakening, 9
Green, 78
Greene, Major, 79, 81
Gregory IX, Pope, 248
Grimm, Baron Melchior von, 269, 270, 271–72, 275, 276, 278, 279
Grotius, Hugo, 332
Guegan, Mr., 156
Guenee, 102

Hagar, 427
Hale, Sir Matthew, 258
Hall, Thomas Cumming, 47
Hamilton, Alexander, 5, 7, 46, 69, 75, 76, 100, 102, 218, 236, 297, 359, 436; biography of, 326–29; on civil liberties, 337–38; duel with Burr, 339–41; *The Farmer Refuted,* 332–33; on hurricane at St. Croix, 329–31
    —letters to: citizens of New York ("Phocion" letters), 337–38, Elizabeth Hamilton, 341–42
    —on natural rights, 332–33; on Quebec Act, 333–37; on religious tolerance, 333–37; will and testament, 342–43
Hamilton, Elizabeth, 329, 341–42
Hampshire County, Mass., Adams' letter to, 100
Hannibal, 250
Harington, Sir John, 10, 235
Harrison, Benjamin, 306

Harrison, W. H., 226
Hartley, David, 264
Harvard College, 76, 156, 160
Haven, Rev. James, 81–82
Haverhill, 349
Hawley, Joseph, 78
Helvétius, Claude Adrien, 142–43, 276
Hemenway, 240
Hemphill (Presbyterian preacher), 36–37
Henry, Patrick, 5, 302, 305
Henschen, Georg, 107, 262
Heresy, Jefferson on, 122–23, 132
Herodotus, 434
Hersey, Dr. Ezekiel, 240
Hesiod, 249
Hevah, 435
Hewet, Mr., 350
Hicks, 282
Hilkiah, 410
History, Thomas Paine on, 433–36
Hobbes, Thomas, 10, 114, 279, 332
Holbach, Baron d', 10, 142, 272, 275, 289
Holland, 323
Holmes, Abiel, 444
Holmes, Oliver Wendell, 17, 444
Holy Ghost, 427, 437 n.
Homer, 99, 114
Hopkins, Stephen, 87
Horace, 253, 267, 282
Horsley, Samuel, 234, 238
Howe, Lord, 40
Huey, Joseph, 42 n.
Huguenots, 9, 115
Hume, David, 10, 114, 230, 234, 253, 274, 329
Humphries, David, 66, 70
Huss, John, 266
Hutchinson, Thomas, 344

Ina, 257
India, religion and philosophy of, 256–57, 260, 261, 288, 415, 435, 436
Indians, American, 49, 54–55; traditions and religion of, 220–22, 226–28
Inquisition, 107–8, 109, 262, 266, 412, 441

Ireland, 10, 67
Isaac, 153, 222
Isaiah, Book of, 434

Jackson, Andrew, 394
Jacob, 153, 222, 245, 427
Jacobins, 363, 393
James, Epistle of, 33
James I, 410
James, William, 17
Jay, John, 5, 234, 326; addresses to American Bible Society, 373–84; on atheism, 364–65; biography of, 358–60; "Charge to the Grand Jury," 361; on distribution of the Bible, 373–384; on Episcopal Church, 385–88
—letters to: John Bristed, 364–65; John M. Mason, 365; Jedidiah Morse, 362–64; John Murray, 365–73; Uzal Ogden, 361; Benjamin Rush, 361–62; Trinity Church Corporation, 385–88
—on Thomas Paine's ideas, 361; on religion, 362–64, 365; on David Rittenhouse, 361–62; on war and its justification, 365–73
Jay, William, 360, 373
Jefferson, Martha, 148
Jefferson, Thomas, 5, 6, 7, 12, 14, 15, 20, 21, 47, 75, 76, 101, 107, 295, 297, 302, 304–6, 308, 315–16, 319, 327, 328, 359, 360, 365, 440 n., 442, 444; addresses to religious bodies, 135–36; *Autobiography,* 118–20; biography of, 114–18; on Christianity, 145–47, 157–58, 160–62; on Church and State, 134–137
—letters to: (and from) John Adams. See Jefferson-Adams letters; William Canby, 140–41; Peter Carr, 127–29; Charles Clay, 171–72; Thomas Cooper, 131–33, 163–64; E. Dowse, 166–67; James Fishback, 138; Samuel Kercheval, 139–40; Miles King, 144–45; Thomas Law, 141–44; Thomas Leiper, 138; on *Life and*

Morals of Jesus, 164–73; Levi Lincoln, 134; James Madison, 121; Samuel Miller, 136–37; Jeremiah Moor, 130; Timothy Pickering, 157–58; Joseph Priestley, 130–31, 165–66, 171; Benjamin Rush, 168–71; William Short, 148–54; Mrs. Harrison Smith, 146–47, 364; James Smith, 159–60; Jared Sparks, 156; Ezra Stiles, 147–48; Isaac Story, 133–34; John Taylor, 154–56; Charles Thomson, 145–46; F. A. Van der Kemp, 172–73; Benjamin Waterhouse, 160–63; Thomas Whittemore, 158–59
—*Life and Morals of Jesus,* 117, 173–216 (text); on morality, 141–44; *Notes on Virginia,* 121–25; on Quakers, 139–41; on religious education, 127–29; on religious freedom, 163–64; religious position of, 118–25; on religious unorthodoxy, 130–33; on revelation, 144–45; Statute for Religious Freedom, 114, 116–17, 120–21, 125–27, 296, 297; syllabus of doctrines of Jesus, 167–71, 246–48; on Unitarianism, 158–60
Jefferson-Adams letters: Adams to Jefferson, 226–37, 238–41, 246–57, 259–62, 263–66, 267–71, 273–77, 278–79, 280–81, 282–83, 284, 286–87, 288–89, 292, 293; on aristocracy, 232–33, 243–46; on atheism, 269–70, 272; on authority, 264–65; background of, 217–19; on belief, 249–53; on Christian philosophy, 233–35; on free inquiry, 293; on future, 263–64, 265–66; 287–88; on general principles of Christianity, 229–31; on Indian traditions and religion, 220–22, 226–28; Jefferson to Adams, 219–25, 237–38, 241–46, 257–59, 262–63, 266, 271–73, 277–78, 279–80, 281–82, 283–84, 284–86, 287–88, 289–91, 292, 293–94; on kings, 292; on law and Christianity,

259–62; on metaphysics, 284–86; on morality, 241–43, 279–81; on party differences, 223–25; on Plato, 262–63; on Joseph Priestley, 235–38, 253–57, 259–62; on religious reading, 280, 281–83; on Supreme Being, 239–41, 289–91; on syllabus of doctrines of Jesus, 246–48
Jehoshaphat, 364
Jenner, Edward, 160
Jerome, St., 107
Jerusalem, 248
Jesuits, 10, 107, 265
Jesus Christ, 3, 19, 42, 43 n., 47, 55; John Adams on, 79, 81, 82, 104, 229, 234, 262, 263, 268, 288; Jay on, 364, 366–67, 368; Jefferson on, 117, 120, 128–29, 138–40, 145, 149, 151–54, 156, 157–58, 160–61, 241–42, 273, 283, 286, 290–91; *Life and Morals of,* 173–216; Paine on, 397, 404, 427, 429, 437
Jews, 21–22, 61, 62, 103, 104–5, 148, 153–54, 160, 166, 169–71, 221, 241, 243, 261, 272–73, 288, 291, 318, 320–21, 395–96, 409, 431, 433–35, 438; and Ten Commandments, 247–48
Jezirah, 241, 248
John, Gospel of, 251, 290–91
Johnson, Samuel, 252, 253, 265
Jones, Joseph, 307
Jones, Sir William, 436
Joseph, St., 437 n.
Joshua, Book of, 128
Jude, Epistle of, 257, 260–61
Justin Martyr, St., 112

Kames (Kaims), Lord (Henry Home), 144
Keith, Sir William, 24
Kentucky Resolutions, 363
Kercheval, Samuel, 138–39
Ketocton Baptist Association, 136
King, Miles, 144–45
Kings, Book of, 433
King's College, 326, 332, 358
Kingsley, J. L., 444

Knox, Henry, 63–64
Knox, James, 329
Koran, 412, 430, 431, 433

Laban, 245
Lactantius, 251
Lafayette, Marquis de, 70–71
Lafitau (Lafitan), Joseph François, 220–21, 226
La Fontaine, Jean de, 263
La Harpe, Jean François de, 110, 235, 252, 276, 279
Lalande (*pseud.* of François Noel Babeuf), 269, 275
La Rochefoucauld, François, Duc de, 261, 268
Laud, William, 352
Law, Thomas, 141–44
Ledyard, John, 272
Lee, Arthur, 350–51
Leibnitz, Baron G. W. von, 10, 272
Leiper, Thomas, 137–38
Leland, John, 234
Leo X, Pope, 253, 267
Leonard, Daniel, 89
Lespinasse, Julie de, 279
Lessing, Gotthold Ephraim, 10
Levi, 272–73
Lewis and Clark expedition, 272
Lightfoot, John, 248
Lincoln, Benjamin, 65
Lincoln, Levi, 134
Lindsey (Lindsay), Theophilus, 222, 229, 231, 233, 235, 236, 265
Lipsius, Justus, 129
Livingston, Robert R., 94–95
Livingston, William, 326
Livy, 128, 152, 232
Llandaff, Bishop of, 407, 417
Locke, John, 10, 95, 114, 132, 230, 240, 253, 285, 286, 329, 332
Lord, Henry, 435
Lord's Prayer, Franklin's version of, 20–23
Loyola, St. Ignatius of, 156, 252, 266
Luke, Gospel of, 22, 232, 251
Luther, Martin, 250, 253, 267, 439
Lycurgus, 288
Lyons, William, 20

Lytton, Peter, 341 n.

Mably, Abbé Gabriel de, 95
Maccarty, Rev., 78, 81
Machiavelli, Niccolò, 97, 99, 247
Madison, James, viii–xii, 66, 69, 120, 121, 138, 154, 164–65, 218, 327, 360; on assessments for religion, 302–4, 306–14, 322; on belief, 321–22; on Bill of Rights, 315–17; biography of, 295–97; on Episcopal Church, 301–2, 304–6, 317–18; on freedom of religion, 301, 320–21; on government and religion, 298–301, 314–15, 319–20, 322–25; *Journals,* 301, 314–15
—letters to: Rev. Adams, 322–25; Frederick Beasley, 321–322; William Bradford, Jr., 298–301; Thomas Jefferson, 302, 304–6, 308, 315–16; George Mason, 322; James Monroe, 304, 306–7; Jacob de la Motta, 320–21; Mordecai M. Noah, 318; Edmund Randolph, 307–8; Robert Walsh, 319–20—"Memorial and Remonstrance," 308–14
Malone, Dumas, 116
Manilius, 227
Manning, James, 87
Manotte, 252
Mansfield, Lord, 258
Marblehead, Mass., 349
Marius, 282
Mark, Gospel of, 251
Marmontel, Jean François, 276
Mary, Queen, 23
Mary, St., 437 n.
Maryland, 2, 9
Mason, George, 64–65, 322
Mason, Rev. John M., 365
Massachusetts, 3, 9, 87–88, 244; and the clergy, 89–90; religious freedom in, 293; Indians in, 228
Mather, Cotton, 23
Matthew, Gospel of, 22, 251, 437 n., 442
Maury, Rev. James, 115
Mayhew, Rev. Jonathan, 79, 82

Mazzei, Philip, 307
Medford, 349
Mennonites, 5, 310
Methodist Church, 59, 116, 163, 319
Middleton, Arthur, 86
Middleton, Conyers, 238
Mifflin, Thomas, 87
Milan Decree, 219
Miller, Samuel, 111–12, 136–37
Milton, John, 93, 114, 235
Mishna, 241, 248
Mitchell, Mrs., 341
Mohammed, 97, 161, 233, 288, 363, 404, 430, 431, 433
Monotheism, 151
Monroe, James, 103, 304, 306–7, 318
Montesquieu, Baron de, 10, 114, 228, 332
Monticello, 7, 114, 118, 129, 138, 146, 160, 165, 328
Moor, Jeremiah, 130
Moore, Bishop Benjamin, 436–38
Morgan, John, 86
Morgan, Mrs. John, 87
Morgan, Thomas, 78
Morison, Samuel Eliot, 358
Morris, Gouverneur, 5
Morse, Jedidiah, 362–64
Moses, 153, 233, 239, 241, 410; and the account of creation, 405; historical existence of, 433, 434; the Law of, 409; and the Ten Commandments, 247, 248, 257, 366–67
Motta, Jacob de la, 320–21
Motte, Richard, 140
Mount Vernon, 67–68
Murray, John, 365–73

Naples, 287
Napoleon Bonaparte, 132, 265, 270, 292
Natural rights, 6, 13, 218, 327, 329, 332–33
Naturalization Act, 130
Nebuchadnezzar, 433, 435
Necker, Jacques, 276
Negroes, 118

Nelson, Stephen S., 135
Nelson, Thomas, 54
New Church, Baltimore, 48, 62
New England, 8–9, 18, 23, 122, 134, 268, 269, 316, 324, 350
New Jersey, 323
New Rochelle, N.Y., 392
New South Church, 344
New Testament. See Jefferson, Thomas: Life and Morals of Jesus
New York, 9, 124, 287, 359, 392
Newell, Graham, 343
Newenham, Sir Edward, 66–67
Newton, Sir Isaac, 7, 230, 234, 418
Nicaea, Council of, 132 n., 286 n.
Nicholas, George, 308, 322
Nicholas, Robert Carter, 119
Niles, Hezekiah, 77
Noah, 222, 373, 409
Noah, Mordecai M., 318
North, Lord, 344

Offa, 257
Ogden, Uzal, 361
Orrery, 397
Otis, James, 5
Ovid, 93

Paine, Robert Treat, 222
Paine, Thomas, 7–8, 12, 14, 42 n., 74, 88, 99, 101, 217, 227, 359, 365; Age of Reason, 395–403; biography of, 389–94; on blasphemy and the Bible, 404–14; on Deism, 396, 401–2, 430–31, 437–42; "Dream" essay, 424–28; on existence of God, 417–23; letter to Thomas Erskine, 404–17; on miracles, 400–1; on mystery, 399–400
—Prospect papers: to Bishop Moore, 436–48; Connecticut Sabbath, 432; Deism compared with Christianity, 430–31; Deism and writings of Paine, 438–42; future state, 442–43; history and religion, 433–36; religion and other words of uncertain significance, 428–30
—religious beliefs, 395–403; on

revelation, 401; on science, 402–3; on Theophilanthrophy, 414–17; on universe, 397–99, 417–23
Palladio, Andrea, 114
Palmer, Elihu, 428
Papebroeck, Daniel, 107, 108, 262
Parrington, Vernon, 18, 154
Patterson, Dr. Robert, 145
Paul, St., 150, 221, 370
Paulding, James K., 72
Paulinus, St., 107
Pearce, William, 67–68
Pemberton, Israel, 87–88, 140
Pendleton, Edmund, 119
Pendleton, Nathaniel, 342
Penn, William, 445
Pennsylvania, 9, 87–88, 124, 162, 163, 323, 392
Perry, Ralph Barton, 8
Persia, 431, 435–36
Peter, St., 369
Peter, Second Epistle of, 260–61
Philadelphia, Washington's letters to, 58, 63
Philadelphia Public Library, 117
Philippians, Epistle to, 26
Philo, 226–27
Physiocrats, 7
Pickering, Timothy, 156–58
Piedmont, 287
Pilate, Pontius, 369
Pillnitz, Convention of, 219, 267
Pinckney, Charles, xi, 5, 102 n.
Pinel, Philippe, 292
Pitt, William, 392
Pius VI, Pope, 39–40
Plato: Adams on, 226–27, 254–55, 260, 355; Jefferson on, 149, 152, 161, 170, 262–63
Platonism, 145, 162, 237, 242
Pliny, 282
Plutarch, 152
Poland, 266, 267
Pomham, Aaron, 228
Pomham, Moses, 228
Pompey, 250, 282
Pope, Alexander, 94, 114, 442
Portal, 292
Porter, Mr., 77
Prat, 289

Prayer, Franklin on, 18, 20–23
Presbyterian Church, 8, 59, 60, 360, 384; Adams on, 102; in England 334; Franklin on, 25–26; Jefferson on, 132–33, 151, 163; and Jefferson's Bill for Religious Freedom, 116, 121; Madison on, 306, 307, 308, 319
Price, Richard, 10, 95, 157, 240
Priestley, Joseph, 10, 102, 117, 130–31, 149, 157, 159, 162, 164–66, 167, 168, 171, 223, 224–25, 229, 231, 233, 234, 251, 259–62, 264, 272, 444
Princeton University, 296, 298
Prisot, Sir John, 258
Protestant Episcopal Church, 23, 45, 59, 62, 102, 163, 296, 297, 308, 319, 360, 430; Jay on, 385–88; Madison on, 301–2, 304–6, 317–18; and the Papists, 428; Samuel Adams on, 350
Psalms, 243, 246
Pufendorf, Baron Samuel von, 332
Puritanism, 8, 12, 75, 84, 296, 349–50
Putnam, James, 78–79, 82, 93
Putnam, Mrs. James, 78
Pythagoras, 29, 165, 169, 238, 254–55, 256, 260
Quakers, 2, 360, 390; Adams on, 87–89, 265; history of, in England, 10–11; Jefferson on, 121–22, 138–41, 161, 237, 289; Madison on, 310; Paine on, 396; Samuel Adams on, 345, 352, 428–29, 440, 441
Quebec Act, 46, 333–37
Quesnay, François, 10
Quincy, Samuel, 93–94
Quintilian, 282

Raleigh, Sir Walter, 118
Ralph, James, 20, 24
Randolph, Edmund, 307–8
Randolph, John, 109
Randolph, Thomas J., 293
Read, Deborah, 24
Reformation, 23, 74, 267
Reformed German Congregation, 48, 57

Reformed Protestant Dutch
   Church, 56
Rhode Island, 163, 287, 323
Rittenhouse, David, 361
Rivanna River, 120
Robbins, Ephraim, 135
Robespierre, Maximilien de, 270,
   393, 410
Rodgers, John, 56
Roman Catholic Church, 2–3, 61,
   67, 80, 94, 102, 111, 345, 363;
   and John Adams, 250–52, 269;
   in Canada, 46, 48–49, 333–37;
   and Franklin, 40–41 and Paine,
   404, 428, 438, 441
Roosevelt, Theodore, 14
Ross, Robert, 107
Rousseau, Jean Jacques, 114, 230,
   265, 269, 272, 276
Rush, Benjamin, 5, 101–2, 117,
   150, 165, 167–71, 222, 233, 236,
   252, 361–62
Rutledge, John, 87
Rutledge, Edward, 87

Sabbath, Connecticut, 432
St. Asaph, Bishop of, 354
Sainte-Beuve, Charles Augustin, 18
St. Croix, 329–31
St. John, Oliver, 235
St. Peter's, Rome, 267
Saint-Pierre, Jacques-Henri Bernar-
   din de, 252
Salem, Mass., 349
Sallust, 282
Samson, 429
Samuel, 222, 427, 440
Sanchoniathon, 233, 256
Sarah, 427
Saunders, 282
Savil, Dr., 240
Scarron, Paul, 249
Scipio, 250
Scollay, John, 351–52
Scot, Rev. Douglas A., 115
Scotland, 10, 115
Search, Edward, 234
Secret societies, 363
Seixas, Moses, 61
Selden, John, 235

Senate, 244
Seneca, 149, 165, 169, 282
Servetus, Michael, 151, 155, 162
Sewall, David, 112–13
Shaphan, 410
Shastra, 256–57, 260, 270, 431
Sheppard, 258
Sherman, Roger, 5
Shippen, William, 86
Short, William, 148–54
Sidney (Sydney) Algernon, 95
Simplicius, 235
Slavery, 41, 84, 119, 147, 265, 319,
   373, 375–76, 391–92
Small, Dr. William, 115
Smallpox, vaccination against, 160
Smith, Abigail, 91
Smith, Adam, 114
Smith, Mrs. Harrison, 146–47, 364
Smith, James, 159–60
Smith, John B., 301–2
Smith, Polly, 91
Society for the Suppression of Vice
   and Immorality, 404
Socrates, 149, 152, 154, 165, 167,
   169, 170, 235, 236, 243, 250,
   256, 263, 404, 412
Sodalitas Club, 84
Sohar, 241, 248
Solomon, 288, 367–68, 429; Prov-
   erbs of, 30, 249
Solon, 97, 288
Sparks, Jared, 47, 156
Spinoza, Baruch, 289
Stamp Act, 348
Sterne, Laurence, 127
Sternhold, Thomas, 243
Stiles, Ezra, 18, 41, 43 n., 147–48,
   444
Stoics, 146, 149
Story, Rev. Isaac, 133–34
Strange, 258
Stuart, Dugald, 284, 286
Suetonius, 250
Supreme Court, 359
Swift, Jonathan, 270, 282, 412
Sydenham, Thomas, 78
Sylla, 282

Tacitus, 99, 128, 220, 232, 267, 282

Talmud, 241, 248
Tate, Nahum, 243
Taylor, John, 105–11, 154–56, 261
Tea Act, 344
Tecumseh, 265
Ten Commandments, 247–48, 257, 281
Tertullian, 291
Thacher, Rev. Peter, 352
Thanksgiving Day Proclamations: Samuel Adams, 355–57; George Washington, 71–72
Thayer, 81
Theism, 272, 429
Themistocles, 288
Theocritus, 223, 234–35
Theognis, 245, 249, 415
Theology, 8, 148, 412–13, 418, 420, 421
Theophilanthrophy, 390, 394, 414–23
Thessalonians, First Epistle to, 436–37
Thomas, St., 251
Thomson, Charles, 145–46
Thomson, James, 30–31
Thucydides, 220, 234
Timaeus, 238, 254, 265, 270
Tocqueville, Alexis de, vii
Tories, 352
Torrey, John, 249
Tracy, Destutt, 279–80, 284, 286
Transubstantiation, 441
Trinity and Trinitarianism, 125, 151, 157, 159, 160, 163, 229, 234, 237, 255, 260, 429
Trinity Church Corporation, 385–88
Trowbridge, Edmund, 78
Trumbull, Jonathan, 66, 70, 270
Tucker, 234
Tudor, William, 111
Turgot, A. R. J., 10
Tyndale, William, 10

Ulster County, N.Y., 361
Unitarianism, 75, 155, 156; Adams on, 231, 234; Jefferson on, 158–60, 161, 162, 163–64, 237
United States National Museum, 165

University of Virginia, 114, 118, 131, 151, 154–56, 164

Valleau, Theo. B., 343
Van der Kemp, F. A., 102–5, 172–73, 235
Van Ness, William Peter, 340
Van Swieten, 78
Vassall, William, 274, 277
Vaughan, Benjamin, 20
Veronica, St., 108, 262
Virgil, 246–47, 273, 274, 282
Virginia, 2, 245, 300–14, 316, 319–20, 322, 324, 350; Resolutions, 363; Statute for Religious Freedom, 114, 116–17, 120–21, 125–27, 259, 296, 297
Virtues, moral, Franklin's enumeration of, 27–36
Vishnu, 256, 288
Vives, Juan Luis, 250, 251, 257
Voltaire, François Marie Arouet de, 10, 101, 102, 114, 230, 234, 252, 253, 265, 269, 270, 274–75, 276

Waldenses, 9
War, John Jay on, 365–73
Ward, Samuel, 87
Warwick, 87
Washington, George, 2, 5, 6–7, 14, 74, 99, 117, 141, 156, 236, 295, 297, 327, 328, 359, 391, 392, 394; addresses and speeches, 54–55, 56, 66, 69–70; biography of, 44–48; General Orders, 50–52 —letters to: Benedict Arnold, 49–50; John Parke Custis, 52; Bryan Fairfax, 53; governors of states, 55; Henry Knox, 63–64; Marquis de Lafayette, 70–71; Benjamin Lincoln, 65; George Mason, 64–65; Thomas Nelson, 54; Sir Edward Newenham, 67; William Pearce, 67–68; John Rodgers, 56; Jonathan Trumbull, 70; Samuel Washington, 52 —and Providence, 53, 54, 70; on religious observation, 50–52; on religious tolerance, 49–50; on Supreme Being, 72–73; Thanksgiving Day Proclamation, 71–72

Washington, Lawrence, 45
Washington, Samuel, 52
Waterhouse, Dr. Benjamin, 160–63
Waterland, Daniel, 234, 238, 321
Webster, Daniel, 10–11
Wells, T., 353–54
Wesley, John, 252
West, 240
West Indies, 376
Whig party, 358
White, Hugh, 87
Whitefield, George, 37–39, 252–53
Whittemore, Rev. Thomas, 158–59
Willard (au. of *Body of Divinity*), 111
Willard, Dr. Nahum, 78
William and Mary College, 115, 148, 151
Williams, Roger, 445
Williams, Thomas, 404, 409, 411, 417

Wilson, James, 5, 316
Wingate, 258
Witherspoon, John, 296
Wollaston, William, 141
Wood, 258
Woolman, John, 445
Worthington, 78
Wycliffe, John, 267

Xenophon, 149, 170, 232

Yale, Elihu, 41
Yale College, 41–42, 43
York, Mass, 349–50
Young, Arthur, 10

Zaleucus, 255, 256
Zedekiah, 435
Zend-Avesta, 431
Zoroaster, 233, 256, 431, 438